EZRA POUND
and music

Ezra Pound, from a portrait believed to have been painted c. 1922 by Stowitz.

EZRA POUND and music

The Complete Criticism

Edited with commentary by **R. Murray Schafer**

A NEW DIRECTIONS BOOK

Copyright © 1918, 1920, 1926, 1935, 1948, 1950, 1955, 1956, 1960, 1965, 1966, 1967, 1968, 1970, 1971, 1972, 1973, 1976, 1977 by The Trustees of the Ezra Pound Literary Property Trust
Copyright © 1965, 1971, 1973, 1976 by New Directions Publishing Corporation
Copyright © 1977 by R. Murray Schafer
Copyright 1927 by Pascal Covici, Publisher, Inc.

All rights reserved. Except for brief passages quoted in a newspaper, magazine, radio, or television review, no part of this book may be reproduced in any form or by any means, electronic or mechanical, including photocopying and recording, or by any information storage and retrieval system, without permission in writing from the Publisher.

Manufactured in the United States of America
First published as New Directions Paperbook 33 (NDP33) in 2008
Published simultaneously in Canada by McClelland & Stewart, Ltd.

Library of Congress Cataloging in Publication Data
Pound, Ezra Loomis, 1885–1972.
   Ezra Pound and music.
   (A New Directions Book)
   Includes index.
   1. Music—Addresses, essays, lectures.
I. Schafer, R. Murray. II. Title.
ML60.P925E9   780'.8   77-9609
ISBN 13:978-0-8112-1784-2

New Directions Books are published for James Laughlin
by New Directions Publishing Corporation,
80 Eighth Avenue, New York, NY 10011

To the memory of Agnes Bedford,
friend of the poet,
friend of the editor

CONTENTS

Preface	ix
Introduction	3
1. England: The Early Reviews 1908–1917	23
2. England: *The New Age* Music Critic, "William Atheling," 1917–1921	57
3. France and Italy 1921–1927	242
4. The Rapallo Years 1928–1941	321
5. Postscript 1942–1972	464
Appendixes	
The Developing Theories of Absolute Rhythm and Great Bass	467
Glossary of Important Musical Personalities	481
"Why a Poet Quit the Muses," by George Antheil	513
Index of Proper Names	517

PREFACE

The most disappointing thing about the bulk of criticism dealing with Ezra Pound is that music has not been given the attention it deserves. Although Pound's interest in music had been passionate and lifelong, it has often appeared capricious, jammed together with commentaries on politics, economics, history, art, and the thousand other subjects which swarmed about in his pantechnicon mind.

The purpose of this volume is to bring forward Ezra Pound's musical theorizings and criticisms in sequence. A projected second volume will deal with his chief attempts to realize these ideas in musical compositions. Some of the material to follow is being presented for the first time; other important material has been collected from newspapers and magazines now almost inaccessible. Absent from the present collection are only interposed remarks on music from the published books and letters, though many of these will be mentioned in the editorial notes.

Few commentators have attempted a serious study of Pound as a musician. Ned Rorem's "Ezra Pound as a Musician" (*London Magazine,* January, 1968) and my own "Ezra Pound and Music" (*Canadian Music Journal,* Summer, 1961) are two early examples, to which one might add the perceptive chapter entitled "Words and Music" from Noel Stock's *Poet in Exile*. Later additions of special value were Stephen Adams's *Ezra Pound and Music* (doc. diss., University of Toronto, 1973) and the collection of articles that appeared in the *Paideuma* music issue (Vol. 2, No. 1, 1973). Nevertheless, the curious paradox mentioned by Ned Rorem seems still to be true: poets and scholars all seem to know that Pound wrote operas, but very few know about his music criticism and theories, while musicians may have "hazily heard" of the harmony book or *The New Age* reviews but are quite ignorant of his compositions.

This presentation of the musical writings should serve two purposes. First of all, literary scholars will be able to study the informed significance of music in the poet's life. This ought to dispel the ignorant and casual chatter about music that has spoiled a lot of criticism to date. Secondly, musicians will then want to investigate the compositions, and they will want to read the criticisms as unusual commentaries on historical musical events. If I can anticipate some conclusions, I think they will discover in Pound's spicy and debunking *New Age* reviews material rivaling G. B. Shaw's of a few decades earlier. They may also find in *Le Testament* an unduplicated little masterpiece of musical composition. In other ways they will be disappointed. Enthusiasm for music does not excuse technical ineptitudes, and it will be up to them to point this out.

This book contains all Pound's music criticism arranged in chronological order. The reviews, like Shaw's, may be dipped into at random; they will always excite and amuse. But only the patient reader will be able to see the gradual maturation of the poet's musical ideas from the casual confections of the first reviews to the important theories of Absolute Rhythm and Great Bass developed three decades later. At first there are a few scattered London reviews, followed between 1917 and 1920 by the important fortnightly column written for *The New Age* under the pseudonym of "William Atheling." It was after moving to Paris in 1921 that Pound's musical ideas began to consolidate in the *Treatise on Harmony*. At this time too he did his propaganda work for the American composer George Antheil, and wrote his most important composition, the opera *Le Testament*. After taking up permanent residence in Rapallo in 1928, his musical interests took another turn. Vivaldi was discovered and some original research on this master was conducted by Pound and his friend Olga Rudge. During these years the *Cavalcanti* opera was composed. A unique series of concerts was established in Rapallo by the poet, and the reviews and promotional pieces he wrote for them in the local newspaper, *Il Mare,* constitute, next to *The New Age* pieces, the largest integrated collection. This work in turn culminated in the musical theories ultimately defined in *Guide to*

Kulchur (1938) and in the musical practices of the later *Cantos*.

The editor accordingly found it desirable to introduce various special sections of the music criticism with some preliminary commentary and to provide continuity between the reviews. Aside from this he has stayed at the bottom of the page. All the footnotes are his unless otherwise indicated.

In Appendix I an attempt has been made to show the gradual consolidation over the years of the ideas of Absolute Rhythm and Great Bass. Although influential musical personalities are introduced chronologically in the notes to the texts, Appendix II is a glossary of the most important of them, together with additional facts concerning their own work and musical accomplishments. Several of the reviews were reprinted by Pound himself in different collections of his work. Frequently these were abbreviated or altered in other minor ways. I have chosen in all cases to reproduce the original reviews and have noted later printings which differ. Nothing has been changed in the reviews with the exception of a few spelling mistakes and the italicization of some foreign expressions, in order to observe conventions Pound elsewhere adopted. The considerable variation in the forms of proper nouns has been retained.

The editing of the musical manuscripts has presented the greatest difficulties. As Pound lacked formal musical training he had to rely on the help of friends and collaborators, and the task of sorting out the definitive Pound utterance from numerous manuscripts in different hands could never be totally successful; but these special problems I hope to explain in detail in the second volume devoted to Pound's compositions.

It remains to thank numerous people for assistances of various kinds. First of all, the late Agnes Bedford, to whose memory the editor has taken the liberty of dedicating the present collection. It was she to whom Pound always turned for musical advice during the London days and to whom he returned years later for help with the scoring of the *Cavalcanti* opera. It was also she who spurred the editor on in his preparation of *Le Testament* for the BBC Third Programme and his first attempt to measure the significance of music in Pound's poetry. Without the memory of her gracious hospitality and enthusiastic conversations, the whole present undertaking would have been a much less pleasant task. Her voice continues to animate many of these pages.

I shall never forget the generosity of Ezra Pound himself, particularly during a visit to Brunnenburg in 1960. These times spent together extended my knowledge of the man and poet and opened up a whole world of musical interests and enthusiasms, which have not only resulted in this book but have undoubtedly left their mark on my own work as a composer. Mrs. Dorothy Pound too, whom I have had the pleasure of visiting a number of times, has always proved delightful and helpful.

Two graduate students contributed numerous insights and hours of work to this volume: Brian Fawcett of Simon Fraser University and Stephen Adams of the University of Toronto both have revealed repeatedly that they knew more than the editor about much of the subject matter, and many of their ideas and suggestions have been incorporated in the text. Stephen Adams, now a distinguished scholar in his own right, followed the text in the final stages approaching publication and helped in many more ways than can be adequately expressed here.

For the translations of the Italian reviews I am indebted to Miss Maria Chiara Zanolli, who did the first draft, and to the poet's daughter, Mary de Rachewiltz, who read these drafts and made numerous stylistic suggestions. The editor, of course, accepts all responsibility for the final form in which they appear.

The poet's son, Omar Pound, must be thanked for his letters and hospitality. Miss Helen Ford was kind enough to place all Agnes Bedford's posthumous Poundiana at my disposal, and Miss Raymonde Collignon allowed me to consult some yet unpublished letters. Other friends and acquaintances of the poet contributed advice, assistance, and hospitality: John Drummond, Dr. Frieda Bacigalupo, Ronald Duncan, Domenico de' Paoli, Violet Marquesita, Vanni Scheiwiller, Tibor Serly, Yves Tinayre, and Virgil Thomson.

Noel Stock's *The Life of Ezra Pound* was a constant companion, and when it failed Professor Stock was always prompt in supplying additional editorial details from his personal files and memories. Hugh Kenner's books and correspondence were also always inspirational. Pound's German translator and editor, Frau Eva Hesse, helped frequently with facts and insights. But above all I must thank Donald Gallup. Not only was his *A Bibliography of Ezra Pound* my most thumbed reference book, but the charm and graciousness of the man himself made consulting him on all matters a true privilege. He allowed me to consult the Beinecke Library's Pound holdings and replied with alacrity to the most finical inquiries. I am also indebted to him for allowing me to quote from some unpublished Pound/Harding correspondence in his private collection. Robert Hughes's important 1971 revival of

Le Testament gave me an opportunity to engage in a lively exchange of letters and to profit from his ideas and discoveries concerning Pound's music.

For checking details I am indebted to numerous other librarians: A. H. King, Superintendent of the Music Library of the British Museum; Brian Trowell, Chief Assistant, Opera, of the BBC Music Library; Michael Short, Secretary of the United Kingdom Section of the International Association of Music Libraries; Mrs. G. Carlton, Biblioteca Internazionale, Rapallo; Miss Jean Lavender, the Music Library, University of Toronto; Harold Spivacke, Chief of the Music Division of the Library of Congress; and to the following libraries in general: the Sächsische Landesbibliothek, Dresden; the Biblioteca Universitaria, Genoa; the Biblioteca Nazionale Centrale, Florence; the Biblioteca Nazionale Centrale, Rome; the Biblioteca of the Accademia Chigiana, Siena; and the Asociatia Oamenilor de Artă, Bucharest. I am indebted, too, to the Yale Graduate Department and University Library for permission to quote from unpublished letters by Pound on the subject of music.

Others who helped trace elusive details or who provided additional facts were: Gladys Deutsch, Ingrid Buch, Robert M. Walshe, Derek Carr, John Peck, Dr. Raf Ravaioli, Francis Rizzo, Vladimir Golschmann, the late Professor W. K. Rose, Prof. Dott. Pietro Berri, and Grace Edie.

Professor G. C. Trowsdale of the University of British Columbia, with whom I have shared an ardent interest in Pound's poetry since our student days together, was kind enough to read the entire manuscript, and it has profited enormously from his detailed observations. All this meant that the manuscript had to be typed out repeatedly, and this whole task fell to the graceful hands of Mrs. Judy Barker, who combined digital celerity with an endearing smile that did much to brighten the days of the moody editor. Beverly Matsu also assisted during the final weeks of typing and checking. Financial assistance for preparation of the manuscript is acknowledged gratefully to the President's Research Fund of Simon Fraser University.

It remains to thank the person most responsible for this book, James Laughlin. Not only was it his idea in the first place, but his perpetual kindness and encouragement enlivened the work from start to finish.

R. M. S<small>CHAFER</small>

INTRODUCTION
The Music in Pound's Poetry[1]

In one of the poet's earliest poems there is a line,

> And viol strings that outsing kings,

which reproduces precisely the silver resonance of the viol string under the bow. A viol is not a violin or a cello, and Pound knew it. He listened.

Pound had always been associated in one way or another with music. He wrote much criticism, including some extremely important remarks on harmony as well as on the relationship of music to poetry. He is the author of an aesthetic known as Great Bass which, taking its roots in music, has multiple significance for all the arts. He is also the composer of several pieces of music, including an opera, *Le Testament,* which, if better known, would have been one of the most controversial pieces of music of its epoch. And all these things had a profound influence on his poetry, both in its sound and in its shape and structure.

A poet's attitude to music will be conditioned by his profession. He will come at music through the word, through *melopoeia,* as Pound called it. He distinguished three kinds of poetry: *logopoeia,* roughly poetry of ideas and precise expression; *phanopoeia,* poetry of images; and *melopoeia,* "wherein the words are charged, over and above their plain meaning, with some musical property, which

---

[1] The Introduction is in large measure a reworking of my essay "Ezra Pound and Music," from *The Canadian Music Journal,* Summer, 1961, pp. 15–43.

directs the bearing or trend of that meaning."[2] This is an early distinction, of course, and while in the *Cantos* all three forms interpenetrate greatly, in the early poetry they achieve more unilateral individuality. He remarks further that in *melopoeia* we find "a force tending often to lull, or to distract the reader from the exact sense of the language. It is poetry on the borders of music and music is perhaps the bridge between consciousness and the unthinking sentient or even insentient universe."[3]

It is rare when a poet gets beyond appreciating music as just one feature in the poetic universe. His interest in *pure* music is generally limited, often nonexistent. In this respect Pound is exceptional, for he came to appreciate the value of much music which has nothing to do with poetry: Vivaldi's concerti, for instance, or the sonatas of Mozart. And in the case of Vivaldi he appreciated their value long before most musicians. This understanding, however, probably came with his middle years, for he speaks of "pure" music much more frequently in his *Guide to Kulchur* (1938) than in earlier critical writings. Previously, he had been dedicated to the idea that in order to ensure the highest fruition of both arts, music and poetry must in some way be wedded together.

Music may have two kinds of relationship to poetry: it may figure as an accompaniment to words, a means of giving them delineation and vitality; or it may provide an extension of communication, an attempt to get beyond or under verbal language. Its service is then mood painting, suggestive propaganda for the poetic idea. These views are not compatible, and it is natural that while the poet clings to the former, in which the words control the situation, the musician approaches the latter. The first tradition comes down as far as the time of the troubadours and Minnesinger, when with occasional exceptions it promptly disappears. Pound's early inclinations drew him quickly to the perfect blending of *motz el son* which was the troubadours' art, and he argued vehemently for this natural symbiosis of the arts. "It is not intelligent to ignore the fact," he wrote, "that both in Greece and in Provence the poetry attained its highest rhythmic and metrical brilliance at times when the arts of verse and music were most closely knit together, when each thing done by the poet had some definite musical urge or necessity bound up within it."[4] Elsewhere he remarked that "... the divorce of the two arts had been to the

[2] Ezra Pound, *Literary Essays*, New York and London, 1954, p. 25.
[3] *Ibid.*, p. 26.
[4] *Ibid.*, p. 91.

advantage of neither, and that melodic invention declined simultaneously and progressively with their divergence. The rhythms of poetry grew stupider, and they in turn affected or infected the musicians who set poems to music."[5]

Pound is probably right when he asserts that technical brilliance in poetry stimulated invention in music, for the Provençal musicians, under the spell of their richly varied texts, produced an equal variety of song forms, standing in high contrast to the stereotyped forms of later periods when composers were content with second-rate verse. In any case, it is easy to lament the passing of that exquisite blending of *motz el son* of the troubadours, for nowhere since have we seen such an unstrained and selfless tradition of artistic dependence and interplay. The divorce of the arts may even have been to poetry's disadvantage, but one could offer no plausible argument that music did not benefit by its freedom. In fact, it was only through the discovery of the motif as an abstractable idea in itself, independent of words or anything else, that true possibilities for musical inventiveness were opened up. The whole physiognomy of the art of music as we know it today may be traced to this discovery. It was a selfish gesture, but it led to achievements which could never have been realized if words and music had always been chained together, matching forces for the same end. Where it would have once been unthinkable to debate the pre-eminence of the arts in collaboration, today there are hierarchies.

Pound expressed his view of the perfect song: "The perfect song occurs when the poetic rhythm is in itself interesting, and when the musician augments, illuminates it, without breaking away from, or at least without going too far from, the dominant cadences and accents of the words, when the ligatures illustrate the verbal qualities, and when the little descants and prolongations fall in with the main movements of the poem."[6] There are few enough examples of successful songs of this kind today. Tagore's music to his *Gitanjali* is one and Pound's settings of Villon's words is another; both, therefore, by poets. Against this, a composer looks at a poem as a stimulant for a discharge of lyrical music. If his work is to be successful as music, many subtleties of the poetry will have to be overlooked. The composer tries to capture the essence of the poem, but verbal details will be subordinated to musical invention. Many contemporary com-

---

[5] *Criterion*, March, 1924, p. 321.
[6] *The New Age*, November 7, 1918, p. 12.

posers have expressed this view. Schoenberg, for example, confessed that for many years he had not known, had not even been curious about, the texts of his favorite Schubert songs. Yet he believed he understood the content of the songs as well as or better than if he had known the words, a perfect case of the view that music goes beyond verbal language. It is worth reminding ourselves how uneven the balance is in what is today taken to be the perfect song, for certainly no one will dispute that Schubert's melodies are more memorable than Müller's or Rellstab's or even Goethe's words.

This does not imply that the arts cannot, should not profit from interplay, or that an intimate understanding of another art will not benefit an artist in the execution of his own. Pound believes that the poet can learn from music. He puts it bluntly: "Poets who will not study music are defective."[7] He asserts that "poets should never be too long out of touch with musicians"; and this, to the credit of his poetry, Pound never was. In fact, since the scattering of the arts probably no poet has profited so much from an intimate study of musical phrasing, forms, and rhythm—not metronomic rhythm, but the individual rhythm of masterpieces that adjusts itself according to the demands of the material, which Pound was to call *absolute rhythm* and incorporate in his theory of Great Bass. Obviously other poets have been influenced by musical sounds, but few have been influenced to such an extent by musical shapes. None has understood so well the real significance of musical forms and the literary uses that might be made of them. As early as 1912, he had written that he was attempting "to compose in the sequence of the musical phrase."[8] During this period he was intimately involved with his Provençal studies. Provençal to Pound did not mean poetry alone, but rather poetry bound to music. Soon he was collaborating with Walter Morse Rummel in bringing out an edition of troubadour songs, for which Pound not only provided the English translations but actually located some of the manuscripts from which the music was drawn. This practice of working at poetry with music directly before him became an important exercise; it was by getting at the "sequence of the musical phrase" that he was led to develop the unusual verse techniques which were to release English poetry from the cramped meters and forms that had imprisoned it for so long. Possibly no poet at any

---

[7] *Literary Essays*, p. 437.
[8] *Ibid.*, p. 3.

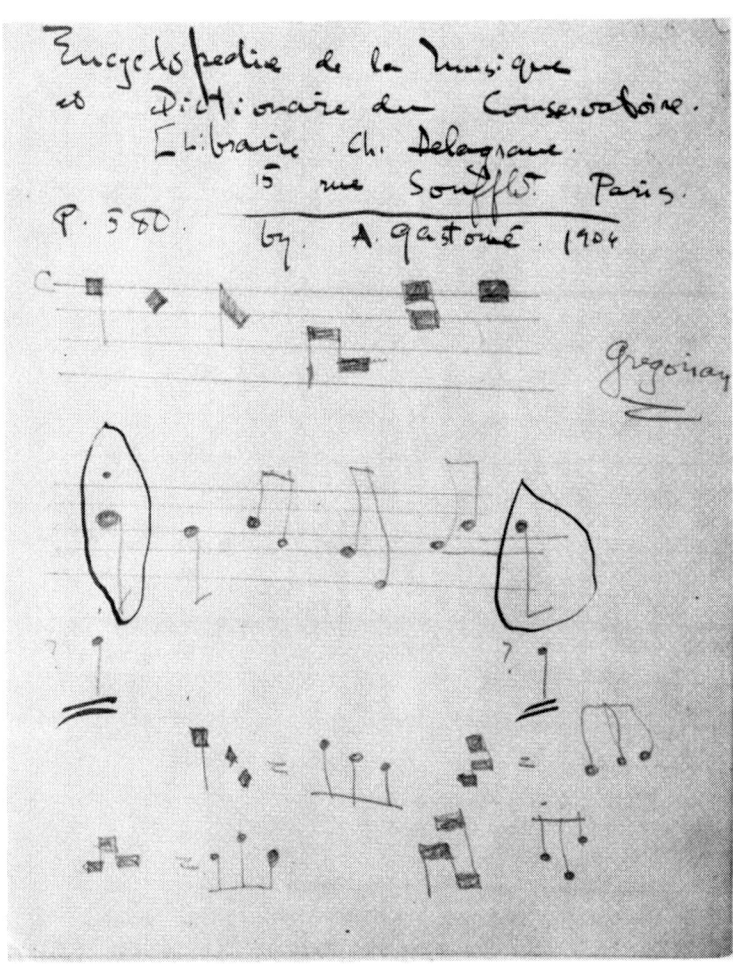

A page from one of Pound's copybooks showing how he taught himself to read medieval musical notation in preparation for his troubadour transcriptions.

An early transcription by Pound of the text and melody of a song by the troubadour Gaucelm Faidit.

time has produced the abundance of technical innovation that Pound did.

It is not surprising, therefore, that of all the troubadours Arnaut Daniel intrigued him the most. Had not Dante called him *il miglior fabbro,* praising his technical expertise? This same phrase Eliot in turn used for Pound in his dedication of *The Waste Land.* Daniel is not generally taken to be the greatest of the troubadours, at least not from the musical side, though this may be due to lack of evidence; but the service he performed for *langue d'oc* by inventing new words and constructions in many ways parallels Pound's own achievements for English verse.

Pound learned the aesthetic of sounds from Daniel; clear sounds (*l'aura amara*), opaque sounds (*sols sui qui sai lo sobrafan quem sortz*), tintinnabulations (*cadahus en son us*); and the effects to which *shaggy* rhymes (*letz, becs, mutz*) might be put by muddying the anticipated sound to produce echo or antiphony. He learned the difference of legato phrasing and stacatto, and all that lies between. Not the least, he learned the function and effectiveness of rests. His translations of Daniel's canzoni are matchless for their sound, the way they reproduce the notes of the original.

Pound studied Provençal for all it could teach him about cadence. He argued against a too exact acceptance of the rhythmic modes alleged to govern troubadour music, for surely the poetry shows no "hefty swat on alternate syllables." It was these studies, too, that made clear to him the way in which a poet might build up counterpoint, or a clever illusion of such, by playing on the memory and the residuum of sounds stored up in it through suspending, anticipating, or curtailing the expected. He speaks of this in relation to Oriental music, where the situation is analagous (and perhaps more than accidentally so, for the troubadours may well have acquired some of the complexity of their versification from Arabic models via the Crusades or North Africa).

> In especial one notes the "extraordinary" length of the rhythm pattern units [in Oriental music], comparable to the mediæval rhyme-scheme of Provençal canzos, where, for example, one finds a rhyme pattern which begins its six-ply repeat after the seventeenth different terminal sound. In this Arabian music, as in the Provençal metrical scheme, the effect of the subtler repetitions only becomes apparent in the third or fourth strophe, and then culminates in the fifth or sixth, as a sort of horizontal instead of perpendicular chord. One might call it a "sort of" counterpoint;

if one can conceive a counterpoint which plays not against a sound newly struck, but against the residuum and residua of sounds which hangs in the auditory memory.

In the two cases, Arabian music and Provençal verse, where there was no musical "harmony" and no counterpoint in Bach's sense of the word, this elaboration of echo has attained great complexity, and *can* give great delight to ears which are either "trained" to it, or which have a natural aptitude for perceiving it. In Europe this aptitude or perceptivity lasted at least until Dante's time, and prompted in him several opinions on the relative merit of Provençal artists, which have puzzled thick-eared "modern" philologists.[9]

What Pound's Provençal discoveries meant for his own verse is immediately discernible by turning to his early collections, *Personae*, *Ripostes*, and *Lustra*. Space does not permit the study one would like to make of the music in these early poems, but "Na Audiart" may be partly quoted here for its illumination of the remarks on verbal counterpoint. Note the delicate rhythms and the way a melodic refrain is built up, echoing from stanza to stanza, so that some phrases are never resolved and others are shortened, cut by an abrupt change of rhythm.

> Though thou well dost wish me ill
>   Audiart, Audiart,
> Where thy bodice laces start
> As ivy fingers clutching through
> Its crevices,
>   Audiart, Audiart
> Stately, tall and lovely tender
> Who shall render
>   Audiart, Audiart,
> Praises meet unto thy fashion?
> Here a word kiss!
>   Pass I on
> Unto Lady "Miels-de-Ben,"
> Having praised thy girdle's scope
> How the stays ply back from it;
> I breath no hope
> That thou shouldst . . .
>   Nay no whit

[9] *The New Age*, April 15, 1920, pp. 387–88.

> Bespeak thyself for anything.
> Just a word in thy praise, girl,
> Just for the swirl
> Thy satins make upon the stair,
> 'Cause never a flaw was there
> Where thy torse and limbs are met
> Though thou hate me, read it set
> In rose and gold . . .

And concluding:

> Thou wert once she
>   Audiart, Audiart,
> For whose fairness one forgave
>   Audiart,
> Audiart
>   Que be-m vols mal.

The dull quiver of the last line, a dissonant arpeggio, is reminiscent of the Minnesinger whose song comes to a premature end, owing to a broken string.

>   . . . nu hei!
> des videlaeres seite
>   der ist enzwei!

Arnaut Daniel's dexterity with complex verse forms is especially evident in the sestina, a form invented by him. Here the six-ply scheme, in which the terminal sounds are constantly reshuffled to form new patterns, creates an intensity which Pound has described as "a thin sheet of flame folding and infolding upon itself," adding that such a form can only be well judged when recited or sung. Pound revived the form in his "Sestina: Altaforte." Here a reader can gather the mood of the poem simply from the aura of the six terminal words. Their constantly shifting reiteration builds like an angry chord which comes to a crashing halt on the last word of the poem, the snarl *peace!* Here is the first stanza:

> Damn it all! all this our South stinks peace.
> You whoreson dog, Papiols, come! Let's to music!
> I have no life save when the swords clash.
> But ah! when I see the standards gold, vair, purple, opposing
> And the broad fields beneath them turn crimson,
> Then howl I my heart nigh mad with rejoicing.

Although Pound once passed an entire year writing a sonnet a day for practice, that form never became a favorite with him. He considered the sestina and the other forms used by the troubadours and Cavalcanti to be superior to the sonnet, and for musical reasons. "The sonnet occurred automatically when some chap got stuck in the effort to make a canzone."[10] He was seeking a tighter, more disciplined poetry. And after having spent so much time with Arnaut Daniel or Cavalcanti, whose "Donna mi Prega" binds fifty-two out of every one hundred fifty-four syllables together into a pattern, it is not surprising that he was impatient with anything as rhythmically unbending as the sonnet.

It is important that Pound, in revitalizing old forms, should have emphasized their singability. He was familiar with many of the original melodies of the Provençal lyrics he translated or adapted. One or two of his poems, like "Winter is icummen in" ("Ancient Music"), show that, like Goethe, he worked side by side with music, following its meter and inflexion.[11] If there is any contemporary poetry ready-made for retransposition into song, it is Pound's early work; and it is both surprising and regrettable that it has not attracted more attention from composers.

There is a kind of poetry which, though thoroughly musical, cannot take song. To be set to music, verse must be versatile, for song attentuates it and blunts its articulation. Song also imposes simplicity; complex ideas, uncommon words, even the most deliberate devices of verbal music, including rhyme, are largely wasted. A poem like Yeats's "Had I the heavens' embroidered cloths" ("He Wishes for the Cloths of Heaven") could not be subjected to the new time-law music imposes, for its tempo is too well-defined in the music of words alone.[12]

[10] *Literary Essays*, p. 168.
[11] In his Provençal notebooks Pound transcribed the text *and the music* as a preparation for translation; also, in his translations of songs for recitals and publications during the early London years, he worked with poetry and music before him on the same page. Fitting the rhythms of poetry to the curves of a musical line was, for him, a habit. Some time ago Loisann Oakes, in *"An Explication of 'Canto LXXV'" (Wisconsin Studies in Contemporary Literature,* Volume 5, Summer, 1964), tried to show that the lines of this Canto match the Janequin transcription which accompanies it. But in this case the results are indigestible. "Stretching the rhythm a bit or condensing it here and there," as Oakes admits has been necessary to get the article written, is indeed very un-Poundian.
[12] Pound recognized this in Joyce's poems, "All day I hear the noise of waters" and "I hear an army," for he wrote: "In both these poems we have a strength and a fibrousness of sound which almost prohibits the thought of their being 'set to music' or to any music but that which is in them when spoken. . . ." *Literary Essays*, p. 415.

By the time Pound had composed "Mauberley" he had reached a similar stage, and from here on it becomes increasingly difficult to imagine his verse in song (though naturally with the odd strong exception, such as the latter part of Canto LXXXI). In "Mauberley" Pound's language reaches such precision and his motivating ideas are so elaborate that there is no question of setting any part of it to music. The shapes defy attenuation or readjustment; the intricate rhythms and rhymes—English against Greek or medieval French—would be quite lost in song. Hugh Kenner says that Pound "asks for complex acts of discernment, not for immolation."[13] *Mauberley* is the first poem of which this is wholly true. It is not a mood piece, but a word-jewel cut clear and hard. Nothing in it wobbles; there are no loose ends.

If most musical devices in poetry lose their point in song, the one exception is rhythm. Every composer knows the values of a line in which the arrangement of tensions and relaxations is so precise, so true to the ideas it expresses, that it suggests its own music effortlessly. Pound's sense of rhythm has been called his greatest gift, and the service he did English verse by uprooting iambic pentameter and offering innumerable alternatives has perhaps had an indirect significance for contemporary music.

It ought to be possible to show that verse meters and patterns have at all times influenced the music of composers interested in song. Certainly the iambic meter was so much a part of the poetical mores of English-speaking peoples that it shaped not only the phrasing of sophisticated art songs, but even that of the blues! Just as certainly the contemporary composer's interest in asymmetrical texts, in order to attain freedom for his vocal line, may be largely traced to the *vers libre* adventure in poetry.

It may take careful and repeated reading of Pound's early work to become persuaded that it is not merely an exhibition of brute force, and one can well understand why his early critics found Pound a disturbance; for while there was no denying the charm of a line like

> Eyes, dreams, lips and the night goes . . . ,

the critics were confounded by its lawlessness. Pound has said he does not believe anyone could use to advantage rhythms more subtle than those he has used. Even when he works within the limits of the iamb, scarcely two lines measure alike.

[13] Hugh Kenner, *The Poetry of Ezra Pound*, Norfolk, Connecticut, and London, 1951, p. 20.

Early critics of Pound were slow to realize that rhythm is not something to be imposed on poetry, but rather something demanded by poetry in its material and situations. With his *vers libre* Pound forced this issue. To the old schools *vers libre* was an escape from discipline; to the new it was an added discipline, for it meant divining the precise meter and shape of each individual poetic thought. The shapes of his lines, their disposition on the page, the placing of punctuation and spaces, were all as much ubiquitous concerns with Pound as the craftsmanship of ryhming. When he breaks up the shape of verse, the impact is oral as well as visual. In the opening of "Provincia Deserta"—

>   At Rochecoart,
>   Where the hills part
>   in three ways, . . .

—we have the outlines of the hills traced on the page, and any reader will instinctively make the appropriate divisions in the tempo of his reading as well.

And what would be the proper tempo for reciting the three-line poem "Papyrus" where we are left to invent on our own?

>   Spring . . .
>   Too long . . .
>   Gongula . . .

If, as Stravinsky suggested, there are two kinds of musical time, one running with the clock and one running counter to it or away from it, this is also true for poetry, and especially true for Pound's. One must turn to the later *Cantos* for the most accomplished examples of this.

>   Here are lynxes   Here are lynxes,
>   Is there a sound in the forest
>   of pard or of bassarid
>   of crotale   or of leaves moving?[14]

This is no matter of fancy typography; it is the tempo of the breathing forest.

The freer spacing of contemporary poetry has its parallel in the preponderance of rests in contemporary music. It is perhaps

[14] Canto LXXIX.

not accidental that while Pound and his associates were investing English poetry with new rhythmic life (*c.* 1910) the same service was being performed for music by Igor Stravinsky. Perhaps Pound had him in mind when he defended *vers libre* with the following words:

> No one is so foolish as to suppose that a musician using "four-four" time is compelled to use always four quarter notes in each bar, or in "seven-eighths" time to use seven eighth notes uniformly in each bar. He may use one ½, one ¼ and one ⅛ rest, or any such combination as he may happen to choose or find fitting. To apply this musical truism to verse is to employ *vers libre.*[15]

Music played a strong part in convincing Pound of the necessity of the reforms he was initiating. He had made the acquaintance of Arnold Dolmetsch (the God Pan, as he calls him), and Dolmetsch's book *The Interpretation of the Music of the XVIIth and XVIIIth Centuries* made a profound impression on him. When opposition to *vers libre* was strong he found it to his advantage to draw on remarks made by Thomas Mace, Rousseau, and Couperin to support his point that verse ought to be composed in "the sequence of the musical phrase." The regular appearance of old music on paper was a deception commented on by all theorists. As Couperin put it: ". . . we write differently from what we play." And again, ". . . I find that we confuse Time or Measure with what is called Cadence or Movement. Measure defines the quantity and equality of beats; Cadence is properly the spirit, the Soul that must be added."[16] Such remarks exposed the paradox of previous English verse techniques to the poet. Speech, which was of necessity unequal in stress and articulation, had in the highest form of poetry been constrained by arbitrary systems of quantitative meter. Music, on the other hand, which appeared equal on paper due to its awkward method of notation, came alive in performance, gaining its true freedom and *cadence.*

Thus, for Pound rhythm was not, could not be, a matter of mere footstamping. He had frequently spoken of a kind of superior rhythm which he called *absolute,* a rhythm which was part of the poetic idea itself, not a discipline over which the poem was strung.

---

[15] *Literary Essays,* p. 93.
[16] "Vers Libre and Arnold Dolmetsch," *The Egoist,* July, 1917, pp. 90–91.

> I said in the preface to my *Guido Cavalcanti* that I believed in an absolute rhythm. I believe that every emotion and every phase of emotion has some toneless phrase, some rhythm-phrase to express it.[17]

James Joyce has also defined rhythm in a way which emphasizes the contribution of parts to an indivisible whole.

> Rhythm ... is the first formal esthetic relation of any part to part in any esthetic whole or of an esthetic whole to its part or parts or of any part to the esthetic whole of which it is a part.[18]

Both poets are concerned with the function of rhythm in form; thus each has in turn been led to apotheosize music as the art in which rhythm is purest and assumes its greatest responsibility in building form. In fact, no poets of any period have shown such a keen interest in putting musical techniques to work for their own art as have Joyce and Pound, though of course each has achieved this in his own way.

It might be advisable at this point to note a distinction in the kind of form each art exhibits. Music, as an abstract art, turns inward, seeking its precise definition through self-exploration; its ideas are rotated, superimposed, and extended in an attempt to balance them convincingly. In literature all abstract ideas must be externalized, that is, turned loose to register on nature and society. It is this essential difference that has shaped the principles of form peculiar to each art. Repetition in music is both necessary as a mnemonic aid and desirable as a method of achieving balance. Literature, on the other hand, is through-composed, gaining its coherence through narration, action, and characterization. The refrain in poetry could never be as relentless as it often is in music, for the reason that it arrests the natural growth and development of the work.

Joyce's most concentrated attempt to utilize the formal techniques of music occurs in the "Sirens" chapter of *Ulysses*. Before the chapter opens two pages of fragments from what is to follow are given. Taken alone they are meaningless and have purely

---

[17] Ezra Pound, *Gaudier-Brzeska: A Memoir* (New York, 1970, p. 84). Hugh Kenner points out that the phrase *absolute rhythm* may have been suggested to Pound by Rémy de Gourmont's *Le Latin mystique*. Although the precise phrase does not occur there, this is indeed a plausible suggestion (see Appendix I).
[18] James Joyce, *Portrait of the Artist as a Young Man*, New York, 1928, p. 241.

musical or sensory value. The clanging opening, "Bronze by gold heard the hoofirons, steelyringing,"[19] is quickly followed by a kind of muscle-bound mumble, "Imperthnthn thnthnthn." Other notes are sounded, "Jingle jingle jaunted jingling," and the dulcimer of this is smothered by, "Boomed crashing chords. When love absorbs. War! War! The tympanum." As the chapter unfolds each sound is given context and meaning. Thus the clatter of hooves and marching feet of the vice-regal procession is followed by Blazes Boylan's jaunting car carrying him to his rendezvous with Molly Bloom, while in the pub Ben Dollard's bombarding piano chords accompany Simon Dedalus' rendition of "When love absorbs my ardent soul." There are cross references and overlappings of these sixty-odd introductory fragments, producing a polyphonic effect that makes for a vivid illustration of the kind of verbal counterpoint Pound has spoken of. Going a step further, Stuart Gilbert has built up an elaborate study of the "Sirens" episode as a *fuga per canonem;* but I suspect Mr. Gilbert's otherwise excellent study of *Ulysses* has been betrayed here by his musical virginity.[20] If we are to take the opening fragments as subjects and countersubjects, we must then expect them to behave as normal fugal subjects and countersubjects do; that is, to exercise complete control over all the ensuing situations. As it is, Joyce's fragments contribute strongly to the flavor of the chapter, but no one could say that the important developments in the "Sirens" is the jingle of Boylan's jaunting car or Ben Dollard's gusty keyboard performance.

The problem resolves itself, I think, to this: is a fugal subject a heterogeneous collection of notes or is it an idea? If it is more than a collection of notes, then it must be the basic motivating power in everything that develops from it. Joyce undeniably creates the illusion of musical timbre and texture in the "Sirens" episode, but this should not be mistaken for musical form. No art has a monopoly over its terminology, but once defined by practice, the meaning of terms should be respected by all who take them over. Too much literary criticism has been written in recent years in which musical terms have been used casually or inaccurately.

---

[19] James Joyce, *Ulysses,* New York, 1934, and London, 1937, p. 242 *et seq.*
[20] Joyce himself referred to the "Sirens" episode as a fugue. See his letter to Harriet Weaver, August 6, 1919. Whether Joyce ever discussed his fugal concept with Pound is not known; but Pound refers to it in a letter to Joyce (June 10, 1919), in which he criticizes the chapter, pointing out obliquely that the climax with which it ends is contrary to the nature of the fugue.

Pound himself claimed his *Cantos* would display the structure of a Bach fugue.[21] He declared to Yeats that there was to be no plot to the *Cantos*, "no chronicle of events, no logic of discourse, but two themes, the descent into Hades from Homer, a metamorphosis from Ovid, and mixed with these, medieval or modern historical characters."[22] This means that when introduced the themes may have little significance, may in fact be as unassuming as many of Bach's fugue subjects, but that with each subsequent re-entry they would be progressively revealed until they stand consolidated at the end of the vast tapestry of events and reflections. It seems to me that Pound is more correct in applying the term *fugue* to his work, for despite the externalization of his themes, they themselves remain unchanged throughout the long poem. There are also subsidiary motifs, but they too remain intact: the usury motif, for example (and incidentally, has anyone else managed to treat the question of money with such cunning that the didactic intent is indivisible from its verbal lyricism?), or the lengthy stretches of the "Thrones" *Cantos* dominated by variants of the line, "The temple is not for sale," enforced by its ideogram. These are truly like the subjects of Bach's fugues; ideas, not mere profusions of sound.[23]

This is not to disparage Joyce's gifts of minstrelsy, but only to make clear the essential difference in the approach of each poet to music. Joyce's musicianship ran more to details, to isolated sounds. He was interested in the tinkle of words. He was like Helmholtz listening to his tuning fork. His gift was for charging individual words with an expansive power to hang on bell-like in the auditive memory.[24] Although his musical devices were numberless, the majority had to do with single words or pairs of words: alliteration, assonances, onomatopoeia, neologisms, infixes,

---

[21] There are numerous stray comments along this line from conversations and letters. One illustration will do, from a letter to John Lackay Brown (April, 1937): "Take a fugue: theme, response, contrasujet. *Not* that I mean to take an exact analogy of structure." *Vide*, incidentally, Zukofsky's experiment, possibly suggested by my having stated the *Cantos* are in a way fugal.

[22] W. B. Yeats, *A Packet for Ezra Pound*, Dublin, 1929, p. 17.

[23] The latest word on this subject is Stephen Adams's "Are the *Cantos* a Fugue?" (*University of Toronto Quarterly*, 45, Fall, 1975) in which a more restrained argument is put forward.

[24] This is most true of *Finnegans Wake*, the first book created for the phonograph. Pound realized this when he wrote of the author: "He has sat within the grove of his thought, he has mumbled things to himself, he has heard his voice on the phonograph and thought of sound, sound, mumble, murmur." ("E.E. Cummings Alive," *The New English Weekly*, London, December 20, 1934, pp. 210-11.)

morphologies, spoonerisms, anagrams, palindromes, to name only a few of the most obvious, are all of this kind.

A lot has been made of Joyce's musicianship, so much in fact that it is sometimes supposed he was in reality a brilliant musician who strayed over into language. Actually, Joyce's musical interests were elementary and got little beyond Puccini and John McCormack. If he composed a song or two, as he is said to have done, they must certainly have been of that rather bathetic Irish variety of parlor song.[25]

It is interesting to compare Joyce's musical tastes with Pound's, for the latter poet's are much more sophisticated. Janequin, Vivaldi, Bach, Mozart, Dowland, Bartók, and Antheil rank among his enthusiasms. If we leave out the minstrels, we see that all the others were great musical craftsmen, master builders of their art. As remarked earlier, such an advanced musical taste is rare among poets, but Pound had special reasons for paying close attention to the best in music. His theory of absolute rhythm governs the proportion of the elements of masterpieces; a second concept, that of Great Bass, links the elements into an indivisible whole.

Pound does not imply a bass in the present-day musical sense of the word, but rather a basis which exists like the keel line of a ship, exercising centripetal pull over everything above it. It, too, is a temporal, not a formal concept; or more correctly, a temporal concept governing the form. Its rudiments were formulated as early as the preface to his Cavalcanti translations of 1910, where he had said: "... it should be possible to show that any given rhythm implies about it a complete form, fugue, sonata. I cannot say what form, but a form perfect, complete. Ergo, the rhythm set in a line of poetry connotes its symphony which, had we a little more skill, we could score for orchestra." In the *Guide to Kulchur* Pound deals with Great Bass more comprehensively, this time stressing its musical roots.

> The wobbling about by deficient musicians, the attempt to give life to a piece by abundant rallentandos and speedings up, results in reduction of all music to one doughy mass and all compositions to the one statement of the performing executant, said wobbly time is due to their NOT divining the real pace of the segment.

---

[25] Padraic Colum writes me that Joyce did in fact make a setting of Yeats's poem, "Who will go drive with Fergus now?" ("Who Goes with Fergus?"), but that this appears to have been lost.

> The 60, 72, or 84, or 120 per minute is a BASS, or basis. It is the bottom note of the harmony.[26]

Great Bass, therefore, is the exact tempo at which masterpieces must be performed or assimilated. It is not a tempo imposed on the elements; it is demanded by them. It is Great Bass that indicates to us the proper tempo of Bach's unedited fugues. It is Great Bass, too, that defines the pace and form of Pound's *Cantos*, for these are not, it cannot be emphasized too strongly, two features, but are one and the same thing. This can only be fully grasped by illustration. Examples are numerous and one may go right to the beginning. Cantos I and II are enacted against a backdrop of seascape. Its presence is ubiquitous and provides both the movement and the shape of the expression. Canto I (a paraphrase of Book XI of the *Odyssey*) begins:

> And then went down to the ship,
> Set keel to breakers, forth on the godly sea, and
> We set up mast and sail on that swart ship,
> Bore sheep aboard her, and our bodies also
> Heavy with weeping, and winds from sternward
> Bore us out onward with bellying canvas,
> Circe's this craft, the trim-coifed goddess.

The strong sweep of the waves carries us off right at the outset. In the sixth line the ship rolls slightly on the word "bellying." During both cantos the subsequent transformations of the water under the keel are always audible, whether they are described or not. In Canto II a stronger wind seems to have caught the sail. The lines are shorter, often ending in one-syllable words to mark the swifter pace.

> Ship stock fast in sea-swirl,
> Ivy upon the oars, King Pentheus,
>   grapes with no seed but sea-foam,
> Ivy in scupper-hole.

But at the conclusion of Canto II a remarkable transformation comes over the water at dusk.

> Then quiet water,
>   quiet in the buff sands,

---

[26] Ezra Pound, *Guide to Kulchur*, New York, 1952, and London, 1960, p. 233.

> Sea-fowl stretching wing-joints,
> > splashing in rock-hollows and sand-hollows
> In the wave-runs by the half-dune;
> Glass-glint of wave in the tide-rips against sunlight,
> > pallor of Hesperus,
> Grey peak of the wave,
> > wave, colour of grape's pulp,
>
> Olive grey in the near,
> > far, smoke grey of the rock-slide,
> Salmon-pink wings of the fish-hawk
> > cast grey shadows in water,
> The tower like a one-eyed great goose
> > cranes up out of the olive-grove,
>
> And we have heard the fauns chiding Proteus
> > in the smell of hay under the olive-trees,
> And the frogs singing against the fauns
> > in the half-light.
> And . . .

The fact that actual music does make an appearance in the *Cantos* should surprise no one. In the second of the *Pisan Cantos*, Janequin's celebrated motet, *Les Oiseaux*, is reproduced in an arrangement for violin. The circumstances should be kept in mind. The scene of the *Pisan Cantos* is Italy at the end of the war. The stench of war has just given way to the arrogance of the victors. Yet through it all comes the clear, incisive voice of the poet.

> > As a lone ant from a broken ant-hill
> from the wreckage of Europe, ego scriptor.

Then he is joined by another voice, then by many voices. It is the inextinguishable sound of Janequin's birds. They are perched on the telegraph wires above his cage. From the word we have been drawn over to music with a movement almost imperceptible. A further slight stir and we are drawn over into the fascinating world of Pound's own music, but that is a story in itself, and it will be told in another volume.

The *Cantos* have aroused criticism. They are said to lack form. Perhaps what they lack is the kind of form with which the literary critic is familiar. I have suggested they might be better appreciated by measuring them against musical forms, especially the fugue. Strictly speaking, the fugue is not a form at all, but rather a procedure. Unlike the sonata, where the length and shape of the exposition determines the development and recapitulation sections, the fugue regenerates itself constantly from its own motivic material, according to the invention of the composer. And it is judged by the craftsmanship of its texture rather than the boldness of its form. Certainly nothing like the tripartite structure of Dante's *Divina Commedia* ever emerges from the *Cantos,* and the final drift into oblivion of the fragments up to Canto CXX is very discouraging for the critic who wants to see a structure he can draw on the blackboard.

The fugue can end anywhere. Not with a cadencing chain of fireworks, not with climax, as Pound knew when he criticized Joyce's "Sirens" episode from *Ulysses;* rather with an unpretentious device, often as brief as half a bar—the pedal. When the pedal sounds in the fugue, we know the composer is getting tired and intends to stop. In the notes for Canto CXVII we encounter a confession we have for some time been expecting.

> M'amour, m'amour
>   what do I love and
>   where are you?
> That I lost my center
>   fighting the world.
> The dreams clash
>   and are shattered—
> and that I tried to make a paradiso
>   terrestre.

It is a confession of humility and failure. A tired old man has decided to give up the fight. A pedal point? And as with Bach, who never lived to complete *The Art of the Fugue,* the final cadence is a reverberant silence.

1
England: The Early Reviews 1908–1917

In 1908 Pound made his way from Venice, where he had just published his first book of poems, *A Lume Spento,* to London, where for the next dozen years he was to make whatever living he could writing columns and reviews for an assortment of periodicals on a variety of subjects. Among these activities music criticism grew to be a special preference. The young poet had few credentials for the job. He had not had the benefit of very much music in his family or school background, and he never did pick up enough skill in the subject to protect himself from occasional serious blunders of fact; but there is, over the years, a growing certainty of what he felt the function of music to be and enough general understanding, picked up from his many musical friends, to fill his reviews with numerous discussions of the subject at a level well above that of which most big-paper journalists are capable.

London was a center of world importance in literature when Pound arrived there, but such claims could hardly be made for its musical life. Then, as now, London concert life was vigorous and variegated, but the main thrusts of new musical thought were arising in Paris and Vienna, and affected London only tangentially. It is true, British music had recently been raised to new levels by Edward Elgar, whose Symphony in A-flat was given its première the year Pound arrived in London. Elgar had undoubtedly restored the confidence of the British in the value of their own creative abilities, not only by capturing performances in Europe and America (a thing few other Britishers had achieved) but also by making it possible for young, creatively endowed Englishmen who followed him—Pound's contemporaries—to think of themselves as composers and not merely as musicians who composed. But Elgar's vision was firmly rooted in the traditional schools of the German masters. It was a type of music-making which never won Pound's interest, even when Vaughan Williams, John Ireland, and the others, whose music the young critic heard frequently, attempted to modernize these traditions by coupling them with British folklore and with the more advanced orchestral scoring techniques of the French impressionists. In his musical tastes as well as his literary tastes, Pound inclined even then to the medieval (unknown to the British musicians of that time) and the modern, the best of which was at that time unknown to Pound. It was only later, when he made the important friendships of Arnold Dolmetsch and George Antheil, that he was able to become a well-informed spokesman for these two edges of the avant-garde.

Pound also loved the Elizabethans, particularly for their high achievement in song; but he was quickly to discover that Lawes and Campion were by no means concert material in prewar London.

> There is no copy of Henry Lawes' three volumes of "Ayres and Dialogues" at the little second-hand music shop in Great Turnstile, but the kindly proprietor is good enough to look up old sale catalogues. The last set went for £49. Dolmetsch's arrangement of some of this music is out of print. Only in a nation utterly contemptuous of its past treasures and inspired by a rancorous hatred of good music could this state of affairs be conceivable. I have bought Waller's poems for a shilling. Yet Lawes' position in English music is proportionally much more important than Waller's position among English poets. (*The New Age,* June 5, 1919)

What London did offer was a plethora of concerts and recitals of main-line repertoire by the oustanding artists of the day. The famous Promenade Concerts had been launched in 1895 in the Queen's Hall. The Queen's Hall, which has been described as "the color of the belly of a London mouse," must have been frequented by Pound from time to time, if only because it was here that the most important orchestral concerts were given. "One retains vivid memories," Robert Elkin was later to write, "of the mirrors all around the stalls, the medallions of famous composers at the sides of the platform, a great deal of ornamentation, and a rather depressing color scheme (largely gray and terracotta), only somewhat relieved by the Venetian red of the seats, carpets, and lampshades."[1] One of the Queen's Hall highlights of these years was the February, 1913, English première of Scriabin's *Prometheus*, repeated the following year with the composer at the piano. Scriabin was at that time enjoying considerable success in London. He had given numerous piano recitals there, and in 1910 Serge Koussevitzky had given the première of his *Poème d'Extase*. We know that Pound must have heard this work for he comments on it bitterly in one of his *New Age* columns. Another composition of historical importance made less impression on the Queen's Hall audience; this was Schoenberg's *Five Pieces for Orchestra* (Opus 16), premièred in 1912 and conducted in 1913 by the composer himself. The London première of Ravel's *Valses Nobles et Sentimentales* was also given in 1913, and the same composer's *Pavane pour une Infante Défunte, Introduction and Allegro,* and *Rhapsodie Espagnole* had already been given in the years between 1907 and 1911. Bartók's music had been performed in London as early as 1914, and Stravinsky's *Le Sacre du Printemps* was given as a ballet in 1913 as part of Sir Thomas Beecham's Russian Season. Debussy, of course, had also been performed frequently in London, often also by Beecham. How many of these important pieces of literature Pound may have heard at that time we do not know, for although Omar Pound, the poet's son, has a note from Sir Thomas Beecham permitting the poet free access to all his rehearsals, there is certainly no evidence in the first music reviews to suggest that any of this music, if heard at all, made any special impression. On August 29, 1916, Pound wrote to Iris Barry, "My present pinnacle is sponged stalls at the Beecham opera. Malheureusement." At this time he had just undertaken a translation of the libretto of Massenet's *Cinderella* for the Beecham company, but though he completed it by the end of the year, it was never used.

He spent more time in the small recital halls, such as the Steinway, Bechstein (later Wigmore), and the Aeolian, where he could hear solo recitals by singers and instrumentalists. Of these Bechstein Hall, seating about six hundred, seems to have grown to be a special favorite. A contemporary account of the Aeolian and Bechstein halls states that throughout the entire concert season they were occupied twice daily by recitals, giving us an idea of the volume of the traffic.

[1] Robert Elkin, *Queen's Hall 1893–1941*, London, 1944, p. 18.

Aside from these concerts, there were the innumerable soirées given in drawing rooms of private homes, followed by supper. Pound seems to have attended a good many of these, for some of the artists he later reviewed frequently, such as Stroesco and Cernikoff, seem to have appeared more frequently in these surroundings than on the stage. A contemporary of the poet recalls him at such functions during these years, coughing critically—"he had a frightfully sharp cough"—and explaining expansively during the intervals how the compositions should have been performed by blocking the air vigorously with his arms and hands.

Fully at home with singers, Pound was always ambivalent about pianists. He had many of them as close friends, even though the piano repertoire never interested him much. His first apparent interest in music after his arrival in Europe was a short letter he wrote on June 21, 1908, to the Paris edition of *The New York Herald* concerning his American friend, the pianist Katherine Ruth Heyman.

> *The Event of the Coming Piano Season*
> Katherine Ruth Heyman, whose American tournée is predicted as the event of the coming piano season there, may give certain concerts in Paris on her way West.
> Her playing in London before sailing is also to be announced.
> E. P. Venice

This was followed on December 8, 1908, by a poem, celebrating one of Miss Heyman's Venetian concerts, which he submitted to the *Evening Standard and St. James Gazette* of London.

> Blue-grey and white and white-of-rose
> The flowers of the West's fore-dawn unclose.
> I feel the dusky softness whirr
> Of colour, as upon a dulcimer
> "Her" dreaming fingers lay between the tunes,
> As when the living music swoons,
> But does not quite, because of love of us—
> Knowing our state, how that 'tis troublous—
> It will not die to leave us desolate.[2]

The poem "Scriptor Ignotus" from *A Lume Spento* is also dedicated to Katherine Ruth Heyman. She was fifteen years Pound's

---

[2] This poem was included in Pound's second volume of verse, *A Quinzaine for This Yule* (1908), under the title "Nel Biancheggiar."

senior and a notable interpreter of the music of Scriabin. Among her papers is a note reading "Pound 1904," presumably referring to their first meeting in the United States. When they met again in Venice, Pound acted for a time as her manager. She must have provided him with some introductions in London, for he later wrote to Iris Barry (August 29, 1916), "I entered London more or less under her wing." In the same letter he jokes about his managerial duties for Miss Heyman in Venice. From her book *The Relation of Ultramodern to Archaic Music* (Boston, 1921), one gathers that the pianist and the poet must have had much in common, notably an enthusiasm for old music and an awareness of the differences between rhythm and meter in art, and the pre-eminence of the former.[3]

Throughout his life Pound experienced a restless love-hate relationship with the piano. Though he repeatedly denounced the instrument, as will become evident, he nevertheless cultivated the friendship of numerous excellent pianists. One of the most notable of his early musical acquaintances was the Franco-German pianist Walter Morse Rummel, whom he seems to have met first about 1908, perhaps through an introduction by Kitty Heyman, and whom he saw frequently during the early London years. "I lived with Rummel several times for months at a stretch in Paris," (letter to Iris Barry, August 29, 1916). In 1912 he collaborated with Rummel on a collection of troubadour songs, for which he not only provided English translations but located some of the original musical material.[4] Rummel was a pianist of great distinction in his day. A German by birth, he developed an un-

---

[3] When Pound drew up a "Preliminary Announcement for the College of Arts," (*The Egoist*, November, 1914), Katherine Ruth Heyman was listed as a member of the music staff, together with Arnold Dolmetsch. Other teachers were to include Wyndham Lewis and Edward Wadsworth in painting, Gaudier-Brzeska in sculpture, and Mrs. Dolmetsch in dance. Faubion Bowers has put together an affectionate article on Katherine Ruth Heyman in which he describes her relationship with Pound. (See: "Memoir within Memoirs," *Paideuma*, Vol. 2 No. 1, 1973, pp. 53–66.)

[4] Rummel's collection was published in 1913 simultaneously by Augener (London), Max Eschig (Paris), and the Boston Music Company (Boston), under the title: *Haesternae* [sic] *Rosae, Serta II, Neuf Chansons de troubadours des XIIième et XIIIième Siècles pour voix avec accompagnement de piano.* Adaptation française par M. D. Calvacoressi. Adaptation anglaise par Ezra Pound. In the introductory note Rummel writes: "The first volume [i.e., Serta I] is here followed by a collection of Nine Troubadour Songs of the 12th and 13th Centuries.... The two Daniel melodies are here published for the first time to the writer's knowledge, and he is indebted to Mr. Ezra Pound, M. A., for communicating them from the Milan Library. ... The writer with the help of Mr. Ezra Pound, an ardent proclaimer of the artistic side of mediaeval poetry, has given these melodies the rhythm and the ligature, the character which,

common insight into French keyboard music, and became an intimate of Debussy's circle, giving the première of Debussy's "Twelve Studies" in 1916, to the approval of the composer. It is obviously to Rummel that we may ascribe Pound's leniency toward this composer whose artistic philosophy was so unlike his own. To Rummel's playing Pound dedicated his "Maestro di Tocar" in *Canzoni*.

> You, who are touched not by our mortal ways . . .
> Have but to lose the magic from your hands
> And all men's hearts that glimmer for a day,
> And all our loves that are so swift to flame
> Rise in that space of sound and melt away.

Richard Aldington gave a colorful account of a visit the two young men paid to Rummel's studio one spring day in 1912.

---

from an artistic point of view, seems the most descriptive of the mediaeval spirit."

Actually Rummel is mistaken; the Arnaut Daniel melodies had been published earlier by Antonio Restori in "Per la storia musicale dei Trovatori Provenzali," (*Revista Musicale Italiana*, 3, 1896).

The two Daniel melodies were located by Pound in 1906 while, as a Fellow in Romantics from the University of Pennsylvania, he visited the Ambrosiana Library in Milan. I have in my possession thirty-six photographs of troubadour material which Pound obtained at this time or shortly afterward. Most of these have been traced to the chansonnier Mss. Ambrosiana R, 71, sup., in the Milan Biblioteca Ambrosiana, and are the sources Pound mentions discussing with the philologist Emil Lévy in Canto XX. That he researched in other libraries at this time is evident from the fact that at least one of the photographs has been traced to the Biblioteca Chigiana.

The Ambrosiana R, 71, sup. has now been published in an edition by Ugo Sesini: "Le melodie trobadoriche nel Canzoniere provenzale della Biblioteca Ambrosiana," in *Studi Medievali* n. s. 12 (1939), 1–101; 13 (1940), 1–107; 14 (1941), 31–105; 15 (1942), 189ff.

Apparently it was not until 1918 that Pound heard his Rummel collaboration in performance. On January 29 he wrote to John Quinn: "I have finished my Arnaut, and now Raymonde Collignon is really going to sing the old music, the reconstructions Rummel and I made six years ago. It means a new start on the whole thing (Provençal XII Century music), and probably the resurrection of as much of it as is worth while. We've been held up for lack of a singer WITH the right equipment, intelligence, etc."

Pound's association with troubadour music was not limited to the Rummel collaboration. In 1920 he collaborated with Agnes Bedford, using the same collection of photographs as source. The texts he adapted on this occasion were not translations but arrangements of Chaucer's poetry (except for the song "Fort chant oiaz," which is his own condensed translation of Faidit's lament for Coeur de Lion). They were published as follows: *Five Troubadour Songs*, by Agnes Bedford. Original Provençal words and English words adapted by E. P. from Chaucer. Boosey and Co., London, 1920. The original manuscript of this work, together with Pound's introductory notes, is now in the Beinecke Library at Yale University.

As Rummel was in his working clothes he retired to change, and by way of passing the time Ezra started playing Debussy with one finger on the open grand piano. Suddenly Rummel, dressed only in his underclothes, rushed furiously in, shouting: "Ezra! Ezra! If you touch that piano once more I'll throw you out the window!" I expected an explosion, but Ezra merely blinked and desisted.[5]

Pound's mother had also played the piano, and as a student his friend William Carlos Williams, who played the violin, had frequently come over for sessions of family music-making around the Pound piano. Williams relates that "Ezra couldn't even carry a tune,"[6] a fact which Pound himself is quick to corroborate, for he mentions his poor singing voice frequently in letters and conversations with friends. Typical is this from a letter to Joyce, who had an excellent tenor voice: "I am glad you have got your voice, or part of it back. I have the organ of a tree toad, fortunately, for if I had been able ever to sing 'My Country tiz of Theeee,' without going off the key four times in each bar, I shd. have warbled & done no bloomin' thing else—che peccato & wot a loss to litterchure."[7]

One of Pound's earliest and closest associates in London was W. B. Yeats, with whom he was able to share his interest in music and poetry, *motz el son,* as the troubadours called it. In a letter to Lady Gregory (December 10, 1909) discussing music for one of his plays, Yeats also spoke of "this queer creature Ezra Pound, who has become really a great authority on the troubadours, [and] has I think got closer to the right sort of music for poetry than Mrs. Emery[8]—it is more definitely music with strongly marked time and yet it is effective speech. However, he can't sing as he has no voice. It is like something on a very bad phonograph."[9]

In 1911 the young medievalist began a series of articles for *The New Age* under the title *I Gather the Limbs of Osiris.* An editorial note explained: "Under this heading Mr. Pound will contribute expositions and translations in illustration of the 'New Method in Scholarship.' " Most of these articles dealt with

---

[5] Richard Aldington, *Life for Life's Sake,* London, 1968, p. 107.
[6] *The Autobiography of William Carlos Williams,* New York, 1967, p. 65.
[7] Letter of June 20, 1920, in Forrest Read, *Pound/Joyce,* New York, 1967, p. 65.
[8] Mrs. Emery, an actress, whose stage name was Florence Farr, made a reputation by reciting to the accompaniment of a Dolmetsch psaltery.
[9] *The Letters of W. B. Yeats,* London, 1954, p. 543.

the problems of translating medieval texts, though in one the columnist turned to the relationship of poetry to music, the first of a long series of ever more precise reflections on the subject.

I GATHER THE LIMBS OF OSIRIS
On Music[10]

I.

The reasons why good description makes bad poetry, and why painters who insist on painting ideas instead of pictures offend so many, are not far to seek.

I am in sympathy equally with those who insist that there is *one* art and many media, and with those who cry out against the describing of work in any particular art by a terminology borrowed from all the others. This manner of description is objectionable, because it is, in most cases, a make-shift, a laziness. We talk of the odour of music and the timbre of a painting because we think we suggest what we mean and are too lazy to undertake the analysis necessary to find out exactly what we do mean. There is, perhaps, *one* art, but any given subject belongs to the artist, who must know that subject most intimately before he can express it through his particular medium.

Thus, it is bad poetry to talk much of the colours of the sunrise, though one may speak of our lady "of rosy fingers" or "in russet clad," invoking an image not present to the uninitiated; at this game the poet may surpass, but in the matter of the actual colour he is a bungler. The painter sees, or should see, half a hundred hues and varieties, where we see ten; or, granting we are ourselves skilled with the brush, how many hundred colours are there, where language has but a dozen crude names? Even if the poet understands the subtleties of gradation and juxtaposition, his medium refuses to convey them. He can say all his say while he is ignorant of the reality, and knowledge of the reality will not help him to say it better.

I express myself clumsily, but this much remains with me as certain: that any given work of art is bad when its content could have found more explicit and precise expression through some other medium, which the artist was, perhaps, too slothful to master.

This test should set to rest the vain disputes about "psychological" and "poetic" painting. If "Beata Beatrix," which is more poetic than all Rossetti's poetry, could have occurred in any other medium but paint, then it was bad art to paint her, and the painters should stick to chromatic harmonies and proportional composition.

[10] *The New Age,* February 8, 1912, pp. 343–44.

This principle of the profundity of apprehension is the only one which can guide us through mixed or compound media; and by it we must form our judgments as to the "limitations of an art."

II.

After squandering a good deal of time and concentration on the question of the relation of poetry and music, it seems to me not only futile, but very nearly impossible, to lay down any principles whatever for the regulation of their conjunctions.

To join these two arts is in itself an art, and is no more capable of being reduced to formulæ than are the others. It is all very well for Plato to tell us that μελος is the accord of rhythm and words and music (i.e., varied pitch). We find ourselves in the same case as Aristotle when he set out to define poetics—and in view of the fact that "The Stagirite" is, by reason of his admirers, become a Shavian holiday, let us observe that he—Aristotle—never attempts to restrict the working artist; he, and Dante after him, merely enumerate the means by which former artists have been successful.

Let us then catalogue, if possible, the simplest and briefest set of rules on which we may assume that intelligent musicians and poets are alike agreed:—

First, that the words of a song sung should be intelligible.

Second, that words should not be unreasonably distorted.

Third, that the rhythm of poetry should not be unreasonably ruined by the musician setting it to music.

I say "unreasonably" because it is quite certain that, however much this distortion may horrify the poet who, having built his words into a perfect rhythm and speech-melody, hears them sung with regard to neither and with outrage to one or both; still we do derive pleasure from songs which distort words most abominably. And we do this in obedience to æsthetic laws; do it because the sense of musical period is innate in us. And because of this instinct there is deadly strife between musicians, who are usually, in the poet's sense, fools, and poets who are usually, in the musician's sense, unmusical.

When, if it ever was so, the lyre was played before the poet began his rhapsody, quantity had some vital meaning in the work. The quantity of later Greek poetry and of Latin is a convention, an imitation of models, not an interpretation of speech. If certain of the troubadours did attend to the strict relation of word and tune—*motz el son*—it was because of the strict relation between poet and composer, when they were not one and the same person. And in many an envoi we find such boast as So-and-so "made it, song and the words."

It is my personal belief that the true economy lies in making the tune first. We all of us compose verse to some sort of a tune, and if the "song" is to be sung we may as well compose to a "musician's" tune straight away. Yet no musician comes to one with a melody, but rather he comes wishing to set our words to music. And this is a far more subtle manœuvre. To set words to a tune one has but to let the musical accents fall upon words strong enough to bear them, to refrain from putting an over-long syllable under an over-short note, and to leave the word ligature rather loose; the singer does the rest quite well. One is spared all the finer workmanship which is requisite for good spoken verse. The stuff may not make good reading, but it is still finished art, suited to its purpose.

If, however, the verse is made to speak, it may have in it that sort of rhythm which not only makes music unnecessary, but which is repulsive to it; or it may have a rhythm which can, by some further mastery, be translated into a music subtler than either poetry or music would have separately attained. Or the poet may have felt a plucking of strings or a flurry of instrumental sound accompanying his words and been unable to record them, and be totally dependent on the musician for a completion of his work. And there may linger in his words some sign and trace of a hunger for this completion.

The musician working from here is apt to find barriers in the so-called "laws" of music or of verse. The obvious answer is that none of these laws are yet absolutely discerned. We do not know whether the first neumes indicated a rise or fall of voice by definite gradations of pitch, or whether they indicate simply rise or fall. The music of the troubadour period is without bars in the modern sense. There are little lines like them, but they mean simply a pause, a rest; the notes do not register differences of duration—i.e., halves, wholes, quarters are written alike. One reads the words on which the notes indubitably depended; a rhythm comes to life—a rhythm which seems to explain the music and which is not a "musician's" rhythm. Yet it is possible to set this rhythm in a musician's rhythm without, from the poet's feeling in the matter, harming it or even "altering it," which means altering the part of it to which he is sensitive; which means, again, that both poet and musician "feel around" the movement, "feel at it" from different angles. Some people "see colour" and some "line"; very few are in any way conscious of just what it is they do see. I have no desire to set up a babel of "post-impressionists in rhythm" by suggesting a kindred searching of hearts with regard to the perception of sound.

Yet it is quite certain that some people can hear and scan "by quantity," and more can do so "by stress," and fewer still feel rhythm by what I would call the inner form of the line. And it is this "inner form," I think, which must be preserved in music; it is only by mastery of this inner form that the great masters of rhythm—Milton, Yeats, whoever you like—are masters of it.

"Nel mezzo del camin di nostra vita." Let me take this as an example. Some people will find the movement repeated in—

> Eyes, dreams, lips and the night goes.

And some will find it in—

> If you fall off the roof you'll break your ankle.

Some people will read it as if it were exactly the same "shape" as the line which follows it—

> Mi ritrovai per una selva oscura.

So eminent a scholar and so noted a lover of poetry as Mr. Edmund Gardener reads the sonnets of the *Vita Nuova* as if they were bad prose, and thinks me an outrageous liar for saying so. A certain Dalmatian loose upon the town reads Dante with no sense of epic line and as if it were third-rate dramatic dialogue by the author of "La Nave." Any reporter feels at liberty to object to the way a great poet reads his verses, yet it is not reported that men tried to tell Bach or Wagner how to play their own music, or that they offer like suggestions to M. Debussy.

"Quo tandem abutere?" Can we have a more definite criterion of rhythm than we have of colour? Do we any of us really see or hear in the same register? Are we made in groups and species, some of us capable of sympathetic audition and vision? Or is Machiavelli right when he says: "L'Uomo" or "L'Umanità vive in pochi"?—"The life of the race is concentrated in a few individuals."

III. Pitch

The preceding paragraphs have had to do with rhythm; the other limb of melody is the pitch and pitch-variation, and upon this our sole query is to be whether there is in speech, as there is in music, "tone-leading." We know that certain notes played in sequence call for other notes, for a "resolution," for a "close"; and in setting words to music it is often the hunger for this sort of musical apparatus that leads the musician away from the rhythm of the verse or makes him drag out the final syllables. What I want to get at is this: in the interpreting of the hidden melody of poetry into the more manifest melody of music, are there in the words themselves "tone-leadings"? Granted a perfect accord of word and tune is attainable by singing a note to each syllable and a short or long note to short or long syllables respectively, and singing the syllable accented in verse on the note accented in the music, is there anything beyond this? Does, for instance, the voice really fall a little in speaking a vowel and nasal, and is a ligature of two notes one half-tone lower than the other and the first very short, a correct musical interpretation of such a sound as "son," "un," "cham"? And are there other such cases where a ligature is not so much distortion as explication.

Song demands now and again passages of pure sound, of notes free from the bonds of speech, and good lyric masters have given the musicians this holiday with stray nonsense lines or with "Hallelujah" and "Alba" and "Hey-nonny-nonny," asking in return that the rest of their words be left in statu.

No one man can set bounds to this sort of performance, and a full discussion of the case would fill a volume, which I have neither time nor inclination to write. The questions are, however, germane to the technique of our art.

A discussion of Arnaut Daniel's music—and Daniel is the particular slide in our microscope for the moment—would be, perhaps, too technical for these pages; but this much may be said, that his words, sung to the tunes he made for them, lose neither in beauty nor in intelligibility.

My questions may seem to be shot at random, but we are notably lacking in "song-literature," and if it is at all important to make good this deficit we must have first some consideration of the basic questions of mediation between word and tune, some close attention to the quality of our audition, some reasoning parley between the two people most concerned—the poet and the musician.

Not long after this article was written Pound discovered the man who among moderns most closely approached his ideal, the great Indian poet-musician Rabindranath Tagore. They met for the first time at a "Tagore evening" on July 7, 1912, organized by the painter William Rothenstein. Pound's enthusiasm for Tagore's poetry and his singing was uninhibited and immediate. On September 24 he wrote to Harriet Monroe, for whose magazine, *Poetry,* he was acting as foreign editor:

> Also, I'll try to get some of the poems of the very great Bengali poet, Rabindranath Tagore. They are going to be *the* sensation of the winter.... W. B. Y. is doing the introduction to them. They are translated by the author into very beautiful English prose, with mastery of cadence.[11]

[11] D. D. Paige ed., *The Letters of Ezra Pound,* New York, 1971, p. 10; London, 1951, p. 44.

The December issue of *Poetry* contained six poems from *Gitanjali* with an essay on Tagore by Pound. When the complete *Gitanjali* collection was published, Pound wrote enthusiastically about it in the *Fortnightly Review* (CXIII, March, 1913, pp. 571–79). He was quick to point out the relationship between Tagore's practices and those of the medieval poet:

> Mr. Tagore is their [the Bengalis'] great poet and their great musician as well. . . . Mr. Tagore teaches his songs and music to his jongleurs, who sing them throughout Bengal. He can boast with the best of the troubadours, "I made it, the words and the notes." Also he sings them himself, I know, for I have heard him. . . . The hundred poems in the present volume are all songs to sing. The tunes and the words are knit together, are made together. . . .[12]

Though Pound found companionship among the literary avantgarde of London during his early years there, he seems to have stayed away from the British musicians. And with good reason, for British musical minds in those days had little interest in the very new or the very old. They were spellbound by the Teutonic heritage from Bach to Brahms. Their own two leading composers, Elgar and Stanford, were cast from this mold. Their critics and historians squatted in this mainstream of musical thought and contemptuously dismissed everything outside it. Typical, for instance, is the book *The Growth of Music,* by Henry Cope Colles, chief music critic of the London *Times* in 1911, in which the music of the middle ages receives a diffident and reproachful seven pages before the reader is led forward to the "sweeter" sounds of the Renaissance. Pound's quaint interest in medieval sounds would have found precisely one pair of sympathetic ears in England at that time, and about 1914 he did, in fact, seek out their eccentric owner: Arnold Dolmetsch.

ARNOLD DOLMETSCH[13]

"I have seen the God Pan." "Nonsense." I have seen the God Pan and it was in this manner: I heard a bewildering and pervasive music mov-

---

[12] A full account of Pound's relationship with Tagore, including his disenchantment with him after his success and Nobel Prize, is chronicled in Harold M. Hurwitz's essay, "Ezra Pound and Rabindranath Tagore," *American Literature,* Vol. 36, 1964, pp. 53–63.

[13] *The New Age,* January 7, 1915, pp. 246–47. Reprinted with some minor stylistic changes in *Pavannes and Divisions,* 1918, and again in this form in *Literary Essays,* 1954.

ing from precision to precision within itself. Then I heard a different music, hollow and laughing. Then I looked up and saw two eyes like the eyes of a wood-creature peering at me over a brown tube of wood. Then someone said: Yes, once I was playing a fiddle in the forest and I walked into a wasp's nest.

Comparing these things with what I can read of the earliest and best authenticated appearances of Pan, I can but conclude that they relate to similar occurrences. It is true that I found myself later in a room covered with pictures of what we now call ancient instruments, and that when I picked up the brown tube of wood I found that it had ivory rings upon it. And no proper reed has ivory rings on it, by nature. Also, they told me it was a "recorder," whatever that is.

However, our only measure of truth is our own perception of truth. The undeniable tradition of metamorphoses teaches us that things do not remain always the same. They become other things by swift and unanalysable process. It was only when men began to mistrust the myths and to tell nasty lies about the Gods for a moral purpose that these matters became hopelessly confused. When some nasty Semite or Parsee or Syrian began to use myths for social propaganda, when the myth was degraded into an allegory or a fable, that was the beginning of the end. And the Gods no longer walked in men's gardens. The first myths arose when a man walked sheer into "nonsense," that is to say, when some very vivid and undeniable adventure befell him, and he told someone else who called him a liar. Thereupon, after bitter experience, perceiving that no one could understand what he meant when he said that he "turned into a tree," he made a myth—a work of art, that is—an impersonal or objective story woven out of his own emotion, as the nearest equation that he was capable of putting into words. That story, perhaps, then gave rise to a weaker copy of his emotion in others, until there arose a cult, a company of people who could understand each other's nonsense about the gods.

As I say, these things were afterwards incorporated for the condemnable "good of the State," and what was once a species of truth became only lies and propaganda. And they told horrid tales to little boys in order to make them be good; or to the ignorant populace in order to preserve the empire; and religion came to an end and civic science began to be studied. Plato said that artists ought to be kept out of the ideal republic, and the artists swore by their gods that nothing would drag them into it. That is the history of "civilisation," or philology or Kultur.

When any man is able, by a pattern of notes or by an arrangement of planes or colours, to throw us back into the age of truth, a certain few of us—no, I am wrong, everyone who has ever been cast back into the age of truth for one instant—gives honour to the spell which has worked, to the witch-work or the art-work, or to whatever you like to call it. Therefore I say, and stick to it, I saw and heard the God Pan; shortly afterwards I saw and heard Mr. Dolmetsch. Mr. Dolmetsch was talking volubly, and he said something very like what I have said and very different; of music, music when music commanded some 240 (or some such number of) players, and could only be performed in one or two capitals! Pepys writes, that in the Fire of London, when the people were escaping by boat on the Thames, there was scarcely a boat in which you would not see them taking a pair of virginals as among their dearest possessions.

The older journalists tell me it is "cold mutton," that Mr. Dolmetsch was heard of fifteen years ago. That is a tendency that I have before remarked in a civilisation which rests upon journalism, and which has only a sporadic care for the arts. Everyone in London over forty "has heard of" Mr. Dolmetsch, his instruments, etc. The generation under thirty may have heard of him, but you cannot be sure of it. His topical interest is over. I have heard of Mr. Dolmetsch for fifteen years, because I am a crank and am interested in such matters. Mr. Dolmetsch has always been in France or America, or somewhere I wasn't when he was. Also, I have seen broken-down spinets in swank drawing-rooms. I have heard harpsichords played in Parisian concerts, and they sounded like the scratching of multitudinous hens, and I did not wonder that pianos had superseded them. Also, I have known good musicians and have favoured divers sorts of music. And I have supposed that clavichords were things you might own if you were a millionaire; and that virginals went with citherns and citoles in the poems of the late D. G. Rossetti.

So I had two sets of adventure. First, I perceived a sound which is undoubtedly derived from the Gods, and then I found myself in a reconstructed century—in a century of music, back before Mozart or Purcell, listening to clear music, to tones clear as brown amber. And this music came indifferently out of the harpsichord or the clavichord or out of virginals or out of odd-shaped viols, or whatever they may be. There were two small girls playing upon them with an exquisite precision; with a precision quite unlike anything I have ever heard from a London orchestra. Then someone said in a tone of authority: "It is nonsense to teach people scales. It is rubbish to make them play *this* (tum, tum, tum, tum tum). They must begin to play music. Three years playing scales, that is what they tell you. How can they ever be musicians?"

It reduces itself to about this. Once people played music. It was gracious, exquisite music, and it was played on instruments which gave out the players' exact mood *and* personality. "It is beautiful even if you

37

play it wrong." The clavichord has the beauty of three or four lutes played together. It has more than that, but no matter. You have your fingers always en rapport with the strings; it is not one dab and then either another dab or else nothing, as with the piano; the music is always lying on your own finger-tips. This music was not theatrical. You played it yourself as you read a book of precision. A few people played it together. It was not an interruption but a concentration.

Now, on the other hand, I remember a healthy concert pianist complaining that you couldn't "really give" a big piano concert unless you had the endurance of an ox; and that "women couldn't, of course"; and that gradually the person with long hands was being eliminated from the pianistic world, and that only people with little, short fat fingers could come up to the technical requirements. Whether this is so or not we have come to the pianola, which is very like professional playing. And one or two people are going in for sheer pianola. They have the right spirit. They cut their rolls for the pianola itself, and make it play as if with two dozen fingers when necessary. That is better art than making a pianola imitate the music of two hands of five fingers each. But still something is lacking.

Oriental music is under debate. We say we "can't hear it." Impressionism has reduced us to such a dough-like state of receptivity that we have ceased to like concentration. No, it has not; but it has set a fashion of passivity that has held since the romantic movement. The old music went with the old instruments. That was natural. It is proper to play piano music on pianos. But in the end you find that it is no use, and that nothing less than a full orchestra is of any use.

That is the whole flaw of impressionist or "emotional" music as opposed to pattern music. It is like a drug; you must have more drug, and more noise each time, or this effect, this impression which works from the outside, in from the nerves and sensorium upon the self—is no use, its effect is constantly weaker and weaker. I do not mean that Bach is not emotional, but the early music starts with the mystery of pattern; if you like, with the vortex of pattern; with something which is, first of all, music, and which is capable of being, after that, many things. What I call emotional, or impressionist music, starts with being emotion or impression and then becomes only approximately music. It is, that is to say, something in the terms of something else. If it produces an effect, if from sounding as music it moves at all, it can only recede into the original emotion or impression. Programme music is merely a weaker, more flabby and descriptive sort of impressionist music, needing, perhaps, a guide and explanation.

Mr. Dolmetsch was, let us say, enamoured of ancient music. He found it misunderstood. He saw a beauty so great and so various that he stopped composing. He found that the beauty was untranslatable with modern instruments; he has repaired and has entirely remade "ancient instruments." The comfort is that he has done this not for a few rich faddists, as one had been led to suppose. He makes his virginals and clavichords for the price of a bad, of a very bad piano. You can have a virginal for £ 25 if you order it when he is making a dozen; and you can have a clavichord for a few pounds more, even if he isn't making more than one.

Because my interest in these things is not topical, I do not look upon this article as advertisement writing. Mr. Dolmetsch was a topic some years ago, but you are not *au courant,* and you do not much care for music, unless you know that a certain sort of very beautiful music is no longer impossible. It is not necessary to wait for a great legacy, or to inhabit a capital city in order to hear magical voices, in order to hear perfect music which does not depend upon your ability to approximate to the pianola or upon great physical strength. Of the clavichord, one can only say, very inexactly, that it is to the piano what the violin is to the bass viol.

As I believe that a certain movement in painting is capable of revitalising the instinct of design and creating a real interest in the art of painting as opposed to a tolerance of inoffensively pretty similarities of quite pretty ladies and "The Tate," the abysmal "Tate" generally, so I believe that a return, an awakening to the possibilities, not necessarily of "Old" music, but of pattern music played upon ancient instruments, is, perhaps, able to make music again a part of life, not merely a part of theatricals. The musician, the performing musician as opposed to the composer, might again be an interesting person, an artist, not merely a sort of manual saltimbanque or a stage hypnotist. It is, perhaps, a question of whether you want music, or whether you want to see an obsessed personality trying to "dominate" an audience.

I have said little that can be called technical criticism. I have perhaps implied it. There is precision in the making of ancient instruments. Men still make passable violins; I do not see why the art of beautiful-keyed instruments need be regarded as utterly lost. There has been precision in Mr. Dolmetsch's study of ancient texts and notation; he has routed out many errors. He has even, with certain help, unravelled the precision of ancient dancing. He has found a complete notation which might not interest us were it not that this very dancing forces one to a greater precision with the old music. One finds, for instance, that certain tunes called dance tunes must be played double the time at which they are modernly taken.

One art interprets the other. It would almost touch upon theatricals, which I am trying to avoid, if I should say that one steps into a past era when one sees all the other Dolmetsches dancing quaint, ancient steps of Sixteenth Century dancing. One feels that the dance would go on even if there were no audience. That is where real drama begins, and where we leave what I have called, with odium, "theatricals." It is a dance, danced for the dance's sake, to a display. It is music that exists for the sake of being music, not for the sake of, as they say, producing an impression.

Of course there are other musicians working with this same ideal. I take Mr. Dolmetsch as perhaps a unique figure, as perhaps the one man who knows most definitely whither he is going, and why, and who has given most time to old music.

They tell me "everyone knows Dolmetsch who knows of old music, but not many people know of it." Is that sheer nonsense, or what is the fragment of truth or rumour upon which it is based? Why is it that the fine things always seem to go on in a corner? Is it a judgment on democracy? Is it that what has once been the pleasure of the many, of the pre-Cromwellian many, has been permanently swept out of life? Musical England? A wild man comes into my room and talks of piles of turquoises in a boat, a sort of shop-houseboat east of Cashmere. His talk is full of the colour of the Orient. Then I find he is living over an old-clothes shop in Bow. "And there they seem to play all sorts of instruments."

Is there a popular instinct for anything different from what my ex-landlord calls "the four-hour-touch?" Is it that the aristocracy, which ought to set the fashion, is too weakened and too unreal to perform the due functions of "the aristocracy"? Is it that nature can, in fact, only produce a certain number of vortices? That the quattrocento shines out because the vortices of power coincided with the vortices of creative intelligence? And that when these vortices do not coincide we have an age of "art in strange corners" and great dullness among the quite rich? Is it that real democracy can only exist under feudal conditions, when no man fears to recognise creative skill in his neighbour; or, are we, as one likes to suppose, on the brink of another really great awakening, when the creative or art vortices shall be strong enough, when the people who care will be well enough organised to set the fine fashion, to impose it, to make the great age?

Born in France in 1858, Arnold Dolmetsch had studied music in Brussels and at the Royal College of Music, London. His father was a piano maker. After being aroused by the collections of old instruments in the British Museum, he had begun to build his own clavichords and harpsichords, first for Chickering of Boston, then for Gaveau of Paris. He later built and revived the playing of almost every instrument of the fifteenth to the eighteenth centuries, training the members of his family to play them. He established his workshop in Haslemere, Surrey, and later opened an annual festival there. His book, *The Interpretation of the Music of the XVIIth and XVIIIth Centuries (1915)*, is a landmark in the revival of the performance practices of ancient music.

Pound must have met Dolmetsch about 1914; at least on November 30 of that year he wrote to his father (unpublished letter): "Dolmetsch is about to have concert." Of their meeting Mrs. Dolmetsch wrote:

> Ezra Pound, then a budding poet, of rather flamboyant appearance, was immediately attracted to Arnold Dolmetsch; and through their continued intercourse he became deeply interested in the English music of former centuries. He delighted in listening to Arnold's performances on the clavichord. For this reason he became possessed of one.[14]

Pound asked Dolmetsch to make him a duplicate of his own clavichord, but Dolmetsch sold him the original.[15] In September, 1915, Pound wrote to Joyce: "So here I am with a clavichord—beside me, which I can't afford, and can't reasonably play on."[16]

Three musical personalities have had cardinal influence on Ezra Pound: Walter Morse Rummel, Arnold Dolmetsch, and George Antheil. Of these perhaps the most important, certainly the most seminal, was that extended to the poet by the personality and teaching of Arnold Dolmetsch. From Dolmetsch's theories of music Pound inherited embryo principles that profoundly affected his own theories of poetry: most immediately, they assisted him in his crusade for *vers libre;* but more than that they instructed him in the philosophy of chronometry—for music bends and twists clock time in mysterious ways—a matter he was to develop further in the *Treatise on Harmony* (1924), and ultimately these speculations were to lead to his own theory of Absolute Rhythm and Great Bass as the breath-pattern of an entire composition.

---

[14] Charles Norman, *Ezra Pound,* New York, 1969, p. 124.
[15] The Dolmetsch clavichord accompanied Pound later to Rapallo and finally to the castle at Brunnenburg. In 1959 he wrote to Dolmetsch's son, ordering a new set of strings.
[16] Read, *op. cit.,* p. 46.

41

VERS LIBRE AND ARNOLD DOLMETSCH[17]

Poetry is a composition of words set to music. Most other definitions of it are indefensible, or, worse, metaphysical. The amount or quality of the music may, and does, vary; but poetry withers and "dries out" when it leaves music, or at least an imagined music, too far behind it. The horrors of modern "readings of poetry" are due to oratorical recitation. Poetry must be read as music and not as oratory. I do not mean that the words should be jumbled together and made indistinct and unrecognizable in a sort of onomatopœic paste. I have found few save musicians who pay the least attention to the poet's own music. They are often, I admit, uncritical of his verbal excellence or deficit, ignorant of his "literary" value or bathos. But the literary qualities are not the whole of our art.

Poets who are not interested in music are, or become, bad poets. I would almost say that poets should never be too long out of touch with musicians. Poets who will not study music are defective. I do not mean that they need become virtuosi, or that they need necessarily undergo the musical curriculum of their time. It is perhaps their value that they can be a little refractory and heretical, for all arts tend to decline into the stereotype; and at all times the mediocre tend or try, semiconsciously or unconsciously, to obscure the fact that the day's fashion is not the immutable.

Music and poetry, melody and versification, alike fall under the marasmus.

Vers libre has become a pest, as painting and regular verse had become pests before it, as rabbits are a pest in Australia. One does not, however, wish to exterminate sonnets merely because sonnets have appeared in the *Century*. Bad as the versi libristi may be, the anti-versilibristi are worse. If I counsel the versilibristi to study music, I can also counsel the anti-versilibristi to study Arnold Dolmetsch's book. Bad as they may be (either the free or the tight), little as they may be able to do after the study of music, they would do less and worse, lacking it.

It is too late to prevent vers libre. It is here. There is too much of it. One might, conceivably, improve it, at least there appears room for improvement, and one might stop at least a little of the idiotic and narrow discussion based on an ignorance of music. Bigoted attack, born of this ignorance of the tradition of music, was what we had to live through.

The Interpretation of the Music of the XVIIth and XVIIIth Cen-

---

[17] *The Egoist*, July, 1917, pp. 90–91. Reprinted with some slight stylistic changes in *Pavannes*, 1918, and in *Literary Essays*, 1954.

turies, by Arnold Dolmetsch (Novello, London, 10s. 6d.; H. W. Gray and Co., New York).

I.

Arnold Dolmetsch's book is full of what we may call either "ripe wisdom" or "common sense," or "those things which all good artists at all times have tried (perhaps vainly) to hammer into insensitive heads." Some of his dicta are, by their nature, applicable only to instrumental music or melody, others are susceptible of a sort of transposition into terms of the sister arts, still others have a direct bearing on poetry, or at least on versification. It is with these last that I shall concern myself. Dolmetsch's style is so clear and his citations of old authors so apt that I had perhaps better quote with small comment.

Mace, *Musick's Monument* (1613):

(1)

... you must Know, That, although in our First Undertakings, we ought to *strive,* for the most Exact Habit of *Time-keeping* that possibly we can attain unto, (and for severall good Reasons) yet, when we come to be *Masters,* so that we can *command all manner* of Time, at our own Pleasures; we Then *take Liberty,* (and very often, for Humour, and good Adornment-sake, in certain Places) to *Break Time;* sometimes Faster, and sometimes Slower, as we perceive the *Nature of the Thing* Requires, which often adds, much *Grace,* and *Luster,* to the Performance.

(2)

... the thing to be done, is but only to make a kind of *Cessation,* or *standing still* ... in *due Place* ... a very Excellent grace.

Again, from Mace, p. 130: "*If you find it uniform, and retortive* either in its bars or strains" you are told to get variety by the quality of loud and soft, etc., and "if it expresseth short sentences" this applies. And you are to make pauses on long notes at the end of sentences.

Rousseau, 1687, in *Maître de Musique et de Viole:*

(1)

... At this word "movement" there are people who imagine that to give the movement is to follow and keep time; but there is much difference between the one and the other, for one may keep time without entering into the movement.

(2)

...You must, however, avoid a profusion of divisions, which only disturb the tune, and obscure its beauty.

(3)

...Mark not the beat too much.

The accompanist is told to imitate the irregularities of the beautiful voice.

François Couperin, 1717, *L'Art de toucher le Clavecin:*

(1)

...We write differently from what we play.

(2)

...I find that we confuse Time, or Measure, with what is called Cadence or Movement. Measure defines the quantity and equality of beats; Cadence is properly the spirit, the soul that must be added to it.

(3)

...Although these Preludes are written in measured time, there is however a customary style which should be followed.... Those who will use these set Preludes must play them in an easy manner, WITHOUT BINDING THEMSELVES TO STRICT TIME, unless I should have expressly marked it by the word *mesuré*.

No one but an imbecile can require much further proof for the recognition of vers libre in music—and this during the "classical period."

I have pointed out elsewhere that the even bar measure was certainly NOT the one and important thing, or even the first important thing, and that European musicians, at least, did not begin to record it until comparatively late in the history of notation. Couperin later notes the barring as a convenience:

...One of the reasons why I have measured these Preludes is the facility one will find to teach them or to learn them.

That is to say, musical bars are a sort of scaffold to be kicked away when no longer needed.

Disregard of bars is not to be confused with *tempo rubato,* affecting the notes inside a single bar.

II.

Dolmetsch's wisdom is not confined to the demonstration of a single point of topical interest to the poet. I have not space to quote two whole chapters, or even to elaborate brief quotations like: "You must bind perfectly all that you play." The serious writer of verse will not rest content until he has gone to the source. I do not wish to give the erroneous impression that old music was all vers libre. I state simply that vers libre exists in old music. Quantz, 1752, in so far as he is quoted by Dolmetsch, only cautions the player to give the shorter notes "inequality." Christopher Simpson, 1659, is much concerned with physical means of getting a regular beat. His date is interesting. The movement toward regularity in verse during the seventeenth century seems condemnable if one compare only Dryden and Shakespeare, but read a little bad Elizabethan poetry and the reason for it appears. (I shall try to show this in later essays.) On the other hand, Couperin's feeling for irregularity underlying "classical" forms may give us the clue to a wider unexpressed feeling for a fundamental irregularity which would have made eighteenth-century classicism, classicism of surface, tolerable to those who felt the underlying variety *as strongly as the first regularizers* may have felt it.

These are historical speculations. If I were writing merely a controversial article I should have stopped with the first quotations from Couperin, concerning vers libre. (I have never claimed that vers libre was the only path of salvation. I felt that it was right and that it had its place with the other modes. It seems that my instinct was not wholly heretical and that the opposition was rather badly informed.) Old gentlemen who talk about "red riot and anarchy," "treachery to the imperium of poesy," etc. etc. would do well to "get up their history" and peruse the codices of their laws.

Pound continued to write about Dolmetsch. In August 1917 he briefly reviewed Dolmetsch's book for *The Little Review,* and also wrote another longer piece on him for *The Egoist.*

THE INTERPRETATION OF THE MUSIC OF THE XVIITH AND XVIIITH CENTURIES BY ARNOLD DOLMETSCH[18]

ARNOLD DOLMETSCH'S book has been out for some time. No intelligent musician would willingly remain without it. No intelligent musician is wholly without interest in the music of those two centuries.

---

[18] *The Little Review,* IV, 4, August, 1917, pp. 10–11.

But this book is more than a technical guide to musicians. It is not merely "full of suggestion" for the thorough artist of any sort, but it shows a way whereby the musician and the "intelligent" can once more be brought into touch. If Dolmetsch could be persuaded to write a shilling manual for the instruction of children *and* of mistaught elders it might save the world's ears much torture. Dolmetsch's initial move was to demonstrate that the music of the old instruments could not be given on the piano; any more than you could give violin music on the piano. His next was to restore the old instruments to us. There is too much intelligence in him and his book adequately to be treated in a paragraph. I am writing of him at greater length in *The Egoist*. His citations from Couperin show the existence of vers libre in early eighteenth-century music. I do not however care unduly to stir up the rather uninteresting discussion as to the archaeology of "free" verse.

ARNOLD DOLMETSCH[19]

It was better to dig up the bas-reliefs of Assurbanipal's hunting than to have done an equal amount of Royal Academy sculpture. There are times when archæology is almost equal to creation, or when a resurrection is equally creative or even more creative than invention. Few contemporary composers have given more to today's music than has Arnold Dolmetsch.

His first realization was that music made for the old instruments could not be rendered on the piano. This proposition is exceedingly simple. You may play the notes of a violin solo on a piano or a banjo, but it will not be the same music. You may play the notes written for clavichord and harpsichord on the piano, or the pianola, but you will not make the same music. The first necessity, if one were to hear the old sounds, was a reconstruction of instruments, a multiplication of reconstructions; and this, as every educated person well knows, Arnold Dolmetsch has effected.

The next step was the removal of general misunderstandings of the old musical notation. This Mr. Dolmetsch has also triumphantly done in his *Interpretation of the Music of the Seventeenth and Eighteenth Centuries* (Novello, London, and H. W. Gray Co., New York). Not only this, but he has opened the way for a reconciliation between musicians and "the intelligent." This last act is extremely important; the reconstruction of old music is an activity which might end in itself. A possible re-fusion of intelligence with that other curious thing com-

---

[19] *The Egoist*, August, 1917, pp. 104–5.

monly known as "musical intelligence" contains many possibilities for the future; for the immediate future, the part of it chiefly concerning us and our mortal enjoyments.

All people have terms of abuse. Among artists and *literati* it is customary to excuse a man's stupidity by saying "He is a musician." Among musicians they say "Oh, that is a singer," implying depths of ignorance inconceivable to all but musicians.

Dolmetsch strikes at the root of the trouble by showing how music has been written, more and more, for the stupid; how the notation or rather the notators have gradually ceased to trust to, or to expect, intelligence on the part of interpreters; with the result that the whole major structure of music, of a piece of music, is obscured; the incidental elements, the detail show on the score equally with the cardinal contentions of the composer.

The neophyte is taught notes one by one, is taught scales. In the old way he would have been given the main structural points, he would have played the bare form of the piece, and gradually have filled in with the details.

There is more in Dolmetsch's "Section 14, on Divisions," than in a long course of practice and exercises; more I mean for the intelligent person to whom the mysteries of music have always seemed rather a jumble; a sort of pseudo-psychism practised by, and practicable for, people otherwise mentally inefficient.

I cannot demonstrate all this on a page. If Dolmetsch would write a shilling manual, simply dogma, leaving out his proofs and his explanations, and if people would use it on children and on themselves, we might have an almost immediate improvement, for a big book travels slowly, and few have the patience to understand anything, though many will obey a command.

The technical points I can scarcely go into, but they are there in Dolmetsch's book for musicians, and for those who have unsatisfied curiosities about music.

The general reflections stirred by his writing I may, however, set down.

First: It seems to me that in music, as in the other arts, beginning in the eighteenth century, and growing a poison from which we are not yet free, greater rigidity in matters of minutiæ has forced a break-up of the large forms; has destroyed the sense of main form. Compare academic detail in one school of painting, and minute particularization about light and colour in another.

Any work of art is a compound of freedom and order. It is perfectly obvious that art hangs between chaos on one side and mechanics on the other. A pedantic insistence on detail tends to drive out "major form."

A firm hold on major form makes for a freedom of detail. In painting men intent on minutiæ gradually lost the sense of form and form-combination. An attempt to restore this sense is branded as "revolution." It is revolution in the philological sense of the term.

The old way of music, teaching a man that a piece of music was a structure, certain main forms filled in with certain decorations, stimulated his intelligence, spurred on his constructive faculty. You might play the same lute-piece as many others, but you thought about playing it differently (i.e. with different notes), of playing it better. In a sense that is true of any performer, but the contemporary way of approach lays stress on having a memory like a phonograph; the reflex centres are as highly thought of as is the main conception. Thematic invention has departed.

Naturally the best musicians escape the contagion, a few good artists in any period always do escape, whatever contagion may be prevalent. In any age also, a few learned men must always support the poet against the music-teacher; the artist who creates against the machine for the vending of pictures; the inventive writer against the institutions of publishing and distribution. The modus is exceedingly simple. Some one must know that the fashion of the last forty years is not the eternal law of the art, whatever art it may be.

The heretic, the disturber, the genius, is the real person, the person stubborn in his intelligent instinct or protected by some trick of nature, some providential blindness, or deafness even, which prevents him from being duped by a fashion; some stubbornness, some unsocial surliness which prevents him from pretending to be duped, from pretending to acquiesce.

When I, for emphasis, say above, "providential blindness or deafness," one must remember that in the case of the artist—if there be some such trick played on him by nature for the preservation of art, the blindness or deafness or whatever apparent protective insensitiveness there may be—there is always a compensating sensitiveness or hyper-sensitiveness, enforced it may be by some voluntary or half-voluntary concentration, which keeps him interested, absorbed in the art.

Nature and humanity will never in the long run be bilked by the music-teacher and the academician. They, nature and humanity, abhor an unreasoning setness; haste is also in their abomination. There also the artist scores, for the "most brilliant," the most apparently sudden great artist is always a plodder. He alone can afford to wait. The singer of late nineteenth-century ballads must get through with his job at once: ditto for the actor, for the successful society portraitist.

In nothing has invention been slower than in the notation of music; it took centuries to find even a Notker, a Gui d'Arezzo. Today the man who desires to comprehend first and make his noise afterward comes upon the idiotic mess of unexplained, unexplainable scale-playing. The days when a *consort* arranged itself while you waited your turn at the barber's appear purely legendary. Our ears are passive before the onslaught of gramophones and pianolas. By persuading ourselves that we do not hear two-thirds of their abominable grind, we persuade ourselves that we take pleasure in the remainder of what they narrate. We feign a deafness which we have not, instead of developing our faculty for the finer perception of sound.

We pride ourselves on having exact transcripts of Arabic and Japanese and Zulu and Malay music; we take a sentimental pleasure in being reminded (in spite of the drone and wheeze, in spite of shriek and squeak), that we once heard the voice of Chaliapin. And as for the structure of music! ...

We turn to the printed page; the eye is confused by the multitude of ornamental notes and trappings, lost in the maze; each note is written as importantly as any other. And "Modern" music is so much a fuzz, a thing of blobs and of splotches—sometimes beautiful, and probably the best of it is more beautiful to those who know exactly what fixed lines it avoids.

But the structure of music? ... "Technicalities" ... "Artists don't enjoy their art as much as people who just enjoy it without trying to understand." That last quotation is one of the prize pieces of buncombe that the last generation indulged in. There is no comparison between the artist's enjoyment and the enjoyment of the layman. Only the artist can know this, for he is an artist in his own art and layman in all the rest, thus he can get some sense of proportion. He knows the difference between enthusiasm with vague half-comprehension, and enthusiasm plus an exact understanding. If the expert rejects 95 per cent. of all examples of an art presented to him, he has more pleasure in the remainder than the layman can get from the lot with vague and omnivorous liking.

What we know of any art is mostly what some master has taught us. We may not know him in the flesh, but the masterwork, and only the masterwork discontents us with mediocrity, or rather, it clarifies our discontentment; we may have suspected that something was wrong, been uninterested, worried, found the thing dull; the masterwork diagnoses it.

Dolmetsch has also made a fine diagnosis. He has incidentally thrown a side-light on metric, he has said suggestive things about *silence d'articulation,* about the freedoms of the old music. When I say suggestive, I do not mean that we are to get a jargon out of these things, to use for artistic controversy; but there is enough in them to prevent fools from interfering with, or carping at, rhythms achieved by the artist in his own way. Art is a departure from fixed positions; felicitous departure from a norm. It is a fight against mechanics. In music the trouble may well have begun with an attempt to write music for the insensitive and the blockhead.

If we are to regain a thematic sense, or a sense of thematic invention or of structure, if we are to have new music, or to have the old music beautifully played; if we are to have a clearer comprehension of what we do hear, we may owe a good deal to Mr. Dolmetsch.

The majority of Pound's musical reviews dealt with individual musicians or solo recitals. He seems to have been less interested in covering opera and ballet. "Je connus the London mondo musicale, at least the concert-hall, recital part of it." (Letter to Iris Barry, August 29, 1916.) *The New Age* music critic "William Atheling" rarely went beyond the recital halls. The following four articles are printed slightly out of chronological sequence to allow the "Atheling" material which follows them to appear without interruption.

In 1919 Pound wrote for a short time—until he was fired—a column entitled "The Drama" for the periodical *The Outlook,* signing himself "M. D. Adkins," and in 1920 he undertook a similar drama column for *The Athenæum,* this time under the pseudonym "T. J. V." From these columns those few reviews which deal with musical theater have been selected.

GILBERT AND SULLIVAN[20]

The cult of little stuffed birds (starting, as *The Athenæum* obligingly tells us, in Mr. Sickert's studio) may be regarded with some suspicion, as may also the cult or "revival" of Ingres *and* David in France, and the Victorian Renaissance as hinted by prophetic dealers in "Pictures and Works of Art." France wants money, and has on hand a great many more examples of pseudo-classic painting than of, let us say, Clouet; and the British families whose ancestors have provided them with abundance of stuffed birds in glass cases are undoubtedly ready for a change (to machine-made art nouveau or something else than has just been in fashion); but the Duke of Plaza Toro is immortal; he is not part of this factitious flurry of dilettantism; he dates in one sense from the latter, not the middle, Victorian era; he has persisted uninter-

---

[20] *The Outlook,* October 18, 1919, pp. 389-90.

ruptedly through the thirty years of his immortality, and the roars with which he is greeted at Prince's Theatre could only be explained to a foreigner on the grounds that the audience "knows he is coming."

It would be an error to take Gilbert and Sullivan more seriously than they were ever intended to be taken; we may leave that form of precocity to the *Athenæum* and the collectors of Victorian wax. The Gilbertian stage art *is* related to the sort of painting stored in the Tate Gallery and to the "art" of *Pears' Annual,* but it is not detestable, as Victorian painting was, for the most part, detestable. The work of Gilbert, and especially of Sullivan, lacks vigour, but Sullivan's music is inoffensive; the clear, reedy voices of Sydney Granville and Helen Gilliand make it delightful in spots; and there is so much "trade" in the whole production; so prevailing an effect of neatness and finish, such freedom from the impressionist sloppiness not always absent from our more ambitious operatic productions. Mr. Toye conducts very neatly; the chorus does its little gigue-steps and shuffles so neatly; there is in it the finesse which we find in the engraved illustrations to early editions of Byron; there is really, underneath it all, an inheritance of eighteenth-century restraint, a gallicism, or a quality which loose criticism has taken to be not "frenchy" but the exclusive property of the French. Neither musician nor librettist ever attempted anything beyond his range, and in this moderation lies the permanent value of the work. This virtue is supported by a less commendable "secret of success," namely, that the authors have put in a little of everything, a sop for those who like Mozart, and a sop for those who like the sentimental ballad (absolutely without merit), and even a sop for those whose taste was going to lead them later to *adore* "Floradora." There are good choruses, or at least choruses which permit excellent chorus work; there are bad choruses, and the harmonic arrangement will seem impoverished to anyone who has ever heard a group of Russian army officers sing to amuse themselves; but Sullivan does not spoil Gilbert's words. Here, again, we have the triumph of moderation and a pious example to many conceited musicians; Sullivan is extremely clever in places. The opera is "carried" by the main characters: The Duke, Luiz, Don Alhambra, The Duchess, and Casilda; Henry Lytton's execution is impeccable, the fun stays funny because it never tried to be too excruciatingly funny; and the propriety, the perfect propriety, of the performance almost supplies a basis for a defence of the "pudique d'Albion." This propriety is so inoffensive that one does not perceive its existence; yet by the whole tone of moderation it attains the dignity not only of a social but also of an artistic convention, as defensible in its way as is the alleged restraint of Corneille or Racine (who is not so very restrained).

Some people are bored by all opera, and to them there is no use of recommending any opera in particular; if they are bored by "The Seraglio" they will be bored by "The Gondoliers." The economy of material in the latter is such that there are several points at which one expects to be bored in five minutes' time, but in each case the situation is saved, either by a denouement of wit or by an improvement of the music. The political allusions are only a little dimmed; the archæologist will learn that Mr. Lytton Strachey was not the first man to wink at the solemnity of the era. The tradition of "a little for everyone" is followed in the scenery—i.e., the first act, the traditional stage set, the kind which is decidedly better under some calciums than under others; in the second act the moderately "modern" is charmingly done. We tender our congratulations and commendations to Messrs. D'Oyley Carte and Gordon for production and to Mr. Lytton for the disarming grace of his acting. With two such voices as those of Mr. Granville and Helen Gilliand the season should not lack the support of the more exclusively musical audience.

RUSSIAN MATINÉES[21]

Bull-baitings, *loas* and *entremeses* have given place to the arts of the theatre, and the spectre of Bolshevism has driven the Spectre of the Rose and the Russian æsthetes to London. We have, therefore, a chance for honourable exploitation of the sorrows of Moscow and "St. Petersburg." Messrs. Comisarjevsky and Rosing have opened their season a little before they are really ready, but the venture is a brave one, and deserves support on the quite selfish basis that if they go on they can quite probably purvey very enjoyable programmes.

For the moment Mr. Rosing himself is the only "unique attraction," the only "one and original" of their repertoire; but given the "high" ideals, the definite and visible intention to refuse nothing because it is "too good for the public," the Russian Matinées at the Duke of York's should serve as a focus for much of the known and latent talent in London—talent that is for scene, for ballet-invention, for music-drama, and for both decorative and poetic devices.

The devotees of ballet of the Pavlova-Nijinski period will for the moment find their pleasure in the current bill, though Miss Bedells is a nervous rather than a sinuous dancer, and though her capacity seems limited to an expression of "the lighter emotions"; and though she has a playful girlishness, a rather faintly coloured eroticism, none of the

[21] *The Athenæum,* March 12, 1920, pp. 348–49.

Slavic "surge and thunder," none of the "Oriental" richness of the old Russian performers. She is, in brief, one to dance Dobson rather than Swinburne, but able to captivate her audience in the old story "Valse Caprice," and certainly able to fill a good quarter of the afternoon if not called upon to be the mainstay of three quarters.

She had a sympathetic rôle in the second ballet, though we have as yet no authentic communiqués to fortify the implication that Dutch costume has been adopted in Riga, Vladivostock, or any other typically Russian or Slavic seaport.

The corporation needs enriching; it needs more brain, new inventions, old bits of "Swan" and "Bow and Arrow" can sink into memory. Dolls also have been somewhat fully exploited; Comisarjevsky's performance contains, however, some novelty, and Margot Luck has just the touch of personality which might "make" a dancer. The doll movements are not maintained with the consistency which solidified "La Boutique Fantasque." If this laxity gives a chance for some pretty moments, it is, nevertheless, a weakness of æsthetic; it leads nowhere, and cannot, in the long run, succeed.

The kidnapping of the smallest doll child by the ogre at the end of Scene Two leads nowhere at all; it is merely a piece of byplay having no structural function. There are probably better-written ballet scenarios lying in various juvenile desks.

But the important thing, and what might, with a reasonable measure of success, become even a significant thing, is that an art theatre has been started, under some auspices other than imbecile. Here is a company to whom the finest perceptions are welcome rather than unwelcome. This potentiality should not be neglected.

Of the announced programme for next week, two items have already been performed at the Lahda (Russian art society). The Nursery is frankly a bore, but the Russian Folk Scenes were an uproarious success on the restricted Wigmore Hall platform, and should gain greatly by their transfer to more commodious quarters, providing M. Rosing continues to act as "The Showman."

MUSICAL COMEDY[22]

Musical comedy is a convention, and therefore permissible; it is a convention which has never quite decided on itself, and is therefore without standards. To an uninitiated but analytical Tibetan this form of theatricals would, perhaps, appear to be the eternal balcony scene from

[22] *The Athenæum*, April 2, 1920, p. 457.

melodrama, enhanced by a corps de ballet which does not, and is presumably unable to, dance. The joke is interpolated, that is to say a musical comedy contains about enough jokes to fill one issue of the *London Mail*. The tones are about the same.

Musical comedy obviously does not aim at pleasing the dramatic sense of the audience; nor yet the musical sense. Thus, in the specimen presented for our dissection we find the same old tunes out of "Florodora," the familiar rhythms of the "Rajah of Bong," and other heteroclite reminders of songs which are but a confused familiarity, dating back twenty years. There seems, however, to be no reason why musical invention should, or even would, be excluded if it were discoverable. It might be against the commercial economies to employ better musicians, but there is, so far as we can see, no reason preventing their entry into this field. The serious song about the brave T.B.D.s was, for one hearing at least, quite as good as the art-settings of Kipling which one hears in the "serious concerts." The versification of musical comedy is presumably the only active stage versification in England, unless we, with considerable tolerance, include the occasional translation of a more "serious" opera libretto. Τάδ' ὡδ' εχει. I do not pretend to say whether or no this is what may be called a "hopeful sign."

The remaining convention of musical comedy is the journey; this, I believe, exists as a convention in the classic plays of Japan, whence it can hardly be derivative, but it has no regular prototype in European drama. The curious mind may assign its contradiction of the unities to some obscure influence of the picaresque novel; we take it as we find it: musical comedy and much melodrama insist on transportation *en masse* of the characters.

In fine, the musical play appeals neither to ear nor to dramatic sense, it is moreover conservative in *décor*. It inclines to garden scenes, beach or nether-abbreviation scenes and mannequin parades, but without appeal to the critical eye of the connoisseur or the artist; its scenic novelties must be "lovely" in the majorities' acceptance of that term, the bold experimentalist is not wanted. Neither, apparently, are the strict sculptural or decorative senses, for if repetition is the essence of pattern, these senses would demand a certain strictness of application. The limbs, for instance, of the non-dancing chorus should, if the whole effect is to bear comparison with Greek vases, repeat, not contradict the given curves of the accepted type. The value of multiplicity on the stage is the same for these group scenes as for ballet; it follows the simple æsthetic principle that when the single object is not interesting enough to retain the eye, the entertainer must provide so many objects that no eye in the audience can quite exhaust its analytical process, the search for perfection must not receive a convincing negation. This profusion of variety should alternate with exactness of pattern, *i.e.*, the silhouettes for this latter should be uniform or at least similar or graduated; if the chorus is made up of a job lot of varied types, the costume should have a unifying effect, when pattern is intended. Also the given costume should be applied to suitable types; it is not every group of eight young women who can wear poke-bonnets becomingly. Carelessness of these details has led many people to suggest that there is in musical comedy some other motive than strict appeal to the optic sense.

I am convinced that in England many discrepancies are tolerated and even unnoticed which would merely stir guffaws at La Cigale. With these restrictions "Society, Ltd.," is a "high-class musical comedy." Miss MacVane has a rich contralto voice, which she should use ever for song, never for speech. The national caricatures by Bromley Challoner, T. Ryley, A. Roberts and H. A. Meymott are not unentertaining.

Marie Dainton is the cleverest member of the cast, or at any rate the part of Lady Whyte-Chappelle gives her greater opportunity for entertaining one. Miss Waring supplies the Vernon-Castle touch. The shadow of democracy or the resurgent ghost of Figaro casts in an occasional allusion to current events, and the serious five minutes devoted to the young sea rover are a more dignified allusion to the war than is to be found in several of the "more serious" current plays. The audience gave repeated signs of approval.

PAVLOVA[23]

Pavlova, that bright bird of memory and fair flower of recollection, that image of whom no one was privileged to speak who could not compass blank verse, has returned in exquisite whiteness, in a shower of artificial snowflakes and the traditional Degas *décor*. She is well advised to begin her programme with a piece of technical bravura and to make her reappearance with sleights of foot which no inexperienced ballerina could perform. A decade ago it was Pavlova, it was her own delicate and very personal comment of emotion upon the choreographic lines of Fokine which won her the myriad hearts; to-day it is the mastery of her technique, chiefly the stillness of her pose and poise and the surety of her balance, which distinguish her from her competitors. And she does well to demonstrate this *maestria* during the first section of the programme.

[23] *The Athenæum*, April 23, 1920, p. 553. Pavlova had appeared in London as early as 1911 in Diaghilev's Russian Ballet, and it was there that she settled after the First World War to establish her own company.

As a mime she is without merit, and despite the steps in her *pas seul,* "Amarilla" is a dreary effort; it is also a stupid effort to mix two incompatible elements: expressionist dancing and the formal "classic" toe ballet. Volinine is delightfully elastic, but Pavlova's confusion when trying to seek sisterly consolations without giving up the modus of the old-fashioned love dance is distressing. On the whole, the sooner this ballet is scrapped the better for her artistic reputation. The black-gowned "marchioness" who decorates the north corner of the stage is a danseuse of promise.

It, however, bodes ill for the management that, having such great resources at their command, they are so lacking in initiative and so mentally lazy that they do not even attempt to stage a third ballet. They give us a divertissement of scraps. Admitting that the youngest generation wants to see "The Swan," and that the Syrian dance is a decorative abbreviation or shorthand rendering of "Scheherazade," and that Mlle. Butsova is very supple and that Mlle. Brunova has talent, still the inclusion of "divertissements," when there are thirty men in England perfectly capable of designing new and really interesting ballets, is sufficient to dry up most of one's sympathy for the Pavlova-Clustine-Volinine enterprise. They are not so artistically serious as Massine, and if they are not very careful, they will be classed among historic revivals.

2
England: The New Age Music Critic, "William Atheling," 1917–1921

On January 24, 1918, Pound wrote from London to his father: "Am doing art and music critiques under pseudonyms, paying the rent. Rather entertaining work."[1] Although Pound had written voluminously for periodicals ever since his arrival in London in 1908, often serializing his work over several weeks or months, it was not until 1917, when he assumed the joint responsibilities of music and art critic for A. R. Orage's Guild Socialist weekly *The New Age*, that he had anything like regular journalistic employment.

The fate of a casual reviewer was then, as ever, risky. During the first year of his marriage, November 1914 to October 1915, Pound's "gate receipts" from reviewing had amounted to a mere £42.10.0. The "demon pantechnicon driver," as Wyndham Lewis called him in those days, may have been "busy with moving the old world into new quarters," but he was not being paid much for his performance. To augment his reviewing income he had frequently undertaken the translation of texts for song recitals and music publications.[2]

In December 1917 he began a fortnightly music column for *The New Age* under the pseudonym of "William Atheling," alternat-

---

[1] Unpublished letter.
[2] For example, *Collection Yvette Guilbert*, English translations by Ezra Pound, Augener Ltd., London, 1912. See also Donald Gallup's delightful detective pursuit in search of translations Pound did for a vocal recital in 1910, "The Search for Mrs. Wood's Program," in *Ezra Pound Perspectives*, ed. Noel Stock, Chicago, 1965.

ing this with an art column under the pseudonym of "B. H. Dias." In *Antheil and the Treatise on Harmony,* Pound described Atheling as follows:

> "William Atheling" wrote fortnightly in the *New Age* from 1917–20; he sympathised with Arnold Dolmetsch' opinions, he might very well have thought that music ended with Bach. He existed in order that I might study the actual sounds produced by performing musicians. He wrote in the hope of making it possible or easier for the best performers to do their best work in public rather than their worst or their middling. By this he meant that he liked hearing Moussorgsky, he preferred Russian bareness to the upholsteries of XIXth century Europe. He liked music with a strong horizontal action, preferring it to music which seems to steam up from the earth. He shared my interest in the fitting of *motz el son;* i.e. the fitting of words and tunes.
>
> He found the Kennedy-Fraser's Hebridean research of great interest, he approved of Le Roi Renaud; and of French folksong, if rigorously selected, as late as Le Pauvre Laboureur, and La Carmagnole. He regretted the lost culture of Henry Lawes. He enjoyed without much audible, though with a good deal of mute, opposition, the writers of Bel Canto: Caldara, Durante, and Carissimi.[3]

William Atheling, who had elected himself enemy of "the pigheaded insularity of the British Association of Musicians," was a blustering and often irritating critic whose reviews are saved, like G. B. Shaw's, by their wit and by the driving spirit of their author. A host of performing musicians passes under Atheling's pen, most of them solo recitalists, the majority now forgotten. It would not be fair to say that Atheling had his finger directly on the pulse of London musical life, for he ignored many of the great international performers of his day, a feature of his reviews which some of his readers did not forgive. Nor was he accepted as an "important" critic in musical circles. I have spoken to several British musicians of Atheling's vintage who never heard of him. Some of the performers he championed, such as Constantin Stroesco and Vladimir Cernikoff, seem to have been more "drawing-room" celebrities than front-rank artists. The amount of attention given certain singers, such as Vladimir Rosing, Raymonde Collignon, and later Yves Tinayre, resulted simply from their

---

[3] *Antheil and the Treatise on Harmony* (reprinted), New York, 1968, pp. 67–68.

having featured Atheling's favorite music on their programs; they later became friends of the poet. While Atheling was vitally interested in the composition of programs, he was often casual in his descriptions of the music he heard. One reads of "the Purcell" or "the Beethoven" without ever discovering which composition is under discussion. Although he was a careless critic who often showed not the slightest intention of discussing what it was his duty to discuss and whose reviews have a jerky confectionary quality, he did have a cogent sense of mission, and when the slightest opportunity presented itself he would be off on one of his fixed themes.

As he says, his abiding preference was for music with a "strong horizontal action," as opposed to that which "seems to steam up from the earth." Throughout the reviews there is a growing insistence on "pattern music, as opposed to impression music, colour music, programme music," a theme which had emerged clearly in the earlier Dolmetsch reviews and was to resound plangently in the promotional material written for George Antheil later in Paris, stiffened obviously by his discovery at that time, through Antheil, of Stravinsky.

Another of Atheling's chief concerns was with the diction of singers, a matter in which the poet's genius for accurate rendering of the spoken language in print was constructive and often humorous.

> If Madame D'Alvarez will draw her tongue back just a little farther into her mouth she will be able to avoid this Peruvianisation of Italian.

> To sing (*sic*) "O had I a HELL-met and doublet and hose"; to repeat this with increasing volume, such as cannot be rendered by any capital letters at our disposal, must be regarded as purely comic by any vigilant listener.

> Purcell was murdered, and singing "forget my feet" for "forget my fate" is no embellishment of the verbal text.

The frequently deprecatory character of Atheling's reviews should not be misunderstood. When he was impressed with an artist, he would consider a detailed fault-finding worth his trouble. When he was unimpressed, he would dismiss the whole affair quickly in order to get on to more interesting topics.

"Dettmar Dressel's violin playing does not matter." Or, "Mark Hamburg's piano playing at Aeolian Hall was wholly without interest." But he also took off at composers whose music fell into the second class, often with amusing results. Speaking of Tschaikovsky, he reminded his readers that "a certain cheapness is imminent in this composer. He is not cheap all the time, or even, perhaps, most of the time, but he keeps one in a state of anxiety." Another time he suggested renaming Scriabin's *Poème d'Extase:* "... we think Scriabin would have been kinder to his audience if he had labelled this *poème* 'Satire upon an Old Gentleman' or possibly 'Confessions of Trouble'...."

Atheling was always blunt. He accused Liszt of being "stupid...; he would try to make a watch go by beating it with a potato-masher." He chided his readers not to be "scared at the great name of Beethoven" and pronounced the Moonlight Sonata "a bore." A concert of Elgar's music is also dismissed with whimsy: "... several cuckoos have laid their eggs in Mr. Elgar's nest and he has patiently hatched them all."

Atheling's opinion of British music in his own day was low. John Ireland, Frank Bridge, Arnold Bax, York Bowen, Walford Davies—then the serious young composers of musical Britain—were summed up as "usual 'école' of 'Narcissus' ripple, etc." The only British composer who impressed Pound at all was Bernard Van Dieren. It might be pointed out that during the First World War the British were rather ostentatiously pushing the home product. For a time German music was actually banned and "A War Emergency Entertainment" committee had been set up. "A specialty was the first performance of new works by British composers, of which two hundred were given."[4] Only in 1920 did music by "enemy composers" begin to trickle back into concert halls.

For Atheling, as for Dolmetsch, his mentor, British music ended effectively with Lawes, Campion, and John Jenkins. Agnes Bedford, Pound's musical friend and amanuensis, recalled how the poet tried once to organize a John Jenkins evening, instructing her to bring musicians to perform and discuss the music of this important Elizabethan. The musicians assembled, but no one knew anything about Jenkins. Finally a young man got up and played his latest piano composition, much to the poet's fury.

In one of the *New Age* reviews Atheling describes how he tried

---

[4] Percy A. Scholes, *The Mirror of Music*, (2 vols.) London, 1947, Volume II, p. 888.

to buy Henry Lawes's "Ayres and Dialogues" without success because this composer was out of print in his native country. In order to appreciate the subsequent expansion of Pound's musical horizon it is important to realize that throughout the London years the poet remained faithful to his idea that supreme musical expression was to be found in song. In 1934 he could still write, in the *ABC of Reading:*

> The great lyric lasted while Campion made his own music, while Lawes set Waller's verses, while verses if not actually sung or set to music, were at least made with the intention of going to music.[5]

For this reason the Kennedy-Frasers interested him, also Yves Tinayre's revival of medieval song; and it was only much later that a true appreciation of instrumental music developed, of Vivaldi and Mozart. Thus one can appreciate Atheling's contempt for the piano, *the* instrument which replaced the human voice. It also typified the desertion of "pattern music" for mush, since the new keyboard and pedal techniques of the impressionists did not compare favorably with the crisp initial transients and clean polyphony of the harpsichord and other older instruments. The intensity of the abuse heaped on the piano at times reached such frenzy that readers became exasperated.

One is disappointed that Atheling heard so little music of the great and then arriving composers of Europe. Apparently he was present for the English première of Stravinsky's *Le Sacre du Printemps,* and he later heard his *Three Pieces for String Quartet,* which he tells us were performed from manuscript at a concert, April 9, 1919. He liked them—at least by comparison with the offering of the bright young Britisher, Joseph Holbrooke, who shared the program.[6] His attitude to Debussy was mixed. He regarded him as "a beautiful and bewildering heresy.... It is no mortal use trying to play his music as if it were 'pure,' as if it

---

[5] Ezra Pound, *ABC of Reading*, New York, 1960, and London, 1961, pp. 60–61.

[6] He mentions attending the *Sacre* première in a retrospective article "Throttling Music," the *New English Weekly,* March 28, 1935, p. 495. By 1919, when the *Three Pieces for String Quartet* were performed, Stravinsky was the acknowledged pacemaker of new music, even in England. These same pieces were performed again in an all-Stravinsky program in September, 1920, at Wigmore Hall. The music was prefaced by a lecture on Stravinsky's aesthetics by Ernest Ansermet. The audience, which a contemporary observer describes as consisting of "earnest musicians and painters with their families," was most enthusiastic.

were simply 'sound' arranged into time and pitch patterns for the expression of emotion." But on the whole his attitude to this master was benevolent, obviously the result of his close association with Walter Morse Rummel, who had been a member of Debussy's intimate circle. Of Schoenberg or Bartók, both of whom had visited London to perform their music during these years, we hear nothing.

Atheling may not have been the most informed music critic of his day, but he had contagious enthusiasm and he never sank to inutility from cowardice. And who could quarrel with his credo?

> The function of musical criticism ... is to make it possible for the best performers to present their best work; for them to give concerts under present conditions without making any concession whatsoever to ignorance and bad taste.

LE MARIAGE DE FIGARO[7]

No feeling is more typical of the conscientious Englishman, and few feelings are more annoying than the feeling that if one does not take a hand in things actively, the constituted authorities will make a mess of them. This feeling and its inevitability have perpetually ruined our artists and musicians, and drawn them away from their work, for they, too, are English, and subject to personal human infirmity.

I write this note in annoyance, on returning to London and finding the opera officially over, that is to say, I write on November 20 with the announcement staring me in the face that the opera will end on the Saturday of this week. All things considered, this is a rather serious indictment of the London public and of the London musical critics. It means either that the critics are stupid and have not urged the audience, or else that they have ruined their credit with the public by a long period of weak criticism, and are no longer believed.

It is not intelligent to blame the war for the lack of public support. The aristocracy turn out to patronise basket-work and peasant-industry, dilettante pottery, and that sort of thing, during the war, and music is

---

[7] *The New Age*, December 6, 1917, pp. 113-15. Of this production of *Figaro* Sir Thomas Beecham, who masterminded it, later wrote: "It was generally allowed that this production topped a peak so far unscaled in the annals of any native organization. . . . Certainly nothing has appeared since to excel it. And yet the cast, which had been selected more for appearance than voice, contained hardly one of the better vocalists of the company, although the singing was both adequate and stylish." Sir Thomas Beecham, *A Mingled Chime*, London, 1944, p. 160.

no less important, and the number of people employed in the opera have as much claim to be supported, to be allowed to support themselves, as have the weavers of embroidery. The less commendable theatres on Shaftesbury Avenue can go on giving the same third-rate plays month after month, year after year, and every night in the week. I have never fancied myself as a critic, and have preferred to sit quiet in my seat, but if the existing musical critics can do no better for both the opera and the public, they will have to endure my presence amongst them.

In any other country in Europe the intelligentsia would have gathered around and supported the Beecham production of "Figaro." Even those among them who had no musical sense would have been drawn by the free spirit of the piece, in a time when the liberties of the Press are in danger, and when the traditional reticences of Victorian speech are in danger of being revived, and when the eighteenth century virtues have been pushed into a corner. The wit of Beaumarchais is more fresh than the jokes of the music-hall, and is to-day quite as full of significance for any one who will hear it. The time is as appropriate for a restoration of "Figaro," not only to the pride of its original libretto, but for incorporating in the libretto more of the original Beaumarchais. "It is not necessary, my Lord, but it is customary." Beaumarchais' play was performed in Spanish costume, and the English version has now been rendered in French costume of the late eighteenth century, in which the singers look rather better than in any other costumes they have worn. For all sorts of costume do not become opera singers.

We owe a debt to the Beecham management that the freedom of English speech, and allusions to the *droit du seigneur,* are restored. With the realities of war about us it is high time that the Victorian hypocrisy should depart.

These things are not the essential matter; but only general reasons why the "Mariage de Figaro" should have drawn to it a section of the public not specifically interested in music. But to a musician, to one who has for long watched the opera with a sort of despairing hope, the Beecham production of "Figaro" is historic. For years the idea of opera in English has been derided. English musicians who have attended any concerts save their own will remember the Beecham beginnings; they will remember the old days at Queen's Hall with Henry Wood conducting with a sort of Teutonic sloppiness; they will remember why ten years ago we preferred to listen to continental conductors; they will remember the new note of exactitude when Thomas Beecham first appeared with the baton, his energy, his most talented feeling for rhythm, and his precision which seemed at that time foreign. In one man at least the English heritage from Purcell was not extinct. Nevertheless, in 1909, the white-headed and grey-headed English writers on music still sneered at "Master Tommy." During the succeeding years he trained an orchestra. A few years ago we began to have the seasons at the little Aldwych Theatre. Robert Radford had a voice, and Mr. Mullings the power of acting. That was all that felicitous accident seemed to have given by way of assistance to the leader and creator of the company. Mullings, despite his unwieldy appearance, was impressive in "Tristan," and his very hugeness and the shortness of his arms and his stillness helped in the effect. One felt the man, the fictitious man of the play, the victim of fate, the immobile mass of humanity, beaten by blow after blow, unable to shield himself. This also again in "Othello," again the victim, but this time an hysterical victim, adding, not only at the Aldwych, but even more on the large stage of Drury Lane, magnificent motion to his other theatrical attributes, as, for example, the way he used all of the stage, rushing full across it in an access of frenzy.

Mullings' acting was memorable, but it by no means made the opera wholly satisfactory. Verdi had indeed dramatic sense, and the drama held one's attention, and even distracted one from the music. The English libretto lost the magnificent line of the Italian, the complete tragedy of the fall of voice in:—

> E come sei pallida
> E tacita
> E mor-ta.

Even Mullings was unable to cover the defect of the English at this particular spot. In the "Tristan," whatever one had felt in the first acts was a little worn away in the last act; the Jæger of Tristan's dressing-gown distressed the eye; and then the opera is not built right. However, I cannot at present go into the whole problem of the virtues and defects of Wagner as a musician.

I am thoroughly convinced that the better musician a man is, the more fully convinced he is that the opera belongs to the Mozart period. In "Don Giovanni" and "Figaro" we have the stage and the music sharing the art in the right proportions. I would have all opera done in the costume of this period and in the form of this period. Even in the "Seraglio" and the "Magic Flute," which are not, to my mind, anywhere nearly so fine as "Don Giovanni" and "Figaro," the musical form is right. Whatever one has felt about the individual passages, the gradual sweep up to the finale of each act gives a major form to the opera, and this can but be effective in a way not shared by opera in which the major form is the form of drama, not that of music. The proof of this is that one can sit through these Mozart, or musically formed, operas time after time, whereas in a dramatically formed opera, as in the Wagnerian, which has an emotional rather than musical structure, the effect of the piece diminishes the more often one hears it.

The historical thing is that Sir Thomas Beecham has in a remarkably short space of time accomplished the impossible. He, in English (though that is in some ways a minor matter), has put on an opera that is æsthetically satisfactory. He has, with little or no exceptional assisting talent at his disposal, without either star singers or performers, so welded together his cast and his orchestra, so imposed his own sense of the fitness of things on all the component parts of his huge machine, that the "Marriage of Figaro" has been a work of art, not merely an evening's entertainment; and those who have seen it will remember it as they remember other works of art. The scenery was not remarkable, but it was adequate; it did not thrust itself between the audience and the piece, either as an annoyance or a distraction. It was reasonably plain, as scenery should be, for costumes should be elaborate and interesting, thus to concentrate the eye on the actor, the moving figure of the action. Mr. Nigel Playfair is to be congratulated on the whole arrangement of the stage, and the singers on their acting, in which nothing grated on the audience. (Of what opera for years can one say this?) If I criticise the one performance of last week in lieu of a series, I only refrain from calling it a perfect performance because no one will believe such absolute words. The flaws were too slight to mention; Licette grew tired toward the third act; the programme calls attention to the aristocratic manner of the count, and this was not on the stage sufficiently contrasted with the manners of Figaro; but neither of these flaws was perceptible until one had said to oneself, "this is a perfect performance," and then tried to find a possible flaw. Has anyone considered the difficulty, well-nigh the impossibility, of controlling such a complicated machine as a stage and an orchestra all together? The mastery of these difficulties is to Sir Thomas Beecham's credit. We all know he can lead an orchestra, that he alone in these years has broken us of the habit of thinking we must have foreign conductors. Who else, in the "Figaro," would have given the pianissimo with such delicacy, with such exact articulation, would have preserved in the huge Opera House the fine charm, as of chamber music? Who else so plays the whole orchestra, reaching the instruments, all of them, through the performers?

SOME RECENT CONCERTS[8]

After a ten years' lapse one takes up a systematic attendance at concerts with a mixture of curiosity and trepidation. Will one's ears and one's patience stand it? Will the occasional discoveries and the very occasional pleasures repay one for the hours and half-hours of boredom, and for the moments of nervous crisis which expel one from the concert hall in the middle of the first number?

Miss Kathleen Brown led off with a Beethoven Sonata (C Major, Op. 53). She is a very clever young lady. The sonata as played was a mixture of prettiness and of bumps. She had thought a great deal about it, but it was full of dull stretches; that is to say, it was dull wherever her invention had failed. The rendering was dramatic rather than emotional; it suggested event, not imagination. Of the feeling for music as music there was scarcely ever a trace. There were smacks on the high points of rhythm, and a demarcation into passages; but the quality of the instrument, if it had any, was not transmitted. The time for sound, the real rhythm, was not taken into account. Let me explain this term if it be unfamiliar.

The tempo of every masterwork is definitely governed; and not only the general tempo of the whole work, but the variations in speed, the tempo of individual passages, the time interval between particular notes and chords. The actual sound of a given note or chord needs a certain time to round itself out before the next sound is imposed or shot after it. The masterly rendering of a piece depends almost wholly on the exact instants chosen for this imposition or suite of the arcs or spheres of succeeding sounds one on another. This affects not merely the rhythm of the piece, but it affects, more than people usually realise, the quality of the tone. This is doubly true for the piano, which depends for its effects so much on the sound of a lot of notes struck together, and is so poor, compared with a stringed instrument, in its ability to make much of single notes.

The sense of the real tempo may be instinctive and incommunicable. At any rate, Miss Brown made her Beethoven very much a matter of punches and ripples, obliterating the real sound, using the piano not as a means of interpreting the emotion underlying the music, but rather as a means of attracting attention. Her Chopin was perhaps better, but however good the "Golliwogs' Cake Walk" of Debussy may be in its way and in its place, it should not be taken as a model for the rendering of earlier composers. The Scherzo (Op. 31) is too beautiful to be

---

[8] *The New Age,* January 3, 1918, pp. 189–90.

monkeyed with in this fashion. At her worst the pianist suggested fireworks and the cinema.

Miss Lulu Juta, "the South African dramatic soprano," began with a burst of high shrapnel. Stupidity, volume; airs and graces, in the fashion-paper sense of the terms, dullness, defective rhythm, drag, boredom, doux baisers, not a fundamentally bad voice, if it could be trained from the mind outward. It is easy enough to make a great noise in a small place like Wigmore Hall.* The singer is presumably aiming at opera, but less squall and a perception of the nearness of the roof at the Wigmore would have made her present performance more enjoyable. She might have noticed that she was not on the veldt, and that less noise and more understanding would have served her to better purpose.

Giovanni Barbirolli gets a pleasant tone from his 'cello in the simpler passages. He and Miss Ethel Bartlett were decidedly over-ambitious in attempting a "sonata recital."

Miss E. G. Knocker's pupils' concert was a good solid affair, assisted by Frank Bridge and Felix Salmond in the Chausson Concert in D. Miss Knocker's crop of rising violinists may be differentiated as follows:—Evelin Cooke gave her Händel with sufficient spirit to atone for a certain roughness. Edith Abrahams attacked her Bach Fugue in C in vigorous Mosaic spirit, and finally got the better of it. Miss Murray Lambert was extremely nervous; she was rather obviously starred for delicacy; one noted the temperament that would as lief listen as play. She had completely forgotten her audience at the end of the *Grave* movement in the Tartini concerto. One sympathises with this temperament a good deal more than with the temperament to which a piece of music is only a chance to make a display to an audience. But these naturally solitary people are bound to find a public career doubly hard. The "Navarra" of Sarasate gave Misses Cooke and Abrahams a fine chance to display bravura and energy. Miss Rhoda Backhouse is advertised as specialising in chamber music, but she does not display the precision either of ear or of tempo that should lead to distinction in this branch. Miss Sybil Eaton played with a firmer tone, but it is unfair to compare the performance of her simpler pieces with the performance of the tours de force by Misses Abrahams and Cooke. Mark Hamburg's piano playing at Æolian Hall was wholly without interest.

Raymonde Collignon

Raymonde Collignon has made the first great discovery, namely, that there is a difference between music and noise. Edwin Evans is to be

---

* "Ef you want ter hear all the operas, just put John Bowers in the bath-tub, an' turn on the hot water" (Atheling).

thanked for having set the fashion of holding concerts at a convenient hour (5.45). One had always known that folk songs have authors, individual authors, and that they are not the spontaneous outbreak of communal rural stupidity. It is, however, a comfort to hear this said on a public platform. Mr. Evans' discourse on folk song was brief and to the point, and his accompaniments were charmingly played. But his discovery or presentation of Raymonde Collignon is notable.

That anyone, after Yvette, should dare appear in a crinoline takes one's breath away. That a young woman should appear in a crinoline, with a simper, without any of Yvette's sweep and surge and élan, shows, to say the least, rare audacity. The finished artist can do almost anything. So great is the variety of emotional effect produced by the apparently slender means! So perfect the articulation of Miss Collignon's singing. The voice, as someone said, was about the size of a postage stamp. With that slender sound Miss Collignon gave us the effect of great spacing. From within that apparently narrow scope, which was nevertheless not narrow, there came proofs of her capacity for tragedy, for *gaminerie,* for *simplesse,* the most dangerous of all qualities.

One is instinctively drawn to compare her with Yvette, but the comparison is foolish and superficial. They are both *diseuses,* and there the similarity ends. Miss Collignon has infinitely more music in her. Her effects are musical, whereas Yvette's effects were those of passion and drama. She was a much larger and more energetic instrument.

With Miss Collignon one turns back and again back to the words: fineness, scope within an apparently limited volume of sound; perhaps the greatest variety one has heard in so slender a sound, precision, perfect articulation. In fact, all the things which by being lacking make ordinary concerts a bore, were here in her performance. I am criticising music and not the art of acting, in which she is perfect also; or, perhaps, we should call her art the art of the suggestion of acting. I want to put this aside, and concentrate attention on the detailed fineness of her actual notes, the variety of their colour, the diversity of their quality. Why, why, and again why will only one musician in three hundred recognise the fact that it is by relativity of sound and not by loudness that music is constructed? Is there no moral to be drawn from a surpassingly delicate performance, in which the singer makes no false accent, commits no excess, a concert where the critic stays to the end, and joins the audience in applauding and wanting more music?

Miss Collignon's "secret" is not much of a secret; it is perfectly easy to analyse. She has a true sense of rhythm, an exact ear for pitch, she strikes each note with precision, and is herself interested in each note (and, indeed, in each gesture, though this aside from my musical analysis). She therefore makes each note interesting to her audience, and the audience being interested note by note does not undergo long stretches of desiccating boredom, during the concert. Miss Collignon knows her voice, knows exactly what it will do, plans, or would seem to plan, her whole performance from beginning to end (either consciously or by instinct) and therefore repeats nothing, not even in the simplest folk song. Her art is as delicate as the art of the cutter of intaglios, and as firm.

In the rendering of old music this delicacy is authentic, or should be. Arnold Dolmetsch has delighted us with his instruments and his renderings, and done much for musical scholarship. Miss Collignon must be one of the very few contemporary singers who could by any chance please an ear so fastidious.

Memento: Miss Jessie Bristol is a quite good pianist. She at least recognises in some degree the nature of that not very satisfactory instrument, and takes some account of its after-sounds.

This was the first review of Raymonde Collignon, a singer Pound was to remember with affection for many years. In 1931 she was to perform the song "Mère au Saveur" in the first BBC performance of *Le Testament*. As mentioned in the review, she was first "discovered" by the critic and historian Edwin Evans, who employed her to illustrate his lectures. She later gained great celebrity in London, particularly for her interpretations of French folk songs, which she performed in costume.

A few days after the above recital, on January 24, Pound wrote to his father (unpublished letter): "The new *diseuse*, Raymonde Collignon is, I think, going to do Walter's [Rummel's] settings of the troubadour songs." In fact she did perform them and Atheling reviewed the concert (May 16). Collignon belonged to that special *genre* of artist trained in song, gesture, and speech. In an article written for *Theatre Craft*, the poet expressed his admiration for such artists.

> The *diseuse* or *diseur* is a medieval personage; is the touring company of one actor. A few dozen skilled soloists would be excellent material for a company "nearer the heart's desire." At present there is no critical standard and no technical skill sufficiently specialized save on the music-hall stage, where one actor must hold the audience. These "artists" have a technique, and by a technique often unintelligible to the "intellectual" they succeed.[9]

---

[9] "To Discriminate," from *Theatre Craft: A Book of the New Spirit in the Theatre*, ed. N. MacDermott, H. Ould, and H. Shipp, London, n.d. (Gallup ascribes it tentatively to spring, 1919).

Pound inserted a short announcement under the name of Raymonde Collignon in *The Little Review:*

> There is a new *diseuse* loose on London. She will go to France after the war, and heaven knows when she will get to America, but she will sometime. She is singing folk-song without the vegetarian and simple-life element. She is the first singer to work on Walter Rummel's reconstructions of XIIth. century Provençal music. Her name is Raymonde Collignon. Verb. sap. She is really a consummate artist. —*E. P.*[10]

FRANCESCO VIGLIANI AND OTHERS[11]

If I again find one supremely interesting musical event to record, it is not because I intended to do so. I have no preconceived notion that an article on Music should star an artist, and group the rest of the critique around him.

The performance by the Vigliani String Quartet was really remarkable. We know that quartets and orchestras are supposed to play in time, and that under tolerably good conducting the end of a bar is, more or less, the end of the bar for most of the instruments. The difference between mumbling group-music and superlative group-music is largely a matter of the perfect coincidence of the tempo. This coincidence, however, is so rarely perfect that the normal concert-goer forgets to look for it; and when it happens it partakes of magic. In the case of the Vigliani quartet I was unable to distinguish the instruments but for the volume of sound, and if I had not known that the deeper notes must come from the 'cello, I should have been quite able to think I was listening to one performer. I find it very difficult to describe otherwise the difference between a reasonable amount of precision, and the overplus, the superlative exactness, which makes music worth listening to.

The Debussy quartet opens with fine mimetics of a theatre with events. The orchestration is exquisite. My complaint against Debussy is largely that he writes so much for the piano. His greater distinction becomes apparent, on the other hand, the instant he writes for strings or for voices; for voices, as in the choral settings of Villon and Charles D'Orléans; and for strings, in the four great passages of music that are set in D'Annunzio's appallingly stupid and pretentious "St. Sebastian."

---

[10] *The Little Review*, March, 1918, p. 60.
[11] *The New Age*, January 24, 1918, pp. 248–49.

Debussy, the minor poet in music, is now well known to us, but the great musician is known so little. How can he be, indeed, until one has heard his string music, or, in less degree, his settings for voices and strings?

His work in this quartet is remarkable; every combination of sound in it is, if not discovery, at least alive; the Mozartian padding has been taken out of it (for there are undoubtedly passages in Mozart in which the composer has just run on without particular attention to his business).

The second movement of the quartet opens with a superficial banality of 1840 and Murger. The banality, I think, is on the surface, but one is, nevertheless, puzzled by it, ultimately to grant that perhaps the opening of this movement has its function in the form; but is by no means as delightful as the rest. The third movement is exquisite and superb, from the silvery tone of the opening, following through in the clarion to the gold-brown and the slender. The fourth movement is rich, with a sort of ripe sinuous richness. To hear all this perfectly rendered is worth a month's prowling in concert halls.

In Debussy's piano work, that is, in the music by which Debussy is generally known, there is a charm which is also a weakness. When Debussy was new to us, those of us who "heard" him at all found in the "Sunken Cathedral," in "Sails," in "Gold Fish," in the "Granada," and, indeed, in all this type of work, suggestion of colours, suggestion of visions, and, with good pianists, a new use of the sound-residue, the aftertone and the overtone. And this visionary revel was a delight. By his very titles it was hinted to us that the composer wished to suggest scenes and visions and objects, and, to a great extent, he succeeded. He succeeded, I do not wish to be paradoxical, in writing music for the eye, with the result—as in a different way with Wagner and the middle XIXth century musicians who wrote for the solar plexus, and as must be with any composer who writes music for anything beside or for anything in addition to the ear—the effect of his music diminishes on repeated hearing.

Even in the opening of the quartet there is a remnant of this eye-music, or music for the imagination's eye; but in his string work Debussy gives us so much for the ear, and for the ear exclusively, and so great an interest in the actual sound, that I think there will be no diminution of interest in his quartet, however often one may hear it. But I do not expect to hear it as well played until Messrs. Vigliani, Dubois, Greenbaum and Mancini choose to perform it again.

The next event in their programme was an ordeal for us. Their singer, Miss Mulligan, was in constant strife with the perfect quartet. She had what might have been a good voice, but no sense of co-operation. She is evidently accustomed to singing with a piano accompaniment, and feels the need of drowning the rest of the music, of competing and overcoming it. The concert audience does, I dare say, prefer some sort of squall. But it was impossible to consider the merits of Catalani's music under these circumstances. The Vigliani quartet might trust to its own abilities in the future, and not call in outside aid to diversify the performance.

Mr. Frank Bridge's "Novelleten" is a sort of pee-wee-pee-wee sound, with a hang and drag in it. It is largely made of left-overs with a little new stuff in it. The new music of living composers ought to be performed publicly, but I do not want to hear this particular piece again, and the fault was not in the players. The third division is most bearable, probably about 1870 Vienna, slightly desiccated. There is no interest of theme or of orchestration.

The opening bars of the César Franck quintet place that composer in his noticeably bourgeois or épicier element, but he indubitably understood the piano as an instrument. The part here is not particularly interesting in its repetitions. Miss Myra Hess was admirably in scale with the strings, and in this she afforded a pleasing contrast to the singer who preceded her. Franck belonged to the period when musicians believed that if you could only keep up some sort of bim-bim-ation long enough you would end by exciting the auditor. This thesis is also provable with a tom-tom. Franck's period, of course, respected renaissance architecture, the mass of La Salute, of St. Paul's; Si monumentum requieres, etc.... The piano is really part of this quintet, and not an excrescence; it is not by any means easy to render this in performance, and Miss Hess deserves commendation. Bits of the quintet are rather better done in the original Chopin, and, on the whole, it is designed to induce postprandial feelings. It even sups a little "Contes d'Hoffmann." Franck is bread and butter in orchestration.

Miss Muriel Foster in her concert displayed a pleasant mellow voice, with ecclesiastical traces. She rather mouthed and muffled her Purcell. She was well accompanied, seemed to have a little phlegm in the throat, but was good when clear. The opacity of her tone was probably intentional; she prolonged her time intervals a little too much. "Nigrocella" was good at the end. After that, the performance accommodated itself to the Chappell Ballad concert level. Mr. John Ireland's lyrics were not stimulating—slush and the Victorian school, an attempt at dramatics, on the part of the singer. In short, she is one of the better sort, with all the current faults of the afternoon concert singer, all there but somewhat subdued and toned down. In this Victorian style there is a struggle to make emotion apparent, not violently, but still apparent; and this interferes with the music, or would if most of the music of the school did not depend, almost wholly, on some such dramatic executive bluff.

Sammons and Murdoch were dull after Vigliani; they lacked just the superlative qualities which made the quartet so refreshing. We were glad, however, to have three sonatas, Brahms (D minor), Franck (in A), and the "Kreutzer," evenly laid out before us. It was a very convenient focus for one's thoughts on these three composers. The performers gave the Brahms rather slenderly, with some temperament and a few squeaks. The piano performance seemed to have no special bearing, though there was obviously some inter-relation. The second movement was given more robustly. It is, however, erroneous to imagine that physical vigour will make up for musical vigour. A slender noise and precision are the musician's means, for in mere volume he cannot compete with even the lightest howitzer. There is resin in Brahms, but this error was as much his as that of his interpreters; the piano drowns the fiddle now and then.

Franck is a shade more theatrical; he suggests a stage scene with drop scenes, wings, etc., whereas Brahms suggests a back parlour with heavy curtains, probably puce-coloured. We recall a period when Pater and Fiona McLeod wrote long purple paragraphs about music. Sammons got his tone somewhere in the Franck sonata, and Murdoch handled his piano well. The sonata has moments of vacancy; it is a search for emotion in music. In its period people longed to be affected by music. Despite one's feeling of duty toward the performers it was easier to go on scribbling one's own thoughts. These mid-nineteenth century composers have about as much form as so many armchairs; and it is about as easy to define the difference between one and another as to define the billowy and bunchy difference in armchairs.

The violin opening of the "Kreutzer" is exquisite; then the piano jabs in, and jerks on the violin, tum, tum, ti, ump, tum, tum, ti ump. One wonders if it would go better with an harpsichord. There is then a monotony and a waggle back and forth. It is the great fight of solar-plexus versus ear. This sonata is a summary of the whole musical history of three-quarters of a century. The second movement is most beautiful when it is reminiscent of the classic style. Then comes the XIXth century, during which the defects of the composer were left to be made up by the sweat of the player. The jijijige jijiji recalls the classics. Then the music kicks up and goes off in tiresome bits and pizzicato. It is pre-Wagnerian, pre-Tannhäuser; and then it is second-class Tannhäuser; and then it is simply all the orchestral overtures that one has since heard in all theatres. It is extraordinary that the whole of a century's, to me, at least, wrong, subsidence in music should be outlined in a single sonata. It is undeniable that Beethoven was greatly to be pitied for the deafness that came on him in later life. He was without doubt a great figure, or all of a half century's musicians would never have set that deafness on a pedestal and imbibed it and revelled in it. He was probably the Paschal lamb and the symbol of the suffering or decadence of the European ear, and the general triumph of loudness.

However, a bad period in an art does not mean the final end of the art. Tasso and Ariosto were long worshipped.

René Ortmans with his orchestra and his indistinct leading managed to take all the quality out of Mozart's symphony in D. He made it sound as if it had been written in 1860. He has taught his strings to produce an organ tone very nicely. He was assisted by an excellent Oboe and Bassoon in the playful Ethelbert-Nevin-like "Paysages" of B. Hollander.

In affairs of tempo the *beat* is a knife-edge and *not* the surface of a rolling-pin. Vigliani and his three friends have discovered this, but a great many musicians have not.

D'ALVAREZ, THE INDISCRIMINATE[12]

The Peruvian lady is a very considerable artist without being quite a musician. Nature and art have conspired in furnishing her with a voice. She is unrivalled in her pianissimo, in all the graces of glide and approach, incomparable in all the little trills and appoggiature. But, immortal gods! What a programme! She began, a little throaty, in Bach's "O Golgotha," with a curious *mat* tone, great art in the descents; she sang as if painting the song with deliberate brushstrokes. (In "Di Veroli" she had an accompanist whom we do not cease to commend.) In "Caro mi Ben" she searched, perhaps a shade too markedly, for an original rendering of a very familiar song. The centre of her talent is not in rhythm. Neither is "ben" pronounced "bain," nor "te" "thé." If Madame D'Alvarez will draw her tongue back just a little farther into her mouth she will be able to avoid this Peruvianisation of Italian. It is quite easy not to "thethear" if one go at it mechanically. In the Handel one noticed a tendency to make great gaps of contrast, a leap constantly from very loud to very soft, rather than a shading. This leap is by no means debarred, but if done too often it betrays a paucity of thought. In "Rispetto" we had the perfect fit; the singer was obviously just in the centre of the composition.

"Dernier Vœu" was a little over-dramatic. "Kisses," by Cox, was not chosen for its musical value. In "Nebbie" we had again the gap of con-

[12] *The New Age*, February 7, 1918, pp. 292–93.

trast, and in "Homing" things descended to the level of Madame Tussaud. The "Girl with the Auburn Hair" used to do this sort of thing on the music halls, with a transparent church, snowstorm, and, I think, gauze angels as a finale to "The Holy City." There was a momentary delirium on the part of the audience, while the piano looked like a hearse covered with bouquets. However, the better part of the company soon began to resent the insult. We presume Madame D'Alvarez hopes to be heard at the Coliseum. In "Air des Cartes," from "Carmen," the interest was dramatic rather than musical, and there is no reason why "Bonjour Suzon" should not win Madame D'Alvarez a success in any café chantant.

Gorgeous voice, and no taste. She is the servant of the public, of any public. There were great depths in her voice in the "Carmen." There was always the skill and the charm, the charm unrivalled in its quality whenever she made her soft glides and approaches. If anyone had doubted her great capacities she reassured them with a group of Debussy songs. "De Rêve" was exquisite (but dramatic). In "De Soir" we again wish to commend her accompanist. In "Massenet" it was further borne in upon us that, apart from the natural endowment of her voice, D'Alvarez's real art or real interest is dramatic, or, at least, a shade more dramatic than musical. "Air de Chimène" was thus perfectly given, for Massenet's own artistic centre is as much in drama as in the music. As long as this singer gives us a certain percentage of beautiful music in each programme we shall go to listen, and we shall listen with a reasonable and delighted rapture—we will endure the slush for the sake of the beauty. We would on the contrary give thanks to whatever gods exist if she would employ some person of taste to select her songs, all of them, for her. Her voice is so beautiful, and at her best her art is so fine that we feel at perfect liberty to find all the fault we like, and to dwell on details which in a lesser singer we should pass over without notice. (Æolian Hall.) D'Alvarez next recital, February 21, at 3 o'clock, in the Æolian Hall.

The London String Quartet gave the Debussy G minor quartet with less resonance, with less colour of tone, than Vigliani. They, in fact, dragged Debussy back about thirty years. One felt that four musicians had just sat down to play a piece, not, as with Vigliani, that one was hearing a prepared and thought-out performance. No executive imagination had gone into the thing. They opened the third movement with exquisite feeling, but got lost in the middle, the lack of plan becoming only too apparent. At no time had we the illusion that we were listening to a single instrument; this was due mostly to lack of leadership, and in part to the 'cello. They are, however, to be complimented on attempting the piece at a concert officially labelled a "pop." Mosiewitch, in the Schumann Toccata, came very near to convincing me for the eightieth time that the more a piano is "played," and perhaps the better it is played, the more it resembles a railroad train or a pianola. Mosiewitch's mastery of the instrument is no mere digital dexterity; one felt that his little soft strips of sound overlaid the monotony of the Toccata, and they were indubitably arranged in a design completely under Mr. Mosiewitch's control. Opening the Schumann Romance in F sharp, he exhibited the piano as a musical instrument (even if sentimentally). Still, we long for a movement that will drive the piano permanently into back parlours, and reserve the stage for real instruments. As for the Mendelssohn Scherzo, we had hoped that this composer had finally followed Rubinstein and the author of "Bubbling Spring" into the limbo of young ladies' seminaries. If, however, Mosiewitch, with his incontestible technique and capacity, chose to give a recital of the less frequented portions of Chopin, we would only too willingly listen. For this he has, I think, an almost complete equipment.

Holbrooke's Impression is well written, and was carefully rendered by the Quartet. Murray Davey has an even control and finish; he understands the capacity of his voice and stays well within it. It is seldom that an opera singer breaks into composition. He is to be complimented on his "Harmonie du Soir." The piano is well with the strings, though I cannot say that the voice with the five instruments at all times produces the effect of being part of an artistic unity. (Queen's Hall.)

La Signorina Nina Garelli is a very attractive young lady, but musical accent is not put on with the eyebrows, nor will any manipulation of these facial ornaments make up for singing flat. She was cold in Caldara, trusting to the music, but not putting life into it. In the Cimarosa she was exquisite, and di Veroli as accompanist was again welcome. Campion's "Oft have I sighed for him" is very charming, but the English word "still" is not pronounced "steel," and such pronunciation does not enhance the charms of the author. A setting of something called "The Cuckoo" was evidently laid by "Killarney's Rocks and Fells," and hatched by something not naturally designed as a parent. Garelli was at her best in the "Stornello," which she perfectly well understood. She has various faults of certain Italian singing systems; she has not, as yet, any grasp on French music. In trying to sing the impossible words of "A Dream" there was, we admit, nothing to do but add Italian terminal vowels to English. There are, however, lyrical qualities inherent in English, even though they have been obscured for nearly three centuries by the laziness and stupidity of English poetasters and librettists.

No singer can be blamed for refusing or making a botch of most English song since Campion. In the line, "What is the night within the mind," in "Isobel," Frank Bridge gives us a prize example of how not to set words to music; all the emphasis of the verbal phrase is destroyed and obliterated. It is impossible to sing his notes without ruining the sense of the line (not that the lyric itself is of any great value). In periods when the art of song was in health, the music intensified the verbal emotion. In Reynaldo Hahn's "Seule" we have by contrast an excellent and commendable placing of words to music. Despite di Veroli's excellent work at the piano, Signorina Garelli emphasised her lack of grip on French singing in Fauré's "Fleur Jetée."

It is to be hoped she listened behind the curtain when her accompanist sang us two songs set by himself. She would at least have had an illustration of how to make the most of a voice, a voice in di Veroli's case having a few soft velvet notes in his lower register.

The musical phrase to his finale "E l'Universo ti dira ch'io t'amo," is inadequate, and the large noise of the accompaniment does not conceal this defect.

Signorina Garelli finished with a scrap of Rossini, having in it a few fine phrases. It begins with a Brighton pier sort of prelude. The tragedy of Rossini's life was to have died before the invention of the cinematograph. He would have written most happily for that instrument.

The song ends, needless to say, on a high note in a yell. (Æolian Hall.)

Atheling was now jabbing confidently against the tonnage of contemporary musical opinion. His summary of the celebrated opera singer Marguerite d'Alvarez—"gorgeous voice and no taste"—may be compared with the more felicitous appraisal of the same recital in *The Musical Times:* "Madame d'Alvarez, the Peruvian singer, gave a recital on January 22. The highly-gifted lady has now made a great reputation, and it may be said at once that at this recital she generally fulfilled the highest expectations of her numerous admirers."[13]

From the correspondence column of *The New Age,* March 7, 1918:

> Sir,—The condescension of Mr. Atheling is sublime; his capability as a critic is doubtful, judging by the cheapness of his satire and the crudity of his suggestions: why call upon "the immortal gods"—they would care as little for the programme as Mr. Atheling's criticism of it!
>
> The song "Homing" is unknown to me, but what can it have to do with the harmless and defunct Madame Tussaud? The description of the piano as a decorated hearse is in questionable

---

[13] *The Musical Times,* London, March, 1918, p. 120.

taste, as surely the admirers of D'Alvarez may offer her flowers without being accused of delirium. Probably the artist would be delighted to sing "Bonjour Suzon" in a café chantant if we could boast of one. I entirely agree with Mr. Atheling when he states that he has the right to "find fault," but to write that D'Alvarez is "the servant of any public," that "one endures the slush for the sake of the beauty," is more in the nature of vulgar abuse than decent rebuke.

I contend that honest criticism should be expressed according to one's conception of the good and the beautiful, and be inspired by a genuine attempt to instruct the public without any deliberate intention of hurting the feelings of the artist. Some of us who criticise are apt to forget the labour, self-denial, and anxiety of those who provide the pleasures of a fickle public: all the more, then, let us be generous and just: we need not, in consequence, stultify our opinions. Perhaps Mr. Atheling is lacking in sympathy —courtesy is obviously absent.

Ernest Wilton Schiff

Atheling replied with a letter of his own to the correspondence column.[14]

> Sir,—Mr. Ernest Wilton Schiff, not having heard the song "Homing," and apparently therefore not having attended the concert, or at least having absented himself from that part of it, is doubtless *the* person most entitled to an opinion of my opinion of the performance. I congratulate him on the telepathy of his perceptions.
>
> The critic does not attend concerts in order to sympathise with or commiserate the performers. Some performers doubtless need sympathy, but the exercise of bringing one's feelings into exact tune and accord with these performers would end by ruining the critic's capacities for perception.
>
> The critic is the agent of the public. His praise is equivalent to advising his readers to spend anything from 2s. 6d. to 12s. 6d. for the privilege of hearing a fine performance, and his credit is ruined if he advises them to waste their admission fees. Madame Alvarez' second performance was of a nature to make me regret having praised the first one of her present series.
>
> The critic presumably has, or should have, heard a certain amount of really excellent music, and he should hold up some

[14] *The New Age,* March 14, 1918, p. 403.

standards of perfection, in the hope either of assisting or even of forcing inadequate performers to improve. His fidelity to perfection and to excellence is far more important than any camouflage of flattery, or, as Mr. Schiff calls it, "courtesy," that he might spread over his notices. These drawing-room manners have little place in a search for exactitude, and they can very well be left to dilettantes who have no other occupation, and who have never sought gradations of language in which to convey the quality of a performance, or the gradations of quality between one concert and another.

What I deplore, and what Mr. Schiff apparently cannot understand anyone's deploring, is that people should labour to please an imbecile public which never does and never can know its own mind, instead of spending an equivalent effort trying to produce excellent art, to which the more intelligent members of the public are always, in the end, gathered.

William Atheling

DÄMMERUNG OF THE PIANO[15]

Conductor Capt. A. Williams, M.V.O., Mus. Doc., Oxon, in a red sash, sword, white gloves, etc., opened the concert of the Grenadier Guards Band, with no perception of the roof or enclosing wall of the building (Queen's Hall). I have inspected the savage rites of our little Island; for twenty years nothing like it has happened to me. (I write this almost immediately after the operation; I hope my ears will be in condition to hear the concerts next week.) Still, one does *not* want to hear chimes from inside the belfry. Mr. Harry Dearth sang his comic song (serious ending) with clear enunciation. The singing of Miss Lett is a sort of combination of "Deutschland über Alles" and Sunday Service in a thoroughly Presbyterian village. Her attack on the Italian language was, without qualification, distressing. Captain Williams made heroic efforts, and in great measure succeeded in keeping the band almost quiet during Felix Salmond's 'cello playing. Salmond can do anything he likes with the 'cello. He is one of the rare artists who are really worth hearing (I had almost written "even with a band in the background"). For the rest these rites of Boadicea are beyond my comprehension; they are an imperial or political manifestation; the performance was obviously creditable of its kind, but the language is one to which I have lost the dictionary.

The first impression of Miss Annabel McDonald is that she is in some

---

[15] *The New Age*, February 24, 1918, pp. 334–35.

ways competent, sings in tune, and has learned correctly to pronounce Italian; then appear traces of the Christmas festival manner. Her defect of passion is only too apparent when she attempts the Kennedy-Fraser interpretations of Hebridean Songs. These things were painted in woad, but Miss McDonald gives them swathed in blue baby-ribbon. One can only pray that the original wilderness of the songs will be apparent at a performance to be given under the indefatigable collector's own supervision at Æolian Hall, March 11th, at 6 p.m.; for the melodies are among the finest of our national heritage, as Wagner found out rather before the English musicians, gaining no inconsiderable advantage from the priority of his knowledge.

The McDonald afternoon was relieved by Salmond's 'cello, resonant, fully mastered, but impeded by the accompanist. Mr. H. Samuel was determined that the audience should realise to the last drop of gore that the Rachmaninoff op. 19 in E minor is entitled "Sonata for the PIANOFORTE and Cello." "Cello" is really printed in the same size type as Pianoforte, but we must admit that the word "pianoforte" comes first in the title. As Mr. Samuel's piano playing is, to put it mildly, without the least vestige of interest, his insistence on the order of words in the title was at times rather trying.

The programme had been chosen without any musical significance and descended to simon-pure suburbania in the second group of songs. I fled before Mr. Samuel was permitted to reach the section labelled Pianoforte Solos. We should be profoundly grateful if Mr. Salmond would give a recital by himself.

THE PIANO

Why, indeed, the piano? This instrument has many sins on its keyboard. I leave aside the unending bickering over the tempered scale, even though one interiorily protests against the argument that it is no use bothering over an accuracy of pitch that only one person in two hundred can perceive. People without absolute pitch-sense do, and do very often, get a certain definite pleasure from correct playing even if they are incapable of detecting a single error, or even a series of errors save by a vague dissatisfaction or by an even slighter and more vague diminution of pleasure.

All keyboard instruments tend to make into performers people not born to be musicians; and the very fact that one can play a keyboard instrument quite correctly without in the least knowing whether a given note is in tune or is correct in itself, tends to obscure the value of true pitch. What is the first requisite of any player upon strings is therefore left perhaps wholly unconsidered by the piano student. The piano-tuner is responsible for all that. His services are inexpensive.

This argument could be used against the earlier keyboard instruments, but they were never sufficiently loud to drive out and predominate over the rest of the instruments. They did not "fill the building."

From carelessness about pitch the piano has gradually progressed to a carelessness about actual sound. The attention centered, in earlier music, upon purity of tone, upon sound quality, has been weakened and weakened, till I have seen a composer of no small talent utterly impervious to the quality of noise he was making. The notes were in the right order; they followed each other as he intended; he was satisfied.

I long, perhaps not too vainly, for the day when the piano shall be as the hansom, which vehicle it not a little resembles; and when the pianist shall be as the cab-driver, so far as the concert hall is concerned. The instrument will abide with us yet, for there is the pianola attachment, and if for some time it is necessary to train acrobats to play Bach-Busoni for pianola records, surely human invention will lead to, and has already discovered, a means for making the records direct. The future composer will do his work, not with a pen but a punch. "You couldn't pack a Broadwood half a mile," says Mr. Kipling, but there is always the gramophone.

But the platform pianist? These remarks are not all due to the last performance I suffered, but that performance has nevertheless been unable to arrest them. She opened, indeed, with delicacy, with prettiness, getting a good variety of sounds out of her instrument. She had no *forte*. I recalled indefinitely some Berlin critic's outburst to the effect that the piano was not a "Schlaginstrument." Then we had the "Stimmung" of the studios; and the "Ahnung" in the stealthy on-creeping bass notes. She was really doing quite well. At least "it took me back twenty years." Have we not all, with the shades of Murger, with the well-known death mask gaping at us, and with the plaster cast of the drowned girl hanging in the other corner, have we not all of us known the charm? (The Schumann quality that has been read into Chopin by generations of conservatoire young ladies to the obscuring of Chopin's austerity.) The pathetic thing is that the pianist had thought about music, and had considered the art, to some extent. It was the studio "mood" as opposed to the piano of Sir Frederick Leighton and the Leightoniania, the instrument at which the very young mother sits with her numerous well-washed, fresh offspring clambering about her, receiving the cultural rudiments. The pianist in this case had merits; so has the cab-driver.

In the next piece there were fireworks; the pianola would have compassed them. Attention faded. I left the hall. I observed the more distinguished critic sitting patiently in his seat, his nose deep in a French book.

I do not say that I am above the studio manner; that I would not willingly recall the past, forget my bald spot. "Four and forty times would I," as Mr. Kipling has it, listen to the wailful note as the more reserved couple wait until it is time to walk home, and the less reserved, or more "bohemian" couple hold hands under the sofa cushion, —Jugend, Jugend, Jugend! and the inefficient illustrator (aged sixty) who once hoped to paint like Raphael, looks at the ceiling or the performer.

But what has all this to do with the concert hall? A certain crop of female pianists always hoped to produce in the concert-hall the atmosphere of the studio; to bring to the hoarse old gentleman from the Thames valley and to the large-waisted lady from Roehampton a "breath of the real meaning," to "show them that life . . ."; and sometimes the female pianist succeeded . . . after the final uncalled-for encore, when all but her dearest friends had left the building.

Nevertheless, the concert-hall is not the studio. Some musicians may actually play better in studios; they may get some force from the "atmosphere"; or the general state of emotion and personal sympathy in the company may merely blur the critical senses; but these things do not concern the concert-hall. The magnetic theory is invalid. No performer can rely on emotionalising the audience. Music in a concert-hall must rely on itself and the perfection of its execution; it is, as it were, under glass. It exists on the other side of the footlights, apart from the audience. With apologies to the language, the audience are spectators, they watch a thing of which they are not a part; and that thing must be complete in itself. They may be moved by the contemplation of its beauty. They are not moved, or at least can be moved only in an inferior and irrelevant way by being merged into the action of the stage.

I labour this point rather heavily, but it is not a trifle, and hundreds of musical careers have been muddled simply because the performers have not understood how entirely the music must lead its own life; must have its own separate existence apart from the audience; how utterly useless it is to try to mix up audience and performance.

A PROGRAMME, AND THE MALADMINISTERED LYRIC[16]

A concert in a concert hall is a performance, a presentation, not an appeal to the sympathies of the audience. It is, or should be, as definitely a presentation or exhibition as if the performer were to bring out

[16] *The New Age,* March 7, 1918, pp. 377–78.

a painted picture and hang it before the audience. The music must have as much a separate existence as has the painting. It is a malversion of art for the performer to beseech the audience (*via* the instrument) to sympathise with his or her temperament, however delicate or plaintive or distinguished. That is the gist of what I wrote in my last criticism of the studio-method, Stimmung, and "atmosphere."

From the "studio" manner (in concert halls), from the domestic manner, from the rural church manner, and from the national festival manner, may the surviving deities protect and deliver us! They have not, they do not, but we do not cease to pray that they may achieve it.

Having written the above paragraph I went to hear Miss Daisy Kennedy. She understands perfectly well the principles I have laid down. She kept her music on the stage, independent of the audience. It was a presentation, it had its own existence, an existence as distinct as that of painting. Moreover, there was some intelligence used in the arrangement of her programme. We are tired of the aimless programme, the programme that is made up of just the pieces the musician happens to know; we are tired to death of the programme, *sic:* 1. Ancient. 2. Less Ancient. 3. Fusty. 4. The Last Thing. Miss Kennedy treated us and music as if music were an art with what is called "its literature," a thing one might take seriously. The programme was Bach and as follows:

> Concerto in E major (Allegro, Adagio, Allegro assai).
> Adagio and Fugue in G minor (unaccompanied).
> Aria on G string.
> Chaconne in D minor (unaccompanied).
> Gavotte in E.
> Andante in C (unaccompanied).
> Prelude in E.

Despite the fact that there were several points in the Chaconne at which the composer "might have stopped but didn't," and despite Miss Kennedy's lack of certitude in execution, this programme served fully to demonstrate that Bach is *not* monotonous; and that the people who find him monotonous do so on the same principle that a man finds a foreign restaurant monotonous having, in his ignorance of the language of the menu, attempted to dine off six soups. Here we had an hour-and-a-half of one composer, and I would have gladly sat through another hour.

I want to be explicit in my commendation, for I take this programme as an example of what an intelligent programme can be. I commend also the manner of Miss Kennedy's playing, the "no nonsense" attitude. Her execution is another matter. It is useless to blink [at] the fact that she is not certain. In one place her tempo is good, but the tone not quite satisfactory; in another place she attends to the quality of her sound; but never during this recital did she show herself in the same class with a player like Salmond. One's pleasure is rather ruined if one has always to hope that the player will do the next passage in a satisfactory way. Most, perhaps all, the elements of playing were present seriatim.

The Aria disposes once and for all of the contention that Bach is lacking in romance. It was quite beautifully played. Considering how much the composer has put into it, one is inclined to ask how much "liberty" is needful in music? Miss Doenau accompanied excellently, and gave the opening passages of the second movement in the Concerto with great beauty. (Wigmore Hall.)

Madame Kirkby Lunn's song recital demonstrated by contrast, if demonstration were necessary, that a lyric is not invariably good, merely because it is dated "sixteenth century." An era of bad taste probably gathers to itself inferior matter from preceding periods. An indiscriminate rummaging in the past does not help to form a tradition. Moreover, there was nothing in the setting or rendering of these Old English songs to show that they had not been done in the heyday of the Oxenford period under the eye of the respected Prince Consort. Madame Lunn began "Westron Wynde" rather throatily. Her voice sounded as if it were being strained through a bag. She did not add to our pleasure by dragging "can rain" into "kerrain"; "kiss" into "kees"; "queen" into "kuh-ween"; "my" into "hmi"; "she's" was blurred into "shees" (as in "backsheesh"); "love" turned into "lav." The opening of "Lover's Complaint" was either ill set or ill rendered ("greeneh willow," "garland" or "barland"). The singer continued producing a placid and mournful sound. The idea that all old music was sung at a crawl has been successfully disposed of. We now know that it was not. But if singers of established position will not keep up to time in these matters, who can be expected to do so? Though Madame Lunn is for the most part above it, I caught a faint trace of the church choir manner in "Fortune is my foe." By the time she got to "Chanson de La Mariée" it was evident that the whole programme was likely to continue in the same placid manner. Exit the critic. (Æolian Hall.)

Miss Carrie Tubb sang with spirit. Her concert may well serve to illustrate that a sense of rhythm covers many defects. One can listen to a singer who possesses this sense; one can listen to her for an hour or so, without exhaustion, even though she be unable to take a high note *forte* without an uncontrolled squall (and Miss Tubb appears unable to do so). The pain caused to the ear by occasional horrid sounds is quickly obliterated in the succeeding flow of the music. Singers hoping for platform success will do well to notice this. A drag, a lack of the wave force, deadens, tires, utterly wears out the audience. Rhythm-sense is not merely a *temps mesuré*, it is not merely a clockwork of the bar-lengths. Measured time is only one form of rhythm; but a true rhythm sense assimilates all sorts of uneven pieces of time, and keeps the music alive.

The next thing that strikes me is the appalling state of the lyric as presented in current concerts. Both the arrangers of words and the arrangers of notes appear inexcusable. Miss Tubb enunciates her English words clearly; and she dared to sing her Schumann, Schubert, Mozart, Brahms in English translations. But despite her abilities it is, in the second verse of the English version of "Mein Ruh ist hin," utterly impossible to sing "His hand's dear clasp" to the notes given. The Mozart melody was exquisite and the words inadequate. (I omit to mention the exact points at which the singer elected to squall.) The Beethoven song was an apparently needless concession to the supposedly low taste of the audience, but it provided the first moment of real enjoyment to the accompanist (Sir Henry Wood). To sing (*sic*) "O had I a HELL-met and doublet and hose"; to repeat this with increasing volume, such as cannot be rendered by any capital letters at our disposal, must be regarded as purely comic by any vigilant listener. We fared no better when lyrics of confessed verbal quality were exposed to our contemporary composers.

> "Let those which only warble long,
> And gargle in their throats a song,
> Content ourselves with UT, RE, MI;
> Let words and sense be set by thee."

wrote Waller in conclusion of his poem to Henry Lawes, and, with Lawes' work and example at the disposal of any of our springall composers who have the patience to inspect it, there is no excuse for the repeated botches, and for the particular sorts of botches continually poured upon us.

In this programme, in a setting of A. E. Housman, the words were clear but not enhanced: in the last line the emotion of the music had no connection with the emotion of the words. Matthew Arnold's verses were over-sentimentalised by the music; and what sense is there in accenting the line, "And sometime by STILL harder fate"? The setting of Blake was rubbish. Stanley Hawley was encored, which perhaps served to show that the singer was at any rate commercially right in singing down to "the public." Vaughan Williams was immeasurably better than the setters who had preceded him; he had at least grasped the spirit of Christina Rossetti's poem. Bantock was experimenting with Arabian exoticism.

When I say the words were clear but not enhanced, I distinctly point out that words of no particular import or value may become part of a complete and excellent song, as was illustrated by the group of Bel Canto songs, by Monteverde, Lotti, Marcello, Pergolesi, Durante, though Miss Tubb is not artist enough to do them credit. Perhaps she can only "get into" songs in her native language. At any rate, her interpretations showed no depth of comprehension. It was curious to note the substitution of the sentimental rendering for the proper emotional quality of the Italian. She was better in the Old English, but I think she is wrong to judge by the volume of applause. People who hear Lawes with slight defects are put off thereby and do not burst into cheering, but it is not necessary to suppose they are fewer than those who clap for a poor thing bawled out lustily. Again, I would point out Lawes as an example of how the words of a poem may be set and enhanced by music. There are different techniques in poetry; men write to be read, or spoken, or declaimed, or rhapsodised; and quite differently to be sung. Words written in the first manners are spoiled by added music; it is superfluous; it swells out their unity into confusion.

When skilled men write for music, then music can both render their movement, as Lawes does often, tone by tone, and quantity by quantity; or the musician may apparently change the word-movement with a change that it were better to call a realisation. Music is not speech. Arts attract us because they are different from reality; yet differ in some way that is proportionate to reality. Emotions shown in actual speech poured out under emotion will not all go into verse. The printed page does not transmit them, nor will musical notation record them phonographically; but, for all that, a certain bending of words or of syllables over several notes may give an emotional equivalent.

This is an art by itself, differing from poetry, and from the art of harmony or of counterpoint. Nevertheless, it has occasionally and triumphantly appeared in the world, and is well worth an effort to recover. Lawes was English of the English; he was no obscure man in his day, being a king's musician and a man lauded of poets. He was English of the English, but he did not fall a prey to the pig-headed insularity of the British Association of Musicians; he did not shun foreign competition. He set Anacreon's "Εἰς Λύραν" in the Greek, and he set songs in Italian and Latin. He was, for all that I know, the last English composer to know Greek. Our decadence may be due to the fact that the educated are now too stupid to participate in the arts. This lack of lineage shows in modern art in all its branches. As a French singer said to me yesterday: "When these people (English artists, composers, etc.) have done (i.e., written, painted, composed) anything, they seem to think that that is the end, and that there is nothing more to be done about it."

MUSIC[17]

HERBERT FRYER (Wigmore Hall) belongs to the blurry and rippling type of pianist; he has variety and liquidity of sound, but it is tiring to wait for the beat. He was doing (or attempting to do) something with sound-retention, but the effect did not reach the Press seats. It sounded at times as if he were beating a pile of feathers; the apparent tiredness of the performer transferred itself to the critic. From his performance one might argue (I should be glad to do so, as it falls in with my own views) that even the pianists are tired of the piano, disillusioned; that the practical inconvenience of admitting this is the chief reason for keeping the admittedly sound article of commerce so to the fore on the platform. With Fryer one felt a constant effort to express *via* the piano a greater musical comprehension than the piano will express. This limitation *by instrument* is never felt with violin, or with the better wind instruments. Digital dexterity will not supply the lack of emotional depth. Fryer began his transcriptions from Purcell with charm. I thought I should have to swallow my condemnation, but his tiredness made itself apparent before he reached the end of the Minuet. He went off into cinema-twinkle in his own composition, and Bridge is of the ripple school.

Margaret Fairless, the rising flapper violinist, is giving a series of three recitals at the Wigmore, with what is, and in this case may very well be, called great promise. The performance opens most of the questions concerning the treatment of students and talented young musicians. It is unfair to criticise this sort of performance in the same terms that one uses for a mature musician, though the praise of "Little Eyasses," whose future is problematic, is more fascinating than the measurement of riper performers who will obviously never be any better than they are at the moment of observation.

Little Miss Fairless was quite good in her Mozart. Nothing but the music occupied her attention, and she had no assistance from her accompanist; but the Bach fugue was too much for her. On the other hand, the Corelli was satisfactory and admirably in her grasp.

She needs, of course, to be "restrained," not in the repressive sense. I mean she needs a master who will insist on the finer precisions, a

[17] *The New Age*, March 21, 1918, pp. 412–13.

master highly pedantic, but pedantic with the pedantry of over-sensitiveness, not of conventional fixedness. The value of pre-Bach music for such young players cannot be over-estimated. They should begin with the old, for modern music (except the most recent) is but a relaxation of it. Its freedoms, to be effective, must be based on a full sense of the forms underlying. The apparent chaos of modern music is a real chaos in practice unless both composer and performer have the form-sense within them, and this sense both of the major forms and of articulation is best developed by study of the earlier "regular" music. To set so young a musician to doing Wieniawski pyrotechnics before an audience is merely a crime against her future. The exactitudes which are included in masterly playing should be learned first. After a man reads Latin with a fluid but passable inexactness he will not go back and learn conjugations (even though they would often save him many a misunderstanding of his author), neither do middle-aged musicians go back and learn musical fineness. The more remarkable the pupil's general temperamental or talental equipment, the greater the crime of encouraging her to make splurges.

Vide, in the last connection, Madame Alvarez, making splurges. In her second recital (Æolian Hall) her voice was not in good trim. All the exquisite pianissimo, all the graces of approach were lacking; she was singing against her voice, forcing the sound the whole time. Nothing is more frail or tricky than a beautiful voice supplied by nature, and subject to being snuffed out by a slight hoarseness. A fine vocal artist has all sorts of resources, but Madame Alvarez was excited by the applause, and her gestures à la Bartholdi did not help her. "Nebbie" is over-dramatic, but justifiable as a display of vocal magnificence. Alvarez's lower notes were in order. There was no need to sing "I dreamt that I was weeping" three times, nor with such sentimentality. Her words in "De Rêve" were not clear; and, lastly and chiefly, one is convinced, above all things, that the Peruvian lady, richly dowered by nature, has not only never desired to improve, but that even the thought of improvement or the idea that improvement is possible has never entered her head. How much the absence of Di Veroli from the piano and the unfortunate substitution of Kiddle contributed to the general inferiority of her second recital I am unable to say. A singer of mental resource would not be so subject to her accompanist.

The Catterall Quartet gave a solid business-like opening to their Beethoven (Quartet in E flat Op. 127. Wigmore Hall). Beethoven was doubtless, in his day, a relief from too many trills; he towered as a colossus over the delicate derivativeness of Steibelt; he was a Titan, but he is now rather too much the daily (or pre-war daily) roast beef of music. The effect of deliverance that he may have given his contemporaries is no more to be had from him. He seems verbose, not nonsensical but verbose. He makes a beautiful appeal to the mediocre intelligence. He should be put away for a time and only taken out again when he shall have regained a certain strangeness. There was nothing uncommon to the usual theatre orchestra, or unsuitable for restaurant performance in the playing of the quite efficient Catterall Quartet.

WINIFRED PURNELL

As for flagrant and obvious errors of inexperience: to begin with Chopin's Twenty-Four preludes, played without intermission; and half the audience, having arrived at 3.5, 3.15, 3.20 waiting in hall till 3.40 and decidedly out of temper! What shall be said for the reckless rashness of musicians who make their début in this manner? I heard through the doors a brilliant, hard technique and a magnificent rhythm. This girl's playing is clear-cut, not mellifluous; it is calculated to annoy the four-by-six Beethoven-Wagner musician, who has from childhood seen above the old family double length grand piano the large photo-reproductions of Haydn and Handel and Mendelssohn. Note that she grasped the rhythm division of the big Liszt sonata; she had the sense of aftersound; she made this rather heavy work interesting. It was not, what it so often is even in presumably accomplished performance, a mush and a mess. The clear, hard, metallic properties of the piano were *applied,* not ineffectively disguised. I am the last to say that Miss Purnell is a safe pianist to recommend to the public; she has a touch of that quality which makes primitive folk believe in voodoo and witch doctors; this is sometimes called genius; it is always disturbing and distressing, if not to the public, at least to the stock-sized practitioner of music, and the stock-sized regular attendant.

Her playing was, if you like, strident, but no part was not clearly thought out beforehand. I here put down my thoughts as they came to me during her Liszt: She will probably be quite intelligent on subjects apart from piano playing. (It is rash to think in this manner about musicians.) This is the first piano-playing that has moved me this season. She is of the first rank among women pianists. At any rate, the music does take up its own life and live and proceed in its own entirety; her playing is not a laborious clawing at the outside of the music. There is a profundity of musical feeling.

The Macdowell sonata is not an unquestionable work; it served, however, to display her bass control. The treble runs are inadequate, and the fault is, I think, the composer's. I do not believe they can be played effectively. Miss Purnell's interpretation was well articulated. She got from the piano not an imitation of orchestral sounds, as do some skilled pianists, but, what is much more interesting, an equal variety of peculiarly pianistic sounds, and she built up, all through the concert, these noises into a sequence and alternation of their own. The performance, lasting two hours and a quarter, including Chopin and the two sonatas, was in itself a great proof of energy.

Her interpretation of Debussy was personal, puzzling but ultimately powerful and impressive, if not, in one or two points, conclusive. I have never heard the bass-rumble near the end of the Sunken Cathedral so effective, and I have heard this piece excellently played (played to Debussy's own pleasure and satisfaction).

Miss Purnell's magnificent rhythm-sense and the definiteness of her articulation lift her far out of the ruck of performers. I do not by any means say that she will ever be popular, or that she will please the present concert-going audience, or that any one of the "established" critics will agree with my estimate of her work, but I do think it possible that she may, in time, build up an audience of her own, and that she will interest any auditor who does not arrive at the hall with a determination to hear each piece of music performed exactly as he has heard it before, and who foams at the mouth at every new or strange interpretation.

OPERA

The Beecham opera has begun again; as it is largely Sir Thomas Beecham's personal gift to the public, and as he knows more about it than any of his critics, and as he is steadily improving the production, probably as fast as circumstances permit, stricture is discourteous and suggestion probably a superfluity. There may be occult or practical reasons for giving "Samson et Delilah"; nature may have intended Webster Millar to sing through his nose, and I must conclude that Edith Clegg is, for the present, an indispensable part of a very large mechanism. "Figaro" is being given, and two other Mozart operas. Few people can go more than twice a week, and it is up to them to select the better operas. That is the public's own critical duty; one cannot perform it for them.

THE GAELIC[18]

There is music which reminds one of great forests, of wind and unbridled ocean; there is music, by no means inferior, which reminds one of gilded chairs and the court of Le Grand Monarque; and there is music which reminds one of nothing so much as of too much underwear

---

[18] *The New Age,* March 28, 1918, p. 434.

and too many waistcoats. Lest the casual reader accuse me of harshness, I will not name the individual cause of this last reflection. The bow in violin-playing should not sound as if covered with a mixture of glue and treacle.

In contrast, I am almost beginning to believe that Philip Ashbrooke's name (as manager) on a concert programme is a fair guarantee of quality. I have been let down rather badly once or twice, but the Goldsmith-Haley concert was not a let down. (Wigmore Hall.)

Miss Katie Goldsmith gave her Purcell delightfully, with taste, discretion, temperament, firmness, causing no anxiety to her auditors. The Pugnani Præludium and Allegro might have been chosen to illustrate the decadence of music during the first half of the 18th century. Not that it is a bad piece, but there is in it more talk and less meaning than in the Purcell selected. Mr. Rowsby Woof accompanied excellently, and the piece was excellently played.

The Glazounov Concerto in A Op. 82 opens with a pleasant moderato, goes into a cheap Andante and ends in the restaurant manner. It is not good enough. (And, damn cadenzas!) In her final selection Miss Goldsmith made Woof's "Scherzo" more interesting than Cui's "Orientale," and the Smetana was excellently chosen for a finale. Woof is a young man of talent, and worth keeping an eye on.

Miss Haley's first move should be to get another accompanist. She has herself a delicate softness of voice, and an art adequate for the rendering of Legrenzi. One noticed a slight clipping of words in her Italian, there was ease and grace, and this tendency, in so far as it makes for clarity, is a good one, but it was just a shade overdone. In the English her singing was like little jets of breath, and she did not close her words at the end; her accompanist (Mrs. Haley) was constanly an annoyance. The Colson song is bad, and the other English composers did not show well against Legrenzi and Fauré.

If I have dwelt more on faults than on virtues, I do not wish to give the impression that faults were, in this concert, predominant. I shall go to hear both Miss Goldsmith and Miss Haley as often as they choose.

Gladys Moger (Wigmore Hall) produced a caterwaul with a few mellifluous spots in it; a mannered squall, the words utterly smeared into a compost; but there was beauty in the melody, and the actual sound was not bad. She began with Henry Lawes' music for Comus with atrocious accompaniment, and finished the critic before she had finished her first selections. This was all the more unbearable as I had heard Stroesco's carefully thought programme (Æolian Hall) the day before, and had noted the admirable contrast he gets from varying the apparent distance *from which* the sound proceeds. I did not understand what he aimed at with his rhythm system, which was to my ear, defective. He was admirably accompanied by Di Veroli. The voice is most pleasing, and, a by no means daily occurrence among singers, thought had been expended on the presentation.

Plunkett Greene brought his faithful audience once more together, and one saw various grey and iron-grey heads not seen at other recitals. He wastes himself on second-rate modern poems set without mastery, but when he gives us something with body to it, as for example "Kerry I Am" or "Mistress Maguire" or " 'Twas in the Month of May" the old fire is still there, and one need not fall back on the fine manner, somewhat Tennysonian, and somewhat a reminder of what was once the best taste.

KENNEDY-FRASER

Marjory Kennedy-Fraser has brought out another volume of "Songs from the Hebrides." These traditional melodies of the Gael are among the musical riches of all time, and one need use no comparatives and no tempered adjectives to express the matter. They have in them the wildness of the sea and of the wind and the shrillness of the sea-birds, and whether they will pass away utterly with the present industrious collector I am unable to say. Miss M. Kennedy-Fraser sang "with no voice" but with a magnificent comprehension of the whole rhythm-structure: The Death Croon, and "Of Donnan of Eigg":

> Early puts the sun greeting on Stroa,
> Early chant the birds the beauty of Donnan.

It is just possible that this curious "Figure eight" rhythm cannot be conveyed to the contemporary musician by contemporary musical notation.

> Eárly púts the sún   gree̋ting on S̄trōā,
> Eárly chánt the bírds   the béauty of D́onnan.

At any rate, the wildness of these chants has not been transmitted to Miss M. Kennedy-Fraser's understudy, Miss P. Kennedy-Fraser, who has a lovely voice, and sings to her own pleasant harping. She gets, in the Seal-Woman's song, a rhythm, and in the mouth-music for dancing a decidedly lively rhythm, but she has none of the elder woman's fire and wildness.

Arthur Jordan, their male singer, has a honied voice and a temperament which cannot tell a bag-pipe from a soft-cushion. He purred through "Kishmul's Galley" and his other wild numbers with a placidity which would not have disturbed the knitting circle in any Victorian vicarage. One's sole desire was to move him with dynamite.

Miss P. Kennedy-Fraser was, however, satisfactory in "Aillte," for here the song is narrative, after the event, and is not an expression of the singer's emotion, but only a telling of happenings or emotions of others. For this she is fully equipped, and here, if ever, one heard the epic note. If anything can be, this is the sound of the Ossianic bards, and Homer would have been sung in such manner:

ἀλλ' ὅτε τόσσον ἀπῆμεν, ὅσον τε γέγωνε βοήσας,
ῥίμφα διώκοντες, τὰς δ' οὐ λάθεν ὠκύαλος νηῦς
ἐγγύθεν ὀρνυμένη'λιγυρὴν δ' ἔντυνον ἀοιδήν.

So much for the performance (Æolian Hall). Of the actual work done in collecting and preserving this Gaelic music we cannot speak too highly or with an excess of appreciation. The only trouble is that it needs some singing. I do not quite know who is to sing it. Mullings is stated on the programme to have sung it. Mullings is a splendid actor for opera, but I doubt if even his voice is the ideal one for this work. Robert Parker may have sufficient savagery at his command, for the men's songs.

The Mouth-music for dancing: "Hin, hin, hàradal O" !, makes interesting comparison with the African syncopation, and both in the Gaelic and African there is the curious and splendid figure eight, or fold-over of one rhythm-end into the start of the next. But my impression is that the melodic line is finer in these Gaelic things than in anything African. At any rate, it is not inferior, and with all the talk of modern music, I cannot see that the "freedoms" have amounted to much more than a rather timid reaching out from, let us say, Mozart, toward a few rhythms older than Gregory, older than the pietising and general taming of music during the Middle Ages.

A few danse-du-ventre tunes did survive among the people, and are occasionally discoverable in early manuscripts, but with these Gaelic airs before us we must conclude that the best melodies stayed unwritten.

This was the first of Atheling's several reviews of Marjory Kennedy-Fraser, whom he seems to have known personally at least since 1912. In her book, *A Life of Song,* she tells us she had been invited to one of W. B. Yeats's evenings of poetry-reading as early as 1909. Perhaps they met there. Though he was sometimes critical of her stage performances, in his review of March 20, 1919, he called her frankly "a genius," in acknowlegement of the great service she had performed for song by collecting Hebridean folk music (*Songs of the Hebrides,* texts in Gaelic and English, 3 vols., 1909, 1917, 1921).

Patuffa was Marjory's daughter and co-collector. "In March of that year (1917) Patuffa, having returned from France, joined me in recitals at the Aeolian Hall. This was her first appearance in London, and we met with such success that we have continued the London recitals every since. Every season we have endeavored to introduce fresh programmes of the material recovered. For some six years we confined our recitals to the Chamber Music Hall (the Aeolian), but in the end had to move to the large Queen's Hall to accommodate our audiences."[19]

ROSING, THE MAGNIFICENT[20]

Miss Evelyn Arden (Æolian Hall), not, for the moment, chasing the snake in "The Magic Flute," sang Gluck with a trace of the water-bubble bird in her voice. The voice has both volume and sweetness, but its possessor small sense of gradation. There is scope but no great mentality. The rhythm is very limp. Again we must repeat that the word "ben" in Italian is not pronounced "baim" as in the second strophe of "Spiagge Amate," nor yet "baahn" as it was sung in the third strophe of that lyric. In Duparc's "Elegie" the singer displayed sweetness and restraint—for two lines; Baton is far from the best of song-setters, but her art was inadequate for his "Soupir," less adequate for Debussy. We were again reminded of the potency of her voice, and Gounod's slop was adequately exposed in her rendering.

I have been patiently awaiting the "younger British composers." Miss Arden's next group of numbers showed a few bad poems worse set. ("Still onward" was sung as "Stlonnward.") Arnold Bax's setting of "To Eire" shows that he has not even considered the ABC of his business. The singer was given about half a yard of note for finale on the short *e* of "Unrest." J. Ireland usually shows up better than his contemporaries in these mêlées, but his song showed gaps, and we had the usual piano rubble-rumble to cover up vagueness of melodic conception. Eugene Goosens, at any rate, does fit his notes to the words. The singer was so careless that she did not even trouble to sing "veux" but sang "vais" at the end of his setting to "Chanson de Fortunio."

Vladimir Rosing

Vladimir Rosing (Æolian Hall) has small French and less English, but, in a case like his, what does it matter? He is, without varnish, a great artist. The voice is there, the volume surrounding the songs; he is

---

[19] Marjory Kennedy-Fraser, *A Life of Song*, London, 1929, p. 181.
[20] *The New Age*, April 18, 1918, p. 486.

superb in rhythm, and he has complete comprehension in all the variety of his repertoire. He began with "Robins m'aime" of Adam de la Halle, he passed through Beethoven to the Russians. He has the great style, from the most delicate notes to the strongest. However fine he was in the mediæval songs and in Wagner's "Rêves" we did not have "all of him" until he reached Moussorgsky's "Serenade" from "The Cycle of Death." Before that he had managed tenderness without sentimentality in the "Cradle Song of Yeremoushka." Nowhere was there a solecism; but the serenade gave us major art.

It is always extremely hard to write eulogy. One can only keep on repeating "Here the thing was done right." Rosing knows, and knows emotionally, what to do, and his power is adequate to deliver the effect. Again we can only say: here is the great artist. The voice is under and above and all around the subject. The song is perfectly graded. The depth of feeling, the contrasts—nothing is lacking. And the magnificence of the interpretation is no mere formal correctitude. He was accompanied by Di Veroli, which, also, was as it should be.

I might also call the attention of young composers to the union of words and music in the Moussorgsky "Trepak." This union is so close that with the English translation before me, but being wholly ignorant of Russian, I was never in doubt of which line Rosing was singing in the original. The music simply was the word-meaning. This last statement may be open to dispute, but there can be no doubt whatever about the quality of Rosing's performance.

Francesco Vigliani (Æolian Hall) is too valuable as leader and organiser of his quartette to be lost to us as a soloist. He gave his Corelli-David delicately, but with over-caution; it was clear, but a shade too reedy, the bowing but tentative. Saint-Saens abounds in phrases expressing nothing whatever, and having no inherent beauty. Vigliani was at his best in Lalo's "Guitare," and his personal fineness was here of most use to him. Of course, violin and piano are dangerous in conjunction, and it is difficult to conceive anyone's playing the former to Mr. Kiddle's key-smacking. There was too much piano in the Schumann. Yet Vigliani was very exact in the third movement, and it was worth waiting for. His playing was delicate, but in the rest of the Sonata there was not enough of it to dominate the piano.

Miss Winifred Lawson is an amiable amateur. She has a certain clear sweetness of voice, no *forte,* no sense of her limitations, poor trills. Chaminade suited her best; though she perhaps gave us more pleasure in the quieter moments of "Ah, fors è lui," which was, as a whole, beyond her compass. Madame Ilma Adowska (Æolian Hall). Not exciting.

DEBUSSY[21]

With the death of Claude Debussy we lay our wreath on the tomb of one of the great minor poets of all music. For those who can estimate a man's work by quality rather than by gross output, Debussy has long outweighed all his contemporary composers in western Europe. There is no scale of measurement between a few brief magnificent compositions, such as "Sails," and the "Sunken Cathedral," and "Granada Evening," and a large wolloping-lolloping façade like "Samson and Delilah." Debussy had the grace to recognise that to be a great exponent of a limited number of moods was a far finer thing than to be a fourth-rate pseudo-colossus, and, in consequence, he has left us no small permanent heritage. His music is like that of no one else. It is supremely delicate; it is full of fantastic colour-suggestion, as no other music. There is no "printer's fat" in it. His orchestration for strings is unique. In the "San Sebastian" he has shown that the "great," the major forms were within his grasp. Only during the last ten years of his life did he cease to be regarded as a *specialité,* as a sort of side-issue, a delicacy for the æsthete; an obscurity due in part to the need for intelligence on the part of his interpreters. How few are the performers who have pleased him with their renderings of his music, and how generous have been his praises for those few! There is not room for a detailed appreciation of him in this column. To gauge with any right-

---

21 Claude Debussy died in Paris on March 25, 1918. At the time of his death Debussy enjoyed great popularity in England; his biographer, Edward Lockspeiser, writes:
> The early impressions made by Debussy's music in England revive the worlds of Pater and Beardsley. The symbolist movement, which had taken its rise in Paris, soon became known in London, particularly in literary circles, and in the early years of the century Debussy's music became as fully understood in London as it had been in Paris among the followers of Mallarmé. In 1908 Arthur Symons declared that a performance of Debussy's Quartet enabled him "at last to enter into the somewhat dark and secret shadows" of what he called "the wood."
> (*Debussy: His Life and Mind,* London, 1965, Vol. 2, p. 120.)

It was undoubtedly Debussy's adoption by the Symbolists that obliged Pound to feel a certain diffidence toward him.

In the last sentence of his obituary review Pound mentions that he had seen the composer conduct. He was, in fact, present at the première of *Le Martyre de Saint-Sébastien* in Paris in 1911, and found the music "wonderful," though D'Annunzio's libretto did not please him. In the article "Ca' Rezzonico" (*Delphian Quarterly,* January, 1937, p. 3) he tells us: "I once heard Debussy insuperably leading a chorus in Paris in his Charles d'Orléans songs, and I heard the first performance of San Sébastian. . . ." Debussy was in London in 1908 to conduct *L'Après-midi d'un faune* and *La Mer* at the Queen's Hall, and again in 1909 to conduct a concert of his own music and to supervise rehearsals of *Pelléas et Mélisande,* which was given at Covent Garden in May. Whether Pound ever met Debussy through their mutual friend Walter Morse Rummel is not known.

ness his volume, one must think of his unique work for the piano; of his absolute mastery in arranging for voices and strings, of his unique orchestration, his originality in the best sense of that term. One must remember that a man's fecundity may be greater than at first sight appears. An acute critical sense keeps down the output, but does not diminish the actual invention. Deprived of his subtle intelligence, of his subtle emotional criteria, Debussy would possibly have produced voluminous works; his discoveries and revelations would have been scattered about instead of assembled. He would have exceeded Saint-Saens in bulk, or been a megatherium like Beethoven or Wagner. Only a few people ever attempt to appraise the great energy required for a little very excellent work, as against the lesser force shown by a great bulk of "almost good" production. Thus to gain appearance of reason one must label Debussy at the start, a *minor* poet, before one can be heard explaining that given his time and his era, this was the finest course open to him. He showed himself an exquisite but moody conductor when he left his study and consented to appear in the minor public capacity; unforgettably.

Note.—Raymonde Collignon's recital of old French and Troubadour songs is announced for 3.15 p.m. Saturday, April 27, at Æolian Hall.

ROSING[22]

Miss Jean Stirling Mackinlay (Æolian Hall, April 6) is not acceptable in her present form; there is too much of the jump through the hoop, the grin and smirk at the audience. As a music-hall performer she "isn't a patch on Lauder"; it is not, however, in this rôle that she approaches us. Possibilities she has, indubitably . . . and she ruins them . . . which is a pity. The worst tricks of the appalling theatre are dragged onto the concert stage, and they are "put across," carried off, to the satisfaction of her audience, such as it is, by the vigour of her rhythm.

Given her equipment, for if she has not got a great deal of voice she has quite enough for her purpose, given her rhythm sense; if she would but add to it a little art-sense, she might have almost the best of our praises. A sudden shock, a month's meditation, might turn her into a fine performer. If, even as she is, she would sing "The Bonnie House of Airlie" without gestures it would be almost a good performance. I take it that other critics are already weary and regard her gestures and costumes as a camouflage, for the better known among them did not attend this performance. If, however, she wishes to wear costumes and

[22] *The New Age*, May 2, 1918, pp. 10–11.

make gestures, she should not use the identical arm flingings as if in expression of so many different emotions. If, for instance, you use all possible physical activity, all the largeness of motion in rushing about the stage in imitation of Argyll's men setting fire to "Airlie," what have you in reserve for expressing the final emotions of the Laird of Airlie? The singing was good *up to the last verse,* which was simply inadequate; demonstrating that Miss Mackinlay just sings along without adequate planning of her songs as a whole. There is in her no sense of scale and proportion ... which things can be learned. She has ideas, quite a lot of them, good, bad and indifferent, but they are not fitted into a whole. Art simply *is* combining things into a whole; it is establishing some convention or proportion or idiom in expression. In the "Epitaph on Salathiel Pavy" she was quite good, the song was beautifully sung, and the movement, or rather lack of it, was right, up to the final bow which was exaggerated and ridiculous. Her gesture was probably at its worst in "Les Trois Sorcières." It is one thing for a foreigner to sing to us in broken English; he may be doing his best to be verbally comprehensible; but one should discourage singing in unassimilated foreign tongues. I am under the impression that she would have been hissed for "Une Perdriole" in any Parisian Café Chantant. Her sense of rhythm availed her in "Weaving Lilt," and she showed vocal technique in a way not to be minimised in her decreasing of the sound into nothing with a perfect evenness in the fading.

A man must be wholly without viscera not to be moved by parts of her "House of Airlie" despite the faults. Her performance was painful and infuriating because her vigour and élan and rhythm-sense are of a quality so much needed, and because any violence of criticism would be justified if it could startle her into self-criticism, stimulate her to a consideration of scale and proportion, make her realise that, as she cannot be a whole theatrical company presenting an exact imitation of "life," she must find some possible modality of suggestion, and must *grade* her action from quiet up to some attainable maximum. Each gesture would gain in significance if she would not throw in gestures so over abundantly. She could do with about a fifth of her present supply. One must compliment Mr. Kenneth Mackinlay on his tactful and skilful accompanying.

Myra Hess, the excellent, steady, highly standardised pianist (Wigmore Hall) gave us Bach (Bk. 1, 15 Preludes and Fugues) with surety and good grading. One enjoyed the firm texture of her rhythm lines. In the next prologue there was reverie, romance, and a moodiness usually denied to the composer. Her opening of the Brahms Sonata (Op. 5) was, I think intentionally, rather anarchic—probably the proper manner for this composer. Miss Hess has not quite enough variety of tone quality, or "orchestration." Her possible development would lie in discovering more kinds of sound producible via the piano. More depth would leave her less need of bordering on pyrotechnics. In the Brahms a heavier bass and a greater richness of sound would not be wasted. These suggestions are marginalia; the reader must remember that Miss Hess is an excellent player, one of the best to be found on the English concert platform. The worst thing that can be said of her is that César Franck suits her rather better than other composers. That is a measured statement. Franck understood the piano. I admit that in his "Finale" she was reduced mostly to percussion and a few clever whistles, but I do not wish to belittle her efficiency, her reliability as a performer, or the fact that you could trust her to play anything anywhere with a complete freedom from amateur flaws. If people are interested in piano playing, if they like good piano playing, she is one of the players to hear.

The week's treat, the feast of soul, was needless to say, Rosing's recital (Æolian Hall, April 13). This gorgeous vocalist managed an atrocious sore throat with almost as much mastery as he did the intricacies of an ineffably difficult programme. He gave us the delicacy and pure reedy quality of a wood-wind in Tscherepnine (the composer had provided a rather scrappy accompaniment). Both Tscherepnine and Glazounov seem French-Russian, and Bagrinovsky seems rather Teutonised. Rosing's purity of high notes showed in the curious "Nereida"; in the "Give me this night" he displayed the great variety of his tone quality (may we call it voice-orchestration). He is full of sudden surprises, unexpected richnesses of expression. In Petrides' "Greek Lullaby" we had the folk-rhythms wherein Rosing is perhaps at his finest, though this programme gave him no such chance as he had at the preceding recital in Moussorgsky. In the face of folk-rhythms, and of the persistence of these rhythms in Russian music, one wonders how long the tenuous and highly intellectualised disjointed almost imperceptible motions of the modern French school will hold their vogue. They are of our time, they are perhaps the only means in which our music will come, the best of our composers are given up to them . . . and yet . . . ?

Debussy's "Noël des Enfants" is an interesting experiment; it shows the composer's unsurpassed comprehension of the relation of rhythm to emotion (chiefly in the accompaniment), it depended equally on the great skill both of Rosing and Di Veroli. And what can one say of war-art, anyhow, when the reality is out of all proportion to any human expression? The "Noël" has emotional intensity, but perhaps no other art-value. F. Bridge's good setting to verses unspeakably bad was properly phrased. The best of the recital was in the Tosca Aria and in the Vassilenko and Nevstruoff and Gretchaninoff songs, especially the "Wanderer." One would prefer Rosing to sing in his native tongue (save perhaps when he does "Adam de la Halle"). There is no need for him to bother with inferior English versions; the audience will take him only too gladly in Russian.

His next recital is at Æolian Hall on May 14. (I suppose at 5.30, the hour is not yet announced). One can't hear too much of him, or of Di Veroli's ministrations.

VARIA[23]

Handel's "Hear me, ye winds and waves," is a good hymn tune, and impressive if one likes church music for opera. We reserve our personal grudge, however, against the Near Eastern influence.

M. Rodolphe Gaillard (Æolian Hall) has a largish, mellow voice. He sang the extremely badly written libretto of Handel with affected enunciation, such as "legiontz" for "legions," and "wein-tess" for "winds." That he had to sing "glo-reee" for "glory" is due to the stupidity of the librettist. The sense of fitting words to notes, fitting them so that they fit, has not greatly shone in this island since, as we continue to repeat, the era of Lawes and Tho. Campion. The last line, "I pray for death alone," is well done, and there is something to be said for Samuel Butler's taste. Handel was not a pernicious influence in English music. English music had already gone to pot and Meinheer von Handel was the best man of his time. He did not reattain the best style of his earlier English predecessors, but neither did his English competitors.

Gaillard got emotional force into "Vision Fugitive," and the accompaniment was good; he warbled or caterwauled in "Though I am young"; there was some charm and richness, but this singer has not the neatness requisite for Ben Jonson or "old music." His work is rather of the popular sort: rather better than the Chappell ballad school, emotional rather than finished, a style quite happy in "Au Pays." There is a pleasant high part of the voice; he grazes the sentimental, and is altogether of the romantic school. The "Chant Hindou" was well sung, the solemnity rather suiting him, but a better artist would have made a greater distinction between the sorrow of the Hindoo whose love is dead, "à jamais," etc., and the sorrows of the Kipling-Ed. German gentleman, who laments that he has "never seen a jaguar nor yet an armadillo," and who hopes to roll to Rio some day. The two griefs are scarcely in the same register. We cannot accept the armadillo matter as heart-rendering; and Gaillard has taken the Ed. German comic, cheap, music-hall stuff a great deal too seriously. We have also heard "Bonjour, Suzon" often enough for one season.

[23] *The New Age,* May 16, 1918, pp. 44–45.

Emanuel Compinsky (Æolian Hall) played his violin with temperament and solidity, was a little hard, had no mannerisms, a few squeaks and a squawk; he made the cuts in the rhythm fairly and clearly, showed not the least messiness, but some harshness, perhaps even a certain roughness, as of a good apple unripe, unripe but a good apple. He should be above the average, quite well above it, if one is to take the risk of a prophecy. He had already found delicacy, if not finish, and before the end of the Scherzo in the Beethoven Sonata he had got the music up on to the stage. I find that I hear Wieniawski's music, its wailing and wallowing, with an increasing dislike, and I saw no good purpose to be served by sitting through the D minor Op. 22 Concerto of this restaurateur.

Miss Margaret Cooper (Æolian Hall) has far more personal charm than the pictures on her ads. would lead us to expect; she has magnificent arms and a figure the Greeks would have envied. She brings the British sentimental ballad as near to art, perhaps, as this highly autochthonous product is capable of being hoisted. Her Sterndale-Bennet was done as well as possible. The absence of Ed. Germans music from all programmes or from any programme in particular would cause me no personal pangs. The real nature of Miss Cooper's programme was not wholly apparent to us (it is a matter for psychology) until the fourth song on her programme, "Because my love has come." This revealed, really revealed to us "how far this sort of thing *can* go"; or perhaps it didn't; perhaps we didn't get the gist and the core until she began on the limericks, and on that exhilarating novelty, the verset wherein the rhyme-scheme leads one almost to suspect the fair creature is about to soil her lips with an expletive (Cam, cram, etc.), and ends to the utter bewilderment of the tittivated audience in some phrase like "Oh, horrors!" Some people like it, and laugh, laugh right out in public. Mr. Gervase Elwes was fittingly included in her programme. His mellow, not to say dulcet, voice protruded in the sentimental manner, oh, yes, in all its honeyed saccharescence.

The Walenn and Munro concert (Æolian Hall) gave a general impression of feminine chaos and indistinctness; there was plenty of technique in detail. The Walford Davies sonata may perhaps be itself this general sort of welter, a clouded emotional welter with various musical clichés interspersed. As given, the effect was rather that of queerness than of governed production. Miss Monro put forth a sort of pleasing Chinese gong tone in her Brahms, but the whole was also confused. Her Liszt was done with a maul; however, it was done her own way. Both these ladies obviously play as they like. One's difference would in the end be found to be rather personal. As with the Walford Davies sonata, one couldn't, from a single hearing, swear there was nothing in it; but one wouldn't be in the least convinced that the content amounted to much.

Raymonde Collignon's delicate and exquisite art (Æolian Hall) was taxed to its utmost with a rather spineless and monotonous programme. Moullé, to her credit, suits her better than Bax (we should hope so). Of her first group the Weitz "Lorsque j'étais petit" is worth keeping. In the second group the Campion "Jack and Joan" was so infinitely above the rest of the songs that one would pray her to keep to the masters; considering that it is nearly impossible to get this old music sung with due precision and delicacy and that she is really equipped for it. It is rather a waste for her to do even the Mignardise, though "La Pêche des Moules" was delightful and the best of the Harold Scott pieces given.

We were delighted with the exquisite melodic line of the Rummel reconstructions from the Troubadour music, and it was a comfort to find words in some relation to notes, a treat not commonly granted us. In the Ventadour song the last line should be sung with the words more separate and distinct, since it is the whole point and climax of the song. Whatever may be written in a modern text, the notes in this mediæval music emphasise and illustrate the words, and the words must stand clearly. Likewise in the Uisel song the effect would be greatly enhanced if the voice gave more the effect of a pluck and tang of the strings. In work as fine-wrought as this one can afford such close criticism of detail; we so seldom get within sight or reach of the perfect that the narrowed margin of difference becomes almost more a grievance than would the normal and wider gap between the achieved and the wholly desirable.

Some of Mlle. Collignon's gestures were exquisite, though the whole programme was not as well contrived as that of her folk-song concert. But what do we ask or expect; is the really exquisite effect so common that we should grumble if we only get a dozen perfect moments in an hour? Mlle. Collignon's art is there, even if this particular performance was not in all points wholly felicitous. It is one of our most precious bibelots.

NOTA BENE.—Felix Salmond's 'cello recital, Wigmore Hall, Tuesday, May 28, at 3 o'clock.

'CELLISTS, ETC.[24]

The "Anglo-French Society" is to be congratulated upon its concerts at Steinway Hall. It is no small treat to hear the Ravel "Septuor"

[24] *The New Age*, May 30, 1918, pp. 72–73.

exquisitely presented, and it is nonsense to talk of the decadence of contemporary music at a time when such work is being written. Defauw is a delightful violinist and gave his Marin Marais solos with evenness, finish, discretion, clean bowing, no pretensions, no airs, simply the music.

Yvonne Yorke (Aeolian Hall) gave her Tartini Sonata with temperament; opening with a veiled or slightly blurred tone, not categorically to be condemned . . . for there is a certain range of taste in the matter of the crystalline and the opaque. I have a personal desire for crispness, for the crystalline in violin tone, and I cannot remember ever having heard this quality so overdone as to constitute a fault. There was a good deal of pleasure from the Tartini and great beauty in the Larghetto. Leopold Ashton kept the piano out of way, reducing it to a means of keeping time; perhaps the best thing to do with it in any (almost any) Violin-Piano Sonata. The excitement that comes in playing does not help Miss Yorke; her advance must be by control rather than by enthusiasm. Her playing improved whenever she consciously "gripped herself"; and a slight decline in quality in proportion as she began to "enjoy herself." The balance, however, was in her favour, i.e., shall go to hear her again on our next opportunity. Charm and depth were in her slow passages, a charm not due to any remarkable exactitude of pitch. In "Gaillard" she was not so successful; there is more to be got from it than by the *tip-tip* style she employed. "Boree," ditto; crystalline —precision being *just* what *is* required in this old English music. She was on her own job in the J. Field Waltz; with temperament to her rescue. Chanson Louis XIV, acceptably done but sentimental romantic. Elgar "Capricieuse" reminded one of schoolboy's Latin verb "fleebo, fleerie, itchee, scratchum." Ashton's Oriental Dance was an improvement, but reminiscent of "Hitchee-coo." Next item, Saint-Saens Concerto (Departure of the critic, as is his custom when threatened with any quality of M. Saint-Saens' productions).

Violet Hume (Aeolian Hall) showed respect for the music, is dramatic, but never uncontrolled, voice firm but not large, kept rather in the throat. Not so pleasing in the kittenish mode. Adolph Mann acceptable at the piano.

W. E. Whitehouse, firm crisp bowing ('cello), one of the artists to whom we can give unreserved commendation; delightful in the Purcell-Warren group; and we must regret the loss of this composer in battle. Whitehouse is pleasing in his own "capriccio."

Ada LeMarchant (Aeolian Hall) began on Bach Cantata, delightful firmness in the themes, and in Mr. Hinchcliff's oboe. The singer's voice does not "come out," seems to be in two rather disconnected sections. Victorian school. Clipped words, no enunciation. In Aria the words do not fit the notes. I don't know why publishers go on pouring out uncorrected botches. Here we have, as commonly, long notes on final vowel in "unconfest" (*é-ést*) vowel both short and closed. Even the deified Purcell is not up to Lawes' (First Book of Ayres, especially) in these matters. John Ireland beat a very firm tempo on the piano for his Romance and Rondo. I am still to hear any of his compositions which demand judgment by any standard save that of current English composers, of whom, be it said, he stands well in the foremost rank.

Zoia Rosowsky (Æolian Hall) immature, even callow; usual "Italian" opera manner, nothing *put into* "Quella Fiamma" of Marcello, beyond what would have been taught in any academy; no more *personal* talent, supposing certain continental training (direct or indirect), than has been shown by various English singers whom we have disparaged in these columns. The Cavalli, pleasantly done, with some technique. Voice production, rhetoric of pretended emotion. Rachmaninoff's "Ne Chante Pas Beauté" is a charming song; here Miss Rosowsky came to something she understood, displayed rhythm, good grading. Small artists can often perform quite well what they understand racially (as distinct from personally) when the racial quality is good, or of a good period. The attempted encore of this same song was not so good. Very likely the performer is not an artist, but just a young lady who sings. The Krein, wordless effort, pseudo-Debussy, throat clearing exercise reminiscent of various odd themes from yon and hither. Singer has not art enough for Rimsky Korsakow, though she got some emotion into the first song. The Poldowski songs, accompanied by the composer, were seriatim; popular music—café chanson rather elevated, pyrotechnic, etc., sort of music to compare with Pierre Louÿs, or "La Femme et le Pantin." Are we still expected to have a scared and ecstatically naughty thrill at hearing "un divin éclair montre Pannyre nue"? Is a disrobing still a literary dénouement? Scarcely in a metropolis.

Arthur Williams began nervously, to a scrabble of piano accompaniment. Ah, but a fine 'cellist. A fine penetrating tone, almost, if we may use the phrase, a fine raucousness; wholly different from Salmond; almost a horn tone, peculiar clarity and distinction. The 'cello is in his hands so different an instrument from what it is for the quiet Whitehouse or for Salmond, that one almost wants to hold over one's criticism until one can group him with the latter. . . . only for the difficulty of holding to any accuracy of comparison through a fortnight with other concerts intervening. Williams has charm in his bass, almost a violin tone in treble, a great variety in his sounds. And the 'cello is a magnificent instrument. A magnificent instrument. I want to state that my interest was wholly in Williams' playing, not the least in J. Holbrooke's "Fantasie, Op. 19," though it gave the performer more chance to display his tone than did, perhaps, the Beethoven variations.

The Monologo of Monteverde's "Orfeo" is a capital song. G. Fergusson began it a little preciously, with a rich voice, sound coming free and clear, not accurate in pitch. Beginning of "C'est un torrent" too fast for him; he was interesting in the end. Did an excellent diminuendo in "Vision Fugitive," but kept getting worse till we had Tennyson's *"and twitter twenty million loves," "Swall' swall' swallow,"* etc. Affair for psychologist not for critic of music. One *had* forgotten the utter asininity of the Laureate.

FELIX SALMOND, EXCELLENT 'CELLIST[25]

VLADIMIR ROSING's programmes are always of music carefully sought out, and no recital is without some rare bit of scholarship. Of the old French songs (May 14, Æolian Hall), the Tiersot was in descant, a little baroque, and by no means as pleasing as the style of Adam de la Halle, content to keep closer rapport between the words and the notes. La Romanesca, XVI century anonymous, is in a fine popular mode. Rosing's scholarship was most clearly emphasised in the Air of Prince Sinodale; who else would have dug out of Rubinstein something worth hearing? The Scenes from Eugene Onegin were interesting, though the transposition of the orchestral part for piano is very unsatisfactory. It improves, however, in Sc. 5, where Lensky's song is well termed the "great aria." The interplay of the voice parts later in the scene is full of interest.

The French words for the Schubert and Schumann songs are appalling, but the Brahms "Strophes Saphiques," despite the shift into another language, was exquisite; what McKail has called the Sapphic lustre was present. More than ever I felt that Rosing's art is an art of his intelligence; it is a beauty that comes from knowledge, from emotional knowledge, not from any unusual vocal equipment, not from some hyperdevelopment of the thorax.

His concerts are the main musical interest of the season. No lover of music and no one with any musical curiosity will willingly miss them. Julien Bonell assisted with an unaffected bass, a fine simplicity. The Borodin Peasant Theme has humour, and is in that yeowl or wail in which this composer has probably approached closer to the folk intonation of a hoarse and frozen country than West European composers would have tried to. I suspect the Igor song needs to have a

---

[25] *The New Age,* June 13, 1918, pp. 107–8.

good deal put into it by the singer. Rosing later sang the "Prince Vladimir" song from the same opera, and one's faith in the composer ascended. His (Rosing's) singing of "The Sea" made one wish he would make a few experiments with the Hebridean melodies which we have been vainly hoping to hear given with magnificence.

MANLIO DI VEROLI (Æolian, May 17) is an excellent accompanist, and it is, perhaps, a sign of something like civilisation that so good a performer is content to contribute to fine effects, rather than trying to star alone, à la prima donna, contending with other pianists who know less of the instrument. It is also laudable that Italian music should be given in special concerts, but Sig. Di Veroli has not yet found an effective corps of assistants. Garelli and Stralia were both distressing. Rosing, latinised for the nonce, displayed in most trying circumstances a sense of humour and devilry comparable only to that of Nikisch.

LIONEL TERTIS (Wigmore) is most graceful in his execution with the long bow. The viola is a slightly more sylvan, or "wood-wind" violin, or call it the oboe of the strings. It is not so good an all-round instrument as either the violin or the 'cello, it has a curious lack of resonance in certain parts, but it has also its own peculiar and incomparable qualities. If people wish to play violin music on it the music should be largely rewritten. Unless this is done certain passages may stand out, may be even an improvement on the fiddle, but the whole composition will not be. The Londonderry Air set for the Viola by Tertis did fit the instrument, and was demonstrably better than it would have been on anything else. Other violin pieces were, perhaps, in the nature of stunts "first time on the viola," etc. The Ireland sonata was most enjoyable where the strings were *least* accompanied by the piano (composer *at* same); was most charming where the slow viola gave most attention to individual sounds, i.e., where the *writing* of the music was not the sole resource of the listener. The third movement opens with cliché, scrabble, goes on in potted Beethoven, and yet more clichés from varied, familiar canneries somewhat later than Ludovico Magnifico. The Sammons "Air with Variations" is not bad; Wolstenholme remembers the "Olde Oaken Bucket." McEwen's "Chaleur d'Eté" opens with sham Debussy, and continues in derivations from earlier sources mixed with pseudo Debussy. Tertis gave it with great delicacy of sound. York Bowen accompanied his Sonata No. 1 in C minor; there is no particular limit to the number of people who might have written this Sonata. A personal and distinguishable style is perhaps more than we should demand of composers, but it is extremely difficult to give any explicit praise to the works until they have attained it. The thing is well placed for the viola; one sits on as through the inter-act music at a theatre; the second movement is not without rubber-stamps. Miss

Ellen Tuckfield accompanied the short pieces rather better than either of the composers.

Felix Salmond (Wigmore) was firm and clear in the firmest and clearest of C. Franck, and showed surety in the approach and recede of sound. Murdock was also up to it; I have never heard him play better, and hope he will keep to good company. Salmond has a little the quality of the controlled *somnambule* who simply cannot go wrong. The music moves the 'cello. It is there first. It pre-exists; does not wait for the bow to drag out an approximation (which waiting is exactly what makes many concerts unendurable). This kind of playing is the nearest thing we have to evidence for Plato's concept of "ideas." Contact with this "reality" is genius; or, at least, the highest pleasure we can get from instruments is in some sort of sense of such contact. I forgot to analyse the Franck. There is great beauty in the second movement after the scrabble of the opening.

Ultimate conclusion on the A major sonata: 'cello excellent Burgundy, and C. Franck not a great genius. Frank Bridge, mediocre in opening piano part of Sonata in D minor, Salmond can make any simple phrase beautiful, but this does not reflect any credit on the composers he chooses to present. Almost any sequence of notes would serve him. There is no particular reason for this sonata. Nor do I think there is among performers any wide-spread desire to discriminate between excellent music and mediocre.

Edwin Evans (series of illustrated lectures at Æolian) is to be thanked for trying to weed out contemporary English composers. Their works should certainly be tried on the public, but English music is suffering, and will continue to suffer from a long attempt to boom Elgars and Parrys as men of commanding genius and of international significance. The only way to improve an art *anywhere* is by maintaining the strictest standards of judgment.

Silvia Parisotti's voice is pleasant enough, but throaty, phlegmy, indistinct, good deal of nonsense. No beauty added by singing "querele" as "querwahahah," or "Penare" as "penahwuh," "penawoh," or even "penahweh." Single beautiful sounds may invite the critic's amiability, but they "are not enough." Albanesi's "Mer" shows that Debussy invented some new sonorities for the piano which other writers may turn on ad lib.

Fresh, we presume, from operatic triumphs in Citta del Castello, Perugia, Saragossa, or, perhaps, it is East Orange, N.J., La Donzella floribundissima Felice Lyne bursts upon us with trills, twirls, tooloodles, Rossini, bulls-eye (Ping-Wok!!) on the last note, not necessarily the note indicated by the composer, but why stop for details?

Keeping to the "ah-ah-ah" method she does rather content herself with "Ut-re-mi," as Waller advised bad composers; but this thing has to be extremely well done to be interesting. Old Twinkle's "La Danza" served to show that the lady had no real technique, though "Una voce poco fa" may require some educational prelude. A lot of camouflage over *nothing*. The great intrinsic beauty of "Deh vieni non tardar" was not wholly concealed. Purcell was murdered, and singing "forget my feet" for "forget my fate" is no embellishment of the verbal text.

MUSIC[26]

MISS LILIAS MACKINNON has in her piano bass a curious softness, a curious *mollesse,* if one may use that term without odium. The playing is individual; is a unification of sounds into a flow, an absorption; a fluid, not an architectural manner; it is not a confusion. Technique does not stick out to the general detriment of the whole. The effect is of metal poured into a mould rather than of something carved, built or constructed. César Franck was made emotional by her playing. I cannot say I have heard him so before. But the playing is perhaps an emotional rather than a musical pleasure; and one's enjoyment is perhaps that of soothed emotional antennæ rather than of a discriminating audition. It is possible to contend in favour of such emotional as opposed to strictly musical presentations.

Chopin did not gain by the method, as Franck very possibly had. The Chopin demanded both more architecture and more passion. Chopin is a major musician, although this is often concealed by his romanticism and by his having written a large number of brief pieces which can be given to young ladies in schools. The D minor prelude was blurred, muffled, confused; playing with temperament not with maestria.

Y. Bowen prelude designed for the four-hour touch. J. Ireland "Chelsea Reach," inspiration negligible and individuality not apparent. "Ragamuffin": four-hour touch. Miss Mackinnon's method mollifies the edges of too harsh and gawdy composers. B. Dale "Night Fancies": clichés in opening, and too long for what he had to say. This fourth section of programme was wearing.

Glazounow "Sonata in B flat minor" (école de Chopin) sounded much the same as the Franck; at this point the danger of the fluid method became apparent, the danger of banking on temperament as opposed to banking on architecture. The emotional flow first soothes, but at last one merely waits. Structure is needed to hold one's attention *after* the first hour. (Miss Mackinnon, let me not forget to say at once, is one of

[26] *The New Age,* June 27, 1918, p. 146.

the few pianists one will risk hearing again.) The Glazounow would, I think, have been immensely effective if it had come immediately after the Franck. There need have been no alteration in the manner of playing it. This may be psychological rather than musical criticism, and all criticism must be tentative as soon as one gets beyond a discussion of rudiments and the castigation of elementary faults. Whether one can discuss music as apart from the effects of music I leave to dialecticians. (Wigmore.)

ROSING exhibited perfect gradation of value and quality in the serenity of his opening Bach song; his lack of English does not seem to matter. Di Veroli was exquisite in the Beethoven accompaniment, but the voice part is not up to the Bach and the English words are rubbish. In Glinka's "Virtus Antiqua" Rosing got his throat more easily open than usual. One wishes to goodness he would stick to Russian and not try rubbishy translations in languages unfamiliar to him. The Yeremoushka Cradle Song is perfection and was perfectly done; "Savichna" is a grotesque and its performance an amazing tour-de-force (present critic loathes village idiots, Wordsworthian or other, but expresses his respect for the technique both of composer and singer). Moussorgsky is, I think, the greatest of the Russian composers, certainly the greatest in writing for the voice. The first, third and fourth of this group of his songs are great art, certainly great art as Rosing gives them; note the command of rhythm in the Yeremoushka, the gradation of the values and qualities in the variety of the pianissimo (clearly heard to the back of the hall), fading into an audible silence. Consider the actual writing in the Sorotchinsky, the exquisite diminuendo of the voice into the final note of the piano part. Consider how flat it made the ensuing Wagner. Moussorgsky is not full of stereotyped passages; of "printer's fat." It is all very well to say the Wagner sounded dull because one was more familiar with it, but there simply is no interest in the melodic line of the notes for the seventeen words beginning "Donne lui donc si Dieu, etc." The composer has used the same set of effects in his Lohengrin, in the "Rêves" which followed and in Tannhäuser; usual intervals, patches lacking in interest, composer so little absorbed in his subject and so intent on being the colossus that he does not keep his hand on the tools. Wagner's "position" is in part due to the XIXth century lust for great figures; its domination by rhetoric. Rosing simply was not into the Chant de Concours. Early in the programme I was optimistic about the public. I said, "No, they will swallow the bad, but the good must win through; look how they take this Moussorgsky"; the enthusiasm over the Meistersinger song, as given, merely showed that if there is one botch in a fine programme the crowd will pick it for applause. Next group stirred again the prayer that Rosing would stick to Russian. If we are to have German music, let us say "The world has got and will get nothing out of these anthropoid apes save a few decent songs and a little music; let us grab what we can get, swallow the whole and be thankful"; but to sing the melodies to bad verbal approximations instead of to the Hun words *that fit the notes* is stupid; let us either eschew the melodies, or sing them to fit sonorities, *or,* wait until the songs are well translated into French, English, Italian or Serbian, or some other Allied speech (perhaps Yiddish would be phonetically nearest the original).

The next song, from Moussorgsky's Cycle of Death, put an end to one's quibbling. This Cycle is a specimen of the real thing as contrasted with Wagner's rhetoric about it and about. It is pure folly for any music-lover to miss Rosing's singing of Moussorgsky. No other composer is within measurable reach of expressing the tragedy of the present. Like all great art (war-art or other) this Cycle was not written to order; it was not an attempt to be topical. Events have followed the artist. (Æolian.)

My next ITEM had several virtues; in fact, she had *all* the virtues compatible with a complete lack of interest. First means of taking all interest out of programme: drag the rhythm; second means: sing Neapolitan, Scotch, Flemish and several other varieties of music as if it *all* had exactly the same character, or, rather, lack of character. If the text reads "Cantando è grato vogare, Vogando è bello cantar" trust to English translator who neglects to translate; refuse to note author's suggestion that the swing of the oars helps the swing of the song, and that the song helps the rowing. Eviscerate Malcom Lawson, and the Skye fishing song, soap down the lot to a single monotony of placidity.

BELGIAN STRING QUARTET (Wigmore) Ravel F Major Quartet, well done, not the best Ravel, bits of intentional novelty mixed with unintentional reminiscence, traces of fat, not up to Ravel's Septuor, but still charming. Defauw, Tertis, Emile Doehard, R. Kay, fine quartet.

PHILHARMONIC QUARTET (Æolian) good firm quartet, no need of any special superlatives to describe them. First movement Schumann F Major, Op. 41, 2, probably as good a piece of work, or better for its time than the Ravel, possibly, even, more inventiveness. Languishes in Andante, Scherzo rather vacuous, Finale improves.

STROESCO IMPROVED, NEVADA, PURNELL[27]

DOROTHY MOULTON (Aeolian Hall) adds no personal art to her renderings; a firm, traditional manner, unaffected, a little rugged, but orderly;

[27] *The New Age,* July 11, 1918, p. 168.

words clear in the Bach song. The essentially non-song quality of W. B. Yeats' "Cloths of Heaven" is illustrated by Dunhill's setting. Contrast this with the essentially song quality of A. P. Graves "I'll rock you to rest" where the words have absolutely *no* literary value whatever. The setting of some poems to notes is pure malversation. Miss Moulton might listen to Plunket Greene with advantage if she contemplates performing "Aghadoe" in the future.

STROESCO (Aeolian) was at grips with his subject from the first note. He has the quality of passion and made a fine firm opening in "Cosi fan tutti" (Di Veroli contributing his share). Donizetti's "Don Pasquale" is an inferior song but offered opportunity for certain technical display. The Liszt was soft in texture after the Mozart, but variations in kind help to keep a programme interesting. The words in Berlioz's "Air de Faust" were clear. Stroesco shows a determination to be intense at all cost; this is not a self-consciousness, and much less a pose, though one may mistake it at first. There is in it a praiseworthy seriousness of intention. Strain appeared in the Franck, especially in the line ending "nuit transparente"; this is purely a matter of rhythm, not of propulsion of voice from throat tubes. The "Manon" was given with great charm; it was finely sung (these two statements supplement each other; they are not the duplication of one statement). The fine quality of voice showed in "Oh, non, Tout est la triste et morose," the ring of clear, thin, pure metal. Debussy: good. Stroesco does not "play it safe," there is a personal addition to what he sings. No artist at his age can bring this off every time; if he has a personal way of doing a song it is bound to irritate someone nearly always, and most people now and then. I find a danger of drag in his renderings of the modern French school, and prefer him in Italian (or in the Massenet, if you like, but Massenet has in himself an Italian quality). There was promise of the future in the second Duparc song. I found the drag in the opening strophes, but the final four lines showed, more than anything else I have heard, that Stroesco "has it in him"; is capable of any amount of development. The "Guitares et Mandolines" is not right. Di Veroli and Stroesco did all they could with the thing, but neither words nor notes were worth the effort.

Hué, on the other hand, had taken the work of a true poet (Klingsor) and set it exquisitely (note lines ending in "Bassora" and in "sur le pré"). The Quilter and C-Taylor songs could have been omitted, though the Quilter does perhaps contribute to the public education in displaying a poor scrap of Browning as the dayspring of E. W. Wilcox.

Willingly we would have had more Roumanian folk-songs. Stroesco must not forget his birthright and there is no one else here to sing "Vine, Leana" and other songs of its sort. It and the Roumanian encores are not of the tame back-parlour variety. The singer may have introduced the Quilter for the sake of setting them off. If so, it was justified. The final Hahn was exquisitely sung, with the sense of meaning in every one of the well-known words. I do not expect to hear it done better. Debussy's "Clair de lune" in encore deserves notice. The upshot of all this is that we have a new Stroesco to cope with; four or five songs in the programme were done so as to give one a really unusual pleasure. Stroesco is no longer trusting to temperament, romance, youthful élan, etc. He has buckled down to work, he is definitely taking the art of singing as a fine art. He has got certain definite results; certain songs finished to a point beyond which I do not think they can be improved. In other songs he showed indubitable capacities for expansion. There is a great gulf between this recital (June 14) and that of a few months ago which gave no such indications. One is exceedingly glad of another singer whom one can treat as a serious artist.

MIGNON NEVADA, (in Edwin Evans Concert-Causerie series at the Aeolian) has *attaque,* that is, she starts plump on the note (the right note), and proceeds with perfect clarity, delicacy and precision, with articulation and a comforting surety. I am inclined to think she has the best woman's voice I have heard since I started these criticisms, and more real technique than any of the women now singing here in opera (contrast, for example, Licette sliding and slippering over everything). The demand for *forte* and for the vocal burst is, of course, a pest and the ruin of singers. Of the early Opéra Comique composers Grétry is perhaps the most pleasing and "Rose Chérie" worth resurrecting for more than one performance. N-Isouard is applied art rather than creation; perhaps there is no reason why an opera shouldn't be full of cribs; it is huge canvas and one can scarcely expect a work-a-day composer to fill the whole of it with novelty, any more than Metastasio, the only librettist who can be read apart from the music, can be expected to be very original, although he has managed to put a few quite good lyrics into his opera work—by accident, possibly. For the rest, the programme was largely in the nature of interesting archæology.

Vivien Hughes, violinist (Aeolian) Jeune fille bien pensante. Admirals Gaillard played too slow, in accordance with now discarded XIX century superstition. Good deal of the smaller technique, displayed. Pergolesi "Air" was the only pleasure in the programme.

WINIFRED PURNELL (Aeolian): Bach-Blanchet, distinct, definite in detail, complete grasp of larger structure; great volume in apparently effortless bass. Altogether satisfactory, no desire to leave the building, no irritation with the piano as an instrument. I had from her first concert the feeling of weird genius; here there was full control, no trace of the amateur; no sign of that merely mechanical proficiency which turns the playing of competent professionals into boredom.

Miss Purnell keeps her composers distinct, does not melt them into a uniformity. She gave a romantic quality to the Beethoven (Op. 81); perhaps read a certain amount of Chopin (who is not her composer) into it. Individual notes were well globed, and given with different flavours and with tang. Schumann (Toccata Op. 7) served as a demonstration of certain sorts of ability but might be left to other performers; a good deal of it can be done on the pianola and does not require the human addendum. Debussy's "Vent d'Ouest" can *not* be left to automata. He is no minor poet as Miss Purnell gives him. Here the music went mad with a madness which is not a dilettantism. Philipp "Deux Follets," pièce de lycée. Pierné "Nocturne" graceful Chopinese, more suited to private than public performance. Liapounow "Ronde" omissible. Chopin, not this pianist's best ground. One can however count on her for variety and personal rendering, and the audience sat for a second encore after end of the programme. There is, emphatically, something in her.

(*Rosing's next concert: Aeolian Hall, Tuesday, July 16, at 8 p.m.*)

ARTHUR WILLIAMS ('CELLO)[28]

ARTHUR WILLIAMS (Æolian Hall, June 24) plies a discriminating bow and gave the Beethoven Sonata (V.2.) in a manner which left no suggestions to be made. At no point did one wish to *explain* to the 'cellist where his insight into the text might be improved. As I have before indicated, there are three 'cellists whom I hear with pleasure: Whitehouse has style and decorum. The Wagnerians do not like it. Salmond has a sort of somnambulistic genius and, as I have said, little apparent care whether he plays good music or mediocre. Williams has, as I hear it, the greater intellectual grasp of music, of the whole of it. He is at once the most discriminating and the most daring. (I regret not having heard Lebell, as I hear, on what I believe to be good authority, that he has greatly improved, and that his concerts (in connection with Mosiewitch) have been interesting.)

Williams gave the Chopin "Introduction and Polonaise" with distinction. He is one of the very few fine musical intelligences now here on the platform. In the Beethoven I found, now and again, a little too much piano. It seems to me also that Beethoven can be "improved" by the clarity of the performer, whereas Chopin does not leave quite

[28] *The New Age,* July 25, 1918, pp. 205-6.

the same sort of gap. Williams added something, added a sort of neater articulation to the Beethoven, and had not the chance of so doing in the Chopin. There is no dogma applicable in such nuances, but it seems to me that the Beethoven could have been correctly played without being nearly so fine-wrought; whereas if the Chopin had not been so fine it would have been *incorrect*.

George Fergusson sings with the style of a suburban soprano doing "The Holy City."

VLADIMIR ROSING is, as the reader now knows, one of our rare delights; but he should hatch his chickens in private. It is a gratuitous offence to the better part of his public that he should jointly recite with Signora Felice Lyne. People desiring to hear the music of one cannot conceivably care to hear the performances of the other. Gounod is for the most part dispensable. Possibly Miss Lyne has been improved by association with Rosing, but his divided attention, his male-hen-ish care for the chick under his wing, interfered with his singing; not that one wanted any more "Isobel" ranted or otherwise. In any case, he overshot his mark in this displeasing ditty.

Duparc's "Extase" is not musician's music; it is the weakness of the modern French school that they have shifted the centre of interest; Debussy from sheer music, often, into suggestions of colour (colour for the imaginative eye, not what is called "tone-colour"). The song-setters try to give a poetic interest. This may charm for a few hearings, but the interest in any work of art wears out quickly when the centre of that interest is not essentially *of* the particular art into which the subject is cast. "L'Invitation" further illustrates the tendency to seek "poetic" music rather than musical music.

Miss Lyne next appeared—Donizetti, florid spots, melodic patches, not enough. Give the girl ten years' training, some unified conception of a complete presentation of a song as a unit, as a work of art, not an exercise.

The Brahms "Strophes Saphiques" needs no praise; the piece is among Rosing's best numbers. Korsakoff's "Southern Night" was art, given as art. In the Aria from "Dubrovsky" was seen Rosing's danger in violent shifts from loud to very soft, the danger of overdoing it. Moussorgsky's Serenade from Death Cycle was magnificent. One still felt that Rosing was labouring to get back into his stride. As he is perfectly capable of filling the hall by himself, there seems no need of his jointure.

M. le Comte de Croze gave a very nice lecture for school-children: "Chançons de Mer." Yves Tinayre did not turn up; M. le Comte's own bursts of sea-chanteys were spirited. Madame Blanche Marchesi gave evidence that she had had a fine and crystalline voice and a precise and magnificent technique; clarity in method and surety. Some of the chanteys are of interest, but the artificising of them is not always pleasing; Charpentier turns out "sob-stuff."

Austen Carnegie (Wigmore Hall) has in his voice volume and quality; he should guard against sentiment, is of the English-local school, perhaps not wholly embedded; should take care not to rant. He showed no special interest in any song in particular; and it is rather foolish for a singer not to realise that each song must be a creation if a series of them is to hold the interest of the audience. His concert was like a school recitation *unprepared*. (Critic declines to hear any more "Isobel.") Dettmar Dressel's violin playing does not matter.

Oriana (Æolian Hall): With an atmosphere of faded "Liberty and Co." green, an air of depressed sprightliness, the Oriana Madrigal Society blossomed upon the Æolian stage and spread through the auditorium. They sang Savile's "Here's a health to his Majesty" with an ecclesiastical drag. This song is not a dirge, and half the time would have fully sufficed for its presentation. They came not to bury Cæsar but to drink his health "with a fa la la." The liquor had run very low.

Suburban chapel feeling then dominated the "Cuckoo." No air of gutter-snipe impertinence was left to that feathered songster, no suggestion of connotations. "Cease sorrows, cease," wailed out like a neo-Celtic keening. The words do not, perhaps, demand an excess of gaiety, though they may be summarised as "Cheer up, we'll soon be dead." But it would have remained a dirge at double the tempo employed.

The slowness in singing all these old songs is probably due to sheer ignorance; to the society's being too lazy to get up their subject; and to the usual hatred of technique common in such bodies.

In the choral work in "Hark, all ye lovely saints," we heard too much machinery, too much sh-sh-sh, and grr-grr, never the fine light bell-tone which results from skilled manipulation of combined voices.

Mr. O. Collier had some quality, but the sloppy enunciation of his support produced "The hunt is *ouh*" for the "The hunt is up." There was a drag in "Three Ravens," and not much vigour in "Tomorrow the fox will come to town," which should be a rough-and-ready and out-of-doorish affair. "Sweet nymph, come to thy lover," was not a pleasure as given. Nor would that horny old lecher, Henry Tudor, have found due robustezza in his composition, "Pastime with Good Company."

Miss Murray Lambert appeared to work against a slight drag, but gave the opening of Handel's Sonata in D major purely, though with small help from the piano. Her violin-playing has improved since I last heard her. The Sonata has traces of nonsense in the two movements allegro.

MUSIC[29]

From what I could hear through the door (Steinway Hall), Mr. Harold Craxton appeared to be giving his Bach with considerable vigour and virtuosity. Certainly he gave his arrangements of Purcell with delicacy, and with a sense of his subject. He had sufficient intelligence not to hammer; a sense of proportion and rhythm. The Minuet and Courante put one in a good humour which lasted well on through the recital. Purcell's dates are 1658-1695; Dr. Arne's, 1710-1778. Dr. Arne's sonata exhibits the gradual substitution of speed and floridity for melodic invention. Noise was beginning to come into its sovereignty; a multitude of notes usurped the place of notes carefully contrived. Still, Mr. Craxton gave the sonata with charm. The cross-rhythms of the final Minuet movement are good Arne; are one of the Doctor's most felicitous flights.

Beethoven C sharp minor, Op. 27, No. 2, or "Moonlight Sonata," followed. This Purcell-Arne-Beethoven sequence might well have been devised to illustrate the decadence of music during the eighteenth century. The Beethoven adagio is *soft,* in the bad sense. People are scared at the great name of Beethoven, and suppose it to be above question; but parts of it are not above Ethelbert Nevin, author of "Narcissus." There is a cheap opening to the Allegretto, and the Presto agitato is largely a shindy; to split the plexuses of the groundlings, etc. It has no real passion, or, at most, a mere trace toward the finale.

A critic must take the risk of such iconoclastic judgments now and then if he is not to sink into utter inutility from cowardice. At any rate, the sonata was a bore.

Craxton's own "African Dance" opened without any savagery; a sort of Delphi via Debussy; its opening might even have been labelled "Shepherdess in porcelain," like the next piece. The African effort was, however, quite graceful, of Debussy's school, and not the worst example I have heard. At the end it breaks loose into Africa. There are some bars which Debussy had not written. His idiom is applied to a different subject-matter. The "Shepherdess" was unimportant.

Craxton got through the "Claire de Lune," scrambled the "Jardins

[29] *The New Age,* August 8, 1918, pp. 241–42.

sous la Pluie"; had no grip on the "Sunken Cathedral," no unified concept, *mollesse*.

Manlio di Veroli's pupils held forth on the same evening (Æolian Hall). It is, however, impossible for me to be in two places at once. All I can say is that Miss Ethel Peake showed care and concern for her music on the one previous occasion when I have heard her.

STROCKOFF (Æolian Hall) should some day be a very prosperous and popular violinist. There is something of the juggler in his art, at which he is extremely proficient. He has the trick of attracting attention. He has firmness, a clear whistling tone which carried him through the rather larky and affected Veracini sonata with by no means a gummy bow. But I could not free myself from the impression that Mr. Strockoff was more concerned with his effect upon the audience than with the subject-matter of his music. Art should be more skilful, not less skilful, than it appears. One felt a constant emphasis on "This is the way I do it," rather than the more advisable, quieter "This is the music."

The first statement is interesting for a certain time only. Still, Strockoff is in the running for the large audience.

ROSING, and damn an audience that prefers "Isobel" to Moussorgsky, anyhow. Damn an audience that prefers "Isobel" to Moussorgsky! Patriotism in music consists in getting the best; it does not consist in a demand for the local product.

Rosing's programme (Æolian) was said to be chosen by vote, a "plebiscite programme." At the preceding concert ballots were given us, with a request to mark the numbers desired for July 16. It is impossible to tell who voted, or on what system the result was managed, but it obviously does show in some way the taste of the people sufficiently concerned to pass in their ballots.

There was very little rubbish included in the "plebiscite programme," but then there was very little rubbish in Rosing's repertoire, so that in voting for twenty numbers there was no great likelihood of much very bad stuff being chosen. However, "Isobel" was preferred to a third Moussorgsky; that much is obvious, and the result was loudly applauded. Rosing made heroic efforts with the autochthonous product. He did more for it than he has done before, but was unable to counteract the nullity of the librettist or the general commonness of the piece. After all, the singer can seldom, by his talents, wholly obliterate the efforts of the composer. The more vacant the written notes the more the singer can put into them.

I am inclined from the applause to think that Rosing is making almost a minimum of compromise with bad taste, and that at least 48 per cent. of his audience would prefer him to sing rubbish. On the other hand, there are a few people of distinction seen regularly at his concerts; they are more worth singing to, and in the end perhaps a firmer support. I do not see them at poor concerts. Neither do I believe that Rosing would be wholly deserted or even greatly impoverished if he kept a high hand and gave us nothing but his best.

No one else can do the Field-Marshal from Moussorgsky's "Death-Cycle." It is great art, in every sense of the word, as I have written before. It is also full of uncountable difficulties; it needs both technique and intelligence. All Rosing's Russian songs were delightful, from the mellow *matt* voice in the Tschaïkowski lullaby, the charm of the Yeremoushka, to the Wanderer of Nevstruoff. The Pergolesi "Se tu m'ami" was flecked by mispronunciation of words, but still delightful (Di Veroli deserving his share of the credit).

In both the Brahms "Strophes Saphiques" and "Serenade" the French words do not ruin the music. The Serenade is turned into some sort of Watteau effect, but this is not to be deplored. The Schumann "J'ai pleuré en rêve" is damaged by translation. It is also an open question whether a *song* should be so completely dependent on the accompanist for its conclusion. Di Veroli has to exercise very great discretion to round out and finish off this piece.

At last Mr. Rosing has sung "charme" not "farme" in Wagner's "Rêves." It is a bagatelle, but one will begin to prod him about his words sooner or later. Another point was the intelligence used in arranging the order of the programme, the placing the soft Duparc setting of Baudelaire's "Invitation" after the Moussorgsky. Musically one would have feared an anti-climax. Rosing went from his great drama to a French song in which the beauty of the words counts for as much as the music. These touches of thought all contribute to the full effect of a concert. He also lifted Puccini a good distance toward the fine.

MUSIC[30]

The wear and tear on one's nerves has been rather less than I had anticipated. Had I tried to write musical criticism for a "daily," I might even now be in that snug grave where certain fond readers have several times cordially wished me; but my conclusion, after a year of selective attendance, is that there is a certain amount of pleasure to be had from London concerts, even in war-time.

At any rate, with an irreducible minimum of about three concerts a

[30] *The New Age,* August 22, 1918, pp. 271–72.

week, I do not feel the need of *all* the sympathy which has been poured upon me by my sympathetic acquaintances. It is, after all, possible to escape from an unbearable concert. Three minutes' scraping are enough to demonstrate that a given concertist is an ass, a duffer, a card-board imitation, a stuffed shirt, a pupil of promise, a pupil of no promise, a performer with possibilities, *or* a musician. And, having once learned that a certain performer is bad, worse, or just dull, the writer for a weekly has sufficient liberty to avoid him.

Without looking over my notes, with memory alone for my guide, I can recall certain "pleasures" of the season:

Notably, Vladimir Rosing, of whom I have written repeatedly and at length, and of whom I have no more to say at this moment, save that I hope to hear him next season, and that I hope he will give his concerts *alone*, and with Di Veroli as accompanist.

I have pointed to three different 'cellists: Salmond, Williams, and Whitehouse, each excellent in a quite different way. I have tried to define their difference. Williams has the best head; Whitehouse, orderliness and composure; Salmond a sort of genius, somewhat somnambulistic; he does not seem to care whether he plays good music or bad, and he appears to be on excellent terms with a party, or faction, or group of people who are *not* the best influence in contemporary British music.

Raymonde Collignon's art is exquisite and her own, minute as the enamelling on snuff-boxes (of the best sort). Her first programme was rather better than the second that I heard. This *diseuse* is very young, but she shows herself capable of perfectly finished work, and if she is not deflected or bribed into doing cheap work she should maintain her distinct place on the concert-stage with songs by Adam de la Halle, French anonymous folk-songs, troubadour reconstructions, etc.

Winifred Purnell has something to her, abundant piano technique, a sense of major form. Mosiewitch has complete control of the keyboard. Myra Hess is decidedly competent, and so, I believe, is Irene Scharrer. Constantin Stroesco woke me up at his final recital of the season. He has shown himself capable of serious and wholly satisfactory work; obviously knows good music from bad, and is capable of presenting the best. Provided he sticks to the best, he should be sure of solid support from the discriminating part of the public for, let us say, Roumanian folk-song, Bel Canto, Mozart, Massenet. I do not mean these hints as strict limitations. Rosing has shown great enterprise in research and Stroesco might well continue the process. There is a good deal of excellent music not included in Rosing's excellent repertoire.

I have had occasion to commend Mignon Nevada for technique, to deplore Madame Alvarez' lack of discrimination while taking delight in her voice. I trust the Vigliani quartette is a permanent and not an ephemeral part of London's music.

Some weeks before I began my notes in this paper I attended a curious concert at the Wigmore. Mr. Van Dieren was rather vaguely conducting a not wholly indoctrinated small orchestra through the curiosity of his own music. The concert had the misfortune to be announced in a rather eccentric, not to say, florid, manner, but one should not judge a man's work wholly by the tone of his impresarios. I was not moved by the music, but I am perfectly willing to believe that this immobility was personal, was due to the unfamiliarity of the subject matter, or to the conducting, or to the imperfectly trained state of the orchestra. I have forgotten the titles of the individual members. I am not convinced that they are successful compositions. This is no condemnation of Mr. Van Dieren. My impression, for what it is worth, is that he is absorbed in his technique. All serious composers, and, I think, most other artists of the better sort, are liable to these periods of absorption; the work produced during such periods is ultimately cast on the scrap heap, but men who have passed through them attain later an interest, or even a mastery, which the lazier type of "inspirationist" or "bird-like" artist does not attain. That Mr. Van Dieren had done a certain amount of hard work was, or should have been, obvious.[31]

[31] Atheling was to return to the curious music of Bernard Van Dieren (November 14, 1918) to point out: "All that the most open-minded critic can say at present is that here is a composer seriously interested in his art. . . ." Although Van Dieren (1884-1936) lived most of his life in London his music received only rare performances. The concert Atheling probably refers to here was given on February 20. There were two works, *Diaphony for Chamber Orchestra and Baritone Solo,* introducing three sonnets of Shakespeare, and *Overture for Chamber Orchestra.* "The *Diaphony* went on without a pause or a cadence for nearly an hour," a contemporary reviewer reported. "The *Overture,* too, was very long, and although somewhat more intelligible than the *Diaphony,* was puzzling and dull. Van Dieren's music seemed to have so laboured a surface that its inner meanings were obscured."

Atheling's reference to the "eccentric" and "florid" promotion of Van Dieren perhaps referred to pronouncements by Philip Heseltine (Peter Warlock) and Cecil Gray, who were among a tiny but enthusiastic group of supporters. A statement from *The Musical Times* (April, 1917) was perhaps authored by one of them.

> While most contemporary composers rely almost exclusively on the harmonic or vertical aspect of music, Van Dieren might be said to be the first composer since Bach to employ a purely contrapuntal texture. . . . The repose, the classic dignity, the calm of his art have few parallels in our time. Indeed, to find his spiritual kinsmen we should be compelled to search, not in the great European schools of thought, but rather in the East—in China.

Atheling did not like Van Dieren's music, but he realized at once that it was more substantial than that of many contemporaries, an opinion supported again more recently in a 1961 statement by Sir William Walton.

I range myself against a good deal of current musical opinion in preferring Ravel's "Septuor" to his string "Quartette" as performed here. For the rest, so far as contemporary compositions have come under my notice during the last months, it seems to me that the archæologists have the better of it; that the Kennedy-Fraser Hebridean songs are a permanent part of music, and that the few frail reconstructions by W. M. Rummel have a certain enjoyable charm.

At the opera: Mullings is a fine actor, apt to shout till he "comes through the tone," thus imperilling the durability of his voice, and diminishing the pleasure of his audience. Radford is enjoyable in the "Seraglio," as elsewhere. Parker shows progress. Some of the singers might be conveniently scragged.

I have also attended recitals by Haley, Mackinnon, and by various other artists whose names I do not wish to recall, or whose performances melt into an indistinguishable compost. Plunkett Greene preserves a gentlemanly tradition.

THE AVOIDABLE[32]

Treatises on music have not been lacking since the days of Gui d'Arezzo; from the time of Couperin composers have not wholly refrained from telling people how they want their compositions played. We have even Dictionaries of Musicians, music publications, romantic biographies of composers, etc., and also novels about musical life, together with scholarly research, and before spending twelve guineas renting a concert-hall the intending performer might do well to look over some few of these works—preferably those written by good musicians, or people familiar with good music, and treating of the structure and the development of music, and of the right ways of playing.

Arnold Dolmetsch's "The Interpretation of the Music of the 17th and 18th Centuries" is both compact and clearly written, and full of valuable hints and citations. It does not much matter where a musician learns his historical facts, so long as he gets into his head the idea that music is a structure; that occidental music, which is about all he is likely to be asked to play to an occidental audience, has developed along certain lines (not the only possible lines).

The works of Bernard Van Dieren deserve to be resurrected. He is never performed today, but he developed a style of free dissonance altogether his own, contemporary with Schoenberg's early work. (Murray Schafer, *British Composers in Interview*, London, 1963, p. 81.)

[32] *The New Age,* September 5, 1918, pp. 302-3.

There was a certain amount of liberty of detail permitted in the playing of early "classical" music. A musician attacking music "historically" will feel the relation between embroidery or optional filling and the essential structural features. He will have the sense of larger form in a higher degree than the musician who treats music as an affair of the last sixty or hundred years, and who "gets it" as an impression.

One finds a decided lack of structural sense; of the sense of main structure, on the contemporary English platform.

Some liberties can be best understood as breaks from certain fixed orders. It is poor economy for a performer not to recognise this.

In any art, whenever "academic" or theoretic "laws" become too cumbersome, or too detailed, the "genius" breaks from them. That is to say, he evolves his own criteria and decides for himself what are really the essentials, i.e., for the most part, what notes have really the emotive power; what regularities under apparently irregular foliage give most effectively the sense of order without which there is no lasting art.

All this is a plea for pattern music as opposed to impression music, colour music, programme music; but it is also advice to performers of whatever predilection not to neglect the study of their art, of its structure and history, in too careless a manner. Pattern may not be pattern in imitation of J. S. Bach, nor anything that he would have recognised under that designation.

The most general faults of contemporary London instrumentalists seem to me to be (a) a neglect of main structure (b) a tendency to melt all composers, or at least very diverse composers, into a unity; to impose on rhythms written in diverse manners a sort of personal uniformity (probably bound up with the performer's own physique).

These two faults beset singers also but are, in them, possibly less apparent.

Both singers and instrumentalists fail in the construction of their programmes. A programme cannot succeed merely because it is well arranged; but bad arrangement can almost spoil it. It was a comfort to find, I think it was, Miss Daisy Kennedy treating music "as if it were a serious study, with a literature." There is not only a tendency to huddle a lot of odds and ends unplannedly into a programme, there is a tendency to forget that members of the audience *may* later have the opportunity to hear some other concert, that they need not be taken from Bach to Scarlatti, etc., Beethoven, Brahms, Wagner, Debussy, every afternoon in the week.

Concerts devoted to a single composer may require more care and thought than those spread over three centuries. They may also serve to fix the performer in one's memory.

There is a decided lack of enterprise in hunting up mislaid music; in finding really good things which everyone is not singing.

As to the setting of words to music, I can but repeat for the eleventh time that contemporary composers seem to have a horror of doing this well. There are excellent models if not in super-abundance at least in sufficiency.

It is only too easy to ruin fine words with a poor setting, but it is quite possible to preserve their beauty, and even possible to enhance them; to emphasise their speech-beauty by a very slight exaggeration of the sound-quality, *keeping* in each case the quality of each word-sound but, as it were, dwelling on it, holding it to the ear, as a good poet might conceivably do in composing it; as for example it is apparent in such a line as

En casque de crystal rose les balladines.

Lawes has done this in setting some poems by Waller. (One of the rare cases where a poet has commended his setter.) Since that date English musicians and poets have, I believe, kept themselves rigidly segregate; though Robert Browning did study music, and Tom Moore played his own accompaniments at the piano.

Serious young performers, even though they had attained little skill, might command a certain attention if they showed a determination to give only the finest sort of music, and if they began with simplicity. I do not mean in the vegetarian manner.

Other faults or virtues should be found listed in any primer. Clear enunciation; study of the individual character of each number (sub. heading under (*b*) in faults of instrumentalists); singer must make different kinds of song different in his performance; must actually create something during performance.

Deficient rhythm-sense presumably cannot be supplied to people afflicted with this deficiency. People who are tone-deaf *can* play the piano by remembering which key corresponds to which black blob on paper. People who are insensitive to sound-quality are, alas, so abundant among all ranks of performers and listeners that this insensitiveness might almost be reckoned an asset (financially); but if a performer have not a sense of rhythm he may as well leave the platform, and if he cannot learn to make clean cuts and segments, and to divide compositions into their larger structural parts, he will never be much worth hearing.

All of these points are very simple and obvious, and one would expect them to be familiar to every child student of music.

PROM[33]

The "Prom," or a prom, or let us call it a specimen prom, began with Mozart, Tziganized or Wognerized (printer please leave the spelling as it is); it was, at any rate, spritely. It was a body of rhythmic sound, but the peculiar fineness of Mozart was undiscoverable. Pur-up-up, pur-up-up. It was followed by Lalo, the spirit of the Holy City, or let us say the spirit of "Nearer my God to Thee" mingled with that of "God Save the King," the manner being peculiar to the late Victorian era: Tup-er-up-up, *skeek*. Followed by up-cheek, up-cheek.

There was the charm of the large and atrociously decorated interior of the Queen's Hall, the stimulus of the crowd, the general spirit of that novel called the "Kreutzer Sonata" and all "Ganz mit Stimmung." Quite enjoyable, but no place for a critic.

It does not disturb one, it simply does not concern one. I do not, as a rule, go to "proms." This was, at any rate, my first "prom" for eight years, for by 1908 or '09, I had learned that no native conductor save, the then, Mr. Thomas Beecham, interested me in the least. Sir Henry Wood wobbles his bâton about in the air; no orchestra can be expected to know what part of the vague wafty movement is intended to mark the beginning of the bar, neither does he appear to consider the orchestra as an instrument of divisible parts. There is no endeavour to stimulate any particular section of it at any particular time. He has *made* the "prom" concerts, and both deserves and receives the gratitude of the audience which enjoys them. He keeps a cheery rhythm in motion. The orchestra produces queer sounds. The plug is taken out of the barrel near the end of Lalo's "Divertissement" (1st movement). Hell broke loose in the Allegro con fuoco. Pat-at-ty wump, pat-at-ty wump. Chee-chee-weecheechee WIP.

Miss Carmen Hill sang "Kennst du das Land" in French, quite good French for an English singer. She sang with clear enunciation and delicacy. Her voice needs the Queen's Hall, and is surprisingly pleasing there. She is bothered by a small auditorium.

Howard Carr was a pleasant surprise. To be told that one is to hear music about three Heroes, two of them heroes of the present war, is a little alarming. Carr had written quite good programme music, though the bombing of a Zeppelin needs a noise perhaps a little more unusual

[33] *The New Age*, September 19, 1918, p. 335.

than that by which he represented it. He has done his orchestration quite carefully. The "O'Leary" is quite good martial music.

He conducted the orchestra excellently and with great firmness, with such firmness, indeed, that one suspects him either of genius or of being an experienced military bandmaster. I am not to be tempted into rash prophecies, but if Mr. Carr can conduct any music save his own, or anything more complicated than his own rather simple rhythms, we should soon rejoice in one more orchestra leader, and, heaven knows, we are in need of conductors. He cut his bars clean and looked after the separate parts of his orchestra. The orchestra woke up, and the audience noticed the difference.

I am inclined to think the "prom" audience would accept better conducting than Sir Henry's without any rebellious murmur. I don't know about their taking better programmes. After all, Sir Henry gave them something labelled Overture to "Le Nozze."

He was jogged out of his Wagnerization in the MacDowell Concerto, but a concerto for piano and orchestra is a diabolically unpleasing form. It is conceivable that an orchestra *might* be used to develop and reinforce a piano composition; it is hardly desirable, but it is a *conceivable* feat. The piano will not share even, it cannot balance an orchestra, and it is not a sufficiently *cantabile* instrument to take the orchestra as an accompaniment. It is, indeed, a little sham orchestra, *or an accompaniment,* and one wants neither a real orchestra against it, nor a redundant accompaniment of an accompaniment.

Miss Purnell made her third piano entry into the general sound rather well, but the piano part here is not of much interest. Wood managed the orchestra rather well in the first part. Miss Purnell got a certain "crystalline-metallic" sound from her instrument which fitted into the scheme; she showed digital celerity. The second piano speciality was at first faulty, but improved; there were certain blurrs in the bass; and the young player was obviously unfamiliar with auditoriums of such magnitude. The sound of her piano, however, carried, and she did good bass work in the largo.

But the orchestra is one medium and the piano is another. I doubt if really good composers will write for this combination in the future. The Piano concerto marks the apogee of the piano-intoxication of the nineteenth century. It is perhaps no worse than trying to combine the piano with a smaller number of strings. The piano accompanies, at the best.

An art becomes, perhaps, undignified when it depends upon too great a mechanical element in its execution. I think the organ has given way to the piano very largely because the organ is too mechanical. The pianola is worse, and should be relegated to seaside dance halls, or to people who, being half familiar with long compositions, want to study their general structure. It is not pleasant to listen to. Music is, after all, a means of expression, a means of human expression. There is more æsthetic satisfaction in a few simple notes played by a person who *intends* something, than in a procession of notes shot through a punched sheet of paper, but unintelligible to the executant.

An orchestra is the conductor. That is to say, it can do nothing and express nothing save what the conductor understands. It cannot convey any emotion beyond those to which the conductor is sensible. There is no use in trying to criticise an orchestra apart from its leader. Thus, though the "Proms" occur nightly, one's criticism of them can be no more extended than one's criticism of any obscure musician who appears once at a smaller hall.

One cannot even make criticisms of the compositions presented, for all the compositions are Woodized or Wagnerized, or, at any rate, melted down to an agglomerate.

Memories arise in the Queen's Hall; one is prompted to ask: What has become of "Henderson, the drummer"? but we are not a correspondence column. Did the Börsdorf family arrive with the Hannoverian dynasty? Let us hope so.[34]

MUSIC[35]

I have, despite experience, again put my ears in peril, but this time I finished my dinner in peace. The powerful organ of the charming Miss Thelma Peterson was tympanating through the corridors of the Queen's Hall when I entered.

Then the composer, Cyril B. Rootham, conducted the overture to his unperformed opera, "The Two Sisters," which has a "leading," if rather depressingly vegetarian, theme based in some way or other upon the "Twa Sisters o' Binnorie." This, however, does not compare in any overwhelming manner with Brahms' treatment of the "Edward" ballad; and for some reason, unexplained even by the voluble Mrs. Rosa Newmarch, expositress in extraordinary to the "Proms," the doleful dumps soon give way to a bright, cheery and wholly uninspired section (presumably "Allegretto 2–4 B major"). Later, Mr. Rootham performs the by no means difficult feat of getting some pleasant sounds out of an

---

[34] Atheling's reference here is to the celebrated Bosdorf family of musicians—Adolf, Emil, Oscar, and Adolf junior, all orchestral performers. Adolf Bosdorf had been first horn at Covent Garden and was one of the musicians responsible for the formation of the London Symphony Orchestra in 1904.

[35] *The New Age,* October 3, 1918, pp. 364–65.

orchestra. There are some excellent bars, *but* the function of a composer is to shape a composition which will remain interesting all through. The noise of oboes and 'cellos playing softly is quite pleasant. Musicians given a key and told to improvise should be able to make quite pleasant sounds. The "consorts" in Elizabethan barber shops are said to have proceeded in this manner.

As conductor, Mr. Rootham marked his bars clearly, but showed no further particular talents in orchestral leadership. The whole effect was rather arty. There were contrasts violent in sound, but not particularly definite in intention.

One gets very tired of feeling that the music of an orchestra may "go off" at any moment into the Old Oaken Bucket or the National Anthem. The audience was enthusiastic. The Puh-pur-up-up-paw opening of the Grieg Concerto was carefully modulated by the pianist, De Greef, who was in his element with the essentially light, and possibly icy, tinkle. Wood was in good form. De Greef showed a suave skilfulness, obviously very experienced. The effect was unified, and this is not a despicable feat in the performance of the piano cum orchestra combination. I had even moments of enjoyment during the first movement. The clarity of the piano went well against the resinous quality of the strings. De Greef's strong point is not his bass, nor is Wood's the fortissimo blare. Later parts of the composition were, or were given as, fireworks and no more, and the long piano passage went off into cinema. In the second movement De Greef lost attention, and I found myself wondering how long the Russian flag would remain in the bevy of colours over the organ.[36] "Prom" music is perhaps very good for tired people who want a rest and lethargic anodyne rather than an extension of life, a vivification of life, in the arts.

Walford Davies' "Solemn Melody" was respectable but not wildly original; W. Evans got good 'cello tone; and one prefers, oh vastly prefers, Kiddle at the organ to Kiddle at the piano. As for the Faust Ballet Music, what *can* be said of it as performed? It was doubly interesting. One felt its orchestral pandemonium beating upon one's ears, and one was also aware of its *fortes* by the vibration of the floor under one's boot heels. We should, perhaps, be doubly grateful to the conductor for tickling us through one sense while he paralyses us through another. The music itself is perhaps well enough, or would be well enough if one had a ballet to watch. Its significance is quite simple, and it ends in the usual clashing and thunderous *frisson*.

[36] Sir Henry Wood, organizer of the "Proms," was greatly interested in Russian music. He was married to a Russian noblewoman and used the pseudonym "Klenovsky" for his own compositions.

The Finnish:—

Mr. Landon Ronald, "born on 7th of June, 1873, Studied at the Royal College of Music, 1890, Engaged by Sir Augustus Harris as maestro at piano and second Conductor at Covent Garden Theatre," etc., etc., etc., showed sentiment and great delicacy in his piano accompaniment to Mr. George Pawlo. The first song was "Dedication," words by W. E. Henley, music by Landon Ronald.

The Edward Oxenford, greatly with sentiment, Twickenham Ferry old Victorian manner, forbade one's giving much attention to the vocal quality of Mr. Pawlo.

By the beginning of the second number one was prepared for this effort, but the caterwauling of

"And you,"

followed by "ni'ite," followed again by a still more rending

"aand yuuu,"

wringing the thirty odd feet of mucous piping which still remain to us from the antediluvian period, was followed by the exit of the critic.

It is a curious indication of the temper of the public that anyone should approach it in this particular month with professedly "Anglo-Finnish" "art-song recital." Finland is electing or not electing a German king, and is, at any rate, an ally of our enemies.

If Mr. Pawlo had worn a V.C. and the collar of the "Garter" I should not have stayed any longer in the Wigmore Hall, on the occasion in question; but it is odd that he should choose this particular heading for his announcement. It should be said in fairness that he used it all last season, and is presumably in no way to blame for the conduct of his country, but courtesy demands at least some sort of formal disclaimer on the part of any alien enemy who appeals for popular support. One does not know that Mr. Pawlo is a Finn. He may have been born in Brixton of Anglo-Welsh parents, but, we repeat, the form of his announcement is curious.

Announcements for the opening autumn season include Vladimir Rosing, Saturdays, October 5 and October 19, at 3 o'clock, Wigmore Hall.

Moiseiwitsch, six recitals on alternate Saturdays, beginning September 28, 3 o'clock, Wigmore.

Muriel Foster, October 3 (at 5.30); November 16 and December 14, 3 o'clock, Wigmore.

A new series of classical concerts, Wigmore, dates not given.

MOISEIWITSCH; ROSING[37]

Moiseiwitsch's success is due to ten years' solid work and he deserves every scrap of it. The crowd at the Wigmore Hall, on September 28, amply testified that he has passed the point where Press praise or Press criticism can affect him. His position is perfectly and deservedly solid. Neither would there be any use in criticising his technique. Whatever a man could be *told* to do with a piano, Moiseiwitsch does and does admirably. He is armed cap-à-pie. There is nothing for one to suggest, but that "something-beyond," that something which the artist should reveal to the critic, baffles one by unanalysable absence. I refrained from writing of Moiseiwitsch last season because I could find so little to say; because there was so patently nothing I could tell him, or tell the reader about him. So good a performer needs one's closest attention and that attention I gave him on September 28 for about an hour and a quarter. The result is solid respect.

The work is so solid that one has to *try* to find fault, and one is inclined to doubt perceptions of such fault when discovered. I thought in the first fugues that there was just the suspicion of the "whirr of wheels," of a residue of sound faintly like the scratch of quills to be heard in bad harpsicord playing. Then there was a certain hardness which did not seem quite masterly, perhaps due to the quality of the instrument used, or quite possibly introduced for some purpose of main structure not apparent to me during a single hearing, but in which Moiseiwitsch is much more right than I could be. Has he a personal interpretation of Bach? Has he any particular commentary to make on that master? Admirable presentation of fugue but *senza fuoga*. Bass runs excellent. Would not, perhaps, a personal manner in presenting Bach border on eccentricity? Yet a less "classic" modus might be the more accurately historical. Chromatic Fantasie, triviality, tone due to instrument? Then great charm and processional stateliness. Prelude and D major fugue; gaiety of many waving small flags, developing into solid charge. Fugue B flat, richness, reward of years of hard work. Volume of sound good. Anything one could suggest is there; but the "element of surprise" lacking from the attack on our susceptibilities. Repose, detachment, impartiality toward his subject-matter—all this is excellent. And to hold one's attention unflagging through five fugues, excellent.

The Liszt Sonata in B minor opened with such charm that I resolved to attend Moiseiwitsch's whole series of concerts to see what he had to say about Beethoven, Brahms, Chopin, Schumann. Then passage of

[37] *The New Age*, October 17, 1918, pp. 395–96.

fireworks. Again I found myself thinking of Moiseiwitsch's music in terms of achievement rather than of revelation. If this is a dangerous metaphysical borderline for the critic, I was soon ready to leave it and say "brava" for many a thing well done. Certainly the pianist showed Liszt the equal of other piano composers, and I think the people who refuse to see Liszt among the great figures of piano-music probably suffer from an hyperæsthesia. (Not but what there is plently of Liszt which one does not want to hear once, twice, or often.) It is an artillery instrument, and Moiseiwitsch, in the Sonata, made it convincing. Still it was not Moiseiwitsch who started me speculating about tone-colour, variety, orchestration of the instrument. I had to get these questions out of my recollection of other, even of other much less proficient, performers. Yet Moiseiwitsch's absence of personality keeps one's attention on the music actually being produced. It is only by strong effort that one can wrench one's mind on to the possibilities of its being produced differently. His playing is, emphatically, *not* hollow virtuosity: there was no effect, or I think scarcely any effect of showing off, of juggling. It was sober, serious, of an even excellence; the man so master of the keyboard that he *seems* to forget it completely. I was pleased, I was approbative, I was even a little apologetic for not being swept "off my feet," or off my seat or whatever the suitable phrase is. The Sonata was so well graduated to its climax, so well graded in its fortes, there is such skill in all of his technique.... There was German sentiment-to-sentimentality in "Waldesrauschen," the thing is definitely "dated." "Liebestraum" is a better thing, but "dated." I felt an obscure irritation coming on me, and left the hall to keep my meditation on the Sonata from being further disturbed or effaced.

Moiseiwitsch's concerts continue at the Wigmore, Oct. 12, and alternate Saturdays thereafter at 3 p.m. My only further criticism would be queries: whether Moiseiwitsch might not have presented Bach with greater variety, shown much more the scope of the composer: whether he has not one mood for Bach, and one mood for Liszt, and possibly a similar moodal or "modal" category or mind-division for each other composer, a sort of Globe-Wernike system of mental drawers, cupboards and boxes.

The other consolation for unsuccessful and over-sensitive musicians with "no memory to speak of," is that memory is one of the least interesting mental attributes; it is one of the first faculties to develop in childhood; it is said to be excellent among elephants; it is shared by many forms of mechanism. It is indeed purely mechanical. The human addition is the faculty which leaps into memory and snatches up this or that at the moment. The Muses are not memory but the Daughters of Memory. By them the creative artist seizes the elements of his composition from the labyrinths of his mind; by them the elements are assembled.

Even the repeating artist brings life into his work by such extra addition and assemblage, adding his own emotional knowledge and imagination experience to the set line of his text.

Vladimir Rosing

His first recital of the season was an agonising duel between Mr. Rosing's remarkable art and a remarkably villainous throat. The programme made no compromise with bad taste. Beethoven's "In questa tomba" suave in opening, given with mellowness and ease, save for a burst of coughing. Despite the throat trouble the singer's art asserted itself in the gradation and arrangement of qualities. Delicate articulation in "Dalla sua pace." Tschaikowsky's "Nights of Madness" was exquisite in its opening. Hoarseness interfered later. In the beautiful Lensky aria from the "Onegin," both the fine quality of the composition and the intelligence of the performer were audible; the stiffness of the throat prevented Rosing's usual cohesion. Art seemed to triumph in the Farewell, but the stronger notes were not at their full, and necessarily affected the scale and proportion of the whole. There was voice enough for the Tschaikowsky Lullaby, in encore. Strophes Saphiques were exquisite, the Brahms' serenade, Watteau or Verlaine; no matter what physical state Rosing is in, one always takes something memorable from his concerts. Here it was "l'ombre de mon âme, l'amour qui dort" from "Au Rossignol."

Where the bawling "lyric" tenor trusts his effects to his fortissimos or his high-note-burst, one finds that Rosing does not. When the memorabilia are not whole and perfectly graduated compositions conceived in unity, and given under favourable conditions, they are lines and phrases in middle sound or sung softly. He got fine comedy into "Serenade Inutile"; and one thought he had finally come into voice in "Hoi, my Dniepr," the magnificent Moussorgsky; the long second strophe bringing the audience to customary enthusiasm. The novelty of the programme was the biting political satire of Moussorgsky's "Song of the Flea." Rosing finally broke down and had to stop in the middle of an encore to the "Hopak." People who think they like music and who go, or can afford to go, to concerts are very foolish not to go to Rosing's concerts, for, voice or no voice, there is no one in London to interpret Moussorgsky as he does, and Moussorgsky is the greatest of song-writers.

Next Rosing concert, including Korsakoff, and Czeck and Siberian songs. Wigmore, Oct. 19th, at 3 o'clock.

Stroesco, Æolian Hall. Oct. 25, at 3.15, with extremely interesting programme.

FUNCTIONS OF CRITICISM[38]

The second season must be worse than the first for any critic who desires impartiality. If a performer has once bored you to death it is, in the first place, very difficult to drag yourself to hear him again; and if this reluctance be overcome it is still difficult not to carry with you a touch of resentment for the initial annoyance. Conversely, it is difficult when one has been delighted by a player not to arrive at his second performance with a certain readiness to attribute all faults to chance. Even so we may take it as unlikely that any performer over 45 is likely to receive a wholly new musical intelligence or to develop a new and ravishing charm. If a man is going to change from an egoistic temperamental impresser of school-girls to a serious musician the change should happen before he is much past 35.

The function of musical criticism, or rather of fortnightly criticism of performances, is to make it possible for the best performers to present their best work; for them to give concerts under present conditions without making any concession whatsoever to ignorance and bad taste. Beyond that one might have ambitions, both of developing the discretion of a possible public, and of actually enlightening young or untrained musicians (or even elderly amateurs) concerning their own shortcomings, and their possible avenues of improvement. (Do bad musicians attend good concerts?) In several cases where great proficiency and obviously great experience in public performance are coupled with overmastering dullness, one would suggest that every piece of music worth presenting in public has a *meaning*. The composer presumably felt something, and equally wished to express something by his fugue, étude or sonata. My statement is simple, and platitudinous; but correct detail and even that rather rare thing, correct architectonics, will not hold the better attentions unless the performer have, beyond a concept of the composers' style, and a style for representing it, some intention to express the unifying emotion or emotions of the particular piece. It is by no means necessary that these emotions be the same as were the composer's, the performer must think both "Bach" and "Ciaconna" if he is to give the piece with effect. He must unite his general feel of the composer to his particular concept of the piece to be given.

II.
There is a prevalent superstition or tradition or condition among performers that they "must give work by living English composers *if* they want press-notices." With devilish cunning they not only give these

[38] *The New Age,* October 31, 1918, pp. 428–29.

works—songs for the most part—but they plant them in the geometrical middle of their programmes. And in explanation of this frightfulness they say that if they put them at the beginning people won't come till they are over; and *if* they put them at the end, people will go *before* the end of the concert. I have not yet verified the existence of the hidden hand in British music. The "Daily Telegraph" is popularly supposed to consult the war-map for the week before deciding on the merits of foreign composers. Practical justice demands that whenever a singer does one the ill turn of sticking his C. Scott, Dunhill, Ireland, V. Williams, F. Bridge smack in the middle of his programme, his concert should be judged on the singing solely of these composers. Mr. ——— was impossible even in the possible part of concert.

ROSING, AND LAUREL CROWNS

The sensitive ear was charmed with anticipation; Rosing's programme (Oct. 19; Wigmore) was wholly uncompromising. His voice was at its best, in all its exquisite variety. Through the opening group of French songs from thirteenth to sixteenth century the singer used the greatest possible diversity of his shading. In this ingle of range, this, at first sight, so small part of his repertoire, he was far too interesting to permit the critic to take notes. I mean exactly that—the orchestration of the voice was so subtle that one could not scribble and listen at the same time, there was too much going on. The four by six performer imagines, or rather does not imagine but takes if for granted, that the scale contains thirteen tones and half tones, and that to sing consists in hitting (or approximating) the note set down on the page. It seemed to me that Rosing never repeated the *same sound* through all the six songs of opening group. The simplicity of de la Halle and Marot allowed an elaborate art of colour, and of recede and approach. "Plus ne suis ce que j'ai été" was taken rather fast, but with a very personal interpretation, and one might in time come to prefer Rosing's speed to one's own concept of the tempo.

The Schumann, which would have been the highbrow gem of a popular programme, sank into scale. Both Schumann and Heine were in perpetual danger of sentiment. "Mes Larmes" grazed the danger. There was a little too much fuss in "En Rêve." This Schumann is "very queer in French." "J'ai pardonné" was drama; one realised after a time that it was "Ich grolle nicht"; once rendered in English as "I do not growl, when thou the heart me break, I do not growl." We might almost lay it down as axiomatic that a song must be sung in its original language. It is probably impossible to sing even Heine (the Kaiser's pet detestation) in German just at present; but the perfect union of word and note is so subtle and so rare a thing that, once attained, no substitute is likely to give satisfaction, unless the translator be a great technician, able to support treble the *technical* difficulty which faced the original poet. In this case the French sob was a shade too sobby. Audience naturally more vociferous than at any other stage of the programme; which, however, made a *volte face* into reality with the Rimsky Korsakoff group of songs. Di Veroli's accompanying had been valuable all along, and showed particularly in "On the Hills."

One comes to believe that the mass of even so good a public as Rosing's is bewildered by anything unfamiliar. "Come see your garden" was perhaps the finest of the four Korsakoffs. The Aria from "Christmas Eve" is great fun, drollery, magnificent singing.

Note that the programme was arranged, built as skilfully as a good play, first the suave subtle old French music, then the florid and sentimental touching the popular heart, then the *real,* in Korsakoff, applause less excited but persistent, the determined clapping of the connoisseurs who had paid their money and were determined to get all the Russian music they could.

Here Rosing executed a *tour de force* of pedagogy. All but the leather-eared had seen the difference between the translated Schumann and the Korsakoff. The Christmas Aria was excellent, a model of how an aria should be set, words and the notes perfectly wedded. The encore was Moussorgsky's "Song of the Flea," and with it the augmentation for climax, for here one felt instantly the hand of the greater master. The song is a satire, but the fullness of the great artist was there.

Moussorgsky has his place beyond all other Russians. You cannot compare Music since Beethoven with the early thin music, which is like delicate patterns on glass. Since Beethoven people have thought of music as of something with a new bulk and volume. Beyond all the floridity and pretence of Wagner are these Russians, and beyond them Moussorgsky, like the primordial granite. It was excellent to have the Schumann in the programme to give this sense of proportion (even though the Schumann was not given in the best possible condition). It was as if the singer had said, You like Schumann—well, here is the real thing, Korsakoff. You take it. Then there is something beyond that— The titan.

After the climax in the third group, the play worked to its end with four Siberian convict songs, eerie, dramatic (not in the bad sense), the rough material on which Moussorgsky built his achievement. In the "Escaped Convicts" we had the peculiar Russian negation, sinister in the opening. Di Veroli gave an excellent frozen accompaniment to "Cold Winter." The audience does not get up at the end of Rosing's performance.

Rosing's next concert wholly devoted to Great Russian Composers.

Aeolian Hall. Nov. 2 at 3. I do not care how much music anyone may have heard, this Russian concert should be part of his musical education.

Kennedy-Fraser, Hebridean Songs. Aeolian Hall. Nov. 6, at 8 p.m., worth hearing.

STROESCO, VIOLINISTS[39]

I noted with approbation that at his final recital, last season, Constantin Stroesco had begun to take singing as a serious art. Again (October 25, at Æolian Hall) I find enough in his singing to make a detailed fault-finding worth while.

Were our musical life more organised, more coherent, we should insist on a greater specialisation by performers. We should not have Rosing singing French translations of German songs when he could just as well, or rather better, give us Russian. We should note that Tinayre (notice next week) has a certain subtlety in his enunciation of French which non-French tenors have not. We should probably want M. Tinayre to leave Italian to someone else, not because he sings it badly, but because his French is better than his Italian. Were there a really critical audience, it would insist on each performer doing the thing he does best—at least in public; one does not wish to interfere with people's private diversions.

Stroesco gave us fifteen songs by fourteen different composers. It was in the main a good programme. A man should not begin his work on too narrow a basis, but Stroesco's next step should be to decide what he does best. This limitation of one's art is perhaps a French gift; the artist should find himself in some mode in which he can use all or nearly all his gifts to the best advantage, and where his limitations will least affect the complete presentation of his subject-matter.

I said before that Stroesco seemed well fitted to render old Italian music on the one hand, and his native Roumanian folk-songs on the other. This is not a Medic and Persian decree that he shall touch nothing else. The first four lines of Debussy's "L'Enfant" were exquisitely given. But this does not convince me that modern French music is "good for him." Does it not interfere with his original élan, and slightly affect his singing of "Muger, Mugural"? Does he do this folk-song any better for having to a great extent mastered an exotic? At any rate, there is something in his singing of modern French songs which raises this uncertainty in my mind.

There was a certain opacity in his tone, perhaps phlegm and tiredness

---

[39] *The New Age*, November 7, 1918, pp. 11–12.

toward the end of his programme, but there was nothing in his singing of the older music which made one feel that it was unsuited to him. "Giorni" was not in academic mould. It was individual in interpretation; it was constructed, painted, with full use of liberties (these liberties are historically correct). Stroesco got variety into his tone, and the interpretation showed thought. I am all for his singing composers of this period—Pergolesi, Cesti, Caldara, Paisiello, Paradies, Del Leuto, Legrenzi. I would gladly hear three-fourths of his next concert given over to work of this character.

On October 25, his close to "Dalla sua Pace" was exquisite, his diminuendos excellent, Moffat's "Lovely is your Mien" given with charm. Not as harsh condemnation, one should note that Mozart's song has the movement of music, not the accent of speech. The singer is bound to follow this. Chausson in "Amour d'Antan" respects the words. Moffat is florid; he follows the accent of the poem, but he cannot resist the temptation to put in little descants too often. The temptation is considerable. He has the grace to put some of his descant on "Ah, ah, ah." Shakespeare put in "Hey-nonny-nonnys," so that the musician might have his fun without upsetting the poetry. Mozart was much more important than his librettist (more important even when he had Metastasio to write words for him). But there is a certain kind of emphasis and there are certain effects of veracity which cannot be given by music of this school.

The perfect song occurs when the poetic rhythm is in itself interesting, and when the musician augments, illumines it, without breaking away from, or at least without going too far from, the dominant cadences and accents of the words, when the ligatures illustrate the verbal qualities, and when the little descants and prolongations fall in with the main movement of the poem. The Debussy song was well set. Easthope Martin tries to follow the words of a poem called "Beauty," but their rhythm is without interest and his setting shows neither talent nor inspiration. Pizzetti da Parma opens his accompaniment with rehashed Debussy, but he is setting one of d'Annunzio's most felicitous poems, and, having therefore a different language from that usually set by Debussy, he adds an Italian element which breaks up the clichés of the modern French school. The song is excellently set, save for the twelfth line. Da Parma shows true restraint in not repeating the final line of the poem, which a fourth-rate musician would have done.

Wagner in French, with the label "Souffrances," opened well, but the second strophe still reeks "Deutschland über alles." Brahms' "Serenade" brought most applause from the audience. I preferred Di Veroli's Mozart accompaniment to the manner of his Brahms accompaniment, which latter gave me no satisfaction.

I think there might with advantage have been more Roumanian on the programme. The Pastoral was very interesting; "Cantec" excellent.

VIOLINS

Evelyn Cooke, Æolian Hall, October 26. César Franck Sonate, pale, "poetic," or moonlight effects, piano accompaniment unduly sentimental (between ourselves, a bore). If the first movement was "allegretto" as announced, it was certainly very, very moderato. The young lady gets a clear tone from her fiddle, failure of interest in second movement possibly due to her having had no definite intention of making it mean anything in particular. Rejoicing of Christmas-card angels, Franck's usual stage sets, executant's technique in detail unexceptionable.

Sascha Lasserson, Wigmore Hall, Oct. 28. Full, rich tone, temperament, rhythm sense, virility. I am not absolutely sure of his pitch sense; acoustics play one odd tricks.

The Bach Ciaconna is a bore if it be not played with considerable ability; Lasserson was well above that danger line. There was perhaps a slight drag at the start, but it improved as he proceeded; one had no very distinct sense of partitions, none of the clean-cutness one rather expected; it was as if the music had been written fifty years later than Bach; but there was clear bell tone in places and a very considerable beauty, an excellent close, and passages showing thought.

Of the two melodies by Achron, the first has a badly written piano accompaniment and no particular interest; in the second the tom-tom for the piano is better, some interest in the harmony, violin part negligible. Tor-Aulin an improvement, but I should prefer the "King's Dinner Music" as given by any native café orchestra in Tangier.

Lasserson should have a very considerable public success. Virtuosity in Hubay "Zephir" a little empty, not good enough to be repeated in encore without boring the more intelligent members of the audience.

The Chopin-Sarasate "Nocturne" showed the violinist's limitations; he should have got more out of it. Sarasate "Spanish Dance" went without a slip.

Kennedy-Fraser second Hebridean recital, Æolian Hall, Tuesday, November 12, at 3 p.m.

VAN DIEREN, TINAYRE, ROSING'S ALL RUSSIAN PROGRAMME[40]

Miss Helen Rootham has a voice clear, pure, largish, rather too cloistral to be convincing in Serbian folk-song as given at her Serbian Red Cross

[40] *The New Age*, November 14, 1918, pp. 27–28.

recital. The songs were interesting but appeared to possess neither the wildness nor energy of either Russian or Gaelic traditional melodies. The concert might have had some æsthetic interest had it been devoted wholly to the works of Van Dieren. There is in his instrumentation a closeness of workmanship which deserves examination. He still suffers from having had an unfortunately blatant introduction two years ago. One is inclined to doubt announced Messiahs, but in "Levana," in the midst of what we were once told was the new revolutionary revelation of octuple counterpoint, there is a wandering, apparently aimless air, theme, motif, at any rate melodic line, like a thread of pale lavender. One is not convinced that Van Dieren is a man bursting with things to say, with messages to deliver, with a new content forcing the music into new manner, but there is abundant fineness in detail, and in combination of sounds made simultaneously. (The ear really listening will not stop to define "harmony" in orthodox or unorthodox manner; it will merely desire to listen.) The main form and the rhythm construction did not appear particularly original. It was rather like a picture made of solid small objects cunningly joined; it was as if the metal had not been molten at the time of the casting. This effect may, of course, have been due to the quartette of performers who seemed much more at home in the piece of clowning by A. Bax which ended the programme.

The setting of the Villon ballade is daring. It is, however, not original in scheme, for Debussy "set" "San Sebastian" by merely inserting four chunks of music: result, one wishes to burn the rubbishy libretto, hang the actors, and have the music by itself. Van Dieren's prelude to the ballade is a little long; the ballade is then recited on the pervading tonality of the music, and during the envoy the music again exquisitely begins, stealing on as if from a distance. The musical postscript is about the right length and exquisite, at least in its beginning. This beautiful effect could just as well take place several times between the strophes of the ballade and would be more likely to hold the audience. Thirty and more lines of perfectly familiar poetry with no surprise and no musical revelation demand a fairly enduring auditor.

This is a matter perhaps of taste. The thing to rub in is that Van Dieren is a serious composer. One would like to hear enough of his work to form a firmer opinion of its merits.

Miss Frida Kindler, "the famous Dutch pianist," is certainly unique in her Chopin. Never have I heard the Etudes given with such elephantine wobs, thuds, and thubs as on Monday. There were school-girl-sentimental soft notes interlarded. If the thub-thob method prevails in Holland, one does not wonder that Meinheer Van Dieren has taken to the attenuation of attenuations in a post-Debussy refinement. One can come to no judgment of it from so meagre a display. It certainly deserves some sort of adequate exhibition. At present all one can do is to hazard the quite unsupportable conjecture that he is possibly at least as important as Ravel, and this may be either a gross underestimate, or an equally gross exaggeration. It is ridiculous for a man to expect public recognition on unperformed, unpublished work. All that the most open-minded critic can say at present is that here is a composer seriously interested in his art; a statement which it would be impossible to make concerning the author of the last movement of the Quartet in G major performed also on Monday.

TINAYRE[41]

M. Yves Tinayre is a charming and delightful singer. He began (Wigmore, Oct. 29) nervously. Dr. Pepusch' Cantata Alexis is a little too late to join good words with good music, but Mozart has, to all appearance, cribbed from it without stint. The melody keeps carefully to the words. Webbe also was a little too late and wrote long notes for "the."

Th. Ford, Attey, Dowland are a different boiling: early enough to find good verse their contemporary. Here we had Tinayre's charm to advantage. Attey's setting of the alba, "On a Time," is the fine fruit of an age erudite in the perfect taste of its medium. Tinayre made an effective change of manner in turning to the Dowland. It is seldom that one can correct the misprints of the programme from the clearness of a foreign singer's (or, for the matter of that, of an English singer's) enunciation. One did in Tinayre's singing "Fine Knacks." Excellent as he was in the old English he was still better in the old French encore.

For all its virtues, the modern French school of song writers will not hold its own when sung with really good art of good periods. It glows by comparison with modern Italian and modern English settings. Fauré's "Nell" was well sung, but vilely, *vilely* accompanied. As a singer is more at the mercy of his accompanist in this modern French stuff than *anywhere* else, I prefer to postpone further discussion of Tinayre until I can hear him to better advantage. The public should welcome a recital of old French songs by him. But this modern school with its eternal twiddle-twiddle, scrabble-scrabbles, becomes tiresome. "Lamento" was dull. "Coucou" sung with excellent diminuendo close. "Le Fou" clever tour-de-force. Tinayre appeared to strain and sing against the voice both here and in the Chausson.

Continuing the afternoon at Æolian Hall: George Parker has a fine

[41] This is Atheling's first review of the French tenor Yves Tinayre, a figure to whom he was immediately attracted because of the singer's intelligence and interest in reviving medieval music. Tinayre was later to sing in the première of Pound's own quasi-medieval opera, *Le Testament*, in Paris, 1926. He also incorporated "Mort, j'appelle" from that work into his repertoire and sang it on his tours during the years following.

robust voice. I hope to hear him in something interesting. As John Ireland both wrote the music and played the piano he has only himself to thank for the xylophonic hash wherewith he utterly devastated and obscured Shakespeare's "When Daffodils." Parker ends the word "notes" with "tss," "floats," ditto. The beginning of Ireland's second song was purely comic; the third song was of Oxenford school. Miss Marjorie Hayward I think the best woman violinist I have heard since beginning these notes. Almost converted me to F. Bridge's music with delicate firm tone in "Gondoliera." Sauret in "Farfalla" appears to have thought violin had been bitten by 94 healthy fleas and was in immediate necessity of being scratched at all points of its surface simultaneously.

Rosing

The readers who absented themselves from Rosing's recital (Nov. 2, Æolian) have only themselves to thank for missing what was probably the most serious Russian concert ever attempted in London. Rosing's voice, especially the lower register, was in excellent condition, and I have already said enough about his art in these columns to omit discussion of it in the few lines that remain to me. He attempted to give, so far as possible in one afternoon's singing, the music-portrait of Russia's subjectivity ("soul" is, I think, the term used). He succeeded admirably. Items: Five folk songs from the splendid collection by Philipoff, harmonised by Korsakoff. Rather "Gregorian" feel in "Red Sun." Chantey, in "Sitting on Stone." Satiric in "Bright Swallows." The next four groups illustrated Oppression, Love, Suffering, Gaiety and Satire, admirably. Kalinnikov, full of race quality. I think we may call the "Ancient Mound" great art. Rubinstein showing as really a Russian in "Prisoner." During Bleichmann's "Convicts" one realised that the "difference" between this music and the usual, was that we were having unexaggerated concern with the real, that it was not cooked up for a concert hall. (Rosing is lucky in his accompanist, Di Veroli.)

Came then three masterpieces, but in especial we note in the oriental quality of Moussorgsky's "Foire de Sorotchinsky," the light that never was on sea or land, the Coleridge-Keats ambition, the casements on seas forlorn. Moussorgsky has always some mastery to distinguish him in whatever company he is found.

Nevstruoff's "Poor Wanderer" is excellent, but from it one comprehends the Russian desire for foreignness, for French neatness, and even German upholstery. Russian music is not all of music. It has a greater place in world-music than is yet accorded it. The Moussorgsky "Trepak," the drunk dying in the snow in delirium, is a marvel. His "Goat" a gorgeous satire, the Borodine "Spes" excellently made, good *"facture."* The imitation of the old man in the "Goat" was capital. Rosing has "got" his audience. He need have no fear of their refusing from now on to take the best he can give them; and let us hope that at least half the next programme will be given up to Moussorgsky.

I stop for reasons of space, not because I have no more to say of the Russian music.

HEBRIDES, KENNEDY-FRASER[42]

There is a certain satisfaction in a concert which knows its own mind and which gives you some one thing in sufficient bulk to provide basis for an opinion; thus in Rosing's all-Russian programme we had Russia, from Nevstruoff who is so "Russian," who is so the bleak spirit of the steppes that he makes you understand the Russian reaction toward all sorts of gew-gaws and floridities, bright colour for costume, admiration of Wagner or Parisianism; we had Russian music from this bleakness of Nevstruoff to Moussorgsky who, to my mind at least, lifts Russian music above all other music of the epic tone, Moussorgsky, who is "of the heroic mould" without any sham heroics, without Wagnerian padding and rhetoric. We had Russia from the steppes to the part of Russia which is oriental, a land-locked people in the main.

The Kennedy-Frasers in the Hebridean music gave us equally an epitome of a whole racial civilisation (with whatever deprivation of luxury you like, the people who produced such art must be termed a civilised people). This music is as full of sea-slash as the Russian is of plain-bleakness and winter-bleakness. It has the wave-pull and wave-sway in place of the foot-beat of the hopak. It has also its mouth-music for dancing (Hin, hin, halla lal a) to match any present-day Jazz that Afro-America has sent over to us. It has its rhythmic validity and variety in labour songs, not to be read by the metronome, but which have their diverse beats and pauses determined by the age-lasting rhythm of the craft, cloth-clapping, weaving, spinning, milking, reaping. And in this connection, damn the young gentleman who said, "I don't go in so much for rhythm. I'm temperamental." Another chance phrase in a corridor, "Very interesting, but it needs the Kennedy-Frasers to sing it."

These phrases are a fair summary of the blight on English music since it has been a genteel, suburban accomplishment. I have walked about London streets before, during and after "peace night." The sense of rhythm is not dead in this island. I have heard costers singing not only with rhythm but also with true tone, as true as you would find among boasted continental peasant singers. An "artistic" nation would have taken its singers from the donkey-barrows and coster carts. Even

[42] *The New Age*, November 28, 1918, pp. 59–60.

La Duse still calls herself "contadina," and once wore the Venetian black shawl. But no, the black curse of Cromwell, and the anathema of Victoriana and genteelness have put a stop to that sort of permeation in England, and the concert-performer is chosen from the exclusively eviscerated stratas of the community.

The result is that these women come down here from "North Britain" and drive one to learning Gaelic. These Hebridean melodies are the only "English" music possessed of the needful vigour. Mrs. Kennedy-Fraser's settings are not the vegetarian school of folk-song.

In execution, Miss K.-Fraser's voice is greatly improved, there was last year a slight heaviness or dulness, but now the due keenness has replaced it, and the more emotional, more passionate songs are given their proper value by her interpretation. I am perfectly convinced that the precision of her pitch, and some of the clarity, are due to work with the harp, *not* with the tempered piano, but with an instrument set true in its scale.

Mrs. Kennedy-Fraser has, as last year, "no voice"; but her singing gives me one of the few, one of the very few occasions in the season of concert-going when I am veritably moved. I sit day after day as a critic. I make my analysis with very little interference; but "Island Herdmaid" or "Sea-gull of Land under Wave" were sung with too great validity to leave one any margin for talk about epiglottis and thorax.

The Shieling Song has run in my head for seven years. I wrote last season that the "Aillte" carried me to the halls and harping of bardic times, and since then Mr. Pound assures me that he has fitted several passages of the Anglo-Saxon "Beowulf" to this music, and that he is certain the "Beowulf" was sung either to this tune, or to something "so near it that the difference isn't worth counting." This would date the music to the eighth or ninth century, and it may be centuries older.[43] One need but try to fit English words to it to see how unlikely it is that words would fit it by accident, and I am assured that it does not

---

[43] Compare: "The Kennedy-Frasers found some music in the outer Hebrides that fits the Beowulf, or at any rate that some of the Beowulf fits. It is the 'Aillte.' I heard it in concert, and racked my mind to think where it fitted. It wouldn't go to the Seafarer. Two lines fitted a bit of the Beowulf, then the next wouldn't fit. I skipped a line of the Beowulf, and went on. The Kennedy-Frasers had omitted a line of the music at that point because it didn't seem to them to have an inherent musical interest." (*ABC of Reading*, New York, 1960, pp. 54–55.) Pound also began making notes for a booklet to be entitled "The Music of Beowulf." A page of this is reprinted in *Ezra Pound Perspectives*, ed. Noel Stock, Chicago, 1965, p. 187. But even on the first page he veered off to discuss "snivelling war profiteers, object lackeys etc.," and other matters equally remote from the admittedly hazy subject of the title. The essay appears not to have been completed. At any rate it was never published. The "Aillte" song may be found in Marjory Kennedy-Fraser's *Songs of the Hebrides*, London, 1917, Vol. II, pp. 80–83.

"simply fit any poem in the Saxon alliterative measure."

At any rate, we have in these Hebridean songs a music which has escaped the mediæval ecclesiastical enervation; other modern music in western Europe has had to work its way slowly and in attenuation from the dominance of "harmless" and innocuous modes. And even now the academies which resurrect south-European mediæval melodies furnish them with proper four-square under-pinnings à la the most approved Johann-Sebastian.

These Hebridean songs, like such Russian songs as Rosing gave us, have subject-matter. They are not cooked up for a concert hall. Every song is about something. Thus there is a difference between one and the next.

The "Sea Gull" and the "Sea-Tangle" are, perhaps, the height of the "art," but there is no choosing—"Kishmul's Galley" is a great song. And for the simpler numbers, "modern" conditions prevent our getting the full effect, for we should go on listening to the repetition of the melody for half an hour or more, not merely to "three verses." Indeed, as a "performance," as an "entertainment," there is more to be done with this music than the Kennedy-Frasers have yet attempted. Ideally speaking, one should not see the hat of the lady in front of one. I loathe "æsthetic" and monkey lighting in concert halls, but for this work I do want a dark auditorium, and I want no explanatory interruption of the singing (even though some of the songs are, perhaps, more effective when one knows the "story"). I want a continuous harping from beginning to end of the show, brief explanations could be given with harp accompaniment as in cante-fable. I want one superb male voice, at least, in the company, *and* I want some of the narrative tunes, and some of the labour tunes repeated often enough to weave their proper spell over the emotion of the whole audience, not merely to excite the few who are specially ready to admire them or to note intellectually the interest of the melody. All of which may be asking a great deal, but what is the critic here for if not to demand the greatest possible pleasure?

(Even with the Rosing all-Russian programme, if one comes to consider it as an entertainment or performance, rather than a revelation, I should have changed the order of the groups of songs, and put the last group in place of the third or fouth.) For the auditor seriously concerned with music this question of "performance" is a trifle, but for meeting the practical question of giving the best possible music under to-day's concert-hall conditions these details are worth considering. It is the artist's and critic's place to see that the best can compete advantageously with the vulgarest.

Madame Alvarez is, this season, accompanied by Mr. Fredk. B. Kiddle.

Unable to attend Thursfield recital, as it conflicted with second Hebridean recital.

Stroesco, Saturday, December 7, 3.15, Æolian Hall. ROSING, December 14, 3 p.m., Æolian.

MISCELLANEOUS[44]

DOROTHY GRIFFITHS (Æolian), ease, grace, clarity in Scarlatti's Sonata in D. Mr. Liddle was in better form as accompanist than was Mr. Plunkett Greene. Arne repeated too many phrases in setting "Come Away Death." There were remains of fire and savagery in the singing of "Mally O," Bullock's setting of "Brittany," exploited naïveté; Chas. Wood's setting of "Ethiopia Saluting the Colours" well sung; a curiosity —music, I suppose, as good as the chosen passage of Whitman, not wholly satisfactory, full complement of various crudities. "Bells of Clermont Town," Mr. Belloc's little joke, was set without distinction, and was sung so fast that the voice had no resonance. Herrick's "Corinna" was hashed both by singer and composer. All but the last four lines were utterly unintelligible. Even if Mr. Greene is a monument to the best taste of the eighties he might take a few lessons in enunciation from M. Yves Tinayre. This jabble, jabble, jabble was a very poor substitute for Herrick's lyrical outburst.

York Bowen, Romance in G flat, usual "école" of "Narcissus," ripple, etc., played with suavity by Miss Griffiths. Hinton's "Fireflies" was labelled "first performance" (trat auf und wieder ab). I seem to remember fireflies, butterflies or some other winged denizen of the æther by this compositor, but it doesn't much matter one way or the other. Miss Griffiths was still varying her G theme variations when I dismissed myself from the hall.

AMY HARE, Chamber Concert, Wigmore, November 18. The slightly anarchic and immoderato "Allegro" of the Arensky Quintet, Op. 51, was given with a good deal of volume and spirit. Arensky is the most German, perhaps we should say the most Viennese, of the Russian composers. His exact meaning in this first movement was not very discoverable. In the second movement, so far as I could make out, Madame Hare created no particular interest in her touch or in the timbre of the piano. Madame Suggia's 'cello was resonant in the bass and firm where it sounded above the other instruments. This Quintet is the kind of music that gives a general bemazement, rather than conveying any

[44] *The New Age*, December 12, 1918, pp. 91–92.

definite impression of meaning or developing any emotion to a super-usual intensity.

As for the third movement "Scherzo," we have heard it, have we not, or we have heard something so very like it, in the First Class salon of a Norddeutscher Lloyd boat approaching Hamburg. It is not quite the Tzigannes. It calls up associations of marine interior decoration. In the Finale the piano emitted various heavy and well-timed booms; one felt that it was the motive force, the donkey-engine inside the merry-go-round.

KATHLEEN PARLOW followed with the Vitali "Chaconne" delicately accompanied by Charlton Keith, whom I should like to encounter more frequently in my inspections. The violin began a shade shrill, or, at least, so it sounded if one were near the platform. There showed at once distinct ability hampered by distressful acridity. It was as if the indisputable concept of beauty were interrupted by fits of annoyance, a sort of personal annoyance on the part of the performer. Miss Parlow is one of the very, very few English (?) violinists who puts any passion into violin-playing.[45] The performance of the "Chaconne" gradually improved, and, as a whole, it was, as she played it, worth hearing, quite distinctly worth hearing.

ÆOLIAN HALL (November 19). The London Trio was, as I entered, performing the late Sir Hubert Parry's "Trio in B minor" with clarity and distinctness. The late composer wrote to Madame Goodwin that she, assisted by Albert Sammons and W. E. Whitehouse, performed the trio most brilliantly. "Full of go and warmth, and everything that is gratifying to me," were his words. I have no doubt that the three performers are still up to that level, and that they were getting out of the music quite all that the late composer put into it. Still, there seems to be no particular æsthetic reason why one should play that "B minor trio" in preference to anything else. I was soon horrified to discover that I had entered in time for the second movement, and that I had been listening to the "Andante," not to the final Maestoso. The third, "Allegro Molto," or jabber movement, drove me into the outer courts of the building, from whence I returned to hear

MISS NIN NEVINE. There was a certain richness in her voice, somewhat opaque but pleasant. The English Church mode has been *almost* eliminated; there seemed to be possibilities; at least, she was by no means hopeless; though the singing was *trop mesuré*, there was not enough binding force in her rhythm. Rousseau wrote in 1687 (in "Maître de Musique et de Viole"):—

[45] Kathleen Parlow was a Canadian violinist.

"At this word, 'movement,' there are people who imagine that to give the movement is to follow and keep time; but there is much difference between the one and the other, for one may keep time without entering into the movement."

It takes centuries for these simple ideas to get into the heads and executive faculties of performing musicians. "Vien, Approche-toi" was not shaped up to the finish. Adolph Mann accompanied adequately. "Se tu m'ami" was given too gently, too twinkingly; possibly this was due to nerves or lack of experience.

KATHARINE ARKANDY (Wigmore, November 20), has a voice of great charm and a sense of singing the *meaning* of the words, and a clear enunciation. I am not so sure of her pitch-sense, but do not think her singing would bore one. In the last lines of "Voi, che sapete" she was not so intent on the meaning. Neither do I think she quite caught the manner for the fall of voice in the *tu* and the *ami* of "Se tu m'ami." An old composer complained that music was not written as it was intended to be played.[46] The singer had not in this song much concept, the end was school-girlish, *but* the under-voice, or what we might call the second layer of the voice, or second colour, or speech-quality, was good. She is not yet ready for such aria as "Ah, fors' e lui"; technique is lacking. If she wants to do this sort of thing she should study Madame Alvarez. There were moments of distinct pleasure, some lines good and some bad; she has a future if she works, but the *if* is very emphatic.

EMILE DOEHARD'S 'cello was clear, reedy, expressive; he had the intention of showing the meaning of the composer's (Rachmaninow's) phrases, and succeeded in doing so. I regretted having to leave in mid-performance. I have often enjoyed M. Doehard's playing in quartettes and ensembles.

CLAUD BIGGS (Steinway Hall, November 20), was clean, distinct in his Bach, and formed it from within. He was intent on difference in the qualities of individual notes in the counterpoint. One felt the old music would have been really effective if Mr. Biggs had been employing his talent on the harpsichord, for which this music is more fitted. With an harpsichord one might have felt ready for a full hour of Bach.

The performer gave the Schubert-Liszt "Wayside Inn" personally and effectively. He does not play like a fool, but rather as a man who might compose music himself. Of the early Scriabine it is, I think, the 15th prelude, which is most exquisite with its careful manipulation of overtone effects. The De Séverac was daintily done, but the following Chopin seemed to have contracted the mood of the music preceding it, and sounded insufficient in weight. I want, however, to give full em-

---

[46] François Couperin, viz., "We write differently from what we play"—a statement Pound picked up from Arnold Dolmetsch and repeated frequently.

phasis to my feeling that Mr. Biggs, if meticulous to a degree that might make it seem that he was merely meticulous, does satisfy one with the sense that he is making something when he plays and that the music is shaped out with a design from inside itself. One feels, Here is a pianist with whom one might discuss the matter, a pianist with interesting ideas about music, and a potential composer, a craftsman with care for his craft, the furthest possible remove from the poseur and "impresser."

MUSIC[47]
"Les pianos, les pianos, dans les quartiers aisés!"

LILIA KANEVSKAYA (Æolian Hall, November 26) displayed animation, conservatism and a certain liking for Brahms; she was soothing and restful on a day like this day of idleness; the playing was meditative, not theatrical. It was, I think, her rhythm-sense that kept it from being a bore. There was a good beginning to the Romance in F. She had not the weight or gross tonnage to deal competently with the Rhapsody. She made a good deal of noise in Palmgren's "The Sea," was graceful in "Rococo," but the "Bird Song" is rubbish, and she had better go back to Dacquin if she wants to do "this sort of thing" pleasantly.

She inclines to the pale-pink school in the "interpretation" of Debussy. It is, of course, admirable that she should wish to play good music, but she should practise the French virtue of recognising one's limitations and keep off "Jardins sous la pluie" until her insight is deeper.

The Chopin Etude (A flat) was very pretty, delicate, and unsatisfactory, though she showed temperament and even an adumbration of the significance. My chief puzzle was to discover why, with obviously no more distinction in the playing, I was not more annoyed. Madame Kanevskaya appears to be fairly young; she labels her performance "First Recital"; she is perfectly within her rights to appear; I do not mean to imply by the harshness of my foregoing sentences that she should go back to the school-room. She is even, according to many standards, "quite good."

There are people whose life is not complete until they have played the piano-part of a piano concerto (preferably the Concerto by Grieg) with orchestra in the Queen's or the Albert Hall. This is, perhaps, one of the conditions of modern life, or modern musical life in London. After all, London is the largest city in the world, and the Queen's Hall, while not so large as the Albert, is one of the largest concert halls in

[47] *The New Age*, December 19, 1918, pp. 107–8.

this city. The Germans have destroyed many things, but they neglected the piano concerto.

Miss CHILTON-GRIFFIN (Queen's Hall, Nov. 28) began the Grieg dashingly, with perhaps a touch of the theatrical manner. Landon Ronald conducted neatly. Miss C.-Griffin's playing is suited to a large auditorium; one had not the feeling that the subtlest part was being lost. One felt her floating somewhat lightly upon the top of the music (rather than working to create it); there were no special ice-tinkle or Norse-frigid effects as when De Greef presented the same composition a few weeks ago. The cadenza? "Oh, Love, what shall be said of thee"!! "Pum, pum, ti pum pum."

I doubt if this music has any very intense emotion concealed in it; at any rate, none emerged.

The one point in the pianist's favour was that her playing fitted the size of the hall; this point is worth noting. It is, if you like, Aristotelian, but the musician should gauge his sound volume and sound-reach to the size of hall he is playing in.

We reserve, on the contrary, our opinion that the kettle-drum is more suited to co-operation with orchestra than the pianoforte; the kettle-drum blends and forms part of a demonstrable æsthetic unity. (The drummer in Mr. Ronald's orchestra on Nov. 28 happened to be a very bad drummer, but this does not affect the general and main proposition.) "Pally-wally-wally wink chin," continued the piano.

The Bizet-Ronald suite for orchestra by itself was lifelessly opened by Mr. Ronald, but livened up when the harp (quite good) and flute took hold of it in duet. (We shall perhaps get ourselves further disliked if we begin trying to sort out the good and bad players in the established "organisations," but what, after all, are we here for?)

Of the piano solos, the first prelude by Corder was given with the same airiness and wide spacing which had been employed in the Grieg; "walking on the waves" very aptly describes it; the second prelude was rather cinema. In the Liszt, Miss Griffin was solider; there was a certain amount of interest in one or two timbre effects, or in the orchestration of the instrument, giving the impression of several instruments of different quality. Here there is an element of promise, but not in the high runs, or indeed in any of her treble. The fortissimos were mostly obliteration.

ADA FORREST (Wigmore, Nov. 28). Phlegm in throat, voice strained through veil or caul, Victorian manner intolerably, indistinct wording, squawk. Constant sound of "cla cla cla," or possibly "gla gla gla," in place of "Since I live not where I love." As Morley and Lawes scarcely preserved a trace of their beauties in the path of her assault, I fled before she began singing modern settings of Tennyson. I should have fled in any case.

Miss MONIQUE POOLE (Æolian, same afternoon) must be likewise rejected. Concerts for charity should not demand so much. The violinist had one virtue, and that unavailing: she was obviously anxious to do her best for the audience.

Miss Helen Wilson approached with a beaming smile; she presented Dvorak's prose declamations in an Anglo-operatic wholly depressing manner. As the words have no interest either in content or rhythm, the composer had not been able to do much with them nor did the singer. The declaration: "I will sing songs of gladness" did not carry conviction. The next attempt was Grechaninow's "Dreary Steppe." I conducted myself to the portal.

My third experience on this drizzling Friday was somewhat more successful. Miss MARGUERITE MEREDYLL (Steinway Hall) showed interest in the general subject of music by ensconcing her piano behind M. Doehard's 'cello and Marjorie Hayward's violin.

Beethoven's Trio (Op. 70, No. 2) is as gracious as anything he has written; there is enough going on to keep the attention of the auditor; Beethoven retains here a rather Mozartian charm. The structure is open to criticism; the different movements begin well, but do not perhaps develop very convincingly; there is, however, a pleasing current.

Miss Meredyll's only point is the tympanum quality of her lower bass notes; she seems to draw blanks or strike with ligneous fingers in the upper bass; there is by no means enough variety in her treble timbre. Chopin étude trivial in the extreme. There is no condemnation strong enough for people who act as if Chopin were solely for young ladies in seminaries. The Polonaise had just enough in it to remind one of what it can be. Miss Meredyll had ample chance for her one ability, the bass boom; but one becomes distinctly angry in remembering the performance.

Notwithstanding this, the concert was not wholly displeasing. Miss Hayward is a good violinist; one wishes she would play something more interesting than Glazounow's "Meditation" or the catch-penny cheapness of the Tschaikowsky "Scherzo." The first movement of the Brahms' trio Op. 8 is excellently written; one had pleasure in hearing it, due to Miss Hayward and M. Doehard. The piano played nicely during the opening bars.

"Les pianos, les pianos, des casinos!"

MOUSSORGSKY[48]
Rosing, Stroesco, Haley

Guilhermina Suggia, with New Queen's Hall Orchestra, Nov. 30, chaotic.

Gwen Mathers, Aeolian, Dec. 3, was excellent in her intention to be expressive, but should not confuse intention with result. Naive, vegetarian *joie de vivre* is not enough. The singing was buttered rather than sculptured; physical equipment satisfactory, and Miss Mathers might do something if she were sufficiently worried, persistently worried, and worried for a long enough time. The bass-voiced bulbul, the words of the late A. Tennyson, and other objectionable features, including the cute, were obtruded.

ROSING gave a full Moussorgsky programme at the Aeolian on Dec. 3, insufficiently announced. There is very little need of the critic in a case of this sort. The opinion of a Russian diplomat that "Moussorgsky might have developed into a Russian Wagner if he had lived" is the most succinct explanation of the fall of the old Russian regime that I have, up to date, encountered. An aristocracy holding such views was certainly too far from reality to weather any social disturbance.

One really wants some strong form of commendation for a man who will give twenty Moussorgsky songs (numbers and encores) in one programme, following his solid all Russian programme of the previous month. This is heavy work, seeing that it contained the Hopak, and three of the Death Cycle songs: Trepak, Serenade, and Field Marshal. The rich semi-low tones showed in the Yeremoushka; Savichna was, I think, better done than even Rosing had done it before. The matt-colour, the mode verging on speech, and the soft notes were never better than in "The Soul." The "Sorotchinsky Foire" is of the most exquisite both in melody and in the economy of notes used. Rosing may have been a shade tired in the "Hopak." If there were any adverse criticism to be made of his manner during the whole programme it would be that he did not seem to be quite at his maximum of physical energy, but there were no errors of feeling, and only one slip in judgment: an epigram like "The Goat" should not be used as its own encore. Encore the audience would have, and rightly, at this point, but it should have been a different song. A "point" loses with repetition. "Is it honourable for a Boyar" was a new piece of irony, broad noted. Specially to be commended was the mastery of the longer and less apparent rhythm-lengths in "Serenade" and all through the programme one observed

[48] *The New Age,* January 2, 1919, pp. 142–43.

how Rosing takes with faultless instinct the central significance of each song and how the right details are magnetised to it (even when he forgets or neglects certain paginal indications). In short: a fine artist, singing great music, a concert unique in the season, and wholly commendable.

STROESCO (Aeolian Hall, Dec. 7) gave a recital charming save for certain selections, and justifying the interest we have taken in him. There were, however, tactical errors, concerning which we may set down certain "laws" of the concert programme for the salvation of any and all singers, irrespective of their natural talent or demerit.

1. In a recital consisting of four groups of songs, the third group must be the climax; it must contain the most important pieces. Stroesco's third group was the weakest in his programme. *If* he had put his fourth group third, used his "Manon" encore for a fourth, and sung perhaps most of his third group in encore he would not have seen so many people leaving the hall. Observe that Rosing used his three songs from the Death Cycle as his third group, and followed them by the satires.

The fourth position is often used for popular numbers by singers not sure of their audience. Note that Rosing avoids this, without making his fourth group an anticlimax. One time he will give folk song or Siberian convict songs; on Dec. 3 he gave the satires; Stroesco's fourth group, folk songs, beginning with the best thing in his programme, Ravel's setting of the Greek song "Wake, my dear," would have been an admirable fourth group *if* he had sung a third group of sufficient magnitude.

Obviously there is no use in a singer's announcing a masterpiece for his third act, *if* he cannot keep his audience in the hall during the first groups; or if he is unable to sing the "big" song. Art consists here in his recognising his own scope, and *grading* his concert from some simple and quiet opening up to his greatest achievable work.

2. A concert should not consist of songs "all the same size and shape," or even all in quite the same mood. Also a series of songs all sung softly at the beginning and ending in a fortissimo squall, becomes monotonous.

A concert should not, on the other hand, be all shreds and patches. There was more variety in Rosing's concert of one composer than in Stroesco's containing songs by twelve.

3. There are divers roads to variety. The surest is that of realising the meaning of each song. Most songs worth singing have something which distinguishes them from other songs. Careful study reveals this. Rosing omits details, forgets or mispronounces his words, and nobody minds, *because* he has in every case a vivid concept of the main emotion or main situation of the song.

4. On the other hand a close study of the words will save errors. If Stroesco had been more possessed by the speech quality of

Il sole imbionda si la viva lana

he would not have accented it wrongly. (Note that the mistake was not Da Parma's who has followed D'Annunzio's speech cadence at this point with exactitude.) This same set of cautions concerning detail would apply with great force in a more detailed critique of the Mathers' recital.

A poem to be worth setting to music must either be of some interest, or it must permit a beautiful sequence of notes. If singers, in singing the first kind of song, would first study the poet, they would get over more than half the difficulties of singing well-set songs. (Ill-set songs they should, we believe, eschew.) The voice is more favoured than the oboe *because* it can articulate words. One should not surrender this asset too lightly. If one is not intent not only on the word-sounds but on their meaning one should sing beautiful arias on open vowels, where the mood and meaning is fairly simple. Modern French song-setting is supposed to have specialised in the literary values. It probably demands closer attention to the meaning of the poems than does Bel Canto.

If a singer has decided that a song means something in particular, even if his concept is wholly "wrong," he will probably make something of it.

5. Granting that the singer has got at the essential meaning of each song, he should not make a programme of songs "all the same size and shape," all sung in the same way, *or* all in the same mood, or with the same meaning, or with meanings too similar, even though their shapes and sizes be different.

6. The singer should never sound as if he was making *all* the noise possible. He must always sound as if he could if necessary sing louder. Mullings yells in opera and spoils one's pleasure. Stroesco's piano and pianissimo notes easily reach the last seats of the Aeolian; he should grade his volume of sound up to a *forte* which *appears* easily taken. I have marked four places when he exceeded this to the detriment of his effect. One must "leave some water in the bottom of the bucket." One wants to feel that the singer can go on singing next morning, not that he is splitting his weasand.

If *Mrs. Edward Haley* really loved the young lady who is, we presume, her daughter, she would not play her accompaniments publicly. Miss OLGA HALEY has a fine voice, as we have noticed before; she sings the ends of her words more distinctly than she did last season; she should pay a little more attention to the pronunciation of her French and Italian, and she might concentrate more attention on the *meaning* of the words she sings, but how any one could keep their mind on the meaning of anything with Mrs. Haley at the piano passes my imagination. Neither can I conceive how "Seguidille" could have been worse sung, or more abominably played. Miss Haley should avoid for a while songs demanding temperament, and those with complicated rhythms. The Rummel experiment was interesting but unconvincing, the accompaniment very cunningly made, but the words and voice-part open (wide open) to question.

Notice of Rosing's recital (Dec. 14) held over. But I cannot close without a special word of praise for Di Veroli's remarkable work in the Moussorgsky recital.

Raymonde Collignon whom we have praised here at various times is now at the Coliseum, and we hope that the grace and precision of her art will not be lost in that great and horrible auditorium. She deserves every success and has all the good wishes at our disposal.

MR. ROSING EXPERIMENTS[49]

Mr. Rosing's programme on December 14 (Æolian) was like an illustrated lecture on music with the lecture left out. The public is badly in need of these implied disquisitions, but does not appear very apt in learning from the physical demonstration; one feels that the prompter should have stepped forward now and again and enforced the points of the argument.

The "Invocation" by Cyril Scott was a blank cheque ably filled in by Rosing and Di Veroli; the composer had done very little to interfere with either singer or player. Handel's "Recit from the Messiah" was a bore in the manner long since shelved and parodied in the Oratorio "Blessed is the man that sitteth . . . etc. . . . blessed is the man that sitteth . . . etc. . . . on a red hot stove (bis. ter. et quatuor) for he shall RISE again." This solemn manner is just a musical bluff. Sterne's definition of gravity, lately quoted by one of my colleagues, fits the matter. Gravity is a mysterious carriage of the body to conceal the defects of the mind. Samuel Butler tried to vamp up some interest in Handel's harmonies, but it would require a greater genius than Butler to put interest into Handel's melodic faculty.

The old French Chanson de Noël instantly demonstrated the difference between the real and the pretentious. Here the perfect melodic sense charmed one without cavil. Tschaikovsky is at his absolute best

[49] *The New Age,* January 9, 1919, pp. 159–60.

in "Garden of Christ." The graceful infantility of Mozart's "Berceuse" does not need a Rosing to present it; of course it was quite well done, but he might leave it to one of his young lady pupils. There is a fine opening to Napravnik's "Aria from Dubrovsky." The Brahms Sapphics were not sung so well as usual, though the meaning was perhaps better accented. Di Veroli was exquisite in the Duparc, but the singer's jumps into pianissimo were rather too great; one feels also that there are a number of people who can sing this modern French stuff and who cannot or will not sing anything else. There is no need for Rosing to cover all the topics listed in the musical encyclopædia.

The danger of a concert made, as this one was, from test samples of different composers grouped according to general subject matter is, first, that it may not be built into the necessary musical unity, with beginning, climax and end; secondly, that the singer cannot get out of the manner of one song into the proper manner for the next. The constant shifting from one kind of music to another confused Rosing, as well as the audience. (I do not mean that the audience analysed the trouble. The hall was crowded, and even the platform filled, as a result of the enthusiasm over the complete Moussorgsky recital; but, on the fourteenth, the enthusiasm was considerably less spontaneous, *not* because Rosing was not singing as well, but simply because of the non-musical structure of the programme.) Thus the Duparc stained the opening of the "I Love you, Olga"; *but* having got into the Tschaikovsky mode, Rosing sang the encore Tschaikovsky much better than the Olga. The accompaniment to Olga was inadequate. They tell me it *can* be presented on the piano, but I am rather in doubt about this.

The Brahms "Rossignol" is not bad in French, and was excellently sung up to the first "tais-toi" which was a bit too sobby. The Moussorgsky "Star" was a different matter altogether. "J'ai pardonné" was sob-stuff, a desperate and slightly comic attempt to do "Ich Grolle Nicht" in French. This bathos highly delighted the audience.

It was a thorough demonstration, if any may still be considered needful, that the audience will stand the best but is wholly incapable of selecting it. The whole programme was interesting to the critic as showing what will and what will not do; but there is need of a very strong arm of protest to prevent artists from following the indications of public applause. I want to insist upon this. The large audience was due to the uncompromising Moussorgsky recital, where the enthusiasm was genuine. Here the enthusiasm was really less; there were fewer people who went away resolved not to miss the next concert. Rosing has his audience where it will take whatever he chooses to give it, but he has still need to solidify this grip. The public is wholly fickle, only those who really care for the best music can form the solid basis of support.

The part of the audience which only comes in order to appear cultured is quite as much afraid of applauding the wrong thing as of showing lack of appreciation for the better.

Rosing did all that is possible with Wagner's "Rêves," but one rather wishes he wouldn't. "O give me this night" was beautifully done. Schubert's "The Dwarf" is the best kind of Rathskeller Romanticismo. Given this kind of thing it could not be better written, or have been better sung; but it needs psychoanalysis or a "Daily Mail" article on the Hun. The dwarf is an example of sadism and sexual perversion; the queen is the ideal and Teutonic female full of submission. Art which cannot get its effects out of more normal conditions is not art in its halest condition; it is art running on cocaine and heroin. Some of the patho-drama of this song carried over into the opening of the "Dame de Pique" aria.

"J'ai pardonné" had given us the first dose of German slop and hysteria. French translator had been avenging, we presume, the war of 1870. I am all for peace with punishment, but this sort of thing is no more needed, thanks to le Mareschal Foch. Chant de Concours not particularly welcome. Virtus Antiqua is in the tone of Macaulay. The Bizet Carmen is well made, French cleverness and good facture, possibly due to influence of Mérimée's commonsense prose.

The Moussorgsky "Flea" was a relief in final encore. But the programme had seemed a little long. I am convinced that this was due to the snipping and the inclusion of too many diverse modes of music. Things should be given in slabs, enough things of one sort to establish their own mood or mental tonality. It is most interesting to have Rosing making these experiments or disquisitions—for once; but they are not to be adopted as a permanent sort of programme. He announces a series of six recitals, January 18 to April 5: Human Suffering, Soul of Russia, God and Nature, Moussorgsky, Love, Historic and Fantastic Legend. (There will be no better thirty shillings worth of music on the market during that season. Profiteers may hear the same for three guineas, from seats slightly nearer the stage.) Two of these programmes are examples of perfect programme-construction, perfect from the point of view of combining a set of different pieces of music into an æsthetic unity. Three are untried.

The error, if one is to call it such, of the programme grouped about a topic is that it substitutes a metaphysical or intellectual unity for a strictly musical unity. But this sort of shake-up is very interesting *as an experiment*. One does not ask the singer to fall into stereotype or to stick only to the songs one critic happens to prefer. Personally, I could be content if he confined himself almost wholly to old French and Russian, though I hope he will find space for the Hebrides when he comes to a presentation of "legend."

ROSOWSKY, ROSING, DI VEROLI[50]

Two concerts (Æolian), Saturdays, January 11 and January 18, bring Tschaikovsky's limitations into the field of one's consciousness. A certain cheapness is imminent in this composer. He is not cheap all the time, or even, perhaps, most of the time, but he keeps one in a state of anxiety. The Gretchianinoff opening duet (January 11) was given with the exquisite blending of two good voices; it is very Russian, for the plus and minus of that national quality, and is on the border of being tiresome, just on the border. Di Veroli was in excellent form; but there is some "fat" in the Onegin accompaniment, some "western Europe," or perhaps some Mittel-Europa. There was a certain blankness in "Tatiana's Letter," "as if the bottom had dropped out of the cup," though it was rendered unaffectedly and with technical excellence by Rosowsky. She is "quite good," enunciates clearly, and is not remarkably interesting.

The Fountain Scene from "Boris" is Moussorgsky's tremolo stop; rumour says the scene was written in after the opera was completed, because the opera house management insisted on an emotional duet between some pair or other of lovers. Even so, one was instantly very much aware that the singers had shifted from Tschaikovsky. There was splendid largensss and capacity in Rosing's low notes in the opening passage.

The "Marina" was thin. True, the character is shallow, but one doubted if the interpretess would have managed any greater profundity. Rosing seemed at the top of his form until the end of the passage beginning "Hush, Marina," where he came through the tone; the duet ended rather chaotically; possibly the orchestra is needed to fill out the conclusion.

Dorgominsky's "Vineyard," and the Rachmaninoff were acceptable; in the first Korsakoff one granted voice, and was tempted to add "præterea nihil," but there was more than that in the Korsakoff encore. Rosing was not at his best in the "Sorotchinsky Foire," but came to in the "Flea" and stole the concert with that and his Korsakoff encore. Despite its obvious merits *as done,* I can add nothing to my opening sentences in regard to the Queen of Spades and Tschaikovsky in general.

[50] *The New Age,* February 6, 1919, pp. 227–28.

Rosing

Rosing's own concert is the first of his implied lecture series. I have already demurred from the non-musical structure of these programmes, however interesting they may be in a given case. The opening Tcherepnin gave fine effects in a veiled and smoky colouring, due, I think, as much to interpretation as to the composition. Despite the persistent mispronunciation (to the point of altering the meaning of the French) I wish Rosing would do more music of Tiersot's period; even though he was over-dramatic for the simplicity of the mode at one point of the "Plainte."

Bach's "Dearest Jesu" belies its words in all but the last three chords. The fine triumphant processional might just as well accompany some remarks about the victorious entry of Cæsar's troops into Bithynia as any wails about bringing anyone *"to despair."* The Chopin "Chant Funèbre de la Pologne" is puzzling in its opening, the Polish quality perhaps verging, or being interpreted to verge, on the Russian; from the words beginning "Varsovie. . . ." it was excellent Chopin, and excellent Rosing; but needed, perhaps, restraint later on, where there was too apparent an attempt to make it expressive. One wants to hear it again, and repeatedly.

Rosing was in his element in the folk song, the frozen convict song, and the Nevstruoff with a sort of double tone in his high notes. The Sahnovsky "Clock" was Di Veroli's piece accompanied by Rosing's voice. There seemed to be a slight obstruction of the singer's rhythm, but the piano part is a tour-de-force with overtones, and Di Veroli worked with the precision of an optical instrument. Tschaikovsky Aria: vide supra, general topic of Tschaikovsky.

I have no intention of making any apologiæ whatsoever for French versions of Hun; neither the Schubert nor the Brahms Translations were satisfactory. Rosing's throat began to trouble him in the Moussorgsky Death Cycle songs; but there were fine effects in "Field Marshal."

The Gretchianinoff and Dorgominsky satires were not quite important enough to fill their niche in the programme. Borodin's 'Spes" is another matter; and in it the musical value predominates over the mimicry. Rosing's voice was tiring when he came to the encores. My only new point in regard to these programmes centralised by a general literary theme, applies equally to all programmes. A concert lasts an hour and a half; it is not an organic composition like the act or the whole of an opera or a symphony. The element of main form must be supplied. I have already written about various means for variety. Beyond them, one should introduce a certain number of songs with more or less symmetrical wave lengths; something with a discernible and regular metric. Rosing, on the 18th, erred rather in giving too many songs with irregular or unobvious rhythms. The element of "regular" rhythm is often (probably without consciousness or design) supplied by the "classic" numbers familiar at the beginning of concerts.

In response to correspondents: Moussorgsky's music is, or was, obtainable from J. W. Chester, 11, Great Marlborough Street, W.1. Beyond that I can supply no special information.

While I should deplore any ambition which might deprive us of the pleasure of Sig. Di Veroli's accompaniments, and difficult as it is to judge from a man's accompaniments how he will play as a soloist, I think there is now sufficient interest in Di Veroli's piano playing to warrant his giving a concert on his own ... in which he should abjure the compositions of his personal friends and contemporaries.

Mr. Frederic Lamond's managers request us to state that Mr. Lamond was born in Glasgow, and that at no time during his internment at Ruhleben did he contemplate changing his nationality; Scotch he was and British he remains, and a master of his instrument, notice to follow. FULL BEETHOVEN RECITAL, Wigmore Hall, February 8, at 5.50, not to be missed.

Raymonde Collignon, Steinway Hall, February 8, at 3.

Rosing, series, Saturdays, February 8, Russian Programme, 22, etc. Æolian, at 3.

THE ALLIED STRING QUARTET (Désiré Defauw, R. C. Kay, L. Tertis, Emile Doehard), Wigmore, January 20, began the Mozart Quartet in F Major, in exquisite accord, kept the main form and governed the relative volumes of sound most commendably, with the general tone of old instruments suitable for this composer. Excellent in Moderato and Allegretto they became just a slight degree vague in the final Allegro. The Debussy Quartet was done well, but, on the whole, perhaps not quite so convincingly as the Mozart, though both quartettes were worth hearing, as also the Brahms, Intermezzo.

D'ALVAREZ (Æolian, January 21). Madame D'Alvarez preserves all the traditions of the Prima Donna; she should have flowered in the spacious 1830's. Auditors who dislike waiting should arrive 15 minutes late. The cantatrice began the XVIIIth century monologue with the bravura of 1850, but the loveliness of her voice is undeniable. Scream she will, but the softer notes are delightful; the "Déploration" was almost unalloyed pleasure, displaying the fineness and full richness of the voice. Even the accompaniment was not bad, though Mr. Kiddle began the next song à la Brighton Pier. D'Alvarez sang it delicately, and there were excellent and exquisite effects in the Cesti.

F. D'Erlanger's "L'Abbesse" is dull modern Frenchness, ideas of poem based on clichés of forgotten ethical struggles—well sung. Still, one cannot be expected to sit through the poems of E. W. Wilcox whoever set them or sing them. Besides the Wilcox, one was threatened with Saint-Saëns and "Isobel."

M. Yves Tinayre, vocal recital at the Wigmore, Wednesday, January 29, notice to follow.

LAMOND, TINAYRE, COLLIGNON[51]

Lamond is the real thing, the old style *maestro* in full charge of his instrument. January 25 (Wigmore), he gave the Franck Prelude, Chorale and Fugue with clear-cut detail, depth, solidarity of construction and met with deserved enthusiasm. As he continued one forgot preconceived ideas of Franck, "critical positions," etc. The delicate trestle work was suspended from solid piers, and one sank into that comfort which envelops one on finding that a man knows his business. Lamond has tone-proportion; and the unified sounds of his heavy bass are a composite tone not a chaos. The Beethoven Andante Favori opened with lofty delicacy: criticism obviously was to concern itself not with strictures but with direction of praise.

His quality was most apparent in the thunders of the Appassionata, this work of fine bass, and—in places—a just adequate treble. I think his main distinction is his clarity. I think also that he cares more for Beethoven than for Chopin, though the B flat minor Sonata was opened with sounds craftily blunted, and there was a fine mood-forming wildness in its progress; the velvety deeps of the third movement were magnificent, orderly, magical.

There was virtuousity ad lib. and policing of amateurs in the Liszt Tarantelle, given on regulation "popular finale to concert" system. If it was a concession Lamond had no need to make it. The Beethoven was the best done number, and was greeted with the most convincing applause I have yet heard in a London concert hall. Lamond had drawn an attentive and critical audience.

It is ten years since I last heard Busoni at the Wigmore, and during the war there has been so little major piano-playing in London that one's critical machinery is rather rusty; one is only certain that Lamond is the chief pianist now in England. [Notice of Beethoven recital held over.]

THE CHARM OF TINAYRE

Yves Tinayre (Wigmore, January 29) was at his delightful best. Perfect tone and clear enunciation with a rich quality in the lower notes began

[51] *The New Age*, February 27, 1919, p. 281.

in the opening notes of "Mercy Clamant." In nothing is M. Tinayre better than in the very old French and in the old English modes. I deeply regret having missed his recital of early music. Coming from the XIIth century in the first song to the "Légende des Pèlerins," the suggestion of wood-wind remained. "Duc du Maine" is lively, of the XVth century, not in the same class with the Coucy song, Tinayre improved it in encore. The two Noëls, which had been charmingly arranged by Leopold Ashton, who accompanied delightfully and with sympathy, were sung with placid beauty, deep feeling, and, above all, with consummate command of rhythm, by Tinayre, than whom no singer has more constant and perfect taste.

One cannot demand that he confine himself wholly to the antique, neither can one pretend to as deep a satisfaction with the modern French school, interesting as it may be in special cases. The Franck "Procession" was given in perfect manner, and with delicious vocal quality; it is as good as a musical version of a descriptive poem can well be. Malipiero had been thoughtful in setting "Chanson Morave," but Debussy's style was by far too personal a gift to be easily followable. In the next setting, Malipiero's weakness was more apparent. He has a perfectly ordinary 1880 sort of mind, is always in danger of clichés, as, for example, in the melody at the end of the first line of the poem. On top of this ordinariness he has spread a thin veil of post-Debussy. The Fauré was dainty, and also improved in encore. "Phidyle" is of Duparc's best, and was sung with crystal clearness, Ashton accompanying exquisitely; throughout the concert Tinayre's fortissimos were well controlled and the tone pure. Cras' setting was simple and unpretentious, satisfactory, unoriginal; the Defosse, charming; Bréville had contracted sentiment from J. Lorain's poem; but was accomplished in the setting of Benedict.

The weakness of these modern French musicians is that their music rises and falls in value exactly in proportion with the literary quality of the words; they cannot hide or improve a banality in the poets whom they use. You can always tell from words on the programme whether the music will be interesting; this is not a fatal defect, but it demands a double care for literature on the musician's part. The concert came back to the Coucy level with the final Debussy songs; here the intensity of the originator of a mode contrasted with the laxness of imitators, it is difficult to say just where the quality Debussy's setting of the words "déguisements fantasques" escapes his followers. If Tinayre will always sing as well as he did on the 29th, few people will be willing to miss his recitals.

Coming Concerts. February 19 and March 12. (Wigmore.)

ROSING triumphed (Æolian, February 8) in improved "Soul of

Russia" programme. His histrionic "realist" method is the antipodes of Tinayre's lyric method, but his histrionics are no mere affair of acting. Somewhere in a discussion of the Japanese classic stage I have read that the *voice* of the actor should express the character portrayed, and although it cannot really be the voice of an old woman yet, remaining the actor's own voice, it must give the quality of whatever part it represents, be that old or young.

Rosing does this, the mood of the song, and the character of the supposed singer are conveyed by changes in vocal quality not by stage acting. In this his method keeps well within the province of his art; it is not an evasion of music. Detailed critique of this recital held over. Further recitals: Love Songs, February 22; Moussorgsky programme, March 8.

RAYMONDE COLLIGNON sang in illustration of Edwin Evan's lecture at Steinway Hall (February 8). The delicate silvery voice has perhaps gained a little in volume, and only by such delicate vocal qualities as she possesses can the charm-in-simplicity of the old French Légendes be conveyed. She is a clavichord among singers. "Juif Errant" could be taken as example of song by verbal effect; we may make a division of the singing methods into four: acting, histrionic or impersonating (e.g., Rosing); lyric (e.g., Tinayre); verbal, method of *diseur* or *diseuse:* the story or subject-matter holding the attention and air and vocal purity used only to augment this interest; lastly, the vocalised; interest of the singer being mainly on the melodic line (? e.g., Stroesco, or possibly Alvarez), words subordinate to music; supposed character of the singer subordinate to the chances of purely vocal effects.

Naturally, any singer mixes these methods, but one may note a preference. In "Sainte Catherine," exquisitely accompanied, one's sympathies were perhaps with poor father. Mlle. Collignon's vocal tintinnabulation was at its best in the Pèlerins, the voice silvery in "Trois Canards"; a maximum verbal effect obtained in "Juif Errant," but in "La Pernette" one realised the youth of the performer and the chances lost. Mlle. Collignon gave the story in the words only; Yvette would have made a complete drama in her variation of each of the *Tra la la* refrains, they would not have been merely uniform interludes. The tone quality was charming in "Je m'en vais par le monde," but the singer had nothing like Tinayre's grip on the "Grand Duc du Maine"; none of his fire and entrain; though she scored in the pathos of her

"Je crois bien que j'en mourrai."

MUSIC[52]

The main new point I had to make in connection with ROSING's performance on February 8 was the impersonation by voice. Gestures, acting with the arms, legs, etc., are no concern of the music critic. They may be superfluities, additions, or camouflage, but this variation in the character of the supposed singer is part of the art of singing. One sings instead of playing a flute, oboe, recorder, or trombone, because the voice is capable of various modulations and variations, consonantal and vowel changes, etc., not possible on the most sensitive brass or woodwind.

The Gretchaninow "My Beloved Country" was clearly produced. It is very "Russian" in its draw and quick beat, and the accompaniment is of interest. The folk songs collected by Philipoff and harmonised by Korsakoff are excellent; the Kalinnikoff "Ancient Mound" was suave and finely shaped to its conclusion; Bleichmann good, Dorgominsky of less interest. Moussorgsky's "Steppe" mounts out of whatever company it is sung in; the "Orphan" is on the dangerous borders of uncontrol, and a song almost impossible to sing without spoiling. It was not spoiled. Rosing was at his best in Hopak and in the encore "Hoi my Dniepr," and gave the "Goat" better than any time previously. The Glinka "Joys of Journey" is a three ring circus tour de force, perpetuum mobile virtuosity; the singer retired apparently to ingurgitate a little realism before the final Drinking Song from "Igor."

I regret that I was prevented from attending: the Rosing performance, Feb. 22; the PHILHARMONIC STRING QUARTETTE's first performance of Stravinsky's Three Pieces for String Quartette, Feb. 13 (next performance March 27); ANNE THURSFIELD's song recital, Feb. 21; and TINAYRE's recital of new French songs, Feb. 19—all of which promised considerable interest.

LAMOND'S BEETHOVEN (Wigmore; Feb. 10). By way of preface and apology I would point out that the second row of the stalls, whence one views the instrument's underside at an upward angle of 60 degrees to treble and 30 degrees to bass is *not* the most advantageous position from which to judge a master pianist's larger structural treatment. Certain unifications and certain constructive qualities which I noted at Lamond's former recital were certainly present in his Beethoven, but less audible to me; still, ardent students who bring scores to the concert and turn pages of same (audibly) might, when finding themselves so under the scenes, turn their attention to other technical details of execution with quite as much profit as is to be had from ferreting in

---

[52] *The New Age,* March 6, 1919, pp. 295-96.

the "text." The piano is an instrument played with both hands and feet, and Lamond's pedalling in the opening Fantasie and later was worth the professional pupil's close attention.

(I write this, of course, out of malice, as I cannot read a score fast enough to follow the player and annoy my fellow-auditors simultaneously.)

To hear Beethoven played by Lamond is to hear Beethoven under test conditions. The programme contained (I do not say consisted of) three sonatas. He was playing the Appassionata as an encore when I was dragged off to an appointment. The C minor, Op. 111, has a fine later manner romantic movement opening. The construction is questionable, and there are trivial repetitions in the Allegro con brio. Lamond displayed brilliance and mastery in his graduation of the high trills.

The Sonata in E flat, Op. 31, No. 3, is early, and full of classic remains. It is a tenable opinion, and a perfectly proper opinion, that all that is good in Beethoven is classic remains. One is dealing with a great musician, one should not be too flippant in anathema. Lamond is a fine player, and Beethoven has an eminently fair chance against the most carping critic when Lamond presents him. Whatever was wrong was Beethoven and not Lamond. The Scherzo was given with rich 'cello tones. The Menuetto was exquisite, and the best part of the afternoon, until the encore Appassionata; but does the Menuetto movement in this sonata hold its own against the fine work of Beethoven's predecessors? Did the thickening and making heavier of music by Beethoven compensate for the loss of the earlier finesse and precision? The hearer must decide for himself. There is no papacy and no Mr. Leo Ward in this department.

The presto con fuoco is full of senseless repetitions, and Lamond was very clever in playing the Ruins of Athens variations immediately after the Sonata, as its opening rather supplies or suggests what the fourth movement of the sonata might have, or ought to have, been. This statement is probably an exaggeration, but in criticising the arts one must sometimes make an overstatement in order to express or suggest anything at all.

The Rondo, Op. 51, No. 2, has an exquisite opening, and is not over important.

Any real criticism of a player of Lamond's magnitude would have to consist in purely technical marks bar by bar. He showed maestria in performing the Waldstein, notably in the softs after fortissimos, crafty diminuendos, sweeps into the final conclusion. I don't know that one can say more. Here is the thing done as it should be. Beethoven is Lamond's composer; every man has a right to his own gods. Another careful auditor leaves the hall saying, "Beethoven makes Chopin seem rather inadequate"; which is to me like saying that St. Paul's makes Santa Maria Miracoli seem inadequate. I can think of things in Chopin that no other composer could have written so poignantly; I can think of no single quality of music in which some other composer is not more intense than Beethoven. These are matters of personal predilection.

FERNANDE KAUFFERATH, the Belgian 'Cellist (Wigmore, February 11), opened with firm, sure tone, not very large, but seeming to carry to the back of the hall; on moving forward one found that there was a whole range of subtle effects too faint to be perceptible to the whole audience. The piano was not always quick enough in effacing itself, but Mme. Kaufferath is the ideal 'cellist for a small hall or for those in the front seats. She has a firm tempo, all sorts of precision and discreet fingering; she is more than a fine musician. I dislike the metaphysical term "soul," and "temperament" is too often used to describe musicians who neglect their notes in careless and unlaudable raptures. The Bruxelloise is the meditative type of musician, thinking apparently more of the music than of the audience. This is a fault in the right direction. She has what, in the coldest terms possible, we must call emotional grip and vividness of an unusual sort, and a musical comprehension both firm and delicate. There was no nonsense, no sentimentality. The Fauré was exquisitely done, the Bach and Lalo were equal to it; the Davidoff not good enough for its company; the greatest resonance attained in the Boellmann, with fine *extase* in conclusion. An unusually sensitive musician and worth hearing ... only this question of "big tone."

Rosing's next recital Moussorgsky, Æolian, March 8, at 3.

Kennedy-Fraser concerts, Æolian, March 4, at 8; and (assisted by Rosing) March 15, at 3.

POT-SHOTS[53]

For some time it has been "growing upon me" that (from the purely professional or journalistic angle) I must, for a while, give up my strictly private enjoyments and launch out into the relatively uncharted realms of uncertain concerts. We will therefore assume that LAMOND'S recital (March 1, Wigmore) was all right, quite all right, and that any other concerts he gives will be equally all right, and that anyone who wants two hours of solid, well-built A1 piano playing cannot go wrong in taking an afternoon of Lamond.

[53] *The New Age,* March 20, 1919, pp. 329-30.

KATHARINE GOODSON (earlier, the same afternoon, Wigmore) has a graceful and fluid style and no inconsiderable charm, bringing a sort of cantabile or vocal quality from the piano, in gentler passages. There was atmosphere in her version of the first intermezzo, Brahms Op. 119; the third did not display her to such advantage, and the rhapsody needs more weight than she was able to apply; it is a manmade affair and needs a more masculine handling; Miss Goodson struggled nobly, as frail power striving to lift something too heavy for it; patches were rendered with beauty, with "feeling." She is in the super-amateur class, pleasant to hear; there is a quality of contact with individual notes and with melody which lulls the severer critical senses; she knows perfectly well what noble or furious emotions the composer intended to convey and strives with a sort of maidenly gallantry to convey them.

In HELEN SEALY, JOAN WILLIS, RENEE BENSON, violin, 'cello, piano respectively (Æolian, thirty-five minutes later), I found a competent 'cello doing Davidoff's "At the Well" with piano in no way remarkable. I am defenceless against 'cellos unless they are tortured by utter mattoids, or used as levers for pretentiousness. At any rate, I enjoyed the Davidoff.

The piano began in the Beethoven trio rather dry and hard; the music was orderly and approached the borders of the pedagogical. I descended the gradient. At first I thought the playing did not transgress these borders; then I said, "This is neither irritating nor remarkable... but gradually it loses hold on one's interest;... this classical sentimentality is the only bearable kind of sentimentality... but perhaps it is more implied than inherent... in fact, these passages might... in fact, this is becoming a bore"... exit.

THE SUNDAY CLASSICAL CONCERTS AT THE ÆOLIAN HALL opened their series under good auspices with four Bach sonatas for flute and piano. Miss Elsie Hall knows her Bach and delivered her subject-matter with great competence and no nonsense. The Elwes-Kiddle numbers could have been omitted with advantage.

We have before now been constrained to compare MISS AMY HARE'S piano-playing to the donkey-engine inside the merry-go-round. This simile only assumed its justness in the third movement of the Brahms quartet (March 3, Wigmore). It must, or, at any rate, may, be said to Miss Hall's credit that she likes (or *likes to play*) some good music, and that she ensconces herself behind better musicians, instead of trying to arrange quatuors of players of her own calibre. The Brahms, which is a charming Brahms, A Maj., Op. 26, was good in parts, i.e., in the woodwind quality of TERTIS viola, and in ARTHUR WILLIAMS' 'cello. For the rest it is borne in upon me that the female player may get a melodic line with some charm, but only in the rarest cases does the woman achieve main structure and architectonics. Miss Hare surpassed herself with the *bobble-boble-bob-bolb* and the superlative finale to the second movement. She has a touch like an Army boot.

We were next submitted to some songs of Miss Hare's composition. We have long heard of the New England lyrist, Emily Dickinson, said to be greatly prized by Americans too intellectual to bear E. W. Wilcox. Miss Hare has revealed Miss Dickinson to us in

A REVERIE

I held a jewel in my fingers
    And went to sleep.
The wind was soft, the air was drowsy.
    I said, " 'Twill keep."
I woke, and chid my honest fingers,
    The gem was gone,
And now an amethyst remembrance
    Is all I own.
               —*Emily Dickinson*

Miss Hare has, most unfortunately, caught the very spirit of these words in her musical setting, and Mr. John Coates' vocal trajectory did nothing to disturb the spiritual unity of versifier and setter. Mr. Coates seemed equally at home amid the terrors of "I crown thee, Love," and we sought refuge in the attempting drizzle of Oxford Street.

Returning to our formula, above used for brevity, "It will be safe to assume" that a KENNEDY-FRASER concert will have certain glorious moments, moments unique in the season's concert-hearing. M. Kennedy-Fraser has, definitely, genius. I do not overwork that word in these columns, and I use it to denote a certain profound intuition and emotional knowledge of subject. P. Kennedy-Fraser's voice, with its harp-like quality, develops from season to season, there is no better voice to be heard here at present. She was most effective in "Barra Love Lilt" and "Uist Croon"; the rhythms most interesting in Dunvegan, Seal-Woman, Rassay, and "Mouth Music for Dancing," especially in the encore of this last. Even if space permitted me I could but reiterate praise of this Gaelic music. The final benediction in "Sea-Tangle" is sheer genius; it has the eternal unexpectedness of great art, however often one may have heard it. M. Kennedy-Fraser made her greatest effects (Æolian, March 4), in it, and in the "Tiree Tragedy." Marjory Kennedy has sung south British XIXth century lyrics, and shows it in her vocal delivery.

Æolian, March 5. FERRUCCIO DINI displayed a good full voice, and sang in simple and unaffected manner, although no great art was shown in his rendering of the Pagliacci Prologue. His companion, Umberto De-Villi, comported his voice in what the harsh and ill-minded critic might have termed the gatto amoroso modality. We content ourselves with observing that his style is very, very Italian operatic, and that the strain or tensity in the higher reaches may have been due to a cold.

The habitual reader of these columns will take it for granted that the ROSING "Moussorgsky Recital" (March 8, Æolian) was worth hearing. The beauty of melodic line showed best in "The Star," and the "Sorotchinsky" song, the "Orphan" was improved, but in this song the histrionic effects tend to over-balance the strictly musical effects. There was fine singing in the "Dnieper," the Death Cycle songs, the first two satires, and the encores, although the singer's voice was only in B2 condition.

There is a peril for Rosing in such songs as the "Orphan," and also in too long a period of singing songs in free rhythms; the danger is as yet latent, but after he has finished the present series of concerts he would do well to refresh himself with the classics; all fine artists must take these baths, not "baths of the crowd," as Baudelaire called his curious plunges into multiple magnetisms, but "baths of the different," to get their ear or their rhythmic sense "in," as a painter would "get his eye in." The music of free period; of a constantly varying phrase-length and rhythm-length is a freedom from fixed lengths, but the symmetry must underlie, and the sense of this symmetry must be kept fresh and vivid, if not in the consciousness, at least in the sub-consciousness of the performer. Rosing showed admirable restraint in not repeating "The Goat," despite the insistence of the audience. The pitfalls of enthusiasm, particularly of irresponsible other-peoples' enthusiasm are numberless, numberless and ubiquitous. Next recital, Æolian, March 22, at 3. Chambard, Piano recital, Wigmore, March 20, at 8.15. Myra Hess, and Yves Tinayre, Wigmore, March 21, at 8.15.

MUSIC[54]

I have been to more interesting concerts (Czernikoff, Nevada, Stroesco, Tinayre-Hess, Rosing) during the past fortnight than I shall be able to discuss on this page; but there are two pests of the contemporary concert stage ripe for internment or deportation.

FIRSTLY, there is the species which thinks that when it has got half

[54] *The New Age,* April 3, 1919, pp. 359–60.

a dozen engagements at the Queen's or Albert Hall, and has the prospect of six or a dozen more, its career is made, that it has nothing more to learn about music, that the art presents no opportunities not already exploited. All countries contain this kind of idiot, and for this reason good musicians in *any* country are often foreigners.

SECONDLY, there is the illiterate song-setter. The give-away, or at least one give-away, of this tribe is the frequency with which the same poems from certain anthologies are set and reset, while poems concealed in volumes of particular authors persistently escape musical notice. A comic detail appeared last week, when one of the double star "younger composers" set two "verses" of a familiar three-strophe poem by one of the best known living poets. He is now worrying the publishers for permission to publish the setting of the fragment, naïvely making the excuse that he didn't know there was any more of the poem. The accident *might* have happened to an artist; but it appears very much like a symptom of the general slovenliness of the British Georgian composers. If there is a literate class in England, which one is sometimes inclined to doubt, it does not go in for music. And if there are English musicians with anything like general culture, they are screened from the public gaze with an amazing assiduity.

Thematic invention in music has coincided with periods when musicians were intent on poetry, intent on the form and movement of words. Thematic invention is the weakest spot in contemporary music *everywhere*. The rhythms of French are less marked, but only in France do we find a careful study of the verbal qualities. I do not think I have shown any delirious or unbalanced appreciation of modern French music, but among their song-setters are practically the only contemporary song-setters whom one can respect.

English contemporary poetry is, I suppose, very dull, and there is very little rhythmic invention in it; but, even so, writers intent on melody would, if they were serious in their technical intention, make greater effort to combine with musicians, and musicians would attempt to learn something from authors about the meeting-points of the two arts. As it is, the musician's attitude towards the lyric is too apt to be "Get me something that I can end on a high note. Got to make some money." Players will not practise for trios and quartettes; there is no place or company where any number of writers and musicians meet to try new experiments of an "unpractical nature." I recently met a poet who wanted a poem set to cymbals and 'cello in order to develop or illustrate the tonality of his words. The man is "of course" a lunatic. No Chappel-Ballad-minded aggregation would tolerate such departure from suburban custom. A "song" is words set to py-ano music. It doesn't matter what words. It is not the business of the business-like song-setter to express anything, or to find poems worth further musical development, or poems in which the verbal rhythm contains the germ of larger musical structure. All of which is very lamentable.

CZERNIKOFF

I have heard Vladimir Czernikoff under all, save concert, conditions during the past ten years, and I have long promised myself a fairly careful analysis of his work. I have heard Czernikoff in a cabaret, playing as suited a cabaret; I have heard him among fat-heads giving fat-headed effects; and I have heard him among connoisseurs playing as only connoisseurs can. I arrived at the Wigmore (March 15) with a ready-made theory, to the effect that Czernikoff is the tolerant connoisseur. There is certainly no one among us who knows more or cares more about music. Czernikoff's "error" is the error of the "human" as opposed to the "intolerant" or "inhuman" temperament. Czernikoff has never been able to hurt anyone's feelings by hurling at them something which they cannot understand; or by cursing a second-rate composition for its shortcomings when he is perfectly aware of its merits. I think the first, and possibly the second, of these processes is wholly or very nearly unconscious. Czernikoff unwittingly absorbs the temper and mental aroma of his surroundings and fits his music to them. For this reason you never can tell how he will play on any given occasion, and for this reason his success, by no means negligible, is still, and will probably remain, incommensurate with his fine musical comprehension. Sympathy is in some cases an artistic faculty, but in Czernikoff the capacity has got out of hand. He would be a better artist and a surer performer if he preferred something, it does not matter what, to something else. The artist must have a faint touch of fanaticism *somewhere* in his nature. Heaven knows that fanaticism in excess is worse than garlic in excess, yet both the quality and the herb have their uses.

I do not know that my theory found much confirmation on March 15 (Wigmore) save in so far as one might predicate that the audience decidedly got on Mr. Czernikoff's nerves. He began the Bach Chromatic Fantasia and Fugue with a slight dullness of impact, then sharpness and flat sound; one thought it was going to be a fiasco, but it became interesting in a sort of literary way, if one is permitted the term. He began to make the instrument "talk"—that is to say, he was intent on the meaning of each phrase, on the vocal or almost "verbal" meaning of each statement of the music, and by this he took one's mind off the actual sound quality. Then when the fugue developed, the more strictly musical qualities crept into the playing, and the technical grasp of the form was increasingly apparent. I don't know whether the early plainness of tone was intentional restraint or not, but the whole performance of the piece was extremely instructive. I cannot recall hearing a piece of Bach more thoroughly *analysed;* and I am inclined to think the plainness of colour at the start was justifiable whether done by design or not; it would be perfectly defensible on the ground that if the early statements are made too mellifluous one would get one's pleasure from accidents and incidentals and not from the main contrivance of the piece. Czernikoff's resonance and his ability to get thunderous noise out of the bass notes were amply demonstrated later, and his arrangement of Arne and the Mozart were given with delicacy. I cannot remember hearing more sound driven from a piano than was expelled during the Liszt "Funérailles." We observed how hard Czernikoff can hit; and we noticed also how STUPID Liszt was, and how little he knew about chords. Czernikoff did all or nearly all that was possible with this piece, and the composer let him down, let him down through sheer stupidity. Stupidity is not an asset in the arts. Passion is as blind as you like, and it sweeps over intellectual subtleties in the drive upon its own truth, but there is a fundamental stupidity in some natures, and, alas! in many composing and writing natures, against which no perseverance or labour is any avail. Liszt was stupid. You can make impressive sounds on the piano while playing Liszt, but you cannot completely conceal his fundamental and congenital and ineradicable lack of intelligence, his lack of susceptibility. He would try to make a watch go by beating it with a potato-masher.

In his second group Czernikoff ran to virtuosity, almost to trick-playing, and only re-ascended to his Bach level in the sub-aqueous tide and colour of the Scriabine "Désir Caresse." Scriabine was just brushed by too great a desire to be unusual. One can, perhaps, have no advance and no artistic discovery without this. It is the peril of inventors, and one should not grumble at its spoiling or damaging part of their work if the other parts attain ultimate beauty. I made nothing of the second Scriabine piece.

WINIFRED PURNELL (Steinway, March 11) showed resonance and volume of bass, but none of the more unusual qualities which we have noted in former recitals.

MAINLY STROESCO[55]

ALFREDO NARDI, the blind composer and violinist was warmly received (Æolian, March 12). Various singers and instrumentalists, also a "chorus of ladies and gentlemen," participated. Nardi's compositions are

---

[55] *The New Age,* April 17, 1919, pp. 396–97.

roughly école de Verdi; Misses L'Anson and McLelland displayed clear soft voices. Nardi's music was carefully rendered by the instrumentalists. Mr. Clapperton was by no means unusual.

The indivisibility of the human body prevented my attending all of both the Czernikoff and KENNEDY-FRASER concerts on March 15. Czernikoff I have dealt with in earlier notes. The sign "HOUSE FULL" greeted me as I arrived for the end of the Hebridean concert, and I had the pleasure of feeling that fine work was at any rate in one instance receiving its due reward. Both the K-Frasers were in excellent form; and ROSING, although he had not wholly assimilated the Sea-Rapture (Kishmul) Song, at least demonstrated that the song will hold its place beside his best renderings of Moussorgsky. He is the first singer who has been adequate to the music, and we may expect the thing done with full mastery at his later recital. The swing, the spirit and savagery were already in his version of it, and the combination of his forces with those of the Kennedy-Frasers is a fortunate one for the public. Miss Patuffa K-Fraser showed her rhythmic skill delightfully in the "Ceol Brutha" and "Raasay."

MIGNON NEVADA (Tuesday, March 18, Æolian) devoted herself in the main to second-rate music; I mean definitely second-rate, *not* third-rate or fourth-rate. Miss Nevada represents the taste of her mother's generation; much of the music was well enough in its way, but "the world" has read Henry James; and Laforgue has replaced De Musset and the easy tolerance of the operatic era is waning. Opera is a diffuse form; it was made to cover light, after-dinner conversation; the exigeant audience which concentrated its attention on careful Mediæval canzoni had given way to eighteenth century fluster. Miss Nevada's programme was in part pleasant enough; even Mr. Kiddle accompanied several passages passably well; but it was a programme without any masterpieces; it was a programme which showed that master-work had not been sought. Let us admit that Purcell's descant on "Hark, Hark, the ech'ing air," was pleasantly done, and that Grétry's "Rose Chérie" is the best bit of Grétry that Mr. Evans had resurrected for his lecture on early light opera; let us admit that it is a good thing for singers to get off the beaten track and hunt up music that is lying in desuetude. All of which things being so, this ferreting in odd corners should lead us to a stricter and not a looser critical standard. Opera was best in court conditions. It is for an audience that drifts together for social reasons and which wishes the social pressure to be loosened, the necessity for conversation to be diminished. Concert conditions are much more the conditions of song-competition "Preislied." One, indeed, wanted to compare the icy tinkle of Miss Nevada's voice with the rich barocco of D'Alvarez, without the fortnight's interval (D'Alvarez, Æolian, April 1, at 8.15). In detail: Kiddle performed the first four lines of the Gluck quite nicely; then something broke loose. Nevada showed charming acuteness in the Prière, but the line of the melody has nothing in particular to do with the supposed meaning of the words; it is eighteenth century artifice. There was technical grace in "Il mio ben quando verrà." We have praised the Purcell, yet the voice was a little clouded, or misted; "stellis nebulam spargere candidis." "Casta Diva" was excellent in the first three lines, and later in spots, but cold, and here one began to speculate as to the possible value of D'Alvarez' equipment, despite its fuss and tropic excitement, and desired a comparison of vocalisations. The Delayrac has its moments, but is not really good enough, save as an illustration to a lecture on musical history. The voice was a shade too thin. In the third group the concert went to pieces. V. Thomas was twaddle after the Hebridean music of a few days before. The words were ill set, and with poor melodic line. Szulc is not the preferred setter of Verlaine. Delius' setting is the sort of thing one would expect from such words as "With perfume heavily laden, the roses droop their heads." "In the Seraglio Garden" (Turkish Bath seraglio)—the composer has not observed the sonorities of the words, and this shows in the way the music tends to make the singer sing "Minarits" and "Torrkish." Delius had, it is true, bad verse to set, but this is only another sign of the blunt-wittedness of contemporary musicians, and their general incapacity for literary choice and selection. Cyril Scott in "Sleep Song" had observed the verbal qualities. Let us mark this to his credit, even though the song is wholly without interest or importance ("Hush-a-bye, Hush, the wind is fled," etc.). Also the final "sleep" is set as "sleeeeeeeeep." Pierné's "Boutique Japonaise" is just music "en toc." That term has been evading me for some months, but "Music in stucco" is certainly the proper designation for a great and damnable category. "Magdalen at Michael's Gate" is post-Tennysonian re-hash balladry, music on a par with the words, after which even in "Canzone della Piovra" by Il Eggregio Signore Io-sono-Mascagni,-mi-pare-che-basta came as an improvement. It is "all sheer nonsense," or "all my eye," or whatever substitute for "Tell it to the Marines" is permitted the serious critic of æsthetics.

STROESCO (Æolian, March 18, evening) gave the best concert he has yet given—a series of clear and finely cut intaglios. Obviously he had intended a full programme of the finest possible work, and only in the case of the Pierné did he commit any error; even this song had the excuse of being fitted into a group of Oriental subjects for unity. A little of the horrible drizzle of Tuesday evening had clouded the singer's throat at the start, but he "sang through" that and gave us a memorable evening. Those are the only flaws. And if he can give three or four concerts of equal merit there will be no justice in his not having a firm and constant support. When he puts his mind to it, he is one of the finest vocal craftsmen we have; he had definitely put his mind to it for Tuesday's performance. I have used the term "intaglios" with intention; there is no other expression for the firm delicacy of his workmanship. Tinayre is an exquisite singer; if I had to discriminate between their two totally different styles I should say that Tinayre is, in sort, an embodiment of lyric joy, a sort of green grass and open air nature. Stroesco is a man in love with his art, innamorato. The term is much abused, but here we have the real thing, a Latin passion with its apparent excess and exaggeration, but real; and, my God! in what glorious contrast with the domestic content wherewith most English singers contemplate their music, or with the domestic satiety of the "type" Elwes.

I record the programme in full, because when a man makes as rigorous a search for perfection as Stroesco obviously had made, and when a singer takes such a strict line in presenting his best to an audience, one should notice the fact. Sic.: 1. "Pur Dicesti," Lotti; "My Lovely Celia," Monro; "Languir mi fais," Enesco; "Air de Joseph," Méhul. 2. "Quatre Poèmes Hindoues," Maurice Delage; "Boutique Japonaise," Pierné; "Sadko," Korsakow. 3. "Pescatori di Perle," Bizet; "Les noirs nuages," Korsakow; "Le Steppe," Gretchaninow; "D'une Prison," Hahn. 4. Roumanian songs, set by Jassy and by Dina. The encores were chosen with as much skill as the songs, and all exquisite.

There was suave and lovely voice in "Pur Dicesti"; this time Stroesco did not over-force his fortissimos (a danger in his earlier concerts). He showed exquisite sense of verbal values in "Lovely Celia." The Enesco setting of Marot's poem a mélange of modern French, and music of Marot's period, ends in an exquisite little cadenza that might be either thirteenth century French or Roumanian; despite these varied elements it attains charm. The Méhul is the mode of pomps and circumstance; it was forcefully and faultlessly presented, and took its place admirably in the programme structure. Di Veroli's sympathy and comprehension were admirably employed in the dénouement of the evening, Delage's "Poèmes Hindoues," which are like painting on silk. The second is more markedly Oriental than the first. The third opens with vowel intoning, and here Stroesco was glorious and unique. This intoning is old as Egypt, it is full of meaning, it still lasts in the synagogues, and takes part in Roumanian folk song. We do not recommend Delage's songs to amateurs. Those who have not heard Stroesco's opening to "Naissance de Bouddha" have missed something, and we counsel them to make good their loss at the earliest opportunity. There are just some things which Stroesco does all by himself without any dangerous competition. Even the Pierné was elevated by Stroesco's sense of verbal values. The "Sadko" is vital Orient; Stroesco had the rhythm, and in this and in the succeeding Korsakow and Gretchaninow he carried the war into the "enemy's country" with no inconsiderable interest and great applause from his audience. We shall soon have a duel of tenors, and Rosing must look to his monopoly. The French translations will doubtless upset the strict Russophile, but the results have a charm of their own. Stroesco was exquisite and passionate in the Bizet, and there was no room for improvement in the Hahn-Verlaine or in any of the encores. The Jassy was perhaps the most interesting of the Roumanian folk songs, absolutely authentic; and this mixture of Latinity and Orient has its definite place and lure.

Dolmetsch concerts, April 16th and 30th, at 5.15, at 6, Queen's Square, W.C.1. (Inquiries to A. Dolmetsch, "Jesses," Haslemere, Surrey.)

MUSIC[56]

JEHANNE CHAMBARD (Wigmore, March 20) gave us a slice of art life. Brisk, brilliant, obviously talented; clear, thin, metallic, interesting in the Allegro of the Bortckiewicz Sonata, an unfailing kinesis with clear-cut detail. It requires a certain nerve to appear in religious dimness with a futurist lamp-shape and to play from the printed page. Memory is not, however, the supreme faculty; and if a performer can use printed notes instead of memory without detriment to his or her performance I see no reason against it (horror of all academic and established heads of musical seminaries!). Chambard's appeal is not universal; we did not, for example, observe il Maestro Lamond in the audience. The playing was modern and feminine, and brilliancy was its main characteristic both in tone and execution; it was all of a piece, not the least patchy. The second movement (andante) was, I am afraid, Deutsch sentimentalisch. The pianist has not much sense of structure, but produces a fascinating current of music.

Scarlatti is to be played with the fingers, and not with graceful loops and arm-sweeps from the shoulder. The second exquisite Scarlatti piece was, however, better presented. Grieg suits the lady. (This sentence being not wholly complimentary, let us say that she perhaps adds emotion to Grieg, while Chopin's music more than contains any she can bring to it.) She has, however, some claim to rank among the leading female pianists; and certainly should not be missed by those who attend feminine instrumentalists. She has what I think is called personality—

[56] *The New Age*, May 1, 1919, pp. 12–13.

a quality more apt to enrich one's private life than to draw swift and easy public success. The Chopin was, we must confess, Chambarded rather than presented. There was not a fundamental atom of Chopin left, but still the performance was enjoyable on the principle of "Very pretty poetry, Mr. Pope, but not Homer." I have before propounded the theory that Chopin was *not* the De Musset of music. The third movement was graceful, clear, and felt; the finale over excited.

This report aims, in the main, to be favourable. This pianist does not bore one to death. There is a good deal to be said for the art-life despite the stern mæstros and épiciers; the dim light (highly inconvenient for the critic who has arrived without an electric pocket-lamp and who wishes to make little notes) might help one to concentrate one's attention on the music, were not the performer so busily engaged in deflecting a portion of said attention toward herself. Members of the audience capable of mixed pleasure, not insisting on a strictly auditory æsthetic, will not, perhaps, object to this diversion of interest. After all, the young lady expresses herself... and gives one a charming evening. Middle-aged women from the suburbs will be reminded of "what they have lost." And all of this is in the main very commendable.

Rhadamanthus, chien de métier, sums up the case: brilliant, fluid, pleasing, the player holds the attention, but has not much solidarity or sense of structure. Go and hear her, mes enfants, ça vous apprendra à vivre.

MYRA HESS (with Tinayre, Wigmore, March 21) opened with a Rameau Minuet, perfectly orderly and in the precise mode suited to the subject. There was no interposition between the music and the audience. Paradies' music was given with equal charm, and Miss Hess showed exquisite suavity in presenting the Bach Chorales, Bk. I. 5 and 7 as splendidly deciphered by Busoni. These pieces are among the best piano music we possess and were given with great richness of tone.

Miss Hess is among our most able executors. Not so skilful as Moiseiwitsch, there seems at times to be more body in her playing. Franck suits her, as we have said before. This is both a commendation and stricture. Debussy shows her limitations with merciless clarity. Franck is pianistic, and in the performance of his somewhat empty music, as in the fine, early music, Miss Hess is at her best. During the Franck "Prelude, Aria and Finale," it was perfectly easy to let one's attention wander from the music. I found myself looking at the ceiling, wondering when it would end, and then as often was recalled to realise that I was in the presence of very good playing, and that there were spots of no inconsiderable beauty. Then Franck ran near to the danger zone where music verges into noise. One remarks on his ability, and then, to get it into some sort of scale and proportion, one thinks that Chopin would have expressed an equal amount of whatever this series was intended to express with half the number of digital impacts.

But Debussy is not Miss Hess' métier. The Sunken Cathedral (encore) just wasn't there. And her "Gold Fish" didn't swim, and the music didn't loop where it should. Debussy, as I have indicated before, was a glorious heresy. He writes for the excitement of phantasmagoria, for the evocation of visual imaginations, and in just so far as he does this his work is unorthodox and off the true track of music. It is definitely an heresy, a beautiful and bewildering heresy, which should have its own converts and enthusiasts; but it is no mortal use trying to play his music as if it were "pure," as if it were simply "sound" arranged into time and pitch patterns for the expression of emotion. And if the player be not initiate into this realm of evoked images, he or she will never play Debussy as anything but an outsider.

If Miss Hess were a mæstro, like Lamond, she would concentrate on the music she best understands. Even Ravel's "Alborada" has more in it than her highly clever martellation gave to the audience.

TINAYRE in his first group was memorable, perfect, was anything that you like; I am, in connection with such singing, unafraid of any hyperbole. In the Monteverde, Pergolesi, and Old French dance songs he showed himself not only a tenor, but a musician. You cannot brush aside such work by calling a man a "mere singer." The voice seemed larger than before; the enunciation clear and accurate, the delivery firm, and with nothing left to chance; suave in "Lasciate mi morire," in "Tre Giorni," with its admirable lyric line, the voice was remarkable with its delicate lift and float, perfect in tang and in passion. In the Gavotte especially, he showed himself a musician. I could go on listening to these songs for hours: "Comme elle est légère." Ashton (Leopold) helped him ably in accompaniment. "Le lierre au chêne s'unit toujours" gave opportunity for exquisite glide. And the beauty of the Pavane was flawless. Consider also (Oh, ye retrograde and abominable and altogether disreputable song-writers and setters!) the technique in the Tambourin, the tripping speed of the words which do not entangle the tongue or spoil the timbre of the music.

And, alas! Tinayre is welcome to most of the rest of his evening. French translations are not good for Russian, nor was Ashton in sympathy with the music. We have already declined Malipiero. Neither Prudhomme nor Victor Marguerite were poets of first rank; and the modern French composers are utterly at the mercy of the poems whose words they set. One does not grumble at Tinayre's experimenting with new songs, but a certain amount of experiment could be profitably performed in private before half a dozen trustworthy and acid friends. Dupin was an engine-wiper. His work does not take one on first hearing.

I am inclined to think that it has a vigour more apparent when taken in contrast with his etiolated contemporaries than when contrasted with authentic wild music. Klingsor also was a poet of second or third order; "Berceuse Triste" was not one of his happier bursts into really good writing—Hüe's setting of his "Ane Blanc" is, as we have noted, quite charming. But the Tinayre who showed himself in the first group is a Tinayre insuperable. (And have I not had the "Duc du Maine" ringing in my head since he sang it a month ago?)

MUSIC[57]

Last year, during the fuller part of the season, I skimped my analyses of various concerts in an attempt to keep my notices up to date, and I was then left with empty weeks in the summer. This year, seeing that this occasional page is not used to attract managers' "ads.," and is intended much more to inform the reader what different musicians "are like" than to advertise concerts, I am going to let the news element go by the board, save perhaps for single line announcements.

Tinayre, Stroesco, and Rosing are all, as I have indicated repeatedly, worth hearing and totally different. Tinayre, I think, you might hear on a country road doing his whole repertoire with rather more pleasure than it will ever give him in a concert hall. Stroesco I have discussed recently and at some length. Rosing has had a reasonable share of space; the fifth concert of his series was, however, the least felicitous, and, indeed, dangerously near to being an æsthetic failure.

Tschaikowsky's "Garden of Christ" was suave, clear, and acceptable. Handel is no part of Rosing's job. His "Thy Rebuke" is, in any case, not particularly worth preservation. It is flat prose; a musical fuss is made over it, but there is no particular rhythm in the words, and the marriage with notes does not imbue it with any great interest. We have already said that there is no reason why Johann Sebastian Bach's processional should be saddled with words stating that he has lost his Jesu. The song results in a fine, jocund, robust proclamation that the obviously *bien portant* and untroubled protagonist is brought "to despair." Every note calls the author a liar. Bach of course had to play his music in church, and it was but natural that he should enjoy himself.... I can still recall a village organist in similar plight doing "Lamb, lamb, lamb!" at a choir practice, it was not the celebrated "paschal" lamb, either. Rag-time is quite fine on a pipe organ. Still the ecclesiastical censorship does not pertain to music performed in Bond Street,

[57] *The New Age*, May 22, 1919, pp. 68-69.

and one might have some honestly secular words set to that Guard's march.

The Tcherepnin and Gretchianinoff nature poems were pleasant enough, but not very important. The best poets have been nature poets only incidentally. Nature appears here and there in their work, but is not singled out for their subject-matter. Whatever "religion and Christianity" may still mean to the populace and to the modern heath-dweller, religion as exploited by artists of the last century has been mostly exploited as convenient furniture and not from any inner necessity.

Mendelssohn put some sort of melodic line into the "Recit" of "Rend Your Hearts," and a deal of sentimentality into the aria, and *anyway* he might be left to the Albert Hall.

In Rachmaninoff's "The Christ has Risen" Rosing, thank God, got back to his own proper level. This song was magnificent and redeemed the rest of the concert. Bizet in "Agnus Dei" has produced a good verbal line and added a futile and frivolous accompaniment. Di Veroli did his part nobly during all the performance.

THE CLASSICAL CONCERT SOCIETY seems to offer its musicians a sober and unenthusiastic audience well worth pleasing. The pleasures on March 26 (Wigmore) were the second movement of Brahms' Quintet in G maj., op. 111, Tinayre's singing of "Le Pauvre Laboureur," and three movements of Bordes' "Suite Basque." The second movement of the Brahms (allied string quartette: Defauw, Kay, Tertis, Doehard with R. Jeremy added) is in its perfect draw and swing as satisfactory as any piece of late-mid XIXth century music I can recall, though the definition of it as "tragic melancholy" by the writer of the programme-explanation seems somewhat excessive. It is a firm elegiac; the third movement opens without significance and settles later into its beauty. The finale is "for the Tzigannes." The violin was a little shrill. John Ireland's "Trio, No. 2" opens cautiously, but soon sinks, or at any rate sank, with the composer's insensitive *bam-bam* at the piano performing notes as uninspired as those written for the violin. The piece does not whet the appetite for rehearsing, and the programmitist raised false hopes by terming it "comparatively short."

TINAYRE showed suave certitude in "Jerusalem Mirabilis," though there are various points in note-length that one would like to take up in detail with Weckerlin or whoever reconstructed the XIth century air. Beautiful it is in its present version, whether or no this be the only possible way of interpreting the original melody. Tinayre was at his finest in the bravura and passion of "Le Pauvre Laboureur," said to be of the XVIth century, a finer re-Marseillaise, with a detached or impersonal, dispassionate passion, a stasis inciting to no action, yet with deepest feeling in its melody.

> Le pauvre laboureur
> L'a deux petits enfants,
> Ils menent la charrue,
> N'ont pas encore quinze ans! . . .

And the magnificent finale:—

> Il n'est ni roi ni prince,
> Ni ducque ni seigneur,
> Qui n'vive de li peine
> Du pauvre laboureur.

The poignancy and the simplicity of poetic statement are matched with the formulation of the music and when I compare this with the utter tosh of sentimentality in four out of five of the lyrics set by Brahms I can but wonder again at the vogue of XIXth century favourites. I have been forced to look anew at Brahms during the past few weeks, and I can only suppose people have accepted them because they have always heard them in a foreign tongue and taken no account of verbal meanings. But they are really much worse than I had ever suspected . . . with exceptions which can be very fine.

The Laboureur song dated to XVIth century reminds us, or might remind us, that democracy did not begin with the French Revolution; and that earlier authors had thought of the labour problem, for this song is not a song by a labourer, but by an observing and indignant poet of no mean attainment. Even Spain was not always a land of inquisitions, and there was democracy south of the Pyrenees, before the suppression of the Cortes in the ill days of Charles V.

Ashton was at his best in accompanying the "Jerusalem" and the "Labourer"; he is not really in sympathy with much of the modern French school. The Quartette were charmingly assisted by V. Borlee's flute in the Chas. Bordes. This "Suite Basque" opens with fine low resonance, no waste of notes, excellent economies, and though of the XIXth century style, it escapes most of the typical XIXth century faults, musical rhetoric, and the like. The second movement is in the main gay, but not unusual; the third "Paysage" is grave and exquisite, and for this movement alone the piece would merit much more frequent performance than it receives. In the fourth movement the folk-dance hurdy-gurdy is applied with consummate good workmanship. The *first* artist to take up any neglected folk element has, historically, nearly always scored a success. At any rate, Bordes has given us a quintet with three excellent movements and one which is not detrimental. There are not too many such, especially since 1807.

I return again to the apparent insensitiveness of the modern audience to the word-value of songs. Since Lawes and Waller collaborated, the technique of English settings has been appalling. German, with its capacity for taking extremely heavy musical accent on thick and heavy syllables, has furnished the "lieder" and the lieder were emotionally effective ... at least people "adored" them, and I don't know that anybody has taken the trouble to make a critical examination of their construction. A few fine poems, folk songs, poems of Heine, served as a cover for the rest. The modern French ran a counter movement, but were reputed to suffer etiolation. We want more discontent with our lyrics, and a stricter examination of claims.

POST-MORTEMS[58]

To make an interim summary of the season to date, I should have to repeat what I have said of Rosing and the Kennedy-Frasers last year; to add that Tinayre and Stroesco give me unusual pleasure and that I never voluntarily miss hearing their work; that Lamond is a master pianist; that Jehanne Chambard is, to a point, interesting. Perhaps one's most difficult problem is the treatment of music which is not outrageous enough to merit condemnation nor yet quite good enough to stir interest. The finer shades and varieties of this mediocrity are more bother to the critic than either the execrable or the excellent.

MLLE. YVONNE ARNAUD with A. Mangeot and G. Pitsch opened the weeping camembert of Schubert's Trio in B flat (Æolian, March 28). Mangeot had a tolerably pleasant middle tone; Mlle. Arnaud showed moderation and kept the piano in register with the other instruments; the music was played as most of Schubert deserves to be played, namely, with that air of the "better" restaurant or "usual" theatre orchestra, more or less brisk and more or less tearfully sentimentalisch. It is impossible to deny a certain amount of proficiency to the performers, and with food or under some propitious emotional circumstances the music might have assisted in keeping one stationary. I am not in a position to report the remainder of the afternoon's playing.

HELEN EGERTON, assisted by Alice Dessauer and A. Williams (Wigmore, March 31), attempted the difficult feat of presenting Beetho-

[58] *The New Age,* June 5, 1919, p. 103.

ven Trios for violin, 'cello and piano; also piano and violin sonata, with a null violin. Music written for three instruments cannot advantageously be rendered with two, especially if the leading instrument be left blank. The 'cello tone was pleasing where heard, but it was usually (as the composer intended) kept under the violin; as for the piano, when it remained subservient it was insufficiently audible in the back on the main floor; when the pianist got excited and "took hold" of the piece one was more agreeably entertained; one even felt that the pianist might be worth hearing in conditions more favoured.

WINIFRED BARNES (Æolian, April 3) deserves special commendation both for the quality of the music selected and for the modesty and self-effacement of its arrangement. There are very few performers, female *or* male, who, having engaged a couple of "draws" to assist them, would so carefully put the "draws" at the beginning of the afternoon's work and leave their own songs, nearly all of them, for a single concluding group. On April 3, the Allied String Quartet showed firm attack in the Franck, the first violin was a bit shrill, with knife-edge coming through at the beginning; there was a general pressure against the music, keeping up the feel of advance. The quartet displays just that difference of art from pastry-cooking, which we did not have in the Arnaud trio; just the difference as it were between sculpture and cake-icing. The 'cello is probably the basis of the Allied Quartet's stability. The Franck, at any rate, is not sentimental as the Schubert trio, and the playing improved with the progress of the piece. Di Veroli was at his charming best in accompanying Stroesco, who, despite the atrocious condition of his throat, gave a perfect example of singing in Caccini's "Amarilli": exquisite in his balance and weighting; in the millimetric time measure of syllables, and in the tensity, and varying tensities, and in the flow of phrase:

Dubitar non ti vale
A primi il petto a vedrai scritto, etc.

Here he managed to overcome the opening roughness of his voice, though it hampered him in the songs following, which were quite beautiful, but unsatisfactory to anyone who remembered his singing them when in voice. For encore he chose a modern Italian "Primavera" with which his hoarseness did not interfere.

Miss Barnes deserves a literary rather than a musical study. She should be assured of popular success; there is a curious ecclesiastical timbre mixed with a Coliseum timbre and puzzling vowel quality, any of which would have engaged Henry James for a fortnight. The same colours appear in some of the members of the Beecham opera company; apart from this there is abundant evidence of training, considerable technical equipment, and let me repeat, excellent taste in the choice of programme.

STROESCO (Æolian, April 8) scored his chief triumph in the opening Gluck "Iphegenie en Tauride," giving it with rare robustness and richness. Di Veroli was charming in the piano interlude. Stroesco showed greatly his sensitiveness to the verbal meaning and made an excellent final cadenza. All through he was stronger in the lower notes than he has been before. The programme, however, declined. The Schumann in English was not very acceptable. The whole *lieder* school is wrong, and it needs only a slightly unfavourable condition to rub in the fact. The whole *genre* is wrong. This does not prevent there being a certain number of acceptable lieder, but the more one examines them the less satisfactory they appear. The Victorian ballad is the natural result of trying to bring the lieder into English, and a very lamentable result it is, too. Stroesco was rather unreined in the finale of "Nuit de Mai."

"L'art ne joue pas," and never was this truth more apparent than in the settings of Stevenson's baby songs. Stroesco did exactly what the composer and poet had intended, but the stuff is not good enough. The settings obviously intend to appeal to silly people, in large numbers. Hahn does some trick programme music, but won't even be popular. To be popular a song must not only appeal to the silliness of the populace but it must be do-able without skill or effort. . . . Not that these songs needed Stroesco to sing them, any young female professional would have done, but they are not easy enough for the average amateur.

Stroesco should reserve himself for the real thing, for Gluck and the old Italians; for such work as he gave us in the Chants Hindous of Delage, or for the chef d'œuvre of operas and of the modern French school. In this programme the Gluck was memorable, and it alone repaid one's attendance.

JOSEPH COLEMAN (Æolian, April 10) showed some firmness, but is one, I ask you, gentlemen, *is* one to sit through a whole concerto by Wieniawski?

Anathema

There is no copy of Henry Lawes' three volumes of "Ayres and Dialogues" at the little second-hand music shop in Great Turnstile, but the kindly proprietor is good enough to look up old sale catalogues. The last set went for £49. Dolmetsch's arrangement of some of this old music is out of print. Only in a nation utterly contemptuous of its past treasures and inspired by a rancorous hatred of good music could this state of affairs be conceivable. I have bought Waller's poems for a shilling. Yet Lawes' position in English music is proportionally much more important than Waller's position among English poets.

This condition of things is more eloquent of the debasement and utter contemptibility of British music publishers and the slovenly ignorance of British so-called musicians than the laws of libel permit me to attempt to express in these columns.

This whilom "nest of singing birds" is apparently on its last roost.

VARIA, DOLMETSCH[59]

THE PHILHARMONIC STRING QUARTET, as now composed: F. Holding, T. Peatfield, R. Jeremy, C. Sharpe (April 9, Wigmore), is worthy of considerable commendation. They played the Borodine D major with fine robustness; and they are to be thanked for their introduction of Stravinsky's "Three Pieces for String Quartet" (mss.), which they have now done three times. The first of these is excellent; the second "curious," emotional, "Russian"; both these being music definitely of the first grade and proving Stravinsky a composer of the first order. The third piece is "wholly mad." It might, it would seem, stop at various places where it does not, and this feeling is hardly compatible with a conviction that its structure is very good. It is a justifiable piece of stunting, but not important as the two first pieces are important.

Joseph Holbrooke was charming in piano prelude to his songs, but Betty Sharpe has the most horrible voice and manner I have been called upon to hear, and I trust the ordeal will not occur a second time. Words were wholly obscured, and as they were not printed on the programme I am still ignorant of their supposed subject-matter. When a few of them ultimately emerged I judged the content to be in the "If-doughty-deeds-my-lady, etc.," manner. We suppose Holbrooke is well to the fore among the younger British composers; he can scarcely be a musician or he would not permit, or at any rate abet, Miss Sharpe to sing his compositions. The second of his songs was most painful; the third, grave-yard groaning. Holbrooke is a possible pianist. The Quartet, aided by Wm. Murdoch, next assailed the Dvorak, A maj., Op. 81, and rendered the popular, bouncing, prancing, and slightly bumptious exhilaration of the piece quite effectively. How often have we been cheered for entrée or the Punch Romaine by this familiar and not unacceptable gaiety. The rocky rattle of its pianistics "gets" the plain man right on the solar plexus (as a well-advertised correspondent of

[59] *The New Age*, June 19, 1919, pp. 135–36.

this paper has recently said all art should do). There is no desiccating intellectuality; no narrow appeal to the intelligentsia; the music is a little incomplete without food. It was "well played" and with good juicy fiddling, a bounding finale; in short, a real challenge to the encroachments of jazz.

MANLIO DI VEROLI (Æolian, April 11), backed by the gratitude which a considerable audience acknowledges for his fine accompanying of our best singers, ventured a full programme of his own compositions, ably aided by Stroesco, Z. Rosowsky, and Oscar Lansbury, each well chosen for the particular numbers assigned them. Unfortunately Sig. Di Veroli has not yet made up his mind whether he wishes to be a "younger" Italian, a "younger" French, or a "younger" British composer, and this indecision, together with an apparent lack of study of the best and closest-wrought periods, has not fostered a unified or developed even a personal style. "Le Gemme" in the Italian, manner after Mascagni, Puccini, and co. (largely and co.), and "Eveil," manner of contemporary Paris, were the most serious works and would not come amiss in some of our passable recitals. The final English lyrics were a hash of 27 familiar ingredients. The first is full of Eng. ballad boredom.

The only excuse for the songs is the hypothesis that the composer wrote them at the age of 15, but if one must make a compost of

> "I want no tum-ty where thou tum love,
> I want no tum to make me blest,
> If within thy tender, etc., love, thou, etc,"

and the Sheltering Palm song from the once popular operetta "Floradora," one should conceal the fact from the public.

Di Veroli presented gay, veiled archaism in his piano "Menuet Rustique." The "Song of Freedom" would do for the Queen's Hall; Lansbury has a good bass voice, combination good for official proclamation manner of the opera heralds in any mid-nineteenth century production. All the old familiar lines. In "L'Après-midi," the tone intervals are too great. Stroesco was a little rough, but the fault is also in the music. Di Veroli, if he intends to progress, should make a close study of a "close" period. His sound retention was good in "Alba Romana," and he had made a slightly new variation on Debussy. The "Diamante" is the best of the "Gemme." This series and the "Eveil" might be retained by the composer. There is lack of skill in the tone intervals of "Chanson." He should scrap the rest of the songs.

ARNOLD DOLMETSCH (6, Queen's Sq., April 16 and 30). It is a good thing that Mr. Dolmetsch was not at the Di Veroli concert; for he would have stood up and cursed audibly, and with some justification during various parts of the programme. It would, on the contrary, be an excellent thing if Di Veroli and other junior composers would attend Mr. Dolmetsch's rare performances *and* read his instructive writings. There is no use in Mr. Dolmetsch's trying to interest all of even his small circle in ancient dances. These belong to archæology, are interesting to the special student of the period (perhaps), but one does not want to see them repeated. At least there is a considerable audience which would be much happier if the playing of Lawes, and Lancare, and the pieces for viols were not punctuated by homage to Terpsichore.

I can only reiterate what has, I think, been affirmed before in these pages. Dolmetsch has plunged deeply into this past era, he has thrown a deal of light on the manner in which the old music should be played. There is exquisite precision in the playing of his domestic orchestra; no player now in London can afford to miss the stimulus to the auditory imagination which comes from hearing the pure tones of the old viols well played; or which at any rate should and would come if the hearer's eardrums were not made of leather or dripped.

The value of the old instruments, harpsichords, spinets, clavichords, viols de gamba, is more in that they induce the player and hearer really to listen to the quality of sound produced than in that they render the old music with veracity. This latter advantage is, however, far from negligible. No one really understands counterpoint who has heard it only with the blare of modern instruments or the plugging of the piano. Neither is there any means so effective for developing a pianist's sense of sound-quality as practice on the clavichord.

Chopin presumably excels all piano-composers of the nineteenth century because his memory embraced the sound of the earlier keyboard instruments. A person *learning* piano-playing on the piano is simply ignorant of a great many kinds of sound, *some* of which can be rendered on the piano by a person whose mind and imagination contain them.

The advantage for ensemble playing is that the harpsichord and spinet "go with" the strings, whereas the piano does not, but is practically always an inruption. For the fortieth time we repeat that the curse of modern playing is the general inacuteness of the performer's audition. Sensitiveness to sound-quality is no less important than sensitiveness to true pitch. We should be just as intolerant of people who make horrible noises "on the note" as of people who cannot sing in tune, . . . at least we should be as intolerant of soloists who so annoy us. In a choir or orchestra the bad noise is swallowed in the general resonance or counteracted by other noises. (This applies to soundquality. It is not an academic objection to what were once called "dissonances.")

Dolmetsch is to be thanked for making his firm stand for soundquality. In the first programme we commend especially the Coperario, and in the second the Lute song, "Puisque Robin j'ay nom," the Couperin "Musette," and the Clerambault. If, if, ah if!!! some of our more frequent singers and players would only go to Mr. Dolmetsch for advice when choosing their programmes!!!!![60]

MUSIC[61]

The difficulties of transport prevented my hearing Moiseiwitsch, but I have not the least hesitation in assuring the reader that Moiseiwitch's concert at the Queen's Hall on Saturday, September 27, was a well-deserved success, and that the pianist played with great skill. I do not believe that I should have been able to add a single line to what I have already written of this musician even if I had got to the hall.

Winifred Macbride (Wigmore, Sept. 30) presented Bach with blurs and with a general suburbanity; the blur was inside the smaller elements of the pattern, and did not obscure the elements just a size larger, and although there was no grasp of the main structure, the performance was not so distressing as might have been expected, and may possibly have given a good deal of pleasure to the not quite musical ear. We can imagine a really erudite musician like Czernikoff leaving the hall in fury at once, but the postprandial inertia of the critic retained him further into the programme.

A perfectly plausible and explicable dislike to Beethoven's "Appassionata" might lead a performer to play something else on the same notes; I do not know that there was any such dislike at the bottom of Miss Macbride's softly sentimental Debussyisms, or her sort of blunt, cotton-wool fireworks, of the blatancies of her treble; and it would not explain the lumpiness of the ensemble even if it did elucidate some of her detail. I sat in intellectual puzzlement, wondering whether I had gone a little—just a little—bit daft, or whether it *was* the pianist; or whether vacation had ultimately unfitted me for my job. Then gradu-

---

[60] As an addendum to this review Pound published the following in the "Letters to the Editor" column of the *New Age,* July 24, 1919: "Sir,—We note that there are two Mr. Holbrookes who participate in British music—Mr. Joseph and Mr. Josef. Of those, the Mr. J. Holbrooke now resident at Harlech, in Wales, desires with a zeal worthy of the ancient denizens—Men of Harlech, Pibroch of Donildhu, and the rest of it—utterly to dissociate himself from the performance of songs rendered by Miss B. Sharpe at the Wigmore Hall on April 9 of this year. Anyone who attended that performance, and no one more feelingly than myself, will readily understand the earnestness of Mr. Holbrooke's (of Harlech) wishes, and heartily compliment him thereupon. WM. ATHELING."
[61] *The New Age,* October 9, 1919, pp. 396–97.

ally into my bewilderment as to *what,* just what, might be going on there crept the suspicion, the more and more clearly defined suspicion, that it should not.

The lady has intentions; so far so good. She has perhaps "something to express," though she herself is not perhaps quite sure what it is. Out of the wuzz there came finally the standardised Beethoven "Stimmung." Yet from the blur of this Beethovo-Bochian swarmishness I sighed for Lamond, I sighed for the school of playing which recognises music as a structure. I am not crushing the glowworm on the wheel. Miss Macbride is at the beginning of her career, and she would do well to recognise that her method of playing falls flat, will go completely to pieces because it depends, apart from some digital ability, upon emotional energy, always a tricky possession, and not on sheer comprehension of music. It holds her audience *now,* but it is wholly undependable. The opening of the Brahms Capriccio was trite and intolerable; the method for the Debussy was perhaps more successful than a more frigid approach would have been, but the lady must use her head if she hopes for more than a third-rate public.

The real events of the week are the Gilbert and Sullivan Opera and possibly the Russian Ballet. The music of the "Gondoliers" ranges from thin Mozart to Floradora, *via* Messrs. Chappel and Co. It is adequate for what it sets out to do. It conveys no emotion and but a frail sort of sentimentality or spritely activity. The performance is well carried out, Mr. Toye conducts very well, the chorus behaves very well, the company acts very well along conventional lines, and Mr. Lytton acts with distinction. D'Oyly Carte scores over Beecham by the superior polish of the ensembles, staging, etc.; there is one good piece of duet writing; Sydney Granville and Helen Gilliland save the musical situation by the pure quality of their voices; there is no strain for effect, just very beautiful singing of the by no means unusual matter provided for them.

When Sullivan's music is bad, it is not so much that it is wrong as that it is "like good music with something left out." He is perhaps a tradesman giving just as much as the contract requires; just enough good music to carry the show, just enough harmony (in places) to keep the impoverishment of other choruses from getting on the nerves of the audience. If he had had anything better than Gilbert to set he would presumably have ruined it; as it is, the "When You Marry" song is bad Chappel ballad, other numbers are satisfactory but unoriginal; but contemporary song-setters would do well to observe how ably he seconds his librettist, how well Gilbert's point and points are enforced by the supple compliance of the music.

Not that there is anything *musically* memorable in the performance.

The opera is carried by its libretto; the songs, such of them as are remembered, are remembered by reason of Gilbert's wit. This wit is in the "Punch" genre, and is the acme of the Victorian titter, the keynote being a sort of unserious compliance with what cannot be altered. Which things being so, the performance as a whole is acceptable to those who like opera. The opera has a main form; it, indeed, complies with the sensible specifications of operatic classical structure. And certainly the producers and performers get every scrap out of both music and libretto. The success of the season is assured, both by the efficiency of the company and by the solid affection of the public for this Simon-pure-British mode of entertainment. It is also certain that we shall never see Gilbert and Sullivan better done, and that the D'Oyly Carte season is "an opportunity," an opportunity emphasised by the presence of Mr. Lytton, Mr. Sydney Granville, and Helen Gilliland.

The Ivan Yorke-Yvonne Phillopowsky concert (September 29, Wigmore) was successful.

Rosing's season of recitals begins October 4 at the Æolian, and continues on alternate Saturdays (three o'clock) until December.

The London Symphony Concerts begin on Monday, October 27 (Queen's Hall), and Rosing appears in that of November 24.

Adrian Boult is conducting impeccably for the Russian Ballet, and "La Boutique Fantasque" is not to be missed.

AT THE BALLET[62]

A person of fixed and meticulous habits, it is easy enough for me to listen to a singer or player and to write down my little mementoes; it is, on the contrary, very annoying to lose the stage for the sake of

---

[62] *The New Age*, October 16, 1919, p. 412. The Diaghilev Ballet had been performing in London regularly since 1911, appearing in evenings of dance, in performances of Russian opera at Covent Garden, and even in music-hall performances. The 1919 season at the Alhambra Theatre opened in March with a new ballet, *La Boutique Fantasque,* with choreography by Massine and sets by Derain and with Rossini's music, orchestrated by Respighi. The production evoked "exceptional enthusiasm," according to the company's biographer, Grigoriev (*The Diaghilev Ballet: 1909–1929*, London, 1960, p. 155). "It culminated in a most brilliant, animated *finale,* which was invariably drowned in overwhelming applause." *The Three-Cornered Hat* was also being given for the first time, with choreography by Massine, sets by Picasso, and music by Manuel de Falla. In September the company moved to the Empire Theatre and this was where Pound saw them. Another new ballet, Eric Satie's *Parade,* was also being given its London première at this time. (See Atheling's review, December 18, 1919.) One might have hoped this sportive anti-impressionistic work would have made a more concrete impression on the poet. As Cocteau, who wrote the scenario, put it: "Eric Satie's orchestra charms without the use of pedals." Pound was later to meet both Cocteau and Satie in Paris.

scribbling one's comments, and I cannot pretend to record the Russian ballet as closely as I might a recital. My main point is that for the present one gets one's best value, simply as music, and regardless of "extras," at the Empire. To criticise the orchestra of the ballet, as one criticises concerts, one would have to go every night, and specify that on Tuesday Mr. Boult conducted in such and such fashion, and that on Wednesday, Thursday, Friday, etc., such and such things were done. An orchestra is not a cinema-film, and it does not run off its effects with equal uniformity. Let me record that I have heard Boult conduct the orchestrated and exquisite Chopin for the rather faded ballet "The Sylphides," in altogether delightful fashion. It was perhaps the best played music I have heard this season.

The Rossini which has been illustrated by "La Boutique Fantasque," has found a true complement in the decadent art of Derain and Massine. I do not use the term decadent as disparagement. Common usage leads one to employ this term for a certain sort of sophisticated or over sophisticated work. Rossini needs some such completion. Note that the Chopin does not need anything; one would, and indeed does, delight in the orchestra independent of the dance.

"La Boutique Fantasque" is altogether so delightful that one does not, and could hardly, separate its components. The music fits; it performs all the needful functions of ballet music. I think my colleagues (Messrs. Hope and Dias) will support me if I say that the miming is excellent, and that the costumes and staging give one more of the spirit and "message" (or whatever they call it) of modern (very modern) art than all the dozen shows of greenery-yallery that a contemporary art-critic is called upon to see in a year.

Musically the "big thing" of the Russian Ballet is the "Igor." This Borodine is stupendous, the surge and thud of the music, complete without any stage, is yet carried on and enforced by the dancing tumult as a complete sound might be enforced by an echo, by a series of resounding repercussions.

The spirit of the music moves this flood of physical rhythm; the "Igor" has a force, where "Carnaval" or "The Sylphides" has but a delicacy, and where "The Three-Cornered Hat" has but a cleverness. The "Igor" grows in an integrity, it is welded, where the Picasso ballet is merely glued.

The "Igor" is moving, and repeatedly moving (we have had it with us for years) whereas "The Three-Cornered Hat" is merely interesting in parts. Manuel de Falla is alert and his music, especially the overture, is the best element in this ballet. I leave Picasso to Mr. Dias, but I can see nothing in his drop-curtain; there seems to me no common denominator between scene and costumes. The scene, indeed, becomes tolerable only under the "night" calcium. All I could note from the costumes was that the long triangles and stripes did develop a sort of kaleidoscopic interest when the dancers whirled or massed. The whole thing seemed the work of a man lacking intention, but who had had clever ideas here and there.

Not so the Derain, where from the opening one felt the homogeneity. Scene, gestures, costumes, are all part of a new idiom; Rossini fitted in perfectly, but was given new life, and the dancing exposed a new emotional violence.

Karsavina is merely silly in "The Three-Cornered Hat"; she has no gift of representing emotional energy in any case; Szolc has what would certainly be called genius if it were displayed in any other interpretive or creative art, or if the term be very applicable to a merely interpretive artist. Tchernicheva has some temperament. In "The Three-Cornered Hat" the choreography has merely added a few frills to Aragonese folk dances, and in every case these merely weaken the intensity of original models. Note that in the "Igor" one has the real thing. The Russian-Spanish is vastly inferior to the Russian-Russian.

The "Boutique" is not Russian; out of its Parisian sophistication it has created a sophisticated intensity. It is the most intense of all the ballets, not built on a pure Russo-Oriental basis. It is full of an intellectuality which a folk-creation like the "Igor" does not need. Both it and the "Igor" are vastly superior to romanticistic refinements like "The Sylphides" and "Carnaval."

"Carnaval" is unimportant, Schumann's music not being very interesting, a collection of scrap impressions, giving a scrappy ballet when "interpreted."

The Rossini and the Derain has design. The Borodine is superlative. Weight, bulk, impact, splendid drumming, magnificent orchestration. I make little of the Zolotareff "Fête Villageoise," but it is a very fitting lead-up to the Picasso ballet. The "vocalist" in this latter was excellent; I thought it was an anonymous talent, hitherto unknown; it had the real gatto-appassionato Hispano-Italian quality. I mean the real thing, the song of the Sirens who mean business effect. If it was Zoia Rosovsky, as announced on the programme, then let us pray that she will continue to sing behind a curtain and that she will keep to the Spanish mode; for the effect was certainly infinitely preferable to anything she has given us on the concert platform.

The "Boutique" seems to me worthy of a permanent place in the art of the ballet. It has stuff in it, it is not merely a triumph of novelty, and certainly no one interested in the mixed art of the ballet will miss it. The Picasso ballet should go with the season. "Petrushka," "Scheherazade," the magnificent "Igor" we have all known, and there is no new element in them for the critic. The point is that they do not grow old and the music is worth hearing... if one have the knack of listening while so much is happening on the stage. And a fair test of the real art of the ballet, as distinct from fortuitous conflict of several arts in one performance, is whether one does hear the music. In the "Boutique" the music is there; one knows it is there, half-consciously; one is satisfied that it should be so. In "The Sylphides" one can neglect the stage; the music permits one to be aware of a vague blur of stage daintiness; but in the "Igor" there is a surge of sound, dominating one, and dominating the stage-tumult. Every foot-beat but marks the integral rhythm. The music has come out of savage emotion, it is one with the dance; the two things play into each other.

Moreover, I have heard grumbles about the new prices, but the Parterre is extremely comfortable (5s.) and judging from the concerts people do go to, there is many a crown worse spent. The Empire is a place that gives you room for your feet. We are in favour of a society for the suppression of theatres which do not.

MUSIC[63]

London, October 16.—Perseverance is the order of the day, and I hope that before it becomes my painful duty to carry this article into its second paragraph I shall have or 'ave a bit uh luck. Rosing, on October 4, was too ill to appear, but valour overcoming discretion he displayed a very nice voice, and very little wit in its employment. The throat was easier than last season, and he pulled the concert together by substituting Glinka for Mozart in the middle of it. Constance Izard showed conscientious endeavour in her laborious fiddling on October 6. Mischa-Leon has a rich and even fruity tone-product. He did not quite supersede Plunkett Greene as a ballad singer in his rendering of the Loewe-Zedlitz ballad. The cute and cunning roguery of Rückert's Poëm (with two dots over the e, *sic* ë) drove the undersigned to the most instantaneous relief possible, and the remainder of the concert was reported by other members of the Press, at least, I left several behind me. I perceive that this season my capacity for being bored is going to be vastly inferior to what it has been during preceding autumns.

On October 18, Rosing showed himself in his old form, sang Tschaikowsky with interest and again demonstrated that his voice is in much better condition than last season, his production more easy. There is,

[63] *The New Age,* November 13, 1919, pp. 28–29.

however, a limit to human endurance, and to the most admiring patience. I do not propose to sit through a French travesty of "Ich grolle Nicht," not again, not ever again, not if it is sung by Gawdamity with seraphs doing a banjo accompaniment.

It is sheer pig-headed stupidity to pretend that there are no other song-writers than Brahms, Schumann and Schubert; it is quite possible to fill programmes without German music; it is rank bad art to use his German music with foreign words which have no relation to the melody or the spirit of the originals. In the case of Brahms, the best of the three, the lieder words are in nine cases out of ten such muck that *any* translation would be insupportable, and it is only by reason of the audience *not* understanding the German that they are able to enjoy the singing.

The slop of Victorian balladism is due in large part to these German lieder. People imitating the translations of ninth-rate Deutsch zendimendalisch gedichte, adding two quarts of dish-water and removing the weight of the originals, produced the Chappel standardised English song. If singers want these tunes they might, at least, since German is still taboo, sing them in Russian or Yiddish. If Rosing wishes still further and yet again to declaim "j'ai pardonné," let him make it clear that it is the translator he is pardoning, we cannot do so, our magnanimity has its limits, but the sight of his Russian large-heartedness may do us good in a world tinged with misanthropy.

"Sir Henry Wood's orchestral arrangement of Debussy's La Cathédrale Engloutie." O Gawd! O Montreal!!

Elsie Cochrane (Æolian, October 22) was ably abetted by P. Mavon Ibbs on the organ. She sang with pure tone for the few opening notes of "Panis angelicus"; then I think she ceased to sing plumb on the note or to hit the tone in the centre, and with simple long notes this is the chief desiderium. The late Sir Hubert Parry did, I believe, dispense with an accurate sense of pitch, but it is not a good practice.... The Philharmonic Quartette then favoured with Dvořák. This is tziganne music, and the quartette lacks the tziganne zip; also they failed to cohere. I felt that I, we, you, most of us, had all heard it better done at the Pré Catalan; I then felt it too painful, I then sought refuge in the well-carpeted passages of the Æolian Hall, and returned to the auditorium only upon receiving an "all clear, sir," from the trusty guardian of the portals.

Miss Cochrane then squalled on her high notes, especially on the terminals of "aimée," but she is by no means hopeless, and if sufficiently hammered may turn into a very acceptable singer. Her voice has probably been "placed" too high; at any rate, all the timbre and beauty are flattened out of the voice when she attempts her topmost notes; she might gain a good deal by giving up the three or four highest and adding a few to the lower reach of her singing. She sang her next group of songs correctly and on the notes, but in the higher notes failed to articulate her words. . . . I should like to have heard Fransella, but was bunkered by two threats of the quartette.

Bessie Rawlins (Wigmore, October 22) has a future, and despite her youth is possibly having a present; she is the most satisfactory of the younger violinists. She has been well taught by Wm. Sachse, and plays without any nonsense. She was most ably accompanied by Ethel Hobday; the First movement of the Brahms D major concerto was given with admirable firmness; the violinist has an excellent ear and handles her fiddle in a business-like, rather male manner; the music was given in cold purity in the serener passages. Miss Rawlins seems free of the objectionable features of the usual female talents; may we pray that she steer clear of the prima donna manner in future as now. The finale of the Brahms was excellent.

She displayed a softness and mournful richness in the Tschaikowski serenade which one would not have anticipated from the harsher tone used (and rightly used) in the Brahms. In nautical phrase there are "things which a man should be able to do blind, drunk or asleep." The spirited Porora-Kreisler appeared to bear this ratio to Miss Rawlins. We heave several sighs of gratitude for a new artist to whom we can listen with genuine pleasure.

Anne Thursfield (Wigmore, October 23) presented a well-chosen list of songs, and presented them from an angle much more musical than is usual on the London platform.

The rendering of Marcello's "Quella Fiamma" was careful, the ear exact, the tone full of sweetness and clarity, the accompaniment lacking in fire, and for the later songs now passable, now quite inadequate. "Plainte" was exquisitely done; "Cigale et Fourmi" is a *diseuse's* piece; there was good graduation and good characterisation; there is not much music in it.

The singer did not manage "On a Time"; did not find the bravura of gallantry the song requires, and also sang it much too slow. It is inexact to term "The Lass with the Delicate Air" old English; we shall soon be having Gilbert and Sullivan dished up as "old English," if this sort of loose terminology goes much further.

The weakness of the photographic or Rosing method showed in "Au Coin"; if you are going to give *exact* imitations of the imagined speaker or singer, you cannot break out into clear impersonal song just when the fancy happens to strike you. The three Moussourgsky child-pieces are entertaining and very clever. The songs from the Chinese might better have been sung in the original, for the English is in three cases un-lyric. Bantock has made a very careful setting for "The Celestial Weaver," modern French manner, not much melodic line, but nice chords à la Debussy. "To a Young Gentleman" has the best words for singing but the setting is commonplace. Mrs. Thursfield deserves praise for painstaking and well-finished singing; for confining herself to good music and excluding rubbish from her recitals. We shall hear her again with pleasure.

Rosing continues on alternate Saturdays at 3. (Æolian.)

The Kennedy-Frasers appear Wednesday, November 12, Æolian, at 8.

Tetrazzini, Albert Hall, November 6, at 8, with Cellini and Cimara; the latter announces a first performance for England of Mancinelli's symphonic poem "Frate Sole."

MARQUESITA[64]

Violet Marquesita (Æolian, Oct. 27) presented a remarkable assortment of the "component parts of an artist" without, however, causing them to cohere into an wholly convincing composition. She began with "Wraggle Taggle Gipsies," a sort of version of the "Flight of the Duchess." She has a good voice, pleasing use of the throat, her gestures were exaggerated, contrasts too violent to be effective, but she has a true capacity for the tragic, and as hardly anyone else has this capacity, it is too precious to be let pass without strict critical comment.

In the second song there were fine odd moments. One could have made a good series of photographs of the various poses, but the thing was not grasped as a whole, and did not carry conviction. She does not understand *scale;* she does not know that certain things which carry in a drawing-room will not carry in a hall. "La Glu" went better; for the first time she showed restraint; she began with the arms folded, kept them so for a time, and then managed a proper crescendo of gestures. In this song the rhythm is good enough, and was well enough managed, to aid the unity. The gaminerie in the song by Ashton needed restraint, but the use of the voice was excellent. Thus in the first four songs the *diseuse* had managed to demonstrate her capacities, i.e., her voice and a real gift for gesture, but showed no art in combining these into the small and unified drama that each song-with-gestures must be if one is to take it seriously as art.

"St. Nicholas" was beautifully *sung;* one, however, received more from it if one kept one's eyes off the performer; the *voice* made its graduations properly, and with great variety. The "Ronde" showed de-

[64] *The New Age*, November 20, 1919, pp. 42–43.

lightful vocal range. "Jack Hall" would have been better omitted; and the fourth song of this group is buffoon balladry. Comedy must not try to be too comic.

In "Mort Renard" we had the same gestures which we had had already ad plenum. This is very bad stage-management. Miss Agnes Bedford[65] was excellent in her accompaniment. "La Perla" has great charm and got the audience as none of the earlier numbers had quite done. One retained no doubts as to the beauty of the *voice*. "Zohra" is interesting and Salvador Daniel probably a musician, and certainly a scholar of exotic music, worth study, but it cannot be said that this song, as given, was convincingly Arabic. "La Paloma" was intended as the "necessary" popular number. "Whistle, daughter," is sheer music-hall, and a bad version of one of Yvette's songs. "Rosa, Rosa," was café chantant or, better, buccintoro, good café chantant with a touch of art added a-top of it. The "Bossu" has a good rhythm circle. The next piece was Harry Lauder; "La pêche aux moules" was very neat, and "Mon père m'a donné un Mari" was in the same gamut. The singer had by now got to the end of her programme and also got under way; the audience was ready for more; they got cabottière.

Net conclusion: Marquesita has more good faculties going to waste than any other performer I have heard and seen for some time. Again, to enumerate: she has a charming voice; she has quite enough vocal technique to sing the best Bel Canto, Caccini, Vivaldi, Caldara. She has temperament, but she has also the taste of any suburban back-drawing room; and in this she presumably follows her teacher, Madame Marchesi, who sings the best music quite perfectly, and then "favours" with unadulterated bilge, without qualms, and in accordance with the once accepted and arrantly cowardly theory that the public insists on its bilge. I do not know Mlle. Marquesita's theories on public taste and chanteuse diplomacy, but if a singer wishes to combine serious art with music-hall farce it is necessary to employ the neglected art of programme

---

[65] It was following this review that Agnes Bedford, the gifted coach and accompanist, was to meet Pound—a most important meeting, for she became the poet's musical amanuensis for the first sketches of his own opera, *Le Testament*, and a person to whom he turned throughout life for musical advice. Their collaborative work began with *Five Troubadour Songs*, arranged by Agnes Bedford with "Original Provençal words and English words adapted by E. P. from Chaucer" (Boosey and Co., London, 1920). Soon Pound was dictating his own music to her, and he sent her the first draft of *Le Testament* for comment, thus providing an invaluable second source to the later Antheil edition of the work. Even after he left England Pound kept in close touch with her by letter, sending her also the score of his second opera, *Cavalcanti*, for criticism. Their correspondence extended to 1959.

Pound also became quite well acquainted with Violet Marquesita, and in 1931 she sang the part of Villon's mother in the first BBC production of *Le Testament*.

construction. There are certain principles of this art displayed, or violated, month in and month out, on the concert platform.

As said on numerous occasions in these columns, a concert is like a play; it consists usually of four groups of songs; of these the third group must be the climax. The fourth can be farce after the drama, it can be a change of tone, it can be a curiosity, a bit of research; or simply a diminuendo.

Marquesita could have held her audience simply by singing, *if* she had chosen songs with sufficient musical interest. She chose to be a *diseuse,* that is, to act songs. This is a different art; fine singing is only part of it. A number of the pieces chosen, little narratives of action, with same melody repeated many times, have not enough musical interest to grip without action. There is really nothing to be said against the singing. In the art of gesture, Marquesita has gifts, but she is all over the shop. One movement is used about 60 times, another about 40; there is little graduation. She does not realise that a human being with its arms spread out to their widest is large enough to "fill" the whole stage at Covent Garden. Neither does she realise the effect of a contemporary evening dress on various gestures. If one could hammer into her head the fact that "art" in gesture, to be *art,* a-r-t, art, requires quite as much nicety and technique as the art she uses in the actual singing; the same sort of graduation, of minor contrasts, the same variety from one piece to another, one would have served both her and her public. For this art each gesture has got to mean something, exactly as the particular quality of voice has got to *mean* something. The little dramas must each be constructed; and the lot of them must be built into a programme.

It would be exceedingly simple for this singer to give a concert which would have more than a clique success. Let her begin, piano-piano with fine and delicate music: Marcello, old Italian, what you will, but something depending entirely on the musical interest. (She had such numbers in her programme, but stuck in without thought of the main form of the concert, and therefore without due effect.) She could hold any audience with good music for at least four songs; probably for sixteen. But let us say we have four songs, simply as songs; the second group could be songs with quiet gestures, and about a fifth the number of movements Mlle. Marquesita would naturally use. The third group must be the heavy work, the real tragedy, the full-blast emotion. And then, if needs must, she might apply the nonsense in the finale.

It is a case for the critics and the public; this artist will not wholly make herself from inside. Yvette had in the first place a receptive intellect; and, secondly, she had about her some of the finest critical taste of her time. In her present condition La Marquesita would set nerves as fine as Tinayre's on edge. The Collignon with one tenth of Marquesita's equipment manages to do certain things perfectly, and to leave a perfectly ineffaceable memory. La Marquesita is a very mixed bag. If the public insists on her best; if the critics insist on her best; if she can take her art seriously—we ought to get something very satisfactory.

If, on the contrary, she wants to "get on" at the Palladium she must devote herself to music-hall technique. This exists. I have never had time to study it, but I believe it to be quite as complicated as, and rather less satisfactory than, the art required by "good taste."

There is no use wasting fine technique on bad songs. *L'art ne joue pas.* There is possibly no use in telling these things to people who don't want to know the difference between the good, the half-good and the no-good; between the best and the mediocre; between real art and sham art. It will, however, be a great shame if the faculties of this singer are not put to worthy employ.

MUSIC[66]

ROSING was again "magnificent," in his third recital of this season (Æolian, Nov. 1). He took his old command of the audience in the firm and passionate declamation of the lines from "Manon"; the tone was rich amber, and the meaning of the text given with effect and "intention." Zoia Rosowsky was full-lunged and inexpressive. Puccini is stupid, and his stupidity is fully apparent when given thus after the finesse of Massenet; there are singable lines in Puccini, but his inferior *mentality* glares from every bar of the opera. In the Boris Godounoff "Fountain Scene" the piano rattled, and the absence of the orchestra was unpleasing; Mlle. Rosowsky is *not* made for the part of "Marina." Rosing sang well in his last two numbers, and the blessings of intelligence were distributed through his part of the programme. One had the sense of his being the character of the singer and meaning the words of his text, not merely being a section of tubing through which were poured variations of melodic sequence. Mlle. Rosowsky was a contrast, an antipodes, a black nadir to this zenith.

All last year's winners seem to be opening this season badly; the KENNEDY-FRASERS were no exception (Æolian, November 12). Certain family calamities, like the murders in classic drama, should take place *off* the stage; Mrs. K.-Fraser has discovered inestimable treasure in the Hebrides, but treasure-trove is not legally the sole possession

[66] *The New Age,* December 4, 1919, pp. 78–79.

of the finder, and there is no reason why Margaret Kennedy should sing these songs publicly. There are plenty of people who would like to sing well, and who suffer, even acutely, from inability so to do. We admit that this elderly lady made most touching and gallant efforts, and in her first numbers succeeded better than heretofore, but the assassination of the "Aillte," one of the finest of all the Hebridean heroic pieces, was an exhaustion of all possible patience or toleration.

Some of Mrs. K.-Fraser's new reconstructions seemed rather as marginalia; they were interesting philologically, rather as foot-notes and by-forms to some of her earlier presentations, but did not add much to our knowlede of the scope of Hebridean song. The Tale of the Skir of St. Kenneth is an exception; here the island genius has succeeded in putting wild life into the dulness of Christian hymn-mode. Mrs. K.-Fraser herself succeeded in giving atmosphere "as never was on sea or land," and her voice was in better condition than usual. In the "Two Cronies" she gave genuine satire and matched Rosing at his own photographic game; the song ranks with Moussorgsky's humour. Patuffa K.-Fraser was singing rather listlessly, and without her usual driving power; she warmed up somewhat for the encores: "Islay Reaper" and "Raasay Lilt."

It is refreshing to find four nice young men with good ears, who will ascend a platform and sing part-songs without the accompaniment of the distressful, perpetual, confounded, ubiquitous, iniquitous, unavoidable, unescapable, damnable, and ineluctable rattle of the py-anoforty; and there is, therefore, plenty of room for the Templars Quartet (Æolian, November 14), Messrs. Stone, Dixon, Hastwell and Halford. The reception of Dixon's arrangement of Morley's "Month of Maying," and of the Volga Boatman's song ought to convince the quartette that good music pays, and ought to divorce them from Elgar.

If there is any worse song-setter than Walford Davies, we are unaware of the fact, and if any such can be discovered he ought to be stuffed down a drain, and there held by the trousers until dead of the odour. Kipling's poems may not be very great literature, but the "Fighting Men" is at least broad and simple enough to be made into a good song. Davies' silly exaggerations of pitch-interval, etc., etc., banality, triviality, cheap musical rhetoric utterly destroy such merit of the poem as a sober and honest setting might have enhanced.

H. E. Darke should follow Waller's advice to poor musicians, and content himself with "Ut, re mi"; Bridges' words being undistinguishable in his hurly-burly. On the other hand, we owe the quartette a distinct debt for introducing us to the work of Lieut. Paul Edmonds. At last we have a contemporary song-setter who *fits* notes to the words, who does not ruin poems by the affixture of melodic imbecilities. PAUL

EDMONDS, let us print the name large, place it firmly in our memories, and then pray that Mr. Edmonds may go on; pray soberly and earnestly that he be really the musician awaited; the musician who will search out other poems as beautiful and as singable as Herrick's "Fair pledges of a fruitful tree," and put to them notes either for four voices or for one voice. We are sick to death of stunting and imbecile musicians; sick to death of "composers" who tack a little pseudo-Debussy to any words whatsoever, and then bleat about "Modern English Composers." There is a wealth of fine English poetry unset, there is crying need for a musician who can think more of the beauty of the poem than of his own pustulent egotism and of his desire to be the leading "modern British composer." Time was when a musician was content, like other true artists, to be the servant of beauty. Paul Edmonds has made a good beginning; if he cannot find friends among the musicians who like a dabble of piano mist obscuring the words of a song, he will certainly find friends among men of letters, and they may be just as good company.

The idea that no poem becomes a song until you have some unrelated piano music in the offing is interred by Mr. Edmonds' setting of Herrick. This is really a cause for rejoicing. It is really a blessed thing that a living musician should set a good poem without spoiling it. Edmonds must develop his literary sense; "Land of Heart's Delight" is not really a very good poem; but the man does put one note under one syllable, and his quartette-writing does not obscure the meaning of his words. The singers gave both his songs with clear enunciation. They did an encore, "Bonnie Braes," in the "not a dry eye in the house" manner; they should steer clear of sentimentality; they should utterly eschew Walford Davies' Dailymailism, his PhillipGibbism in music; they should develop a critical sense; they should notice, as they possibly did not, that their Irish folk tune was fitted to words less singable than the "Month of Maying." They need not become exclusively high-brow; no one asks them for æstheticism. We compliment them on singing as a quartette, and on putting the piano in the intervals by itself instead of having it as accompaniment; more power to their throats and their elbows, renewed thanks for singing Paul Edmonds, and let them, in conclusion, develop selective power. The public will take the best music they can find for it.

ROSING (Æolian) on November 15 stirred the usual enthusiasm with his Russian numbers. He sang "Lord Randall" much too slowly, and in his zeal for realistic method he has overlooked the spirit of old English balladry: the sort of sardonic and gloomy gaiety with which folk-tales and children's fairy-tales present horrors; the force lying not in a Zolaesque photography but in the contrast between the subject and the aloof unfeeling motion of the telling. Rosing's present series of recitals professes to instruct us in the development of singing; but as very few people in the audiences connect one concert with another this schematisation is not very effective. The fervour for actualism has carried him rather past the mark even in the Moussorgsky death songs; his acting of them was excellent, but in all arts one wearies of the non-centric element, and Rosing in his realist programme reduced the singing element to a point where one cannot defend him against anyone who happens not to like the method. One felt he would do well to sing nothing but early and formal music for a time; one knew that the insouciance of rhythm in some of the dramatic numbers would have been more effective, would have been less of a strain on the auditor, had it been embedded in a different sort of programme, and given in contrast to distinctly measured songs.

There were fine moments; and also moments when no control or shaping power was evident; and, as he intended, a general impression of acting rather than singing. This is imprudent. "A fig for your prudences," says our impulsive Russian. He sings or acts again on the Saturdays, November 29 and December 13 (Æolian, at 3 p.m.).

STROESCO returns Thursday, November 27, Æolian, 3.15.

DOLMETSCH, 6, Queen's Square, Bloomsbury, December 3, at 5.15.

MUSIC[67]

Maggie Teyte has what is usually, and can without irony be, called a "divine voice"—fluidity, charm, ease, and notably the quality of seeming to fit snug into all the corners and crevices of the hall; whereas most voices, even quite good ones, seem to fill only a sort of amorphous area ending a yard or so from the edges of the room and leave the auditor with a sense of strain, or strained attention. Miss Teyte (Æolian, December 4) began with Méhul and Grétry, plausible archæology, and suitable for opening a programme if she had gone on to something more worth her metal. Unfortunately, Novello and Poldowski were about the height of the remainder of the performance. Debussy's Villon setting is interesting, but not wholly a triumph. Holbrooke's music to "Lake and Fairy Boat" is a prize example of how to spoil a poem in setting, by neglecting the author's climax. E. Martin (we apologise to Mr. Easthope Martin if some other homonymous person is here concealed) has set the utter serenity of Wordsworth's opening lines—

    I wander'd lonely as a cloud

[67] *The New Age,* December 18, 1919, p. 112.

to a musical St. Vitus' dance, thereby displaying the typical mentality of the average and detestably incult "Younger British Composer." Two drops of horse-sense or a little use of the sjambok are the only suggestable remedies for this sort of botching. All whereof is all the more annoying as Miss Teyte is one of the exceedingly few singers who could give us a whole programme of masterwork without the least inconvenience to her greatly talented self. Meliora speramus.

There is no reason why anybody should go to the Picasso ballet called "Parade," save possibly that Karsavina is for once given a part she can fill. (Apologies due to her performance in "The Good Humoured Ladies," which succeeded the "Parade.") There is also no reason why Diaghileff should not withdraw the "Sylphides," which has become an utter bore, more especially as the present corps de ballet is either too fagged, jaded, aged and worn out to do it, or else too uninterested. They present but the dead shells of gestures which once had a meaning, most of them leaping about with a grim ferocity of expression not exactly in the original spirit of the piece. The "Good Humoured Ladies" is more to their talent, a pleasant show to see once.

Dorothea Webb (Æolian, November 26) gave a soggy, devitalised and thoroughly lady-like rendering of various unexceptionable songs. The substitution of depression for heart-break may be "true to life," but it is not stimulating to an audience. In the case of the "Croppy Boy," if one is going to be purely photographic, one must cease to trouble the imagination with the convention that the unfortunate lad expressed his dying emotions in any form of verse whatsoever. "The Lord of the Isles" was too suave.

We all owe Arnold Dolmetsch a great debt for his book on 17th and 18th century music, for his continued researches and labour for revival both of old music and of old instruments, but at his last concert (December 3), his zeal as archæologist had somewhat outrun his prudence as a performing artist; only the most faithful and enthusiastic inner circle of devotees can be expected to sit through a two-hour performance consisting of one hour and a quarter of "intervals." It is likewise an imposition on the strictly musical part of the audience to insert reconstructions of Old English dancing; these could be put at one end or the other of the programme, for however pleasantly they were done, they were not done with anything approaching maestria, and whatever use they might be as a basis for modern ballet they were not, as presented, of any great interest to any but a student of terpsichorean history. We would commend the viol playing of Miss Nathalie Dolmetsch, and the ensemble in Coperario's piece for five viols.

Miss Jelly d'Aranyi (Wigmore, November 26) showed considerable talent and accomplishment in execution, but less in analysis. In the

Bach concerto she seemed somewhat confused and hampered by Miss Knocker's orchestra. In the first movement one got no impression of the fine joiner's-work which is distinctive of Bach; later, when the violin had a more separate part, the quality of the whole improved. The piano was distressing in the first part of the Mozart sonata; the violin charming in easy lift and fall. Later the piano became infuriating, the violin adequate, but hampered by increasing volume of piano noise. The limit of our interest in the violinist is not, I think, due anywhere to actual use of bow at the moment, but, we repeat, to lack of analytical power expended beforehand. Miss d'Aranyi probably gives considerable comfort to other musicians who play *with* her in ensembles; she is free from all, or very nearly all, the nameable faults of performance; and her limitations would not be perceptible to another musician actually thinking and playing the same piece of music, and subjectively sustained by his or her concept of it; at least, it is to this that I must attribute her considerable reputation among musicians. But for the listener who is only listener, the case is different. Each bar is correctly and spiritedly played; but each phrase and passage is not played as if it were a distinct statement, forming part in a series of distinct statements making in all the whole composition. The temperament is adequate, the concentration of intelligence might be, with advantage, augmented.

Rosing (Æolian, November 29) presented his Russian programme; which is the best of all his programmes save the all-Moussorgsky. Di Veroli was in good form, especially in the opening Gretchaninow. The "Weeping Herb" went best of the village songs collected by Philipoff; Di Veroli again scored in Kalinnikoff's "On an Ancient Mound," which Rosing delivered with suavity and with broad evenness of tone. It was good to hear again the "Foire de Sorotchinsky." Rosing made a good climax in the "Bleichmann," but in the "Onegin" I think, that the singing again betrayed the tendency which I remarked at his concert of two weeks before this, namely, that his constant singing of songs in very free rhythm has led him to carry freedom a little too far. A freedom of detail can only be durably effective if the sense of inner form is strong; one cannot hammer upon this too often; the musician or verse-writer who has the sense of form ingrained may take liberties in some safety, liberties which are fatal if the sense of form is not imminent, hovering, present without being obvious, but still present.

Again, Rosing's mimetic method is not free from danger; the songs he acts rather than sings lose their element of surprise, an element on which much of their initial effect depends; one would almost prescribe the drastic measure of having Rosing sing only formal music for, say, three or six months at a stretch; but popular favourites are not given to taking such strong purgatives on journalistic advice. The "Drunkard" was very well sung, the "Trepak" no better than last year; but, then, it couldn't be any better than it used to be, and the "Cui" encore was excellent.

I regret having missed the Coleridge-Taylor concert, Wigmore, December 7. The outlook for the rest of this month is not over exciting.

TINAYRE, Kent House, Knightsbridge, Friday, December 19th, at 3.15 p.m.

THE PYE-ANO[68]

The Pye-ano, Ge-entlemen, the PYE-ano is the largest musical instrument known to man, with the possible exceptions of the Steam Calliope Whistle or Fog Signal and the three-barrelled pipe-organ; of which the pipe-organ has one chief and especial merit—namely and to wit, its stability—I mean, "Where it is, there it rests," whereas the pye-ano may, with four fat men and considerable difficulty, be moved from one spot to another (Mr. Kipling to the contrary notwithstanding); all of which is no reason for pye-ano recitals outnumbering all other concerts three to one, or seven to one, or seventeen to one in the damp season.

Messrs. and Mesdames Leo Livens, Frances Coopman, Bryden Monteith, Harold Craxton, Anderson Tryrer, Margaret Tilly, and William Murdoch are all giving piano concerts as I write this (to say nothing of Mr. Vladimir Czernikoff, whose manager has, in apparent consideration of the multitude of other opportunities of my hearing piano music, refrained from drawing my attention to the Great Vladimir).

The future of piano music lies in the Jazz, and we may soon expect a much louder and more varied contraption with xylophone, whistle, and gong attachment in the treble octaves and solid steel bars in the bass. This new and forthcoming implement should, from present indications, present most of the advantages over the pye-ano that the original forte-piano did to its predecessors.

ANNE THURSFIELD (Wigmore, December 9) gave a serious song-recital, hindered by stiff crank-action and ligneous thudding of piano accompaniment. She was correct but inexpressive in "O cessate di piangarmi"; she displayed great delicacy of tone quality, but no fire, in "Pur dicesti"; her pianissimo tones were, in especial, delightful, but the drawing-room manner and the Christian village soprano qualities kept intruding upon the *"godor," "amor,"* and *"bacio"* of the text. Mrs. Thursfield became even more moral in "Sleepe," and for general

[68] *The New Age,* January 1, 1920, pp. 144–45.

remedy we can suggest nothing but a complete severance from respectable society. Technically, the flaw lies in not recognising that rhythm is made not merely by a correct division of music into bars of equal time-length, but also by a pluck and impact of accent; this applies to her rendering of "My Lovely Celia."

The "Pastoral" was another matter; in the trills and graces of this song Mrs. Thursfield gave impeccable pleasure, and one cannot too highly commend the quality and neatness of the runs and graces; she is perhaps better at singing la-la-lahs than in imparting a meaning to sung words; the final note of both strophes was perhaps a shade too strong; but, apart from that, the "Pastoral" was almost perfectly done. I use perfect in the strict sense, for here the singing gave unquestionable pleasure.

Jean Sterling Mackinlay has eminent capacity, but she does not steer by the pole-star of good taste; she often infuriates, but never quite bores one. Thus the "Souling Song" arranged by F. Maitland was nearly idiotic. The "Cherry Tree Carol" (Aeolian, December 9, in aid of Caldcott Community) is a fine thing, and was given with dignity. Mrs. Mackinlay definitely convinced one of her fine voice and her great capacity in this song. Her bad taste is puzzling, for it goes with a very considerable diligence of research. Her choristers followed her with Willbye's "As Fair as Morn," one of the finest of English part-songs, after which Baildon's "Once in England's Age of Gold" was anticlimatic. The rest of Mrs. Mackinlay's songs were mixed—one infuriating, one rubbish, one at least ("Il était une bergère") presented so that the subject-matter was clear to the audience.

Queen's Hall, December 10. Mr. Hamilton Harty conducted the Berlioz overture with firmness, possibly with a certain stiffness. Mr. Henry Coates' printed analysis informs us that it is somewhat curious that Berlioz was "unable to produce a successful opera"; yet, considering that the first five minutes of the "Benvenuto Cellini" make one feel as if one had been listening to it for half an hour, and as if it would take one three weeks to "get anywhere," we find the "somewhat" an extremely diminutive *quantum*. Mr. Coates also tells us that an "effect" is later "heightened" by tympani played with sticks covered with sponge. I could not, from the grand circle, see the little spongeous coverings, but I sincerely hope they were not left out or left off. Berlioz was indubitably competent, and one might be interested in his technique if Wagner hadn't buried him full fathoms fifteen. The bassoons are "augmented by two" for this overture, and one knows it. "The conventionalities of the operatic school of the period rather overshadow," etc. Yes, Mr. Coates, they do. Then concertos!

Piano concertos! At its birth the forte-piano seems to have turned people's heads; even so sensible a man as Thomas Jefferson ordered a forte-piano. Apologists claim that the earliest pianos preserved some of the qualities of the harpsichord. The present instrument is a sort of cheap substitute for an orchestra, the one instrument with enough variety and range to give a sort of shorthand account of music too complicated for a fiddle or 'cello or cornet. But to play a piano *with* an orchestra is anathema maranatha; it is the sum total of fatuous imbecility, and to prove it there is in Beethoven's "Emperor" concerto, in this Commodus of music, not one single and solitary motif or melody or salient line given to the piano which would not be more effective if it were played on any other instrument in the orchestra. Violin, oboe, flute, 'cello, tympani, any, absolutely *any*, of these instruments lifting a significant phrase from the body of the orchestral sound would be more effective; and there is demonstration of it whenever any other instrument or instruments is or are given a phrase to themselves. Part of the highest praise one can give to a piano soloist is that he or she gets varied *orchestral* effects from the piano; why the substitute when the richer medium is at hand? If a mania for pianos swept over Europe during an unfortunate period, can we not forgive, or at any rate forget, and let the piano concerto go to the proper scrap-heap of experiment, meritorious in its day, but no longer fit for conservation?

En passant, Mr. Anderson Tryer is perfectly competent; we cheerfully give him his certificate of capacity for playing with orchestra; only we wish he would realise that it is not the place for a piano.

Escaping from the Beethoven concerto, I found Mr. Bryden Monteith playing Bach at the Wigmore, with delightful fluidity and clearness, notes well sphered, phrases intelligent and sympathetic, and my wrath against all pianos was melted; then he abandoned Bach for a Schumann sonata which required more "dreaminess" and resignation than can be expected from any man who has to face three pianos between his dinner and breakfast.

At the Aeolian, Harold Craxton was playing his excellent arrangement of Arne's Sonata in B flat with great neatness, and Arne's precision came as an improvement on Schumann. Conventions he had, but after the "conventionalities of the operatic," etc., there was no eighteenth century convention of Arne which was not dew-fresh and full of pleasurability.

John Booth's chief difficulty seemed to be that he could not sing two hundred and forty-seven words per Pelman minute without losing tone quality. He sighed and sobbed through a sentimental George Macdonald, with the proper "not a dry eye" intonation; but in the more rapid songs one was conscious chiefly of vocal strain, bad production. He is mature enough to have learned to let out his voice.

Psychological speculation, or, rather, pathological, the pleasure of *playing* a piano with orchestra as opposed to *hearing* a piano played with orchestra, is explicable on the grounds of exhilaration. The feeling that one is being so accomplishedly agile, so rippingly and dashingly efficient as to get one's fingers onto all the notes in good time with the conductor probably sustains the *player;* he gets the same physical pleasure as he might from quick and clever use of the foils in a fencing bout; he has no attention left for auditory sensation. Parallel case that of the inebriated or excited talker who imagines he or she is being "brilliant" merely because of rapid trajectory.

But as the player receives this pleasure, he ought to pay the audience (on the official "classic" Greek system), not they him.

From the correspondence column of *The New Age*, January 15, 1920:

> Sir,—I am one of your regular subscribers, but together with several of your other readers with whom I have compared notes, I have been constantly exasperated by the articles of your music critic. His effort last week has really gone a bit too far. I do not know who Mr. Atheling is, or what your reasons may be for maintaining him on the staff of your paper, but he gives himself away in every article he writes as an ignoramus of the first water where music is concerned. One might overlook his repulsive flippancy if his judgment were correct, and if he knew how to criticize impartially.
>
> How can you employ a musical critic who avowedly dislikes the piano and ridicules everything to do with it?
>
> The present article is the first for many weeks on the subject of piano-playing. Mr. Atheling deigns only to mention the least distinguished pianists and completely ignores the three supreme artists (supermen of the piano)—Busoni, Cortot, and Arthur Rubinstein, whom we have recently had in our midst. His remarks qua the pianoforte concerto are preposterous. I am sure that if every member of the audience at Queen's Hall this afternoon, who heard de Greef's masterly performance of the Grieg Concerto, were confronted with Mr. Atheling's article, they would relegate it and *him* to the "scrap-heap" which he himself recommends.
>
> Rose G. Morley

MUSIC[69]

London has, as is well known, a new star among orchestral conductors. Mr. Albert Coates, the much-discussed, has evolved a style. At the Queen's Hall (December 17) the Overture to "Le Nozze" was presented with the bar divisions clearly marked. Mr. Coates seemed to have ingurgitated the music on the basis of those little perpendicular lines, and the idea of music as a structure of larger pieces of rhythm did not emerge, nor did the underflow of the work become apparent. Marguerite Nielka seemed to find certain Balkanic impediments between herself and "Voi che sapete"; the words were indistinct, the singing good enough to have passed in a performance of the whole opera, but lacking distinction, and not interesting enough to stand being sung apart from the context. In "Non so piu" the words were not heard; they were too faint and swallowed, but the voice was capable of filling the hall with ease and sweetness.

In these arias Coates got the real pull of the music, as differentiated from the mere division of rhythm. He carried the music over the singer, or imposed it upon her. The double basses did excellent work. In the Gluck "Orpheus" Coates showed his authority over his orchestra. In the "Iphigenie" the violins were excellent. Madame Nielka's French was difficult to follow; she pronounced père peire, yelled slightly in one or two places, and was up to the general level of English opera; toward the end of the recitative she missed a number of chances. Perhaps Coates' best conducting was in the exquisite introduction to the "Air."

The last movement of Korsakov's Scheherazade suite is a triumph of orchestration. The mastery is everywhere present; one notes the perfect scale and graduation from one instrument, from the delicacy of the solo violin, to the massed thunder of the whole ensemble of instruments; here for once one has the whole demonstration of causes why the orchestra has superseded chamber music, why this huge instrument has swept away so much of the fine work made for instruments of smaller calibre. In the "Alabief" which was not worth singing, but which gave a chance for technical display, the voice seemed older than the woman producing it.

The starred number was the Scriabin "Poème d'Extase." Here, as in the Korsakov, Coates showed his realisation of the capacities of his orchestra, but the *extase* is senescent; it is manifestly not the *extase* of youth; the long beginning is like the prose of its era, heavy as Henry James or as Charles Louis Phillippe, fin de siècle, of an extreme and laborious sophistication, Coates doing admirably, Scriabin conscientiously avoiding the obvious in everything save the significance, and

[69] *The New Age,* January 15, 1920, pp. 175–76 .

treating one of the oldest topics with anatomic minuteness, though possibly unconscious of his humour, anatomic even to the notes given on the triangle, spurring one to quotations from Gautier's "Carmen." The double basses superb, but one longed, possibly, for the older spirit of English May-day. It is too late to emend the title; we quarrel with no work of art because of title lightly or sarcastically given, but we think Scriabin would have been kinder to his audience if he had labelled this poème "Satire upon an Old Gentleman," or possibly "Confessions of Trouble," supposing all the time he "knew." We entertain doubts, however, as to just how far his awareness extended.

While the public can find orchestral concerts, price the same, it is a little difficult to discover why they go at all to piano recitals, and with the flow of time one rather wonders at young men taking up the piano as a profession. The onus upon the solo-pianist is very heavy; if he divides his concert with a vocalist, he becomes, at once, second fiddle; and to entertain an audience for an hour or more with nothing but a piano is exceedingly difficult, and it grows more and more difficult as the public becomes more and more familiar with piano repertoire.

Ivan Phillopowsky (Wigmore, December 15) held the attention of the company, though the first three Scarlatti sonatas sounded a little too familiar. In the D minor (fourth in the series) he maintained the movement with delicacy, making a firmer advance and getting the maximum effect in the fifth. The sixth was of less importance and interest. He showed a good deal of ease and power in the Schumann F sharp minor, with richness and breadth in upper bass and enough drama to keep one awake; there was a slight break at beginning of scherzo; he picked up the intermezzo, though the railroading in the allegro was not commendable.

Yves Tinayre (Kent House, December 19) gave a wholly delightful presentation of French war songs from the Middle Ages to the present. In the "Mort Renaud" there was roughness in transition from narrative to dramatic passages. It is difficult to maintain the unity in these ballads unless one either act the whole or give the whole in formal narration; at any rate, one should not break *too suddenly* from formalism into realism. Tinayre sang the song, and indeed the whole series of songs, very finely with larger and easier voice than last year. "Jerusalem Mirabilis," the fine movement in "Gentle Soldier of France," the development of rhythm in "Trois Jeunes Tambours" with its superb climax, the élan of "Gallant Soldier," the "En Passant par la Lorraine," combined to make a memorable afternoon, and should have served as demonstration to any doubter that the maximum emotional effect of singing is gained by presentation and not by sentimentality. The "Trois Jeunes

Tambours" especially in the suddenness of its turn to the climax is a model of how to make a brief narrative, and Tinayre's singing of it beyond cavil.

The discomfort of the audience when he left the wars in lace and sang "La Carmagnole" was still further tribute to the reality and conviction of his work; the spirit of 1793 arose and breathed all too vividly for the Knightsbridge gathering.

Tinayre had admirably chosen his songs to convey France of the Middle Ages, France of the Grand Siècle, and the France of revolution and democracy. "Le Chant du Départ" was splendid, and had all the vigour which faddists and sentimentalists, during the Dostoievsky craze, used to attribute solely to Russia. "Au près de ma Blonde" and "Fanfan la Tulipe" were typically French popular art, and the "Marseillaise" is possibly the only national anthem that can be raised to the status of music by competent singing.

It is a great shame that one does not hear the "Carmagnole" more often, though it is perhaps just as well for established order in general that music of this sort should be reserved for polite surroundings.

Rosing (Æolian, December 13) showed superb suavity in Glinka's "Ask not a Song," the voice rich and subtle in graduations, Di Veroli in excellent form. The vocalist then managed to transform our English Purcell into a totally new and unknown Russian composer, and "Thy Hand Beloved" into vers libre; there is nothing to be said against these innovations *if* the new composer turns out to be better than the old one. Personally I prefer Purcell as he was. The Wagner "Rêves" opened with fine moderation. Strain showed in "Rossignol." The Moussorgsky "Star" by itself was worth the price of admission, and the "Hoi, my Dniepr," superb, bravura, distance, rhythm. Both Rosing and Veroli showed great delicacy in the Korsakov encore.

Rosing next gave a splendid rendering of the Countess's death scene from "The Queen of Spades," but in the Aria one knew again that Tschaikovsky does not hold after Moussorgsky.

The three groups made a noteworthy concert. I should have stayed for Albert Coates' "Cossack Song," but for an unsurmountable obstacle, announced brazenly in the programme.

Those who shared our high opinion of Constantin Stroesco's capacities will not be surprised to hear that he has received a two years' engagement to sing the difficult rôle of Pelléas at L'Opéra Comique in Paris. His absence from London is to be regretted. There are singers who have received warmer receptions in London who could not possibly hope for entrance at L'Opéra Comique, and one cannot help rather enjoying such confirmation of one's own estimate in this particular case.

MUSIC[70]

The London Trio (A. Goodwin, piano; Pecskai, violin; Whitehouse, 'cello), essayed (Aeolian, Jan. 6), the Schubert Grand Trio in E. flat. In the opening Allegro we had the piano wooden, but in its proper place, with the graduations of softness and loudness well considered. The Grand Trio is a fine example of the typically Schubertian, and, as rendered, was well starched and neat; music of the dress-suit and shirt-front variety. Mr. Whitehouse, temperate in his use of the 'cello; total result that the first movement neither bored nor greatly encouraged one; it suggested theatre rather than life: stage savannahs.

In the second movement Whitehouse dragged at the opening; Pecskai was not up to his old form; there was also a drag from the piano, on which instrument the notes were played but insensitized. It was "British Official" piano playing, with jerks rather than sinuosities; eminently not sloppy, but, with equal certainty, neither music of seraph nor siren. At times the piano part might have been managed by beating a barrel-head with a mallet; and at times it was musical.

The player seemed to stop dead at the end of every bar. It is probable that bar-ends should be clearly marked, but this line of demarcation is geometric; it should have no thickness; above all, it should not be a dead stop stock-still, requiring each time a subsequent heave to "start 'er agayne."

Muriel Brunskill has no Italian and no expression; she has a large voice, but no graduation; she jumps from loud to soft. This may have been due to "nerves," but we doubt it. She needs three years' training before her next public appearance, she really knew nothing, absolutely and utterly nothing, about Gluck's "Che faro"; but she has a voice that should repay arduous labour, really a fine voice. We hope sincerely to hear her again after a long, a really long, interval.

MISCHA-LEON (Aeolian, January 10) was rich and moderate in the Gluck Recitatif and Cavatine, but with a slight sappiness where the music may be held to require a curious sort of dryness (granting the reader can conceive a species of dryness which is a virtue) for its finest interpretation. Any criticism which seeks to carry the analysis of musical qualities beyond banality must plunge into words easily ridiculable by gentlemen of ill-will. We will accept emendation of the term dryness from anyone who will find a better term for the difference between the eighteenth century "soul" of Gluck and the rather nineteenth century mode of Mischa-Leon's interpretation.

Felix Fourdrain's "Le Papillon" is the usual and stereotype modern

---

[70] *The New Age,* February 5, 1920, pp. 220–21.

French; Rhené-Baton's "Au Désert" is the almost equally stereotyped modern-French melodramatic mode. Leon got delicacy and sweetness into Baton's "Berceuse" without much finesse or tensity; again we found a slight roundness where an edge or a sense of clean rectangles would have helped one. Albert Roussel's "Bachelier de Salamanque" was the usual Debussy playfulness. The general and, perhaps, the sole defect of this group was that Mischa-Leon was singing derivative poetry set to derivative music. There was nothing definitely very bad, but nothing superlative.

We were then subjected to Elgar's setting of "Speak, Music," arranged for quartet accompaniment by A. H. Behrend. ("Augier, crinoline, parapluie!") Pastiche of many old melodies all undistinguished, typical English hymn tune phrases for the setting of the line-ends, "bid me rest" and "bright and blest"; words indistinctly sung. Some relief came with the pleasant opening of "Holbrooke's" "Anabel Lee" (Josef, Joseph, or some other member of that talented family, I cannot say.)[71] He was put down simply as "Holbrooke," and he has—for purposes of identification—set Poe's "Anabel Lee," a poem containing considerable excess verbiage and no little sentimentality.

This poem is evidently addressed to the senile, for it begins with a remark that "it was many, many years ago." We are then told that "a maiden there lived," "whom you may know," ergo, q.e.d. age on part of auditor. The maiden who "*there* lived" in line three, patronymic Lee; arrives in fifth line sic: "And this maiden *she* lived."

If anybody but a man with a great international reputation had written this first stanza our literary critics would tell us that it was very badly written, and full of remplisage, of words, that is, chucked in to fill up the metric scheme, and for no other reason; and that these words in no way assist the poetic intensity or any other quality of the poem; and that this remplisage displays no mastery whatsoever on the part of its author.

In fact, if Baudelaire had not translated some of Poe's tales, and if Poe hadn't been a tragic figure, and if the symbolistes in Paris hadn't stewed about the matter, and if Mallarmé hadn't translated the "Raven" into one of the worst pieces of arty prose extant in the French langauge (refrain "Et le corbeau dit 'Jamais Plus' "), and if, above all, the poem weren't a piece of sentimentalism, it might not have been set at all, or sung on January 10, 1920.

Poe, let us record it to his glory, said that some of his poems were exercises built to a formula, but certain people always know more about a man's mind and intentions than he himself does, and many "learned"

---

[71] See Atheling's reply to J. Holbrooke's letter, note 60, p. 186.

and imperceptive professors and publishers' puffers have since contradicted the author of "The House of Usher," no doubt to the profit of themselves and of publishers.

Now, however well Mr. Holbrooke may have set this verbose poem, and he has set it quite well, it is impossible that there should not be some corresponding remplisage in the music; and the whole would, we believe, gain if the poem-scaffolding (which, as sung, bored one to death before the end of the second strophe) were cast aside—having served its turn—and if the remaining musical structure were then purged of all superfluous bits, i.e., of all notes and bars and elements which do not contribute to its entity as a piece of music.

The little squawks in the fourth strophe might go. I believe, however, that a very presentable string quartet could be rescued from the remains.

But for the Holbrooke setting to Tennyson's "Come not when I am dead," we find very little excuse. Leon sang it badly; "not" was sung "notcht"; "sick" as "sickcht," in the old "Shakespearian regular drama" style of ranting, but the composer had done equally ill; there was meaningless acceleration at "upon my grave," an over-emphasis where even the late Laureate had been at least consistent. Then the words ascended into a howl; the music into cliché phrasing.

KENNEDY-FRASER recitals, March 6 and March 30 (Saturdays), at 3 p.m., Aeolian Hall.

CERNIKOFF[72]

While various excited people have been throwing bricks at the commentator for his scepticism, Vladimir Cernikoff has brought the scholarship of a lifetime to the most ample discussion of the piano and of piano music that London has had for some decades. His series of six recitals present the whole argument. With his clear-headed demonstration, his technical finish, and, beyond all, his ability to sympathise with each composer, from the earliest writer for spinets to the last Russian, he is an ideal performer for just this historic survey. He is infinitely better as a demonstrator than a Beethoven specialist like Lamond, or a talent like Busoni, who gives one, often, a magnificent afternoon by displaying how he, Busoni, can utterly transform the notes of a composer into some thing of his own, wholly different and rather better.

On January 26 (Aeolian) Cernikoff had got to 1770. Hummel was shown still running on in the manner of the old writers for pre-piano; Field was shown as a fore-amber of Chopin. Not even the best historic

---

[72] *The New Age*, February 19, 1920, pp. 254–55.

schematisation can infuse interest into the sentimental maunder of Mendelssohn. As a record of what things have existed, two or three pieces of Mendelssohn's should be played annually by Cernikoff at the Royal College of Music, for the enlightenment and warning of students. This would be quite enough Mendelssohn for one year, and even a demonstration in alternate years might be sufficient.

On the other hand, we are firmly of the opinion that Cernikoff ought to give his full course of six recitals every year, and, if not in connection with the Royal College, at least attendance should be required from all students contemplating the "piano as a career"; for, by the time he has completed his series, Cernikoff will have summarised the history and scope of the instrument. He is a very capacious anthologist, and there is little alteration to suggest in his schema, though Steibelt might be added. He would be pleasant to hear—pleasanter than Field or Mendelssohn, but not illustrative as the latter.

The Schumann "Carnaval" was given as literature, and it has the durability of literature. Here one forgot the history and settled in to solid enjoyment of Cernikoff's skill and intelligence. The Brahms B minor rhapsody has a sentimental start, and there is not a great deal of intelligence in it; this in contrast with the Schumann "Carnaval," where one definitely sees the "given concentration of knowledge on the given portion of surface." (Put aside quibbles on terms "knowledge," "intelligence," etc., one does not get the needful *concentration* of these without emotion or passion either present or foregoing.) There is a soft loveliness in the Brahms A major intermezzo, and Cernikoff gathered his very great skill into the rendering of Hungarian dance.

In estimating the piano (not as played by pyanists, but in its capacity) one must admit that it is the only modern instrument upon which the solo player can exercise so much musical knowledge and comprehension. It is louder than the spinet or clavichord, it has mechanical advantages over the harpsichord, and is probably less trouble to keep in order. It will reign supreme in the parlour until the pianola and the gramophone have democratised it out of existence. It is, from the auditor's point of hearing, inferior to the orchestra. Public demonstrations of the instrument are in great part incubatorial, designed for and attended by people who wish to pianise. A great artist can get music out of his instrument. So can some players from a brass string and a cigar-box. A few piano recitals each year are worth hearing. Cernikoff's Schumann was worth hearing—very much so. Further recitals, Saturdays, February 14 and March 13, Aeolian, at 3 p.m.

Returning to my archives, I find that Dorothy Robson (January 14, Aeolian) displayed some merit and insufficient technique, also considerable briskness; that she distorted words, and that in her Brahms songs she trotted out all the sentiment of all the German young ladies since Werther's tears first came into prominence and fell from vicarious eyelids. Mathilde Verne had taken the sub-title "Moonlight" very much to heart, also the direction "adagio" in the Beethoven sonata. I have no doubt that the Mendelssohn (Andante, etc.), announced for a later reach of the programme, was admirably suited to her equipment; but I decided, with no qualms whatsoever, that I had an engagement elsewhere.

Megan Foster showed herself (Aeolian, January 15, at 8.15) to be what is called on the Continent "très anglaise." C. V. Stanford has flattened the rhythm out of Byron's "There be none of Beauty's Daughters." The recital proceeded with cambric tea; one felt it was for an audience which "ought to have been in bed earlier." Then, when Miss Foster got to the air from Robert Jones, one knew that some music-hall manager was waiting, that some Revue was incomplete, and that fortune will certainly dump Exchequer bonds into her lap when once she appears in this milieu.

Of the French songs, the Chausson was beautiful, but requires more art than Miss Foster possesses. For the Debussy she needs three years' study; Moussorgsky has treated the theme to which Ravel has done Nicolette, and with much greater vigour. Rootham has made quite a good or goodish modern French accompaniment for "Noël."

Next arrived Mr. Ivor Foster with heavy sentiment, very male in manner. The music was such as Masefield deserves; also, the singer was the ideal singer to convey the inner inwardness of these "bold bad sailormen abaft the rahn' (round) pon' (pond)" in bashy the Bo'sun ballads. I am not sure that Mr. Foster did not attain a naïveté even a shade naïver than the author could have believed. "The chief" (to quote my colleague, Mr. Hope)—"the voice breaks at the word"! "I ain't never had no schoolin', nor read no books like you," sobs the bellowing Bo'sun, as no Bo'sun has ever sobbed, save when protected by a boiled shirt of immaculate whiteness.

Ethel Hobday and Felix Salmond gave a delightful piano-'cello recital, three sonatas, Wigmore, January 17. Miss Hobday began with good piano volley, and she had been fortunate enough to find a good instrument (Steinway); Salmond, as usual, brought clear amber tone from his 'cello, and one forgets to analyse when he plays, forgets as one only forgets a few times each season. The Ropartz sonata is pleasing, not remarkable, not "modern," probably a permanent part of 'cello-piano repertoire. The familiar Brahms F major, Op. 99 was finely done; one wonders just what vocabulary or superlatives one is expected to reserve for such work—expected, that is, by the reader who wants one to gush over every scraper of catgut. The piano may have been just a little soft (downy) in places; the 'cello just a little too submerged, like phosphorus under sea-water, or the course of a fish half-seen. In the Grieg I think the 'cello was definitely lost at moments where it should not have been, especially in the more rapid passages. But this sonata amply demonstrated the limitations of the Ropartz. These comments are merest marginalia; the whole recital was excellent.

Kennedy-Fraser recitals, Saturdays, March 6 and 20, Aeolian, at 3 p.m.

Rosing recitals, March 27 and April 17, Aeolian, Saturdays, at 3 p.m. Cernikoff as above.

MUSIC[73]

We may add Douglas Marshall to our brief list of enjoyable singers. He has a pleasing manner and is to be heard with some respect. On January 27 (Æolian) he gave the best presentation of Poldowski's songs I have yet heard. There is an excellent end to the accompaniment of "Circonspection." In "Dans une Musette" the composer employs the modern French method with no inconsiderable technique, though the thing is not quite finished, and the singer exaggerated "des cris," etc., in the middle of it. There is excellent melodic accommodation of the words and verbal quality in the first half of "Fantoches." There are good spots in the accompaniment of "Impression Fausse." "Spleen" begins with sentimentalism and ends with a yell. The best of the recital was the Bassani; the singer gargled a little over "sguardo," but the "Che dolente," etc., and the "E, ad altro," etc., were delightfully sung, also the Minuet. One is grateful for someone who will sing music of this quality and who can sing it.

There is not much to be said for Louis Aubert as a composer if the four songs by him were illustrative. The first was a bore, the second showed no compositorial intelligence—tenuous Debussyism and no recommendable features. The songs with accompaniments reconstructed from Dowland's lute tablature were of uneven merit. The first was included presumably out of respect to the period, the second had the aroma; in the third the singer shifted various words like "Care" and "Pain" without much altering the sense of the poem. "Rest Awhile" was sung rather too slowly. "Wilt thou unkind" is well written, and "Away with these self-loving lads" is billed for an encore every time. So also the extra Dowland given as the second encore.

[73] *The New Age,* February 26, 1920, pp. 268–69.

Mr. Marshall should count on very solid support if he will go on giving us Bel Canto and Dowland. We suppose Aubert is a personal friend of the singer's, and in gratitude for the Bassani we should perhaps be willing to waive the matter.

Jessie Snow (Queen's Hall, January 22) was preceded by the London Symphony Orchestra, which discoursed a light and not unpleasing description of "Pippa Passes" by Hamilton Harty. Mr. Harty had got the general date of Pippa; the music can in no sense be called creative. Wieniawski, rather like Harty, but more florid, provided the score for Miss Snow's stiff-arm violining. She has no very remarkable sense of rhythm, and one fled at the first pause in the music.

Arriving at the Æolian, one found Miss *Gwenhilda Birkett* playing a good firm cello with even tone, with a fine time sense, and no mess whatsoever. She put a vitality into Grieg that one does not habitually associate with that composer. She had even galvanised her accompanist, the well-known Mr. F. B. Kiddle, into a temporary musician. (We believe this to be no mean achievement.) Her playing is at once tense and sinuous, and her distinction a sort of Attic severity. She next tried a piece of her own composition. Emphatically we are in favour of performers being sufficiently musicians to be able to compose; there is no reason why Miss Birkett should not play this cello solo in public; there is no reason why anyone else should. At the start the composer seems somewhat unable to "get off the mark." The main impression is of feminine irritation rather than of emotion, and the whole expressed in rather copybook style; but for all that it is of interest that the performer, this performer, any performer, should give the public evidence of being just this much more than a reciter of other men's themes when the performer can do so. One hopes that Miss Birkett will have composed another item and that she will play it at her next recital. In her third number she attempted to be accompanied by both piano and organ simultaneously. By some utterly unforeseen and probably unrepeatable miracle these two instruments were mutually in tune, but the effect was rather that of a stunt.

The concert was shared with Mr. Hubert Eisdell: attar of roses and Twickenham—oh, very, very Twickenham manner. Even more so than Mr. Ivor Foster. Pale, saccharescent, lily pronounced "lee," playful Vaughan Williams on Stevenson (great success with the audience). Jocund pronounced "jukk-und." Sort of singing called "English" by hostile nations.

LAHDA, the Russian arty society, burst upon a Beardsleyised world at the Wigmore, dance and song, the child-naïve, clever stage set, considering the possibilities of Wigmore platform, and Rosing as a Chas.

Chaplin among the eighteenth-century grand dukes, a rippling and contagious success. Also he sang magnificently from beneath his exaggerated shako, Chaplin moustache no impediment.

THE UKRAINIAN NATIONAL CHOIR (Queen's Hall, February 3) gave us the best part-singing I have heard in London. It is like a huge organ with human pipes, and upon it Alexander Koshitz plays with incomparable skill. Technically there seems nothing it cannot perform, and perform with all the subtleties of graduation and of approach and recession. The music of the Ukraine, as exhibited at the Tuesday recital, was not, however, of very great interest either rhythmically or thematically. "Saint Barbara" was just the same old hymn-tune germane to all countries whose music has been watered by Churchianity. Our "Lady of Potchaiv" was the real thing, and the fine solo voice magnificent. The trail of the church was over "Guardian Angel." So also with the Xmas Carols. We suppose the Gladstonian policy has impressed these Ukrainians and that they think it necessary to prove to the earnest British auditor that they are a pious and Christian people. I wish they would choose some other medium than song for this communication. When they get free of Gregory they are more interesting. "Jordan," "Sctchedryk," and "Behind the Mountain" were pleasing. Koshitz arrangement of the "Young Monk" was excellent, also the "Violin Playing in the Street." "Poor Hawthorne" was Christian wail.

What struck one most was the discrepancy between the capacity of the choir, capacity for every vocal effect, and presumably for the rendering of any and every rhythmical subtlety, and the paucity of theme and of rhythm-invention in the music—nothing comparable to Negro or Hebridean music, or to the Russian tunes we have had from Rosing. The actual part writing or arrangement of the tunes for the eighty voices was delightful. Given a more interesting melodic basis one would be wholly enchanted. As it is, one rather regrets all this ability flowing away upon nonconformist religio-sentimental modalities and Moody and Sankey inventions. Even the final "God Save the King" was hardly a musical anti-climax—all of which simply means that an incomparable instrument and a vast amount of performing energy are being more or less wasted. Given better subject-matter this choir could be one of the delights of the world. Their present repertoire is perhaps only one more of the crimes of the nationalist fallacy. We suppose they *must* sing Ukrainian music if they are to remain a "national" choir, but the sooner they internationalise the better we shall be, musically, pleased. No praise is too high for their actual singing.

MUSIC[74]

Cernikoff continued his argument for and against the piano, at the Æolian Hall, February 14; the answer in so far as it concerns Chopin was, and always has been, in the affirmative. It is particularly in the affirmative when we get the real Chopin malely and firmly done. In the Variations we had romance, flowing water, colour of light in water, reflections on Venetian canals; delicacy in the valses, maintenance of the upper and nether wave in Etude Op. 12. After showing us that he could Chopinize à la 1830, Cernikoff took the "Bolero" à la Derain-Matisse, Boutique-fantasque period; it was great fun and a definite Cernikoff creation. There was lucidity in his enunciation of the Etudes Op. 25. Then ill luck overtook him; in the Polonaise the intoxication of kinesis got the better of him. After a splendid opening he suddenly forgot where he was and what he was doing; there was a blank, the notes continued with nothing inside them, he "lost his audience," he awoke to the fact several minutes too late. This is a sheer accident, a sort of aphasia or arhythmodia or whatever the correct term may be, that might happen to anyone. Emphatically Cernikoff is coming into his own, the public is beginning to recognise his remarkable equipment, and one only notes with transient regret a contretemps in this gradual trend. There was no one in the hall, I think, who did not, during the first part of the programme, realise what magnificent music Cernikoff can produce.

The second half of the programme was Liszt, the interest largely historic; St. Francis and the birds is a bore, the Sonata was well interpreted, with emphasis on line, colours heavily defined as if by wide black circumferential lines, emphasis on the construction, the thing divided by a series of brick walls, dull thuds without resonance (presumably with intention), this in contrast with delicate reverie, an interesting reading, and the dead thuds allowed the finale to sink into the tone, for contrast.

As the programme preface stated, Liszt outlived the romantics; he wrote transcriptions of other men's music. He did also a piano version of the Liebestod, and he was a rather heavy-minded individual. He had gifts, but it is questionable how far this is a matter for rejoicing.

Rosing was in form on February 7, interesting pianissimo in opening Korsakoff, with great variety; in the Tscherepnin he displayed several new developments, inventions he had not before given us. There was fine team work between him and Di Veroli in the Wassilenko. Then, if my memory serves me, he sang (exquisitely) a Mozart, a good melodic line with sounds bearing some relation to the English language.

As usual, Moussorgsky rose from its context, a better art, a due

---

[74] *The New Age,* March 11, 1920, pp. 309–10.

melodic weight. Tschaikowsky set a fine poem, "Nights of Madness"; it was dramatically sung, and this term is not unqualified praise. The melody does not "take the voice" as does Moussorgsky's. In the Debussy "Beau Soir" the exquisite text makes a true verbal contribution to the whole effect.

Then Rosing humbly asked if he might sing Schumann in German. The audience greeted the proposition with enthusiasm, but their hopes were disappointed. Rosing sings but two languages: Russian and Rosing. That is to say, he may, for all I know, sing a Rosing-Russian, but in the Russian songs one does not expect to grasp each word clearly, and the present critic, at any rate, has no exact criteria for Russian pronunciation. The Russian numbers are incomprehensible without the libretto; even a libretto is very little guide to the verbalism of the other tongues alleged to be in process of delivery. The Lowenson Serenade was delightful. The Rossini was spirited and full of larks, etc., in all, a good concert. The next is on March 27, Æolian, at 3 p.m.

Douglas Marshall (February 24, Æolian) is, as I have before stated, a pleasant singer. I doubt if he knows of the existence of art. He has a fine voice, likes to sink it into abysmal depths, and his French sounds continental. Mallarmé's "Sainte" is hardly lyric, the first of the Greek "folk songs" has been fiddled up to drawing-room tone by Ravel, much as the 18th century put the classics into lace and silk breeches. It compares most unconvincingly with, for example, Stroesco's Roumanian folk songs.*

"Là bas vers l'église" has an interesting accompaniment which was well played, although Raymer is not a particularly satisfactory accompanist. Quel Galant had some of the real thing in it. The words of Ceuilleuses de lentisques are not lyric, but the music has a beautiful melodic line. "Tout gai" was folk with bravura.

Renaud's "Le Paon" emphasised once more, ah, once, if it were only once more that we should have it emphasised, that the mode Paris 1892-1910 is over. It is as uninteresting as a Paquin model for 1894; Le Paon is playful and has a circus accompaniment.

Then we were let in for a cantata. Now if it is imbecile to sing ring-a-round-a-rosy words with a serious meaning, it is doubly imbecile to sing such words when they do not even give good, open vowel sounds for the long notes and ligatures. In the "Ich habe genug" one might, so far as the notes are concerned, sing, "Two scones and butter were seen on the plate"; the auditory pleasure would be equal to that of hearing "There I too with Simeon the joy," etc. If we were to respect tradition

* Three times, since last writing, people have said to me, "You know Stroesco was," etc., and I have refrained from replying, "A qui le dites vous?" (Atheling).

as some people understand that phrase we should have to preserve every idiocy of mankind. People have got used to Cantatas and therefore they are, for some people, "good." They remind people of their lost youth. All right; but there is no reason why succeeding generations should not be reminded of different lost youths.

The stupid and customary traditionalist always stops at a set year, i.e., the year where his teacher taught him to stop. The customary traditionalist never goes to history when history is likely to trouble his stagnation. We presume that the Sequaire is the ancestor of the Cantata. Mediæval choirs sang in descant on "amens" and "hallelujahs," these decants got longer and longer, it became difficult to remember the long series of notes on mere vowel sounds, various writers, notably Goddeschalk, then wrote in words to *fit* the notes of the descant.[75] This produced the Sequaire and the fruit was a justification. But after the lapse of seven centuries it is no justification of the English translation of "Ich habe genug," which has no merits and does not fit the music. Marshall would have done better to sing do-re-mi. The statement that the protagonist "has enough" is doubly true of the auditor before the singer has forty-seven times bade him "softly sleep." As it is Bach there is naturally staunch melodic line and fine music.

Rounds and part songs are another matter altogether. In them the word phrase holds the musical phrase in the minds of the different groups of singers. The Cantata is merely a superstition, a keeping of structure after its function is gone.

Marshall followed Plunket Greene, at a distance in "Seventeen come Sunday," pleasantly in the third strophe. He succeeded in the Kennedy-Fraser Hebridean numbers and would do well to try some of the more ambitious pieces from that repertoire. "Royal Oak" was the real thing, folk song, not Coliseum, and not in danger of becoming so, as had been "I'm seventeen." This was perhaps his best effect. Bear in mind that he is a delightful singer. He has little Italian, and got no meaning into the second strophe of "I pastori." Again we have heard singers walk into Stroesco's repertoire only to stir memories unfavourable to them-

---

[75] Goddeschalk, better known as Notker Balbulus (d. 912), a monk of St. Gall, Switzerland, was one of the originators of the Sequence, or as Pound has it, the Sequaire. It began as one of the main forms of interpolation in the ordinary of the Roman Catholic mass. As the melismatic character of certain portions of the mass, notably the Alleluia, increased, texts, at first in prose and later in poetry, were fitted to these extended melodies, rendering them again into syllabic types of song. Pound intends to demonstrate here his preference for this syllabic type of song as against melismatic song, typified by J. S. Bach's arias. Goddeschalk, whom he mentions relatively frequently in his writings (e.g., in the *Rock-Drill Cantos*), was apparently first known to Pound from Rémy de Gourmont's *Le Latin mystique*.

selves. In San Basilio he showed the gap between singing, quite nice singing, and art. Fiaba has a bad setting.

On the whole we retain our first impression of Mr. Marshall, but he should house-clean his stock of music.

MUSIC[76]

Anne Thursfield (Wigmore, March 2) again displayed her talents and the folly of not recognising the scope of one's personal aptitudes. Her lace-china effects are all that could be desired, but Doric severities and savage mood are not for her. In Handel and Scarlatti her grace and fine shading were effective, though the verbal sense was not exploited to the full. A credit mark must be given for accenting *"Cosi"* correctly and in contradiction to usual warbler of Monteverde.

The second group of songs was by the "Younger British School," a group of composers in whom we would willingly find some serious consideration of the art of music. A. Bax had chosen a rather good poem by J. H. Cousins, and set it to a simple air, but as the word-rhythm is not very interesting and the music uninspired the result is not memorable. Goossens' "Wild Geese" is trite, with worn pitch intervals, and derivative wash melody. The translation of Tagore chosen by J. A. Carpenter is not lyric; it is provided with pseudo-Debussy accompaniment, in the spirit of "In winter I get up at night," but even so it might be taken as an argument that free word cadences offer more to mediocre musicians than the habitual iambic of fourth-rate versifiers. The danger of making "juice" an homophone for "Jews" in the last strophe should be overcome by the singer.

The Minuet was delightfully done, but Mrs. Thursfield's delicate "vocalisation" is inapposite for narrative ballads, and "Trois Princesses" lacked intensity. The Korsakov was excellent; but the singer had not caught the robustezza inherent in the American Negro songs, and the roll and lap-over of rhythm were absent from her Glory Hallelujahs. The "Ol' Ark" is not a dirge.

Doris Montrave (Aeolian, March 2, evening) illustrates just the difference between pleasant singing like Douglas Marshall's and the art of singing. She has a firm, clean-hitting voice, and gives the sense of her subject-matter, sense of the text. Her songs by Scarlatti, Falconieri and Lully might "serve as communication between intelligent beings"— and this compliment is as rare as it is pleasant to give.

Ill fate also tempted her to sing Parry, Bridge, and Palmgren. She

[76] *The New Age*, March 25, 1920, pp. 338–39.

overshot the finale of the first Parry, the second was "Kathleen Mavourneen" falsified by Parry's top-dressing. "My Garden" was rubbish, and the group continued to deteriorate. There was a little merit in the J. Ireland number, and it was well sung. Poldowski's music at least projects from the ruck of its contemporaries, but "Panyre" is full of overemphasis and blank cartridges. It is too late for anyone to throw a fit over its anti-Victorian climax. A lot of this stuff, including Debussy's "Des Fleurs," is no more master-work than the average novel of commerce is literature.

Hüe's "L'âne blanc," which Stroesco used to give with such fine *ciselure*, was sung like a Poldowski, i.e., without the precise carving and clarity, more through ill judgment in placing it at the end of the group and programme when the singer was exhausted, than through inherent inability to sing it with distinction.

The average of this modern French stuff is poor; now that the novelty is worn off, one is soon bored with the eternal hurry and slow-up, the continued waste of musical means employed by the school. We will hear Miss Montrave with respect, and hope that at our next opportunity she will take subjects worthy of her ability.

Beatrice Eveline, in the same concert, played the 'cello with clear, light, resonant tone; a fine strength and a "reality," with a sense that it is intelligent force not mere muscular energy which makes music. There was passionate lament in the elegy, *gallego* humour and spirit in the "Serenade Espagnol," and, although Cui has not really attained the Arabic feeling in his "Orientale," the work was delightfully rendered.

I wish to make it clear that both these women have distinction. One might wish to alter Miss Montrave's programme (that is easily done), but one did not feel that one was listening to a fool. Certain of her effects cannot be produced without precise knowledge of emotion; this is, perhaps, the basis of all distinction in the arts. It is always "out of the common."

The Kennedy-Frasers (Aeolian, March 6) demonstrated that their supply of Hebridean melodies is not yet exhausted. "Barra Sea-Moods," "Skye Sea-bird," "Eigg Wind on the Moor" were given for the first time, and all worth giving. I have claimed, that whatever limitations there may be in the details of performance, one always has certain memorable moments in a Kennedy-Fraser concert. The moment of ecstasy on Saturday was in Mrs. Kennedy-Fraser's rendering of the "Skir of St. Kenneth."

Miss Kennedy-Fraser seemed to find her voice a little "stiff in tow," like the ancient ox in the Saga; she partially awoke for the labour lilts; for the whirl, whirl and draw-out of the Spinning song, and was at, perhaps, her best for the afternoon in "Dunvegan." She is always enjoyable, but the wildness of the sea-wind was not at its full in the Islay

Reaper, and while her "Kishmul" is preferable to most renderings, it is not really within the scope of her vocal energy, nor was the harp quite vigorous enough for the accompaniment. "Wind on the Moor" has got somewhat away from the seaboard, and the kinship between these Hebridean songs and Moussorgsky is all the more apparent in this tune, with the sea absent, for it is very like Moussorgsky indeed.

The labour lilts illustrate at each Kennedy-Fraser concert the value of some rhythm-base more diversified than English accentual prosody made in not very inspired imitation of mediæval degenerations from the Latin imitation of Greek quantitative metres. The Oriental and African division of music into raga and tala, i.e., rhythm-tune and pitch-tune, is probably more fecund in diversity. The churn, the loom, the spinning-wheel, the oars, all give splendid bases for distinctive rhythms which can never degenerate into the monotony of mere iambs and trochees. They keep their essential difference as even dance tunes cannot. Even so, the real feeling of moving feet which is so often the soul of thematic invention in Bach and Mozart, is increasingly rare in music.

Words help thematic invention only so long as poetic metres are truly alive, and so long as the musicians are sensitive to shades of different verbal quality. The charm of Mozart, if one can analyse it, seems often to lie in a rare combination of notes which have musical structure, musical line, but which suggest, beyond these and simultaneously, dance steps and language.

One is not attacking "modernity," one is not depreciating the value of harmonic colour, or of orchestral colour, when one declines to believe in the all-sufficing power of smears of sound.

One would have a deal more patience with contemporary composers if they showed a little more sense of these matters, and a little more seriousness in their approach to design and the means of it.

Rosing is singing Moussorgsky's incomparable Death Cycle at the eight Russian matinées, Duke of York's Theatre, March 15-28.

MUSIC[77]

I do not know whether we are to be allowed more than a semi-private hearing of Madame Thérèse de Lens, who has been commissioned by the French Government to "maintain the traditional music of Morocco"; neither do I know how far this music is susceptible of record in "occidental" notation. I know from having heard "the king's dinner music" and other traditional tunes in Tangier that Madame de Lens has the

[77] *The New Age,* April 15, 1920, pp. 387–88.

authentic manner; it is indeed impossible not to think that one is hearing the true nasalation of an Arab when she sings, with "shut throat" and many noises offensive to a "narrow-minded" ear.

I have never been able to determine how far various alleged oriental melodies, as concocted for example by Borodine or "recorded" and "arranged" by Salvador Daniel, have been mis-written in our notation, or how far the writing is really sound and *would* indicate the right tune and rhythm to a performer who knew the right manner of presentation. Salvador Daniel, if I remember rightly, scouts the idea of quarter tone, and argues that what insensitive ears have mistaken for quarter tones are really the odd pitches of Greek modalities, modalities perhaps a little worn away with the centuries. I do not imagine there is yet a "paying audience" for Madame de Lens; but the inquisitive musician will feel it no small privilege if he can manage to hear her.

In especial one notes the "extraordinary" length of the rhythm pattern units, comparable to the mediæval rhyme-scheme of Provençal canzos, where, for example, one finds a rhyme pattern which begins its six-ply repeat after the seventeenth different terminal sound. In this Arabian music, as in the Provençal metrical scheme, the effect of the subtler repetitions only becomes apparent in the third or fourth strophe, and then culminates in the fifth or sixth, as a sort of horizontal instead of perpendicular chord. One might call it a "sort of" counterpoint; if one can conceive a counterpoint which plays not against a sound newly struck, but against the residuum and residua of sound which hangs in the auditory memory.

In the two cases, Arabian music and Provençal verse, where there was no musical "harmony" and no counterpoint in Bach's sense of the word, this elaboration of echo has attained great complexity, and *can* give great delight to ears which are either "trained" to it, or which have a natural aptitude for perceiving it. In Europe this aptitude or perceptivity lasted at least until Dante's time, and prompted in him several opinions on the relative merit of Provençal artists, which have puzzled thick-eared "modern" philologists.

For the normal concert-goer the first impression of Arabian singing is that a cat is being strangled in the vicinity. After the "fool in the outer ear" has been put to sleep by the rhythm; after the ear's rebellion against the first *shock to its habit* has worn off, the little whiskers of the ear's interior "miniature piano" begin to wave quite nicely in the ebb and flow of this different sort of sound current; a nostalgia of the sun overtakes one; the music is, and is rightly, an enchantment, and would to what gods there be, that European musicians might return to that concept of music!

March 13 (Steinway), I found J. S. Mackinlay dull, but was perhaps distracted by the news of that afternoon, and incapable of proper attention.

March 14 (Curtain Group, Lyric Theatre, Hammersmith), Raymonde Collignon not in good voice, but gave a truly distinguished rendering of her songs. No one has a more keen perception than she has of the difference between art and life; of the necessary scale and proportion required in the presentation of a thing which is not the photograph and wax cast, but a re-creation in different and proportional medium. As long as this diseuse was on the stage she was non-human; she was, if you like, a china image; there are Ming porcelains which are respectable; the term "china" is not in this connection ridiculous. One would like the ability to express verbally the exact difference between this "sort of presentation" which is art, and the other sort of presentation, which is just Miss Jones of Peckwell singing a song—being half the time Miss Jones, and half the time something, rather indefinite, but more or less en rapport with the music.

March 20. Mrs. Kennedy-Fraser was in better voice than I have heard her for some time; in the "Island Herdmaid"[78] the singing was full of charm, suave wave-water and ground-swell in the rhythm. The weaving song has the sort of "circular" or "curved wall-of-Troy pattern" in it. In the "Spreading the Sea-Wrack"[79] we have the feel of the throw-and-catch of the fork, or whatever implement is used to turn the sea-wrack; there is long-drawn sort of descant in the "Driving Cattle." Again and again I emphasise the value of these different rhythm-roots as above that of a tired and mechanical accent-metric. Miss Patuffa Kennedy-Fraser's "distance" and pure high notes were advantageous in the "Solitary Reaper" and "Sickle Reaper." Rosing assisted in this concert; his Gaelic was perfectly intelligible, though I do not know that real Gaels would have understood it. The songs he elected to sing had not been utterly and absolutely mastered, but he gave a most spirited and interesting version of them. To have him sing them is an added help to one's perception of the curious disjunct and unrelated relation of this Hebridean music to Moussorgsky's.

March 27 (Aeolian), Rosing, in his own full Russian and announcedly penultimate programme, proved once more that he is unique, that he "can do it" whenever he fully determines to. The Moussorgsky "Soul," "Yeremoushka," "Star," were given with suavity, graduation, and the float of the tone, which is different from descant; the voice open, more so than usual, the bass in form. The Borodine "Arabian Melody" was charming, non-Arabian and yet allowing one to guess what Arabic

[78] Cf. *Songs of the Hebrides*, ed. Marjory Kennedy-Fraser, London, 1917, Vol. II, p. 42.
[79] Cf. *ibid.*, Vol. III, p. 123.

quality Borodine may have been utilising or exploiting or trying to reproduce. The concert ended in the "Death Cycle." A fine programme.

Wigmore, March 27. I found Miss Adela Verne playing Liszt about as well as he ought to be played, with sharp-cut colour, femininely yet with rather more than feminine weight. The St. Francis is fundamentally dull, but the player's commentary was good. In the "Walking on the Waters," the mass roll was well managed; the thunder of the surf and the weight of waves was illustrated as it might have been in some rather rhetorical German painting of Liszt's period. Granting the style, Miss Verne was most competent, she had a grip on its spirit; "all trace of the means was obliterated"; yet one has heard of "Schlaginstrument," and rather wonders whether the supreme economy of art would not attain the same result or at least equivalent effect with African drums, demanding far less digital dexterity than the same effects on a piano. The Chopinesque nocturne recalled the familiar reproductions of "The Stirrup Cup" and "The Dancing Lesson."

MIGNON NEVADA, ET VARIA[80]

With London going mildly mad over Raquel Meller, it is a little difficult to tie up one's marginalia into a neat parcel; and it is perhaps a little unfair to the reader who may be presumed to be thirsting for an opinion of, presumably, a great singer, whom it has not yet been my good fortune to hear. The question is whether the gaps made in last year's concert list are to be made good by her and by other imported talent, or whether new singers are to grow here "under our eye."

Douglas Raymer has been the one new home-produced pleasure of the season, thus far, and even he would seem to have had a good dose of the Continent—a pleasant voice and defective art-sense.

Rosing has appeared in a Lhada performance since his announcedly "ultimate" recital. We hope he will continue to give farewell performances for some time, if he can do so as triumphantly as he did on April 17 (Aeolian). We have presumably written enough about Rosing. On the 17th, "Phydilé" was not sung with Stroesco's *ciselure,* but it is a very beautiful song. Rosing was particularly successful in Donizetti's "Furtiva Lagrima"; Di Veroli has not yet got to the centre of the Hebridean spirit.

Th. Stier, who conducts for Pavlova at Drury Lane, is a very acceptable addition to our stock of orchestra leaders. He has not Thomas Beecham's pianissimo, but conducts with precision, with draw and flow. The Pavlova ballets are technically fine when old-fashioned.

[80] *The New Age,* May 13, 1920, p. 28.

Mignon Nevada (Aeolian, April 22) demonstrated marked development. She was in particularly good form, but the condition of the voice was not "all there was in it." Her technique is considerably more spacious than it was even last season, and it has been, for some years, very good. Anything that can be done by control of the voice is indubitably within Miss Nevada's compass. In the Handel "Piangero la mia sorte" we heard clarity and promptitude of opening in the best opera manner. It was as if the singer were perfectly able to do anything she thought of, but as if she thought of nothing that could not have been almost done by an instrument. With the Mozart aria, "Riposa mio ben," she awoke to a more emotional gamut of things. There was charming articulation and an aerial float of the voice, with exquisite and varied pianissimos, wherein, as in much else, she excels. Still, it seemed as if she were chiefly concerned with the perfection of individual sounds rather than with a fundamental or central "something to be expressed." It is not that she actually sings all songs and all composers in one manner, but that one is not conscious of any great change in quality or manner when she shifts from one kind of song to another. Thus she stirs admiration, but hardly emotional enthusiasm. By emotional enthusiasm I distinctly do not mean that one should make an assault on the tear-ducts, such as is made in Norman O'Neill's "incidental" orchestral wailings at the Haymarket Theatre, for example. These latter are of a piece with the performance in which they occur. I simply mean that Miss Nevada, with all her stage experience, does not seem to begin her preparation of a song in some central and dominant emotion and then carry it out, execute it, *by means of* vocal technique. I know only too well that the concert platform is crowded, and that the crowd upon it is as nothing to the multitude who do not even get on to it, and that in this multitude 90 per cent. start with something they consider "feeling." I am not, heaven forbid, wanting Miss Nevada to be sentimental, and I am very grateful for her delightful performance. The ornithological beauty of her "Nightingale" is indisputable.

Yet, as I have indicated, one gets something from Mrs. Kennedy-Fraser, almost voiceless, which one does not get in a Nevada recital. One gets something from the not yet perfect, but indubitably and tragically passionate singing of V. Marquesita which one does not get from Nevada's somewhat "Bond Street" perfection. One must, perhaps, find one's ideal artiste in fragments, never whole and united.

Grétry's "Rose Chérie" would seem to be one of the few permanent bits of repertoire which have resulted from Edwin Evans' search into demoded operas. It gave Mlle. Nevada another chance for technique, for more than technique, for here the mood did develop, and any sane examiner would have awarded her 100 per cent. for art and production.

Yet the Monsigny "Il regardait mon bouquet" would have become a reality had Mlle. Collignon done it, with, of course, infinitely less voice and less vocal bravura than Mlle. Nevada, who in her next number, Purcell's "Ecch'ing Air," showed marvellous *fioritura,* a graduation of small sounds, admirably displaying the spirit of Purcell.

Her Saint-Saëns fireworks were admirably done. Then came the "dramatic" effects in Donizetti, wherein she was extremely effective, yet this and De Lange Dutch, and Granados Catalan, and Goossens' setting of Thomas Wyatt's "The Appeal" were all "unified," were all brought into one and the same category of manner. Goossens has been very careful in making his notes fit the words of this poem.

Ali Khan, in scarlet and fine linen, sang the "Death of Othello" in strong nasal voice, with somewhat dragging rhythm, but with intensity and sobriety, utterly without the fire and feeling that Mullings puts into it, and without Mullings' feeling for the verbal cadence; yet Khan's version compels respect, by reason of his concentration on the reality of scene, by his very earnest and audible endeavour to be Othello and reel the "come sei tacita, e pallida, e mor-ta."

In his presentation of Occidental music he offers interesting antithesis to the Occidentals who have been trying to introduce to us the music of the Orient, and we might do better than call him out of tune when his non-acceptance—possibly involuntary, yet significant—of the "well"-tempered scale, strikes oddly upon ears unhappily habituated to the latter. The last word on the division of the scale has not yet been said.

MUSIC[81]

Stroesco has gone to l'Opéra Comique and one may perhaps be permitted a moment's satisfaction that the precision and fine chiseling which we commended in Stroesco's work have received this higher commendation, this certainly expert approval. The London season will be the poorer for his absence, and for that of Mlle. Nevada, also absorbed by the Comique; of Tinayre, now in America; of Rosing, engaged in one knows not what vague and errant activities. We shall have to find a new set of favourites.

Kathleen Parlow (Æolian, October 1), after twelve years' hard work, has got over her nervousness to some extent, or at least makes her audience less aware of it. Pizzetti, whose Sonata in A she presented "for the first time in England," has attained a style, or at least a personal idiosyncrasy—something to bind his various works together and by

[81] *The New Age,* October 21, 1920, p. 356.

which they may be distinguished from other works. It may be, sometimes, a relief not to know just what a composer is driving at; in Pizzetti's case it often causes one to wonder just why, if he is so anti-classical, he retains certain classical phrasings, on what grounds he accepts, on what grounds he rejects this or that part of the tradition. Here he has joined piano and violin so that the combination is not annoying, but he has hardly discovered a unified musical dialect. The second movement did not retain one's attention; the third demonstrated Pizetti's capacity for dance tune, and Miss Parlow played it very well, but it cannot be said that her effect is of magic, or of emotion, or intoxication, or of exultation, or of maestria, but rather of conscientious struggle creditably brought off, and with a richness which has increased since last year.

Conus' Concerto is one of those things which one feels one has heard before, despite all the rational procedures which one uses to assure oneself that one hasn't. The Beethoven was beautifully begun, but unevenly continued. If Miss Parlow could sustain the quality she attained in the best passages she would start a solid enthusiasm for her work. Mozart is not her composer, and in the Mozart one had perhaps the best clue to the cause—namely, that she was not, and is, perhaps, seldom, wholly absorbed in the music; a margin of her consciousness is ever engaged in a struggle with the audience, a struggle not æsthetic but volitional, a combat of wills. Busoni carries on this sort of combat successfully, but it is not the most advantageous approach; it is at bottom a mistake, and doubly so if one cannot Nietzscheanly "beherrschen" the company.

The New Russian Choir (Wigmore, October 5) contains a good anonymous bass voice, with which it opened Moussorgsky's "Arise, Red Sun," very acceptably, but it is not a choir (as for example the Ukrainian choir was); it is an assemblage; it might advantageously be scrapped and a male quartette collected from the remnants; yet even this would demand some sort of leadership. Mr. Lazare Saminski turned on his company too loud, he proceeded without graduations, and it cannot even be said that he showed any considerable rhythmic talent.

Douglas Marshall has already raised our hopes to a certain (moderated) extent. He intends to sing the best music available. He was delightful in Falconieri's "Cara é la rose," the enunciation neat and distinct. The Aubert songs are unconvincing; French sentiment is perhaps more sentimental than English sentiment, and one never feels it has quite the same excuse (i.e., in unavoidable mental muddle). One was bemazed by the Debussy modes in 1910, and certainly the "modern French school" has produced a number of charming songs, but the manner is played out, it was never really "right," and the more one hears it *now* the more it bores one. The attempt on the Hebridean songs was praiseworthy, the English words fit the music none too well, which leads us to Mr. Marshall's manifesto, p. 2 of his programme: "The presentation of a poem musically in order to interpret its meaning." It is a hopeful sign that one singer at least should print this sort of manifesto, even though some of the phrases are not satisfactory and may not quite accurately convey what the writer may have, by charity, intended them to convey: "Composers have in the past seriously offended poets by neglect of literary accent," etc. The point which Mr. Marshall and his affiliated composer, Mr. Robertson, miss is that there is no earthly use in a composer's following the "literary" or verbal accent of the poet unless the poet is composing "musically." True, Mr. Marshall indicates the existence of poems not suitable for musical rendering, but he does not, and, by the samples presented, Mr. Robertson does not, distinguish between the various sorts of "poetic" composition. A musician's flattery of, or subservience to, the litterateur is of no avail unless the litterateur have reached out toward music. A writer may, obviously, write with the sole aim of exact expression, he may put this composition into prose or into a regular metre, or even into an irregular metre, of which the musical interest is already exhausted; or he may, secondly, try to throw up colours and images, as does Keats in "Endymion," without much singability, or he may as Burns, or as Waller, or as Browning when he writes "songs," or as perhaps some of the modern writers of free verse (for the most part unknown to us), compose his words in such a way that music will further develop their "souls" or meaning or mode. From a recent critical work I take the terms logopoeia, phanopoeia, melopoeia, and even in this latter division the musician is concerned properly only with one of three categories, for a poet writing "musically" may write so as to sound "musical" in speech, or in a sort of intonation, or in song; and, for this latter, the words are fitted together in a manner different from that required in the two preceding categories. All of which emphasises Mr. Marshall's plea for closer co-operation between writers and composers.

An example of Mr. Robertson's error was Mr. Mather's poem, intended to express the quiet of a Chinese valet annoyed with the "twitching faces" of occidentals, so read by its author, with extreme quietness, and then set to a melody which demanded squawks and shrieks. The less said of Mme. Brunel's recitations the better. People who like poems read as she reads them will presumably go on setting them as Mr. Robertson does.

Luigi Rangoni, in his first English appearance, was scared to death. He sang "Incoronazione di Poppea" delightfully; then his throat closed and his pitch became undependable. His accompanist, Mr. Liddle, came most nobly to his aid in "Mélodie de la Basse Bretagne," and restored his morale by one of the best psychological tours de force I have seen on the concert platform, and one for which we lay a special wreath of compliments at Mr. Liddle's plate. Rangoni has a really beautiful voice; he sang the Gretchaninoff "Berceuse" almost as well as Rosing does; he did not maintain this level in "La Steppa," nor did he approach the Stroesco bogey in Pizzetti's "I Pastori." I don't know why Landon Ronald sets "find" as *"fi-i-ind"* on an ascending series of tones. I stayed to the end of the concert and heard Mr. Frank Bridge, "Love went, etc." I shall not hear it again this season, but one should refresh one's memory in these matters, and one would forget how unpleasant some experiences are if one did not occasionally check and verify them by repetition. If Rangoni can manage to sing in tune he will be a distinct addition to the winter's season of concerts.

MUSIC[82]

A month's search for a singer with a conception of song as an art, and capable of putting said art into practice was triumphantly rewarded at the Æolian Hall, October 21. Judith Litante meets the requirements. A song when sung should be a whole composed of elements placed in proportion, etc. During the last three years I have encountered this in rather fewer than half a dozen singers. A song should be sung from a central, main concept of its meaning, and made to express the main passion or mood of its makers; and this occasionally happens in performance when the idea or mood is trivial. After the pastel and chocolate-box voices we find with relief Judith Litante's sense of gradations and of sober colour; the voice almost ugly in the unglazed, unbuttered, iron-coloured tones of the middle register which gave the strength of the Italian songs, in such excellent scale with the delicacy of the head tones. It seriously matters for our winter enjoyment whether she sings one sort of music or another. Her programme was chosen with serious intent; even the four songs by "younger British composers" was, in a manner, negotiated, and if for nothing else she would have deserved our gratitude for singing the five songs of the Dichterliebe in the original and not in the despicable translations to which other performers have subjected us.

Yet I doubt whether the romanticism of Schumann, and of his contemporaries, any longer expresses a modality of mood which is very real to us, in the year of grace 1920; the inner significance of this music

[82] *The New Age,* November 11, 1920, p. 21.

might, perhaps, seem to be nearer that of Tom Moore and the Minstrel Boy, than to the straight art, Bel Canto, of Caldara, and Vivaldi, or the bleak realism of Moussorgsky; or the hard stroke of "Le Roi Renaud" and the old French narrative lyrics. It seems often allied to the terra cotta statuettes of the noble fisherman with his lifebelt, and the noble fisherman's daughter; which do not hold their own against Shang bronzes, or Tanagra. But if singers are going to sing these songs, for God's sake let them sing the words the composers intended. Miss Litante's curious accent showed conclusively that she was not singing her mother-tongue. Neither is French the language of her pays natal; and despite the general rumour that she is "Russian," I do not believe that the Slavic gloom and melancholy really form her spiritual domicile. But by all means let her sing Moussorgsky. The Levenson songs (composer at the piano) permitted her to make two graceful pianissimo endings and one forte ending. They are not bad work, but neither, on the contrary, do they possess unusual interest. Pergolesi, Mozart, and Donizetti gave the best opportunity for her voice and for her art of using it, and neither of these can be judged in the Ed. Oxenfordism of Bantock, or the bad and indifferent vowel sequences of the English or Levenson songs. Miss Litante has the sense of rhythm which should carry her through the Hebridean songs. She has the tang and intensity which bring out the temper of Donizetti's gipsy. She has that quality of bite which one feels fit for singing Villon.

Giorgio Corrado (Æolian, October 11). Solid, vigorous, full of confidence, under-estimated taste of his audience; would have had greater success if he had given whole evening of Rossini; could be most useful if he would stick to "that sort of thing."

Dawson Freer (Wigmore, October 20), an entertainer, delightful low notes (Ciampi beautifully given); has apparently no very strict canons of taste, no art-sense, and certainly no adequate rhythm sense; "Go Down Moses" ruined, and "Sheiling" Song wrenched out of its movement for sake of final sentimental sob.

Roland Hayes, next concert, Wigmore Hall, Saturday, November 20, 3. Worth hearing.

MUSIC[83]

Lilias Mackinnon, the Scriabine specialist, announces a system for training the musical memory, six lessons, and then no more pianistic forgetfulness. We hope it is true; we have felt an even deeper need for some

---

[83] *The New Age,* November 25, 1920, p. 44.

system of inculcating rhythm; some means of teaching the British practitioner that rhythm is not made by cutting a piece of paper called a "bar" into little sections called notes. A rhythm unit is a shape; it exists like the keel-line of a yacht, or the lines of an automobile-engine, for a definite purpose, and should exist with an efficiency as definite as that which we find in yachts and automobiles.

It is possible that if our singers were in early life, or even in their present maturity, given Oriental finger drums, or even common drumsticks, and told to beat out *rhythm-shapes* on the dining-table, they would in time discover an "element" more vital to music than their present training leads them to suspect. I need hardly add that the metronome, distinguished invention of the age which held the exhibition of 1851, and was so renowned for mechanical ingenuity, will not greatly assist the learner in the understanding of metrical form.

Astra Desmond (Wigmore, October 25) displayed a suave and capacious voice; but lacks constructive ability. She has not the centralising energy needed to make each song a whole, an entity, distinct from the song which precedes or follows it; vocally good, artistically undeveloped.

Roland Hayes (Wigmore, October 28), second discovery of the season, which now promises to be of some interest. Rhythm sense unsurpassed by anyone now singing in London. It is not necessary to have a book of the words. Whether English, French, or Italian, Mr. Hayes enunciates each one so that the hearer can understand it. Audience's enthusiasm amply deserved. Mr. Hayes has a beautiful voice; but there are other good voices. The distinction of performance is given by the clear presentation of the words, the rhythmic validity, the utter sincerity of feeling, which saved even the songs of mediocre composers from their inherent banality. I can at the moment think of no singer who employs so many different qualities of voice, from operatic delivery to a singing which is almost speech, as, for example, in Lawrence Dunbar's death-bed poem. It goes without saying that the Negro Spirituals filled the audience with enthusiasm. In every song Mr. Hayes moves from a main concept; the *meaning* of the poem is in him, and the presentation is a unit; it is a considered and proportioned expression. While Hayes' great advantage over the remaining "white hopes" is in his splendid grip on the rhythm-sweep, and while the Spirituals and folk-songs are certainly his castello, his "O Souverain Juge," from Massenet's "Cid," gave ample proof of a considerably wider range of technique.

Olga Rudge[84] charmed one by the delicate firmness of her fiddling

---

[84] This is the first mention in Pound's writings of Olga Rudge, who later in Paris and Italy became such a close and influential musical friend.

when paired with Hela Ziemska, a very alert and promising young pianist, following more or less the Leschetizky tradition. Miss Rudge, however, committed a serious error in changing partners, and was unable to overcome the wooden burden of Mlle. Renata Borgatti's piano whack.

Arthur Rubinstein is one of the outstanding personalities among living pianists, and his art will require more lengthy and special treatment.

The Maharani of Tikari has a voice of exquisite quality, charming in Mozart, breathes badly, should keep to Italian, at least for the present. Production undeveloped.

Gertrude Blomfield is depressing.

Judith Litante, next concert December 9, Æolian Hall, at 3.15. Worth hearing.

MUSIC[85]

Arthur Rubinstein (Wigmore, November 11) began with Bach-D'Albert Toccata in F maj.: a solidity of rhythm, the whole like a set of taut steel cables whirling, seizing and holding the auditor; a barbaric noise, splendidly structural, fit for a decade that has taken up African sculpture. Rubinstein then relapsed into the sickly opening of the Franck prelude, with enormous waste of technique; he showed himself a hopeless sentimentalist pyrotechnic in the Chopin barcarolle, gave the Etude as a speed test, and whatever one may say in praise of his Polonaise, it was anything but an interpretation of Chopin.

Mlle. Taillifer began her valses with a Chopin touch, but that is a parenthesis. Rubinstein came back in the rather shallow alerte of Poulenc, did well in the Prokofieff "Marche" and in the Falla "Dance." The other two Prokofieff numbers were omissible, and as for "Suggestion diabolique," the poor old devil is such a worn out stage prop that one is ashamed to heave rocks at him any longer. "Diabolique" fiddle-sticks.

As Rubinstein is so great a pianist that all the other star-players come out to listen to him, we may as well analyse his "art"; sic. For him the piano is not an abbreviation of the orchestra; it is not the means whereby one performer can express his orchestral thought. His technique is adequate; it is that abundant technique which is required of a master-pianist or a trapeze virtuoso. Beyond a certain point any great concentration of technique is bound to be interesting. But Rubinstein's personality is ordinary; only at one point is he a super performer;

[85] *The New Age*, December 9, 1920, p. 68.

PROGRAMME

I.

Sonata in E flat, op. 31, No. 3 · · · Beethoven
    Allegro.
    Allegretto vivace.
    Minuetto.
    Presto con fuoco.

II.

Sonata in B minor · · · · · · · Liszt
    (in one movement.)

III.

Masques
La Terrasse des audiences du clair de lune
Ondine   ·   ·   ·   ·   ·   Debussy
Minstrels
L' Isle joyeuse

IV.

Alborada del Gracioso · · · · Ravel
Rondena · · · · · · ·
Navarra · · · · · · · Albeniz

ARTHUR RUBINSTEIN
Extra Recital, Saturday, December 18th at 3 p.m.

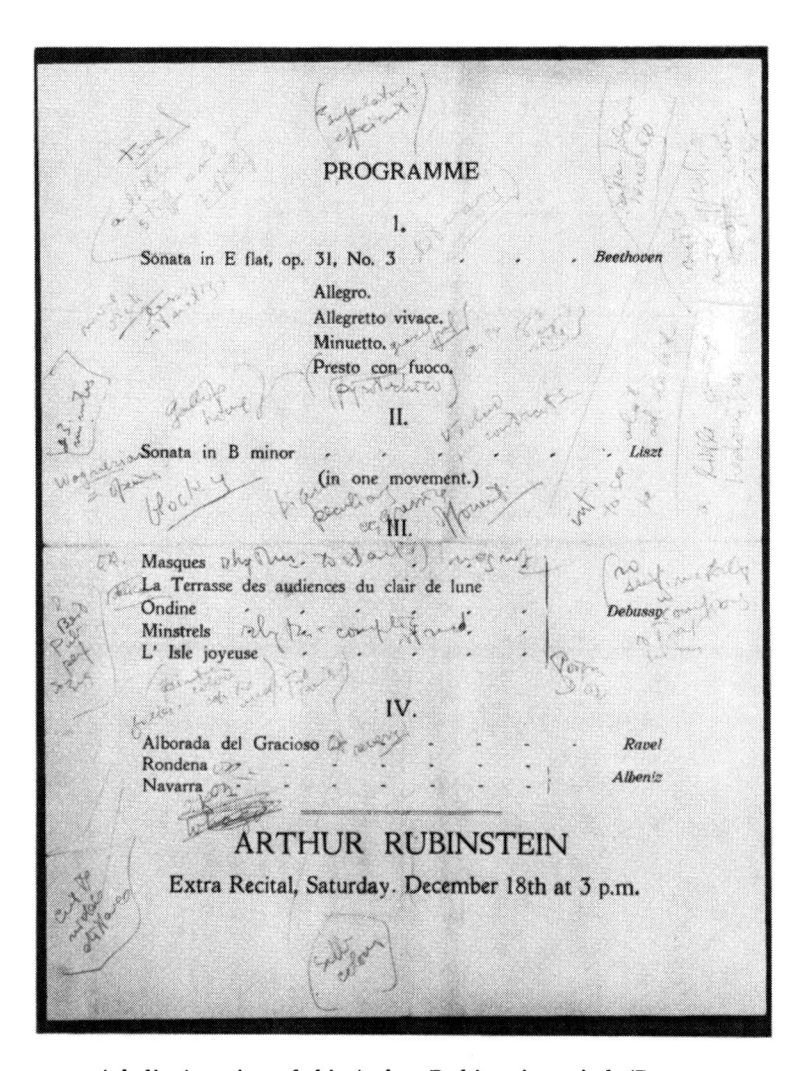

Atheling's review of this Arthur Rubinstein recital (December 7, 1920) appeared in *The New Age,* December 23, 1920. The notes here, and on the following illustration as well, are in Pound's hand.

PROGRAMME

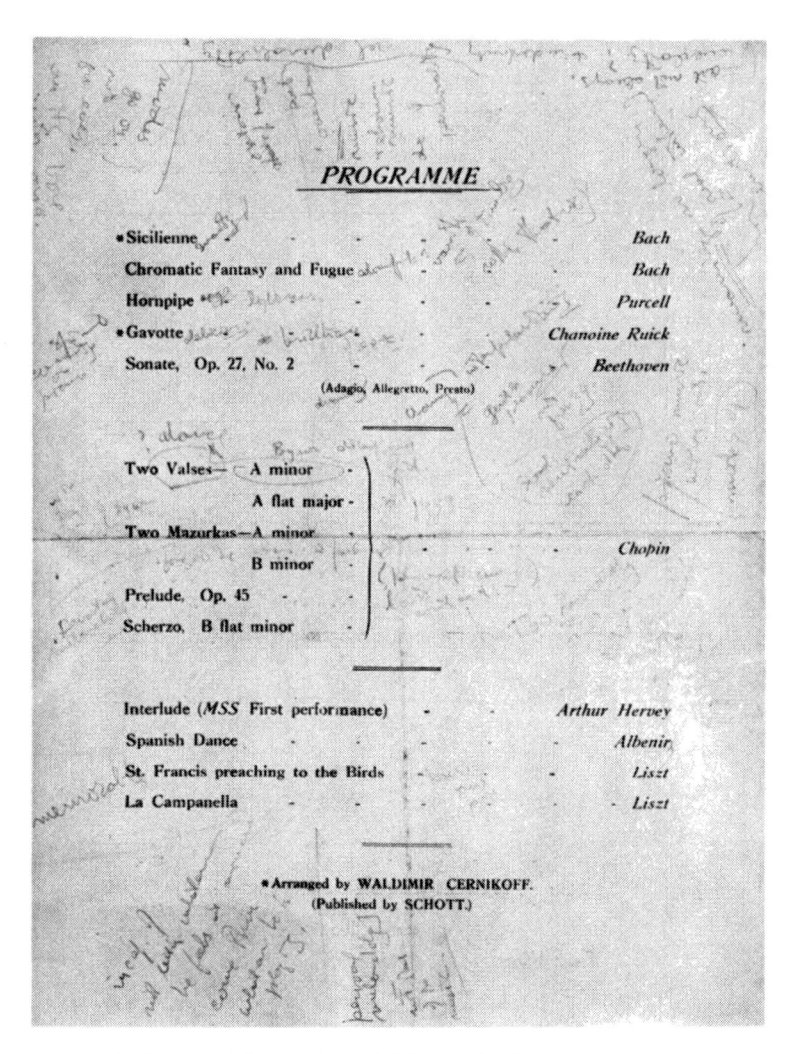

*Sicilienne	Bach
Chromatic Fantasy and Fugue	Bach
Hornpipe	Purcell
*Gavotte	Chanoine Ruick
Sonate, Op. 27, No. 2	Beethoven
(Adagio, Allegretto, Presto)	

Two Valses— A minor	
A flat major	
Two Mazurkas—A minor	Chopin
B minor	
Prelude, Op. 45	
Scherzo, B flat minor	

Interlude (*MSS* First performance)	Arthur Hervey
Spanish Dance	Albeniz
St. Francis preaching to the Birds	Liszt
La Campanella	Liszt

*Arranged by WALDIMIR CERNIKOFF.
(Published by SCHOTT.)

Atheling's brief mention of this Wladimir Cernikoff recital (December 16, 1920) appeared in *The New Age,* January 6, 1921.

i.e., in his rhythm. And the compelling power of this excites the audience, for the same reason that a really great drummer or even a normally good tom-tom player excites. For Rubinstein the piano is a Schlaginstrument; it is not a little orchestra; it is a gorgeously varied drum or series of drums. The skeleton of his work is tympannic, i.e., it is a drummer's skeleton; his variety is not in variation of orchestral colourings, but in drum-shadings, in the light and dark, the approach and recede which a drummer can render.

Note the magnificent effect of the Bach Toccata. Magnificent, barbaric. And note also how it is done—done in a manner effective just so long as the lines of musical structure run longitudinally = = = =, i.e., in the counterpoint.

By playing very fast this line is reinforced and becomes = = = =. Even as a proposition in physics we know that one sound wave may be used to reinforce another. Rubinstein simply drives one note into the back of another; he establishes a solid current of sound and this torrent of notes beats triumphantly into the auditor. But this system is no use whatever when he comes to music which is constructed harmonically, i.e., more or less vertically, sic.: ///////////. The attempt to jam these rising aromas, smoke columns and algæ of sound only leads to a confusion. That part of music which can be expressed by sheer rhythm he gets—the toccata, the March, the Dance; but music to interpret human passion, or reverie, or psychology, no. He expresses either perfectly ordinary and common-place nullities, or sentimental tosh; he does not "interpret" anything of interest. The Taillifer stuff? Most talented young performer, Miss Taillifer, but young-lady psychology.

A full Bach programme of Rubinstein would be a musical event. Played with this solidity the contrapunto has the excitative element of syncopation; it is indeed a much more architectonic syncopation; and, in his Bach, Rubinstein is perhaps the only musician who has succeeded in bringing into musical performance the qualities which Vlaminck and Picasso have admired in African carving. But not Chopin, and certainly not Debussy.

MUSIC[86]

Roland Hayes (November 20) gave a recital for connoisseurs. The Cadman settings of American Indian songs were beautiful, with a beautiful simplicity, yet perhaps too strange ever greatly to please or move an English audience. They will probably remain part of musical

---

[86] *The New Age,* December 23, 1920, pp. 92-93.

scholarship. Hayes in "The Moon droops low" made a very neat cut-off of sound. The Hebridean songs were given with vigour, but not quite assimilated. He was delicate in the Massenet, and imparted more emotion to "J'ai pleuré en rêve" than the French composer had, presumably, thought of. His maximum effect was in the "Spirituals," especially in Burleigh's "I don't feel no-ways tired"; "Peter go ring-a dem bells," and in his own setting of "I couldn't hear nobody pray."

The general lesson both for him and for the audience is that effectiveness attains its maximum when the melody rises out of the actual words. The Indian tunes were beautiful; the Hebridean melodies were both the richest in themselves, and set with greatest richness, of the three folk-song groups; but both Indian and Hebridean tunes were straddled over the words of English translations. The Spirituals grow out of the actual words which they sing.

Only by the greatest cunning and turn of technical force can the librettist make up for inverting this proper process. In the finest lyrics the music so comes from the words and enriches, reinforces, illuminates them. We will recapture this art of illuminating only when we have musicians capable of literary discrimination, capable of selecting *cantabile* words, and of feeling the fine shades of their timbre, of their minor hurries and delays.

Adela Hamaton is a delicate and competent pianist. Phyllis Carey-Foster shows great delicacy of shading and considerable promise as a singer of modern French compositions.

Arthur Rubinstein compels me to eat my words, or rather one word, Debussy, for at the Wigmore (December 7) he gave one of the best *public* performances of a Debussy group that I have heard in England. The rest of my criticism of his work still seems to me correct: wherever he can rely on rhythm he is excellent; it was his grasp of the complications and changes of Debussy's rhythm, and of the activity of the Ravel and Albéniz dance movements which gave life to the programme. To which add his appreciation of Debussy's humour. His tone in the Beethoven sonata was somewhat stiff. We believe $22\frac{1}{4}$ minutes is a speed record for performance of the Liszt B minor sonata, and offer what wreaths are in order. In the Liszt, done in a sort of Wagnerian blockiness, Rubinstein seemed to regard the piano as a peculiarly aggressive opponent, and dealt with it accordingly. He began to enjoy the show in the Debussy and went on from that, triumphantly, into a supplement of several encores in well merited triumph.

Judith Litante (Æolian, December 9) showed again her verbal intelligence; she is there on the note, on the word, on the beat, with fine pianissimo; the voice is still veiled in parts; great art would consist in having more palatal, epiglottal, tonsillar, bronchial technique than Miss Litante yet has, *and* in *suppressing* it *nearly* always. The strongest promise of her future was given in Tchaikovsky's "Adieu Forêts" and in Ravel's magnificent "Kaddish." The woman is not a fool, and this is really one of the essential conditions of good singing; to convey the intensity of a given song the singer must, as first requisite, have some conception of the significance, even of the literary significance, of what he or she is singing; must mean the words sung; this central grasp prevents at least idiocies of rhythm and tone. In Miss Litante's case we have, as stated, the added grace of correct time and pitch. If Mr. Raibin can produce similar results in any other of his pupils he will have proved himself an eminent instructor. In the Bax songs we note a touch of rhetorical melody on the words "endless rue," at other points verbal infelicities had conduced to musical infelicities, as is but natural.

Miss Litante's Schubert and Brahms were received with due enthusiasm. (Next recital January 30, Æolian, 8.15.)

MUSIC[87]

As part of the special inquest on the crimes of singers and contemporary composers, I have raided numerous music shops and find that the *shops* are *not* to blame. Some editions of good songs are difficult to find, or even, apparently, unobtainable, yet with no greater energy than is required to get from Oxford Circus to Berners Street and thence to Gt. Marlborough Street, and the immediate purlieus, to wit, the houses of Augener, Ricordi, Boosey, Chester, and Winthrop Rogers, I have collected a sufficient song-library to save any intelligent singer from bad taste; by intelligent singer I mean one who having been shown a chef-d'œuvre will not toss it aside and sing rubbish. To remove the excuses of ignorance at least from one's few dozen readers, let it stand that the following collections of really good lyrics are obtainable:—

Parisotti's "Arie Antiche" (Carissimi, Vivaldi, Caldara, Pergolesi, etc., the masters of Bel Canto). 3 vols. Ricordi.

Julien Tiersot, Sixty Folk Songs of France (Roi Renaud, St. Nicholas, Joli Tambour, etc.). Rogers. (The "Duc du Maine" is not in this collection but in the Repertoire Raymonde Collignon, published by Chester. The "Pauvre Laboureur" is in another Tiersot collection obtainable at W. Rogers.)

Wekerlin's great collection, "Echos du Temps Passé" (at Augener's) contains Merci Clamant, Robin m'aime, Dieu qui la fait bon regarder,

[87] *The New Age,* January 6, 1921, pp. 117–18.

etc. The only objection to the arrangement of this collection is that the oldest music is scattered over the opening pages of the three volumes. They contain, however, 140 pages each, and are exceptionally good value. Augener also has the Yvette Guilbert collection of songs, and W. M. Rummel's "Hesternae Rosae," of which we recommend the Neuf Chansons des Troubadours.[88]

Boosey has just produced a new collection of Five Troubadour Songs.[89] He carries the famous Kennedy-Fraser collection of Hebridean music, and Arnold Dolmetsch's "Selected English Songs of the 16th and 17th Centuries" (Henry Lawes, Dowland, etc.). Novello publishes Dolmetsch's inestimable work on 17th and 18th century music.

These books are mostly large albums. It would be rash to say that every song in them is a masterpiece; but in their thousand or so pages of music there is enough perfect work, enough great song-art to give the student a permanent distaste for slush, for the soft and sloppy, and for the atrocious technique of the average contemporary or late nineteenth century composer.

The man of letters has also his lessons to learn, and music has saved more than one poet from the worst errors of remplissage. From the direct statements and bareness of phrase in the "Roi Renaud," or from the climax of "Joli Tambour," a writer might learn some of the most precious secrets of his craft. There is (corollary) no greater stumbling block for the musician than the useless word of an author, the word that has no function in the poem. (Evidence in every concert of modern music.)

The books I have mentioned should give the student ample basis for comparisons; one period arms him against another; the discrimination bred from a study of this dozen or so of books, should make him more sensitive to values in lieder and in the modern French songs. Note that an omnivorous diet of lieder or of modern French composers never yet bred discrimination in anyone.

No library is complete without Russian songs, but, then, no library ever is complete; and I have sufficient discretion to limit my recommendations to languages which I understand and where I can really see whether the words and notes fit and enhance each other.

Concerts.—Arthur Bliss has taken Waller's advice; contented himself with ut, re, mi, and attained a unity of effect in his spritely "Rout," not common to his contemporaries. Czernikoff again showed himself incapable of distinguishing between subjective and objective; he is too little the actor and too utterly at the mercy of his own moods to prevent

---

[88] Pound had done the translations for the Yvette Guilbert collection in 1912. For the Pound-Rummel collaborative collection, see note 4, pp. 27–28.

[89] The Pound-Bedford collaborative collection, see note 4, *loc. cit.*

their dominating his performance, ever to receive full credit for his rich musical comprehension. He played Purcell and his own arrangement of Chanoine Ruick with great delicacy. Arthur Rubinstein is the antithesis, wholly the performer; he was magnificent in Bach (Dec. 18) and despicable in Chopin. The rest of the concert is already covered by our previous criticism of his previous concerts, save that he got more orchestral colour into the Fugue, and needed, possibly, more severe condemnation for the Chopin.

3
France and Italy 1921–1927

At the end of 1920 Pound left London for Paris, anxious for new challenges, disenchanted with British letters and publishing houses. In Paris there were literary personalities more to his taste. Joyce had moved there in 1920, Ford Madox Ford was there, as well as a growing community of Americans—Hemingway, Gertrude Stein, Malcolm Cowley. There were also French writers such as Cocteau and Louis Aragon, both of whom quickly became personal friends. Tristan Tzara had come to Paris in 1920 and Dadaism was in full swing.

Paris was also fulminating with new music. Debussy was dead, but Ravel was still active and had just completed *La Valse*. Stravinsky had moved to France from Switzerland in 1921 and was at work on *Mavra* and *Les Noces*. Diaghilev was giving a new production of *Le Sacre du Printemps* at the Théatre des Champs-Elysées and had revived *Parade,* the Cocteau-Picasso-Satie collaboration. The Americans were also beginning to move in. Virgil Thomson had just come and Copland was soon to arrive. George Antheil, whom Pound was soon to encounter with such stimulating results, was touring Europe, performing his boisterous piano pieces.

In 1920 the French critic Henri Collet wrote an article on "The Russian Five" and in it identified for the first time a new group of young French composers of kindred sensibilities which he called "Les Six": Louis Durey, Darius Milhaud, Arthur Honegger, Germaine Tailleferre, Georges Auric, and Francis Poulenc. Their spiritual mentor, Collet suggested, was the eccentric Eric Satie.

"There is no Satie school," Satie said; but Jean Cocteau, jumping to the task of pamphleteering for the new group, christened him "le bon maître" and outlined in his *Cock and Harlequin* an audacious new musical aesthetic. "The nightingale sings badly... MUSICAL BREAD is what we want."[1] The mists of impressionism were dispelled, revealing the hard glitter of "pattern music" —of neo-Classicism and of jazz. It was altogether a vigorous atmosphere; Pound felt at home.

Settling into 70bis rue Notre Dame des Champs, he began almost at once to carry forward the work on his opera, *Le Testament*, which he had conceived in London a year or so earlier. Strangely, an experience with Debussy triggered his enthusiasm.

> Sat through the *Pelléas* the other evening and am encouraged— encouraged to tear up the whole bloomin' era of harmony and do the thing if necessary on two tins and wash-board. Anything rather than that mush of hysteria, Scandinavia strained through Belgium plus French Schwärmerei. Probably just as well I have to make this first swash without any instruments at hand. Very much encouraged by the *Pelléas,* ignorance having no further terrors if that DAMN thing is the result of what is called musical knowledge.[2]

When the singer Yves Tinayre came to tea in 1922 the poet announced: "I have an opera for you." Tinayre later commented to Charles Norman:

> The conception was entirely novel to me.... At that time I was a concert and opera singer, and I had not yet done any medieval research. Pound's idea struck me as fine—for words, Villon's ballades, for music a few trombones and troubadour-like songs. The music was longitudinal and linear. He showed me the "Heaulmière" first, terming it the "fireworks" of the piece. Then he sang it.[3]

It was George Antheil who eventually assisted the poet in the notation and orchestration of *Le Testament*, substituting for the "two tins and wash-board" an idiosyncratic little orchestra

---

[1] In a letter from Paris (April, 1921) Pound recommends the Cocteau book to his musical friend Agnes Bedford.
[2] Letter to Agnes Bedford, April, 1921. Paige, *Letters,* N.Y., p. 167; London, p. 231.
[3] Charles Norman, *Ezra Pound,* New York, 1969, p. 254.

> à mon cher ami Ezra Pound,
> ~~JEAN COCTEAU~~ souvenir de la lecture de son "Villon"
>
> ♡ Jean Cocteau
> Sept 1922

Jean Cocteau's note of September, 1922: "to my dear friend Ezra Pound, memento of the reading of his 'Villon'" of brass, winds, a couple of strings, and mandolin. The opera will be dealt with in detail in a second volume of the work.

In his autobiography, *Bad Boy of Music,* Antheil states that he met Pound in 1923 at a gathering which also included Eric Satie. The two American exiles took to one another immediately. "Ezra asked me to get some of my music and go with him to the home of a friend who had a piano. I did so, went with him, played for hours, and Ezra seemed very pleased with it all."[4]

Antheil in music displayed the same rhythmic toughness Pound had previously admired in the Vorticists and Gaudier-Brzeska. The solid precision of his music achieved its most celebrated expression in his *Ballet mécanique,* premièred in Paris in 1926. As Pound was to put it: "He demanded short hard bits of rhythm hammered down, worn down so that they were indestructible and unbendable." Immediately he took up Antheil's cause with the same disinterested and unflagging alacrity he had shown for nearly everybody else's. It is difficult today to appreciate the extravagant claims made for the young composer. Antheil, who had pioneered forward until about his twenty-fifth year, spent the rest of his life pioneering backward. Eventually he was a great disappointment; he went over to Hollywood. In 1936 Aaron Copland summed up his failings:

> George Antheil, as always, belongs in a category of his own. In 1926 Antheil seemed to have "the greatest gifts of any young American." But something always seems to prevent them full fruition. Whether this is due to a lack of artistic integrity, or an unusual susceptibility to influences, or a lack of any conscious direction, is not clear.[5]

But in 1923 the prospects looked good. On his numerous concert tours Antheil had impressed and outraged the European capitals with the barbaric daring of his pianism. In his autobiography he tells us how, with an obvious flair for showmanship, he placed a loaded revolver on the corner of the piano to intimidate obstreperous audiences. Soon after Antheil arrived in Paris

---

[4] George Antheil, *Bad Boy of Music,* New York, 1945, p. 117.

[5] Aaron Copland, *Copland on Music,* New York, 1960, pp. 157–58. This was a view later also corroborated by Virgil Thomson: "My estimate of him as 'the first composer of our generation' might have been justified had it not turned out eventually that for all his facility and ambition there was in him no power of growth. The 'bad boy of music' . . . merely grew up to be a good boy." *Virgil Thomson,* by Virgil Thomson, New York, 1966, p. 82.

in June, Pound introduced him to his violinist friend, Olga Rudge.

> She was a dark, pretty, Irish-looking girl, about twenty-five years old and, as I discovered when we commenced playing a Mozart sonata together, a consummate violinist. I have heard many violinists, but none with the superb lower register of the D and G strings that was Olga's exclusivity.
> Olga, actually, could lay claim to being an American girl, for she was born in Boston and carried an American passport; but there all resemblance to things American stopped. She had been raised in England and Italy, spoke English with a decided British accent. She also spoke Italian, for all I know flawlessly.
> She had already made a successful debut as a concert violinist, and her name was well known to me. I now consented to write two violin sonatas for her and, looking at her Irish adrenal personality, I decided that the sonatas must be as wildly strange as she looked, tailored to her special appearance and technique.[6]

On December 11 George Antheil and Olga Rudge gave a joint recital in the Salle du Conservatoire at which they premièred the two violin sonatas. A short notice of the event in the Paris Edition of *The Chicago Tribune* (December 13) triggered a typical Poundian reaction.

> GEORGE ANTHEIL PLAYS EZRA POUND'S MUSIC
> Hitting the piano keys with his wrist and his palm as well as with his fingers, Mr. George Antheil, young American composer and pianist, drew from the instrument strange barbaric sounds and created a sensation at his recital given at the Salle du Conservatoire in Paris on Tuesday evening.
> Among the selections played were some compositions by Mr. Ezra Pound, the American poet-composer, who has just switched from the muse of Homer to that of Beethoven. Miss Olga Rudge played the violin.

The following day Pound replied with a letter to the editor of the *Tribune:*

> Sir: Your critic has placed a wreath on my head which is, I regret to say, vastly too large for me.
> The music played by Mr. Antheil at the Salle du Conservatoire

---

[6] Antheil, *op. cit.*, pp. 121–22. Virgil Thomson, recalling the works, says that one of them had a "bass drum laid on at the end," though Antheil makes no mention of this (Thomson, *op. cit.*, p. 78).

on Tuesday evening was not mine but his own. I am sorry that I did not write his two sonatas for violin and piano, but it is too late to remedy the matter now.

When unable to attend a concert in person, the perfect critic should always refer to the printed program.

Respectfully yours,
EZRA POUND

P.S. Miss Rudge not only played the violin but played it extremely well.

The program had indeed included a Pound arrangement for solo violin of a 12th-century air by Gaucelm Faidit, and also a short composition of his own entitled *Sujet pour violon (Resineux)*. What angered him was the misleading title of the notice, for these contributions were played by Olga Rudge. Antheil had played his own music.

Beneath the letter an Editor's Note commented: "The 'Perfect Critic' not only attends the concerts he writes about in person, but he signs his name to all articles he publishes thereon. This little nicety Mr. Pound evidently had no knowledge of or he should have been more guarded in his observations."

On December 15 a review of the concert appeared, signed by Irving Schwerke.

NOTES OF THE MUSIC WORLD

Olga Rudge, the American violinist who gave a concert at the Ancien Conservatoire Tuesday evening, assisted by Mr. George Antheil, American composer, at the piano and Mr. Ezra Pound, American poet-composer, turning pages, should be comforted to come into the knowledge that she possesses a "very pretty sonority bidding fair to develop into virtuosity." We also admired her sonority, it is remarkably ample—"pretty," if you will—but more than that did we admire this young artist for having enough courage to sacrifice on the altars of Mr. Antheil's conceited art, personal honors which otherwise might have been hers. Both her enterprise and her playing merit commendation.

Miss Rudge was the first heard in an unaccompanied group—a J-S Bach *Gavotte* and two pieces by Ezra Pound, *Plainte pour la Mort du roi Richard Coeur du Lion* (Gaucelm Faidit, XIIth century) and *Sujet pour violon*. The chief interest of the two latter was apparently not in their melodic charm and ideational content, but rather in the fact that they had dripped from the pen of one who, only a few days ago, so nobly refused to enter the musical hall of fame via the "34th" note route, preferring to get there by a way much less original and certainly more modest. (On the 13th he again refused an opportunity, emphatically denying, as seen in the letter printed yesterday, that he had composed Mr. Antheil's music.) Mr. Pound, it would thus appear, is a favorite with Opportunity, since she has honored him twice with a knock and both times been turned away. This by the way. Mr. Pound's pieces won their share of applause, and to those who like to push their musical researches into that kind of thing, were extremely interesting.

The Mozart "Concerto in A major" was a flat performance, at least so far as Mr. Antheil was concerned. The violinist's sonority was "pretty," but the pianist's was not. Mr. Antheil's playing, even more than Miss Rudge's, lacked distinguishing charm, limpidity and grace. His Mozart accompaniment could have been better, but hardly worse. In his own music Mr. Antheil may try to "get away" with whatever he wants to, but he really should beware of composers so refined and subtle as Mozart.

Mr. Antheil's *First Sonata for violin and piano* and his *Second* (both first performances) caused the audience to disagree. They did so quite *à la bonne franquette*. While we cannot report any "glissando *of* the piano" or any other similarly astonishing phenomena, we can and do make record of this, viz:—that the tone produced by Miss Rudge and Mr. Antheil in the latter's compositions, frequently imposed a severe strain on the naked tympanum; that both pianist and violinist "threw" themselves heartily into their instruments and their music, and that their strenuous exertions had at least this result,—the ear drank hence a copious draught of sound, which in the memory of some listeners was classified as "music" pure and absolute, in that of others as degenerate noise and crash.

On the same page appeared a second letter to the editor.

FROM MR. POUND

Sir: First you credit me with Mr. George Antheil's violin sonatas, and then you credit me with discretion. It won't do. Let us, by all means, "jump" to perfection so far as the power be within us; but your conclusions are illogical; the habits of your critic, as you declare them, do not prove that, even in time of stress, my statements would be guarded. I leave that sort of thing to more competent guarders; all you prove is that your heading, "George

BUREAU INTERNATIONAL DE CONCERTS
C. KIESGEN & E.-C. DELAET
Télégr. Ciadela-Paris   47, Rue Blanche, 47   Tél. Trudaine 20-62

SALLE DU CONSERVATOIRE
2, Rue du Conservatoire (9ᵉ)

Mardi 11 Décembre 1923, à 9 heures du soir

OLGA RUDGE
Violoniste

George ANTHEIL
Compositeur

PROGRAMME

I

1. *Plainte pour la Mort du roi Richard Cœur de Lion*. . — GAUCELM FAIDIT (XIIᵉ siècle)
   Air déchiffré du Manuscrit R. 71 superiore Ambrosiana, par M. Ezra POUND (1).
2. *Gavotte* . . . . — J.-S. BACH
3. *Sujet pour Violon (Resineux)* . . . . — EZRA POUND

   OLGA RUDGE

II. — PREMIÈRE AUDITION

Première Sonate pour Violon et Piano . . . . — GEORGE ANTHEIL
   Allegro moderato, Andante moderato, Funebre, Presto.

   OLGA RUDGE
   Au Piano : l'AUTEUR

III

Concerto en la majeur. . . . . — MOZART
   Allegro, Aperto, Adagio, Rondo.

   OLGA RUDGE
   Au Piano : George Antheil

IV. — PREMIÈRE AUDITION

Deuxième Sonate pour Violon et Piano. . . . . . . — GEORGE ANTHEIL
   Allegro mechanico.

   OLGA RUDGE
   Au Piano : l'AUTEUR

---

(1) *Cet air se trouve, avec partition pour piano par Agnès Bedford, dans FIVE TROUBADOUR SONGS, publié par Boosey and Co, 295, Regent St., London.*

PRIX DES PLACES :
Fauteuils de Balcon, 25 fr.; Premières Loges, 15 fr.; Fauteuils d'Orchestre, 12 fr.; Fauteuils de Baignoires, 10 fr.; Fauteuils de 2ᵉ Loges, 8 fr.; Fauteuils de 3ᵉ Loges et Amphithéâtre, 5 fr.

BILLETS EN VENTE : A la Salle du Conservatoire; chez Durand et Cⁱᵉ, 4, place de la Madeleine; au Bureau Musical, 32, rue Tronchet; au Guide-Billets, 20, avenue de l'Opéra ; chez Roudanez, 9, rue de Médicis et au Bureau International de Concerts, C. Kiesgen et E.-C. Delaet, 47, rue Blanche. Téléphone : Trudaine 20-62.

For a review of this concert, together with some correspondence surrounding it, see pp. 246–50.

Antheil Plays Ezra Pound's Music," was not written by your "perfect critic" but by your imperfect critic or by some other member of your staff, subject like the rest of us, to human frailty and to error.

EZRA POUND

Pound's music was beginning to be known by 1924. Although his opera was not to be performed until two years later, Rudge and Antheil again played the *Sujet pour violon* together with Antheil's music at an Aeolian Hall recital in London on May 10. On this occasion they also performed Pound's "Fiddle Music, First Suite," part of the autograph of which was published in the *Transatlantic Review* in August. On July 7th Pound, Antheil, and Rudge arranged a concert to celebrate the American Declaration of Independence. Pound's contribution to the program, which was given in the Salle Pleyel, is enumerated by him in an unpublished letter to his father of June 19:

> "XV century piece, I dug up in Perugia. [for violin] Javanese fiddle chunes.
> fanfare, violin and tambourin, by E. P. to celebrate George's entrance."

In addition the concert featured Pound's *Strophes de Villon*, melodies from the forthcoming opera, sung by Yves Tinayre. The remainder of the program was given over to Antheil's music, and featured the première of his *Quatuor à cordes*.

Pound and his wife sent out invitations to selected friends. Sylvia Beach, proprietress of the left-bank bookshop Shakespeare and Company, attended and later recorded the following impressions.

> This concert of two musical conspirators was held at the Salle Pleyel, in one of the small rooms. Adrienne Monnier and I were seated with Joyce and his son, Georgio. Joyce had brought Georgio along in the hope of converting him to modern music, but Pound's and Antheil's compositions were hardly the best choice for that purpose. Margaret Anderson and Jean Heap were present. So were Djuna Barnes and Ernest Hemingway.[7]

In these days in Paris there were two "experts in genius": Jean Cocteau and Ezra Pound. The true test of such a gift was to be able to be the first to identify talent no matter what art its

---

[7] Sylvia Beach, *Shakespeare and Company*, London, 1950, p. 132.

author practiced. Had not Cocteau "discovered" Stravinsky and "Les Six"? Pound fastened onto Antheil as the best musical prospect around. Immediately after their first meeting he began probing Antheil for information about contemporary music.

> He accompanied me back home and asked if by any chance I had written anything about my musical aims, and I said, "Yes, I have"; which accidentally happened to be the truth, for I had purchased a typewriter in Berlin and had occasionally amused myself with typing out pronunciamentos on art and music which would have blown the wig off any conventional musician; among other things I said that melody did not exist, that rhythm was the next most important thing to develop in music, and that harmony after all was a matter of what preceded and what followed.
> Ezra was most delighted with all this and asked if he could keep the "precious sheets" for a while, he would take scrupulous care of them.
> "Oh sure," I said. "I'm finished with them anyhow."
> I was, really. I had gotten this particular sort of adolescent effervescence out of myself by capturing it on paper so that it could be read over once or twice, then destroyed. . . .
> After Ezra's visit, and as the weeks went by, it became more and more apparent that Ezra was working with the stuff I had written. Sylvia [Beach]—who, like Eva Weinwurstel, always got to know about everything first—told me that Ezra was planning to write a book about me, and that a friend of Ezra's, Bill Bird, would publish it in Paris.
> This scared me.
> Two months later Ezra was to bring me proof sheets with big black letters on the front page: *Antheil and the* [sic] *Theory on Harmony.*[8]

[8] Antheil, *op. cit.*, pp. 117–18. In addition to "Why a Poet Quit the Muses," reprinted as Appendix III, the following list of Antheil's published articles gives an indication of his musical preoccupations over the years: "Jazz" (*Querschnitt*, 2, 1922, pp. 172–73), "The Musical Ethic of the Future, Musical Neofism" (*Querschnitt*, 3, 1923, pp. 51–53), "Abstraction and Time in Music" (*Little Review*, 10, 1924, pp. 13–15), "Mother of the Earth" (*Transatlantic Review*, Vol. II, No. 2, 1924, pp. 226–27), "Sample of American" (*Querschnitt*, 4, 1924, pp. 132–33), Correspondence (*Transatlantic Review*, Vol. 2, 1925), "My Ballet Méchanique-What it Means" (*Querschnitt*, 5, 1925, pp. 789–91), "Jacques Benoist-Mechin" (*Transition*, 4, 1927, pp. 166–68), "American Folk Music" (*Forum*, 80, 1928, pp. 957–58), "Jazz Is Music" (*Forum* 80, 1928, pp. 64–67), "Wanted—Opera by and for Americans" (*Modern Music*, 7, 1930, pp 11–16), "Breaking into the Movies" (*Modern Music* 14, 1937, pp. 82–86), "On the Hollywood Front" (*Modern Music* 14, 1937, pp. 105–8).

How much of Pound's writing about Antheil may have been taken over from Antheil's scribblings? Certainly the notion that harmony "was a matter of what preceded and what followed" became the core thesis of *The Treatise on Harmony*. Pound needed no one to tell him about rhythm, but the idea that the history of music is a gradual development toward more and more precise expression and accuracy of notation, this was new, and it came from a Stravinsky-inspired Antheil. The temptation here was to place machines higher than men, a temptation to which Antheil surrendered, along with the Futurists, Marinetti and Russolo; and there are a few rather strained lines in Pound touching on this theme. Somewhat later he planned a book on "Machine Art," though it seems to have remained incomplete. More importantly Pound treated Antheil as a convenient personification for ideas which reflect his own advancing musical theories. Antheil sensed this from the start and was embarassed.

> ...from the first day I met him Ezra was never to have the slightest idea of what I was really after in music. I don't think he wanted to have....
>
> I still do not know why I permitted Ezra to issue his book about myself. Perhaps it was because at that moment I could see no other way of blasting into the otherwise tight-as-a-drum salons. In any case my error and lack of judgment were to cause me a lot of future grief—grief which has not been entirely dispelled even today.
>
> Ezra's flamboyant book, couched in language calculated to antagonize everyone, first by its ridiculous praise, then by its vicious criticism of everybody else, did me no good whatsoever; on the contrary, it sowed the most active distaste for the very mention of the name "Antheil" among many contemporary critics, prejudiced them before they had even so much as heard a note of mine. Nobody could have been a tenth as good as Ezra made me.[9]

Pound later realized this too, and when, in 1962, he permitted a reprinting of *The Treatise on Harmony* (London, Peter Owen), Antheil was dropped.

The original volume, entitled *Antheil and the Treatise on Harmony,* was published in Paris at William Bird's Three Mountains Press, October 1924. Substantial portions of the book had appeared throughout the year in the pages of the *Transatlantic*

[9] *Ibid.*, pp. 119–20.

Review, that short-lived periodical which Pound had helped to found along with Hemingway and Ford Madox Ford (the editor). The Antheil chapter had appeared the same year in the pages of *The Criterion* in March. The book had four sections: I. The Treatise on Harmony, II. Antheil, III. William Atheling (a conflation from *The New Age* reviews "with marginalia emitted by George Antheil," and IV. Varia. The book has recently been reprinted in its entirety,[10] so we are transposing the sections here in order that the Antheil essay may lead to the more important Treatise.

GEORGE ANTHEIL[11]
(Retrospect)

I

The Vorticist Manifestos of 1913–14 left a blank space for music; there was in contemporary music, at that date, nothing corresponding to the work of Wyndham Lewis, Pablo Picasso or Gaudier-Brzeska.

Strawinsky arrived as a comfort, but one could not say definitely that his composition was the new music; he had a refreshing robustness; he was a relief from Debussy; but this might have been merely the heritage of Polish folk music manifest in the work of an instinctive genius.

The article on Vorticism in the Fortnightly Review, Aug. 1914 stated that new vorticist music would come from a new computation of the mathematics of harmony not from mimetic representation of dead cats in a fog horn (alias noise tuners). This was part of the general vorticist stand against the accelerated impressionism of our active and meritorious friend Marinetti.[12]

There wasn't any vorticist music available and our specifications couldn't have, in the nature of things, been very exact at that time.

There had, and has, been extremely little critical examination of

---

[10] *Antheil and the Treatise on Harmony*, Da Capo Press, New York, 1968, with an introduction by Ned Rorem. This is a facsimile of the first American edition, Pascal Covici, Publisher, Inc., Chicago, 1927. The Chicago edition has also been used as the basis for the present reprinting.
[11] The first few paragraphs were added for the book version. The original article (*The Criterion*, II, 7, March 1924, pp. 321-31) begins at the paragraph: "For some years, either over my own name, or...," and here we take up the original *Criterion* version, which differs from the book in tiny stylistic details only.
[12] Pound was certainly familiar with Marinetti's work. The reference to the noise tuners suggests that he was also familiar with Luigi Russolo's *L'arte dei Rumori* ("The Art of Noises"), a Futurist manifesto dating from 1913. Russolo produced a number of howlers and buzzers, and intended to replace the symphony orchestra with an orchestra of *intonarumori*.

music; I mean detailed examination of melodic line, structure, etc; comparable to Landor's examination of Catullus; or questioning as to whether a given work contains rhetoric, padding, undue repetition, etc. There had been a great many volumes of "Lives of Musicians" (usually called "Lives of The Great Musicians") and books on the relation of music to morals, the "Problem ... etc. ..."

This is not to say that there haven't been intelligent musicologues; for example Fétis[13]: Les impressions du chef (d'orchestre) ne peuvent être bien comprises que par des signes extérieurs (Manuel des Compositeurs).

Friedrich Richter; to the effect that actual composition can not be compared with studies which are merely the application of abstract theories (Traité de Contrepoint).[14]

Sauzay on Bach,[15] already cited, to the effect that Bach was doing something other than follow known laws.

Dolmetsch.[16] Take the whole of his book on xviith and xviiith Century Music.

There had been Mr. Corfe's revealing title page[17], a document of very great importance, but no one had noticed it.

[13] There is no apparent continuity in the names of the five celebrated theoists Pound mentions in the following paragraphs (Fétis, Richter, Sauzay, Dolmetsch, and Corfe), but there is a rationale: they were all both practitioners as well as probing theorists. Thus, François Joseph Fétis (1784-1871) was a pianist, organist, and violinist as well as a famous critic and historian. He founded the *Revue Musicale* in 1827 and in 1833 became director of the Brussels Conservatory. His chief work was the monumental *Biographie Universelle des Musiciens* (1837-44) in eight volumes. The full title of the book from which Pound quotes is *Manuel des compositeurs, directeurs de musique, chefs d'orchestre et de musique militaire*, Paris, 1837.

[14] Ernst Friedrich Eduard Richter (1808-1879) had been cantor of the Thomas School at Leipzig (Bach's former position), and was the author of numerous theoretical works, the chief of which were his *Lehrbuch der Harmonie*, Leipzig, 1853; *Lehrbuch der Fuge*, Leipzig, 1859; and the *Lehrbuch des einfachen und doppelten Kontrapunkt*, Leipzig, 1872. It is the last-named from which Pound quotes in a French translation: *Traité complet de contrepoint traduit par Gustave Sandré*, Leipzig, 1892, p. 9: "La théorie pure ne peut et ne doit s'occuper de la pratique, car elle a pour seul but de définir la nature des divers éléments constitutifs de l'art, sans traiter jamais des cas spéciaux, particuliers, qui résultent de l'emploi de certains procédés personnels."

[15] Eugène Sauzay (1809-1901) was a violinist first in the famous Baillot Quartet and later in the orchestra of Napoleon III. *Le violon harmonique* was published in Paris, 1889. In *The Treatise on Harmony* Pound quotes this passage: "Il faut se borner à penser que J.-S. Bach écrivait la musique par certains procédés dont la loi général nous échappe," p. 217.

[16] See pp. 42–46.

[17] Joseph Corfe (1740-1820) was an English organist and composer. He was organist and master of choristers at Salisbury Cathedral, 1792–1804. He composed a treatise on singing as well as the volume to which Pound alludes here: *Thoroughbass Simplified*, London, n.d., (182?).

We had also said that the organization of forms is a much more active and energetic occupation than copying the play of light on a haystack; and, elsewhere, that there is in music a fault corresponding to the fault of verbosity in writing.

There is musical rhetoric.

You may argue that Beethoven committed in one or two sonatas, all the faux pas that were to be the fashion in the days of Wagner and Brahms; you may argue that Wagner, a great musician, in his manner of greatness, produced a sort of pea soup, and that Debussy distilled it into a heavy mist, which the post-Debussians have dessicated into a diaphanous dust cloud.

You can compare Debussy to Manet, you can say that he was an heresy, and that he is less concerned with the mechanics of music than with using music to affect the visual imagination of his hearers.

You may also disagree with any or all of the above statements.

I have found "harmony" defined as a "simultaneous melody."[18]

Some musicians dislike that definition. Let us say that chords are like colour. They are a complex of sound occurring at a given instant of time, a minimum audible of time, as colour is a complex of light vibrations thrown off by a given spot, or minimum visible, of space or surface.

There remains the given succession of sounds; and the given delimitation of points, whence lines, surfaces, volumes. Here endeth our retrospect.

II

The authentic genius will be as touchy, or perhaps more touchy, about the differences between his own particular art and all others, as, or than, he will about any possible analogies with other arts.

And it is a very good sign that Antheil is annoyed with the term "architecture" when this term is applied to music. The sensitive non-musician had been content with this term; the sensitive manipulator of verbal rhythm has been content with the phrase thematic invention; Antheil has emphasized the term "mechanisms."

He has, in his written statements about music, insisted that music exists in time-space; and is therefore very different from any kind of plastic art which exists all at once.

---

[18] Pound is possibly referring to this statement by Francesco Geminiani, quoted in Dolmetsch: "The Art of Accompagniament consists in displaying Harmony, disposing the Chords, in a Just Distribution of the Sounds whereof they consist, and in ordering them after a Manner, they may give the Ear the Pleasure of a continued and uninterrupted Melody." Arnold Dolmetsch, *The Interpretation of the Music of the XVIIth and XVIIIth Centuries*, p. 354.

Just as Picasso, and Lewis, and Brancusi have made us increasingly aware of form, of form combination, or the precise limits and demarcations of flat forms and of volumes, so Antheil is making his hearers increasingly aware of time-space, the divisions of time-space.

From Manet to Matisse the good painters revived and resensitized our colour sense.

Rousseau, Cézanne, Picasso, Lewis, Gaudier revived and revivified our perception of form.

The XIXth century musicians ending with Debussy and Schönberg were occupied among other things with musical colour; in Debussy's case he got it mixed up with visual colour; I mean in his own mind. The arts were in a period when each art tried to lean on some other. Notably painting, sculpture and music leant heavily on bad literature.

All of which means something more than: Picasso was a magnificent draughtsman, Wyndham Lewis is a master of design, George Antheil has a good sense of rhythm. Nobody but a fool will contradict any of these statements; but the point is that Picasso, Lewis, Antheil were or are all doing something rather different in kind from Manet and Debussy; they were or are taking hold of their art by a different extremity.

For some years, either over my own name, or over the signature William Atheling, I have indicated the paucity of thematic invention in music; that doesn't in the least mean that I anticipated Antheil. I pointed out that music and poetry had been in alliance in the twelfth century, that the divorce of the two arts had been to the advantage of neither, and that melodic invention declined simultaneously and progressively with their divergence. The rhythms of poetry grew stupider, and they in turn affected or infected the musicians who set poems to music.

That observation was natural to me, as poet, working for twenty years with a monolineal rhythm. The horizontal construction (or mechanics of music) had gone or was, with increasing rapidity going, to pot.

It was also possible, by study of twelfth-century music, to see that melody wasn't mere improvisation. The Hindoos have given us the terms, *raga* and *tala*, the first for toneless rhythm arrangement, the second for sequence of notes at determined pitches.[19]

Let me say here, in my twenty-fifth or twenty-sixth parenthesis, that there are two æsthetic ideals, one the Wagnerian, which is not dissimilar from that of the Foire de Neuilly, i.e. you confuse the spectator by smacking as many of his senses as possible at every possible moment, this prevents his noting anything with unusual lucidity, but you may

---

[19] The two terms are confused. *Tala* refers to rhythm and *raga* to pitch sequence.

fluster or excite him to the point of making him receptive; i.e. you may slip over an emotion, or you may sell him rubber doll or a new cake of glass-mender during the hurly-burly.

The other æsthetic has been approved by Brancusi, Lewis, the vorticist manifestos; it aims at focussing the mind on a given definition of form, or rhythm, so intensely that it becomes not only more aware of that given form, but more sensitive to all other forms, rhythms, defined planes, or masses.

It is a scaling of eye-balls, a castigating or purging of aural cortices; a sharpening of verbal apperceptions. It is by no means an emollient.

The fulcrums of revolution in art are very small, and the academic recognition of *faits accomplis* usually tardy, sic; Marchetto (of Padua, in the fourteenth century, in his *Pomerium*) "shows that the *breve* can be divided into three, four, six, eight, nine, and twelve parts, but does not admit that these new values are anything but *semi-breve"*; Prosdocimus de Beldemandis, in the *Tractatus Practicus,* shows that fourteenth-century Italians *"faisaient suivre à la semi-brève la minima et la semi-minima et autres notes encores dont la valeur un peu vague ocillait entre la minima et la chroma."*[20]

To grasp the modus of Antheil's procedure one must remember that the development of musical notation has been exceedingly slow; that

---

[20] Guido Gasperini, "L'Art Musical Italien au XIV siècle," in Lavignac and Laurencie's *Encyclopédie de Musique* (Delagrave, Paris). (Pound's note.) Guido Gasperini's article should be read in its entirety by anyone wishing to understand Pound's argument. He is referring here, though not too clearly, to the fourteenth-century period known as "Ars Nova," after a treatise of that name by Phillipe de Vitri (1291-1361). The principal achievement of the Ars Nova theorists was to render the rhythms of musical notation more precise by introducing new signs with *quantitative* durations. This made greater rhythmic variety possible, and indeed fourteenth-century music is noted for its special rhythmic *élan*. Prosdocimus de Beldemandis in his *Tractatus practice cantus mesurabilis ad modum Italicorum,* Padua, 1422, was one of the leading theorists of the Italian Ars Nova movement. Marchettus of Padua, in a treatise entitled *Pomerium musicae mensurate* (written sometime between 1309 and 1343) provided music with a neatly classified system of rhythmic notation. The basis of the system is the *breve* which never alters its value once fixed. He then divides the *breve* into ternary and binary groups, giving units of three, six, nine, twelve, and two, four, six, eight equal parts respectively. The important "fulcrum" of this "revolution" was that it created a notational system in which for the first time quantitative proportional units were expressible. Previously rhythmic notation had been *qualitative*, i.e., one note was recognized as longer or shorter than another but by no fixed ratio. Curiously, this quantifying of time may be traced directly to the introduction of the mechanical clock into Europe in the late thirteenth century. Time then became *audible,* and seconds, minutes, hours became sonic time-cells, each proportional to the others. This development found its parallel in the revived rhythmic consciousness of composers (Stravinsky, Antheil) at the beginning of the present century under the impact of machine technology. Note Pound's later use of the words "mechanism" and "precision."

up to the year 1300 the written notes were *not* an exposition of the melody, they were a mnemonic device. A man who knew the tune or a man with a very fine ear for musical phrase could make use of them.

Couperin complains "we do not play as we write"; Dom Bedos de Celles has to warn his readers against other writers who "have not said a word about ornaments, nor of the combination of silences, held and touched notes to form articulations of the music, etc.; of the distinction between first and second quavers and of the crochets, etc., of their inequality, etc."*

We have all heard of tempo rubato, ad lib., and so forth. To Igor Strawinsky we owe the revelation: "NO, you will *not* find any musical geniuses to execute this music. It would be better for the composer to write down what he wants the performer to play."

Strawinsky's merit lies very largely in taking hard bits of rhythm, and noting them with great care. Antheil continues this; and these two composers mark a definite break with the "atmospheric" school; they both write horizontal music;[21] but horizontal music has been written before; the Arabs have used it for a long time; the troubadours used it; you might have detected horizontal merits in Arnaut Daniel and Faidit.

My own idea is that the horizontal merits faded from music (and from the rhythm of poetry) with the gradual separation of the two arts. A man thinking with mathematical fractions is not impelled toward such variety of *raga* as a man working with the necessary inequalities of words. But the verbal rhythm is monolinear. It can form contrapunto only against its own echo, or against a developed expectancy.

Here we must emphasise the relation of *raga, tala,* and harmony. Any note can follow any other, any ten notes can follow each other in any order you like, but if their arrangement, I mean their *tala*,[22] their tone sequence, is of any interest it will *lock* their time intervals, i.e. their individual durations and the rests between them.

When counterpoint slumped into harmony, Lutheran chorals, etc., and progressively into Schönberg, this fundamental drive in music was obscured. The harmonists gave their attention to the perpendicular values, ending in a technical morass, undefined rhythms, tonal slush.

---

* Arnold Dolmetsch, *Music of the Seventeenth and Eighteenth Centuries.* (Pound's note.)

21 Pound means merely to distinguish between atmospheric music and music with strong lines. The word "horizontal" is unfortunate. Stravinsky's music during the period under discussion was decidedly vertical, i.e., harmonic. The music of Schoenberg on the other hand was contrapuntal (horizontal), which is the direction implicit in atonality and the twelve-tone method. We can probably trace this misunderstanding of Pound's to Antheil, since later in the essay Pound quotes Antheil as referring to [sic] "the vertically-calculated music of Schönberg."

22 Read *raga.*

A purist and an archæologist might have revived the precision of *raga*;[23] he probably would have agreed with Dolmetsch's verbal grumble, "No, music didn't begin with Bach, it ended with Bach." (Mr. Dolmetsch didn't mean this literally, but he got something off his chest, and mine, when he said it.)

What I am driving at is that Antheil has not only given his attention to rhythmic precision, and noted his rhythms with an exactitude, which we may as well call genius, but he has invented new mechanisms, mechanisms of this particular age.

1. His large concerto for piano and orchestra is early work. I have not heard it with orchestra, but the piano part contains at least one good mechanism.

2. In "The Golden Bird" he was not wholly freed of Debussy, but he did succeed in making the "solid object." This term suggests sculpture and is intended to, just as Debussy intended to suggest apparitions in mist.

By solid object "musically," I suppose we mean a construction or better a "mechanism" working in time-space, in which all the joints are close knit, the tones fit each other at set distances, it can't simply slide about. This new quasi-sculptural solidity is something different from the magnificent stiffness or rigidity of Bach's multi-linear mechanism.

3. In the "mechanisms" there are distinct innovations of musical action. An electric power-station has recurrences, differing from those of the minuet.

4. In the series of six piano pieces called "Sonates Sauvages" Antheil gives us the first music really suggesting Lewis "Timon" designs.

Numbers 3, 4, and 5 are interesting experiments, the whole of this music is still in the experimental stage, which does not mean that there are no definite results. Numbers 1 and 2 are accomplished facts. The first of these sonatas "does it," the base is really a basis, the music rises and acts above it, like a projectile carrying a wire and cutting, defining the three dimensions of space.

The sixth of these sonatas seems, after the others, a retrospect. Every solid artist having made an advance by emphasising some cardinal element, returns to examine the other elements of that art. This sonata is, by comparison with the others, soft and "feminine," by its title.

Antheil has purged the piano, he has made it into a respectable musical instrument, recognising its percussive nature. "It is like the xylophone and the cymballo."

5. In the magnificent violin sonata, the most recent of his works, he has tried something of the same sort with the violin, I mean he has

---

[23] Read *tala*.

made the piano sound like a pianoforte, he has used the violin for sounds that you couldn't make as well or better on the flute.

I repeat that the thorough artist is probably more sensitive to the difference between his own art and other arts, than to their resemblances. One of the marks of Antheil's authenticity is his disgust with the term "architecture," and his insistence on the term "mechanism."

Antheil is probably the first artist to use machines, I mean actual modern machines, without bathos.[24]

Machines are not really literary or poetic, an attempt to poetise machines is rubbish. There has been a great deal of literary fuss over them. The Kiplonians get as sentimental over machines as a Dickensian does over a starved and homeless orphan on a bleak cold winterrrr's night.

Machines are musical. I doubt if they are even very pictorial or sculptural, they have form, but their distinction is not in form, it is in their movement and energy; reduced to sculptural stasis they lose *raison d'être,* as if their essence.

Let me put it another way, they don't confront man like the *faits accomplis* of nature; these latter he has to attack *ab exteriore,* by his observation, he can't construct 'em; he has to examine them. Machines are already an expression of his own desire for power and precision; one man can learn from them what some other man has put into them, just as he can learn from other artistic manifestations. A painting of a machine is like a painting of a painting.

The lesson of machines is precision, valuable to the plastic artist, and to literati.

Prose is perhaps only half an art. The medium of poetry is words, i.e. human symbols, conventions; they are capable of including things of nature, that is, sound quality, timbre, up to a point.

They have interior rhythm, there can be rhythm in their arrangement, even tone leadings, and these with increasing precision; but you can not get a word back into the non-human.

It is redundancy, and therefore bad art, to use it where a less conventional humanised means will serve. Words are superfluous for certain things and inadequate for others; we have already said that a painter about to paint a sunset needs to know more about it than an author who describes or refers to it.

---

[24] This remark is uninformed. Satie's ballet *Parade* (1917) had called for sirens, a steam engine, an airplane motor, a dynamo, Morse code apparatus, and typewriters. Pound had heard the ballet in London (*v. The New Age,* December 18, 1919), though probably in a scaled-down version. See also note 11, *sup.,* on Russolo's machine-orchestra (1913).

I am perfectly aware that you can imitate the sound of machinery verbally, you can make new words, you can write

pan-pam   vlum   vlum   vlan-ban, etc.,

there are also mimetic words like *bow-bow* and *mao, miaou,* in Greek, Chinese, Egyptian, and other tongues, imitating the noises of animals; but these are insufficient equipment for the complete man of letters, or even for national minstrelsy. The mechanical man of futurist fiction is false pastoral, he can no more fill literature than could the bucolic man. This is perhaps an aside.

I take it that music is the art most fit to express the fine quality of machines. Machines are now a part of life, it is proper that men should feel something about them; there would be something weak about art if it couldn't deal with this new content. But to return to the vorticist demands:

"Every concept, every emotion presents itself to the vivid consciousness in some primary form, it belongs to the art of that form."

I am inclined to think that machines acting in time-space, and hardly existing save when in action, belong chiefly to an art acting in time-space; at any rate Antheil has used them, effectively. That is a *fait accompli* and the academicians can worry over it if they like.

6. Thorough artists are constantly searching for the permanent elements in their art. This is a very different thing from being interested in embroideries and emollients and wanting to keep up electroplates.

The thorough artist is constantly trying to form the ideograph of "the good" in his art; I mean the ideograph of admirable compound-of-qualities that make any work of art permanent.

I think, too, that all thorough artists at the outset try to put down their ideas about this, verbally, and that their notes are usually in a fairly unintelligible jargon, having a meaning for themselves, and for a very limited number of other people.

This metaphysic doesn't always get printed. Its chief characteristics are extreme seriousness, and *reiteration:* n.b. reiteration of certain sentences which obviously mean more to the artist than to the reader. This mass of verbiage must be taken rather as evidence of mental activity than as exposition of ideas.

The difference between this utterance and similar statements by lunatics is that the artist does attain precise utterance in his own medium. And from that precise utterance the interested reader may interpret, more or less, the artist's ambiguous, or more than ambiguous, verbal statements about life, cosmos, being, non-being, time, eternity, etc.

(These are, often, no worse or no more ambiguous than the general and considered statements of professed philosophers.)

I mean that from such fragmentary and confused writing the intelligent observer will induce the fact that the artist is very gravely concerned with the bases of his art, and with the relations of that to *everything else*. This is very different from preciosity; archæological preciosity; emollients; trimmings; connoisseurship; traditions regarding superfices, or the customs or fashions of the moment.

Hence the permanent resemblances of masterwork, the "revolutionary" nature of genius, the returns to the primitives, and so forth.

Antheil is supremely sensitive to the existence of music in time-space. The use of the term "fourth dimension" is probably as confusing in Einstein as in Antheil. I believe that Einstein is capable of conceiving the factor time as affecting space relations. He does this in a mode hitherto little used, and with certain quirks that had not been used by engineers before him; though the time element enters into engineering computations; and the only lucid remarks on economics have, in our day, come from an engineer.

The x, y, and z axes of analytics would appear to me to provide for what Antheil calls the fourth dimension of music, the "oblique," but technical mathematical language is almost as obscure as Antheil's. The first of his piano sonatas shows perfectly clearly what he means. And a gang of African savages would probably illustrate what he means by the "hole in time-space."

As indication of his attempt to form the ideograph of the art, and *de quoi rêvent ces jeunes gens,* we turn to Antheil's criticism of other composers, the turns of phrase, the abruptness recalling Gaudier's manifestos:

"Despite his great admiration for Strawinsky we find (*Der Querschnitt,* Sommer, 1923) the failure of Strawinsky, the only man who seemed rhythmically and musically gifted enough to reorganise the machineries of music."[25]

"... event of Strawinsky necessary, ... antipode to the anæmic and unmusical but marvellously vertically-calculated music of Schönberg."

"In accepting Satie as a master, ... we see that he [Strawinsky] was

---

[25] Antheil's remarks about Stravinsky should perhaps be prefaced with a brief account of his relationship to that master. He had been an early admirer of Stravinsky, meeting him first in Berlin in 1922. "He was my hero," he wrote in his autobiography. "I worshipped the brain that had conceived the colossal, world-shaking 'Sacre du Printemps'...." Stravinsky, too, seems to have liked the young American. But after Antheil's arrival in Paris, a rumor started that he was going about telling people how much Stravinsky admired his compositions. Stravinsky heard of this, and the next time the two met at a concert Stravinsky

nothing but a jolly Rossini, a real musician of terrific verve and musicality in whose hands every musical machinery had to undergo a transformation, ... a brave and jolly Rossini in an age where composers were occupied with improvising rhapsodically on music paper after the manner of Bartok, Ornstein, Szymanowski, Block, and the too-late-Rachmaninoffs, ..." etc.

So much for your idols, and the china shop. There is in Antheil's notes a constant tirade against improvisation.

Then we come to appreciations, tempered: "Debussy great destructionist, evolved new musical locomotion of time; genius of French salon, inhabitant of pages of Madame Bovary ... ease in which he passes from the ribbon on her dressing-table to the quietness of outdoors, never more than a mile from her house."

"His piano [Debussy's] breathes and undulates with ancestral tinkle ... but soft and persuasive ... can music be 'impressionistic'? is it not a term for painting alone?"

"Debussy is new and forever a great land-mark in musical composition," i.e. because of his "new propulsion of time-spaces." "A what's-his-name Italian and the juggler Satie discovered and unfolded most of his nuances beforehand."

I take it this "what's-his-name Italian" is Fanelli *(Tableau Symphonique,* 1883, etc.), to whom justice has long been overdue.

"Debussy, soul of ardent virgin, clear and sentimental implanted in great artistic nature."

Les Six "charming and fickle people. Everything they imitate with the utmost freshness and understanding."

"Cataclysms: Wagner, Scriabine, Bloch. It is all a little fat. Bloch however has the memory of other things. He wants to be without fat."

"Sound vibrations are the strongest and most fluid space vibrations capable of a tangible mathematic."

(There are a number of pages full of such abstract statements which are interesting only after one has heard Antheil's music.)

"... in musical history names of great men, eventually discerned only through the necessity which they have apart from others to create a new locomotion for their musicality."

---

cut him dead with a monocled stare. The estrangement was not repaired until 1941 when the two met again in Hollywood. We may assume that these events had something to do with Antheil's opinions in 1924. Similarly we may feel inclined to excuse the soft spot he harbored for Ernest Bloch, his own former teacher, without excusing the soft spots in this composer's music. And we may not be inclined to excuse Pound for passing off Antheil's flabby opinions as "very good sense."

"Music, the adventure of time with space."

"Architecture static... impossible term in musical criticism... impressionism, still more imbecile term."

"Has anyone beyond Strawinsky brought forward a new propulsion of time-space, a new comprehension of musical mechanism?"

"Two men who resemble each other in mechanism but are total opposites in sensibility: Ernest Bloch... Debussian-Javanese-Mongolian tonalities... essentially Jewish, voluptuous without being sentimental."

"Szymanowski... [his music] ranges from being infinitely precious to the soul-shattering, fat iridescence of Scriabine."

"Now, emphatically necessary to break forever from the fatness of Wagner."

"'Afternoon of a Faun,' despite his professed enmity toward Wagner, crammed with marvellous alchemised 'Tristan.'"

"Bartok, while sense of time-space in the violin sonata is essentially masterful and probably his own, has done much bird-stuffing with folk-songs of Hungary."

"Two ways music can not go: first, purely vertical—one is no longer satisfied with static sensuality that lacks adequate machinery to move it. Second, the purely horizontal, organisation of time-spaces in single plane no longer interesting."

Schönberg "whose musical machinery is based fundamentally upon Mendelssohn."

All of which appears to me to be very good sense. As to background and general æsthetics, limiting biography to minimum: George Antheil, born Trenton, N.J., July 8, 1901, of Polish parents; taken to Poland at age of four, returned to America at fourteen, already composing canons and fugues, studied with Von Sternberg and Bloch; performing his own compositions with Berlin Philharmonic and other mid-European orchestras in 1922. Possibly the first American or American-born musician to be taken seriously. If America has given or is to give anything to general æsthetics it is presumably an æsthetic of machinery, of porcelain baths, of cubic rooms painted with Ripolin, hospital wards with patent dustproof corners and ventilating appliances. Only when these spaces become clean enough, large enough, sufficiently nickel-plated, can a sense of their proportion and arrangement breed a desire for order, τὸ καλόν, in that arrangement; from which perhaps a beauty, a proportion of painting and architecture. There we must leave it.

But Antheil has made a beginning; that is in writing music that couldn't have been written before. "Interpreting," as the awful word is, his age, but doing it without the least trace of rhetoric. He is not local. His musical world is a world of steel bars, not of old stone and ivy.

There are his analogies to Lewis's "Timon," to the "ice-blocks" of Picasso. There is the break from the negative (in the geometric sense) or suspended, fluid quality of Chopin and Debussy. There is edge. There is the use of the piano, no longer melodic, or cantabile, but solid, unified as one drum. I mean *single* sounds produced by multiple impact; as distinct from chords, which are sort of chains or slushes of sound. That the fifth sonata is built up on memories of peasant violins in Poland doesn't in the least break the unity of this series, or turn the work into romanticised reminiscence. It is the actual sound, time-spacing of this violin playing, i.e. the proper musician's content of it, not its literary associations, that George Antheil has utilised.

POSTSCRIPT, JULY 1924
1. The old harmonists made a wire work, Antheil wants slabs of sound to construct his active time-machines. It may be necessary to fill in the gaps between the wires (the sacrosanct 1sts, 3ds, and 5ths,) even if it cause pain to some ears avid of succulence and insensitive to the major form.
2. "Rhythmic reiteration" as one objector has called it, is of course M. Strawinsky's personal property?
3. Postscript to the treatise, etc. The unsynthesized sub 7th.?

Portions of the "Atheling" section of *Antheil and the Treatise on Harmony* appeared in the pages of the *Transatlantic Review* during 1924,[26] prior to the October publication of the book. The notes are a conflation of remarks from *The New Age* columns, 1918-1920, selected by Agnes Bedford though undoubtedly at the author's instigation. They have not been extracted carefully and many *non sequiturs* result. Pound is guilty here of the very thing he always warned against: ideas are true only as they go into practice, i.e., they must have specific references to the comings and goings on the Jacob's ladder or in the street. *The New Age* reviews were immediate criticism, specific reference. In the following form they are purely notional, fleshed out with no particularities, for all references to historical events have been slashed. Readers already familiar with the original reviews may wish to pass on to page 290 and avoid these oblique ramblings. Neither do Antheil's flatulent "emissions" possess any mordant attraction.

[26] *Transatlantic Review*, Vol. I, No. 2, February, pp. 109–15; Vol. I, No. 5, May, pp. 370–73; and Vol. II, No. 2, August, pp. 220–25 (which also contained the autograph of Pound's "Fiddle Music, First Series").

ATHELING

"William Atheling" wrote fortnightly in the *New Age* from 1917-20; he sympathised with Arnold Dolmetsch' opinions, he might very well have thought that music ended with Bach. He existed in order that I might study the actual sounds produced by performing musicians. He wrote in the hope of making it possible or easier for the best performers to do their best work in public rather than their worst or their middling. By this he meant that he liked hearing Moussorgsky, he preferred Russian bareness to the upholsteries of XIXth century Europe. He liked music with a strong horizontal action, preferring it to music which seems to steam up from the earth. He shared my interest in the fitting of *motz el son;* i. e. the fitting of words and tunes.

He found the Kennedy-Fraser's Hebridean research of great interest, he approved of Le Roi Renaud; and of French folksong, if rigorously selected, as late as Le Pauvre Laboureur, and La Carmagnole. He regretted the lost culture of Henry Lawes. He enjoyed without much audible, though with a good deal of mute, opposition, the writers of Bel Canto: Caldara, Durante, and Carissimi.

In 1922 his marginalia were submitted to a "qualified musician" with the request that any general criticism therein, might be separated from the paragraphs dealing only with the success or failure of particular concerts (à la "Herr Wintergarten im Bechsteinsaal trat auf und wieder ab.," or "At this point the composer has drawn his inspiration from the soda-water font of Mendelssohn, in fact several cuckoos have laid their eggs in Mr. Elgar's nest, and he has patiently hatched them all," or; "M. Mark Hambourg's playing presented no points of interest.")

In 1923 the siftings were submitted to George Antheil with the request that he mark any passages with which he violently disagreed, or which seemed to him far too imbecile to be tolerated.

His scribblings on the edge of my typescript were intended for my eye alone; but it is sometimes more interesting to know what a man thinks than to know what he thinks prudent to say at a given moment. At any rate both M. Antheil and myself are so fed up with the alleged critics who try ever to appear omniscient, and who work not to express their thoughts but to establish their critical position; that we have preferred this extreme imprudence.

The notes can stay here as a manifesto of our angle of attack. There is the result of my twenty years work with monolinear verbal rhythms, my study of mediaeval music; and Antheil's solid fugal, contrapuntal, and harmonic training. There are certain forms of musical padding and rhetoric and mushiness with which we are both equally bored.

Atheling's notes are badly written; heaven knows they are in places platitudinous; but this platitude and the necessity for this platitude may be taken as a measure of certain very simple things which contemporary performers, and not by any means the worst of them only, so often, and often so amazingly, do not know.

NOTES FOR PERFORMERS
by William Atheling, with marginalia emitted by George Antheil

I. THE PIANO, *February* 1918

Why indeed the Piano? Apart from bickering over the tempered scale, though one can hardly accept the argument that it is no use bothering over inaccuracy of pitch that only one person in two hundred can perceive, people without absolute and pitch sense do, and do very often get a certain very definite pleasure from correct playing, even if they are incapable of detecting a single error, or even a series of errors save by a vague dissatisfaction or by an even slighter and more vague diminution of pleasure.

All keyboard instruments tend to make performers of people not born to be musicians; and the very fact that one can play a keyboard instrument quite correctly without in the least knowing whether a given note is in tune or is correct in itself, tends to obscure the value of true pitch. This perception, the first requisite of any player upon strings is therefore left, perhaps, wholly unconsidered by the piano student. The piano tuner is responsible for all that. His services are inexpensive. This argument might be used also against the earlier keyboard instruments although they were never sufficiently loud to drive out, or predominate over, the rest of the instruments. And they did not fill the building.

From initial carelessness about pitch, piano-playing has gradually progressed to a carelessness about actual sound. The attention that was centered in earlier music upon purity of tone, upon sound-quality, has been weakened and weakened till I have seen a composer of no small talent utterly impervious to the quality of the noise he was making.

(I presume the "timbre" is meant. G. A.)

The notes were in the right order; they followed each other as he intended; he was satisfied.

I long, perhaps not too vainly, for the day when the piano shall be as the hansom, which vehicle it not a little resembles, and when the pianist shall be as the cab-driver, so far as the concert hall is concerned. The instrument will abide with us yet, for there is the pianola attachment, and if, for some time, it is necessary to train acrobats to play

Bach-Busoni for pianola records, surely human invention will lead to, and has already discovered, a means for making the records direct. The future composer will do his work, not with a pen but a punch. "You couldn't pack a Broadwood half a mile," says Mr. Kipling, but there is always the gramophone.

(I bow gracefully. Several years. G. A.)

At least "it took me back twenty years." Have we not all, with the shades of Murger, with the well-known death mask gaping at us, and with the plaster cast of the drowned girl hanging in the other corner, have we not all of us known the charm? (The Schumann quality that has been read into Chopin by generations of conservatoire young ladies; to the obscuring of Chopin's austerity.)

It was the studio "mood" opposed to the piano of Sir Frederic Leighton and the Leightonians, the instrument at which the very young mother sits with her numerous well-washed, fresh off-spring clambering about her, receiving the cultural rudiments.

I do not say that I am above the studio manner; that I would not willingly recall the past; forget my bald spot. "Four and forty times would I," as Mr. Kipling has it, listen to the wailful note as the more reserved couple wait until it's time to walk home, and the less reserved, or more "bohemian" couple hold hands under the sofa cushion,—Jugend, Jugend, Jugend! and the inefficient illustrator (aged sixty) who once hoped to paint like Raphael, looks at the ceiling or the performer.

But what has all this to do with the concert-hall? A certain crop of female pianists always hoped to produce in the concert-hall the atmosphere of the studio; to bring to the hoarse old gentleman from the Thames valley and to the large-waisted lady from Roehampton a "breath of the real meaning," to "show them that life..." and sometimes the female pianist succeeded... After the final uncalled for encore, when all but her dearest friends had left the building. Nevertheless the concert-hall is not the studio. Some musicians may actually play better in studios, they may derive force from the "atmosphere," or the company may blur the critical senses, but these things do not concern the concert-hall. The magnetic theory is invalid.

(In fact the concert-hall has nothing at all to do with the studio. It is its enemy, thank God. I prefer the excusable boredom of the classics to the young gentleman who "sketches" Chopin out with the new knowledge of a Cyril Scott. G. A.)

The magnetic theory is invalid. No performer can rely on emotionalising the audience.

(One must try as hard as Brancusi's bird. Finished! Why worry? The hysteria is there. G. A.)

Music in a concert-hall must rely on itself and the perfection of its execution; it is, as it were, under glass. It exists on the other side of the footlights, apart from the audience. With apologies to the language, the audience are spectators, they watch a thing of which they are not part, and that thing must be complete in itself. They may be moved by the contemplation of its beauty, they are not moved—or at least can be moved only in an inferior and irrelevant way—by being merged into the action of the stage.

(Push this a little further and you have my theory of absolutism, ffff and pppp are as sentimental as the insufficient painter nuancing up his messes. G. A.)

Hundreds of musical careers have been muddled because performers have not understood how entirely the music must lead its own life;

(My dear E. P. hundreds of musical careers have been ruined because there was no such thing in the people. G. A.)

must have its own separate existence apart from the audience; how utterly useless it is to try to mix up audience and performance.

(Which all reminds me that I once had a friend who always said "I might have become a great pianist if...." Tommyrot! G. A.)

March 1918

A concert in a concert-hall is a performance, a presentation, not an appeal to the sympathies of the audience *(Yes. G. A.)* It is, or should be, as definitely a presentation or exhibition as if the performer were to bring out a painted picture and hang it before the audience *(Yes, yes, why not? G. A.)* The music must have as much a separate existence as has the painting. It is a malversion of art for the performer to beseech the audience (via the instrument) to sympathise with his or her temperament, however delicate or plaintive or distinguished.

(By the way that reminds me that the emotionalism you speak of is the performer's dramatic disguise. When listening to music why not listen for music. Musical art assuredly can come only out of the very inmost secrets of musical line. Why not come out and out with it and say that music is no Goddamn circus. G. A.)

From the "studio" manner (in concert-halls), from the domestic manner,

(Great mistake to confuse it with music. G. A.)

from the rural church manner, and from the national festival manner,

(Ditto. Politics is no field for a music critic. G. A.)

may the surviving deities protect and deliver us! They have not, they do not, but we do note cease to pray that they may achieve it.

(The studio manner is the kindergarten method for young radical ladies. G. A.)

An era of bad taste probably gathers to itself inferior matter from preceding periods. An indiscriminate rummaging in the past does not help to form a tradition.

(A splendid turn for Mr. Casella, Malipiero, Prokofieff, and the Six. G. A.)

A sense of rhythm covers many defects.

(One might say almost all. G. A.)

The pain caused to the ear by occasional horrid sounds is quickly obliterated in the succeeding flow of the music. Singers hoping for platform success will do well to notice this.

(This is the whole thing in a nutshell, not only of singers, but of all platform artists. Ninety per cent of failures are due to absolute incapability in the primary rudiments of music—rhythm! How can they hope to be musicians—not even an excuse! Printed notes laid before them and keyboard instruments. Everything laid out and planned for the unmusical! Back to the troubadour! I mean ninety per cent are not musicians, trained, born or anything. G. A.)

A drag, a lack of the wave force, deadens, tires, utterly wears out the audience. Rhythm-sense is not merely a tempo measure, it is not merely a clock-work of the bar-lengths. Measured time is only one form of rhythm; but a true rhythm-sense assimilates all sorts of uneven pieces of time, and keeps the music alive.

Lawes' work is an example of how the words of a poem may be set, and enhanced by music. There are different techniques in poetry; men write to be read, or spoken, or declaimed, or rhapsodised; and quite differently to be sung. . . .

(By the way, most songs are written for the wrong kind. G. A.)

Words written in the first manners are spoiled by added music; it is superfluous; it swells out their unity into confusion.

When skilled men write for music then music can both render their movement, as Lawes does often, tone by tone, and quantity by quantity; or the musician may apparently change the word-movement with a change that it were better to call a realisation. Music is not speech. Arts attract us because they are different from reality. Emotions shown in actual speech poured out in emotion will not all go into verse. The printed page does not transmit them, nor will musical notation record them phonographically.

(Ha! The famous Antheil notation to the rescue! G. A.)

But for all that, a certain bending of words or of syllables over several notes may give an emotional equivalent.

This is an art by itself, differing from poetry, and from the art of harmony or of counterpoint. Nevertheless, it has occasionally and triumphantly appeared in the world, and is well worth an effort to recover.

(Yes, it is an end to which both arts are struggling. The future is too dark for a prophecy. G. A.)

Lawes was English of the English, he was no obscure man in his day, being a King's musician and a man lauded of poets. He did not fall a prey to the pigheaded insularity of the British Association of Musicians; he did not shun foreign competition.

He set a poem of Anacreon's in the Greek, and he set songs in Italian and Latin. He was, for all I know, the last English composer to know Greek. Our decadence may be due to the fact that the educated are now too stupid to participate in the arts. This lack of lineage shows in modern art in all its branches. As a French singer said to me yesterday: "When those people (English artists, composers, etc.) have done (i.e., written, painted, composed) anything, they seem to think that that is the end, and that there is nothing to be done about it."

October 1918

The second season must be worse than the first for any critic who designs impartiality. If a performer has once bored you to death it is, in the first place, very difficult to drag yourself to hear him again; and if this reluctance be overcome it is still difficult not to carry with you a touch of resentment for the initial annoyance. Conversely, it is difficult when one has been delighted by a player not to arrive at his second performance with a certain readiness to attribute all his faults to chance. Even so we may take it as unlikely that any performer over 45 is likely to receive a wholly new musical intelligence or to develop a new and ravishing charm. If a man is going to change from an egoistic temperamental impresser of schoolgirls to a serious musician the change should happen before he is much past thirty-five.

(I do not think that young virtuosi should follow the spirit of the older virtuosi either. For instance, the young virtuoso, B., is playing Chopin romantically with both public and critics wildly acclaiming him. Chopin with heavy neo-German-Russian romanticism! Chopin à la Schumann! Chopin in the grand manner! Synthetic calculation that the largest and most colossal manner is the finest! We cannot expect a young man to develop a new characteristic if he is recreating masterpieces, sure-fire, by synthesis. G. A.)

The aim of this present musical criticism* is to make it possible for the best performers to present their best work; for them to give concerts under present conditions without making any concession whatsoever to ignorance and bad taste. Beyond that one might have ambitions, both of developing the discretion of a possible public, and of actually enlightening young or untrained musicians (or even elderly amateurs) concerning their own shortcomings, and their possible avenues of improvement. Do bad musicians attend good concerts?

(Yes, but they don't like them. A bad musician will only admit a name so well-known that there can be no question about it. He is a bad musician because he has no "guts" anyway. G. A.)

In several cases where great proficiency and obviously great experience in public performance are coupled with overmastering dulness, one would suggest that every piece of music worth presenting in public has a *meaning*. The composer presumably felt something, and equally wished to express something by his fugue, étude, or sonata. My state-

---

* i. e., criticism contained in notes on current concerts (Pound's note).

ment is simple, and platitudinous; but correct detail and that even rarer thing, correct architectonics, will not hold the better attentions unless the performer have, beyond a concept of the composer's style and a style for representing it, some intention of expressing the unifying emotion or emotions of the particular piece. It is by no means necessary that these emotions be the same as were the composer's, but the performer must think both "Bach" and "Ciaconna" if he is to give the piece with effect. He must unite his general feel of the composer to his particular concept of the piece to be given.

(I misread this word for "contempt" at first. Why a "style" and "intention"? Why not, instead of an "emotion," a dynamism, a vitality? G. A.)

We might almost lay it down as axiomatic that a song must be sung in its original language . . . the perfect union of word and note is so subtle and rare a thing that, once attained, no substitute is likely to give satisfaction unless the translator be a great technician, able to support treble the technical difficulty which faced the original poet.

(Yes, once the words are polished into the music. G. A.)

Moussorgsky has his place beyond all the other Russians. You cannot compare Music since Beethoven with the early thin music which is like delicate patterns on glass. Since Beethoven people have thought of music as of something with a new bulk and volume. Beyond all the floridity and pretence of Wagner are these Russians, and beyond them Moussorgsky, like the primordial granite.

(I think Moussorgsky is the connecting link between Wagner and Strawinsky. Debussy existed somewhere out of the connection, like Chopin. G. A.)

There is a certain satisfaction in a concert which knows its own mind and which gives you some one thing in sufficient bulk to provide basis for an opinion; thus in Rosing's all-Russian programme we had Russia, from Nevstruoff who is "so Russian," who is so the bleak spirit of the steppes that he makes you understand the Russian reaction towards all sorts of gew-gaws and floridities, bright colour for costume, admiration of Wagner, Parisianism; we had Russian music from this bleakness of Nevstruoff to Moussorgsky who, to my mind at least, lifts Russian music above all other music of the epic tone, Moussorgsky who is of the "heroic" mould without any sham heroics, without Wagnerian padding and rhetoric. We had Russia from the steppes to the part of Russia which is oriental, a land-locked people in the main.

November 1918

The Kennedy-Frasers in the Hebridean music gave us equally an epitome of a whole racial civilisation (with whatever deprivation of luxury you like, the people who produced such art must be termed a civilised people). This music is full of sea-splash as the Russian is of plain bleakness and winter-bleakness. It has the wave-pull and wave-sway in place of the foot-beat of the hopak. It has also its mouth-music for dancing (Hin, hin halla lal a) to match any present-day Jazz that Afro-America has sent over to us.

(I am beginning to get annoyed with Americans who tell me that jazz will be the music of the future. Young prodigy-composers from the U. S. writing classic jazz in four-four beat throughout. My God, the African Negroes have the American Negroes stopped a mile for every kind of rhythmic and musical effect. American whites must have a bad effect upon their Negroes, don't you think? G. A.)

It has its rhythmic validity and variety in labour songs, not to be read by the metronome, but which have their diverse beats and pauses determined by the age-lasting rhythm of the craft, cloth-clapping, weaving, spinning, milking, reaping. And in this connection damn the young gentleman who said to me: "I don't go in so much for rhythm. I'm temperamental." Another chance phrase in a corridor, "Very interesting, but it needs the Kennedy-Frasers to sing it."

These phrases are a fair summary of the blight of English music since it has been a genteel, suburban accomplishment.

(That is exactly what is the matter with American music. Even jazz has lost its bite, the Negroes are upon Broadway and in the Little Review, and everything is becoming genteel. G. A.)

I have walked about London streets before, during and after "peace night." The sense of rhythm is not dead in this island. I have heard costers singing not only with rhythm but also with true tone, as true as you would find among boasted continental singers. An "artistic" nation would have taken its singers from the donkey-barrows and coster carts. Even La Duse still calls herself "contadina," and once wore the Venetian black shawl. But no, the black curse of Cromwell, and the anathema of Victoriana and genteelness have put a stop to that sort of permeation in England, and the concert-performer is chosen from the exclusively eviscerated strata of the community.

(How funny it must be in England. G. A.)

The result is that these women come down here from "North Britain" and drive one to learning Gaelic. These Hebridean melodies are the only "English" music possessed of the needful vigour. Mrs. Kennedy-Fraser's settings are not the vegetarian school of folk-song.

We have in these Hebridean songs a music which has escaped the mediaeval ecclesiastical enervation.

(So has the music of Africa, but should you bring the Negroes to Paris in numbers you would either have them in church or putting little frizzes upon the little French tunes at the "Casino de Paris." Voilà, look at America. We have to look for the corners in our own music. G. A.)

Other modern music in western Europe has had to work its way slowly and in attenuation from the dominance of "harmless" and innocuous modes.

And even now the academies which resurrect South-European mediaeval melodies furnish them with proper four-square under-pinnings à la the most approved Johann-Sebastian.

These Hebridean songs, like such Russian songs as Rosing gave us, have subject-matter. They are not cooked up for a concert hall. Every song is about something. Thus there is a difference between one song and the next.

For the auditor seriously concerned with music this question of "performance" is a trifle, but for meeting the practical question of giving the best possible music under today's concert hall conditions these details are worth considering. It is the artist's and critic's place to see that the best can compete advantageously with the vulgarest.

(Dear E. P. Everybody knows that the business of critics of the great music trade journals is to push the vulgarest music possible. They stop only when the game is taken out of their hands by the ragtime publishers. Criticism, musically, is politics and business. G. A.)

For all its virtues, the modern French school of song will not hold its own when sung with really good art of good periods. It glows by comparison with modern Italian and modern English settings.

. . . In especial we note in the oriental quality of Moussorgsky's "Foire de Sorotchinsky," the light that never was on sea or land, the Coleridge-Keats ambition, the casements on seas forlorn. Moussorgsky has always some mastery to distinguish him in whatever company he is found.

Nevstruoff's *"Poor Wanderer"* is excellent, but from it one comprehends the Russian desire for foreignness, for French neatness, and even German upholstery. Russian music is not all of music. It has a greater place in world-music than is yet accorded it.

February 1919

Tchaikowsky: a certain cheapness is imminent in this composer. He is not cheap all the time, or even, perhaps, most of the time but he keeps one in a state of anxiety.

(Strawinsky imitates him but then one loses all anxiety: as S. says "music need be neither good nor bad." It must be one thing or the other—sic: good or bad. G. A.)

*A concert lasts an hour and a half; it is not an organic composition like an act, or the whole, of an opera or a symphony. The element of main form must be supplied. I have already written about various means for variety. Beyond them, one should introduce a certain number of songs with more or less symmetrical wave lengths; something with a discernible and regular metre. . . . The element of "regular" rhythm is often (probably without consciousness or design) supplied by the "classic" numbers familiar at the beginning of concerts.

*. . . one cannot be expected to sit through the poems of E. Wheeler Wilcox whoever set them or sing them.

*The weakness of these modern French musicians is that their music rises and falls in value exactly in proportion with the literary quality of the words; these composers cannot hide or improve a banality of the poems which they use.

This is not a fatal defect, but it demands a double care for literature on the musician's part. You can always tell from words on the programme whether the music will be interesting.

*"It will be safe to assume" that a KENNEDY-FRASER concert will have certain glorious moments, moments unique in the season's concert-hearing. M. Kennedy-Fraser has, definitely, genius. I do not overwork that word in these columns, and I use it to denote a certain profound intuition and emotional knowledge of the subject.

The music of free period, of a constantly varying phrase-length and rhythm-length is a freedom from fixed lengths, but the symmetry must underlie, and the sense of this symmetry must be kept fresh and vivid, if not in the consciousness, at least in the subconsciousness of the

---

* Paragraphs preceded by * are deleted from Mr. Antheil's typescript copy (Pound's note).

performer... The pitfalls of enthusiasm, particularly of irresponsible other-people's enthusiasm are numberless, numberless, and ubiquitous.

(The fine great-chested virtuosi are never enthusiastic without a system. G. A.)

April 1919

If there is a literate class in England, it does not go in for music. And if there are English musicians with anything like general culture, they are screened assiduously from the public gaze.

Thematic invention in music has coincided with periods when musicians were intent on poetry, intent on the form and movement of words. Thematic invention is the weakest spot in contemporary music *everywhere*. The rhythms of French are less marked, but only in France do we find a careful study of the verbal qualities. I do not think I have shown any delirious or unbalanced appreciation of the modern French, but among their song-setters are practically the only contemporary song-setters whom one can respect.

English contemporary poetry is, I suppose, very dull, and there is very little rhythmic invention in it; but even so, writers intent on melody would, if they were serious in their technical intention, make greater effort to combine with musicians, and musicians would attempt to learn something from authors about the meeting-points of the two arts. As it is, the musicians' attitude towards the lyric is too apt to be "Get me something that I can end on a high note. Got to make some money." Players will not practice for trios and quartettes; there is no place or company where any number of writers and musicians meet to try new experiments of an "unpractical nature." I recently met a poet who wanted a poem set to cymbals and cello in order to develop or illustrate the tonality of his words. The man is "of course" a lunatic. No Chappell-Ballad-minded aggregation would tolerate such departure from suburban custom. A "song" is words set to py-ano music. It doesn't matter what words.

(The difficulty of getting even "revolutionary" musicians to reinstate certain instruments once in good standing, is also of interest. E. P. seven years later.)

It is not the business of the business-like song-setter to express anything, or to find poems worth further musical developments, or poems in which the verbal rhythm contains the germ of larger musical structure. All of which is very lamentable.

The artist must have a faint touch of fanaticism *somewhere* in his nature. Heaven knows that fanaticism in excess is worse than garlic in excess, but ...

*...we noticed also how STUPID Liszt was, and how little he knew about chords.

Stupidity is not an asset in the arts. Passion is as blind as you like, and it sweeps over intellectual subtleties in the drive upon its own truth, but there is a fundamental stupidity in some natures, composing and writing natures, against which no perseverance or labour is any avail. Liszt was stupid. You can make impressive sounds on the piano while playing Liszt, but you can not completely conceal his fundamental and congenital and ineradicable lack of intelligence, his lack of susceptibility. He would try to make a watch go by beating it with a potato-masher.

(I am tired of fire-eaters, ten cent stores, cheap vaudeville.

Sheer brilliance alone is about done in for. Witness Liszt's tone poems, Strauss' "Salomé" and Strawinsky's "Oiseau de Feu." We are gradually tiring of old whisker'd Rimsky-Korsakoff dressed in Johnny's knickerbockers and rolling a hoop. G. A.)

. . .*the easy tolerance of the operatic era is waning. Opera is a diffuse form; it was made to cover light afterdinner conversation; the exigeant audience which concentrated its attention on careful Mediaeval canzoni had given way to eighteenth century fluster.

. . .*let us admit that it is a good thing for singers to get off the beaten track and hunt up music that is lying in desuetude.

Opera was best in court conditions. It is for an audience that drifts together for social reasons and which wishes the social pressure to be loosened, the necessity for conversation to be diminished. Concert conditions are much more the condition of song-competition, "Preislied."

(Today the swifter young crowd are taking up vaudeville in the same way. The most fashionable way is according to the guiding principles in "The Seven Lively Arts.")

. . . the blunt-wittedness of contemporary musicians, and their general incapacity for literary choice and selection.

"Music in stucco" is certainly the proper designation for a great and damnable category.

May 1919

*It requires a certain nerve to appear in religious dimness with a futurist lampshade and to play from the printed page.

*Memory is not, however, the supreme faculty; and if a performer can use printed notes instead of memory without detriment to his or her performance I see no reason against it. [Horror of all academic and established heads of musical seminaries!]

. . . personality—a quality more apt to enrich one's private life than to draw swift and easy public success.

(Anyone with a capacity for grinning has a "pleasing stage personality." G. A.)

I have before propounded the theory that Chopin was *not* the De Musset of music.

Then Franck ran near to the danger zone where music verges into noise.

(Yes, a kind of silvery, angelic, unbearable noise. G. A.)

One remarks his ability, and then, to get one's estimate into some sort of scale and proportion, one thinks that Chopin would have expressed an equal amount of whatever this series was intended to express with half the number of digital impacts.

*Neither Prudhomme nor Victor Margueritte were poets of first rank; and the modern French composers are utterly at the mercy of the poets whose words they set.

Debussy as I have indicated before, was a glorious heresy. He writes for the excitement of phantasmagoria, for the evocation of visual imaginations, and in just so far as he does this his work is unorthodox and off the true track of music. It is definitely an heresy, a beautiful and bewildering heresy, which should have its own converts and enthusiasts; but it is no mortal use trying to play his music as if it were "pure", as if it were simply "sound" arranged into time and pitch patterns for the expression of emotion. And if the player be not initiate into this realm of evoked images, he or she will never play Debussy as anything but an outsider.

(Bravo! G. A.)

*Dupin was an engine-wiper. His work does not take one on first hearing, I am inclined to think that it has a vigour more apparent when taken in contrast with his etiolated contemporaries than when contrasted with authentic wild music.

Tinayre, Stroesco, and Rosing are all, as I have indicated repeatedly, worth hearing and totally different.

*Mendelssohn put some sort of melodic line into "Recit" of "Rend your Hearts" and a deal of sentimentality into the arts and *anyway* he might be left to the Albert-Hall.

We have already said that there is no reason why Johann Sebastian Bach's processional should be saddled with words stating that he has lost his Jesu. The song results in a fine, jocund, robust proclamation that the obviously *bien portant* and untroubled protagonist is brought "to despair". Every note calls the author a liar. Bach of course had to play his music in church and it was but natural that he should enjoy himself . . . I can still recall a village organist in similar plight doing "Lamb, lamb, lamb!" at choir practice, it was not the celebrated "paschal" lamb either. Rag-time is quite fine on a pipe organ. Still the ecclesiastical censorship does not pertain to music performed in Bond Street, and one might have some honest secular words set to that Guards' march.

. . . The best poets have been nature poets only incidentally. Nature appears here and there in their work, but is not singled out for their subject-matter. Whatever "religion and Christianity" may still mean to the populace and to the modern heath-dweller, religion as exploited by artists of the last century has been mostly exploited as convenient furniture and not from any inner necessity.

The *first* artist to take up any neglected folk element has, historically, nearly always scored a success.

"Le Pauvre Laboureur" said to be of the xvi[th] century, a finer pre-Marseillaise, with a detached or impersonal, dispassionate passion, a stasis inciting to no action, yet with deepest feeling in its melody.

> *Le pauvre laboureur*
> *L'a deux petits enfants,*
> *Ils mènent la charrue,*
> *N'ont pas encore quinze ans! . . .*

And the magnificent finale:

> *Il n'est ni roi ni prince,*
> *Ni ducque ni seigneur,*
> *Qui n'vive de la peine*
> *Du pauvre laboureur.*

The poignancy and the simplicity of poetic statement are matched with the formulation of the music and when I compare this with the utter tosh of sentimentality in four out of five of the lyrics set by Brahms I can but wonder again at the vogue of xix[th] century favourites. I have been forced to look anew at Brahms' songs during the past few weeks, and I can only suppose people have accepted them because they have always heard them in a foreign tongue and taken no account of verbal meanings. But they are really much worse than I had ever suspected . . . with exceptions which can be very fine.

The Laboureur song dated the xvith century reminds us, or might remind us, that democracy did not begin with the French Revolution; and that earlier authors had thought of the labour problem, for this song is not a song by a labourer, but by an observing and indignant poet of no mean attainment. Even Spain was not always a land of inquisitions, and there was democracy south of the Pyrenees, before the suppression of the Cortes in the ill days of Charles V.

I return again to the apparent insensitiveness of the modern audience to the word value of songs. Since Lawes and Waller collaborated, the technique of English setting has been appalling. German, with its capacity for taking extremely heavy musical accent on thick and heavy syllables, has furnished the "lieder" and the lieder were emotionally effective . . . at least people adored them, and I don't know that anybody has taken the trouble to make a critical examination of their construction. A few fine poems, folk songs, poems of Heine, served as a cover for the rest. The modern French ran a counter movement, but were reputed to suffer etiolation. We want more discontent with our lyrics, and a stricter examination of claims.

June 1919

Perhaps the critic's most difficult problem is the treatment of music which is not outrageous enough to merit condemnation nor yet quite good enough to stir interest. The finer shades and varieties of this mediocrity are more bother to the critic . . .

(Yes! they bother the "ultra modern" critics fearfully. G. A.)

than either the execrable or the excellent.

. . . the music was played as most of Schubert deserves to be played, namely with that art of the "better" restaurant or "usual" theatre orchestra, more or less brisk and more or less tearfully sentimentalisch . . . with food, or under some propitious emotional circumstances, the music might have assisted in keeping one stationary.

(One must never be suddenly jarred in either a restaurant or a concert hall. One eats food in the first and digests it in the second. Imagine the effect of the Sacre on "The old gentleman who must be careful."

The average concert and "better" restaurant music are identical. Food represents the basic problem of the race. G. A.)

*The whole *lieder* school is wrong, and it needs only a slightly unfavourable condition to rub in the fact. The whole *genre* is wrong. This does not prevent there being a certain number of acceptable lieder, but the more one examines them the less satisfactory they appear. The Victorian ballad is the natural and lamentable result of trying to bring the lieder into English.

To be popular a song must not only appeal to the silliness of the populace but it must be do-able without skill or effort.

(One in the eye for 99% of the "great" public and their "Great" virtuosi. G. A.)

There is no copy of Henry Lawes' three volumes of "Ayres and Dialogues" at the little second-hand music shop in Great Turnstyle, but the kindly proprietor is good enough to look up old sale catalogues. The last set went for £49. Dolmetsch' arrangements of some of this old music are out of print. Only in a nation utterly contemptuous of its past treasures and inspired by a rancorous hatred of good music could this state of affairs be conceivable. I have bought Waller's poems for a shilling. Yet Lawes' position in English music is proportionally much more important than Waller's position among English poets.

This condition of things is more eloquent of the debasement and utter contemptibility of British music publishers and the slovenly ignorance of British so-called musicians than the laws of libel permit me to attempt to express in these columns.

This whilom "nest of singing birds" is apparently on its last roost.

*The value of the old instruments, harpsichords, spinets, clavichords, viols da gamba, is more in that they induce the player and hearer really to listen to the quality of sound produced than in that they render the old music with veracity. This latter advantage is, however, far from negligible. No one really understands counterpoint who has heard it only with the blare of modern instruments or the plugging of the piano. Neither is there any means so effective for developing a pianist's sense of sound-quality as practice on the clavichord.

*Chopin presumeably excels all piano-composers of the nineteenth century because his memory embraced the sound of the earlier keyboard instruments. A person *learning* piano-playing on the piano is simply ignorant of a great many kinds of sound, *some* of which can be rendered on the piano by a person whose mind and imagination contain them.

*The advantage in ensemble playing is that the harpsichord and spinet "go with" the strings, whereas the piano does not, but is practically always an inruption.

October 1919

. . . a fair test of the real art of the ballet, as distinct from fortuitous conflict of several arts in one performance, is whether one does hear the music.

(The dancing ought forcibly to draw attention to the music—or else it is a social affair. G. A.)

The perfect song occurs when the poetic rhythm is in itself interesting, and when the musician augments, illumines it, without breaking away from, or at least without going too far from the dominant cadences and accents of the words; when ligatures illustrate the verbal qualities, and the little descants and prolongations fall in with the main movements of the poem.

Were there a really critical audience, it would insist on each performer doing the thing he does best—at least in public. (One does not wish to interfere with people's private diversions.)

This limitation of one's art is perhaps a French gift; the artist should find himself in some mode in which he can use all or nearly all his gifts to the best advantage, and where his limitations will least affect the complete presentation of the subject-matter.

Shakespeare put in "Hey-nonny-nonnys," so that the musician might have his fun without upsetting poetry. Mozart was much more important than his librettist (even when he had Metastasio to write words for him). But there is a certain kind of emphasis and there are certain effects of veracity which cannot be given by music of this school.

December 1919

*There is a wealth of fine English poetry† unset, there is crying need for a musician who can think more of the beauty of the poem than of his pustulent egoism and of his desire to be the leading "modern British composer".

*A freedom of detail can only be durably effective if the sense of inner form is strong; one cannot hammer upon this too often; the musician or verse-writer who has the sense of form ingrained may take liberties in some safety, liberties which are fatal if the sense of form is not imminent, hovering, present without being obvious, but still present.

† Erasure very vigorous at this point (Pound's note).

January 1920

The Pye-ano, Ge-entlemen, the PYE-ano is the largest musical instrument known to man, with the possible exception of the Steam Calliope whistle or Fog Signal and the three-barrelled pipe-organ; of which the pipe-organ has one chief and especial merit, namely and to wit, its stability. I mean, "Where it is thare it rests," whereas the pye-ano may, with four fat men and considerable difficulty, be moved from one spot to another (Mr. Kipling to the contrary notwithstanding); all of which is no reason for pye-ano recitals outnumbering all other concerts three to one, or seven to one, or seventeen to one in the damp season.

(There is no more fun being a virtuoso. G. A.)

The future of piano music lies in the Jazz, and we may soon expect a much louder and more varied contraption with xylophone, whistle, and gong attachment in the treble octaves and solid steel bars in the bass. This new and forthcoming implement should, from present indications, present most of the advantages over the pye-ano that the original forte-piano did to its predecessors.

(Naturally. The one who screams the loudest is the greatest genius according to the new American standards—but don't get out of four-four time ever—my God. G. A.)

. . . rhythm is made not merely by a correct division of music into bars of equal time-length, but also by a pluck and impact of accent.

(We MUST *have something we can understand and that is* MODERN. *Paint over the tin-lizzy like a Rolls-Royce. G. A.)*

*Berlioz was indubitably competent, and one might be interested in his technique if Wagner hadn't buried him full fathoms fifteen.

*Piano concertos! At its birth the forte-piano seems to have turned people's heads; even so sensible a man as Thomas Jefferson ordered a forte-piano. Apologists claim that the earliest pianos preserved some of the qualities of the harpsichord.

*The present instrument† is a sort of cheap substitute for the orchestra, the only instrument with enough variety and range to give a sort of shorthand account of music too complicated for a fiddle or 'cello or cornet. But to play a piano *with* an orchestra is anathema. It is the sum total of fatuous imbecility and to prove it there is in Beethoven's "Em-

† Ditto (Pound's note).

peror" concerto, in this Commodus of music, not one motif or melody or salient line given to the piano which would not be more effective if it were played on any other instrument in the orchestra. Violin, oboe, flute, 'cello, tympani, any, absolutely *any,* of these instruments lifting a significant phrase from the body of the orchestral sound would be more effective; and there is demonstration of it whenever any other instrument or instruments is or are given a phrase to itself or themselves.

Piano soloists are praised for their "varied *orchestral*" effects; but why use these substitutes when the richer medium is at hand? If a mania for pianos swept over Europe during an unfortunate period, can we not forgive, or at any rate forget, and let the piano concerto go to the proper scrap-heap of experiment, meritorious in its day, but no longer fit for conversation?

Arne's precision came† as an improvement on Schumann. Conventions he had, but after the "conventionalities of the operatic" etc., there was no eighteenth century convention of Arne which was not dew-fresh and full of pleasurability.

The last movement of Korsakov's Scheherazade suite is a triumph of orchestration. The mastery is everywhere present, one notes the perfect scale and graduation from one instrument, from the delicacy of the solo violin to the massed thunder of the whole ensemble of instruments; here for once one has the whole demonstration of causes why the orchestra has superseded chamber music, why this huge instrument has swept away so much of the fine work made for instruments of smaller calibre.

Scriabin, "Poème d'Extase"... Coates showed his realisation of the capacities of his orchestra, but the *extase* is senescent, it is manifestly not the *extase* of youth; the long beginning is like the prose of its era, heavy as Henry James or as Charles-Louis Philippe, fin de siècle, of an extreme and laborious sophistication, Coates doing admirably, Scriabin conscientiously avoiding the obvious in everything save the significance, and treating one of the oldest topics with anatomic minuteness, though possibly unconscious of his humour, anatomic even to the notes given on the triangle, spurring one to quotation from Gautier's "Carmen". The double basses superb, but one longed, possibly, for the older spirit of English May-day. It is too late to emend the title; we quarrel with no work of art because of a title lightly or sarcastically given, but we think Scriabin would have been kinder to his audience if he had labelled this poem "Satire upon an Old Gentleman," or possibly "Confessions of an old gentleman in trouble," supposing all the time he "knew." We entertain doubts, however, as to just how far his awareness extended.

While the public can find orchestral concerts (price the same) it is a

---

† *i.e. in the concert in question* (Pound's note).

little difficult to discover why they go at all to piano recitals, and with the flow of time one rather wonders at young men taking up the piano as a profession. The onus upon the solo-pianist is very heavy; if he divides his concert with a vocalist, he becomes, at once, second fiddle; and to entertain an audience for an hour or more with nothing but a piano is exceedingly difficult, and it grows more and more difficult as the public becomes more and more familiar with piano repertoire.

... the maximum emotional effect of singing is gained by presentation and not by sentimentality.

The Marseillaise is possibly the only national anthem that can be raised to the status of music by competent singing.

Psychological speculation, or, rather, pathological: the pleasure of *playing* a piano with orchestra, as opposed to *hearing* a piano played with orchestra, is explicable on the grounds of exhilaration. The feeling that one is being so accomplishedly agile, so ripplingly and dashingly efficient as to get one's fingers onto all the notes in good time with the conductor probably sustains the *player;* he gets the same physical pleasure as he might from quick and clever use of the foils in a fencing bout; he has no attention left for auditory sensation. Parallel case: that of the inebriated or excited talker who imagines he or she is being "brilliant" merely because of rapid trajectory.

February 1920

It is probable that bar-ends should be clearly marked, but this line of demarcation is geometric; it should have no thickness; above all, it should not be a dead stop stock-still, requiring each time a subsequent heave to "start 'er agayne".

As a record of what things have existed, two or three pieces of Mendelssohn's should be played annually by Cernikoff† at the Royal College of Music, for the enlightenment and warning of students. This would be quite enough Mendelssohn for one year, and even a demonstration in alternate years might be sufficient.

The Schumann "Carnaval" was given as literature, and it has the durability of literature ... one definitely sees the "given concentration of knowledge on the given portion of surface." (Put aside quibbles on terms "Knowledge," "intelligence," etc., one does not get the needful *concentration* of these without emotion or passion either present or foregoing.)

In estimating the piano (not as played by pyanists, but in its capacity) one must admit that it is the only modern instrument upon which the solo player can exercise so much musical knowledge and comprehen-

---

† This from a full article in appreciation of Cernikoff as a connoisseur. E. P.

sion. It is louder than the spinet or clavichord, it has mechanical advantages over the harpsichord, and is probably less trouble to keep in order. It will reign supreme in the parlour until the pianola and the gramophone have democratised it out of existence. It is, from the auditor's point of hearing, inferior to the orchestra. Public demonstrations of the instrument are in great part incubatorial, designed for and attended by people who wish to pianise. A great artist can get music out of this instrument. So can some players from a brass string and a cigarbox. A few piano recitals each year are worth hearing.

March 1920

The average of this modern French stuff is poor; now that the novelty is worn off, one is soon bored with the eternal hurry and slow-up, the continued waste of musical means employed by this school.

The labour lilts illustrate at each Kennedy-Fraser concert the value of some rhythm-base more diversified than English accentual prosody made in not very inspired imitation of mediaeval degenerations from the Latin imitation of Greek quantitative metres. The Oriental and African division of music into raga and tala, i. e. rhythm-tune and pitch-tune, is probably more fecund in diversity. The churn, the loom, the spinning-wheel, the oars, all give splendid bases for distinctive rhythms which can never degenerate into the monotony of mere iambs and trochees. They keep their essential differences as even dance tunes cannot. Even so the real feel of moving feet which is so often the soul of thematic invention in Bach and Mozart, is increasingly rare in music.

Words help thematic invention only so long as the musicians are sensitive to shades of different verbal quantity. The charm of Mozart, if one can analyze it, seems often to lie in a rare combination of notes which have musical structure, musical line, but which suggest, beyond these and simultaneously, dance steps and language.

Now if it is imbecile to sing ring-a-round-a-rosy words with a serious meaning, it is doubly imbecile to sing such words when they do not even give good, open vowel sounds for the long notes and ligatures. In the "Ich habe genug" one might, so far as the notes are concerned, sing, "Two scones and butter were seen on the plate"; the auditory pleasure would be equal to that of hearing "There I too with Simeon the joy," etc. If we were to respect tradition as some people understand that word, we should have to preserve every idiocy of mankind. People have got used to cantatas and therefore they are, for some people, "good". They remind people of their lost youth. All right; but there is no reason why succeeding generations should not be reminded of different lost youths.

The stupid and customary traditionalist always stops at a set year,

i. e., the year where his teacher taught him to stop. The customary traditionalist never goes to history when history is likely to trouble his stagnation. We presume that the Sequaire is the ancestor of the Cantata. Mediaeval choirs sang in descant on "amens" and "hallelujahs," these descants got longer and longer, it became difficult to remember the long series of notes on mere vowel sounds, various writers, notably Goddeschalk then wrote in words to *fit* the notes of the descant. This produced the Sequaire and the fruit was a justification. But after the lapse of seven centuries it is no justification of the English translation of "Ich habe genug," which has no merits and does not fit the music. The statement that the protagonist "has enough" is doubly true of the auditor before the singer has forty-seven times bade him "softly sleep." As it is Bach there is, naturally, staunch melodic line and fine music.

Rounds and part songs are another matter altogether. In them the word-phrase holds the musical phrase in the minds of the different groups of singers. The cantata is merely a superstition, a keeping of structure after its function is gone.

April 1920

I have never been able to determine how far various alleged oriental melodies, as concocted for example by Borodine or "recorded" and "arranged" by Salvador Daniel, have been mis-written in our notation, or how far the writing is really sound and *would* indicate the right manner of presentation. Salvador Daniel, if I remember rightly, scouts the idea of quarter tones, and argues that what insensitive ears have mistaken for quarter tones are really the odd pitches of Greek modality, modalities perhaps a little worn away with the centuries.

In especial one notes the "extraordinary" length of the rhythm pattern units, comparable to the medieval rhyme-scheme of Provençal canzos, where, for example, one finds a rhyme pattern which begins its six-ply repeat after the seventeenth different terminal sound. In this Arabian music, as in the Provençal metrical schemes, the effect of the subtler repetitions only becomes apparent in the third or fourth strophe, and then culminates in the fifth or sixth, as a sort of horizontal instead of perpendicular chord. One might call it a "sort of" counterpoint; if one can conceive a counterpoint which plays not against a sound newly struck, but against the residuum and residua of sounds which hang in the auditory memory.

In the two cases, Arabian music and Provençal verse, where there was no musical "harmony" and no counterpoint in Bach's sense of the word, this elaboration of echo has attained great complexity, and *can* give great delight to ears which are either "trained" to it or which have a natural aptitude for perceiving it. In Europe this aptitude or perceptivity lasted at least until Dante's time, and prompted in him several opinions on the relative merit of Provençal artists, which have puzzled thick-eared "modern" philologists.

For the normal concert-goer the first impression of Arabian singing is that a cat is being strangled in the vicinity. After the "fool in the outer ear" has been put to sleep by the rhythm; after the ear's rebellion against the first *shock to its habit* has worn off, the little whiskers of the ear's interior "miniature piano" begin to wave quite nicely in the ebb and flow of this different sort of sound current; a nostalgia of the sun overtakes one; the music is, and is rightly, an enchantment, and would to what gods there be, that European musicians might return to that concept of music.

... the difference between art and life; the necessary scale and proportion required in the presentation of a thing which is not the photograph and wax cast, but a re-creation in different and proportional medium.

One would like the ability to express verbally the exact difference between this "sort of presentation" which is art, and the other sort of presentation, which is just Miss Jones of Peckwell singing a song—being half the time Miss Jones, and half the time something, rather indefinite, but more or less en rapport with the music.

Again I emphasize the value of these different rhythm-roots as above that of a tired and mechanical accent-metric.

May 1920

I know only too well that the concert platform is crowded, and that the crowd upon it is nothing to the multitude who do not even get on to it, and that, in this multitude, 90 per cent start with something they consider "feeling."

One must, perhaps, find one's ideal artist in fragments, never whole and united.

October 1920

French sentiment is perhaps more sentimental than English sentiment, and one never feels it has quite the same excuse (i. e. in unavoidable mental muddle.)

November 1920

A rhythm unit is a shape; it exists like the keel-line of a yacht, or the lines of an automobile-engine, for a definite purpose, and should exist with an efficiency as definite as that which we find in yachts and automobiles.

December 1920
In the finest lyrics the music so comes from the words and enriches, reinforces, illuminates them. We will recapture this art of illuminating only when we have musicians capable of literary discrimination, capable of selecting *cantabile* words, and of feeling the fine shades of their timbre, of their minor hurries and delays.

Shortly after the publication of *Antheil and the Treatise on Harmony* the "Varia" section of the book was reprinted in *A Magazine of the Arts* (Vol. 4, December, 1924). In it Pound makes reference to the puzzlement of visitors who came to the *pavillon* at 70bis rue Notre Dame des Champs to discover him hard at work on his opera *Le Testament* instead of poetry. One of these was William Carlos Williams, who recalled the following typical visit:

> We talked of his appendix, renaissance music, theory of notation, static "hearing," melody, *time*. I have always felt that time was Ezra's chief asset as a music appreciator. A man with an ear such as his, attuned to the metrical subtleties of the best in verse, must have strong convictions upon the movements of the musical phrase.[27]

VARIA

I

BREVIARY (in parenthesis) FOR COMPOSERS

Nothing but the main form of a work will resist the vicissitudes and calamities of presentation. For your detail you are at the mercy of the executant, and the executant is at the mercy of his endocrines; your melody is at any gland's mercy, but your main structure defies even an orchestra or an operatic soprano.

Sharp-cut rhythm is at the mercy of a singer who fails to observe the exact duration of one note, or who misplaces an ictus; a poor estimate of a carefully figured direction can reduce the whole line to banality.

II

ON THE READING OF MUSIC

The young violinist stood here beside my chair playing arie from Le Nozze, and adding such accompaniment as the instrument permitted.

---

[27] Williams, *Autobiography*, p. 225.

I thought of the horror of concerts; both for the audience packed into rows; and for the performer tortured to the point of perfect production, the bother of memorizing; and for the starting musician the, so often false, public examination, the accidental collapse. To say nothing of the financial bother, etc.

And I thought that here was a perfectly simple way for intelligent musicians to earn a small independence from people who are interested in the extent of music, but who are as stupid as I am about playing an instrument or who read the music page slowly and painfully as a child reads a primer. Lord X used to pay —— — S. to read him books and the morning paper.

III

What is a musician?

1. An instinctive musician?

An instinctive musician is one who knows the *shape* of things, i. e., musical things: to wit; a melody, a raga.

2. A trained musician (i. e., in the contemporary sense); what are these marvelous executants who appear so often to have no intelligence apart from their amazing faculty for synchronized playing?

A trained musician is one who knows the *size* of musical things. They have this marvelous millemetric training; they can count the infinitesimal fractions of the time-inch.

Having been hopelessly bewildered in childhood by idiotic teachers, it has taken me years to find out this simple fact. I used to ask Dolmetsch to write a manual for beginners, seeing how amazingly he had taught his own children to play the delicate ancient music.

He never gave them scales or exercises, they learned the music; i. e., the tunes, the shape of the tunes, and the size seemed to come perfectly and of itself.

But after a century of trained orchestral performers, and of the present system of training, we find "musicians" who are solely sensitive to size. Their ability to count, their metronomic ability, has engulfed them, and they have become insensitive to shape; they don't know what one means when one talks about it; they are amazed that a musical ignoramus can feel it; can tell one form from another, can detect the slightest deformity in a beautiful line of Mozart or Faidit.

It is exactly as if one man were sensitive, amazingly so, to the line of Botticelli; and as if a set of trained painters could tell you, oh to the tenth of a millimetre, the length of Mona Lisa's nose, or of Primavera's.

And this is not to scoff at an amazing faculty in trained musicians. Without it orchestral playing is utterly impossible, and good solo playing hap-hazard.

I wish to heaven I had been taught it in childhood instead of having to acquire it, or at least attempt to, at an age when the pliancy of the senses is waning.

This much seems clear to me: Musical training or learning consists in refining or making accurate the sense of pitch; and of developing the inner metronome; that is about all that can be done by rote; but the pupil should be told of the existence of shape, line, form, etc.

He should be told to observe WHAT he is measuring with his MEASURE.

He must not cut off the noses of his subjects because they don't coincide with the marks on his foot-rule.

MONG DEW; consider these "musicians" capable fellows too, who can't "hear" a melody until it is harmonized;

When, DAMN it all, the melody contains the root of the matter. When the African's drumming contains the root of the matter.

The art of writing music, as distinct from improvising or composing on an instrument: consists in knowing what note you want; how long you want it held; and how long one is to wait for the next note, and in making the correct sign for these durations.

Loud guffaws, from the astute musicians. Mais, mes chers amis, it is for the lack of just such simple statements as this, that the misunderstandings arise between the musician and the well wisher.

Visitors come here (70 *bis*), I am writing verse. It seems a natural operation. They find me stumbling through a line of musical composition and they look at me as if I were committing an incomprehensible act. They assume expressions of awe and bewilderment. Yet I have put into writing poetry, twenty years of work which they do *not* in the least understand; and in music, apart from accommodating notes to words, I am an incompetent amateur.

PROGRESS OF NOTATION ...

... from the times when written music was merely a mnemonic device, through Couperin's complaint: "We do not play as we write" to the modern "composers" who mark it, "rit.," "allargando," etc., and leave their *harmony* to the feel of the players.

(N.B. *they call it movement*)

Even with the best devices there will be enough left to the feel of the great interpreter. A great performer will always have chance enough to show his superiority in the *mise au point* or in the comprehension of his authors.

RETROSPECT

European music up to Bach was usually literary. It was good literature during several centuries when verbal literature was uninteresting.

Bach, we are accustomed to say, was pure music. Hardly any other composer has been able to rely on music alone. XIXth century music is full of BAD literature. Chopin is, I suppose, the best romantic literature that we have. Mozart is perhaps the best literature of his time...*and a charming musician.*

One might perhaps work out one's literature in verbal manifestations and so leave the purely musical components for one's music.... Omitting superfluous notes.

PRIÈRE:
Quelque chose sans chic. The opus must be the expression of an idea of beauty (or order); this is of far more import than skill in the execution. Here fail the clever arts.

THE TREATISE ON HARMONY

We now come to the core of the little book *Antheil and the Treatise on Harmony,* the treatise itself, which originally appeared as the first section though in point of chronology was probably about the last to be written. A short portion of it appeared in the pages of the *Transatlantic Review* (Vol. 1, No. 3, March 1924, pp. 77-81), but it did not appear as an entity until the book came out in October. As has already been stated, the extravagance of Pound's praise for Antheil, which has over the years brought the volume little flattering criticism, has tended to obscure its real achievement, the beautifully succinct and individualistic conception of the purpose and function of harmony. In my original study of Pound's music I stated that "the total number of contributions to the science of harmony in our century is three," and counted them as Schoenberg's *Harmonielehre,* Schenker's *Harmonielehre,* and Pound's treatise.[28] This grouping may seem unusual, for the former two are carefully worked out philosophizings by musicians of great reputation, while Pound's *Treatise* is a scramble of jottings on a subject about which he could be expected to have only the vaguest notions. But they are the *right* notions, and that is why I signaled it as an important text, despite the many practical errors I have dealt with in the footnotes. One must distinguish between a harmony textbook and a theory of harmony. Of the former, dozens appear annually; the latter are rarer than masterpieces.

[28] R. Murray Schafer, "Ezra Pound and Music," *The Canadian Music Journal,* Vol. 5, No. 4, Summer 1961, p. 31.

Schoenberg's *Harmonielehre* is valuable for well-known reasons. The *Harmonielehre* by Heinrich Schenker, though anachronistic, is indispensable to the modern musician for its concepts of *Urlinie* and *Auskomponierung*, through which the biological urge of tones is stressed and a method outlined for a kind of harmony controlled by horizontal rather than vertical considerations. A superior work of theory can alter our entire conception of music just as much as a masterpiece. If this is true, then Pound's book deserves mention along with Schoenberg and Schenker, for no modern book on the subject so cogently forces us to see harmony as a study in movement.

In this respect Pound is close to Schenker, of whose work he had probably never heard. It must be said that by viewing harmony as they did both Schenker and Pound were retrieving an ancient conception of musical composition. In Bach's day the theory of music consisted of counterpoint and figured bass only. What bound them together was the discipline of voice-leading. To consider a figured bass simply as something over which one shoved the appropriate chords would have been unthinkable. It was not until Rameau laid the emphasis on the vertical or harmonic interpretation of music that it was reduced to sequences of related chords. There is in existence a letter by Carl Philipp Emanuel Bach in which he explains his opposition to the Rameau theory and adds that his father shared these feelings. Nevertheless, Rameau's vertical conception eventually won the day and led to the familiar practices of chord stuffing which, by the beginning of the present century, had become taxidermic.

The horizontal or biological nature of the material had been ignored, at least until Janáček once again paid attention to the effects of *time* in chord groupings. But Janáček's theoretical writings were scarcely known (alas, still are), and Schenker's were not much better appreciated, when Pound wrote his own remarks on harmony, so that he may almost certainly be credited with coming on his conceptions simply by the grace of his own good ears.

Pound begins his *Treatise on Harmony* without mincing about. He asks an *élève* what element is omitted from the teaching of harmony, and drawing a blank, gives him the answer.

> The element most grossly omitted from treatises on harmony up to the present time is the element of TIME... The early students of harmony were so accustomed to think of music as something with a strong lateral or horizontal motion that they never

imagined any one, ANY ONE could be stupid enough to think of it as static; it never entered their heads that people would make music like steam ascending from a morass.

Having exposed the disease Pound makes a law:

> A SOUND OF ANY PITCH, or ANY COMBINATION OF SUCH SOUNDS, MAY BE FOLLOWED BY A SOUND OF ANY OTHER PITCH, OR ANY COMBINATION OF SUCH SOUNDS, providing the time interval between them is properly gauged; and this is true for ANY SERIES OF SOUNDS, CHORDS OR ARPEGGIOS.[29]

The factor which determines the propriety of juxtaposed material is time, not academic rulings about consonance and dissonance. Having got this over with, nothing remained but to discuss time intervals or durations, and Pound's subsequent remarks deal with rhythm. We will discuss his concepts of absolute rhythm and Great Bass in detail in Appendix I, but it may be pointed out here that the insistence of the last half of the *Treatise* on conceiving music as a combination of discrete vibrations, so that "the percussion of the rhythm can enter the harmony exactly as another note," is intended to force the listener to realize that rhythm is the root principle of the art, not treacle. Pound's concept of absolute rhythm was well in hand as early as 1910, after he had divined the secrets of Cavalcanti, but now the concept of Great Bass was beginning to be shaped. Rhythm, he continues, "enters usually as a Bassus, a still deeper bassus; giving the main form to the sound." Hence he dwells emphatically on the sixteen-cycle threshold where bass tones can begin to be felt as palpable form. In his own Villon opera there are numerous examples of these ideas in practice, both in the incorporation of percussion directly into the fabric of the arias and in the megaphonic pedal tones on double bass and trombone.

It is not surprising, of course, that a poet should have drawn such conclusions about musical harmony, for he has a natural bias against it in the first place. His concerns are for rhythm and melody alone. What little practical experience Pound had with music was largely with monolinear instruments. He never dis-

---

[29] As we already know (see remark on page 251) Antheil obliquely laid claim to having suggested this idea to Pound. This is indeed possible, but failing Antheil's original notes (the claim was not made until twenty years after the *Treatise* had appeared) such rhetoric cannot diminish Pound's achievement in having given the idea such explicit public expression.

guised his dislike of the "pyanny," and although he owned a Dolmetsch clavichord, the only instruments he ever actually performed on were the bassoon and the drum, the former having been taken up in Paris at about the same time as the writing of the *Treatise*.

CHAPTER I

I

"What, mon élève, is the element grossly omitted from all treatises on HARMONY . . ."
      at this point the élève looks up brightly . . .
               "except the treatise now being composed" . . . ? the élève continues to regard me brightly . . . and blankly. No answer is offered me.
 The answer, mon élève, is:
        "The element most grossly omitted from treatises on harmony up to the present is the element of TIME. The question of the time-interval that must elapse between one sound and another if the two sounds are to produce a pleasing consonance or an *interesting* relation, has been avoided.
 AND YET the simplest consideration of the physics of the matter by almost the simplest mathematician, should lead to equations showing that A SOUND OF ANY PITCH, or ANY COMBINATION OF SUCH SOUNDS, MAY BE FOLLOWED BY A SOUND OF ANY OTHER PITCH, OR ANY OTHER COMBINATION OF SUCH SOUNDS, providing the time interval between them is properly gauged; and this is true for ANY SERIES OF SOUNDS, CHORDS OR ARPEGGIOS.

II

The limits for the practical purposes of music depend solely on our capacity to produce a sound that will last long enough, i. e. remain audible long enough, for the succeeding sound or sounds to catch up, traverse, intersect it.

III

WHY IS THIS QUESTION OF TIME-INTERVALS omitted from all other treatises on harmony?
      Parenthesis for historic survey.
 1. Musical theoricians are exceedingly conventional, for cen-

turies they went on quoting Franco of Cologne instead of listening to sound.[30]

2. Harmony in Bach's time was a vigorous and interesting matter.

Why?

The answer to this question and to the main question of this section, is:

The early students of harmony were so accustomed to think of music as something with a strong lateral or horizontal motion that they never imagined any one, ANY ONE could be stupid enough to think of it as static; it never entered their heads that people would make music like steam ascending from a morass.

They thought of music as travelling rhythm going through points or barriers of pitch and pitch-combinations.

They had this concept in their blood, as the oriental has his raga and his tala. It simply never occurred to them that people would start with static harmony and stick in that stationary position.

IV

Hence it has arrived that the term "Harmony" is applied to the science of chords that can be struck simultaneously; and the directions for modulations have been worked out for chords that can follow each other without demanding a strict or even interesting time-interval between their emission.

In short, Mr. Joseph Corfe produced his
THOROUGHBASS
simplified
and laid open to the meanest capacity;
he did that over a century ago, and no one detected the fact till this year (a.d. 1923.)[31]

I am told that even Mr. Corfe's work contains errors.

But far be it, far, afar from me to contradict Mr. Corfe, or that still more illustrious professor, Dr. Schönberg. All that they have said is, or may be true, and lacking in interest.

Ernst Friedrich Richter has said: "Pure theory can not and should not concern itself with practice, for it has as sole aim the definition of the nature of the divers constituent elements of the art, without ever

---

[30] In his treatise *Ars Cantus Mensurabilis*, c. 1280, Franco of Cologne codified developments in mensural notation, which still survive today as the fundamental principles on which Western musical notation is based.

[31] Joseph Corfe, *Thoroughbass Simplified*, London, n.d. (182?).

treating the special and particular cases which result from the employment of personal procedures."³²

Observation:

Aristotle was not a pure theorist.

Sauzay "Il faut se borner à penser que J.-S. Bach écrivait la musique par certains procédés dont la loi générale nous échappe."

(Sauzay, *Le Violon harmonique,* p. 217.)³³

The secret or part of it probably is that Bach, consciously or unconsciously, never thought of using two chords except as parts, integral parts, of a progression, a rhythmic progression.

I believe in an absolute rhythm. E. P. 1910 with explanations (*).

In 1910 I was working with monolinear verbal rhythm but one had already an adumbration that the bits of rhythm used in verse were capable of being used in musical structure, even with other dimensions.

Treatises on harmony give you all sorts of recipes for getting from one chord to another (this is more or less reduced to a few simple mechanisms) they do not stop to enquire whether the transit by these means is interesting, or, in a given situation, expressive.

That is supposed to be a matter of creative genius. It is.

V

Any series of chords can follow any other, provided the right time-interval is discovered. The interesting sequences are probably those that DEMAND very set and definite intervals.

That is probably all we have to say in this chapter.

CHAPTER II

I

Given proper approach, the progression

is probably perfectly sound. I mean from the point of view of mathematics.

II

Fortunately this theory of harmony can never be reduced to an academicism. At least it seems unlikely that any mathematician will bother. The mathematics of the case might prove discouraging.

---

³² See note 14, p. 254.
³³ Eugène Sauzay, *Le Violon harmonique,* Paris, 1889.
* Preface to translation of Guido Cavalcanti (Pound's note).

You can reduce the line composition of *La Nascita di Venere*[34] to trigonometric equations; it would make a long charming series. The results might be interesting but they would not help you to draw.

"How did you find those four notes?" said X... in undisguised admiration. "Gee, I wish I had found those four notes."

Answer: By listening to the sound that they made, a thing no pyanist has ever done.

That is perhaps all we have to say in this chapter.

CHAPTER III

And possibly the last; for we have probably said about all we have to say. The former treatises on harmony dealt with static harmony, they may have defined harmony as "simultaneous melody" or they may have sought some other definition, but they did not consider that the lateral motion, the horizontal motion, and the time interval between succeeding sounds MUST affect the human ear, and not only the ear but the absolute physics of the matter. The question of where one wave-node meets another, or where it banks against the course of another wave to strengthen or weaken its action, must be considered.

I

The harmony for one instrument is BY NO MEANS necessarily the harmony for another. Good players have always "GOT THE MOST OUT OF" the compositions they played by their subtle seizing of this gaya scienca, and we have said "he has a sense of rhythm" or she "has a sense of rhythm."

II

And again Sauzay*: Le fameux Durante, qui a fait tant d'élèves célèbres, ne leur donnait jamais les raisons des règles qu'il formulait.

Naturally. When Harmony was alive it was merely a personal give away, it was a bundle of tricks of the trade, the fruit of personal experience, it was *A* way of getting over a difficulty or managing a turn of expression; it wasn't intended to cramp anyone's style: It was pragmatic, it worked, and each school worked its trade secrets to death with the magnificence of Bel Canto, of music up to Johann Sebastian. The mechanism was a plus thing, it worked in an open field.

---

[34] Botticelli's *The Birth of Venus*. Compare this remark with similar comments from the end of the *Treatise on Meter*, viz., "Give your draughtsman sixty-four stencils of 'Botticelli's most usual curves'? And he will make you a masterpiece?" (*ABC of Reading*, p. 206).

* *Violon harmonique*, p. 69 (Pound's note).

The mess came when it was set up as a fence, and everyone tried to walk on the rails or climb over it.

They rotted their melodies by trying to find schemes which "harmonize" according to a concept of "harmony" in which the tendency to lifelessness was inherent.

CHAPTER IV

Corollaries and Complications

Continuing, mon élève; you will probably have noticed by now a glaring omission on my part.

A SOUND OF ANY PITCH, ETC. . .

any chord may be followed by any other provided the right time interval be placed between them.

The duration of the resolving chord must also be considered; and the duration of the various chords in a sequence will be subject to mathematical computations, if people prefer mathematics to judging the sounds by ear.

THE HARMONY FOR ONE INSTRUMENT MAY NOT BE THE HARMONY FOR ANOTHER.

Again the competent mathematician could show us that the vibrations of a 'cello where the sound is steadily produced by a drawn bow will combine in a different way from those of a horn, a plucked string or an instrument of percussion.

Everybody knows this; but the time is over when we can give more reverence to a person who can detect slight variations of a pitch, than to one who can detect the difference between

♪♪♪♪♪♩♪ and ♪♪♪♪♪♪♪

It will make a difference what instrument the sounds are played on; it will make a difference if one note or several notes are played louder in the chord; it will make a difference if the next chord strikes the precedent chord while that chord is still being propelled from the instruments or if the second chord strike the other chord as it fades;

and all these things are really in the domain of harmony, that is of active, not static, harmony;

and as for the workings of the latter; this time element may upset them or reinforce them in given circumstance.

The so called "laws" of harmony were useful when they were a bag of handy tools; but if one tries to carry the whole machine shop, one's mobility will probably suffer.

To the above treatise I received four answers:

1.—Antheil: had known for some time that the duration of the notes and the duration of the time-intervals between them made a difference to the way the harmony sounded.

2.—A violinist: had not thought of the matter but tried various combinations of notes and found that my statement applied.

3.—Author of a work on Einstein: approved the treatise; thought it ought to be longer; doubted whether the statement was true for *all* possible combinations of notes.

(This, I take it, was due to his overlooking my restrictive clause.)

Perhaps I might better my statement. Perhaps I should say: There are no two chords which may not follow each other, if the sequence of time-intervals and durations is correct.

4.—Then there was the gent who found the treatise interesting but who (as who should prefer to study the circulation of the blood from corpses exclusively) preferred to study his harmony "separate," i. e. static.

Which might be very nice if it could be done or if there were any essential difference between one part of harmony and the other.

PROLEGOMENA

To make my simple statement even simpler; let us consider the nature of the ear, and of sound.

Sound, we are told, consists of vibrations of from 16 to 36,000 per second.[35]

The ear is an organ for the detection of frequency.

To the best of my knowledge I have always heard the lower notes of the pipe-organ not as pitch but as a series of separate woof-woofs. I don't want to insist on what may be a personal idiosyncracy due to my being so excessively quick on the uptake. The point is that UP to 16 items per second we notice the separate shocks; after that we notice a synthesis of frequency.

Animals probably notice frequencies favourable and unfavourable to their existence. Hence the powers of Orpheus.

Music as the ancient philosophers say, arises from number.

Let us say that music is a composition of frequencies.

---

[35] The human ear extends in its upper limit to about 20,000 cycles per second. Probably this is a misprint in Pound's text and should have read 16,000 cycles, a good practical limit for average adults.

That definition covers all possible forms of music; harmony, melody, counterpoint, form in the fugue, etc.

Some of these combinations of frequency, very simple ones, are academically considered pleasant.

Raphael Socius in a. d. 1556 catalogues a number of them, that had long been considered respectable.[36]

When the frequency of vibration of one note bears the relation of 3 to 2 to the frequency of vibration of another, the combination is considered respectable.[37]

Academicism is not excess of knowledge; it is the possession of *idées fixes* as to how one shall make use of one's data.

The time element affects harmony, sic.

You can hear a note which has 16 vibrations per second.

BUT

You can also beat (on a drum head or other object) 16 times per second.

The ear measures frequency.

If you sound a note whose frequency is 16 per second and start beating, tap, tap, etc. exactly half way between the nodes of your note 16, you will produce a combined frequency of 32, i. e. equivalent to the octave above 16.

If your beats fall 2–3 of a wave behind the inception of the note 16, you will get alternate periods, some belonging to the series 24, i. e. the fifth above the note 16; and others belonging to the series 48, i. e. the octave above that fifth.

So the Negroes in darkest Africa are probably right when they say that from simple beating of their drums they can imagine other instruments.

And the proportions, even very complicated proportions can be established by simple percussion.

I have taken a very simple and understandable case of a note vibrating 16, the number low enough to be thought of easily.

The stiff-necked will say: Oh but for higher notes this beating can't matter; you can't beat 3000 times per second, or even 256 times per second.

---

[36] Pound is in a playful mood. The only figure "comrade Raphael" can possibly refer to is Giosoffo Zarlino, whose famous treatise *Institutioni harmoniche* was published in 1558. In Book III he discussed the intervals available to the composer, laying special emphasis on the major and minor third—intervals which Pound detested, preferring the more grainy dissonance of seconds and sevenths (see his remark a few paragraphs later and also the score of *Le Testament*).

[37] I.e., the perfect fifth.

Responsus est:

The consonances of counterpoint as outlined by comrade Raphael, or of harmony as meant by Dr. Schönberg apply to simple combinations of frequency. Obviously if one note is vibrating 600 per second, and another 1200 there can be six hundred coincidences per second, and you can not strike your drum as often as that.

(There is nothing sacred about the duration of the second, it is merely a convenient and current measure. A note vibrating 221 and ½ times per second is just as conceivable as one vibrating 221 or 222.)

If three notes are sounded at once, the complete coincidences of their wave-nodes may be considered rarer than when only two of them are sounded. You may beat with or against the coincidence: with, to clarify; against, to complicate.

You can use your beat as a third or fourth or N^{th} note in the harmony.

To put it another way; the percussion of the rhythm can enter the harmony exactly as another note would. It enters usually as a Bassus, a still deeper bassus; giving the main form to the sound.

It may be convenient to call these different degrees of the scale the megaphonic and microphonic parts of the harmony.

Rhythm is nothing but the division of frequency plus an emphasis or phrasing of that division.

Why, mon contradicteur, have masters of music specified that certain compositions be played at a certain speed?

(Example, in my copy of Le Nozze, one finds: Presto; half note equals 84; Allegro, black equals 144, etc.)

If anyone is interested, or cares to speculate upon Mozart's indubitable comprehension of the matter, they might do worse than study the time proportions in the opening of the Concerto in A major.[38]

DISSOCIATION A

Percussion can enter:

1. At unison, i. e. at each incidence of nodes of the lower notes.

2. As bassus, i. e. on octaves, double octaves, 12ths, etc., below the more frequent incidences of nodes of the higher notes.

3. (As afore noted), against the incidences, thereby complicating the harmony rather than emphasizing some other element or elements.

There is no fundamental difference between the first two manners, or even between them and the third.

---

[38] While Pound read a good deal of music theory, it is in remarks such as this that he betrays his lack of scholarly integrity. Mozart's *Le Nozze di Figaro* was produced in 1786 while Johann Nepomuk Mälzel did not invent the metronome until some years later. Mälzel was a friend of Beethoven, who indeed employed M. M. markings in his later works. The markings in Pound's Mozart score would have been added later by an editor.

The more complicated the incidences the more interesting the arrangement of percussion may be.

The arrangement of the percussion is probably more important, or more effectively or interestingly employable in a sequence of 2nds, and 7ths than in the simpler relations (listed by comrade Raphael as safe for contrapunto).

Naturally percussion in unison can be used higher in the scale for less simple proportions, than for more simple proportions of pitch-intervals.

If I can only get the mathematics of these relations so complicated that composers will become discouraged; give up trying to compose by half-remembered rules, and really listen to sound, I shall have performed no inconsiderable service to music.

NEXT SECTION
Or: various inconvenient items which the bud should consider before becoming too fixed in its opinions.

I
What applies to the harmony, or the "perpendicular" or simultaneous melody "microphonically," applies also to the melody, i. e. the succeeding notes of a series, to the interceptions of counterpoint, to the statement and answer in the fugue.

There is nothing whatever in music but a composition of frequencies, microphonic and macrophonic.

II
There are 40,360 possible sequences of the eight notes in the single octave, regardless of their duration;[39] if you take eight half notes and add a quarter note, there are nine times as many combinations.

The modern musician says he can't hear a melody till it's harmonized.

This is utter atrophy.

III
Dom Nicholas, inventor of the archicembalo, thought the ear could distinguish difference up to the proportion of 80 to 81 per second, but that its power of synthesis stopped there.

It would notice a difference of 80 to 82, i. e. the proportion of 40 to 41.[40]

---

[39] This should read 40,320.
[40] The reference here may be to Nicolas de Rans, a sixteenth-century lutenist; but the archicembalo, a bowed keyboard instrument, was invented by Johann Heyden and first made known in his essay *Commentatio de musicale instru-*

The academic musician prides himself on his sense of pitch. Sir X. X. of the Royal, etc., sat next to H. in the Albert Hall, the singer sang E. "Ah C," said Sir X. X. "No, E," said H.

A little later the singer sang B. "E," again and Sir X.

So let us refrain from vainglory.

IV

Some people have a sense of absolute frequency, others of proportional frequency.

I. e. some recognize the number of vibrations of the note.

Others recognize only the proportion of vibrations of a note to some other note (pitch) already given.

This proportional sensitivity is called having a musical ear.

V

And the fight between these two kinds of auditives has been going on from the time of Aristotle and Ptolemy to the present. Thank heaven.

That is to say one party (mine) says: You can NOT transpose. That is to say you can transpose till you are blue in the face, but the thing after transposition is NOT the same, i. e. does NOT sound the same as it did before.

Doni in the *Trattato de' modi veri*[41] says that if "I Modi si pratichino separati da una certa e determinata tensione, perdono la meta della loro efficacita, ed anco piu."

(I beg the reader, at this point, to consider that M. Antheil and I have heard all about superpartient sesqui octaval proportion, etc. If anyone wants more mathematics let me refer him to Lemme Rossi's *Sistema Musico overo Musica Speculativa*. [Perugia 1666].)[42]

VI

170 pages of mathematics are of less value than a little curiosity and a willingness to listen to the sound that actually proceeds from an instrument.

---

mento (1605). The whole observation seems to be in error. Latest studies in psychoacoustics show that up to about 1000 cycles per second the ear can hear changes of three cycles per second only. That is to say, a pitch change from 80 to 83 would be detectable, but not one of 80 to 82, and certainly not one of 40 to 41, as Pound alleges.

[41] Giovanni Battista Doni, *Compendio del trattato de' generi e de' modi della musica*, Roma, 1635.

[42] Lemme Rossi (1601–73) was professor of philosophy and mathematics in Perugia. His treatise is a compendium of various musical systems—"tutti i tre generi." Pound may have made his acquaintance in Robert Eitner's *Quellen-Lexikon der Musiker und Musikgelehrten*, 1900–04, which he knew.

Singers transpose because they are thinking of their own throats, not of their ears, or of the ears of their auditors. Pianists think of their fingers, of the gymnastic excitement of their adrenals.

You may reduce the line composition of Botticelli's Nascita to the algebraic equations of analytics, without learning how to paint.

VII

After Dolmetsch tunes a clavichord he has slightly to untune it. Why? That is to say, the proportion of the different notes remains correct but each note is sounded on two strings, and these must *not* be in absolute accord. He says the waves "cut" each other and ruin the resonance.

One may either graph this by picturing two sound waves, the crests of which mutually bump and depress each other, or you may say that the nodes need a certain width, they must meet, but they must meet as if on the knife's back not on the razor's edge.

These prolegomena are not intended as the complete whifflepink to deaf musicians. They are a statement of points that should be considered before contradicting the author.

And to hot tempered sticklers, could we recommend dear old Lavignac's temperance:

"Nous n'entendons pas dire que ce système a été organisé par les mathématiciens ou d'après leurs calculs; il a été créé empiriquement par les musiciens, sans autre guide que leur instinct."

(P. 55, 18th edtn. *La Musique et les Musiciens.*)[43]

P. 52. Discussing some chanting he had heard one Easter: Le résultat était atroce *pour mes oreilles.* Words of a savant.

Before leaving *Antheil and the Treatise on Harmony* we will simply mention that of the few reviews the book originally received, the longest and most competent was the consideration given it by the eminent American musicologist Carl Engel in 1931, republished under the title "Poet as Prophet" in *Discords Mingled* (Freeport, New York, 1967, pp. 172–83). It was a kindly review but contained no special insights.

A month after *Antheil and the Treatise on Harmony* was published, three brief notes appeared over Pound's name in the *Transatlantic Review* (Vol. II, No. 5, November 1924, pp. 566–67).

---

[43] Albert Lavignac (1846–1916) was a French theoretician and historian who taught at the Paris Conservatoire. *La Musique et Les Musiciens* was first published in Paris in 1895.

Ernest Fanelli (1860–1917), subject of the first note, is a curious figure in music history. As a composer he had been overlooked and had earned his living playing percussion in various Parisian orchestras. Debussy was impressed with him as a precursor of impressionism and had written an article about him. Antheil too became intrigued and on impulse one day went to visit his widow.

> I explained to Mme. Fanelli that I was an American music critic (a lie) anxious to write an article on the true worth of Ernest Fanelli. Whereupon they innocently took me into their household, where I was permitted to peruse Fanelli's manuscripts at leisure.
> I soon discovered that Constantine von Sternberg had been right, at least in one regard; the works of Fanelli *were* pure "Afternoon of a faun" or "Daphnis and Chloë," *at least in technique,* and they predated the Debussy-Ravel-Satie works by many years.
> *But,* as I also soon discovered, they were not as talented as the works of the two slightly younger men, although they had had the advantage of being "firsts."[44]

Antheil wrote an article arguing Fanelli's importance for the same issue of the *Transatlantic Review* which included the following notes by Pound.

THE UNPUBLISHED WORK OF FANELLI

The problem of Fanelli, the neglect of him, and its causes, is too complicated for me to go into. It seems established that Debussy was perfectly well aware of Fanelli's work and had had access to the manuscripts. A beau geste would—so far as we can see—have cost him little and been worth a good deal to his posthumous reputation. But then, Debussy himself was in no very strong position in French musical *politics;* a word from Debussy might have got Fanelli talked about before 1912, but would it have secured him performance?

The recognition of the Tableaux Symphoniques, written in 1882, 1883, and 1886 came promptly on their performance in 1912. Their novelty was, let us say, less striking after this thirty years' wait.

Fanelli had begun composing in 1872. From 1894 to 1912 he wrote

---

[44] Antheil, *op. cit.,* p. 129.

nothing. That is to say there were twenty-two years of composition, followed by eighteen years of non-activity. He was playing tympani at the opera, and the piano at Armenonville. One evening Debussy entered this latter restaurant with a couple of "duchesses"; Fanelli began to introduce "curious modern harmonies" into the dance and dinner music. Monsieur Debussy went out. He was a man ever modest. Or let us grant that the position was difficult.

Three of the Tableaux Symphoniques were presented at the Concerts Colonne on March 17th, 1912. I am informed that the performance was followed by about five hundred critical articles and notices. *Le Monde Musical* printed facsimile pages of Fanelli's orchestral score; and analyses of his structure. We suppose something more might have happened if the war hadn't intervened in 1914 (i.e. two years later).

The Tableaux Symphoniques were published. The piano reduction of the first part of the Tableaux (Thèbes) was published (by Max Eschig, Paris 1912). One song (La Vierge de Prompt Secours) was published. The First "Humoresque" for clarinette and piano was published. But the object of this note is to record Fanelli's *unpublished* work, as follows:

THIRTY-TWO songs, dated from	1880 to 1892
(details on application)	
Souvenirs de Jeunesse, piano	1872–78
Souvenirs poétiques	1872–78

ORCHESTRAL WORKS
Impressions Pastorales	1890
L'Ane, Quintette,	
arrangé en double quintette	1894
Suites Rabelaisiennes	1889
Carnaval	Août 1890
Marche Héroïque	Avril 1891
Au palais de l'Escorial	Mai 1890
Mascarade	1889
St. Preux à Clarens	1881
Une nuit chez Sophor	Janvier 1891
(Piano, flûte, clarinettes, 2 violons, violoncelle, contrebasse).	

Humoresques II.	Mars 1892
III.	1893
IV.	1894

Les deux Tonneaux. Opéra bouffe en 3 actes tiré
de Voltaire   1879 (?)
Hérode, non terminé.

The materiel d'orchestre of the Impressions Pastorales exists but has not yet been utilized.

THE FORM
(ou "Je cherche un ami sérieux".)

The form
$d2 = a.dx2 + b\ dy2 + c.dz2 + f.dt2 + ... + 2g.dx.dy + ...$ is too indefinite, it is too complicated. It is uselessly and unnecessarily complicated. But there is no reason why some skilled mathematician should not offer us a form as simple as

$$d2 = dx2 + dy2 + dz2$$

Neither can one see any reason why the equations of a geometry applicable strictly and solely to the components of music should not be as suggestive, and ultimately as useful as the constructions of Euclid or Descartes.

For all I know, such a geometry may already exist, but I should be extremely grateful for enlightenment re its status and loci.

Musical form is perceivable by the senses; people have talked about musical form for centuries. It is amazing that the mathematicians have never attempted to carry their analysis of it beyond the arithmetical phase. Are they as conservative as MM. du Conservatoire?

LONDON LETTER

In quest of the London communique I applied to that rare bird a musician resident in England. And received—verbally—: "Yes, I could write one letter, the first and the last, but you would be unable to print it."

Urging the matter further, I received a personal note giving reasons for *not* writing a critical article on British music at this time. The editor and I are agreed that a mere statement that there is no music of any interest being given in London is not particularly worth printing; even though the statement should be distended to cover several pages, and veiled in somewhat technical language. I offer a few phrases from the letter, bona fide of its existence.

Excerpts from the letter:
"I can't imagine anyone now writing music here whose things are worth putting in the transat."

There follows a detailed list of composers mostly unknown on the continent. These it is therefore useless to insult.

Then follows a short list of imported continental concerts.

Then a statement that Mr. Roland Hayes sang most beautifully at the Queens Hall, two groups of good songs old Italian and lieder, *but the rest was all Quilter,* etc."

Opera: "German and Swedish singers sang Wagner and Strauss; I don't like Wagner and Strauss but the performances were good." Italian season: "French and Italian artists, excellent, *L'heure Espanole* perfectly done. Hislop in *Pagliacci,* sang and acted well, the only good English artist."

British National opera season "too awful". The communicator then expresses the view that *Othello* is the best Verdi and that *Pelléas* is enjoyable "but the British company was terrible, scene production, acting all awful, some of the voices were good, orchestra bad, and conducting poor."

"My impression is that there is no English music, the public grows less and less musical. I can't very well write that and couldn't write anything else. Perhaps Evans has a brighter view, and he is after all the most sensible of the critics, and so far as I know is not writing for any paper at present."

By 1924 the Villon opera was complete and *The Treatise on Harmony* had been published. The first thirty *Cantos* were assuming shape, and Pound knew they were now to become his life's work. He was restless with Paris, and in October he traveled to Italy, to Rapallo on the Ligurian coast, where he was to settle for the next twenty years. Although this removal to a simple Italian town surprised the literary world at the time, it seems to have caused no hiatus in his creative life. He continued with his music and soon began a second opera, *Cavalcanti*. On May 6, 1926, he was in Rome at the Sala Sgambati to hear Olga Rudge and Alfredo Casella give a recital which featured works by Satie, Ravel, and the first performance of his own composition, "Hommage à Froissart".

Throughout these years there were numerous trips to Paris

too, and one in particular is of interest, because on June 19, 1926, he attended the long-awaited première of Antheil's *Ballet mécanique*, and ten days later presided over the première of his own opera, *Le Testament*. The *Ballet mécanique* was performed before a crammed house at the Théâtre des Champs-Elysées, conducted by Vladimir Golschmann. Antheil had originally planned it to go with a film by Fernand Léger, and although the two works had eventually developed separately, Léger provided some décor for the occasion. But the real sight was the orchestra itself, consisting of eight grand pianos and a large battery of percussion, including electric bells and two airplane propellers. This promised to be a festive occasion for the ears and everyone had come. Joyce was there, a patch over one eye. T. S. Eliot arrived escorting the Princess Bassiano. Sylvia Beach recalled the event vividly.

> Up in the top gallery, the centre of a group of Montparnassians, was Ezra Pound to see that George Antheil got a fair deal ...
> The audience was strangely affected by the *Ballet mécanique*. The music was drowned out by yells from all over the house. Objectors on the floor were answered by defenders above; Ezra's voice was heard above the others', and someone said they saw him hanging head downward from the top gallery.
> You saw people punching each other in the face, you heard the yelling, but you didn't hear a note of the *Ballet mécanique*, which judging by the motions of the performers, was going on all the time.
> But these angry people suddenly subsided when the plane propellers called for in the score began whirring and raised a breeze that, Stuart Gilbert says, blew the wig off the head of a man next to him and whisked it all the way to the back of the house. Men turned up their coat collars, the women drew their wraps about them; it was quite chilly.[45]

But Antheil, at one of the pianos, did at least hear the music.

> At the first chord of the *Ballet mécanique* the roof nearly lifted from the ceiling! A number of persons instantly fell over from the gigantic concussion! The remainder of our guests squirmed like live sardines in a can; the pianos underneath or above or

[45] Beach, *op. cit.*, pp. 132-33.

next to their ears boomed mightily and in a strange sychronization.[46]

It was the high point in young Antheil's musical career, and it pushed his name immediately into contemporary music history. Looking back, however, recent analysts have tended to agree with Wilfred Mellers, who has stated that the work has "only historical, not musical interest."[47] The idea of multiple pianos was taken over from Stravinsky's *Les Noces* of 1923, and the incorporation of the noisemakers had its precedents in Satie's *Parade* and Russolo's *intonarumori*. The *bricolage* of the composition is everywhere evident, and even Antheil's notorious rhythmic talent today sounds—square.

The première of *Le Testament* was given in the old Salle Pleyel on Tuesday, June 29, 1926. Yves Tinayre sang the tenor lead and Robert Maitland the bass. There seems to have been a shortage of women; Tinayre also sang the "Heaulmière" aria in falsetto with a shawl over his head. The orchestra was not complete but featured a five-foot *corne* with only two notes, although this instrument is not indicated in the manuscript. Antheil, who had helped with the scoring of the work, was at the keyboard, and Olga Rudge accompanied the singers on her violin. The three-hundred-seat hall was filled and included such notables as Joyce, Hemingway, Eliot (who, according to Robert McAlmon, slipped out before the end), Djuna Barnes, Mina Loy, Virgil Thomson, and probably Jean Cocteau—since a bit of the text of the autograph was changed at the last moment to form a play on his name. Recalling the event, Virgil Thomson wrote, "The music was not quite a musician's music, though it may well be the finest poet's music since Thomas Campion . . . and its sound has remained in my memory."[48]

It has been alleged that Pound played the drum in the performance though Tinayre insists he was in the audience. In any case it is difficult to imagine Pound, who was in the habit of playing drums whenever the opportunity presented itself, resisting the temptation at this exciting moment. Certainly another contemporary Pound-Antheil concert featured some drumming, as Vernon Loggins was later to recall for Charles Norman. The occasion was a small assembly room in Montparnasse, and the program was to include a sonata by Antheil for piano and drum.

[46] Antheil, *op. cit.*, p. 185.
[47] Wilfred Mellers, *Music in a New Found Land*, New York, 1965, p. 159n.
[48] Thomson, *op. cit.*, p. 83.

Antheil, an excellent musician, was, I am sure, improvising, and the drummer—whiskers, grey tweeds—was obviously trying to communicate some sort of narrative with his drumming—maybe a battle, maybe the love act, maybe an encounter of wit. He employed many tempi and I could distinguish no definite rhythmic pattern. The performance was heard respectfully. I recall hoping that the evening might end in a riot. Not so. Pound's seriousness of mien in beating his big bass drum won the day.[49]

The Pound-Antheil association draws to a close with two more reviews written in 1926 and 1927. "Antheil 1924-1926" jumps off with the June 19th affair fresh in the mind and was published in the *New Criterion* (Vol. IV, No. 4, October 1926, pp. 695-99). "Workshop Orchestration" appeared in *New Masses* (Vol. II, No. 5, March, 1927, p. 21). In it, in a footnote, Pound employs the words "great base" for the first time.[50] Together they formed an extension to the "Varia" section of the first American edition of *Antheil and the Treatise on Harmony,* published by Pascal Covici, Chicago, 1927.

ANTHEIL, 1924–1926

I

Thanks to a rare stroke of discretion, or rather two strokes on the part of two patrons of music, it has been possible (Paris, June to July, 1926) to hear most of the work of George Antheil in sequence, and thereby to revise, videlicet augment, one's estimate of this composer.

I see no reason to retract any of the claims made for him in an earlier *Criterion* notice. He has very greatly consolidated his position, and, during the past two years made important advances.

The new works demanding attention are:

1. A symphony for five instruments (flute, bassoon, trumpet, trombone and alto.), the initiation, very possibly, of a new phase of chamber music, with Mr. Antheil in the role of Watteau, or some tonal equivalent.

2. A string quartette, presented by The Quatuor Krettly, rather more difficult of analysis than the symphony, unless one has biographical data

---
[49] Norman, *op. cit.*, p. 271.
[50] But note the spelling and see Appendix I.

as follows: in 1924 Mr. Antheil made a string quartette. It was hastily produced, the author kept tearing it to pieces and re-doing it, up to the day of the concert, and finally "reformed it altogether."

It had, at the start, what his elders (the present writer included) used to regard as form (i.e. as that element is discernable in Mr. Antheil's own 1st Violin Sonata). The said element seemed to annoy Mr. Antheil, and he proceeded to remove it in the interest of some more arcane principle of unity.

This process of elimination had begun in the 2nd Violin Sonata. It continued in the early quartette to the final effacement of same, and the present quartette, now after several performances approved by so good a musician as Monsieur Krettly, is manifestly what Mr. Antheil was driving at two and a half years ago.

Krettly has got used to it. I console myself with the thought that Keats was at first considered incomprehensible because he omitted various moral fervours and axioms which the eighteenth century had got used to finding in poesy . . . in the favour of some element . . . conceivable to himself.

Technically Mr. Antheil has, in this quartette, avoided the smaller clichés. The polyphonic element in his composition continues its development in the Symphony in F (eighty-five instruments), and in this partially conservative work the composer shows his ample ability for dealing with the full orchestra. He avoids various habitual conclusions, and commits numerous innovations in the details of orchestration. It is a symphony on more or less accepted lines (voices from the audience murmuring: "reactionnaire sans le savoir"), a symphony with the usual slush left out, or even "a symphony debunked." We suppose this is what Mr. Koussevitzky means when he complains that, "It is all here" (tapping his forehead), "it has no heart."

It should in any case terminate discussion of Mr. Antheil's musical competence, and has, indeed, largely done so.

If none of the above works would have "made" Mr. Antheil's reputation, they all go to making it solid, and to establish the copiousness of his talents. None of them would give a reason for discussing him in a periodical not exclusively devoted to music; a competent musical chronicle would however record an innovation in chamber music, an addition to the literature of the string quartette, and a new symphony for large orchestra, which latter is a means ready to hand, and needing, probably, nutriment.

II

With the Ballet mécanique we emerge into a wider circle of reference. I mean that this work definitely takes music out of the concert hall, meaning thereby that it deals with a phase of life not hitherto tackled by musicians and freighted before the act with reference to already existing musical reference.

Three years ago Antheil was talking vaguely of "tuning up" whole cities, of "silences twenty minutes long *in the form,*" etc. One thought of it as mere or "pure" speculation, the usual jejune aspiration of genius, and "one" (one, at least, of those who heard the vague talk) dismissed it from his mind.

Now, after the three years, I do not in the least regret any then seeming hyperbole, or any comparison of Antheil and Stravinsky that I then made in the former's favour.

With the performance of the Ballet mécanique one can conceive the possibility of organising the sounds of a factory, let us say of boilerplate or any other clangorous noisiness, the actual sounds of the labour, the various tones of the grindings; according to the needs of the work, and yet, with such pauses and durées, that at the end of the eight hours, the men go out not with frayed nerves, but elated—fatigued, yes, but elated.

I mean that we have here the chance, a mode, a music that no mere loudness can obliterate, but that serves us, as the primitive chanteys for rowing, for hauling on cables; "Blow the man down" and such like; have served savages or simpler ages, for labours, ashore and afloat. And this is definitely a new musical act; a new grip on life by the art, a new period, a bigger break with the habits of acceptance than any made by Bach or by Beethoven, an age coming into its own, an art coming into its own, "and no mean labour."

The "Sacre" stands, but its cubes, solid as they are, are in proportion to the Ballet mécanique as the proportions of architecture are to those of town-planning.

Technically, the fact is, that Mr. Antheil has used longer durations than any other musician has ever attempted to use . . . much longer durations.

"Noces" falls to pieces. After the Ballet it sounds like a few scraps of Wagner, a Russian chorale (quite good), a few scraps of Chopin, a few high notes "pianolistic."

Technically, Mr. Antheil has discovered the Pleyela, and freed it from ignominy; it is now an instrument, not the piano's poor ape. (I skip the details of the innovation.)[51]

---

[51] The player piano or "pianola" had been invented in the nineteenth century. It became very popular in the 1920s and Stravinsky and numerous others had cut rolls for it. Antheil originally intended to orchestrate his *Ballet mécanique* for sixteen player pianos, but had to give up the idea when the piano people were unable to solve the problem of synchronization. But he did

If in the Ballet Antheil has mastered these long "durées," these larger chunks of time, in the third Violin Sonata, he has made a less obvious gain, for this Sonata thinks in time's razor edge. Whether this shows incontestably on its written pages, I cannot say, but it does show in its playing by the composer and by Miss Olga Rudge, who has borne the brunt of presentation in all three sonatas.

This is not a simple question of playing "in time" or even "in time with each other."

It means that, via Stravinsky and Antheil and possibly one other composer, we are brought to a closer conception of time, to a faster beat, to a closer realisation or, shall we say, "decomposition" of the musical atom.

The mind, even the musician's mind, is conditioned by contemporary things, our minimum, in a time when the old atom is "bombarded" by electricity, when chemical atoms and elements are more strictly considered, is no longer the minimum of the sixteenth century pre-chemists. Both this composer and this executant, starting with the forces and iterations of the 1st Violin Sonata have acquired—perhaps only half-consciously—a new precision. There is something new in violin writing and in violin playing. Violinists of larger reputation who looked at the earlier sonata and walked away, those who thought it "bizarre," will possibly awake and find themselves a little out of date, and the initiative of the first performer, may in time receive its reward. There will be a new hardness and dryness in fashion, and the old oily slickness of the Viennese school will receive diminished applause. There may even be found those of severer taste who will prefer the distinct outline of a Ballet mécanique as shown by the Pleyela role alone, or with the meagre allowance of mechanical sound offered on June 19th, to the seducation of cymbals and xylophones (July performance), or who will at least find it easier to comprehend in the former way, at the start, awaiting the composer's next move, and believing that the vitality of music is in its lateral rather than its perpendicular movement.

---

prepare an early version for solo player piano. Sylvia Beach recalls being invited to Pleyel's along with Joyce and Robert McAlmon to hear the première of this version. Everyone liked the music, but Joyce regretted that "'the pianistic contortions" had not been eliminated by the mechanical piano. Incidentally, Joyce felt quite attracted to Antheil's music, and the two had talked about collaborating on an opera around the "Cyclops" episode of *Ulysses*. Antheil claimed that Joyce had written articles about his music, but after a thorough search, Stephen Adams has concluded that this was merely wishful thinking on the part of the composer.

WORKSHOP ORCHESTRATION

Laying aside all questions of technique, new "theory" etc., there is the reason why the MASSES, new or old, should take note of Antheil. I mean that he has taken, or at any rate has found a means that can take, music out of the concert hall.

The savage has his tribal ceremonies, primitive people have ther sea chanteys and labor songs. Modern man can live, and should live, and has a perfectly good right to live in his cities and in his machine shops with the same kind of swing and exuberance that the savage is supposed to have in his forest. The tenement is no more uncomfortable than the cave, and no more verminous. Neither is there any reason why the city intuition should be any deader than that of the savage.

As for the machine shop, the boiler works, Antheil has opened the way with his *Ballet mécanique;* for the first time we have a music, or the germ and start of a music that can be applied to sound regardless of its loudness. The aesthete goes to a factory, if he ever does go, and hears *noise,* and goes away horrified; the musician, the composer hears noise, but he tries to (?) "see" (no, no), he tries to *hear* what kind of noise it is.

"Music" as taught in the academies deals with the organization of smallish bits of sound, of sounds having certain variations inside the second, organized into forms, or bits of form having differences inside a minute or ten minutes, or, in the "great forms," half an hour.

But with the grasp of the *longer durations* we see the chance of time-spacing the clatter, the grind, the whang-whang, the gnnrrr, in a machine shop, so that the eight-hour day shall have its rhythm; so that the men at the machines shall be demechanized, and work not like robots, but like the members of an orchestra. And the work will benefit, yes, the overlords need not worry; a half minute's silence here and there, the long pause of the lunch hour dividing the two great halves of the music; this will not diminish the output or pejorate the quality of the product.

Say there are forty small stamping presses in a room, let them start not one at a time, raggedly, but *kk!* on the snap of the baton; and *stop,* and then the periods of sound grow gradually longer, and the rests ever so slightly longer in proportion, but so graduated that the difference of ten seconds in the rest is a sensible, appreciable division.

Needless to say each shop, each sort of work will have its own compositions; and they will be made by the men in the shops, because no outside orchestral player will *know* the sound of the shop as well as the people in it, or know what sounds lie in the nature and needs of the work.

The actual measurement of sounds, the mathematics of a new theory does not present any great difficulty, I mean it would not if one were dealing with mere theory; it is easy enough to find out how many times an asphalt drill hits the pavement per minute, and to work out its octaves and fifths, etc.* But one is not thinking into a vacuum; the abstract mathematics might give a good scaffolding, or it might not. It probably would; but one is dealing with the effect of these sounds on human beings; and here as in other musical invention, the work must be done by the man who can *hear,* who can hear the time in his head. It is work for the musician *on the floor of the factory.* And the ultimate sound of this percussive music will be vastly better than the sobbing of tubas.

I have said that the germ is in the *Ballet mécanique;* perhaps I should have said it is in Antheil's *First Violin Sonata,* but I doubt if anyone would have found it there. The sonata has still a relation to older music; but after hearing the *Ballet* one can recognize the roots in the *Sonata.*

As a simple and practical tip I suggest that people who want to get at what I mean (that is, to *hear* what I mean) as a further step from merely assenting to a general idea, should listen to the *Ballet* with simply the Pleyela and the "reduced sonority," that is, wood and metal buzzers, and the electric amplifier for the third movement. It may be nicer music with the attendant xylophones and pianos, but after all it was written originally for 20 Pleyelas, and until the perfect synchronization of 20 Pleyelas is obtainable, the main idea, the division of the great time-spaces, shows up more clearly from the bare, austere, rigid outline.

As for the rest: there is no use waiting for millennia; primitive man cries out to god; the proletarius cries out to Social Justice. In the meantime there are certain things that can be done, made, constructed, without waiting for a millennium.

By 1928 Antheil was definitely moving in more conservative directions, so much so that Pound even walked out of one of his concerts. In 1930 he was to have considerable success with his tabloid opera *Transatlantic,* first produced in Frankfurt. Pound attended and took along the German anthropologist Leo Frobenius, though neither was particularly impressed. Somehow the rumor spread that the work was dedicated to Pound. Pound killed it with a letter to the Paris Edition of *The Chicago Tribune,* April 19, 1930.

* I.e., octaves *lower,* for what we will come to call the "great base," vide my book on Antheil (Pound's note).

UNINDIGNANT DENIAL

Sir:—

I think there must be some misunderstanding. So far as I know Mr. Antheil's opera is not dedicated to me. I have not seen Mr. Antheil for some time. I have never heard Mr. Antheil express the slightest intention of dedicating an opera to me.

As long as the American musical world *y compris* the Metropolitan Opera House, the private Philadelphia back garden, and the heavy chested musical foundations remain the pocket boroughs that they now are, I shd. strongly advise Mr. Antheil or any other good composer to refrain from dedicating me anything, or from being seen in my company.

The Metropolitan's flimsy bluff of wanting American opera (? the King's Henchman, etc.) can pass with the other hoaxes. The taste of the Metropolitan gallery, the determination of the arty and literary foundations to limit their benefice to professorial pets, the determination of the music foundations to produce subsidized students and to exclude composers who invent anything, are all marvelous works of the local gawd.

It is bad enough that the first great American opera shd. make its debut in Germany without having it permanently excluded from America on the suspicion of containing music or being handicapped by my approval. Sagacious American musicians are advised (now as in 1870) to change their patronymics by the addition of -ski or -osh, to call themselves Bakerovitch, Brownsky, Jonesosch, to conduct orchestras and to refrain from composing in a contemporary or tomorrowistic manner.

The ang-sax race and its epigens are all right to play tennis with.

Yrs.
E. POUND

Pound continued to recall Antheil with affection. Although in his autobiography of 1945 Antheil was quick to disassociate himself from Pound "now that the poet has fallen into disgrace," the poet was always more generous in remembering the spirit of Paris and the impetuosity with which they had once shared a credo.

> Musical moralists have damned in my presence that very tough baby George Antheil. He has gone to hell and to Hollywood a "sub-Medean talent," he has made himself a motley and then some. He was imperfectly schooled, in music, in letters, in all

things, but he nevertheless did once demand bits of SOLIDITY, he demanded short hard bits of rhythm hammered down, worn down so that they were indestructible and unbendable. He wanted these gristly and undeformable "monads", as definite as the

> All the angels have big feet.
> Hump, diddywin tum. . . . Hump, bump, stunt.

This is in accord with, though not contained in Jean's *Rappel à l'Ordre*. Cocteau there demanded a music to be like tables and chairs.

That goes with Mantegna's frescoes. Something to be there and STAY there on the wall.[52]

As a postscript to Pound's Parisian years, we should mention his 1928-29 translation of Boris de Schloezer's Stravinsky book, printed in seven installments in *Dial*.[53] He was later to call this "the best volume of musical criticism I have ever encountered...."

> I am aware of De Schloezer's mental coherence, and thoroughness. I am delighted by one sentence, possibly the only one in the book that I remember (approximately): "Melody is the most artificial thing in music," meaning that it is furthest removed from anything the composer finds THERE, ready in nature, needing only direct imitation or copying. It is therefore the root, the test, etc.[54]

[52] *Guide to Kulchur*, pp. 94-95. The big-footed angels are Pound's parody of the Virgil Thomson-Gertrude Stein *Four Saints in Three Acts*.
[53] *Stravinsky: His Technique*, translated from French by Ezra Pound, *Dial*, October, 1928, pp. 271-83; January, 1929, pp. 9-26; February, 1929, pp. 105-15; April, 1929, pp. 298-303; May, 1929, pp. 394-403; June, 1929, pp. 463-74; July, 1929, pp. 597-608.
[54] *ABC of Reading*, p. 24. Boris de Schloezer's exact commentary on "melody" from Pound's translation (*Dial*, June, 1929, p. 473) is as follows: "Melody is the form of organizing sonority which is furthest removed from reality, the most artificial, and precisely the form by which the sonorous world acquires a specific character. Whatever be the historic origins of song, even if one admit that it began as the howl, i.e., direct, as you might say, physiological expression of emotion; its development is indisputably due to detaching it from its physiological sources and organizing it according to acoustic and aesthetic principles. Melody is the creation of human intelligence standing up against nature. Nature offers no model but merely imposes certain anatomical and physical conditions which the human mind obeys precisely in order to escape from them and to construct an artificial universe wherein to reign. There is an intellectual part in every melody, and for that reason it demands comprehension from the auditor. It strikes the auditor as melody, succession, only in so far as the auditor is an active collaborator performing a synthesis (as rudimentary as you like)."

4
The Rapallo Years 1928–1941

The Pounds left Paris for Italy in 1924, settling eventually in Rapallo, where they were to spend the next twenty years, with occasional trips back to Paris and to other metropolitan centers. Rapallo is a small town about eighteen miles southeast of Genoa on the Ligurian coast with a population, in the 1930s, of about five thousand. At first the Pounds lived in hotels, but soon they found a little apartment on the fifth floor of the Albergo Rapallo, entered from the Via Marsala, with windows facing out to sea.

Pound's reasons for moving to Rapallo may have been twofold. He obviously wanted freedom from distraction to work on his *Cantos,* now his chief preoccupation. But also—though I have nowhere seen this idea sufficiently stressed—he seems to have felt the need to find a community in which his undisputed leadership as an intellectual and cultural force would allow him to put his ideas into practice, to plant them, watch them grow. When Yeats, Zukofsky, Bunting, Serly, Ronald Duncan, and the rest came to Rapallo, it was Pound they came to visit. The bust which Gaudier had done of him in London now adorned the hotel dining room, and it was here that he read newspapers, wrote letters, and held forth. On the local scene he established himself as "il Signor Poeta," and the cultural life was quickly imprinted with his personality. Probably his largest contribution was his organization of a unique series of concerts which ran intermittently between 1933 and 1939.

The idea for holding modest but unique concerts had come to

Pound when, years earlier, he had attended a concert in Cesena, organized by the librarian Manlio Dazzi.

> My research into the life of Sigismundo Malatesta took me to Cesena and from the library to a concert, managed by the librarian. The program was composed of music of the highest quality and a local lawyer was adding more interest to it (from the piano) than the professional musicians who had been imported for the occasion. Cesena is not numbered among the ten largest cities of Italy; I should say not among the largest 40 or 60. Szigeti had played there a few weeks before . . . Cesena showed me how to have first rate music in a small town.[1]

Two musicians formed the nucleus of the Rapallo concerts: the violinist Olga Rudge and the pianist Gerhart Münch. Miss Rudge, who had been such a close musical associate in Paris and had performed Pound's music, had come to Italy and took a small apartment in Sant' Ambrogio, the village on the escarpment above Rapallo. Gerhart Münch was an excellent pianist who also composed and had come from Dresden. Two other regulars were Luigi Sansoni, a violinist who also conducted the local orchestra and, according to Pound, played "jazz in the *Kursaal*"; and Marco Ottone, a cellist from Chiavari, the next town down the coast from Rapallo.

It was imperative that the concerts should remain modest and should employ local musicians as much as possible. "Civilization begins when people start preferring a little done right to a great deal done wrong," Pound wrote in 1937.[2] They were not to replicate the musical life of larger centers. "I have said several times that it is useless to do on a smaller scale in Rapallo what is being done with magnificence and great means elsewhere."[3] The focus was at all times to be on the music; no star system, no pandering to the public. Pound wanted a laboratory in which to put his ideas into action. "Laboratory" is the word he used in describing the concerts in his *ABC of Reading* and in a 1936 article for *The Delphian Quarterly*, from which the following

---

[1] "Possibilities of Civilization: What the Small Town Can Do," from *Impact: Essays on Ignorance and the Decline of American Civilization*, Ezra Pound, edited by Noel Stock, Chicago, 1960, pp. 78–79.

[2] "Civilization," from *Polite Essays*, Norfolk, Connecticut, 1940, and London, 1937, p. 193.

[3] *Il Mare*, April 11, 1936.

remarks come. "The Rapallo concerts have provided a laboratory for the *objective* (with the emphasis strictly on that word) examination of music. There has, I believe, been very little serious attempt anywhere to establish a demarcation between first rate and second rate music. . . . Very few people have the chance to observe different musical masterworks under uniform (laboratory) conditions, and very few people have really wanted to do so. . . . A small town can provide a laboratory and can specialize in work not being done in the heavily monied 'centres' up to the quality and number of its local performers."[4]

In other words differences in interpretation had to be minimized if the music was to be truly studied: great virtuosi would impose their personalities, obscuring the composer's original thought. Such figures were to be excluded. Later on, when visiting artists did begin performing in Rapallo, Pound explicitly mentions the shift in emphasis their appearances gave the concerts.

In the *ABC of Reading* he prints a couple of the early programs as a demonstration of Fenollosa's "ideogrammic method" of criticism transposed into musical terms. The ideogrammic method consists of a "careful first-hand examination of the matter, and continual COMPARISON of one 'slide' or specimen with another."[5] When the Chinese wish to establish the concept "red" (Pound says via Fenollosa) they put together abbreviated pictures of a rose, iron rust, cherry, and flamingo. The useful concert would then be one in which the program was gathered together to illustrate a particular concept or to understand the precise shades and weightings of a number of like musical thoughts. Thus, one gets a precise idea of Mozart's violin sonata conceptualization only when the *same* artists perform a great number of them in series; or of Vivaldi's concerto form and technique only when they are done in great batches. Bartók's string quartets can be studied in the same way, and for contrast they can be stacked against some Boccherini in the same form. Similarly one understands the more subtly different hues of Debussy and Ravel when pieces in the same form by each composer are executed in close proximity. To Tibor Serly he wrote: ". . . intention to present the music, old *and* new, in manner that would lead to more *exact* estimation of the value of the compo-

---

[4] "Money versus Music," *The Delphian Quarterly,* January 1936, p. 4.
[5] *ABC of Reading*, p. 17.

sitions. Enough of *one* composer to show his scope and limits; his force and his defects."[6]

Father Desmond Chute, a faithful member of the audience and occasional reviewer of the concerts, described the whole undertaking later as "rare and unforgettable. . . . One remembers blocks of music. *Block* in this context was a great word with Ezra: not only did he insist at rehearsals on 'blocks' of light and shade in the performance of old music, he also demanded integrated and consecutive programs."[7]

Even without knowing much music history, the reader of the *Il Mare* reviews—an overview is possible here for the first time—will be immediately struck by the richness and variety of the programs. Medieval music to Chopin, Mozart to Bartók, Satie to Janequin, where could one go today to find such stimulating fare in one series?[8] It is true, the programs tended over the years to oscillate around a fairly consistent body of repertoire, but their configurations were constantly varied—often even between announcement and execution. These differences need to be noticed, especially since Pound laid such stress on the importance of "form" in program building.

If only, one keeps thinking, small towns throughout the world could show half the touch of inventiveness displayed in these concerts, instead of aspiring to acculturation by the unanimous ambition of producing yet another civic orchestra or opera company. Wishing to have pets, they immediately go after the dinosaurs. For the same amount of money expended annually on the average semiprofessional orchestra a small city could have in residence one of the world's great string quartets. This is Pound's argument. The small town is to form an antipode to the mercantile system of metropolitan concert life. "Music in the great cities has been damned and crushed by the overhead. . . .

---

[6] Letter to Tibor Serly, April 1940, in Paige, *Letters*, New York, p. 343; London, p. 443.

[7] Desmond Chute in the *Pound Newsletter 8*, Berkeley, University of California, Department of English, October 1955, p. 13. "Block" was a favorite word of Pound's as early as the London years, and he frequently "blocked" out pieces with his arms and fists to show what he meant. See above, p. 26. Father Chute recalls that Münch gave a reading on three consecutive afternoons of the complete *Wohltemperierte Clavier*, which should be mentioned here for the record since these private recitals are nowhere mentioned in the *Il Mare* reviews.

[8] Parenthetically I will mention one series of concerts closely approximating Pound's ideal. This was the "Ten Centuries Concerts" which I founded a number of years ago in Toronto. Although I didn't know much about Pound's Rapallo concerts at the time, the idea of comparisons, contrasts, and weightings of little-known repertoire across the centuries was also our aim. And local musicians were used exclusively.

There is no cranny of life into which an infamous monetary system has not spread its poison, invisible as chlorine and as deadly."[9]

The economics of the Rapallo concerts were simple. "*All* the proceeds go to the performers in Rapallo save *ten* lire to the janitor and door-keeper and the small printing expenses which are reduced by cooperation with the town paper."[10] The municipal hall came free and a heating system was installed by the municipality. In addition to the reviews, broadsides, and posters he wrote, Pound also sold tickets and distributed programs at the door. "Ezra brought the money home after each concert, dumped it out on the bed, and they divided it up," Mrs. Pound recalled for me in 1968. "Ezra also wrangled money from a local patron to buy a secondhand grand piano. Sometimes he also helped the musicians with money from his own pocket, what little he had."

Concerning the audiences, Dorothy Pound said "they were usually small, occasionally swelling to about eighty people, a small but élite audience, very enthusiastic." When Chiavari started its own concert series and drew an audience of three hundred, Pound was delighted by this amplification of the Rapallo example. Similarly, when the Siena Festival, several years later, decided to concentrate on one composer—Vivaldi—Pound saw this as a further vindication of his ideals, probably with justification, since he and Olga Rudge were in close contact with Alfredo Casella, the festival director.

The Rapallo concerts can be divided into two periods. The first consisted of the two initial seasons, up to Münch's departure in July, 1935. These were given almost entirely by the local musicians, and the program theories mentioned above were of prime importance. The second period, extending up to the war, featured more visiting artists, more contemporary music, and a greater emphasis on the artist as interpreter, though never as star. "When we have had 'celebrities,' they haven't been bribed to come and they weren't there as *celebrities* but as MUSICIANS."[11] Among those who performed were the Gertler Quartet, the singers Lonny Mayer and Chiarina Fino Savio, the pianists Renata Borgatti and Luigi Franchetti, the New Hungarian Quartet, and Pound's close musical friend of these years, the violist-composer Tibor Serly.

[9] "Music versus Money," *op. cit.*, p. 2.
[10] *Ibid.*, p. 6
[11] *Ibid.*, p. 6.

Pound became most anxious to secure leading musicians. To Gerhart Münch he wrote (December, 1936), asking him to try to persuade Paul Hindemith to come to Rapallo. He had heard Hindemith play his own Viola Concerto at the Venice Biennale and had been much impressed. When in the late 1930s the poet Ronald Duncan was trying to arrange for Stravinsky to conduct a concert of his music with one of the London orchestras—unsuccessfully as it turned out—Pound wrote inquiring about the possibility of his coming to Rapallo.

> Dear Ron: As you haven't given me Uncle Igor's address (or, if you did, I can't find it) you might forward this.
>
> This Hall is at their disposal, père et fils, for anything they care to do. This *is* a pleasant part of the coast, rains and cold *should* be over in a week or so. There is *no* population and I can't draw money from the air. A fee for Stravinsky fils; yes, if it be moderate. *If* their glory is strong enough to draw a public from Genova or Pekin or Marseilles, they are welcome to the total gate receipts. I will splurge away in the *Mare,* and Cuneo is ready to go for the rest of the press. Genova papers always have noticed our concerts; before and after.
>
> As you know the only overhead is the ten lire to porter and the cost of programs. This family can cover that as their reward for admission.[12]

Though Hindemith and Stravinsky never appeared, their music was played. Finding new music was, in fact, a task Pound pursued with great alacrity. In the autumn of 1937 he wrote to Joyce, in a letter now lost, to inquire about some Purcell sonatas.[13] About the same time he wrote to Gerald Hayes of Oxford University Press with a similar request for information. The letter is worth quoting in full, as it indicates his intense curiosity about a subject which was interesting few native Englishmen at the time.

> Dear G. H.: I am aiming my muzikfest for the first week in Feb. Hoping to give rather more of Whittaker's 12 new Purcells than W. seems to think advisable all in a lump.
>
> Now about Jenkins: I think I asked you once before, just as you were in confusion of moving house. I hope to have three

[12] Paige, *Letters,* New York, p. 320; London, p. 415.
[13] Cf., *Pound/Joyce,* ed. Forrest Read, New York, 1967, p. 258.

trusty fiddles, Münch at piano, a cello, and at a pinch the members of an untried but recommended quartet. Is there anything of Jenkins (or enough for a whole evening) that could be played as it stands?? Say I have it photo'd white on black 3½ by 4¼ inches—would that be legible? O.R. could then copy out the parts. *Preferably* not more than three fiddles, keyboard and cello. Probably *no* keyboard in original. Do any Dolmetschers want to dechifrer the basses (if so it be) or rejuice something for disponible instruments? I know nowt of Jenk, save what you have told me. Münch should provide the new Vivaldi, and stick to that job.

Heaven knows there is enough. And with the Purcell, we shall have presentation proportional to Englyshe, *but* may as well interjuice Mr. Jenkins if it is possible.

As I haven't yet a projector, the small but not millimetric photos would save time. I don't mind spending a bit *if* it is to effective and immediate end.

Can you tell me who publishes Dowland? Or have 'em send catalog *if* anything possible for 3 fiddles and/or edited to fiddle and keyboard.

P. S. I seem to remember 3 vols of Lawes' songs. Thought it was modern edtn., but may have been in Brit. Mus. Songs, not instrumental stuff. Have never seen any instrumental Lawes.[14]

W. Gillies Whittaker, referred to in the letter above, was a Scottish conductor and editor with whom Pound had been corresponding from the early 1930s. From him he obtained his edition of the eleven sonatas of William Young in December, 1933, and several of them were immediately presented in Rapallo, presumably in advance of their British "première" at Oxford under Whittaker's direction.[15] Sonatas by John Blow and Henry Purcell in Whittaker editions were also given at Rapallo. A further source of neglected old music was the Querini-Stampalia collec-

[14] Paige, *Letters*, New York, pp. 299–300; London, pp. 392–93.
[15] I have been unable to confirm this. Pound suggested in a number of places that all the sonatas were performed in Rapallo, but I can only account for six having been performed there (March, 1934). In his review of that year in *Il Mare* (April 7) Rev. Desmond Chute expresses disillusionment at not having heard all the promised William Young sonatas, but in his retrospective note in the *Pound Newsletter 8* (1955) he suggests they were all performed, adding, ".... absolute priority of execution must be claimed for Rapallo, actually in advance of the 'first' performance under the editor, W. Gillies Whittaker, at Oxford." Whittaker himself, in his letter to the *Musical Times* (December 1938, quoted below, p. 446), was pleased at least to give the Tigullians credit for their enterprise.

tion from Venice. Pound obtained some of this music, and it was featured in a few of the concerts.

Another musicologist of importance for the Tigullian group was the Italian, Oscar Chilesotti. For Lavignac's *Encyclopédie de la musique et dictionaire du conservatoire* he had contributed an elaborate essay on Italian lute music of the sixteenth and seventeenth centuries. Chilesotti's unpublished papers had come into the hands of Gerhart Münch, who arranged much music from them for the Rapallo concerts of the first years. I avoid the word "transcribe" purposely, for it would appear that Münch's work amounted to quite elaborate reconstructions. Pound was aware of this. Writing to the Princesse Edmond de Polignac to thank her for sending an edition of Janequin's works, he added: "I am afraid the fantasia you liked was more Münch than Ign [oto]." One may get an idea of what was involved by comparing Münch's violin part for the Janequin *Chant des Oiseaux* as it appears in Canto LXXV with the original and with the lute version by Francesco da Milano.[16] This was consistent with Pound's theory of the metempsychosis of the spirit of the masterpiece. "Janequin's concept takes a third life in our time, for catgut or patent silver, its first was choral, its second on the wires of Francesco Milano's lute."[17] Now that we can see how frequently this work (in Münch's version) was performed at the Rapallo concerts, it gains a special poignancy when Pound recalls it in his cage at Pisa. "What thou lovest well remains...."

From 1936 on Vivaldi became the chief preoccupation of the Tigullians, and here some original musicological research was carried out. In 1936 Pound sent Olga Rudge to Turin to catalogue the three hundred and nine Vivaldi instrumental pieces in manuscript in the National Library there.[18] Pound initiated the Vivaldi studies with an article in *Il Mare,* March 14, 1936, and Miss Rudge added two more in April and May in the same pages. It is necessary to bear these dates in mind when fitting the Tigullians' research into Vivaldi's twentieth-century revival, which

---

[16] I also have in my possession a Münch arrangement of *Due Arie di Francesco Severi* which "omette le parole delle arie riducendo i due brani dal canto a violino e piano"—a very romantic reconstruction.

[17] *Guide to Kulchur,* p. 152.

[18] Turin has the largest holdings of Vivaldi material. The second largest is the collection in the Sächsische Landesbibliothek in Dresden, from which Pound ordered microfilms in 1937. The Turin manuscripts are in twenty-seven volumes, eleven of which were the gift of the Foà family in 1927; the remainder were donated by the Giordano family in 1930. They were eventually catalogued and published by Olga Rudge after she became secretary of the Accademia Musicale Chigiana in Siena.

really did not begin seriously, at least as far as the actual performance of the music goes, until later.[19]

In 1937 Pound had ordered several manuscripts from the Sächsische Landesbibliothek on microfilm, and he gave them to Count Guido Chigi Saracini in 1938 for inclusion in the holdings of the Accademia Musicale Chigiana in Siena, where Olga Rudge was then working as secretary. Some of these were to be performed during the Settimana Musicale in 1939 under the direction of Alfredo Casella. The rumor seems to have spread that the originals were destroyed during the war and that Pound's microfilm was the only form in which these Vivaldi works survived. This is both true and untrue. A few of the Dresden manuscripts, including those obtained by Pound, were "badly damaged," but the collection as a whole remains intact.[20]

Pound copied out the Dresden Vivaldiana himself, and wrote numerous other pieces celebrating this composer, but his practical research on the subject ended here. Noel Stock is correct in his assessment of Pound's role in the Vivaldi studies.

> Pound's part in the revival may be seen as twofold. He played the leading part as organizer in the early stages, but more important in the long-run probably was his constant support and encouragement of Olga Rudge. To her he communicated his enthusiasm and helped her to overcome various obstacles, with the result that she carried out a difficult and arduous programme of research that was beyond Pound himself.[21]

[19] Pound and Rudge were, however, preceded in the field by the musicologists Arnold Schering, Marc Pincherle, W. Altmann, and Alberto Gentili. A complete account of their work is given in *Vivaldiana*, Publication de Centre International de Documentation Antonio Vivaldi, No. 1, Bruxelles, 1969.

[20] This story seems to have been started by Miss Rudge in her publication, *Vivaldi: Quattro Concerti Autografi della Sächsische Landesbibliothek di Dresda*, Accademia Musicale Chigiana, Siena, 1949, where she writes: "I manoscritti dei quattro concerti qui riprodotti in fac-simile fanno, o purtroppo facevano, parte della famos collezione di autografi e manoscritti vivaldiani nella LANDESBIBLIOTHEK di Dresda che pare sia stata irrimediabilmente distrutta durante le recente guerra." In fact only one of the works in this publication (CX 1045 B) is numbered among those damaged by the war. (Vide: "Die Dresdener Vivaldi-Manuskripte," by Hans Rudolf Jung, in *Archivs für Musikwissenschaft*, Jahrgang, 1955.) That a scholar such as Charles Norman (vide: *Ezra Pound*, New York, 1969, p. 319) has perpetuated the story without checking it out is carelessness that should not go unnoticed. Noel Stock knew the truth when he wrote *The Life of Ezra Pound* (1970) but was kind enough merely to omit the oft-repeated story. A summary of the Pound-Rudge contributions may be found in Stephen Adams's "Pound, Olga Rudge, and the 'Risveglio Vivaldiano' " (*Paideuma*, Vol. 4, No. 1, 1973, pp. 111–18).

[21] Noel Stock, *The Life of Ezra Pound*, New York and London, 1970, p. 338.

Olga was, in fact, to go on to occupy a leading position in the revival; Vivaldi lovers will frequently come across her name.[22]

All the reviews of the Rapallo concerts come from *Il Mare*, the local Rapallo newspaper, no longer published. In 1932 Pound had persuaded the editor to issue a "Supplemento Lettarario," and for it he had obtained some interesting little pieces by James T. Farrell, Robert McAlmon, Basil Bunting, Louis Zukofsky, and F. T. Marinetti. At first the music reviews appeared in this supplement, but later, when it was dropped, they went into the main pages, where they appeared under various titles: *Inverno musicale* (Musical Winter), *Concerti Tigulliani* (Tigullian Concerts), or *Amici del Tigullio* (The Friends of Tigullio). The Tigullian Gulf, by the way, is the gulf on which Rapallo is situated.

It appears that Pound wrote his first few reviews in English and they were translated for him into Italian, but later he wrote directly in that language. All the Italian reviews, and a few longer articles from other publications, have had to be translated back into English. For help in this difficult task I am greatly indebted to two people: Miss Maria Chiara Zanolli, who did the first draft, and the poet's daughter, Mary de Rachewiltz, for numerous further suggestions. Of course I take full responsibility for the form in which they appear. I have tried to ensure that they are musically accurate, but have not tried to force them to speak Pound's own inimitable English. Wherever Pound expressed the same ideas in an original English text, the comparison has been noted in the footnotes. A few of the reviews are unsigned, and while most, even in Italian, are distinctively Poundian, a few are bland enough to be by someone else. In all

---

[22] A partial list of Olga Rudge's Vivaldiana follows: "Antonio Vivaldi," in *Il Mare*, April 4, 1936; "Vivaldi: La sua posizione nella storia della musica," in *Il Mare*, May 9, 1936; "Venice and Vivaldi," in *The Delphian Quarterly*, January, 1938, pp. 7–10 and 56; "Letters of Antonio Vivaldi" in *The Listener*, October 28, 1936, p. 834; "Catalogo Tematico delle Opera Strumentali di Antonio Vivaldi" (the Turin catalogue), in *Antonio Vivaldi: Note e Documenti sulla vita e sulle opere*, Accademia Musicale Chigiana, Siena, 1939; "In Margine ai Mss. Vivaldiani" and "Opere vocale attribute a Antonio Vivaldi nella Biblioteca Nazionale di Torino," in *La Scuola Veneziana*, Libreria Editrice Ticci, Siena, 1941; "Lettere e dediche di Antonio Vivaldi," Accademia Musicale Chigiana, Siena, 1942; "Note sulla opere eseguite durante la prima Settimana sienese Settembre 1939," in *Antonio Vivaldi*, edited by S. A. Luciana and Olga Rudge, Siena, 1947; "Fac-simile del Concerto Funebre di Antonio Vivaldi," Accademia Musicale Chigiana, 1947; "Fac-simile di un autografo di Antonio Vivaldi," Quaderni dell'Accademia Chigiana, No. 13, Siena, 1947; "Antonio Vivaldi: Quattro Concerti Autografi," Accademia Musicale Chigiana, Siena, 1949; and the article on Vivaldi in Grove's *Dictionary of Music and Musicians*, Vol. IX, London, 1954.

cases, however, I have accepted Donald Gallup's *A Bibliography of Ezra Pound*[23] as the final authority, and have managed to hunt up a couple of reviews not mentioned by him but assuredly by Pound. The *Il Mare* reviews are interspersed with articles Pound wrote in English for various other periodicals, though some very slight departures from strict chronological ordering have been made to preserve certain sequences of concerns.

By comparison with *The New Age* reviews, the *Il Mare* material makes less interesting reading, though as documentation of a largely unknown area of Pound's work it is equally valuable. Certainly the repetitiveness is boring. I have eliminated a few of the many redundancies in the matter of dates, times of concerts, etc., but all the programs are intact and the reviews are complete.

There is an important change in tone in the *Il Mare* material, necessitated by writing for a small-town newspaper as opposed to the big-city publication. In a sense perhaps only someone who has had the experience of trying to make something happen in a small town can appreciate what is involved. Concessions are necessary; ideas have to be slowly but emphatically rubbed in. The opacity of the small-town mind cannot easily be pierced. Pound's purpose was to arouse the local citizenry out of a certain ancestral sludge, but to accomplish this even the man with a precise sense of mission must frequently adopt plodding tactics.

In June, 1933, Olga Rudge and Gerhart Münch rented the local cinema house, the "Teatro Reale"—in which, incidentally, Pound liked to watch grade B movies—and gave, in a series of three concerts, twelve of Mozart's violin sonatas. Pound and his biographers have frequently stated that "all" Mozart's works in this form were performed. But since Mozart completed thirty-four violin sonatas and left a number of others incomplete, this is a little wide of the mark. In a letter to Tibor Serly (*Letters*, p. 442) Pound recognizes this but adds: "The rest done privately so that a few of us heard the whole set." Let us simply say that a "block" of sonatas was performed in public, some earlier specimens, some later, and some "which he did, as I like to imagine, at crucial moments of his musical thought, preceding, and holding in his mind the nuclei of, larger compositions."[24] In this way the artists were able to demonstrate "what Mozart *meant* by the form or

---

[23] Donald Gallup, *A Bibliography of Ezra Pound*, The Soho Bibliographies XVIII, London, 1963. Gallup claims the authority for his selection was Olga Rudge.
[24] "Money versus Music," *op. cit.*, p. 3.

what the form meant to him."²⁵ The programs consisted of the following works:

Monday, June 26
1. Sonata in B-flat major (K. 454);
2. Sonata in G major (K. 301);
3. Sonata in E minor (K. 304);
4. Sonata in B-flat major (K. 378).

Tuesday, June 27
1. Sonata in A major (K. 305);
2. Sonata in G major (K. 379);
3. Sonata in A major (K. 402);
4. Sonata in E-flat major (K. 380).

Wednesday, June 28
1. Sonata in D major (K. 306);
2. Sonata in F major (K. 377);
3. Sonata in E-flat (K. 481);
4. Sonata in A major (K. 526).

Pound wrote a short announcement for the series which was published as a broadside, and Basil Bunting, who was intermittently in Rapallo during these years and an active participant in the early concerts, followed this with an enthusiastic front-page review in *Il Mare* for July 1.

> *You and your family are cordially invited to attend the*
> MOZART WEEK
> *which will take place in Rapallo in the "Teatro Reale"*
> *JUNE 26, 27 AND 28 AT 9:00 P.M.*
> *under the auspices of the Fascist Institute of Culture.*

The musical section of the "Amici del Tigullio," taking advantage of the presence in Rapallo of two distinguished artists, has decided to initiate an activity which has long been under consideration.

The section announces a MOZART WEEK which it hopes will become a celebration to be repeated annually.

Mozart's sonatas for violin and piano represent a phenomenon as distinctive in music as Dante's *Paradiso* in the field of literature.

The performers will be the composer Gerhart Münch of Dresden and Olga Rudge of Paris.

---
²⁵ *Ibid.*, p. 4.

At the age of thirteen Münch played the piano solo in Liszt's Concerto with the Dresden Philharmonic, conducted by Edwin Linder, and also performed the same work in Berlin, Leipzig, Munich, Brussels, and Zürich.

Olga Rudge, who was the first to perform many modern compositions and is already well-known in London, attracted the attention of the public to the composer Antheil in Paris through her concerts at the Salle du Conservatoire, Salle Pleyel, etc., and she has also performed in concerts with the Italian maestri Casella and Pizzetti. *Il Messaggero* of Rome says: "An extremely capable artist with an impeccable technique, a clear sound, an ample and secure bowing technique, and talents which have once more earned her a warm success, particularly in the limpid sonatas of Mozart."

On July 8 a double-column announcement in *Il Mare* entitled "Concerto Scriabiano" contained an article "Scriabin" by Basil Bunting, beside one entitled "Anti-Scriabin," by Pound. Neither article expressed much passion for or against Scriabin, though Pound took the opportunity to reaffirm the old suspicions he had about this composer from *The New Age* days. The recital was given on July 12 in a private home, placed at the Tigullians disposal by Father Desmond Chute.

ANTI-SCRIABIN[26]

Having taken such a stand, I must explain myself.

Art, like religion, is a matter of faith. My musical faith tends toward a whole composed of about one hundred substantial composers, some great, some minor. In this pantheon Bach and Mozart reign supreme.

In music after Debussy there are three major figures: Scriabin, Schönberg and Stravinsky.

I have a reasonable amount of faith in Stravinsky's first periods; for Schönberg I have respect, but I can't help thinking he is guilty of too much theory; that is, sometimes in theorizing he believes he is inventing or discovering when he is merely attaching superfluous terminology to combinations which might serve an artist in one or three cases, but which don't constitute a musical pedagogy.

Scriabin is the greatest colorist after Debussy, from the mystical point of view, etc., and may be more interesting than Debussy himself, but precisely like Debussy, being a colorist, I believe he sins against durability; for the life of a work of art, even by a great inventor or artist,

---

[26] *Il Mare*, July 8, 1933; translated from the Italian.

depends on elements belonging specifically to that art and to no other, i.e., no "transfer" from a contiguous art. Thus Debussy, having more visual than aural imagination, was more exciting *in his own time* than today, and today a work by Debussy is more exciting at the first hearing than after the tenth.

I think Scriabin belongs among the heretical composers, but he is a most interesting heretic, and I will certainly be part of the small company that will listen to the presentation of Scriabin's work which Münch will give on Wednesday in the Villa San Giorgio.

And I will listen most attentively with the certainty of learning more than I know today; to augment my musical knowledge and be able to define more accurately to myself my opinion of Scriabin's music.

EZRA POUND

NOTE: To consolidate the effort of the "Amici del Tigullio" and to make our offer to the composer Münch to remain permanently in Rapallo more interesting, the aristocracy of the Gulf of Tigullio has decided to organize a private subscription concert as a solid demonstration to our guest of said interest.

The "Amici del Tigullio," determined to perpetuate the Mozart series, offer their most sincere thanks to the Committee, frankly recognizing that Münch is the real pivot of the affair and that without him (his talents and great general competence) it would be, if not impossible, at least very difficult to continue.

Ladies and gentlemen wishing to assist this effort to achieve a higher degree of musicality in the Gulf of Tigullio are invited to contact the Marchesa Carola Colli di Felizzano, initiator of the patronage, or the Musical Section of the "Amici del Tigullio" through the editor's office of *Il Mare*.

The Hungarian-American composer Tibor Serly first came to know Pound in 1929 when he wrote a "scathing" letter to the poet attacking *Antheil and the Treatise on Harmony*. During the 1930s he frequently stopped in Rapallo on his returns from America, where he was playing viola in various orchestras, to Budapest to see his friends and his old teacher Kodály. He passed periods of several summers in Rapallo and Siena right up to 1938. In August, 1933, Serly visited Rapallo with his friend Geza Frid, on their way back from Budapest. Serly and Frid had studied together at the Budapest Academy, graduating in 1925. While Serly had originally studied with Kodály, his own music was closer in spirit to that of Bartók. He later befriended Bartók during the latter's final tragic years in New York, and in 1945 he completed and orchestrated Bartók's unfinished viola concerto. He is also responsible for introducing Pound to Bartók's music, an auspicious introduction as we shall see later.

To Serly, Pound gave the manuscript of his *Ghuidonis Sonata,* and the composer arranged the solo line for string orchestra and performed it in this version with some friends for Pound when he visited America in 1939. On one occasion, when Serly was looking for an opera libretto, Pound gave him a "large and beautiful edition of Golding's translation of Ovid and said, 'Here are plots for a dozen operas.' "[27]

Pound could never understand why Serly's music could not attract attention in America. To E. E. Cummings he wrote in 1935:

> Why don't them buzzards in Noo Yok play bro Tibor Serly's muzik? Stokowsky keeps *promising,* and then Tibor has to come here or go to Budapesth for concerts (hand made) or orchestrated.[28]

At any rate Pound did *his* best to help get Serly established, and during his 1933 summer visit wrote the following piece for *Il Mare.*

HUNGARIAN COMPOSERS IN RAPALLO[29]

Guests during the past few days, *Tibor Serly* and *Geza Frid,* trained by Kodály. Serly is a brilliant composer of genuinely modern music, based on profound studies—modern for its polytonality but classical in its sobriety and shaping. In fact, he opposes the current opinion about polytonality, maintaining that, at least in practice, polytonality is rather a combination of major and minor together with a common fundamental in the bass.[30]

Whether we accept this theory or not, Serly presents the pragmatic

---

[27] Letter to the editor, July 22, 1968.
[28] Paige, *Letters,* New York, p. 268; London, p. 357.
[29] *Il Mare,* August 20, 1933; translated from the Italian.
[30] Concerning this Serly writes: "It was a time when I felt something was wrong with the expressions polytonality, atonality, and most of all, dodecaphony. They were neither accurate nor the complete solution to the twentieth century dilemma of consonance versus dissonance. Ten years later the answer came to me. Again I can only say that E. P. instinctively grasped the meaning of my attempts (not yet completely formulated) at a solution." (Letter to the editor, October 25, 1970.)

proof in his "Viola Concerto" where the rhythmic life of the instrument passes deftly between two groups of stringed and wind instruments.

Some of us were privileged to attend a private audition at Villa Andreae with a presentation (skeleton) for viola and piano by the composer and his friend Frid, both masters of the deepest secret of music, i.e., that precision with time which distinguishes the best from the competent, that precision which escapes many so-called conductors.

I remember two pleasures of the ear of this kind: one given by Wanda Landowska, the other by a blind beggar singing *Pepina* (or something in *ina*) in the streets of Ravenna.

Sense of rhythm, fine, but there is also this sense of time, the equivalent in "duration" of the great designers' mastery of line in "space."

This is the essence of music, where harmony is but a *corpus vitae*, the *animated* sonority of divisions shaped by duration.

As a study piece Serly has orchestrated Mozart's sublime *Fantasy and Fugue for Mechanical Clock*, which for so long has been inaccessible or, let us say, unperformable. Last year it was presented by the Philadelphia Orchestra. Perhaps more interesting than these works is a sonata written first for woodwinds (Holzbläser) and expanded for full orchestra.

Frid is better known in Europe. Monteux and Dohnányi have presented his *Suite for Orchestra* in Paris, Amsterdam and Budapest; Koussevitzky in New York and Boston. He writes for *quatuor à cordes*, for quintet and for piano; he is a master of the piano as much as Serly is of the viola.

In "Divertissements" for orchestra the texture is clear and precise, a clarity that has almost forsaken music for more than a century.

We hope these two strong talents will come back to Rapallo when our plans mature for public performances of contemporary music.

WILLIAM ATHELING

The first full season of concerts was given in the Rapallo Town Hall and opened on October 10, 1933. The hall still stands; it is very reverberant, seating about two hundred fifty, with painted decorations on the walls and ceiling. The inaugural season was backed by a prestigious group of patrons: Marchesa Solferina Spinola, Marchesa Imperiali, Contessa Gabriella Sottocasa, Conte Nicolis di Robilant, Mrs. Ephra Townley, Grand'Uff. Angelo Sraffa, Sig. George Marshall, Rev. mo Desmond Chute, Sig. Allan MacLean, Sig. Chilesotti, Gentil Donna Bice Berino, Mrs. Romain Brooks, Miss Natalie Barney, Signora Pomilio, Dott. ssa Bacigalupo, Mrs. Watkinson, Mme. Czarada, Miss Gordon, Sig. H. L. Pound (the poet's father), and Mrs. Dorothy Pound.

The organizing committee consisted of Pound, Basil Bunting, and Eugen Haas, a German resident who, according to Pound, had been a music critic in Stuttgart. When, toward the end of 1933, Bunting left Rapallo for the Canary Islands, his place on the committee was taken by Mrs. Ephra Townley, who had been active in organizing concerts on the Paris scene.

From Haas and Bunting's review of the first concert we learn that the series opened splendidly. "Il numero e l'entusiasmo del pubblico è la migliore garanzia per la continuazione di questi concerti." The mayor attended and patronage was secured from the hotels "Rapallo," "Marsala," and "Pensione Lido," which underwrote passes for their guests. Pound wrote a preview of the season for the September 16 edition of *Il Mare*.

EXCEPTIONAL PROGRAM OF MUSICAL EVENTS IN RAPALLO[31]

Accepting Mayor Solari's offer to put the new great Town Hall at the disposal of the Committee, and soliciting the patronage of the Fascist Institute of Culture, we are taking advantage of the favorable circumstances to propose a series of first-rate concerts with programs that would be highly distinguished in any European metropolis.

We have already reported, thanks to the *Mozart Week*, the discovery among us of the musical transcriptions of the late Oscar Chilesotti. Having heard a quantity of this music in private audition, I can certify that it did not disappoint my expectations.

This treasure, as we may well call it, consists of twenty volumes containing, among other things, outstanding works and unpublished music by Francesco da Milano, Giovanni Terzi, Bassani, Josquin, Nic. Nigrini, Gorzanis, Vincenzo Galilei, S. Molinaro, Giovanni Picchi, Lodovico Roncelli, and others.

The presence of the musicians of the *Mozart Week* has been confirmed for the winter, or at least we know that Münch, occupied with his compositions and studies of old music will be with us for several months to come, barring unforeseen circumstances inherent to human destiny. Olga Rudge will be passing through Rapallo, or will never be further away than Venice, and will participate in at least four of the planned concerts.

We will also have Maestro Sansoni, whose merits are sometimes forgotten by those who see him conducting the municipal orchestra in

---

[31] *Il Mare*, September 16, 1933; translated from the Italian.

the open air or playing jazz in the *Kursaal;* but with his pure violin technique and over-all musical intelligence this pupil of Hollander and Serato could pursue a musical career in a milieu more demanding than the local, and his presence is fortunate for our purposes. Prof. Marco Ottone, cellist from Chiavari, has generously promised his help, and we may also profit from the presence of other professional musicians passing through town.

Our aim however is to develop a group of local performers sufficient for our needs and desires, and not to spoil our musical life as in so many countries by trusting and encouraging only the so-called "stars," whose glitter is often based more on publicity than actual competence and musical finesse.

If we can find *sustaining members* we propose—the first week of each winter month—to hold concerts in the Town Hall, performing the following program, subject to a few changes or minor postponments.

OCTOBER: Chilesotti Collection: *Canzone degli uccelli,* Francesco da Milano; songs by Bassani; *Suite di balli,* Giovanni Terzi; et al. Corelli, *Sonata per due violini e pianoforte;* Purcell, *Golden Sonata* for two violins and piano; Debussy, Sonata for violin and piano.

NOVEMBER: Chilesotti Collection. Ravel, a group of pieces for piano; *Les trésors d'Orphée,* edited by Münch; Bach, Sonata for two violins and piano.

DECEMBER: Chilesotti Collection. Lübeck, Fantasia; (to be announced).

JANUARY: Chilesotti Collection. Chopin, piano works; Ravel, Sonata for violin and piano; Mozart, Trio.

FEBRUARY: Chilesotti Collection. *Trio Program;* Pergolesi, Bach, Haydn —probably.

MARCH: Chilesotti Collection. Scriabin, half hour of piano music; Münch, Second sonata, violin and piano.

Alternate numbers include compositions by Eric Satie, Stravinsky, Vivaldi, and Veracini.

PERFORMERS: Olga Rudge, violin; Gerhart Münch, pianist; prof. Luigi Sansoni, violinist. Guest musician: prof. Marco Ottone, cello.

The subscription for the whole series will be 100 liras for *sustaining members* and will admit two persons to each concert. The more members we find, the richer the concerts; and we will also be able to add to the number of performers.

A second promotional article in *Il Mare* on October 7, though not by Pound, gave a similar program outline but substituted the Bach C major violin sonata on the first program for Purcell's *Golden Sonata,* which was to be moved to the second program. According to Haas' and Bunting's review of the first concert (*Il*

Sotto gli auspici dell'ISTITUTO FASCISTA DI CULTURA
COMUNE :: ENTE AUTONOMO :: FASCIO
SOSTENITORI DEGLI "AMICI DEL TIGULLIO

CONCERTI
"INVERNO MUSICALE„

NELLA GRAN SALA DEL MUNICIPIO DI
RAPALLO

STAGIONE INVERNALE 1933-34 A. XII

ESECUTORI :
OLGA RUDGE, violinista; GERHART MÜNCH, pianista; prof. LUIGI SANSONI, violinista. Invitato: prof. MARCO OTTONE, cellista.

SOSTENITORI DEGLI "AMICI DEL TIGULLIO„:

Marchesa Solferina Spinola • Marchesa Imperiali • Contessa Gabriella Sottocasa • Conte Nicolis di Robilant • Mrs Ephra Townley (2) • Grand'Uff. Angelo Sraffa • Sig. George Marshall • Rev.mo Desmond Chute • Sig. Allan Mac Lean • Sig. Chilesotti • Gentil Donna Bice Berino • Mrs Romain Brooks • Miss Natalie Barney • Signora Pomilio • Dott.ssa Bacigalupo • Mrs Watkinson • M.me Czarada • Miss Gordon Sig. H. L. Pound • Mrs D. Pound.

Cover of a brochure outlining the first season (1933–34) series of Rapallo concerts, built largely around the talents of Gerhart Münch and Olga Rudge and organized by a committee consisting of Pound, Basil Bunting, and Eugen Haas. Pound's father and wife were both patrons.

Mare, October 14, 1933) the following program was given: the first two sections of Francesco da Milano's reworking of Janequin's *Chant des Oiseaux* in a version for violin and piano prepared by Münch; a *Suite di balli,* consisting of "Passemezzo in tre tempi," "Gagliarda in tre tempi," and "Villanella in quattro tempi," arranged by Münch for violin and piano from the Chilesotti collection of early baroque material. The "Passemezzo" was by Giovanni Antonio Terzi, "the most celebrated Italian lutenist of his day except, maybe, Vincenzo Galilei," and the remainder was anonymous; Corelli's Sonata in A major for two violins and keyboard; Bach's Sonata in C major for two violins and keyboard; and Debussy's Sonata for violin and piano.

The three following reviews introduced Münch and Olga Rudge to the Rapallo public.

THE PIANIST MÜNCH[32]

We know Oscar Chilesotti was not a composer but a great scholar and authority on music, particularly Italian music of the XVIth and XVIIth centuries. He published a dozen volumes of musical masterpieces he had been digging up in some thirty libraries, but he left unpublished a great number of manuscripts, only partly in modern musical notation. One cannot expect, therefore, that such a treasure could be used in its present state for concert, or that any interpreter, even a great virtuoso, who is not at the same time a scholar in this field, could play directly from the Chilesottian manuscripts.

As members and supporters of the Committee promoting the previously announced *Inverno musicale,* we are not only paying Münch for that hour of virtuoso playing he offers us on the evening of the concert. His real task is different and greater: he must decipher a whole system of abbreviations for old music adopted by Chilesotti, who had for the most part, merely transcribed the *tablatura* used by the composers of lute music. So to give effect to his manuscripts, or at least to provide them with a beauty evocative of their period, frequent checks with the work of the great collector are necessary. One must know how to recognize when a piece is of great archeological value but unsuitable for a concert performance.

The *Suite di balli* from the manuscripts of Giovanni Terzi and other unknowns consists of short pieces because in the XVIth century dance orchestras used to repeat the same melody as they do today in jazz and dance-band music.

[32] *Il Mare*, September 23, 1933; translated from the Italian.

For a concert performance these short pieces must be combined according to their spirit and tonality, just as a piece of architecture is structured creatively. All this is the task of a composer and a conductor, not of a mere pianist, not even of a pianist endowed with the right kind of temperament, and it requires long and conscientious training.

What we do as members of the Committee is contribute to the perfection of European musical culture. Münch does not perform for an hour, but works for entire days, conservatory work, well deserving of a grant, etc.

Those who prefer study and the sounds of instruments above erudition to abstraction, can—should—support our effort, knowing that our guest Münch does not remain idle twenty-nine days a month, that is, from one concert to the next, as do some of the "hippopotami" who pass for patrons of the arts.

We are not begging, but we accept any help sent to ensure the success of our presentations.

We want to hold the concerts here without having to ask for help from the conservatories of Paris or Berlin.

The best known work by Chilesotti was printed in Paris, in the *Encyclopédie et dictionaire du conservatoire* of Paris, but we are now living in another era; we write the years in Roman numbers, and we must do here in Rapallo what could once be done only elsewhere.

THE VIOLINIST OLGA RUDGE[33]

I heard her play for the first time with a pianist whose name I now forget, in a concert at the Aeolian Hall, where a few days later Miss Borgatti, the daughter of our distinguished fellow citizen Commendator Giuseppe, also played the piano.[34]

My review was favorable, but the critic of the *Morning Post,* an old hand at the game, outdid me, declaring openly that he found himself face to face with a new artist of great promise and "a special talent for her chosen instrument."

As a critic I was conscientious, I took the problem of the judgment I had to pronounce seriously, and I tried to find out to what extent it is possible to sit in concert halls year in year out and preserve proper

---

[33] *Il Mare,* September 30, 1933; translated from the Italian. In a footnote in *Il Mare* for October 7, 1933, Pound makes several corrections to the original translation of this article. They have been incorporated in the present English restoration.

[34] See *The New Age* review for November 25, 1920. Pound forgot that Miss Borgatti was on the same program and acted as one of Miss Rudge's accompanists.

terminology. I tried to remember the *relative* merits of all the performers, never giving a "better" instead of a "good," an "excellent" instead of a "better," never confusing the diverse qualities and talents of the artists. I concluded that Olga Rudge was a sober violinist who respected the notations the composer had printed.

In fact, during the following years she illustrated for us more than anyone else the difference between demonstration and execution. To clarify my shade of meaning, I would really need a translator, and even were I to write in my native language, the degrees of such distinction would have to be expressed with great caution. How far does the player present and how far *must* he present the idea of the composer? How far must he take the printed music as a starting point to build or perhaps to improvise something new and of his own?

Is the printed music something "to represent" or must the artist "interpret" it as an actor interprets a rôle?

Hamlet by Shakespeare or *Hamlet* by Booth, Salvini, Forbes Robertson?

Bach by Bach or Bach by Busoni?

A fair answer would be that there are two different activities, and that, according to circumstances, either can give pleasure, arouse interest, augment knowledge, awaken emotions.

Miss Rudge was interested in music as it appeared in the mind of the composer. Taking the longest route (and in that case the most difficult) she did not seem interested in the amelioration of an inferior kind of music. She looked at the page, she played the notes; if the composition was faulty or mediocre, she did not try to titillate the public by making it believe a piece of false music was a masterpiece.

It ended in a cult, naturally, a cult for Mozart. And people were looking for the best known harpsichord "maestra" to study Bach's sonatas for violin and *clavier*.

The artist whom I had seen once from the music critic's seat I later met in Paris in a salon. In Paris there is always "the last salon." For the past half-century every salon has been considered "the last" specimen of an extinct organism from a dead epoch.

I met her in the most picturesque of the many milieux I have known, the ancient abode of Adriana Lecouvreur, a garden with ancient trees, the biggest of which is supported by a wooden structure, the house with classical decorations also supported by scaffolding. A house ready to fall the moment the love and care of the American owner ceases to keep watch over it or gives way for a week to the common sense (or let us call it *avarice*) of the French.

The tiny temple, dedicated "A l'amitié," has been used even in our days for feasts evocative of the past, and is situated, garden included, right in the middle of Paris. As a literary salon it has had as main supporter in our time Rémy de Gourmont, it is not therefore deceiving to call it a "salon." Through this salon many celebrities have passed and even some honest writers. It is no use believing that a salon can be constituted exclusively of serious, honest people, intent on their own business and work, always acting with justice toward others (still with reference to the artistic world), judging each other exclusively on the basis of literary merits.

So for malicious tongues (let us say the malicious tongue of this writer) a salon is "used" or can be used, to create, to determine antipathies and irreconcilable points of view, to verify the correspondence that exists between the flesh and blood writer and his writings, or the asymmetries and mysterious inequalities which appear between them (even if insignificant).

I had an opportunity to "verify" Gide, Valéry, Valette, Rachilde, the women of French literature.

I think it was the hostess of the salon herself who defined the feminine of writer (écrivain) as "écrevisse" (crayfish).

Once she even took me to see Anatole France. People of all sorts arrived in that salon: starry-eyed Americans, etc.

For me the salon represented "a link with the past,"[35] with a generation whose opinions and points of view I wanted to destroy for the most part, though I wanted to preserve five per cent of its intelligence or its verbal manifestations.

Detached also was the person, so much younger, that I met there. I sensed this, but for quite other reasons, as I discovered later.

As a child, accustomed to a different salon, or, let us say, to different surroundings (those of the Gautiers), she felt, I suppose, rather strange in this one. Such is the impression that meeting Judith Gautier, daughter of Théophile, translator of Chinese poetry, made on all those who were introduced to her, at least as far as I have been able to determine.

Judith Gautier's milieu was preserved until 1930, at least as an empty shell. All the furniture, etc., was in its place, down to the very chair of the great Théophile himself in a small detached sitting room.

Here too the musician kept herself aloof with a certain delicate and unemphatic reserve; but as soon as I questioned her she said she was always disconcerted on returning to the salon to find "another woman" where Judith used to sit.

[35] English in the original. The following reminiscence of Judith Gautier reappears in several details of Canto LXXX.

To shift to another set of facts and ideas: Antheil rose from an atmosphere of "gangsters," the "tough guy,"[36] the police hoodlum, perhaps the only composer today who has been able to become an "honorary member of the Paris police," not for services rendered, but because of the warm sympathy he inspired, during a night of cheerful company with some characters out of a thriller, in the chief of the metropolitan police.

The Cagney[37] of music came back from Berlin penniless, possibly without a single farthing, and with the longest record of uproars, fiascos, and hostile demonstrations ever obtained by a musician on tour in Germany. A man of talent, full of talent, a composer in whose defence I was later to publish a book.

The chaos continued in Paris. The Champs Elysées theater, filled to overflowing for a variety show, turned into bedlam five minutes after Antheil was at the piano.

A review in an American monthly, years later, hinted that one voice could be heard above all others, and compared the intelligence of the French public to that of sucklings.

I don't deny it. At this concert, or at the première of Antheil's *Ballet mécanique,* Eric Satie sat next to me applauding, nobody knows why: conviction, a desire to test the audience's reactions, capacity to enjoy anything, pleasure in making the audience or "les Six" angry?[38] Who knows. In 1930, when Antheil's opera *Transatlantic* was presented at the Stadtoper in Frankfurt I saw the other side of the coin. The international audience arrived from Paris, the critics and the impresarios from the other German cities were clapping, calling repeatedly for the composer.

A young man, only one, with fine hair, with beautiful and delicate features, was defying the audience until the arrival of the police, proclaiming his romantic opposition by means of a shrill whistle.

Geheimrat Leo Frobenius[39] judged the opera "not satirical, but naive, interesting as *Kulturausführung."* In fact he argued that Antheil was

---

[36] English in original.

[37] James Cagney, the American actor and Hollywood star of the 1930s and 1940s, famous for his pugnacious roles. Antheil's stormy concert career can best be followed in his autobiography, *Bad Boy of Music.*

[38] It was not at the *Ballet mécanique* première but at a piano recital given by Antheil on October 4, 1923, that Pound sat next to Satie. The incident is related in Antheil's *Bad Boy of Music,* pp. 132-34. "I suddenly heard Satie's shrill voice saying, 'Quel précision! Quel précision! Bravo! Bravo!' and he kept clapping his little gloved hands. . . . By this time some people in the galleries were pulling up the seats and dropping them down into the orchestra; the police entered, and any number of surrealists, society personages, and people of all descriptions were arrested."

[39] The philosopher and authority on Africa who led the latest expedition to the Sahara for the Italian government. (Pound's note.)

using real instruments for proletarian democratic music, and then a few days later he took us to see an electronic mechanism for generating new sonorities.

I started this article to introduce Olga Rudge to the readers of *Il Mare*, not to write my memoirs or to set forth the esthetic history of the last decade.

I hope to concentrate on music in another chapter in which I will explain the part that our violinist played in the history of contemporary music: "Rudge/Antheil concerts in Paris and elsewhere."

THE VIOLINIST OLGA RUDGE[40]
Rudge-Antheil: Concerts in Paris

So things stood. Antheil was a young composer full of talent but ridiculed by the public. Everyone was waiting to see "which way the cat would jump"[41] before committing themselves to his peculiar music so as to receive immediate or future advantage from it.

I stated the facts to the violinist and the following dialogues took place at different times:

SCENE ONE.
Violinist—Has Antheil written anything for violin?
E.P.—Don't know, I'll ask.

SCENE TWO.
E.P.—Have you written a sonata for the violin?
Antheil—No, but I will. When will she give this concert?
E.P.—Don't know yet. I'll ask.

So not one but two sonatas by Antheil were presented in the concert hall of the Paris Conservatoire in December, 1923, performed by an established violinist, Olga Rudge, who had already played with Pizzetti and Consolo in Florence. A new violin technique was born. And it seems to me that while various "names" have promised to perform Antheil's sonatas, nobody has been able to adapt himself or herself to the special technique of this violent music or to the demoniac temperament of the pianist-composer, for that is how he appears when he plays.

Outside Paris Rudge presented these two and a third sonata by Antheil in Rome, London, and Budapest; and Antheil continued his

[40] *Il Mare*, November 4, 1933; translated.
[41] English in original.

career, via Vienna, at the Frankfurt Stadtoper and under the patronage of prestigious American organizations in New York.

In Paris Mrs. Christian Gross gave concerts in her home with marked preference for contemporary American music by Antheil, the author of this article, and others. Olga Rudge was always an indispensable associate in these concerts, interested only in the music and not always asking to play the leading role. She organized a quartet to present other Antheil music, and I think she once even helped to pay for a presentation out of her own pocket after an affluent lady decided she had already paid enough for the musicians.

Now that the Rapallesi and those who frequent the gulf of Tigullio have had a chance to judge the merits of this *virtuosa* of the violin, there is less need for me to continue this report, written in English a month ago and delayed for publication owing to lack of a translator. My critique of Antheil appeared in the London *Criterion,* in several magazines, and in a book which also included examples of my previous criticism and a "Treatise on Harmony."

I am not writing criticism now, but merely giving information. It is an indisputable fact that Olga Rudge has made known two contemporary composers, and maybe more than two, having always had the courage to present new things, experimenting with this music side by side with known classical works.

I will also add that while still an adolescent she was chosen for the first performance of Pizzetti's *Sonata per violino* in London but could not play because of a sudden tragedy in her family.

For many years now she has been fighting for the right of the performer to present to the public the best music of the repertoire instead of cowardly pandering to public taste. Finally I remember the unusual pleasure I experienced in 1927 when she played with Gabriele Bianchi in Venice, in a concert of Mozart, Bach, and Debussy masterpieces. Delicacy, richness in the lower register of the instrument, and a clear concept of the spirit and intent of these extremely different composers emerged from the sonatas she interpreted.

This violinist we may hear again, together with other artists, in Rapallo's Town Hall on the evening of November 14.

E. P.

The second concert of the 1933–34 season was given on November 14. Pound wrote the following promotional piece for it in *Il Mare,* November 11, and then reviewed it, November 18. Notice again the changes from the original announcement of September 16. News of the success of the *Inverno musicale* was beginning to spread around the Ligurian coast, and the Tigullian musicians were being asked to perform in Genoa and Chiavari.

SECOND CONCERT: TUESDAY 14TH NOVEMBER, 9:00 P.M. IN THE TOWN HALL[42]

Change of taste from one generation to another is a useful test for the durability of great masters and geniuses. Perhaps what displeased the venerable Oscar Chilesotti gives the most pleasure to the writer of this article and to his young colleagues. Maybe the Stravinsky-like piece *Branle del villaggio* which delights our editor Münch, would not have been liked by the old man with the white beard who used to bicycle around Bassano and who was asked to teach the lute to Queen Margherita. In Cassini's bookstore in Venice when I mentioned Chilesotti's name I was told, "You saw nothing but hair, beard, and those huge spectacles...."

In any case Chilesotti, in the *Encyclopédie de la musique,* p. 653, accuses the lutenists, *"très bons luthistes,"* Galilei, Terzi, Bésard, of having profaned church music by adapting it for the lute, but at p. 669 he talks of an inexhaustible treasure, the *Thessaurus harmonicus de Jean Bésard de Besançon*. This book was published in 1603, at a time when from the ruins of Siena there arose a glorious monument though little glorified in wisdom: the Monte dei Paschi.[43]

Of this very different *Thesaurus* Chilesotti gives a partial inventory: among the authors mentioned by "Besardo" we recognize Doolandi as the famous Englishman John Dowland.

In the program to be presented Tuesday, November 14, we are conserving chronological order, but without the violent Bach-Debussy contrast, by which in the first concert we illustrated the difference in spirit between the various ages. This contrast did not obscure the structural solidity of the pre-eminent colorist of our time (a period that is already passing away—the intoxication of the 1910s), the heresy of the *maestro* Debussy who wanted to substitute visual imagination for "musical" or mathematically "pure" imagination, or if he did not mean to, at least was so inclined.

In every art there are elements which appear and disappear in cycles. Chilesotti states in the *Encyclopédie de la musique:*

---

[42] *Il Mare,* November 11, 1933; translated.
[43] The famous Italian bank, still in existence, with branches all over the world, an important subject in Cantos XLII through XLIV, on which Pound was working at this time.

> At least three *tablatures* [the lute's] accurately preserve the tradition of the chromatic style of the performers of vocal music in the XVIth century, [today] . . . discussed at such length by those who do not look at it from this point of view.

The meaning of this passage is not clear. We are thrust into a discussion and without specialized knowledge we cannot make a decision, as Bunting would have done, since he has made a specialized study of the lute; but he has left for the Canary Islands.

The lutenists of that time certainly altered the material of music. The lute had chromatic possibilities, but we don't know whether the twelve or the eight tone scale was chosen (some chose one, some the other), nor do we know the exact division.

Francesco da Milano certainly did not try to preserve Janequin's text philologically; that is, he made an altogether different use of his predecessor than does, say, Respighi, whose "ancient airs" give so much pleasure today, evoking the past, recalling a bygone era to the audience. The XVIth century consciousness certainly did not have such respect for the previous century.

It was rather analogous to the spirit of Malatesta, who took marble from Sant' Apollinare to make out of it a "chiexa" of his own.[44] To listen to Francesco is not simply to listen to Janequin on another instrument. Scored today for a single string instrument, listening to Olga Rudge, we hear a more archaic kind of music than that heard by an audience of the XVIth century.

Certainly the contrapuntal imagination is not chromatic, even less is it pure Dorian. It has no tonality, which does not mean it is atonal in the Viennese manner of the day before yesterday; it is modal in a scale of eight steps.

Münch asks me to explain that next Tuesday's audience should not think, while listening to the composition *Branle del villaggio,* that the musicians have suddenly gone mad. They will play the notes of the manuscript as written by Besardo—not hyper-modern or ultra-twentieth century.

E. P.

PROGRAM
Tuesday, November 14, 1933, 9:00 p.m. Second Concert.
1) From the Chilesotti collection ed. by G. Münch:
    J. BÉSARD: *Chorea Anglicana Doolandi*[45]—*Ritornando da S.*

---

[44] Sant' Apollinare, a Byzantine church in Ravenna. The episode is mentioned in Canto IX.
[45] This was a Bésard arrangement of John Dowland's famous "Lachrimae" ("Flow, my teares").

Nicolò—Volte, chiamate la Samaritana—Branle del villaggio Performers: Olga Rudge, Gerhard Münch, Luigi Sansoni.
UNKNOWN AUTHOR OF THE XVIITH CENTURY: *Fantasia contrappuntistica.* Performers: Rudge, Münch.
2) PURCELL (1659–95): *Golden Sonata.* Performers: Olga Rudge, Münch, Sansoni.
3) J. S. BACH (1685–1750): Sonata in E major (Adagio, allegro—allegro assai). Performers: Rudge, Münch.
4) MOZART: Trio. Performers: Münch, Sansoni, Ottone.

GENOA.—First result of the exchange program proposed by the Committee: The three artists of the *Inverno musicale* (Rudge, Münch, Sansoni) have been invited to play in Genoa in the Auditorium of the Fascist Cultural Institute, next Friday, November 17. They will present a concert of music drawn from the Chilesotti collection and of Bach, Mozart, and Debussy. In exchange Maestro Criscuolo of the Paganini Conservatory in Genoa will give a piano recital in Rapallo on November 16, as explained in the program published separately.

ABOUT THE COMMITTEE: Having noticed an exceptional musical awareness and discrimination in one of our supporters, my curiosity drove me to investigate and I finally came up with a program of the "Siohan Concerts," famous in Paris for their finesse and the high quality of their programs. In the lists of the various organizing committees I found the name of our guest Mrs. Ephra Townley, whom I immediately invited to substitute on our Musical Committee for the critic B. Bunting who has left Rapallo.

THE PIANOFORTE

With great generosity two distinguished persons, whose names we are not allowed for the moment to disclose, have started the subscription for buying the piano that will be used for the concerts organized by the "Amici del Tigullio." We have found a magnificent instrument and we hope to be able to have it for the concert on Tuesday evening. Anyone of good will who wishes to support the initiative of the *Inverno musicale* can obtain two free tickets for every concert left in the program by contributing a hundred pro-piano liras. The offer will stand until we have raised the necessary sum. The piano will be presented to the city by the Musical Committee, and will be used only for concerts of distinction.

THE CRISCUOLO CONCERT

As mentioned in the article introducing the second concert of the *Inverno musicale*, Maestro Leandro Criscuolo will give a piano recital in the Town Hall, Thursday, November 16, at 9:00 p.m.; an exchange concert for that which the musicians of the "Amici del Tigullio" will give in Genoa.

The evening will be dedicated to Bach with the following program:

1) *Italian Concerto* (allegro, andante, presto).
2) Preludes and fugues from the *Well-tempered Clavichord*.
3) Bach-Liszt: Prelude and fugue in A minor.
4) Albéniz: "Evocation"—"El puerto," from the suite *Iberia*.
5) Debussy: *Isle Joyeuse*.

Tickets: Ten liras. 30% discount for members of the Fascist Cultural Institute and 70% for musicians from the Tigullian bands.

SPLENDID SUCCESS OF THE SECOND CONCERT[46]

For the second concert of the "Amici del Tigullio" last Tuesday the Town Hall was crowded with the most distinguished clientele, mainly from the tourist colony. Rare music from the Chilesotti collection was received with the greatest attention, special honor going to the *Fantasia contrappuntistica* on a theme by an unknown composer of the XVIIth century, arranged by Münch and interpreted to perfection by violinist Olga Rudge and the arranger himself. Warm applause greeted the *Golden Sonata* of Purcell with Münch at the piano and violinists Olga Rudge and Luigi Sansoni. This was followed by a mature and refined interpretation of Bach's sonata in E major; and the concert concluded with a commendable presentation of Mozart's trio by Münch, Sansoni and the cellist Ottone.

The evening constituted a veritable artistic event.

The audience, the performers' skill, the warm musical emotion every number on the program aroused, the perfect acoustics of the large Town Hall, everything contributes to making our *Inverno musicale* one of the finest and most successful attractions that Rapallo has succeeded in organizing up to now, thanks to the disinterested and commendable work of eminent and distinguished guests.

The efforts of the Committee promoting these musical events have been substantially re-enforced by the eloquent presence of the new Steinway piano, which will be donated to our city by the "Amici del Tigullio."

The third concert, scheduled for December, will offer an even stronger

---

[46] *Il Mare*, November 18, 1933; translated.

program, with Bach's toccata for piano and the concerto for two violins. Music yet to be chosen from the Chilesotti manuscripts will be played.

The *Chorea Anglicana* by Dowland, Francesco da Milano's adaptation of the *Canzone degli Uccelli* from Janequin, and the *Fantasia by an Unknown Author* heard last Tuesday amply justify the efforts of the Committee and its faith in the judgment and expertise of its transcriber, Gerhart Münch.

Münch's talents as composer and transcriber were in evidence on Tuesday. His talent as a pianist will have wider scope in the future concerts when he will play, we hope, Bach's toccata and groups of piano pieces by Chopin, Ravel, and Scriabin.

THE CRISCUOLO CONCERT

Maestro Criscuolo arrived during a storm, without his manager, and with all the odds against him.

A handful of courageous people braved the storm and were compensated with the stark beauty of Bach's *Italian Concerto* and the prelude and fugue for harpsichord.

If this writer were to begin his career all over again by resurrecting the character of William Atheling, Rapallo's new musical life would perhaps explode at the very outset.

Mr. Atheling maintains, and even complains, that Liszt was an ass of elephantine proportions and that he massacred Bach, turning him into a piano orgy. Maestro Criscuolo has vindicated this thesis majestically by demonstrating his personal mastery of the instrument (post-Bachian).

It is my belief that the taste, at least the official taste in Rapallo, is for the moment pure (100%). We prefer Bach unadulterated, we do not ask for concessions from the ideas of the pre-fascist era.

(Incidentally, the loss of 83½% of the music written between the death of Chopin and the first works of Debussy would not elicit a single tear from me, and I would offer the same percentage of Beethoven to the third Eumenides.)   E. P.

WARM RECEPTION IN GENOA FOR THE TIGULLIAN MUSICIANS[47]

Having attended a concert given by our Tigullian musicians on November 17 in the "Cesare Battisti" Auditorium in Genoa, and having attended more as a listener than as an organizer, I have ascertained the difference between a physically warm hall and a cold one.

---

[47] *Il Mare,* November 25, 1933; translated.

That afternoon Münch showed once more his exceptional pianistic ability in a performance of Scriabin. Even an attack of fever, which would have cut the legs out from under the average or temperamental pianist, did not diminish his mastery during the afternoon, nor during the concert.

I believe Bésard's Suite, arranged by Münch from the Chilesotti manuscripts, followed by a development of the eighteenth-century theme by the same musician into a "contrapuntal fantasy," has never been better played by him, Olga Rudge, and Luigi Sansoni. And I declare that the combination of known music such as that of the "Mozart Week," plus the discovery of the Chilesotti collection, etc., has produced not only a musical event but a real addition to the whole body of existing music. In fact, we have a new sonata, obtained via Chilesotti's collection, which would have remained sterile but for Münch's discrimination and enterprise.

In this way Homer's epic material was born, from unknown forerunners, short narrative poems, ballads, which preceded the epic poems.

In the new sonata we have in order the following elements:

I. Bésard's reduction of Dowland's admirable serenity, the *Chorea Anglicana,* in my opinion unsurpassed in the history of music.

II. The less severe component of the movements *Ritornando da San Nicolò* and *Volte, la Samaritana,* supposedly by Bésard himself, or adapted by him to the diapason of the lute, without any indication of the source.

III. Allegro, allegrissimo, the *Branle del villaggio.*

(And it still warms my heart to recall the smile of the old man—I would say a captain of a fishing boat—sitting in the third row of the "Cesare Battisti" Auditorium.)

By Jove and all the other gods, FIRST RATE music touches and moves men regardless of the second-rate and idiotic culture instilled in them by school education. Here men of goodwill received the same food. Here is the common ground between the hyper-educated, the well-educated, the fully-educated, and the good man who has not been perverted by fixed ideas received in school.

IV. The "contrapuntal fantasy" which takes the place of the final fugue.

This is a gift to the permanent repertoire which I will do my best to take to Paris and submit to evaluation by demanding musical experts and connoisseurs.

The rest of the program has already been discussed in *Il Mare:* Mozart's sonata in A major (K. 526); the insuperable Bach sonata in D major for piano and two violins; Debussy's Violin Sonata.

Here I want to point out that the construction of the program MUST be a dramatic form in itself. The public at our concert of October 10 experienced the effects of such a construction. Construction was missing, due to outside circumstances, in the second concert, that of November 14. In Genoa Mozart's sonata replaced Corelli's sonata. The second piece is the least important of four; it must extend the first but on the whole can be forgotten. Given the first, third, and fourth, the second number can be subject to infinite variations; but the great contrast between the Bach for three instruments and Debussy's sonata is perhaps unique in music, at least I don't know of one like it.

And if in our third concert we experiment with Ravel's sonata following Bach's concerto "reduced" for piano and two violins, I don't think that even with demigods and archangels for musicians we could achieve the same strength of construction.

It is now thirteen years since I attended a minimum of four concerts a week. The great majority of modern sonatas oscillated between rubbish and merit, but remained almost always mediocre and wanting.

It is useless for some musicians to point out the value of these sonatas to me. Let's say that many well-known composers arrive at MERIT 30% of the time. They have usefully followed a fashion, they have adapted, etc., have learnt at a school, etc. . . .

Not to be specifically offensive I'll cut this list short. I have no doubt, speaking at a human level, that many "composers" of the pre-eugenic and anti-malthusian era have the right to live. But this has nothing to do with MUSIC.

In parenthesis: In Genoa a lady said to me, referring to Bach: "I like *ensemble* music. The person disappears and only the music remains."

And people have said to me: "In Genoa! But you can't imagine how people are in Genoa, etc., there's no musical taste, there isn't . . . these uncouth Ligurians!"

On the two occasions I have attended a serious performance in Genoa (once a play, the other musical) I have observed a public attentive and curious, in the sense that it showed a strong desire to UNDERSTAND what was going on on stage. And this kind of public is forty times better than a public of "educated" people with closed ears and a "what not"[48] full of preconceived ideas about music in place of a head.

If *Il Secolo XIX*[49] is right in saying that the Tigullians have not been "adequately received," this is in no way exceptional to the relationship between art and the public which has been universal in the world for centuries.

---

[48] "what not"—English in original.
[49] A daily paper still published in Genoa.

In a hall which can seat eighteen-hundred people, a public "adequate" for a smaller hall may not perhaps give the impression of crowding. In the "Cesare Battisti" Auditorium the audience did not want to leave, and resisted until the musicians added two movements of Purcell's *Golden Sonata* to an already substantial program (at least substantial for a London public).

We have read the appeal from Chiavari printed in *Il Lavoro*[50] on the 18th of this month. This appeal will not remain unheard. We hope that our sister city will shortly have the opportunity of listening to the Tigullians.

Perhaps the medieval idea that *le jongleur* has a stomach will rise again over the "singing dispute."

When an English judge asked Whistler: "Sir, you ask five hundred pounds for an hour's work?" the painter replied: "No, I ask it for the knowledge of a lifetime."

FIRST result of the concert at the "Cesare Battisti" Auditorium: an invitation to return on a date to be decided.

SECOND result: tomorrow, Sunday, November 26, the Tigullians will give a concert in the hall of the "Volontari di Soccorso" Association in Genoa at 9:30 p.m.; with music by Chilesotti, Mozart, Bach; then Münch will play Chopin's piano solos *Impromptu II* and *Scherzo I*.

EZRA POUND

"INVERNO MUSICALE"[51]

The third concert will take place Tuesday, December 5, at 9:00 o'clock in the Town Hall.

The third concert of the *Inverno musicale* will take place on the date already announced, Tuesday, December 5, at 9:00 p.m. in the Town Hall, which we hope will be heated by radiators if the work under way is finished.

PROGRAM

The program of the concert is as follows:

From the Chilesotti collection transcribed by Münch:

    SEVERI: *Due arie,* moderato, allegretto (first half of the XVIth century).

    LODOVICO RONCELLI:[52] Preludio, Giga, Passacaglia (second half of the XVIIth century).

---

[50] Chiavari is the next large town down the Ligurian coast from Rapallo in the opposite direction from Genoa. *Il Lavoro* was the local paper, no longer published.

[51] *Il Mare,* December 2, 1933; translated.

[52] Pound spells "Roncelli" as "Roncalli," following a misprint in Chilesotti.

J. S. BACH (1685–1750): Toccata.[53] Soloist: Gerhart Münch.
J. S. BACH: Concerto for two violins.[54] Performers: Olga Rudge, Luigi Sansoni, Gerhart Münch.
MAURICE RAVEL: Sonata for violin and piano (I. Allegretto; II. Moderato, Blues; III. Allegro perpetuum mobile). Performers: Olga Rudge (violin), Gerhart Münch (piano).

Chilesotti has transcribed Severi's music but I cannot say whether he left any notes on it because not all the manuscripts have been examined yet. The learned musicologists to whom I have written have not bothered to reply to my questions.

In the *Encyclopedia Musicale* and in the other books of my modest library, *nil reperunt*. In any case it seems that Severi belongs to the first half of the sixteenth century.

Chilesotti informs us of Roncelli with this note: "In 1881 I had the pleasure of publishing Roncelli's *Capricci Armonici* in their entirety because they seemed to me worthy of consideration for the charming grace with which they developed a succession of various dance rhythms." He then gives the *facsimile* of a prelude with some observations on the nature of "tablatura" and his interpretation of the signs, but no further information on the author except the date 1692, which is perhaps the date of the first edition. Roncelli, it has been deduced, was probably already alive in 1660.

Münch's transcriptions have meticulously respected the old notation.

E. POUND

Comparing the first and third concerts, Pound later observed: "The point of this experiment is that everyone present at the two concerts now knows a great deal more about the relations, the relative weight, etc., of Debussy and Ravel than they possibly could have found out by reading ALL the criticisms that have ever been written of both."[55]

The spring portion of the 1933–34 season included two concerts featuring the singer Chiarina Fino Savio, a singer at the "Casa Reale d'Italia" and specialist in the music of Scarlatti, Pergolesi, and Monteverdi.

Enthusiasm for the concerts seems still to have been running high except for "the inhabitants of the great villas and backward, short-sighted hotels," and Pound was now beginning to seek the co-operation of musicians abroad. One of these was Gillies Whit-

[53] A note in the *ABC of Reading*, p. 24, tells us this was the Busoni transcription.
[54] In D major, *ibid.*
[55] *ABC of Reading*, p. 24.

taker, the Scottish musicologist and choral conductor. Whittaker's choirs were well known throughout Britain. He had made a specialty of Bach's vocal music, but also conducted such difficult works as Thomas Tallis' famous forty-part motet, and had given the first complete performance of William Byrd's "Great Service." Pound appreciated him as an important figure in the revival of the great period of British music, and a correspondence began. Whittaker had just edited the eleven string sonatas of William Young from the sole surviving copy (in the Uppsala Library) of the original 1653 printing. In December, 1933, he had the publisher send Pound a copy of this work.[56] With customary alacrity Pound immediately programmed the sonatas—perhaps without realizing that some of them called for more instruments than the Rapallo committee usually had at its disposal. As I mentioned above, it appears that not all, but six of Young's sonatas were presented in concerts in March, 1934, possibly in advance of the "first" performance under Whittaker's direction at Oxford.

INVERNO MUSICALE[57]
Future Concerts

Program of *Inverno musicale*'s next events, to take place with the participation of the singer Fino Savio, violinist Rudge, pianist Münch, and violinist Sansoni, in the Town Hall in Rapallo:

SATURDAY, January 27, 9:00 p.m.: Fino Savio, Scarlatti and other old arias; pianist G. Münch.
SUNDAY, February 4, 3:30 p.m.: Special feature outside the regular program, general ticket price: 5 liras. Piano recital by Gerhart Münch.
TUESDAY, February 19, 9:00 p.m.: Fino Savio; Münch.
TUESDAY, March 13, 9:00 p.m.: First performance of the sonatas by William Young (XVIIth century), discovered and edited by Dr. Whittaker and just published by Oxford Press. (Rudge, Münch, Sansoni.)

With the exception of the bourgeoisie, the inhabitants of the great villas and backward, short-sighted hotels, there is no lack of encouragement for the Committee of the "Amici del Tigullio." The public can distinguish between first-rate music and mediocre music.

[56] Oxford Orchestral Series (Nos. 81–91), Oxford University Press, London, 1930.
[57] *Il Mare,* January 13, 1934; translated.

From abroad I have received promises and expressions of intelligent assistance that must be sincere because they are objective.

This is what a learned British musicologist, one of the founders of the Dolmetsch Society, writes me:

"God bless you for your news, a flash of light in a darkened world. It is good to know that your work is proceeding. The first program (October) was encouraging. You are lucky to have a musician of Olga Rudge's artistry. The material you present gives the connoisseurs food for thought."

As we announced before the last concert, we have received some books of rare music. The Oxford Press has sent us a magnificent edition of William Young, the XVIIth-century composer.

And the above letter continues: "Your group is certainly a godsend to be able to return Wm. Young to the musical scene."

And we shall not fail to perform this music and to write a critique of it after the presentation.

A noble donor[58] has sent us the Janequin volume edited by Henry Expert which contains among other things the original music of the *Canzone degli uccelli* which Francesco da Milano adapted for the lute in the XVIth century, as performed in the October concert.

Nor is the assistance limited to printed music. Gerald Hayes is offering to copy, or to have copied, or to let us borrow, manuscripts of the great English masters of the XVIth and XVIIth centuries: John Jenkins, Charles Butler, John Cooper; and he will help us choose from the available editions of Orlando Gibbons and other Elizabethan composers.

Our principal aim is to feed our artists, but the local public is not numerous enough to do this decently unless they subscribe to the whole series of concerts. I have already said that Münch cannot work a whole month on the Chilesotti manuscripts and then play them for half the fee of a single concert.

Nevertheless we have been cheered by offers of collaboration from noted musicians. The limits put to such collaboration and to the number of concerts are conditioned by a single factor: *money*.

I apologize for not being able to embellish or elaborate on the field of our activity until more concrete support is offered. To be more explicit, the heading "under the auspices" does not mean under void or blank auspices. The "Ente Autonomo" in Rapallo is one of our staunchest supporters. To it we should add Maestro Ferola, who has

---

[58] The Princesse Edmond de Polignac. See Pound's letter to her in Paige, *Letters*, tentatively dated March, 1934; but December, 1933, would be more accurate since mention is made of the Whittaker/Young sonatas, under way from the publisher.

favored us in the matter of the piano's cost, a praiseworthy act of public spirit.

I hope to announce soon a program with Chiarina Fino Savio. I can assure her right now, thus publicly, that we are ready to welcome her for an evening dedicated to the findings in the Chilesotti manuscripts plus a repertoire of masterpieces by a single author: Scarlatti, Monteverdi, or Benedetto Marcello. We have faith in her reputation and her knowledge of the repertoire of Bel Canto. If Italian criticism and her reputation are not entirely false, her qualifications are undoubted and need not be proved.

Among our more or less realizable hopes we would like to give preference to the "Cantori del Mare" from Savona, who sing not only choruses from well-known operas by composers unfortunately too well known, but also Carissimi, Palestrina, de Vittoria, etc.

We are well aware that Gene Sadero has collected a quantity of regional folklore and that Danina de Witt not only sings Wagner in the festivals, but (for the specialists) can also sing Polish folk music, a study to be placed alongside Chopin's songs and compositions.

Even the question of inviting the great Segovia is a matter of high finance.

E. P.

NOTE: Apropos the third concert, I have received a message from a person who attended it and who a while ago heard Ravel's Sonata played by the composer himself. It says:

"Münch played Ravel better than the composer himself, and Miss Rudge was better than the man who played the violin. Everything clearly incisive, wasn't it? And very intelligent. Wouldn't it be useful to repeat the whole concert?"

We have turned down the request. There is too much other music that we want to hear. In principle we don't want to present works in "reduced" versions, but with the same number of instruments indicated by the composer, which means, better Bach's sonata in C major (as in the first concert) than the orchestral Bach of the third.

e. p.

MEANING AND IMPORTANCE OF WILLIAM YOUNG'S MUSIC[59]

William Young's music is presented in its entirety for the first time since the XVIIth century in a special matinée which will take place in the Town Hall in Rapallo on Sunday, March 11 at 3:30 p.m.; during

[59] *Il Mare*, March 3, 1934; translated.

the last concert (first series) which will take place in the same Auditorium on March 31; and then in concerts of the second series, organized by the "Amici del Tigullio."

The importance of William Young's music is guaranteed by the reputation of the man who revived it, Gillies Whittaker, Head of the Scottish Academy of Music, noted and competent musicologist, not only respected in England, but devotedly loved by a large public in the North of England and Scotland for his conducting of Bach's music. They tell me he directs a great many of the chorales without a score!

Whittaker's genial figure stands out in an epoch of poor composition, of weakness and tolerance for any musical mediocrity. Whittaker belongs to the "no nonsense" school.[60] Musical realities are hard and resistant. First-rate music has no need for excuses and tolerance. Naturally those who have so-called "ear-tolerance" to the highest and lowest and vilest degree have said that the old maestro is an eccentric.

I would like to have a good dose of such an eccentricity! This alleged eccentricity guarantees the quality of any piece of music by any composer that Dr. Whittaker thinks worth bringing to light in our time. His is the beautiful edition of Young that we have received from the Oxford Press. He is now working at an edition of twenty-two sonatas by Purcell for two violins, cello, and piano. And we hope to last, as a Committee, until its publication. We foresee in it substantial food for our future concerts.

Even without Münch's admiration, and without my experience in thematic matters, the following passage from Whittaker's introduction would be enough to arouse the interest of musical connoisseurs:

"On April 1, 1653, William Young, Englishman, published at Innsbruck, the part-books of a set of sonatas . . . dedicated to Ferdinando Carlo, Archduke of Austria. . . . They are the first printed English Sonatas, issued the year in which Corelli was born, and five years before Henry Purcell came into the world. Their surprising freshness and beauty claim our interest apart from historical considerations. Harmonically they are frequently bold, indeed, often defiant, and anticipate traits which we have been wont to consider Purcellian. In the notes to the individual works, attention has been called in detail to examples of harmonic and contrapuntal daring, not from a pedantic point of view, but because of interest to the student and as a defence of the Editor's accuracy of transcription. One noteworthy feature is Young's appreciation of the characteristic qualities of the violin in contrast to those of the viol. The Uppsala Collection is definitely violin music: not until the close of the century do we find that again in English music."

[60] English in original.

Our intention is to present the Three Sonatas for two violins with cello and keyboard at the matinée, and the Seven Sonatas for three violins with cello and keyboard at our concert of March 31.

After this performance Rev. Chute will publish his review, and I hope also to be able to register my praises.

EZRA POUND

Desmond Chute reviewed the two concerts in *Il Mare* on March 17 and April 7. In addition to the three sonatas by William Young for two violins, cello, and keyboard, the first two of which were in D minor and the third in G major, the first program was completed by Matthias Weckmann's Canzon in C minor and Johann Adam Reinken's Toccata, J. S. Bach's Chromatic Fantasy and Fugue, all played by Münch. Olga Rudge and Mario Brizzolari were the violinists, with cellist Marco Ottone and Gerhart Münch performing the continuo. In his review of the second concert Chute mentions his disappointment at being presented merely three more Young sonatas after having been promised seven, but he was pleased when the remainder of the program consisted of repeats of some of the music from earlier affairs, namely: the Janequin/Milano *Canzone degli uccelli*, Münch's *Fantasia contrappuntistica* elaboration on a seventeenth-century theme, the Dowland/Bésard *Chorea Anglicana*, together with Frescobaldi's Toccata in D flat [sic], Veracini's Sonata in D minor, and Bach's Sonata in C major for two violins.

A spring series of concerts under the title *Primavera musicale* was announced in *Il Mare*, April 28, and the dates given were April 27, May 8, 25, 29, 31, and June 5. The April 27 event featured the singer Lonny Mayer, fresh from successes in Berlin, Frankfurt, and Zürich, accompanied by Münch. Music in the concert was by German baroque composers and by Paul Hindemith. Pound reviewed it in the May 5 edition of *Il Mare*, and then passed on to preview the May 8 event.

THE SINGER LONNY MAYER[61]

Irritated by trivial details and unavoidable interruptions during a particularly active year, I have often been on the point of exploding and renouncing my responsibilities as organizer of the concert series by the "Amici del Tigullio." But just when it seems I have had enough, my determination is weakened by some unexpected event. This happened

---

[61] *Il Mare*, May 5, 1934; translated.

a few days ago when Münch played Bach's preludes and fugues for a private audience.

When I retired from the world of vanities, I didn't expect to find musical pleasures in Rapallo superior to those I had already experienced in London and Paris. But life is full of surprises.

Last Friday, Münch and Lonny Mayer provided me with a pleasant surprise. Lonny Mayer is a young singer of superior talents. I don't want to use any superlatives: she is a solid musician without any trace of affectation; she trusts music and music may well trust her. It is a beautiful voice, without artifice. For the concert of last Friday, April 27, she had chosen the program with great insight; a program for real connoisseurs, containing nothing I had heard before.

The seventeenth-century songs by Heinrich Albert and Dedekind show that the German *Lied* had by then already reached the height of its development. They were sung by Miss Mayer with delightful charm.

As an intermezzo Münch had unearthed Lübeck's *Klavierübung* in six parts.

This was followed by a Telemann masterpiece, a magnificent cantata (1725). Here Lonny Mayer showed complete control of the melodic line, using her voice as an instrument, combining it with the other instruments with masterful self-assurance. Telemann's music for the *Annunzio a Maria* showed exactly the vigor and fervor that religious music MUST have, and that religion did have in its great days. This quality was missing in the performance given by the Malines Choir in the cathedral on April 15, in a program of masterpieces by Palestrina, de Vittoria, and Jachet de Berghem. It was missing, not by fault of the composers, but through the shortcomings of the execution, however accurate. It is not a question of harmony perpendicularly conceived, but of rhythm and the maintenance of proper tempo.

Only twice in my life have I heard church music achieve true intensity: once in Burgos, Spain, and again in Cortona, Italy. But it would take too long to explain further what I mean in technical terms.

In this music by Telemann there is real strength. It is clear that the Annunciation indeed brought "good tidings" (*incipit saeculum novum* —the new era begins). It is an alleluia expressing the exultation of celestial forces. "The more perfect a thing, the more active, the less passive." The thrones, spirits, archangels of Dante's *Paradiso* exercise their influence; they are the forces that move the great celestial spheres. Religion is not only depression, sorrow and suffering, it is eternal energy; sometimes even exuberance of energy. This quality is to be found in music, particularly great music, more than in any other art. To write valid music criticism in this area one would require a good grounding in theology.

With a year's study, and by writing a book of two hundred pages, I could do justice to Hindemith's music. It will be enough to say here that Miss Mayer proved herself to be a great artist. The composer has put enormous difficulties into this music, he has written *Das Marienleben* in such a way that it would be impossible for someone who has only a beautiful voice (*vox et praetera nihil*—a voice and nothing else) to sing it. In Miss Mayer, Hindemith could find the singer he needs if he wants to hear his music performed accurately and attractively.

After this Münch performed the cleverly conceived *Klaviermusik* by the same author.

For the concert next Tuesday, May 8, our musicians have chosen an unusual program different from our previous events:

PART ONE
1) Nardini: Concerto in E minor, violin and piano;
2) Münch: two fugues in D minor and C minor;
3) Liuzzi: *La Passione* from the Cortona Missal (XIIth century), four selections;
4) Words by Sordello: "Tos temps serai," "Ailas!"

PART TWO
1) Bach: Partita (three movements) arranged by Münch, violin and piano;
2) Bach: Prelude and Fugue in G minor, piano;
3) Bach: Three religious songs and an aria from a cantata.

The knowledgeable Liuzzi has taken *La Passione* from the Cartona Missal (XIIth century). After dealing with medieval music for twenty-five years I can speak with special competence on this subject. It seems to me that among all the researchers of this music Liuzzi is the only one who has grasped the true and triumphant spirit of its rhythm, the only one who has intuitively understood how the ligatures and series of quick notes are to be approached and deciphered.

Having missed the presentation of this *Passione* two years ago at the Venice festival I had to wait until now for a second performance.

Miss Rudge and Münch will present a concerto by Nardini. The second half of the program will consist of three very diverse items by Bach: Münch will play the prelude and fugue; the violinist Olga Rudge will join him in the presentation of three movements by Bach, transcribed and arranged by Münch; and Miss Mayer will close the concert with a Bach cantata.

The myth that the Germans are a musical people or that they are interested in great music has gone up in smoke, and another Teutonic bluff has been demolished. Up to the time of Bach's death there had been great composers in Germany, we agree on that. But the performance of Telemann's and Lübeck's masterpieces (which cannot be heard in a concert in Berlin or any other German city every day or even every year) was attended by three German people only: two from the Consulate in Genoa, and our personal friend, the critic Haas.

It is certainly not worthwhile then to stimulate the Germans' *amour propre* with great German music if they show themselves to be unworthy descendants of their lofty tradition.

The anti-aesthetic Anglo-Saxons seem, on the face of the evidence, to be much more cultivated and open to cultural opportunities. I swear that the concert of the 27th would have excited me tremendously if I had come across it during my years as a music critic in London; and I also declare that even in Paris, though I seldom went to concerts, and only attended the really exceptional ones, I never heard a better performance or a more consistently sustained program.

Those who were absent have lost a chance that will not be repeated here or anywhere else. It is not easy to get three such artists together, and to find them so totally in agreement on the music to be chosen and on the basic interpretation of sacred music. This doesn't happen even once every three years. We were happy enough with our two soloists, but the law of chemical attraction has brought us a singer who is completely free from vocal artifice, and who fits so beautifully into our plans and ambitions to offer to the public true masterpieces, known or unknown, in original performances and authentic interpretations.

EZRA POUND

There is an interesting enigma connected with Pound's preview of the May 8 concert: "Words by Sordello: 'Tos temps serai,' 'Ailas!' " These were the titles of two arias from Pound's opera *Cavalcanti,* recently completed. This performance by Lonny Mayer of the two songs is presumably the only time any portion of the opera was sung in public. They were offered anonymously. Desmond Chute, in his review of the concert (*Il Mare,* May 19), wrote: "There followed the 'Words by Sordello,' two songs by an unknown author, but who, I imagine, was not far removed from us in time or space. The martellato rhythm of the second piece suffered from the same defect as the interpretation of lauds. It knew more of the metronome than the human voice because it disregarded the requirements of breathing and therefore of those silences which put the words into relief when chanted rather than sung. But the counterpoint of the two instrumental colors—voice and violin—reached the ear agreeably, like a pleasant interpretation, melodically, tonally, and historically, of the Middle Ages, much as Puccini interpreted Japan."

Chute went on to liken the richly varied program to the paintings of Matthias Grünewald. The Bach G minor fugue, a Liszt transcription, was contrasted with Münch's own fugues, which reminded Chute of Schumann. But the real highlight of the concert was *La Passione nelle intonazioni del Laudario 91 di Cortona*, a thirteenth-century example of secular monody edited by Fernando Liuzzi.[62] "No one remained indifferent," Chute wrote, "when these melodies, which were contemporary with Francis of Assisi, were sung."

The May 24 concert featured the preludes and fugues nos. 4, 7, 20, and 21 from the second part of Bach's *Well-tempered Clavichord*, played by Münch. This was followed with John Blow's two trio sonatas, edited only a year earlier by Gillies Whittaker[63] and performed in "la prima esecuzione" by Olga Rudge and Luigi Sansoni with the continuo provided by Münch and A. Simonati. Bach's Sonata in F minor for violin and keyboard completed the program.

The concerts of May 29, 31, and June 5 were given over to a Mozart festival, and Rudge and Münch performed fifteen Mozart violin sonatas.

The 1934–35 season of the *Inverno musicale* promised to be exciting. More contemporary music (Bartók, Stravinsky, Serly, Bianchi) and the remaining William Young sonatas were programmed, though the latter appear never to have been presented. Moreover guest artists were expected: the Gertler Quartet, Lonny Mayer, Tibor Serly, and possibly Yves Tinayre, Pound's old friend from London and Paris and an enthusiast for ancient music. This is all outlined in Pound's promotional piece which follows. The article referred to in the opening paragraph was by Basil Bunting, from *The Musical Times* (August 1934, p. 750), giving a rough outline of the whole Rapallo undertaking. The cultivation of this "the-whole-world-is-watching-us" posture was not only typical of Pound but, as anyone who has ever organized

---

[62] Cf., F. Liuzzi, *La lauda e i primordi della melodia italiana*, 2 vols., Rome, 1935.

[63] John Blow, *Deux sonates pour deux violons, viole da gamba et basse;* publiées par W. Gillies Whittaker, Paris, Editions de l'Oiseau lyre, 1933.

concerts in a small town knows, is frequently necessary to jack up morale, particularly if one is trying to substitute arcane treasures from ancient and modern times for the sentimental treacle of "Columbia Artists presents...."

PLANNED TIGULLIAN MUSIC[64]
Inverno Musicale

In a short time our musicians have received well-deserved praise outside Rapallo, so much so that in its August issue the London monthly, *The Musical Times,* commenting on our efforts and on Münch's transcriptions, states that "Rapallo is challenging the position of San Remo as the musical centre of the Italian Riviera. The Chilesotti music may almost be said to turn the balance in Rapallo's favor."

If we can obtain sufficient funds we plan a musical series for the winter, six concerts more or less, in which the following compositions will appear:

   I. Telemann or Weckmann: Toccate, not yet performed in Rapallo.
      Stravinsky: *Petroushka;* Münch (with violin or cello).
  II. Unpublished music of the XVIIth century for voice, violin, and piano, transcribed by Münch from the manuscripts in the Querini-Stampalia Library.
      Bach: Cantata, "Mein Herz schwimmt"; Lonny Mayer, Olga Rudge, Gerhart Münch.
 III. Contemporary Hungarian music:
      Béla Bartók: Quartet III;
      Béla Bartók: Quartet IV;
      Tibor Serly: Quartet.
      For this concert we shall invite A. Gertler's Brussels Quartet.
  IV. Gabriele Bianchi: Sonata for violin and piano;
      Gerhart Münch: Sonata for violin and piano;
      Stravinsky: Sonata for piano;
      Stravinsky: *Pulcinella* (violin and piano);
      OLGA RUDGE, GERHART MÜNCH.
   V. Mozart: *Sinfonia Concertante,* (violin and viola);
      Tibor Serly: Sonata for viola and piano;
      Other works for viola and violin to be decided; Tibor Serly, viola, Olga Rudge, Gerh. Münch.

[64] *Il Mare,* October 6, 1934; translated.

VI. William Young: Sonatas VIII, IX, X, XI (a.d. 1653), for three and four violins (Whittaker edition).
Bach: Concerto in D major.
Münch, Rudge, et al.

As possibilities or for special concerts:
I. Masterpieces of French song from the XIth century to the end of the XVIIth:
Yves Tinayre.
II. Bach: *Goldberg Variations;* Gerhart Münch.

The possibility of presenting this wide-ranging and colorful program depends on the solidarity of our supporters.

NOTES.
GABRIELE BIANCHI, chosen for our program of contemporary music, was presented at the Venice Music Festival two years ago. Among today's Italian composers he is one of the most serious and worthy of consideration.

TINAYRE has dedicated long years of study to these masterpieces and is very well known in London and Paris for his impassioned and dramatic interpretations of folksongs and the stark melodies of the Middle Ages.

The composer SERLY, who plays in Stokowski's orchestra and passes through Rapallo every year on his way from Philadelphia to Budapest to visit his old teachers, assures me that Bartók's more recent music has a force and richness unknown to the very lively and better known first works of this composer.

E. POUND

Pound reviewed none of the concerts of the 1934–35 season. This task was taken over by Clary Benoit. The poet's prose this winter was devoted almost exclusively to economic and political subjects. But he continued to work actively on the Committee and attended the concerts. A brief résumé of the music presented is therefore in order.

As usual, the actual concerts departed considerably from the original intentions. The first concert (November 8) consisted of a group of Scarlatti sonatas, Tartini's Sonata in A major for violin and keyboard, Stravinsky's piano reduction of *Petroushka,* and Münch's *Music for Violin and Piano* (rag, molto lento, tango, fuga). The performers were Rudge and Münch. The second program appears to have been given as Pound announced it, and

Clary Benoit's review followed in *Il Mare,* November 24. But the third concert, December 11, turned out to be a Chopin recital given by Münch. It was an overwhelming success. "A quando un altro concerto con pubblico più affollato ancora?" asked the reviewer deliriously, now that nineteenth-century romanticism, previously totally denied the Rapallese public, had at last been revealed. The audience at the fourth concert was "non numeroso," to hear Rudge and Münch perform Stravinsky's reduction for violin and piano of his *Pulcinella* suite, based on themes of Pergolesi. The program also included one of Pergolesi's own sonatas and one by Bach (not identified), together with some piano selections by Ravel (also not identified), which closed the program. Clary Benoit reviewed the event in *Il Mare,* February 9.

On January 13, 1935, the Gertler Quartet gave a concert of modern Hungarian music: Bartók's first and fourth quartets and Tibor Serly's quartet. This was the first chance Pound had had to hear any of Bartók's mature music. The music in the February 7 recital by Rudge and Münch consisted of some of the Chilesotti material, a Bach sonata (unidentified), and a selection of Debussy piano solos.

On March 3 Tibor Serly, who was in Rapallo, joined the Tigullian musicians for a concert which featured his *Concerto for Viola* in a viola/piano reduction. The program opened with some keyboard music by Vincent Lübeck, and Serly and Rudge performed the Duo in G major for violin and viola by Mozart and concluded the concert with the same composer's *Sinfonia Concertante.*

I give what details I can of the three final conerts of the 1934-35 season, taken from announcements in *Il Mare.*

March 21
BACH: Suite, sonata and fugue;
MÜNCH: elaborations of seventeenth-century mss.;
STRAVINSKY: *Petroushka.*

April 4
BACH: Sonata for violin and keyboard;
BACH: *Italian Concerto;*
ERIC SATIE: *Choses vues à droite et à gauche (sans lunettes);*
  Chorale hypocrite, Fugue à talons, Fantasie muscolaire;
DEBUSSY: Sonata for violin and piano.

April 25
PERGOLESI: Sonatas;
JOH. ROSENMÜLLER (1620–84)
G. CH. WAGENSEIL (1715–77)
  Rudge-Sansoni-Paterson-Münch;
TIBOR SERLY: Five pieces,
  Rudge-Münch;
STRAVINSKY: *Pulcinella,*
  Rudge-Münch;
STRAVINSKY: Sonata for piano,
  Münch.

For the final concert there was one new musician, identified only as "Paterson ... a cellist from Edinburgh." A review, by Clary Benoit, appeared in *Il Mare* on May 5. Two days later Rudge and Münch gave a private recital in Florence, and returning from there they performed also in Chiavari. An invitation to the Chiavari recital gives the following program:

TIGULLIAN MUSICIANS
Olga Rudge   Gerhart Münch
KALENDAMAJA—(Unpublished manuscripts of the sixteenth century from the Chilesotti collection).[65]
MARZO-APRILE—(Unpublished manuscripts of the seventeeth century from the Querini-Stampalia library).
SONATA FOR VIOLIN AND PIANO—Debussy.
PETROUSHKA: 1. Russian Dance
           2. Shrovetide
                        Stravinsky.

Pound attended both the Florence and Chiavari events and reviewed them for *Il Mare*.

OLGA RUDGE AND GERHART MÜNCH IN FLORENCE AND CHIAVARI[66]

On the seventh of this month our musicians played in the salon of the well-known music patroness Mrs. Dalliba John in Florence, a salon

---

[65] The title "Kalendamaja" comes originally from an *estampida,* or collection of such dances, by the troubadour Reimbautz de Vaquieras. The matter is discussed in Pierre Aubry's *Trouvères et Troubadours,* Paris, 1914, p. 41. "Kalendamaja" is mentioned again by Pound in Canto CXIII.

[66] *Il Mare,* May 18, 1935; translated.

frequented by Pizzetti, Mainardi, and a hundred other celebrities in the musical world.

Mrs. John, a novelist, mother of the poetess Gerda Dalliba, established a musical center in London before the war, noted both for its originality and the generosity of its founder. In fact she kept an open house for a decade (food, lodging, practice rooms, concert hall) where talented students and great musicians—Zimbalist, Gabrilovitch, and many others of international renown—were received, the founder displaying a singular intuition for new and undiscovered talent. And the hospitality was offered with unparalleled tact, in as much as the hostess was for the most part absent or invisible, satisfied simply to be generous.

In Florence the players presented the results of Münch's researches (Chilesotti collection, Querini-Stampalia collection), and their talent proved itself in works by Debussy and Stravinsky; Delfini Cinelli, Eugenio Montale, and other Florentine celebrities were present.

They were enthusiastically received and were immediately invited to give a broadcast for the E.I.A.R.[67]

Chiavari should be proud of the courageous organizers of the "Amici della Musica," and grateful to Messrs. Filippini and Ottone. We must express admiration for the architecture of the great Teatro Cantero which has perfect acoustics.

Finally we must note that three hundred inhabitants of Chiavari have answered the invitation of the "Amici," a figure of which we cannot even dream in Rapallo.

A new chapter in my experience as critic seems to have opened up with the opportunity of listening to the same music in both our Town Hall, an admirable hall, and the Teatro Cantero.

I report my first impression not due, I think, to fortuitousness. Olga Rudge's sound, her tidy technique in Bach and Nardini, the truly aulic rhetoric of her music, had an increased effectiveness. In this music Rudge's technique is set off to advantage in the large space of the Teatro Cantero. I note that this is *linear* music, with a continuous melodic line, with what is called "musical form." Debussy's sonata, on the other hand, is made for a concert hall, not for a large theater.

Perhaps each composition implies in itself a certain optimum space. That is, *chamber* music, a *chamber* orchestra. Debussy's music is called "visual," and perhaps all music made of "blocks of musical color" loses some of its qualities if played in a large theater where "linear" music best asserts itself—and this independent of the execution. In any case I hope to verify these observations at the next concert of our Tigullians, planned for next June in Chiavari.

[67] The E. I. A. R. (*Ente Italiano Audizioni Radiofoniche*) later became R. A. I. (*Radio Audizioni Italiane*), the state-owned radio and television network.

The same phenomenon was heard in the contrast between Chopin, romantically interpreted by Münch, and *Petroushka*. In Chopin[68] it was clear that the effectiveness of Münch's style and his prodigious technique gain in maximum space.

Stravinsky on the contrary merits the hall in Rapallo. The composer created *Petroushka* for orchestra, and an orchestra is what is proper for its execution in large theaters, whereas the piano reduction is suitable for concert halls; a fact which proves Stravinsky's maestria.

A CHALLENGE.

I challenge totally any gratuitous defamation of the Ligurian public. I notice in Chiavari, as in Genoa, the public is predisposed to appreciate first-rate music as opposed to third-rate. The large audience in Chiavari listened to the sophisticated program with the keenest attention: I heard only three or four whispers during the whole evening; the audience was as silent and attentive as our own select group in Rapallo. It interrupted to applaud between the movements of the sonata and the suite, but this is customary. The desire to hear the whole composition before applauding has prevailed only recently in certain places. I report also that the program consisted exclusively of great composers: Bach, Nardini, Debussy, Chopin, Stravinsky. In daring to present such composers the organizers in Chiavari are keeping in touch with the intuition of their public and are showing curiosity and a desire to experiment directly with music that has not yet become traditional.

E.P.

In 1932, A. R. Orage, back in London from America, had launched a new periodical entitled *The New English Weekly*. It was here that the following article on Tibor Serly appeared. It precipitated a letter which I am quoting in its entirety, not only because Pound replied with one of his own, but because it raises the matter of money and music, which is dealt with in the two subsequent articles. Pound now saw clearly the relationship between socio-economic conditions and cultural survival, and with justification was able to boast that the Rapallo experiment had succeeded in "liberating the ability of performers from the noose of international finance." The articles "Throttling Music" and "Money versus Music" provide an informative summary of his first two years' activities and successes as a concert promoter.

---

[68] As there is no Chopin on the printed program this must have been a substitute or an encore.

TIBOR SERLY, COMPOSER[69]

I have been watching Serly's scores for some time. Last year his orchestration of the fantasy which Mozart wrote for a musical clock, was performed in Budapesth under Dohnanyi, and I believe Toscanini approves of this orchestration.

Twelve years ago Serly was moving against clinical thermometer music, against hyper-intellectuality as we find it in Hindemith, that is the writing of music that is "interesting" to musical specialists almost exclusively.

Roughly this music is paralleled in *part* of Eliot's poetry, and in that of his imitators, notably Louis Zukofsky, Schönberg, Hindemith, etc. I don't want to detract from their merit one iota. They both know a great deal of detail that I don't. I only want to distinguish one current from another.

Serly's violin pieces startled no one in 1923. If you hear Haydn *after* Mozart, you will or might notice the lower tension. We, to-day, hear Mozart and notice *no* high nervous strain, but Mozart was not immediately popular. "Zauberflöte" must have been almost as shocking to Haydenites as was the "Sacre" to Ricketts and Shannon, whom I remember seated in front of me at the first London performance, and heaven knows they were a fussy enough pair of æsthetes, and not the "general musical public."

If the curious or enquiring reader will *try* a little Haydn *after* Mozart, he will hear what I mean.

Cocteau, years ago, demanded a "music like tables and chairs," meaning in part a serviceable music that should function in daily life. Serly's music of the decade before last does not suggest tables and chairs, but it does, to at least one auditor, suggest a tension no greater than Bill Williams', it suggests the calmness of a river and trees, with no razor-blade stylisation, its uncommonness being only in not being "common." That is to say: here is something that escapes being sentimental without any apparent effort to avoid feeling.

You might, were it painting, almost pass it a dozen times without seeing it. Sane art grows out of craftsmanship, the very great art, and I think all durable masterwork grows out of craftsmanship.

Haics Geza, in the "Magyarsag" (Budapesth), 1st Aug., 1934, summarises Serly's doctrine—or shall we say Serly's estimate of what has happened musically during the past few decades, and where his own work comes in. Roughly the phases are: decay of melody and consequent flop of music. Harmony dominates half-formed fragments of

[69] *The New English Weekly*, March 28, 1935, p. 495.

melodiousness, as distinct from being generated by a nucleus, that is from a melody strong enough and fixed enough to give tension to larger musical forms.

Accidentals and chromatic notes break loose from all orderly control, producing atonalism, then polytonality, but no new, real technique.

Tibor Serly sees the birth of the new music in the use not merely of polytonality, but in correlation (with due opposition) of two scales, major and minor, of the same key. This movement or phase includes at different tensities and densities, Bartok, Stravinsky and Casella, Bartok being Serly's spiritual father as Kodaly was his actual teacher in the conservatory at Budapesth.

Serly's opportunity, and I ask no man to believe Serly has taken it until he has heard some of Serly's music, lay in the fact that both Stravinsky and Bartok were primarily pianists. Serly, after taking his degree, submitted to playing the viola in the Philadelphia orchestra for seven years, and believes that that amount of suffering ought to bring some sort of reward.

I have heard enough of his compositions, either whole or in fragments, to know that he has a just claim to having invented a new MATERIAL technique. Using the viola as key to the knowledge of the general nature of stringed instruments he has invented along that line, namely in accordance to the conditions wherein, and factors whereby, the sound actually is produced.

His viola line in the viola concerto does not interfere with the *"tutti,"* nor will any amount of noise smother it.

He and I are at a deadlock re the relative status of Stravinsky and Bartok, or rather, my ignorance of most of Bartok's later work (apart from the fourth quartet, done here by the Gertler team) disqualifies me from having anything but a tentative estimate of Bartok and a willingness to lean upon opportunity.

I have heard a great mass or mess of so-called "piano concertos," but I have never heard but one *composition* for piano and orchestra, namely Stravinsky's Cappriccio—there the piano and orchestra are as two shells of a walnut. I sat in the top gallery in Venice, while Igor led and his son played the solo part, and while I have sometimes thought I could hear, or hear part of, the noise of a composition from looking at printed notes, on this occasion I had the mirage of seeing the unknown score from the aural stimulæ offered.

Serly swears that Bartok has attained a comparable sanity. I don't believe it, but I shall be delighted to find it true. Among composers whose work I have heard, Stravinsky is the only living musician from whom I can learn my own job.

I mention Serly's admiration of the LATER work of Bartok as a means of describing Serly. If the B.B.C. would get Primrose to play Serly or if they would perform Bartok's "Wonderful Mandarin"[70] I for one would certainly make a special effort to listen in. They have done Bartok's two piano concertos. Beyond that there is other orchestral Bartok, which we most of us know too little about.

EZRA POUND

From the correspondence column of *The New English Weekly*, April 25, 1935:

> Sir,—So "William Atheling" was Ezra Pound! Who'd have thought it? Now *The New English Weekly* is *really* making things hum.
> Mr. Pound's article on Tibor Serly is promising, first-class innovation in English musical criticism. It is still far too subjective in its approach to those elements in this unique art which really endure, and matter, "biologically"; and in that respect Mr. Pound is still about 10 or 20 years behind the new age. But he is getting warm.
> Artists and other aware and emotionally alive men suffer from the presence of huge volumes of stupidity, personified in enormous tribes of stick-in-the-mud cash hunters great and small, creeping and scurrying all over the place in idiotic and spasmodic confusion. The creative artist, initiated because of his dethronement by the usurping IOU forger and the cheque worshiper, takes flight into abstractionism, leaving the majority to their concrete interests and orientation. The situation is further complicated somewhat by the pranks of objective sexuality—which may be defined as the Caricature of the Abstract, as Money is the Caricature of the Concrete.
> The "critic" should put some order into all this muddle. He is the natural intermediary between the top and the bottom people. His function is most emphatically not the maintenance of standards of value, or the vitality of new "schools" or "movements." No! It is the connecting link between the "concrete" and the "abstract" in the people's mentality. (At present it is often the link between their respective caricatures Money and Objective Sexuality; *vide* the late P. G. Konody: "Romance and Art go hand-in-hand.")
> Let the "critic" cease to criticize, and begin to interpret. Let him first, make sure of the power to wield the language as Orage

[70] Usually anglicized as the *Miraculous Mandarin*.

would have him wield it. Then let him, humbly but urgently, tap at the door of the artist's sanctum, and let him ask his King for wisdom and enlightenment. Let him plead on behalf of humanity, dying of spiritual thirst, blinded by the rude and cruel flashes from the inferno of morbid sex, deafened by the roar of the accursed Money-machine....

Emil Van Loo

From the correspondence column of *The New English Weekly*, May 2, 1935:

MUSIC AND MONEY

Sir,—With due respect to Mr. Van Loo I have for 25 years found the utmost difficulty in getting anything at all into print until it is 10 or 20 years behind what I believe to be the present.

The venerable Wm. Atheling had at any rate the objective merit of persuading a few performers to give better music than they would otherwise have attempted. I would also call Mr. Van L.'s attention to the unique series of concerts given in Rapallo, OBJECTIVELY, by application of abstract Douglasite principles to a concrete situation in space and time.

I will supply the details of the concerts, or of the system, when the editor thinks the traffic will stand it. The reason why critics should "maintain standards" must be investigated orthologically. IF "MAINTAIN" means "petrify," then Mr. Van L. is right, i.e., they shouldn't. But if it means that critics must aid the half-aware public to distinguish real kings from counterfeit, or to emerge from the metaphoric fog where artists have to be called kings, then Mr. Van L. is wrong.

Music is under the dirty boot of the banks in every town where people can afford bad music, and where the performers can't afford to play good music. But, in this, music is perhaps no worse off than literature or any other decent human activity.

EZRA POUND

THROTTLING MUSIC[71]

The horrible boredom promoted by most writings about music rises perhaps from the futility of criticism that closes one eye, one ear and two thirds of the understanding, *id est*, in assuming that public per-

---

[71] *The New English Weekly*, July 11, 1935, pp. 247–48.

formance of music commonly occurs in a state of freedom and that the performers can do as they like.

The black rot of usury has so infiltrated into every region of *thought* that almost no one imagines the possibility either of freedom or of abundance. The giving of concerts in London has long been restricted to performers having on an average £60 sterling at their disposal. It has been a racket whereof the main proceeds did *not* reach the producer (the *composer* as producer hardly enters the financial side of the matter); the performer, for the purpose of concert hall economics *is* the producer. The composer's work is largely cultural heritage.

In 1908 a full blooded British or Celtic, very well-known London singer said to me, "I have to give one concert a year to keep my pupils." The established performers pay expenses, or make a small profit by ca' canny, by appearing as rarely as possible and by mobilising brigades of carefully tended friends.

"Mais j'ai mangé si peu." "M.X. . . . ne peut pas diner ce soir ayant mal au doigt."

There is the other racket of counter blackmail. Whether you get enough music in the home by inviting performers to play for their supper, in return for buying their tickets, once or twice during a season.

All of which arises from black, sodden usury. And at the other pole this penetrates music, as it penetrates brickmaking or pickle-preserving. The economic expert, the technical expert who has made an ass of himself in every bureaucracy, and worse asses of his victims, has got into music. *Vide* the great and glorious B.B.C., with the usurer's tout *inside* killing performers.

Some hell's pimp makes *hours* of labour for musicians, some wart on the back of Beelzebub's dachshund degrades Flesch' pupils and soloists into components of an orchestra at the dictates of Finance (dictates of course filtered down through a heirarchy of pimps, doubtless traversing numerous nice, nice chaps with nice intentions.)

I found in Paris (a centre just as syphilitic with usury as your own jubilant London) that one could *afford* to give concerts of *new* music *if* one invited the public, and did not permit anyone to *pay* to get in.

That is the cursed and vile state of perversion into which the Age of Usury, finally in its most complete Tulip, Mr. Chamberlain, has brought us.

Hence the emphasis which I put on a *local demonstration of credit*, mobilised in a town officially larger than Woergl, but not so overwhelmingly larger, that the difference matters for purpose of demonstration.

Given the presence a few years ago of one Social Creditor (where there are now several dozen) and of two musicians capable of playing the highest type of music in a manner which leaves no great amount of space for critical comment, we have had concerts in Rapallo certainly as good as Wm. Atheling heard during his three years' service on the *New Age,* 1917–1919. As to the *average* quality of the Rapallo concerts, I suppose it would work out to a conjectural 98 per cent as against the 31 per cent or 16.5 per cent of bearable music that Atheling *heard* in London, after he had picked the five or nine concerts per fortnight that offered (to his experienced sorrow) the greatest chance of enjoyment or the probability of the avoidance of pain.

The real praise of performance is that the auditor is put in position to *judge* the composer and the work, when that work is masterwork.

The typical "great success" in performing nineteenth century music was that of the robot who could learn a *few* moving pieces, and who without musical knowledge, could be billed for big halls. Every impresario rolls 'em on his tongue. Tell papa, I once dined with Battling Siki's manager. He was looking for a great musical composition, five hours long, that would fill the Velo d'Hiv and knock Paris endways.

Waaal, bhoys, that was one glorious dinner. And Leon's earlier ambition had been to find a human gorilla for the "ring." At the time I met him, Siki had left or was about to elude him. He wanted a remplaçant.

Opportunity wasted on me, in my strict function as critic of music, perhaps? But what a night, what an *immortal* night for a novelist!

By getting out from under the heel or bum of the usurer we have given in Rapallo, repeatedly, the Mozart violin sonatas, en bloc, 12 and 13 at a time. We have given Bach, Dowland, Strawinsky, we have played I think more William Young, than any English old music society. Gerhart Münch is not only a pianist of first rank, but he is a very able editor and mobiliser of old music and has had Oscar Chilesotti's unedited manuscripts at his disposal. The Kalendamaja, put together from Besard, and using Besard's Dowland, with a missing movement supplied by the transcriber, is definitely an addition to the body of music performable to-day. As is Münch's arrangement of Franceso da Milano's Janequin "Chant des Oiseaux." Il Lavoro di Genova, commenting on a concert in the huge Politeama Cantero of Chiavari notes: Di Olga Rudge, violinista austeramente completa, abbiamo potuto ammirare il senso preciso, impeccabile della tecnica e la cavata composta ... suono cristalino, purissimo. The Secolo notes "secure and ample bowing" and the Giornale di Genova "perfect intonation."

Tibor Serly played here and approved of us before his recent triumph in Budapest, where he conducted the Budapest Philharmonic in a full programme of his own composition. In the presence of Bartok,

Kodaly, etc. (Full length articles in Pesti Naplo, Uj Magyrsag, Pester Lloyd, Uj Nemzedek, Ujsag, Pesti Hirlap, all confirming in more florid language what I said in my article on Serly in *New English Weekly* some weeks ago.) (Fino Savio, Lonny Mayer, the Gertler Quartette, Maestri Ottone, Sansoni, Simonati have all contributed to local auditive pleasure.) The Amici della Musica of Chiavari (with 300 adherents) has arisen in the wake of a Genoese editorial demanding "if Rapallo, why can't Chiavari?"

What we have done, we have done by liberating the ability of performers from the noose of international finance. And that goes for any man who tolerates Neville Chamberlain as an exponent of the meaning and intentions of England.

What Douglasism can do for music in one town (having almost no population) it can do for any and every human activity in any town on this planet.

WILLIAM ATHELING (E.P.)

MONEY VERSUS MUSIC[72]

I have said for a number of years that a group of 500 people can have *any* (I mean positively *any*) kind of civilization they want. With the afterthought: "up to the capacity of their best artists." I doubt if Pericles had more than 80 citizens who knew the worse art from the better.

Music in the great cities has been damned and crushed by the overhead. Years ago I was in the lobby of the Carleton (London) where I sat very seldom in those days. As a tenor then in view told me, I think for the benefit of a detective who called himself an army captain, and who was employed to break the tenor's contract...all of which lent aroma to the occasion...the detective's employer had unquestionably a name in the "world"...the tenor told me of his first great London fiasco when he had no concert, because at the last moment he had not sixty pounds, and his impresario wouldn't wait for the gate receipts but wanted his, the tenor's, watch (last gift from a dying father). As Gourmont says, "Nothing but bad literature ever happens in real life."

For three years, at a later period, as critic I cajoled and bullied musicians to give better programs than otherwise they would have dared. Rosing gave full programs of Moussorgsky, and I believe I had something backstage to do with it. Later in Paris when Miss Rudge

[72] *The Delphian Quarterly*, January, 1936, pp. 2-6, 52.

launched Antheil, we found that one could afford to give concerts if one invited a public, but not if one allowed anyone to pay for admission. That is part and parcel of the usurers' age. There is no cranny of life into which an infamous monetary system has not spread its poison, invisible as chlorine and as deadly. The Rapallo experiment has passed the stage of experiment and I offer it on the chance that some other three people who prefer the best music to the second, or fifth best, may be able to use their critical faculty and to hear what they otherwise mightn't.

By chance an American violinist and Gerhart Münch were overheard from the next villa trying a Bach sonata, and by chance the totally nonmusicianly denizens of the villa expressed their pleasure. The violinist and composer took a chance on playing (in theory "all") Mozart's sonatas (in cold fact, there were twelve), but given in the groups as composed, four from the six composed at first go, four from those Mozart did as a group a couple of years later, and four of those which he did, as I like to imagine, at crucial moments of his musical thought, preceding, and holding in his mind the nuclei of, larger compositions.

Münch and Miss Rudge began in the local cinema house. During the first concert the Podesta offered us the town hall, which we accepted for a later series of concerts.

The public provided a piano, and the municipality put in the steam heating. There is in Italy the "new mentality" distinct from what the new men call "old mentality." Rapallo is a town officially of 15,000 inhabitants, 10,000 being peasants who live up in the hills. I do not say you can do this in every Italian town, nor that every Italian town (any more than every town of similar size in Ohio) would have run us a literary fortnightly supplement in the local paper (at a loss to the paper, which was never mentioned until we suggested dropping the supplement).

If there is any lesson in what we have done here it is this: You can have the highest possible programs when the performers can play them and you can have them *wherever* the public *can't afford worse.*

Pianos are scarcer in Liguria than in America, where Town Halls abound. It is not every village that contains a Chilesotti collection. (You can look up Chilesotti in the Encyclopedia of the French Conservatoire. He was, a few decades ago, *the* great savant of sixteenth century lute music, and had left a good deal of unpublished work, copies of Francesco da Milano, Besard, Severi, none of which were available to the public in an age which does not play the lute.)

Münch is not yet ripe as a composer but he has impeccable taste in transcription. Francesco da Milano had put Janequin's song of the birds into lute music. (See Delphian Text, Part XII, p. 151.)[73] Münch took it out, as you might say, of mothballs, mobilized it, and the violin part is one of the beauties of now-available violin music. I have mentioned this in my *ABC of Reading,* for I think Janequin inherited from the troubadours the fine clear cut *representation* of natural sound, the exactitude of birds and flowers which parallels Pisanello's portrait of the Este, an art that is medieval, in complete distinction from all that comes with the Renaissance.

The Gertlers have been here. Tibor Serly played his *Viola Concerto* here and played the Mozart *Symphonie Concertante* with Miss Rudge, before his recent triumph in Budapest (the first time in years that an American-Hungarian or any other Hungarian or American has conducted the Budapest Philharmonic in a full concert of his own works).

Just why Serly should have dawned on Europe *instead* of America, where he has been for the last seven years, will, I suppose, remain a mystery to those who believe America knows how to use artists.

If I could see the interest in Serly's manuscripts, why shouldn't the "great American *conductors"* who have most certainly seen that manuscript been able to see that it was interesting? A vast pile of Hungarian notices with an equally formidable syntactical rendering into an unknown tongue (derived from English) now shows that Hungary has discovered her prodigal.

Italy is still the land of Puccini, but Italy is also more than the land of Puccini, as evidenced by a comment I heard in the hall after Strawinsky's *Pulcinella,* a voice, rather puzzled than otherwise: "Quella violinista è *intelligente"* (That violinist is *intelligent*). Which indicates what I have been driving at. The Rapallo concerts have provided a laboratory for the *objective* (with the emphasis strictly on that word) examination of music.

There has, I believe, been very little serious attempt anywhere to establish a demarcation between first rate and second rate music. I mean in the way I have attempted to establish such literary demarcation in my *ABC of Reading.* Very few people have the chance to observe different musical masterworks under uniform (laboratory) conditions, and very few people have really wanted to do so.

In America the conductor has been so happy in being the great man of his city, and in receiving popular homage, that composers have not greatly flourished. It is very easy to turn the popular mind from the composition itself to the performance. Perhaps only men who have

---

[73] The reference is to volume twelve of the Delphian Text, prepared for "the exclusive use" of members of The Delphian Society, published in Chicago, 1929. The volume is entitled *Appreciation of Music,* and on page 51 there is a passing reference to the work of Janequin.

composed at least a little themselves see what idiots most composers have been; where composers have bluffed; where composers have missed opportunities; where they have been content with putting it over or with avoidance of reality, for there is musical reality. There are hard facts in music. Chopin knew musical form. Bach obviously could hear his own polyphony, the various lines going on all at once. Bach and Mozart did really know how long they wanted their notes. This matter is relative, but a great many nineteenth century composers simply didn't. Quite often men "write" music long before they understand their own notation.

The terrible severity of listening repels a great many people. Most auditors have neither the desire nor the energy to note the difference between masterwork and a nice piece of music, something beautiful but not able to stand repetition before or after the real composition.

A small town can provide a laboratory and can specialize in work not being done in the heavily monied "centres" up to the quality and number of its local performers. (One of our difficulties has been that as soon as we bring out a local player he gets a job elsewhere for more than we could in any way offer him. All of which helps music as music.)

I don't know that the Rapallo system *depends* on free hall. What actually happened was that Olga Rudge and Gerhart Münch took the cinema theatre for a series of three concerts giving the solid block of Mozart violin and piano sonatas with the aim of demonstrating what Mozart *meant* by the form or what the form meant to him.

The quality of the performance was such that the town (in particular the Podesta instigated by the Segretario Politico) offered us the town hall during one of the intervals of the first concert.

We did not accept it for the two concerts already announced for the following evenings for fear of confusing the public, but very gratefully accepted it for further development of local music.

Undoubtedly we began in exceptional conditions; i.e., the actual presence of two exceptional players in Rapallo, one resident and one temporarily there, plus the presence of three critics, myself, Bunting and Haas, experienced writers on music in London and Stuttgart, respectively, who were capable of certifying the quality of the music.

As a *"system"* to be applied *anywhere,* all the particular town can do is to place its music in charge of its best performer and most knowledgeful local critic—minimum two people with some mutual respect and deference. Quite distinctly the *aim* is the development of a local group of performers. And quite definitely it is to end or instigate the deadly system of getting in stars; i.e., performers often with very limited repertoire, who play the same music everywhere and have often neither wide nor deep musical knowledge, nor even a very great interest in music *as such,* apart from their own success or profit. Given *one* local musician of high capacity, and one player friend who either lives in the town or can without great increase of expenses pass considerable time there, and you have your nucleus.

The development of the *quality* of local music consisted in Rapallo of the encouragement and stimulus given the *other* local musicians. For example, Maestro Sansoni had been in Rapallo 15 years, an excellent musician though not very powerful, a composer who had had a few things published, who lived by leading the small town orchestra and playing jazz, dance music, *anything,* but with almost complete submergence.

He was quite definitely transformed. As he said: "When I play with them I am another man." The chance of playing the Bach concerto and sonata, Purcell's golden sonata and music of that kind, for two violins and klavier, had *not* come to him in 15 years of getting his living by playing the violin.

He (Sansoni) had a 'cellist friend in the next town (15 miles off), a man who had taken degrees, et cetera, but was of old family and had no need to make any money, and in particular not a fighter who could on his own impose high grade music on his home town. The Rapallo example has been more fecund in Chiavari than even in Rapallo. Chiavari has a huge opera house, and when they started their music society last winter, they had 300 members.

Thus to me, as critic, comes the chance of, as you might say, laboratory work; i.e., the chance to test given pieces of music first in a small hall and then in a large one. Note that as a *specific* form of critical examination, this doesn't occur when one is writing music criticism in a large city. The critic gets whatever chance and the commerce of music toss up for him.

Our next excellent 'cellist was from the other end, so to speak. I had seen him about the town but did not know him. He presented himself to me one day when he hadn't eaten since breakfast the day before.

What counts in *developing* the local standard of playing is that an organization like ours not only *permits* but requires the local players to play the *best* music they can understand; instead of perpetually wobbling about and trying to find the medium or low level of what the public likes most easily at first hearing. In the cases of Sansoni and Simonati we had musicians of first grade sensibility, rusty and weakened from lack of performing the finest music. When we came to groups of three and four fiddles, as in the performance of William Young's sonatas, the leaders had largely to carry the supplementary instruments.

There is a limit to the amount of such "carrying." You can only incorporate a certain proportion of weaker and less exact players. It is always a strain on the best players, but not an unbearable one. If they (the leaders) care about *music,* they will stand for quite a good deal of it (within decent limits).

I think I said that the danger *to* such an organization as ours is that when the local performers have been got *out* of their obscurity and given a chance to show their best, they then are noticed and are offered more remunerative jobs elsewhere. That wouldn't happen in a larger town where their pay could be raised.

But if the original organization is conducted in the right spirit, I think you would find, as we did, that the musicians who had moved through it would retain a loyalty to it. I said that Sansoni is now in charge of an orchestra on one of the big liners, but he is always ready to help us out if and when a concert for which we want another violin occurs during his week or ten days' shore leave. (He lands at Genova, and goes to his old father in Lucca, all of which is within reach.)

Any town, having a town hall *and* any public spirit whatever, ought to be ready to use the hall for such a purpose. Where no town hall has a room large enough for concerts; i.e., where the mayor's office is nothing but a shed or the police station, a church, some church, may have a basement.

All the proceeds go to the performers in Rapallo save *ten* lire to the janitor and doorkeeper and the small printing expenses which are reduced by cooperation with the town paper. The paper gets the notice of the concert with the program which is printed as news; this covers the cost of the type-setting and all we (the concerts) pay for is the reprint of the standing linotype.

For extra evenings or intimate concerts you can also hang up a big sheet of paper with the program written out *large* by hand. I dare say this would be too informal for most *American* towns, but a local artist might sometimes volunteer.

When we have had "celebrities," they haven't been bribed to come and they weren't there *as celebrities* but as MUSICIANS. They get the pleasure of expressing approval of the kind of things we stand for, and the satisfaction of our recognition of the fact that they are serious musicians—sometimes more detailed criticism, or at least a variant on the criticism they would get from hurried or tired critics in a larger town, but usually at least the criticism of an unusual program.

The whole aim is to raise the standard of music actually performed in any *given place;* to free this music from the domination of a dying commercial system; and to feed or at any rate assist in feeding a minimum of local first rate musicians and *permit* them to *work* in the highest degree possible to them (*quality* production, not *quantity* production).

The charge for admission in Rapallo is ten lire *to those who can afford it,* five lire to anyone claiming student's privileges—no examination of the claim is made, and this term covers anyone with a serious curiosity—two lire to members of Circolo di Cultura and to members of the town bands of Rapallo and Santa Margherita; and I might add free admission to a few people who deserve it; i.e., who are supposed to be living on less than the performers or to be working for the concerts.

Just compare this with what is true of concert giving in London and Paris—teachers who teach all year and then *have to give* a concert to *"keep their name up";* young musicians agonizing over the $300 necessary to be one among 300 concert givers in the season, with corresponding wear and tear on nerves and program selection, et cetera, and *naturally* no line, no plan in the music *heard* by the concert-goer. *Even* in the case of large conservatories with great resources, the season's concerts are apt to be a mixed bag, leaving the auditor at the end of the year with no more musical *knowledge,* but only aware of the fact that one celebrity is more *celebrated* than another; or at best that certain virtuosos have certain superiorities over others and that one is more highly pepped or dominates his audience, or gets away with it.

No attempt is made to interest the townspeople in the performers. *The interest is focused on the music to be played.*

They are *told* what the music is, and *why* it is of interest to people who know a good deal about *music as a whole.* In the case of Münch and Miss Rudge, it has gradually dawned on the Rapallo public that the music was being played exceptionally well, in fact, so well that they hadn't been worried about *who* was playing it. The performers weren't getting *between* the hearer and the composer. It's *not* showy. When Toscanini does *Fidelio* or *Falstaff, it is not showy,* but you end by knowing all that Beethoven and Verdi had to say in those operas. Whereas when Bruno Walter plays Mozart one has merely a dull rage at hearing what one believes Mozart to have been, being generally smeared over and reduced to the level of sausage and sauerkraut.

Gerhart Münch left Rapallo in the summer of 1935 and did not return until the spring of 1937. Desmond Chute, in an *Il Mare* article (July 27, 1935), rebuked the local public for letting him slip away unnoticed. The musical life of Rapallo, and Pound's concerts in particular, had been dealt a blow. Following a considerable gap, the Tigullians gradually recovered and in the spring of 1936 recommenced their public activities in a new format the study-sessions devoted to Vivaldi; then, little by little, they restored the concerts again, for a time with the substitute pianist

Luigi Franchetti. Other visiting artists began to appear, excellent visiting artists. But this was the big difference: the Tigullians no longer had complete control over the program material, and in a very real sense the most attractive feature of the first two-years' events was lost. In the curious little piece "Marconi's Violins" Pound, while continuing to argue for the balance of power between the metropolis and the smaller towns of the corporate state, realized that just as Rapallo had no claim on the Stradivarius violins, it also had no claim over Münch, who had returned to Dresden, where he was to have some successes as pianist and composer. Certainly in "Money versus Music" he had been in a retrospective mood, recognizing that the most convivial and educative concerts were now probably past. There are also frequent complaints now about the lack of audience.

But new vistas were also opening up. Olga Rudge had begun her Vivaldi researches and Pound was accompanying her enthusiastically in these investigations. In 1936 he encouraged her to go to Turin to compile a catalogue of the Vivaldi material in the National Library there. Agnes Bedford reported later that when she visited Rapallo in 1938 she found the poet totally preoccupied with transcribing the Vivaldi works from the microfilms of the Dresden manuscripts he had recently obtained.

The first Vivaldi articles are groping. A few—not necessarily all—of their inaccuracies have been noted in the footnotes. It is not known precisely what happened at the study-sessions. The review of April 11 is anonymous, and while that of April 25 is signed "E. Pound," both appear to be transcriptions by someone else of statements Pound made at two of these sessions.

TIGULLIAN STUDIES[74]

Rapallo is now a well-known musical center, even if the public avoids our concerts; and since we can't be completely shattered by Geneva's sanctions and plotting,[75] we propose to establish a study-workshop with the immediate aim of examining the Italian musical heritage of the period before Bach, beginning by reading all Vivaldi's works for one or two violins and piano.

We trust those of our "supporters" still remaining in Rapallo will give the same valuable help as in previous years.

[74] *Il Mare,* March 14, 1936; translated.
[75] The reference here is to sanctions imposed by the League of Nations against Italy after Mussolini's attack on Ethiopia in October, 1935.

Antonio Vivaldi (1685–1743)[76]

Music historiographers have testified that Vivaldi was highly honored in his time by Benda, Quantz, and the supreme poet of counterpoint, J. S. Bach. They say that the latter adapted sixteen of Vivaldi's compositions for his own purposes. These historiographers have not fully clarified the nature of this adaptation, which we may well believe was undertaken by Bach mainly for his convenience, that is, in order to play Vivaldi's great "sound strategies" with the musical means at his disposal, viz., four harpsichords, organ, etc., failing a full orchestra.

The enormous "continent" of Vivaldi's work has not yet been explored, let alone catalogued with precision. Fétis lists 28 operas, including the *Dramaturgia d'Allaci* (as an authority), Robt. Eitner *(Quellen Lexicon)* gives 25 titles, La Costanza, Dorilla, Griselda, etc.[77]

The most systematic catalogue of Vivaldi's instrumental works is that by W. Altmann *(Thematischer Katalog, 1922)*.

Contents:

Op. I.	TWELVE SONATAS for three instruments (two violins and violone or cembalo;
Op. II.	TWELVE SONATAS for violin and basso continuo;
Op. III.	L'ESTRO ARMONICO, 12 concerti dedicated to Ferdinand III of Tuscany. Bach's interest is shown by the fact that he used them: No. 3 is Bach's No. 7 (425), transposed into F; No. 8 is Bach's No. 2 (385); No. 9 is Bach's No. 1 (425); No. 12 is Bach's No. 5 (425), transposed into C major;
Op. IV.	LA STRAVAGANZA, 12 concerti. Contains *The celebrated Cuckoo*. Bach used Nos. 1 and 6;
Op. V.	SIX SONATAS, violin and basso continuo;
Op. VI.	SIX CONCERTI;
Op. VII.	TWELVE CONCERTI. Bach used them. Cf. vol. 12 [i.e., of the Bach-Gesellschaft edition] where Nos. 2 and 3 are transposed into C major;
Op. VIII.	IL CIMENTO DELL'ARMONIA E DELL'INVENZIONE, twelve concerti;
Op. IX.	LA CETRA, twelve concerti. Dedicated to His Majesty Charles VI;

---

[76] Vivaldi was born about 1675–78. Later research has also shown that he died in 1741.

[77] This has now been substantially expanded to include at least forty-one operas. See Olga Rudge's article in *Groves Dictionary of Music and Musicians*, Vol. IX, London, 1954.

Op. X.   SIX CONCERTI for flute;
Op. XI.   SIX CONCERTI for solo violin;
Op. XII. SIX CONCERTI for solo violin.

Other works are printed without the "opus" indication. The sources of the most important manuscripts are the MAURO FOÀ COLLECTION, Turin,[78] Biblioteca Reale, Prof. A. Gentili, curator; and the one in DRESDEN, where the 79 manuscripts numbered CX. 1015-1094 are CONCERTI by VIVALDI and those numbered 1095-96 and 1100-1108 contain other instrumental compositions by him.[79]

Today the following pieces for strings are available in print:

SONATAS:
*A major, Op. II, No. 2, edited by F. David, published by Breitkopf;
*D major, Respighi (Ricordi);
 E minor, Salmon (Ricordi);
 B-flat major, Salmon (Ricordi);
 D minor, A. Moffat (Schott).

CONCERTI (violin and piano):
*G. Dandelot (M. Eschig) 1928;
*D major *(Estro Armonico 9)*, Dandelot (Max Eschig), 1928;
 G major (Op. IV, 12), Nachez (Schott), 1912;
*A minor *(Estro Armonico 6)*, Nachez (Schott), 1912;
 G minor, Nachez (Schott), 1912;
 B-flat major, Nachez (Schott), 1912;
*E major *(Estro Armonico, 12)*, E. Borrel (Maurice Senart), 1921; Ms. in the Fitzwilliam Library in Cambridge, England;
 A major, F. de Guarnieri (Ricordi), 1918, from the *Mauro Foà Collection,* Turin, edited by Prof. A. Gentili;
*B minor, Principi-Gentili (Ricordi), 1932;
*G minor, Corti-Gentili (Ricordi), 1932;
*E-flat major, Zino-Gentili (Ricordi), 1932.

CONCERTI for two violins, Op. III:
*A minor, III, 8, Nachez (Schott), 1928;
*D major, III, II, Dandelot (Schott), 1928. This had been transcribed by Bach for organ and had been for a long time attributed to him instead of Vivaldi.

[78] The Foà collection comprises only part of the Turin holdings, which also includes the even more extensive Giordano collection.
[79] The Sächsische Landesbibliothek manuscripts in Dresden have been subsequently renumbered.

SONATAS, for two violins, piano (cello ad lib.):
G minor, J. Peyrot et Rebeffat (Senart), 1921;
E minor, J. Peyrot et Rebeffat (Senart), 1921;
C major, J. Peyrot et Rebeffat (Senart), 1921;
E minor, J. Peyrot et Rebeffat (Senart), 1921;
SIX SONATAS for piano and cello: Morse Rummel-Chaigneau (Senart).

Our study will begin with the compositions marked by asterisk with parallel references to Bach's music and other points of comparison, for example:

JANEQUIN: *Canzone degli Uccelli,* edited by Münch;
BACH: Toccata;
STRAVINSKY: *Pulcinella; Petroushka.*

Our musicians will also transcribe unpublished concerti or those only available in eighteenth-century editions, for example, that by Roger le Cene.

For further details and information write to: E. POUND, Albergo Rapallo. For identification, the card of the Fascist Institute of Culture.

TIGULLIAN STUDIES[80]

Before beginning the study session dedicated to the music of our Vivaldi, Ezra Pound addressed a few words of introduction to the people gathered last Wednesday in the Town Hall in Rapallo. Among other things he said:

"I must explain the difference between these 'study sessions' and the concerts of previous years.

"First: we cannot always do the same thing. Second: we have already given 'organic' concerts, that is, concerts I have been able to quote in my writings (for example, the *ABC of Reading*) as models of structure. I mean to say that they were not only composed of masterpieces but that these masterpieces were combined so as to form a complete cycle, as in a drama, where every piece of music worked to give us the sum total.

"Let us think—to give an example—of the difference in our general culture between music and painting. I say 'general' in the sense of having a knowledge of the history of painting as well as of the aesthetic value of the paintings themselves, as in the case not among artists,

[80] *Il Mare,* April 11, 1936; translated.

but among those of us who do not paint. We know and refer back in our minds to the total qualities of Mantegna, Carpaccio, Botticelli, Dürer, Van Eyck, Leonardo, Pier della Francesca, with an almost precise vision, or at least, I think, with one much more precise than when we make distinctions between Paisiello, Marcello, Viotti, Vivaldi, Caldara, Bach, Mozart.

"We recognize of course the difference between Bach, Chopin and Debussy as between Mantegna, Velasquez and Picasso, but we do this only with music of different periods.

"The system in vogue in the great cities, centers of usury, where greed governs almost every manifestation of art and obscures or slowly degrades and vilifies it, does not permit the freedom that we have achieved here in Rapallo.

"In London and in several great capitals, concerts that devote a whole hour to only one composer are exceptions. Those which give time to an unfashionable composer are very rare. In my three years' experience as a critic in London, a Russian gave whole concerts of music by Moussorgsky; a Frenchman gave concerts demonstrating the development of French song.[81] Vladimir Cernikoff, with great élan and reliance on his extensive knowledge of the subject, tried a series of, I think, six concerts to illustrate the history of piano music.

"But these are memories gathered during a lifetime, they are not usual events.

"I have said several times that it is useless to do on a smaller scale in Rapallo what is being done with magnificence and great means elsewhere.

"The lesson of the fifteenth century, the Italian cultural heritage, teaches us that as far as high culture is concerned the small town is not or should not be a pale (sometimes even clumsy) imitation of the great city, but must do something of its own in its own way. This idea of the healthy, robust, dynamic cell works very well within the concept of the differentiated and well-developed body of the corporate state.

"To the faithful who have supported us for several years and to the traveling music lover who comes to observe our activities we must offer an opportunity that is out of the ordinary.

"The usual bunch of flowers or the usual menu would get lost in their memory, would not do anything to make Rapallo stand out.

"Specifically, this series of Vivaldi events now under consideration will give us the opportunity to form for ourselves, we hope, a clear impression, a sharper insight into the qualities of this great composer.

---

[81] Vladimir Rosing and Yves Tinayre; see *The New Age* reviews.

"In three hours we can distinguish his style with assurance from that of his admirer Bach, from Mozart, who resembles him in certain ways, and from the crowd of minor, though charming, luminaries: Marcello, Paisiello, Pergolesi.

"We will not simply remember 'a' concert but 'the' Vivaldi concert, the first of the series, the second of the series, etc.

"And I say without exaggeration that there are people who still remember, as models of concert structure, the first and second concerts of our first year given in this auditorium.

"I have never tried to defend my musical 'taste' or my opinions. If someone wishes it, I will willingly relate what seem to me to be Vivaldi's qualities, his merits in relation to or in comparison with certain other composers. But words, the literary expression of musical qualities, say little.

"It is possible to 'explain' something. I admit that. But it is almost impossible to choose terminology that does not lead to useless or barely useful distinctions, distracting the attention of the scholar from the essence of the music and from the sound itself.

"Studying Mozart, we have frequently illustrated, by three hours of music, his *idea* of the sonata, exemplifying his first and second periods of violin sonata conceptualization, and have brought to light several landmarks of his career concentrated in this form.

"Such a demonstration is not possible for Vivaldi for the simple reason that his sonatas and concertos are not published or on sale at present. Some of them have never been published. I inform our supporters that we have already spent three-hundred lire for the music, that is, for those fragments that can be bought today, and we now have a collection necessarily small, but bigger than those to be found in the music libraries of many conservatories and 'great and celebrated' academies of music in cities much more populous than Rapallo.

"To illustrate the rarity of the texts and the problems they pose for scholars, I may say I received today six sonatas edited by Chaigneau, with the bass parts deciphered by my great friend Walter Rummel.[82]

"In the introduction to this edition the celebrated musicologist Henry Expert tells us that these sonatas are to be found only in an extremely rare quarto volume engraved by Leclerc and Madame Boivin in the middle of the eighteenth century. It is therefore omitted from the opus catalogue numbered I to XII published in *Il Mare* last March 21."

---

[82] *Antonio Vivaldi: 6 sonates pour violoncelle et piano;* recueillies et annotées par Marg. [uerite] Chaigneau, réalisation de la basse-continue par W. Morse-Rummel, Paris, Editions M. Senart, 1916.

TIGULLIAN STUDIES[83]

Last Wednesday, speaking at the second study session in the Town Hall in Rapallo, our friend Pound said among other things:

"If we discover a painting by an old master, all the papers of Europe will talk about it; if we reveal a piece of old music the fact goes unnoticed. Paintings by Melozzo da Forlì and Botticelli are no longer to be found, but I have known an American in Paris who had a Fra Angelico. He used to say it cost him his whole fortune to buy and he was waiting for a millionaire to pay him double the price for it, but feared finding him because he had fallen in love with the thing. An authentic painting? I don't know, but very beautiful.

"These examples should help me introduce what I have to say. The problem of Vivaldi's position in the history of musical invention would not be resolved even by writing a large volume. I certainly don't intend to explain it in a few lines.

"An article on this problem will be published shortly by Miss Rudge in *Il Mare*, where we keep registering the progress of our studies. I want to mention two things here: the first concerns Vivaldi's so-called 'Program Music,' i.e., not pure mathematical and emotional construction but music which 'depicts.'

"This virtue has been a subject of lengthy discussions in literature since Flaubert. It is the difference I am trying to emphasize. Music can suggest certain things, for example a country fair. With a modern orchestra one can produce imitative sounds, for example a symphony of cats. There exists in the development of music a clear and precise difference between the Middle Ages and the Renaissance—a clear difference, as between the period of Piero della Francesca or Pisanello, and the paintings of Raphael.

"Let us listen to a representative piece of music by Vivaldi, the cuckoo for example. The bird is to be heard clearly among the other sounds. However this is not a discovery made by Vivaldi, it is rather a cultural inheritance. Vivaldi, Couperin, Daquin all did such delightful things. If, on the other hand, we listen to an earlier piece of music, we learn how far this art had gone two centuries before.

"We arrive through this process at Janequin. Janequin wrote music for chorus. I have heard a choir execute the *Chant des oiseaux* but in a way that showed no profound understanding of the author or his precision in notation. Francesco da Milano, wishing to express Janequin's concept without using a chorus of twenty people, edited the *Canzone degli Uccelli* for the lute." (Part of this transcription was

---

[83] *Il Mare*, April 25, 1936; translated.

executed on the violin during the study session of the Tigullians last Wednesday in the Town Hall of Rapallo. For pedagogical reasons the whole composition was not played at first, for the meeting on Wednesday was not a concert but a study session; rather it was performed in its entirety later, after Pound's explanation, to illustrate its complete form.)

"It is said that the first impression of the work of a genius is often unpleasant. Humanity on the whole does not like to change habits; but to understand something new, outworn prejudices have to be abandoned.

"Personally I feel that Münch's version of this song repays me for all the effort I have made over the last three years for the sake of music. I would not have experienced greater pleasure if I had dug up a piece of Greek marble. By analogy I may add that the most interesting book on Botticelli has been written by a Japanese, who has reproduced photographs of fragments of the paintings, giving us an opportunity to see many strange perspectives not visible when admiring the whole.

"By listening to the violin alone we reach back to a period at least three centuries prior to Janequin, who was born towards 1475 and was published in the sixteenth century.

"Arnaut Daniel, admired by Dante, who called him 'Il miglior fabbro,' has left poems where the sound of the birds is registered in the words themselves. The music is lost, but all the great art of the troubadours claimed to join words and notes together. Thus to have been extolled by contemporaries and by Dante (whose knowledge of the Provençal language was profound), the music must have corresponded perfectly with the words. Between Arnaut and Janequin we notice a decline and a development. Arnaut's words are poetry; the meaning is bound into the phrase. For Janequin words have no great importance and are reduced in his choruses to non-articulated sounds, for example, 'gnouf, gnouf' for the stag in the *Canzone della caccia*. This kind of art has been magnificently illustrated in our time in 'Quand j'ai ouy le tabourin' by Debussy, composed to Charles d'Orléans' words.[84]

"The music of the first centuries after 1000 A.D. has reached us in imperfect notation; sometimes the notes are nothing but an aid to the memory and usually only the melody is notated.

"To understand the development of music we must not only notice over-all differences, i.e., clever registrations of the sounds of nature (poetic atmosphere in Janequin, 'ornamentation' during the Renaissance, diagrams of mathematical beauty, etc.); it is also necessary to analyse the means of expression and other material changes such as

[84] Pound had heard Debussy himself conduct this work in Paris.

that of instrumentation. The beauty of the staccato section in the violin solo of Münch's Janequin transcription resides in his use of the lower strings of the instrument, coinciding approximately with the sound of the medieval *viel*.[85]

"As early as 1475 Francesco da Milano could present complicated voicings on the lute, comprising all the dimensions of the chorus. By the time we reach Vivaldi—and the middle of the seventeenth century —the voice of the violin has risen perceptibly over the body of instrumental sound. Think of Vivaldi's memorable phrases, or Mozart's sonatas, which begin on the submediant of the mediant chord. Every conquest in art is obtained through sacrifices and we often lose, at least for a year or a century, some other beauty."

E. POUND

Subject of the next study session: "The problem of the relationship between Vivaldi and Bach."

MARCONI'S VIOLINS[86]

In the July 16 issue of *Italia Nostra,* published in London, we read:

"The great inventor Marchese Guglielmo Marconi has recently inherited a splendid collection of old violins from his brother Alfonso, whose premature death we have already announced.

"Alfonso Marconi was, in fact, a passionate collector of these instruments, which he gathered during his many journeys throughout the world. The collection even includes two 'Stradivari' that Alfonso Marconi bought in London. One of these bears the date 1718 and is considered by the experts to be one of the most perfect violins in existence. The collection, which is now housed in a villa in Rapallo— Alfonso Marconi's home—will very soon be moved to Rome.

"The Marchese Marconi has expressed the intention of donating a 'Stradivarius' to the Academy of Santa Cecilia in Rome. The instrument will be played twice a year by the best student of the celebrated academy at benefit concerts for needy musicians."

As we can see, the great inventor has not failed to show himself a man of the new era, sensitive to the values of our times.

A treasure leaves Rapallo, but nobody can object to the wisdom of the decision and to the greater claim of the Academy of Santa Cecilia.

---

[85] Usually spelled "vielle," a medieval precursor of the viol, but with a more biting tone.
[86] *Il Mare,* July 18, 1936; translated.

Now that the Empire exists, we must consider the relationship between center, periphery, and minor nuclei of the State. An Empire needs a Center in which the intelligence and the strength of the race are concentrated, but from which in turn the light of its civilization spreads across and penetrates the lesser nuclei. This diffusion depends not only on the undefined will of the lesser cities but also on their sensibility and perception. It is not enough to be sensitive to the passive reception of benefits alone; it is also necessary to show ourselves ready to seize the opportunity for constructive work.

The New Order will spread from Rome in ways neither understood nor dreamed of, in ways foreseen only by a few people who have an "ardent imagination," and it will spread not only "geographically" in space, but will also grow in depth of development and concept. The cells and nuclei, whether small cities or large, are not rivals of Rome. The corporate concept has implicit in itself the idea of organic composition. The liver is not the rival of the lungs; the small glands do not repeat the function of the heart but work as complements to it.

In the magnificent body of the Fascist state no one is excluded, but everyone must function according to his abilities, according to his imagination and perception. One's abilities must not be considered as a fixed, immutable, nonextensible quantity, but must include the possibility of growing, developing, and harmonizing with those of others. Rome's heritage is not the heritage of a single era. Rome's power did not cease with the fall of the Empire of the Caesars, it was not the creation of Julius alone, its order was perpetuated in the action of Antonius, Constantine, and Justinian, and later with the canon law of the Middle Ages.

We must not consider the grace of God only as "forgiveness" but also as an aesthetic quality, and we must consider morality not only as an ethical force but also as a deeply intellectual energy. This good can be appreciated in the pursuit of any social and economic study.

E. P.

Over the years Pound kept in active touch with numerous musicians through correspondence. One of these was Yves Tinayre, the French tenor who had performed in *Le Testament* in 1926. It will also be recalled that William Atheling had been an enthusiastic supporter of Tinayre's work in the *New Age* days. Pound had written to invite him to give a concert of early music in Rapallo, though such a concert never took place. The following preview is an introduction to a concert of early music given on July 26, 1936, over the BBC, in which Tinayre was the soloist, with an orchestra and chorus conducted by Anthony Bernard. Tinayre sang two groups:

1. *Milles bonjours vous présente,* Guillaume Dufay;
   Chanson provençale (Danse de la Reine Arvillouse) (with chorus), XIIth century;
   Plourés, dames, Guillaume de Machaut.
2. Scene from *Orfeo (The Despair of Orpheus),* Luigi Rossi.

It is possible that the program also included some "Laudi to San Lorenzo" (XIIIth century). These were all arrangements. Although Tinayre did later edit a great deal of early music, at this period his work was confined to its performance in arrangements by others.

MEDIÆVAL MUSIC AND YVES TINAYRE[87]

The æsthetic culture of the twelfth century, or at any rate the literary and musical culture, was focused in a particularly intense manner on one problem, that is, the joining of word and tune.

This form of civilisation has declined since then in an almost uninterrupted downward curve, relieved by an occasional rise.

Bach was no good at it. One might as well take the largest bull by its most prominent horn. "Music," as they say, "developed," but in *one* way it never got any better.

Whether "song" developed is open to question. There is a vast hiatus in the archives. Troubadour music is preserved mainly on parchment. With very few exceptions, these editions *de luxe,* or manuscripts *de luxe,* were made for dilettantes of the next century or at least the next generation. Of Dante's period we have next to no musical texts.

No form of human record developed more tardily than the written recording of melody. Primitive man records it by ear. The Greeks and Provençals recorded it approximately on paper and parchment, but guided their interpretation of the written signs largely by memory of the rhythm; that is, to such an extent that there can be only approximately "correct" and "incorrect" modern printing of twelfth-century tunes. There can be interesting and uninteresting interpretations.

Great composers record their rhythm *exactly.* Bach, Mozart and Stravinsky write what they want played. But a vast horde of third-rate

---

[87] *The Listener,* July 22, 1936, pp. 187–88.

and second-rate and very famous composers do not. They just put down something approximate.

Having come to music by way of verse, I know all the sorrows of this thorny and rock-strewn path.

The troubadour, as poet, thought the singer would *feel* how the thing *ought* to be sung. And in his record we still have the words as guide to the singing. The notes on the stave represent the rise and fall of the voice, from A to C, from C to B flat, etc., but the amount of time the singer stays on one note, and the length of the pauses, is left largely to his own choice or to the discretion of the modern editor (within reasonable limits).

Tinayre in the forthcoming B.B.C. programme announces one very early song, but it is not a highbrow composition. "La Regine Avrillouse" is a dance tune, and I see no reason to suppose the "chorus" was sung other than in round.

Out of these dance tunes came the grace of European civilisation right up to Botticelli. That may seem like a fairly strong statement, but our editor would not thank me for a four-hundred-page digression into theology and the life of Scotus Erigena. A very lively mind, namely, Leo Frobenius, fed up with the term culture and/or Kultur has dug up a polysyllabic horror which he spells *paideuma*, implying a tangle of ideas, mental habits, predispositions which make the mind of an era.

Let us say that mediæval thought (or *paideuma*) was at its best in an endeavour to find the *precise word* for each of its ideas, and that this love of exactitude created some very fine architecture, and that when it got into song (or, if you like, when it came out of song) it produced a very exact fitting of the melody to the shape of the words. I don't mean just the general flop or wobble of the emotion of a given poem. I mean that the music definitely fitted the consonants and vowels, and in particular it fitted the vowel sequence that stands in the words. Some of the most beautiful single lines of melody known to Europe are to be found in the troubadour canzos.

It is open to question whether mastery of longer melodic sequence developed in Italy after the wreck of Provence in the crusade against the Albigeois. I think it probably did. But there is at least a century's gap in the records. We know that the form of the strophe developed. We can guess that the melodic sequence of 8 to 14 lines "developed," but when the record is again available something has perished. The word and the tune are no longer cut and welded into a unity. "Fol der ol der ol" sings the chorus. "Hey, nonny, nonny" sings Wm. Shakespeare's player. "La Regine Avrillouse" is a dance tune with a chorus, but "A la vi, a la vi, jaloux" means: "Get out, you blithering cuckold." And in the songs of Arnaut and Faidit and in all the contemporary criticism or appreciation of twelfth-century song writers we find *continual* allusion to the tune fitting the word; the word, the tune.

This comes up again in England in the song setting of Lawes and of Campion. But they constantly show irritation at their having to work against the general current.

You can read in almost any history of poetry or music that when the canzone was taken into Italy, the highbrow poets began writing philosophic poems, notably or flagrantly Dante (preceded by Guido Cavalcanti, and Guido Guinicello) and that almost nobody could understand these poems when or if sung. Dante indeed has left very long prose explanations of what he was driving at in certain canzoni.

There must have been a contemporary musical development. The musicians got tired of fitting music to incomprehensible words, and what had been the accompaniment to the canzone "developed into the sonata."

It is impossible to explain this clearly and in detail on half a page. But anyone who has tried to write a canzone according to either the "rules," or rather the specifications of Provence, A.D. 1200 or Italy 1290 or 1310 will be able to identify the corresponding elements in a sonata by Mozart or Ph. Em. Bach. And in like manner any graduate of even the worst musical conservatory should be able to pick out the elements which form the verse structure of "Donna mi Prega," or "Voi ch' intendendo."

But thematic invention declines when the divorce of word and music has persisted too long. I wonder if this statement is due to literary vanity.

Your dyed in the wool musician may turn up his nose at French café chanson. And yet it is the *caf' conc'* that has kept the mediæval tradition, wherein the words of a song matter enormously. Your music hall has at least kept the faith that one or two lines of a popular song must sing themselves, and they "sing themselves" because the tune fits the words like the best possible glove. That is the lesson that Yves Tinayre started teaching the London public back in 1918. And that is at least one reason why the B.B.C. is to be congratulated on having him for soloist in a broadcast. However few or many French mediæval, Italian and French renaissance songs he gives you, you have twenty years' consistent work on his part behind them.

When I say that music both declined and developed after 1290, this must not be taken to mean that it utterly flopped all at once, or that it grew suddenly and marvellously complex overnight. The work of the troubadours reappeared (or at least we, mulling over stuff in the libraries, refined it) in Janequin; but the words and the tune are not all made into one perfect fabric. The tune has learned from what the words, centuries earlier, had taught the music. And when you begin your programme with Purcell you should not take it for granted that he is the father of English music. Before Purcell was Dowland. And if any man wish to understand the history of music, specifically of the sonata form as a means of communicating the composers' intelligence to the players, he must, if not hear, at least read William Young's music. If I seem to drag this sentence in "out of the blue" it is not wholly irrelevant. Mediæval music was made for lovers of poetry, that is for lovers of a meaning. There is a certain analogy in Young's music in that it was, I believe, made more for understanders of music, and actual players of music, than for people who merely go to a concert to be lulled. I have a firm conviction that music gets blobby, obnubilated, gross when people give up understanding it.

On a number of occasions throughout the 1930s Pound attended the Salzburg Festival. In August 1936 he was there and heard Toscanini conduct *Falstaff* and *Fidelio,* and Bruno Walter in a Mozart concert. Since he wrote about these events in *Polite Essays* the following year, it might be useful to give program details of at least the Mozart concert, which he so heartily disliked. Zino Francescatti was the soloist and the concert included the Divertimento in B-flat major (K. 287), the Concerto for Violin in G major (K. 216), and the Symphony in G minor (K. 550). It needs to be added that the fashionable Mozart orchestra of these years would have been considerably more corpulent, and the style possibly more lethargic, than what we should prefer today. In any case Pound's metaphor for Bruno Walter's Mozart is unforgettable.

Nor did he care much for Beethoven's *Fidelio*. James Laughlin, who accompanied him and Miss Rudge to the performance, recalled an unbuttoned incident: "... at one interval Pound sang out, 'What can you expect from a man who had syphilis.' There was a buzz of disapproval from the audience some of whom apparently thought he was referring to Toscanini."[88]

---

[88] As recalled in Noel Stock's *The Life of Ezra Pound*, p. 332.

CIVILIZATION[89]

I

Honesty of the word does not permit dishonesty of the matter.

If in my early criticism I showed a just contempt for the falsity of writers who would not face technical problems, that cannot pass, for much longer, as indifference to *ethos* or to values of any kind. An artist's technique is test of his personal validity. Honesty of the word is the writer's first aim, for without it he can communicate nothing efficiently. His best velleity may be of no more avail than that of blurred men howling for peace, while abetting the murderers and mass starvers.

Orthology is a discipline both of *morale* and of morals.

II

Civilization begins when people start preferring a little done right to a great deal done wrong, as for example to Molinari's conducting, or that sort of thing in Salzburg to which brother Sheean objects. The aesthetic pleasure of hearing Bruno Walter play Mozart is about what one would derive from seeing a bust of Mozart carved in a sausage.

There is another pest, old music re-done for large orchestra: a miniature splodged out as a mural. At least we have had in our village, Rapallo, authentic presentations which gave one a basis for contemplating the composer. In parvo, what Toscanini does in the grand way. To hear Toscanini give Falstaff or Fidelio is part however of education. To hear any other man conduct these operas would probably be intolerable. They are both highly unsatisfactory to anyone with aural discretion of an high order. They are both, if authentically presented, essential parts of the education of anyone who wants to understand the history of OPERA as a form. The beastly Beethoven contributed to the development of the opera.

Let us by all means know it. Let us have the perfect rendering which leaves Ludwig no possible alibi. It is NOT a pleasant way of passing an evening but it is immeasurably instructive. It shows what poor Ludwig suffered.

Ditto Falstaff? No. NOT ditto. Falstaff is vindication of all Verdi's objections to Wagner. It is vindication of all Verdi's drive toward making a unity out of that heteroclite chaos of stage, orchestra, and caterwauling. Everything in it fits and belongs. In needs Toscanini, BUT it is second rate music. Not third rate. Given these two axes of reference

[89] From *Polite Essays*, pp. 193-95.

one can be all the more justly severe on the inexcusable defects of nineteenth-century opera.

For the tenth time of saying it, the nauseous idiocy of composers is beyond anything a man can imagine until he himself has had a try at composing. The grossness of mind, the unending missing of continual opportunities is enough to produce black misanthropy.

Turning to Dr. Whittaker's edition of William Young and his prefaces, we revive. Botticelli's "Zephyrus" placates our parched audition. Young wrote for performers who were not virtuosi, but musicians capable of reading (that is of understanding) the musical line set before them.

Whittaker has blown the tags off the "history" of the sonata. Dry datum, that, for the philologist. But he has also educed music for the auditor of discretion. Young says something in every few bars.

At the risk of thumping the pulpit, I reassert this distinction between art made for USE—that is painting to have painted into the plaster and stay while one lives there—and painting to stick in an exhibition to catch the eye of the passing possible buyer or vendor; music for who can play it and distinct from music made for the least common, and most vulgar, denominator of the herd in the largest possible hall. Having heard the original Janequin sung badly, I am inclined to wonder whether any chorus was ever sufficiently perfect in execution to give the intervals with the clarity of the fiddle, or if F. da Milano's lute could have rendered them as effectively. There is no valid reason for idolatry or antiquolatry. There is no reason why the re-creation of beauty should fall always below the original. The supposition that it does is half the time but fruit of a complex of inferiority in the sterile.

The Venice Biennale had long been a renowned exposition for contemporary art when, in 1930, it also became a music festival, specializing in contemporary music. Pound had visited the Biennale in 1934 and had been profoundly impressed by Stravinsky's *Capriccio*, a new piece, which the composer himself had conducted with his son at the keyboard.

In September, 1936, Pound returned to the Biennale where he heard several more important pieces of music, recently composed: Berg's *Lyric Suite* for string quartet; Alfredo Casella's *Sinfonia, Arioso and Toccata* for piano and orchestra, receiving its world première; Honegger's second string quartet, also a world première; Hindemith's *Schwanendreher*, a viola concerto based on folk material; and Bartók's fifth string quartet. He was unimpressed by the *Lyric Suite;* its sinuous expressionism was bound not to please him; but he was most enthusiastic about Hindemith's composition, which had been played by the composer himself. Hindemith, we should remember, was one of the great violists of his time.[90] Pound wrote to Gerhart Münch to get him to invite Hindemith to perform in Rapallo.

> Dear Gerhart: Do you know Hindemith well enough to be able to find out what is the minimum he wd. take to give an all Hindemith program here with you (or with you and Olga, if there is a trio)?
> I hear he is coming for the Florentine Maggio musicale so he wd. be passing near here . . .
> I think the New Hungarian Quartet is fixed to come. As I wrote they and Hindemith highlight in Venice Biennale, with the Gertlers whom we had here two years ago. That item in case he wd. feel he was [not] in good company apart from you.[91]

The firm pleasures of Casella's triptych also appealed to Pound, but he was much more profoundly impressed by Bartók's quartet, which he was afterward often to say he felt resembled his *Cantos* in the sense that it was the record of a struggle, a revolt against the entanglements of a civilization in decay. Bartók's fifth quartet had just been completed a year earlier and had been premièred by the Kolisch Quartet in Washington. The New Hungarian Quartet had given the first European performance in 1936 at the ISCM Festival in Barcelona and had brought it from there to Venice. It is the largest of Bartók's quartets. The first and fifth movements are related; so are the second and fourth. By comparison with the fourth quartet, which Pound also knew, it is both more expansive in gesture and a good deal looser in form. It would not be wise to push its relationship to Pound's *Cantos* any further than Pound himself did, but perhaps there are stylistic features suggesting affinity; at least Pound sensed an affinity during the several times he listened to it.

As soon as he heard it Pound wanted to secure the work, and the New Hungarian group, for Rapallo. From Venice he wrote to Tibor Serly:

> Dear TTT-borrrRRR: Yer damn right, them New Hungs *can* play the fourtett. I like Palotai vurry much. He can't say much

[90] There is a recording of Hindemith playing *Der Schwanendreher* on 78s with the Fiedler Sinfonietta on H. M. V., 6028/30; also issued in the U.S.A. by Victor, 15922/4.
[91] Paige, *Letters*, New York, pp. 284–85; London, p. 374.

and we have only my limping German. I wd. damn well like to have 'em in Rapallo. In fact am determined to go on with the Rapal. concerts, despite fact that I have no assets save what I can earn. And haven't yet sold the stuff I proposed to shove into 'em.

Pal. sez they wd. be passing thru Italy in Feb. You spose they wd. come for 500 lire and a night's lodging? I can't *tell* 'em the Gertlers did and would again. I don't honestly know which 4tet is the better. Palotai a better cello than Gertler has, I think. Eh bo? Both of the quarts played here last week. Hung. in Ferroud and Bartok Vth. Gertler in Honegger and Berg.

And say bo!! can yr. li'l friend Hindemith play the VI-olahhh?! I'll say he can *play* the viola.

Yunnerstand I can't even *offer* the 500 lire yet. All I can do is to ask you to write Pal in Magyr and ask if they wd. be insulted by the suggestion. I told him I wd. like to have 'em. The date wd. be at their convenience.

What I am doing now is to put together a project on which I might by a miracle raise the minimum necessary cash.

Onforchoonate incident. The Hungs wanted to *eat* at midnight. I have known Venice 30 years but never tried to eat a dinner at midnight. I know that all the good cheap restaurants, the family cookings, etc., close at about 9.55. Am afraid I got 'em stuck with some bad grub, but it was the only place I cd. count on being open. Not having any common langwidge, will you tender my tough apologies and hope they fergiv and ferget. The violer player yenned toward another place, where I thought they wd. git stuck a price. Mebbe they wdn't have been stuck but it is a place on the Piazza where I thought it wuz dangerous for working men like ourselves to risk a bill.[92]

MOSTLY QUARTETS[93]

Few critics have, I believe, succeeded in communicating any musical wisdom to their public save on the basis of actual performances, whereto they have listened not merely with that charmed passivity permitted the dilletante listener, but with at least the double personality of enjoyer and examiner.

In the wings of the Venetian Biennial, Vilmos Palotai, whom the B.B.C. listeners enjoyed last year (he is the rich-toned cellist of the

---

[92] Paige, *Letters*, New York, p. 282; London, pp. 372-73.
[93] *The Listener*, October 14, 1936, pp. 743-44.

New Hungarian Quartet), said to me: "There is so much good new stuff that we don't know what to take next."

Obviously something has happened and is happening in today's composition. Fifteen years ago England's best conductor had torn up all his own work. Music was at a dead end, at least in the opinion of most of the more highly sensitised performers.

Cocteau wrote of the stick of barley sugar, the longer you suck it the sharper the point, but, alas! the child's stick of candy gets shorter, woefully, woefully shorter. Thus M. Jean Cocteau teaching the French by parable the danger of art for the few, fewer, fewest and finally for no one whomsoever.

Some of Hindemith's songs seem to belong to that cycle. The solidest and best critical analysis I have ever read, Boris de Schloezer's *Stravinsky*, takes an analogous line. That book is a marvellous piece of perceptive writing. It is a marvellous logical construction. It is one of the few critical works that has an existence of its own that would remain to it even if all Stravinsky's work disappeared. It is indeed so beautifully constructed in itself that a cynic might claim that it doesn't much matter whether it has any relation to Stravinsky and his work whatsoever. As reading matter I found it delightful. I wish I knew as much about music as does M. de Schloezer, but I do not propose to give up my own little corner, and, as critic, that corner consists in a large block of ignorance of everything save what specific compositions sound like, when played by particular players.

From that savage state of untrammelled nature I move to a platonic belief in the compositions themselves, based on the performers' manifest competence in relating their presentation of them, first, to the total idea of the author, and, secondly, to the co-ordinated details (relatively or totally unimpeded by technical difficulties of execution).

I trust the auditors of the B.B.C. will be able to confirm my impressions gleaned at a comparatively new institution (the Venice Biennial of Music) which has this year grown up to maturity, and can, I trust, henceforth serve as grazing ground or laboratory for first or early auditions of new work from the expanse of which one will be able to predict future broadcasts.

Contemporary composition has suffered two severe losses, Alban Berg at the age of 50 and Pierre Octave Ferroud, born in 1900, snuffed out in an auto accident near Budapest the day before Palotai and his friends were to meet him.[94]

---

[94] Pierre Octave Ferroud (1900–36), French conductor, also critic and composer, principally of ballet music; by no means as significant a figure in contemporary music as Alban Berg, who had died in 1935.

Ferroud's Quartet in C is pleasant music. It is neither classic nor neoclassic nor unconventional. As Symons said in speaking of Whistler, the artist is happy when he neither tries to follow a model nor to avoid one. The basic principle of counterpoint, as distinct from any set of niggling "rules," is that a number of melodic lines carry on and, by carrying on, interact.

It was Sauzay, I think, who spoke of Bach operating according to a series of "procedures whereof the secret escapes us."[95] In which statement I believe there is a fundamental error implied. I do not believe that Bach used a "series of procedures" at all. I think he had a direct perception of the added interest that came into music when two or more melodic lines interact.

Ferroud with four instruments has given four parts and, as there are three kinds of instrument in the quartet, the qualities of fiddle, 'cello and viola are kept distinct. Of course, you have to have executants who know this either by mind or by feel.

I have just heard three very different kinds of contemporary quartet. And it is hard to say whether Ferroud is more different from Bartók than is Bartók from Honegger.

Few of us have heard enough Bartók, that is to say, enough of the Bartók of the past six or eight years, to speak with any final authority. Even in his Fourth Quartet, with its telling pizzicati, one feels (or at least I felt) that Bartók was still sincere but uncertain. You can't get the maximum enjoyment even from an admirable and ingenious work if you, from time to time, feel that the composer is worried. Bartók has always been human, but even up to the Fourth Quartet, he seemed to me worried for fear his listeners should be bored.

I should be prepared to state that Bartók's years of daring experiment in magyarism have, in the Fifth Quartet, brought him to maturity. Here is a work in his own idiom, consistently in his own idiom, built up into a complete and coherent structure. It is like no other known quartet. It definitely adds to the literature or whatever we are to call articulate repertory of work written for four stringed instruments. It projects from the preceding borders and frontiers of quartet composition, and is highly satisfactory in so doing. That means to say it is in a very different category from Ferroud's which adds nothing to our concept of the string quartet and total possibilities of it, but is simply an excellent piece of work inside the known frontiers, a good thing of its kind, which is a known kind.

The Honegger can only be located in relation to the Bartók when one shall have heard both alternatively several times. The Honegger

[95] See note 15, p. 254.

Second String Quartet in A minor, was given publicly for the first time on September 12 of this year by the Gertlers, to whom it had been ceded by the Pro Arte of the Belgian Court.

Like Bartók's Fifth it launches into the unknown, but into a doubly remote unknown. Bartók's work is emotionally known. That is not a condemnation. It is warm with humanity. The only people who will object to it are people who suffer from a musical training, that is the kind of musical training which stiffens peoples' mentality, blunts their perceptions and knocks their critical sense into splinters, because they are always looking for something which they think ought to be in a new composition. They get half their pleasure or whatever they do get, from scolding composers because the whatever-they-are-looking-for isn't there.

Honegger is as Swiss as Bartók is Hungarian. He is a thousand miles nearer Paris. Whether he admires Tchelitchew's paintings I don't know. But everything that the surrealists in ignorance discovered, but might have taken from mediæval Flemish mystics, is common both to surrealist airiness and to this piece of Honegger's music.

The incongruities, the distasteful detail, which these so very, very annoyed young men hurl into painting, and then carry into the ultimate beauties of colour and of line composition, is present in Honegger's A minor Quartet. Not a fuzzy moonbeam, but a razor-edged moonbeam. Not necessarily a bull's legs on a duck, but an aerial mermaid three parts carburetter, with tentacles of an octopus, resolved in pale blue, ash pink and steel platinum.

Probably Honegger and Hindemith can hear this quartet of the former and know from second to second that the "chord of the 17th," or it may, for all I know, be the 47th, is about to resolve into do, mi, sol, by some stellar hat trick.

To the uninitiate I think there will come simply the feeling of cleansing acid, call it cacophony which wakes the hearer or washes his inner ear—possibly scrapes it, so that there is a bit of sensitive nerve ready for the next exquisite set of whispers.

The Crime Club and Edgar Wallace have both and all told us that long fingered Tommy scrapes the skin off his finger tips when he is going to burgle a combination safe.[96] This may be pure fairy tale. But every child of seven in our sophisticated world now believes that such sensitive fingers can tell when the tumblers are falling into place.

Whether it's true or not, it serves as analogy for the function of sharp scraping sounds in this quartet, and in modern music.

The good old hymn tune chords bump on an insensitive callus. The

---

[96] Reading Edgar Wallace crime stories was a pastime shared by both Pound and his wife, particularly during the Rapallo years.

laws of Pythagoras go further than the relations of 2 to 3, 3 to 4, and such simple arithmetic. Honegger has constructed an astrological marvel, he has sent his imagination up past the Gordon-Bennett Cup racers into the high thin air over the breathable air and earned at least more gratitudes than mine in the process.

Alban Berg is regretted. It would be unfair to compare three movements of his Lyric Suite to a solid quartet composition. There are, as they say, moments. I cannot write without conviction. My only conviction about Berg is that Endré Gertler and Pierre de Groote certainly know more about his music than I do, and they believe in these three movements which they find very beautiful.

At any rate, music 1936 is active and various. Berg is nearer to Bartók. You can measure the music geographically. It seems to me a bit weak to call a man "the most talented of Schönberg's epigons," but I suppose it is meant for a compliment.

Budapest, Vienna, Paris! and to measure them you have got to listen to Hindemith. Or put it another way, the richness and abundance of music in 1936 is infinitely greater than it was in the 1920's, when most of us could deeply admire no one save Igor Stravinsky (though a handful, including myself, enjoyed Antheil, whose work from 1922 to '26 still deserves more attention than has been given it).

In Hindemith's own field no one can touch him. I haven't a quartet in my mind to illustrate this point. His Viola Concerto (Der Schwanendreher) was finished last October (*i.e.*, 1935). I wonder has any man ever heard a composition which so grows like a tree in absolute evolution from the lead throughout all of its details?

I heard Hindemith play it. A composer has divine and human right to the best possible execution of his own work. Music that is nothing but music or at least that exists independent of any concurrent arts; that draws the auditor's mind not out of itself toward some further objective, but keeps it concentrated on the actual sound being presented to it! In this kind of music, no one, and least of all his greatest contemporary and our lasting delight Igor Stravinsky, competes with Hindemith. From the viola lead grow all the sounds of the orchestra. My emphasis is on the verb grow.

You hear of instruments following each other. You have the fugue tradition, by name and definition a flight, implying a chase. You have bales of writing about music wherein every page contains some allusion to construction. For the "Schwanendreher" this terminology is inept.

Conscious or unconscious, the composer is impregnated with the sense of growth, cellular, as in the natural kingdoms. From the initial cells of the root-heart out to the utmost leaf of the foliage, in this case the harp notes, the "Schwanendreher" is natural in its liveliness. That dominant fact is worth more than any fragment of it, and if the critic be worth his salt he will want to convey that main fact, above all else, however much he admires specific minor events in the workmanship, as for example the acceptable use of the harp, which is the last instrument other composers ever use with efficiency. There is authentic gaiety in the active movement before the finale. We have had so much spurious gaiety that this robust outbreak is notable, though it is a minor facet in relation to the totality of the work.

MUSIC AND BRAINS[97]

Title chosen in hope of avoiding the usual discussion of music and morals. If the radio has added a few unending and unendable controversies to the problems of music it has terminated none of those that existed in 1850.

When I complain that hundreds of people will discuss painting with a wealth of, often dry, detail, for one who knows the difference between the qualities and characteristics of quite well known seventeenth century composers, I am told: "Oh! yes, but now with the radio they are giving historical programmes."

Which does not in the least affect my main contention.

With or without the B.B.C., performers like Gerhart Münch will demand rigid adherence to the printed or manuscript music before them. And performers like Luigi Franchetti will say more than they mean by insisting that positively any composition played by a great performer is pleasanter to listen to than a masterpiece played by any one else.

The answer to Franchetti is that when Ysaye played a bad piece of music he played a great deal that the composer never thought of. Sarah Bernhardt made similar use of second rate and sixteenth rate plays. I have heard Yeats read poems that had no rhythm of their own, poems that had no more metric force and validity than you can find in a mashed potato, and by imposing a rhythm of his own on the formless verbiage, give it a transient and passing life.

Painting does not have to be remade for every observer. Music has to be remade. A play has to be remade in so far as it is a stage play and not reading matter.

If my criticism of music has ever had value enough to cover printing expenses it has been due to my objectivity. I have wanted to know what

---

[97] *The Listener*, December 3, 1936, p. 106.

the performers actually do on the platform (or, still better, in private when they don't know one is listening).

Of the two types exemplified in Münch and Franchetti, Münch plays best when annoyed. A loose cuff link will put unforeseen energy into a Bach toccata. Münch gets his major effects, as one of the younger *Sunday Times* critics wrote recently of Toscanini, by the cumulative effect of an exact time measure maintained perfect for a longer period than temperamental and moody performers think of attempting.

Franchetti is pleasant to listen to even when doing music that would normally drive me from a concert hall, but the very delicacy and attention given to details creates its own peril. One doesn't know what has been played. One enjoys it while it is going on. That's all right. One does not listen to music as punishment.

And yet one doesn't play tennis for punishment. One doesn't indulge in the vigorous discipline of athletics as punishment.

There are two perfectly distinct and legitimate modes of listening. A tired man has the right to be soothed. He has his right to gentle oblivion. But the active man has also his right to lay up treasures in memory; to hang the walls of his mind with musical masterwork just as he would hang the walls of his visual memory with pictures by Velasquez and Pier della Francesca.

Quite good natured friends complain that I do jump about so. A carpenter has to jump about a little when he puts four legs into the making of a table. What I have just written doesn't lead to what I am just about to put down. But writing the two things in the same article doesn't necessarily mean that I have lost control of my wits.

A considerable liveliness was infused into contemporary poetry along about 1908, 1912, 1915 not by the introduction or reintroduction of any one or two technical changes or technical exacerbations or stringencies, but because several men, often with very different intentions, thought that poetry should once again become a medium for communication between intelligent men. If poetry needed that regeneration what will the gentle reader say about the conditions of music, if he can be got to say anything?

On the one hand we have composers who write only for specialists and on the other hand we have a plethora of performers turned out yearly from hundreds of conservatories in the most abysmal ignorance and unculture. A cry for better programmes may even bring its own punishment. I have heard the most sublime compositions used as a medium for presenting the most abject and hair-oiled vulgarity.

You can't get a four-inch bullet out of a two-inch gun. If the performer is absolutely incapable of feeling Pergolesi or Mozart, one is merely infuriated by a technical display based on a falsification of the composer's meaning.

And when I say meaning I am on the edge of using that most dangerous of all words, that is, "soul," anima, courage.

The term "courage" might better be used; the heroism of a composer to assert a greater fineness, and greater perfection than humanity can in its daily life come to! That is, after all, the sense of great music: that Bach can exclude the boiled cabbage, that Mozart can forget the unpaid tailor's bill and assert a perfection of order above all human attainment in any material manifestation; that is a meaning.

"Without character," says Confucious, "you will be unable to play on that instrument or to execute the music fit for the odes."

The treasure of music from Faidit's time (A.D. 1200) up to Chopin will not be unlocked until musical education has in it at least the romance of a current film, "Casta Diva."

If the prizes of the conservatories and the whole working of the conservatories go to producing monkeys who can do clever stunts with a bow or a keyboard we will not unlock the older and finer music, and the first prizes will continue to end up in restaurants as in their true spiritual fatherland. There are material conditions. There are overworked performers. There are people who don't realise the horrors of an eight-hour day for musicians, but back before that there are remediable defects of curricula.

Heaven knows the amateur can be pestilential, but so can the trained musician who is trained in nothing but solfege and fingering. You don't need to drive your players through a course in philology, but a moderate and brief introduction to at least the fact that poetry has existed, that literature has existed, that a cultural heritage has existed, could be introduced into musical education, with, I think, gain both to players and hearers.

MUSIC IN CA' REZZONICO[98]

Italy's greatest and least appreciated press agent was the late Robert Browning. Admiring, as I do, many Italian events, I cannot praise their unconsciousness at this point. People have dropped violets on Keats' gravestone, and gone on about Shelley's inability to float in the gulf of Spezia and Signor Edmondo Dodsworth has translated Blake, and Mr. Ruskin's maunderings are in a Tauchnitz edition in many shop windows, but the man who found Italy for our time and our parents'

---

[98] *The Delphian Quarterly,* January, 1937, pp. 2–4, 11.

and grandparents' time has left little indentation in the Italian mind. This is all the worse in that he is, I presume, responsible far more than Ruskin for a change from bad taste to good taste, an awakening to Early Italian painting as opposed to the post Renaissance fuzziness. Yet the pilgrims who come yearly from Waco on the Browning tour know more of Italy before they leave Texas, than do the Italians of Browning.[99] There is an eight foot square tablet on the side wall of a palace saying:

ROBERT BROWNING
Etc., Etc.

Whether that palace was a bargain, whether Browning lived sketchily in one corner, or whether Elizabeth Barrett's mahogany furniture filled the vast expanses of the Rezzonico I have no immediate means of ascertaining. "*Ca'*" (pronounced, Kah Ret-zon-eécko) is Venetian for Casa, House. And is used for a big House, a House, as it were, with a capital H.

The Rezzonico Palace is too big for comfort; it is big enough to contain a huge concert room, decorated during the wrong state of Venetian wall painting but at any rate grandiose and by association a fit place for international festivals.

One can assume Browning's benediction of the performance of Baldassare Donato's music (dated 1550); of that of Giovanni Croce who was called il Chiozzotto and who lived at the other end of the lagoon from 1557 till 1609; of Lotti, Vivaldi, Monteverdi, and Benedetto Marcello under his roof.

The news in this item is that the Venetian Musical Festival has established itself, on its fourth round, on a plane infinitely higher than the boring and ill-advised picture shows that occur here in alternate years.

Back before the war Alfredo Casella started educating the Roman, and thence the Italian, public in modern music. At once the most competent of living Italian composers, an unrivaled teacher, an impeccable orchestral conductor and that far rarer thing a creative musician with a wide interest in other men's work and utter impartiality in judging it, Casella gave, first for a handful of Romans, the best modern compositions. I take it that whether his name appears on committees or not, he has been pacemaker for musical performance in Italy.

Italians who go to picture shows have had no such initiator, with the result that an American traveler can learn more of present day painting by spending half an hour in any one of a dozen Parisian art shops than he can by dreary hours, a dozen years running, in the allegedly "International" Expositions in the Public Gardens of Venice.

---

[99] Browning died in Venice in 1889, having made his home in Italy for many years.

Not so with Music. Among a dozen experiences worth keeping in memory, and that one couldn't, if one would, efface, was that of hearing Stravinsky lead an orchestra here two years ago, in his own *Capriccio* with most efficient aid from the pianist, his son. That goes into the reference shelf along with some Russian exiles singing unpaid. I once heard the Ukraine choir, and that was below the exiled regiment, and I once heard Debussy insuperably leading a chorus in Paris in his Charles d'Orléans songs, and I heard the first performance of *San Sébastien* in Paris, and the *Sacre,* which is again Stravinsky, when it was new in London and people still disliked it out loud.

Scandal, in 1934, *said* that Stravinsky only got in at the last moment because Ravel had influenza. I don't care how he got here. Having once heard such music in the Venetian *Biennale* I would cheerfully chance the price of my rail fare, though I would have been here this month in any case. The show two years ago, apart from Stravinsky was mainly an amateur mess, though a horde of celebrities put in an appearance. This year it has been done with less money and a vastly greater intelligence. I couldn't, as they say, have arranged it better myself. If Maestro Lualdi[100] is responsible, he has my compliments and my respect. He and/or the committee took a bold line in letting in young composers and managed it without making the public suffer *too much*. But they also established the maximum level of achievement. Antonio Guarnieri is an outstanding conductor. He can carry a cantankerous and over critical listener like myself not only through certain classics wherewith I don't greatly sympathize but through modern works which I dislike. I don't mean that I object to classics as such or dislike moderns, I mean that I prefer some of each to some others. Guarnieri is a conductor who gives you a new light, or at any rate who gives you a more thorough knowledge of the works he presents. I will never henceforth willingly miss one of his performances when I have a critic's seat or the price of a ticket. The presence of Casella both as executant and composer gives proof of the level of performance intended by the committee. First performances of his vigorous piano *Sinfonia* and of Honegger's string quartette in A minor, the first Italian performance of Ferroud's Quartet in C, Bartok's Fifth Quartet and Hindemith's viola concerto *Der Schwanendreher* (which he finished in October, 1935) proved the show was up to date. There were other novelties less notable. But as a feat of program engineering the festival was as a whole superlatively efficient. It gave enough old music to enable the auditors to measure the innovations, as to their relative qualities; to see what had gone out of music by reason of changing taste and what had gone out because it was worn

---

[100] Founder of the Venice music festival, in 1930.

out. That is to say because it had been said so often, and in so many ways that there was nothing new to be done with it.

If I am telling Delphians what to get, what to apply to New York agents for, when asking for concerts I can say: get the New Hungarian Four (Sandor Vegh, László Halmos, Denes Koromzay, and Palotai; the latter is the kind of cellist whose tone is usually kept for concertos, it sounds from the wood).

Get the Gertlers (Endré Gertler, Pierre de Groot, László Revesz, Marcel Lounon). They also started in Budapest but are now centered in Brussels. Get both these fours as often as possible, then maybe you'll be able to tell which is the better. I don't know. I haven't heard them play the same music, though I have heard both play Bartok. Bartok's Fifth quartet is something new. It is far ahead of his Fourth one.

And GET with a capital G., g, e, t, GET Hindemith. Anyone who hasn't heard Hindemith play his own *Schwanendreher* has something to learn: about orchestration, about viola playing and about modern composition. I mean modern composition that can stand up to any work of the past asking no favors, not being in any way an imitation of any past work, but having its own, 1935, organization, as perfect as the organization of wood fibres is in a tree trunk.

That performance ended the Festival. For contrast there had been Honegger's surrealism. Perhaps if one listended to that quartette of Honegger's long enough one would understand surrealist painting. The Gertlers did it impeccably. They know what it is all about. They also believe Alban Berg, and it may be, probably is, unfair to measure bits from a suite of Berg's against a total composition by Honegger or by Hindemith. Berg's death and Ferroud's would have crippled the music of many a decade less rich than the present one. Ferroud was a gentle, sensitized and skillful composer who respected the qualities of the instruments, Berg's admirers place him among the descendants of Schönberg and Schönberg's work is so little heard outside Germany and Austria that one doesn't yet know how to measure this estimate. You would probably be better advised to accept Gertler's opinion than mine on this subject. At any rate some of Berg's work interests very sensitive executants of first rank.

If I heard Stravinsky tomorrow I would probably think him alone among living composers, preeminent in a realm by himself, but having just heard Hindemith, I am convinced at least for the moment, that he, by reason of the organism of "Der Schwanendreher" stands peer to Stravinsky, as different as Bach is from Couperin. But the German mission in music is again established and valid in Hindemith, as is the French Russian function in world music by the repeated triumphs of Igor Stravinsky—Stravinsky being full of theatre, full of representative pantomime, Hindemith leaving out, you might almost say, all activity save that of sound, and its organization.

The next Venice Music Biennial is in 1938 and I can heartily advise Delphian travelers in that year to arrange their itinerary so as to have at least part of that week in Venice.

LIGURIAN VIEW OF A VENETIAN FESTIVAL[101]

Stravinsky is the only living composer who makes one feel like a dud. If this statement is purely personal and subjective, I excuse it on the ground that any real emotion is kin to mania in that it is concerned only with itself. The moment one brings in questions of relation between inside feeling and exterior fact, or tries to calculate the feeling's relation to, and distance from, other men's verity or from the material world, one enters the domain of thought, worry and intellect.

I mean, by my opening sentence, that Stravinsky's music makes me as workman in a different art want to go back to my own *métier,* overhaul my technique, and be ready to do a better job next time.

The Venetian biennial music feast hit high-water mark two years ago with a family production of "Capriccio," Igor conducting and the junior Stravinsky at the piano. For that notable pleasure I am still grateful.

This year's festival has been constructed with less expense and, I think, considerably greater cohesion and foresight. The problem before the organizers of such a contemporary review is to give a cross-section of living composers' work with enough classic or standard music to provide the auditors with axes of critical reference. That is, to enable them to think or hear how the orchestration or melodic line of to-day's writers compares with the best known music. This year's committee is to be complimented. Two years ago the programme was spotty, all ups and downs, high pleasure in the lucidity and perfect presentation of the Stravinsky and sudden exits when one could not stand vile compositions. I take it you could get a fair majority to agree that Stravinsky is the first living composer, but you would find no sort of agreement as to who is the second. You would have eight or ten or more candidates, all proposed sincerely by people who find Stravinsky inhuman or who prefer some form of musical gumminess to some other.

The ideal programme committee would also try to give as great a proportion as possible of music not being given in "regular" concerts. In one sense no contemporary festival should omit Igor Stravinsky. In Italian circumstance of 1936 the musophiles, at least, will have heard a

[101] *Music and Letters,* January, 1937, pp. 36–41.

good deal of that composer, notably in entire Stravinsky concerts in Milan, so that perhaps only a Ligurian longshoreman like myself will have missed Stravinsky's inclusion in the Venice pageant.

An orchestral programme in the Piazza San Marco taxes any man's critical ingenuity. It is somewhere between a show in an opera house and a show in the open. The sonority is better than that in most over-sized halls, but one has no rod ready to measure by, unless one can try to estimate the fitness of the specific works specifically for the Piazza, that is as to the volume of sound and, more vitally, the relative carrying powers of the different kinds of composition.

Antonio Guarnieri gave a beautifully articulated version of the fifth Symphony. I think there was no detail that did not receive due attention without ever usurping more than its due place in the total. Let us assert that Beethoven with large orchestra has, or can have, for the Piazza, the qualities which the best chamber music has in a small hall or salon. What Aristotle asserted for size in sculpture has a legitimate analogy for volume of sound in music. I assert also that in going from a small hall to a very large one, sonata players and small groups of instruments will find that linear music establishes itself in the larger space and sometimes even gains, whereas music constructed in what are called "patches of colour" loses when you let it loose in too large a building.

Respighi's "Fontane di Roma" stood up as orchestration for the Piazza. It is to my ear the kind of music that owes, I mean has to owe, quite as much to the conductor as to the composer. This can, in a loose sense, be said of most orchestral composition, but grant me the difference between music which the conductor can spoil only if he commit grossness, from sheer lack of sensibility, and music into which he must put a deal of positive constructive work—in some cases as much as two-thirds of the orchestral (as distinct from the thematic or linear) effects, by emphasis, by isolation, by shading—if he is to make it effective and give it reality.

As purely personal impression, which would perhaps differ among equally attentive auditors placed in different parts of the Piazza, I would say that the Richard Strauss and Wagner yielded quite charming moments, but that their instrumentation was not so uniformly effective as either the Beethoven or Respighi. In the Beethoven the violins and double basses maintained their effectiveness better than the brass. Again meaning in relation to the enclosed but unroofed space of the Piazza. Students of acoustic will remember that the "square" of San Marco is not a square and that its sides are nowhere strictly parallel.

The passionate pilgrim will wonder whether Robert Browning, inhabiting the Ca' Rezzonico, passed much of his time in the concert room. Decorations there are. Art is said to exist in other interstices of the edifice. Acoustic has been obtained by turning the chandeliers into inverted May-poles and stretching ribbons hither and yon.

Some notables insulted the players and the ghost of Ferroud by untimely entrance *en masse*. Apart from that unseemly incident the old Italian regime had throughout the festival given place to the new regime.* Illersberg led his Triestine chorus with snap and discipline:

> Viva Vinegia, Viva VIN-E-Gia
> Viva Vinegia
> In terrrr—ah e MAar.

Back of which rose a memory of Wolf-Ferrari in 1908 conducting a Bach chorale in the then Liceo Benedetto Marcello· with each lyrist in his choir attempting a passionate solo aimed at his best gal in the audience. Illersberg has established, at least for the northern border of Italy, the principle that singers in part-songs observe the duration of the notes as written (and how!). The trains leave on time.

The part-singing of that Russian regiment stranded in Souillac in 1919 was another matter. Art and especially song is in some of its more delicate manifestations the fruit of leisure; it just gets there because people like it and have no other way of passing the time. Illersberg was the performance. He got magnificent results from very ordinary personnel, which is a leader's job, and he is by no means at the end of his tether.

Casella in the only piano solo included in the festival proved that there is more to him than the calm Lhote-like constructions of his earlier work. The "Sinfonia" was vigorously presented and makes good use of the (damned) piano as mechanical instrument.[102] Any composer who can still get something out of it deserves respect.

Two of the best quartets in Europe upheld the second and fourth concerts of the series. Having heard the Gertlers in Rapallo two years ago in the first and fourth of Béla Bartók's string fours does not give

---

* The Prince of Piedmont did not enter the third concert in the middle of a composition. (Pound's note.)

[102] The *Sinfonia* was part of a triptych; the other two sections were entitled *Arioso* and *Toccata*. The composer himself wrote that it "was finished in Siena in mid-August and performed in a thoroughly satisfying manner by Ornella Puliti-Santoliquido in Venice the following month. It is apparently my most important work for the piano, not only because of its size, but above all for its musical content.... Whether by compactness of musical substance, by sentiment so in keeping with its expression, or by the form completely freed from every suggestion of the past, the triptych seems to me to mark a decisive point in my production, and a basis on which—God willing—I can build with sureness." Alfredo Casella, *Music in My Time*, trans. Spencer Norton, Norman, Oklahoma, 1955, p. 214.

one a basis wherefrom to compare them to the new Hungarian Quartet in Bartók's fifth, for the plain reason that the fifth string quartet is definitely superior to the other two.

Béla in music found himself in a mess similar to that which writers were in, back in 1905 and 1906. Somebody had to stir round, break moulds, try this, that and the other and generally get out of the slough of a partially dead and generally moribund idiom. Bartók was in the hinterland. There was abundant Magyar material, not quite as unstuck from the exploited European fields as was the Russian, or as the Russian had been forty years earlier, but still good.

Bartók spent years in grasping. The anxiety shows, to my mind, in such of his works as I had hitherto heard. They were a mixture. In the fifth quaret he has, I should say, come out on top of the rubble. I find the work whole, concrete, coherent. I think you could play it before or after or between any music you like and not damage it. It would hold its own and be different.

The Ferroud shows beautiful workmanship and sensibility. Palotai's cello carried one rich vein of sound. Koromzay's viola another, Halmos and Vegh had each a separate function. Both French and European music suffered a loss when Ferroud smashed himself and his auto in August and thereby defeated the Biennial Committee's intention to lead off the first Rezzonico concert with the work of a living and still young composer. Ferroud was thirty-six in January 1936.

Against these two ranking works the Gertlers offered Honegger's Four in C and *"tre tempi"* of Berg's "Lyric Suite." The Honegger is of extreme delicacy. His membership in "Les Six" is everywhere manifest. He is of Paris as the best of it has been in his time. Max Ernst, Miró, Salvador Dali have lived in, and created, this hyper-material world.

By comparison the Berg is sticky and aimless. But one must in justice say that three movements from a suite, however well chosen, cannot by definition stand up against a total and formed composition. Performers must perforce know more about the merits of such a work, or at least about the interest inherent in its specific details than can any auditor after hearing it once. Both Endré Gertler and Pierre de Groote are ready to go to the bat, the stake, or whatever, for Alban Berg's memory. At any rate music is active. There are, in 1936, a lot of different kinds of work being done well, even with the depletion of the creating force by Berg's death in 1935, *aetat* fifty, and Ferroud's.

Out, over and above any event of the season is Hindemith's "Schwanendreher." Here the totalitarian ideal, the corporate ideal contemporary with to-day's musical thought, whoever may ignore it, stands manifest.

As the real Marxist literature is in Flaubert, as the real literature of any "movement" is nine times out of ten done by someone who has never heard of the movement but who lives it in his domain by immediate act, by a congeries of perceptions simultaneous with those of his contemporaries, so all the force of Hindemith's decades, in whatever department human and humane, constructivity impregnates this viola Concerto.

As the plant mind or unity which can be only that kind of plant, so the mind or unity of this composition. Hindemith's music is as different from Stravinsky as Bach is from Janequin, or as Picasso's most cubist and abstract work was from Douanier Rousseau's portrait of Guillaume Apollinaire.

Music that was, in the highest and most laudible degree, representative and objective of the one subject-matter that music can properly represent, namely sound, flowered in Janequin, though it is not always present in choral performance of Janequin. Whether the casual auditor can find it from imperfect performance and whether more than a handful of people will ever hear a choral presentation fine enough, that is precise enough, to convey it, I am unable to say. Francesco da Milano presumably saw it. Gerhart Münch has written it into a violin part.

The heritage from this kind of music has been in our time Stravinsky's. But the Teutonic mission in music triumphs once again in the work of Paul Hindemith. Here is no literary admixture, no vague suggestion of pictorial art, nothing derived from non-musical plastic.

The two kinds of composition are licit. One offsets the other. Only a crank or a graduate from an educational infirmary will want to curtail either kind of creation.

You can use this new work of Hindemith (finished October '35) to measure any modern music whatever. What others have and have not, can be gauged by his musical sapience. The reason why some narrow-minded auditors refuse partial work by highly energized moderns becomes clear when Hindemith turns a light on what organism in music can be. An unsurpassable executant who can hurl his own work at an audience, impeccably, Hindemith, at forty-one is the most formidable fact in Stravinsky's era.

As for the Venetian Music Festival, it has, what the wretched Biennial of painting never has had, namely authority and a knowledge of international work. The whole series of concerts was constructed, it included the heights of contemporary mastery, and was at the same time wide open. Men under thirty had an opportunity, mostly wasted, to show promise. But there was no concert one would have missed. The innocuous interludes fall out of one's memory and I doubt if, counting from any Sunday to any other, the general auditor or the expert detector has heard more notable work in any other one place in eight days.

Mr. Coates admires Shostakovitch. Someone has called the late Berg the "most talented of Schönberg's minor descendants." May they be forgiven. Janigro and Sonzogno ought to be prohibited from playing Vivaldi, though how the public is to know it, I cannot state. Unless the auditors have already a concept of the height and delicacy of a composer's meaning, obtainable by non-performers only from some player's version, the public is completely defenceless against a blunted but pleasant-sounding and well constructed orchestral performance. Imagine that Mino da Fiesole had left a bronze portrait bust, and that some infant had gone at it with a hammer blunting the features. There would remain considerable beauty in the damaged relict.

Porrino proved that Giordano is not the worst composer in Italy. He should be the worst composer in Europe. Certain dead modes of thought ought to be buried.

In December, 1936, Pound had written Agnes Bedford, reminding her to look out for the "Ligurian View of a Venice Festival" in *Music and Letters*.

> It is the next *Music and Letters* that I am in. I think it is called Jan. issue. And the estimable editor REGRETS my deleting a line wherein I referred to GIORDANO as a garbage can. (Age, m'deah; AGE, I am getting mild and tender—I delete) . . .
> *Music and Letters* (Mr. Blom) appears to be too intelligent and 'right' (from my pt. of view) to last.
> What of other music pubctns? I am ready to *write* and have a go at building up reception of the Villon. Critical campaign for intelligence—rights of the word etc. Aiming at really putting over the Villon and Cavalcanti. But also to bring in vogue of Young, Janequin (already under weigh) etc.
> And poke into the operatic blokes (XVI etc.) who meant well— (I am yet too damn iggurant to know what they really did) . . .[103]

The reference in the last line is to the sixteenth-century Florentine *Camerata*, the group which, in trying to rediscover the relationship between music and poetry in ancient Greek drama, ended up discovering opera. Like Pound, they insisted on the primacy of the text in vocal composition, and it is interesting to note that he intended investigating them. In two reviews of 1939 and 1940 he does mention them in passing.

---

[103] Paige, *Letters*, New York, p. 285; London, p. 375.

In the spring of 1937 the Rapallo concerts took on a new life with appearances by a pianist Luigi Franchetti, the New Hungarian Quartet, and the return of Gerhart Münch.

THE ART OF LUIGI FRANCHETTI[104]
The Concert of Wednesday, February 3.

If to write a critique I temporarily abandon poetic composition or the struggle for certain totalitarian ideas which I believe are basic for the peace of Europe and for the civilization of the future, it is certainly not for the pleasure of seeing my name printed at the end of the thousandth article. I may add that this article of mine is part of the struggle which I have been waging for a quarter of a century to defend certain values in the arts and literature. Let me say at once that I am not attacking anyone's tastes. I like listening to Gigli in the Piazza San Marco in Venice singing "O sole mio"; the lady violinist participating in our concerts likes music performed *in piazza,* the trumpets of the First Fascist Band of Milan, etc. To each his own pleasures, to nobody the right of prohibiting others from what pleases them.

Consequently—to come to the point—besides the great auditoriums of the Augusteo, of Queen's Hall, or the Spielhaus in Salzburg, the small but no less valuable auditoriums also have a right to existence. Certain delicate effects in music cannot be achieved with a large collection of instruments. Maestro Piccardi used to tell me: "This music of yours, you can have it with a small group of instruments, not with a full orchestra."

Nevertheless I do attack one thing: the indifference of the maestros, of the professionals who have played everything and everywhere to the point where they have completely abandoned the inner beauty and more delicate and profound meanings of the masterpieces they perform and present. On the other hand I can declare once more that in Rapallo we have heard music of rare beauty, beauty both in composition and in execution. Münch has the rarest sense of the total structure of the great piano compositions.

Luigi Franchetti, who will be joining us, has a sensibility of his own, possesses a large knowledge of music, not only from having read it on the page but from having heard it for twenty years all over Europe and having carefully preserved it in his memory, comparing different interpretations.

Up to now we have talked about the nature of our programs, which

---

[104] *Il Mare,* January 30, 1937; translated.

has given the bass for measuring and judging various compositions. Having established this, let us tackle the question of the interpretations, which vary from connoisseur to connoisseur, even if they are all of them right, even if they throw light on different aspects of the author's mentality. The beauty of a painting by Goya is not and cannot be the beauty of a painting by Mantegna! In art it is impossible to combine all the effects in a single work.

Great success brings dangers with it. The performer who wants to triumph in the musical world at large must be robust and persistent, for this reason alone the most sensitive often collapse in mid-career. The most famous virtuosi can disappoint us because they often have to play in gigantic halls, and for these reasons listeners miss the most poignant effects. The players are not to blame; it is a trade defect. Small endeavours like those of the "Amici del Tigullio" are therefore doubly valuable.

Here we are fighting to defend and sustain a system of values losing ground in the great world of metropolitan publicity. It is impossible to preserve certain precisions and refinements and to work at the same time for monetary reward. Equally justified therefore is the interest shown for the "little laboratory study-sessions" in Rapallo by a restricted but no less important number of specialists and critics around the world from Glasgow to Tokyo.[105]   EZRA POUND

The Program

The "Amici del Tigullio" will present the first musical evening of the season on Wednesday, February 3 at 9:00 p.m., in the Town Hall of Rapallo, with the following program and performers:

    OLGA RUDGE   LUIGI FRANCHETTI

PROGRAM
MOZART: Sonata in B-flat major;
CÉSAR FRANCK: Sonata for piano and violin;
BACH: Sonata in E major.

February 18, 9:00 p.m.:

    NEW HUNGARIAN QUARTET
       in
    Bartók, Haydn, Bartók.

[105] The interest of the Scottish musician W. Gillies Whittaker has already been noted. The mention of Tokyo is probably a reference to Kitasano Katue, the Japanese poet and leader of the *Vou* group, with whom Pound was at this time in active correspondence.

THE NEW HUNGARIAN QUARTET[106]

At the Biennale of Music in Venice last fall there were three events imported from abroad which achieved notable success: Hindemith, viola soloist in his own "Schwanendreher" (viola concerto); the programs of the Gertler Quartet; and the New Hungarian Quartet. Between these last two I have no ground for comparison because I have heard the first twice (here in Rapallo in 1935 and in Venice) and the second for the first time in Venice, and never in a performance of the same work.

In his fifth composition for four strings Bartók greatly surpasses, I think, his previous work; but I must alert the reader that, having lived in Rapallo now for fourteen years, I am not in a position to offer an authoritative evaluation of Bartók's whole production.

My impression is as follows: Bartók is, I think, more or less my age,[107] and like all the artists of my generation he has lived through a period of transition, a period that differs essentially from the one that men who are today forty years old or less have experienced. Some around their fifties, who were slow at the beginning of their careers, in rare and perhaps fortunate cases have escaped the entanglements burdening our adolescence and the first years of our work.

Our first poems or music or paintings were "coagulated"; that is, they contained a mixture of elements and styles that marred their clarity. Bartók's music suffered from this defect, its articulation was not distinct. In some pieces one could feel the composer's effort to avoid irritating or boring the listener.

With the Fifth Quartet it seems to me the great Hungarian finally arrived at full mastery. The basic culture of the Magyars has always been rich, emotional, humane. It exudes the earthiness of this people.[108]

---

[106] *Il Mare,* February 13, 1937; translated.
[107] Bartók was born in 1881, Pound in 1885.
[108] Compare the following comments from *Guide to Kulchur,* written at about the same time: "Bartók's Fifth Quartet . . . is the record of a personal struggle, possible only to a man born in the 1880s. It has the defects or disadvantages of my Cantos. It has the defects and disadvantages of Beethoven's music, or of as much of Beethoven's music as I can remember. Or perhaps I shd. qualify that: the defects inherent in a record of struggle. . . It was impossible to 'marvel' at the cleverness of the performers. By contrast the Bartók was 'too interesting.' Given the fact that 'no one' cd. grasp the whole work at a first or even a second hearing, one did wonder what 'in hell' wd. occur if any other musicians attempted to play it. Koromzay says the 'Kolisch' have played it. He says they were marvellous. That makes two organizations of four men each who can deal with this new musical situation. That is no more a 'culture' than the invention of a new smelting process is 'culture.' It is, or may be, a link in a chain of causation. . . The Vth Quartet may 'go into a culture,' as gold dust may go into a coin." (*Guide to Kulchur,* pp. 134–36.)

Next Thursday, February 18, we will have the opportunity of comparing here in Rapallo—a previous work by Bartók (the Second Quartet) with the last one, as executed by our four friends: Vegh, Halmos, Koromzay (viola), Palotai (cello) who were a great success in Venice (witness this writer) and in many other cities as reported by the critics of the papers in Barcelona, London, Amsterdam, Zürich, Prague, Vienna, Budapest, etc.

The critic of *Ultima Hora* in Barcelona calls this quartet "the best of any we have heard." In Buda the *Nepszava* remarks that "their phrasing and their tone are equally perfect"; *Pesti Hirlap* says that we must consider the "first" performance of Bartók's new creation given by the New Hungarian Quartet as "a memorable date in the history of music."

It may be that this is only chauvinism; but beyond the Hungarian frontier the *Wiener Zeitung* gives further evidence for the N. H. Q., stating it "can compete with the best of our time." In Strasbourg the *Journal d'Alsace* finds "these Hungarians imbued with their mission."

Let us introduce them: Vegh is a disciple of Hubay; Halmos of Waldbauer; Koromzay of Hubay; and Palotai belongs to the school of Schiffer and Becker. Moreover, he has been the first cellist of the Bremen Philharmonic and later a professor in Prague, and he has travelled all over Europe as a soloist before joining the New Quartet.

Between the second and the fifth quartets of Bartók, Haydn's classical composition will bring us an aura of other times and other customs.[109]

Unquestionably it will be an exceptional evening for Rapallo—this Thursday, February 18, at 9:00 p.m. in the Town Hall, when the New Hungarian Quartet will stop here on their way from Lyons to Naples, where they will perform on February 20.

Program[110]

Town Hall of Rapallo—Thursday, February 18, 9:00 p.m.

BARTOK: Quartet II, op. 17—Moderato, allegro molto capriccioso, lento.

---

[109] Compare: "... a Haydn quartette can be ... advantageously sandwiched between two Bartóks as to serve as perfect segment (engine-cooler or whatever) in a concert. (*Op. cit.*, p. 183.)

[110] Actually two programs were given in Rapallo and the dates turned out to be March 4 and 5. The Bartók/Haydn program was to be the second. The first was simply announced as "Mozart-Boccherini, and composers of today." It may be that Pound had these reversed in order to give Bartók first position, for in *Guide to Kulchur*, referring to the Boccherini concert, he gives the date as March 5, and tells us that Boccherini's Quartet Opus 18, No. 5, was performed. By comparison with Bartók's fifth he found it "utterly beautiful. No trace of

HAYDN: Quartet in G minor op. 20, No. 3—Allegro con spirito, minuetto, poco adagio, finale.

BARTOK: Quartet V—Allegro, adagio molto, scherzo alla bulgarese, andante, finale.

We offer our congratulations to the composer Tibor Serly, who was with us in the year XIV,[111] for the success of his Symphony, performed by the Philadelphia Orchestra in Philadelphia on January 19, and in New York on January 26 with the full approval of the competent critics.

THE RETURN OF GERHART MÜNCH[112]
Rudge-Münch Concerts
March 18 & 19—April 1

We expected a reasonably large public. It was bitterly disappointing. It was almost as if the idea of a better and nobler culture was hateful. But I console myself by remembering the gratitude and warm response of the small handful of people who recognize the exceptional importance of the events taking place in the Town Hall in Rapallo. I am of course making an exception for the few people who were not there because of other commitments. I affirm again the excellence of the New Hungarian Quartet. I have already described the music festival in Venice—which took place last September—in three important foreign magazines with large circulations;[113] it was a festival of very high quality at which I was able to observe the exceptional accomplishment of the conductor Antonio Guarnieri. (The art of conducting an orchestra did not end in Italy with the departure of Toscanini nor with the lack of understanding he showed in the political-economic field.)

Notable among the performers in Venice were our skilled friends, the Gertler Quartet, in the execution of Honegger's Quartet, Ornella Puliti-Santoliquido in Casella's *Sinfonia*, the Hungarian Quartet, and especially Paul Hindemith in his own composition *Der Schwanendreher*.

---

effort remained." The contrast of these two composers was useful to Pound in trying to demonstrate the difference between knowledge and culture, the central theme of the *Guide*. Culture comes into existence when one is able to accept and shape an inheritance with grace and nobility. Boccherini had "culture." Beethoven, like Bartók and himself, says Pound, may have had knowledge and competence, but all three are working against the current of their time; they may provide ingredients for culture but they are not enveloped by it.

111 In the Fascist calendar the year XIV corresponds to 1933.
112 *Il Mare*, March 13, 1937; translated.
113 Viz., "Mostly Quartets," *The Listener*, October 14, 1936, pp. 743–44; "Music in Ca'Rezzonico," *The Delphian Quarterly*, January, 1937, pp. 2–4 and 11; "Ligurian View of a Venetian Festival," *Music and Letters*, January, 1937, pp. 36–41.

I can now say after six months continuous work that here in Rapallo the New Hungarian Quartet has greatly surpassed all the performances I have heard in Venice.

With youthful generosity and enthusiasm the Hungarians themselves praise the Kolisch Quartet of Vienna. I haven't heard the Kolisch group for ten years and I have no right to make critical comparisons with musicians I have not recently heard. I can only say that in the field of quartets I have never in my life heard a mastery equivalent to that of the group made up of Sandor Vegh, Laszlo Halmos, Denes Koromzay and Vilmos Palotai.

Notwithstanding the shamefully small audience, the quartet, moved by a love of music and by the keen and enthusiastic attention of those few who did attend, has promised to return next year. This will be the final test for the Rapallo audience.

For those ignorant of Münch's musical integrity I emphasize again this great quality of his. The *suonatore ambulante*[114] has a miniature repertoire so often repeated that every note and inflexion gets into his bones, blood and muscles. Very different is the task of a *stock-company*,[115] that is, of musicians who present to the same public an extended repertoire of music performed (as has always been the case in Rapallo with Olga Rudge and Münch) with seriousness, authority and sometimes supreme beauty. Those who followed our concerts will remember that for four years we have had from these musicians a catalogue of masterpieces performed on two instruments alone. I doubt if any other series of concerts, even in great cities, could surpass what has been done in Rapallo.

Next Thursday, March 18, we will present the last of Bach's sonatas accessible to us in a printed edition. We have already presented the others. In April we will repeat that masterpiece to be found in the edition Suite, sonata and fugue [sic]. We will choose some of the charming sonatas by Pergolesi not yet performed by the Tigullians, and compositions by Matelart, Negri and Giovanni Picchi.   EZRA POUND

Program for Thursday 18th

PERGOLESI: Three sonatas—Violin and piano;
J. MATELART: (1559) Fantasie;
CESARE NEGRI MILANESE: Pass'e mezzo;
GIOVANNI PICCHI: (1620) Padovana (piano);
J. S. BACH: Sonata in G major—Violin and piano;
STRAVINSKY: Serenade and Rag Music.

[114] A kind of wandering folk-fiddler.
[115] English in original.

The "Amici" wish to thank Mr. Andermarcher of the Hotel Italia for his generous hospitality to the New Hungarian Quartet.

CONCERTS OF MARCH 29 AND APRIL 1[116]
The Town Hall, 9:00 p.m.

For the benefit of the numerous unfamiliar faces at the last Rudge-Münch concert, I think this is a good time to recall that the group of the "Amici del Tigullio" was formed several years ago as a general enterprise for the benefit of the whole Tigullian Gulf. For two years it flourished and advertised its activities through a "Literary Supplement" in *Il Mare,* brilliantly directed by Gino Saviotti—author of *Il fratello* and other well-known novels and philosophical writings, together with the generous support of Arti Grafiche Tigullio and the editorial staff of *Il Mare* and with the collaboration of known writers.

As a local public event the "Amici" organized a number of concerts, but these do not represent the principal activity of the faithful Tigullians. Münch, for example, is presently scoring a composition, a kind of Mass for full orchestra, organ, solo voices and mixed choir, which we have reason to believe will arouse great interest. We can also list among his compositions a sonata for violin and piano, a string quartet, a concerto for thirteen instruments, and several adaptations of music by old authors, no longer performable today failing the original instruments for which they were written. Likewise Miss Rudge is continuing her studies on Vivaldi. All this is also part of the activities of the "Amici del Tigullio."

E. P.

Programs of the Concerts

These two concerts, like the preceding one, will be performed by the violinist Olga Rudge and the pianist-composer Gerhart Münch.

Monday, March 29, 9:00 p.m.
VIVALDI: Concerto in D major, Op. 3, No. 9—Rudge-Münch;
J. S. BACH: Concerto in D major, adapted from a concerto by Vivaldi, Five movements—Münch;
J. S. BACH: Concerto in A minor—Rudge-Münch;
CHOPIN: Polonaise Fantaisie (Op. 61)—Scherzo No. 3 in C-sharp minor, Münch.

[116] *Il Mare,* March 27, 1937; translated.

THURSDAY, APRIL 1, 9:00 P.M.
VIVALDI-MÜNCH: Concerto;
J. S. BACH: Sonata and fugue, piano and violin;
HONEGGER: Sonata for violin and piano;
BARTÓK: Sonata for piano. Allegro barbaro.

By 1938 it was becoming exceedingly difficult to maintain the concerts, at least with any degree of regularity. Münch had left Rapallo once again, and even Olga Rudge was frequently absent, dividing her time now between Venice, Siena and Sant' Ambrogio. Pound wanted to stabilize the Rapallo events in order that they might constitute a miniature festival and an annual attraction for visitors to the Ligurian coast. Late in 1937 he announced plans to make February music month in Rapallo. As a prelude to the 1938 series the New Hungarian Quartet were to appear in January in a concert of the new quartet literature.

An attractive broadside entitled "Music in Rapallo" was prepared (the cover was in English, French, and Italian), containing pictures of Rapallo and reprints of the *Il Mare* articles of January 8 and January 22, in an obvious attempt to appeal more directly to the tourist crowd. The February concerts were not reviewed by Pound but by Desmond Chute in a longish piece in *Il Mare,* February 12.

The programs for the February concerts were as follows:

February 1
PURCELL: Sonatas from the "first series," I, II, III.
DEBUSSY: *Suite Bergamasque* (1890);
Etude *Pour les Sonorités opposées* (1915);
Masques (1904).
MOZART: Sonata in A major (K. 526), allegro moderato, andante, presto.

February 2
PURCELL: Sonatas IV, V, VI.
DEBUSSY: Préludes: *Puerta del Vino; Ce qu'a vu le vent d'ouest; La Terrasse des audiences du clair de lune; Voiles; Les Collines d'Anacapri; Les Tierces alternées;*
2 Etudes: *Pour les arpèges composées; Pour les notes répétées.*
VIVALDI: Concerto in D major (Op. 3, No. 9), allegro, larghetto, allegro.

February 3
PURCELL: Sonatas VII, VIII, IX.
DEBUSSY: *Children's Corner; Cloches à travers les feuilles; Isle Joyeuse.*
HINDEMITH: Sonatina.
GALUPPI: Sonata.
BACH: *Caprice pour le départ de son frère.*
MOZART: Sonata in G major (K. 379), adagio, allegro. Tema con variazione;
Sonata in E major (K. 304), allegro, tempo di minuetto.

February 4
PURCELL: Sonatas X, XI, XII.
WILHELM RUST (1739–96)—called by Goethe "the great master Rust"—Sonata in F-sharp minor.
PH. E. BACH: Sonata in A minor.
VIVALDI: Sonata in A (Op. 2, No. 2), preludio, presto, largo, giga.

February 5
Study-session with explanation of the application of microphotography for musical research of unpublished materials, etc.
DEBUSSY: Sonata for violin and piano.

TIGULLIAN MUSICAL LIFE[117]

The date of our "Sagra Musicale"—so we will call our *Inverno Musicale* this year—is provisionally set for the first week of February with the hope of being able to repeat it at the same time each year so that tourists may remember it without the need for special advertising.

The Tigullian studies have continued silently. Münch has written an *enormous* composition for orchestra and voices, and hoped to spend the winter in Rapallo, but has been called back to Germany. But we count on having him with us again very soon, even if I can't deny that this great success may turn into a danger for our manifestations, which will continue nevertheless.

In Venice a Vivaldi Society is being formed, to which the studies we have pursued may be of value. We don't want to call ourselves the

[117] *Il Mare*, December 4, 1937; translated.

"forerunners" of the effort in Venice, but we would like to remind people that we were the first to seek a rivival of Vivaldi's music.

On October 29th our violinist, Olga Rudge, with David Nixon and Giorgio Levi of Venice presented a whole program from the *Estro Harmonico* in that city. Perhaps since the days when Vivaldi himself conducted, there has not been a concert composed entirely of music from one of the volumes of his works. And the Vivaldi Society was planned immediately after this concert.

This month Miss Rudge published an article on new methods of musical research in *Townsman* (a London monthly) and another on Vivaldi is due for publication in *The Delphian Quarterly* of Chicago.[118]

On the whole the program of our week in February will be devoted to the presentation of the Italian musical heritage with particular attention given to the works of those who, though at a distance, have collaborated with us in our musical researches. There is, for example, the edition of Purcell's twelve sonatas for two violins and piano edited by Whittaker.[119] David Nixon and our friend Sansoni will be in Rapallo to help make our February program a success.

We would like to register, however Platonically, our interest in the splendid edition of Orazio Vecchi's *Anfiparnasso* edited by Carlo Perinello of Milan, a work that would unfortunately require resources beyond those of the Tigullians in order to be performed for our public.

I would like nevertheless to point out that this edition has used photography and photographic reproduction, and to emphasize the possibility in the near future of using films and photography to settle unquestionably the authenticity of texts by old composers. At the International Librarians' Congress in Cambridge last September these microfilm methods were discussed at length without, however, sufficient realization of their importance in opening new horizons for musicology and oriental studies, and the economic attractiveness of inexpensively "photographing" the original texts, a development unforeseen until a few years ago and as important as the discovery of printing in the fifteenth century was for the diffusion of books.

EZRA POUND

---

[118] "Music as a Process," *Townsman*, January 1938, p. 21; and "Venice and Vivaldi," *The Delphian Quarterly*, January, 1938, pp. 7-10 and 56. The *Townsman* article was on the benefits of microphotography for musical research.

[119] Henry Purcell, *Twelve Sonatas in Three Parts*, ed. W. Gillies Whittaker, Editions de l'Oiseau Lyre, Paris, n. d.

TIGULLIAN MUSICAL SEASON[120]
January 21—From February 2nd to 5th.

In accordance with the spirit and critical standards now well established, the first concert of the "Tigullian Musical Season" will take place in Rapallo on January 21, in the Town Hall at 9:00 p.m., with the participation of the NEW HUNGARIAN QUARTET (Székely, Vegh, Koromzay, Palotai) and with the following program:

MOZART: Quartet (to be decided);
STRAVINSKY: *Concertino;*
HONEGGER: Quartet;
VERESS: Quartet.[121]

Starting February 1 and continuing all week, there will a concert every evening, presenting twelve sonatas by Purcell contrasted and compared with music by Debussy and Hindemith, and with references to the important forms of the concerto as conceived by Vivaldi, and of the sonata as envisioned by Mozart. The faithful supporters of the Tigullians will remember the beautiful *Golden Sonata* by Purcell performed some three years ago by Miss Rudge, maestro Sansoni and Gerhart Münch.

These twelve other sonatas by Purcell have been lately brought to light by W. Gillies Whittaker, head of the Scottish Academy of Music in Glasgow, and published by the Lyre Bird Press of Paris. We may remind the reader that both Mr. Whittaker and "Lyre Bird" have already aided the efforts of the Tigullians with advice and gifts of rare editions of little-known music. We take this opportunity to congratulate Mrs. Dyer, head of the Bird Press, for the prizes obtained with her editions at the Paris Exposition.

The aim of this year's concerts is to present "the concept of the sonata for strings and keyboard" as it developed in the mind of Henry Purcell (1659–1695), who was among the finest English composers, a great unknown for us, equalled perhaps only by Dowland and Jenkins. In the same way during previous seasons we have tried to affirm Mozart's and Vivaldi's form by presenting blocks of their sonatas.

Performing in these concerts will be Olga Rudge and maestro Sansoni, violins, and the pianist Renata Borgatti. The participation of Gerhart Münch is unlikely, but we hope to be able to remember him

---

[120] *Il Mare*, January 1, 1938; translated.
[121] Sándor Veress (b. 1907), Hungarian composer, pupil of Kodály, much influenced by Bartók.

either by executing one of his compositions or one of his new transcriptions of an old masterpiece.

We will also have with us the fine cellist Marco Ottone from Chiavari.

The Quartetto di Genova will give a concert with music by Boccherini, Cherubini and Mortari, but we cannot be more specific about the date because of their engagements with the Teatro Carlo Felice.[122]

If the quartet can't come for the Musical Week, Ezra Pound will give a lecture illustrated by music, on the microphotographic process as applied to musicology (already mentioned in *Il Mare*) and the opportunity this process offers for future diffusion of the enormous quantities of musical treasures still buried in libraries.

On a date to be decided we hope to be visited here in Rapallo by David Nixon and Giorgio Levi of the Vivaldi Society of Venice.

Those who wish to see the New Hungarian Quartet more frequently in Rapallo are invited to get in touch directly with Ezra Pound at the Hotel Rapallo.

Subscription cards entitling the holder to two tickets for each of the six concerts, 100 liras. Single seats: the usual prices with the usual discounts for members of the Fascist Cultural Institute, the Fascist recreation clubs, professional musicians, etc. We accept any financial help from those who want to encourage musical research, as long as the donor understands the aims of the benevolent and hard-working founders, and the nature or at least the spirit of the work.

FEBRUARY CONCERTS—THE PIANIST RENATA BORGATTI[123]

The pianist Renata Borgatti will also perform in the musical week that will take place in February in Rapallo.

To get acquainted with the pianist of this musical season of ours, it would be enough just to read the newspaper clippings of critics who have written about her over the past two years; but I don't want to miss the chance to add some notes of my own on the strength of my direct acquaintance with this artist and with today's musical world. In this milieu we see, or rather we hear, a considerable number of young people of both sexes who are very brilliant pianists. They appear in

---

[122] The Quartetto di Genova, or as they called themselves "Il Quartetto Silvestri," performed in Rapallo on April 5, 1938, in a program consisting of Boccherini's quartet in D major, Cherubini's quartet in E-flat major and Virgilio Mortari's one-movement quartet in G. Mortari was a contemporary composer born near Milan in 1902.

[123] *Il Mare*, January 8, 1938; translated.

the vigour of their youth, more or less hypnotized by their teachers—I repeat—brilliant, but in reality more like comets than stars.

Gradually they lose the impetus, the stimulus, the novelty of appearing in the great metropolitan concert halls; they disappear, they become hacks, some sustaining themselves by means that have nothing to do with music, others struggling on because of financial necessity. But very few show a consistent development in musical understanding and intelligence.

The first time I heard Miss Borgatti in London I was not satisfied. But not even the pianist herself was satisfied with her work at the time. Then for several years she disappeared from the concert halls and, as happens with a chosen number of performers and creative artists, these years of obscurity were decisive. The Miss Borgatti I listened to five years ago in Paris showed a re-organization of technique and a clear concept of the compositions she was performing. Then one day in 1936 on the promenade in Rapallo I met her father, Grand' Ufficiale Giuseppe Borgatti, who was completely and justifiably proud of his daughter and the recognition she had recently received in Rome. He said: "Now they call her a great artist."

Later on I will quote a critique from a Roman newspaper; others I will mention in due time before the next concerts. But in all these criticisms two points are missing.

Not only has Renata Borgatti been recognized by audiences in France, Holland, England, and Germany, but for years she has also been taking the new Italian music into those countries. With Olga Rudge she gave the first performances of Ildebrando Pizzetti's sonata for violin and piano in Paris and Oxford. And together or separately they have introduced abroad many other examples of new Italian music.

Secondly: Miss Borgatti, having to undergo the hard test of German criticism, was ahead even of us in her determination to present programs of a single composer's work; and in Germany she has performed the complete series of Mozart's sonatas for piano and violin, as we have also done several times. For this reason too, and not only because she has the full approval of the international critics, Miss Borgatti is perfectly suited to collaborate here in Rapallo, in full sympathy with our Tigullians' aims.

And I conclude by quoting a piece of criticism from the *Giornale d'Italia,* signed by L.F.L., which appeared in the issue of May 24, 1936, concerning a concert given in the Sgambati Hall: "The pianist Borgatti has a rich musical temperament which shows itself in an inexhaustible number of unexpected details. Her technique has a stark, precise, intelligent and nervous clarity. Her lively, strong fingers obtain a touch with a clear firm sound, producing an impression of sheer naturalness.

Her sensitivity never results in vagueness, but creates potent sonorities which are never noises, and delicate sounds which never degenerate into affectations. These two qualities appeared first in Vivaldi's concerto in D minor, where Miss Borgatti gave the sense of a strong and impressive crescendo, and then in Galuppi's sonata in C major. They recurred with particular emphasis in the difficult and long *Humoreske* by Schumann, which was executed with richness of accents, exquisite poetry, and above all brilliant variety. Three *Etudes* by Chopin and six *Préludes* by Debussy concluded the program. And in this second half Renata Borgatti again showed herself to be an exceptional interpreter of music. It is rare to hear Debussy played with such strength and feeling. Her success was warm and overwhelming."   EZRA POUND

TIGULLIAN MUSICAL STUDIES[124]
The New Hungarian Quartet
In the Town Hall of Rapallo, Friday, January 21, 9:00 p.m.

They were unforgettable, the two concerts given in Rapallo last season by the New Hungarian Quartet, because of their juxtaposition of old music by Haydn and Boccherini with modern masterpieces. We had two evenings without the interference of secondary music or music unadmired by the performers or alien to their taste. Thus our Hungarian friends have had more success with us than at the Venice Biennale, where they recently played.

I don't know the reasons for the changes that have taken place in the quartet this year, but it is enough for me to note that since Halmos's departure Vegh has given up his role as first violinist to the famous Székely. If I had been free over the past ten years to tour the centers of Germany and Hungary instead of living in Rapallo, I would have known the high quality of this artist by direct experience and not only through his fame.

The New Hungarian Quartet remains a quartet of soloists, each highly talented, who have joined together for the greater glory of ensemble music. After laurels of success in Paris concerts, they will be in Rapallo on March 21, and I am glad to welcome them on behalf of the musicians of the Tigullio.

As has already been announced, the program includes works by Mozart; by two pre-eminent modern composers, Stravinsky and Honegger, one already very famous, the other a master of musical sensitivity; and by a new composer, Veress, unknown to me but recommended by

[124] *Il Mare*, January 15, 1938; translated.

Mr. Palotai, whose judgement is enough at least to arouse my interest and make me want to listen to this work.   EZRA POUND

TIGULLIAN MUSICAL SEASON[125]
The February Concerts

LAST NIGHT'S SUCCESS

We are convinced there should be a place in the world—let us say like Rapallo—where the valiant and enlightened researches of serious musicologists can be listened to by other professors, scholars and music lovers as sound, and not merely read as dry notes on paper.

For this reason, even though we lack the advantage of a distinguished and precise musician like Gerhart Münch in Rapallo and on the Tigullio, we Tigullians are planning to continue our efforts in spite of new difficulties, in the hope of being understood and of receiving further help. The difficulty of attracting artists to Rapallo who can give "authoritative" presentations of the old masterpieces that are being brought to light, will require greater effort from me too, and I am willing to undertake it.

For the benefit of winter guests I have proposed that we have the annual concerts at the beginning of February, and that the date remain the same from year to year, so that guests who want to attend will know the exact time when they can listen to unusual music in Rapallo.

This year we will offer, so I believe, the first twentieth-century presentation of Purcell's Twelve Sonatas from the first series. Miss Borgatti will offer also a sonata by Rust (1739–1796) which I have not yet heard.

The definite programs for the five concerts of February 1, 2, 3, 4 and 5 will be published in next Saturday's issue of *Il Mare*. We can say right now that the main item will be Purcell's Twelve Sonatas executed by **Olga Rudge and Luigi Sansoni, violins, Renata Borgatti, piano, and Marco Ottone, cello**. The other four concerts will include music by Debussy, and sonatas and concerti by Mozart and Vivaldi, with the addition of an unpublished Vivaldi work if the results prove satisfactory.

The first concert of the New Hungarian Quartet took place last night with great success in the Town Hall. The late hour prevents us from publishing the critical review of it. We will present it in our next issue, and it will be written by our eminent collaborator, Prof. Clary Benoit.

A LITTLE HISTORY

The "Tigullian Concerts" were started in 1933, Anno XII, almost by chance, when Gerhart Münch and Olga Rudge decided to perform

[125] *Il Mare,* January 22, 1938; translated.

Mozart's sonatas (for piano and violin) in block at the Teatro Reale of Rapallo. After this first concert the local authorities, with rare foresight and consideration, offered the Town Hall as a place better suited to chamber music and more convenient for the economic success of the initiative.

Later we acquired a piano, bought partly with subscriptions from a group of Rapallo inhabitants, but mainly through the generosity of the Marchesa Imperiali. During the following years the continuous support of the Marchesa Solferina Spinola and other subscribers, both Italian and foreign, was registered and appreciated. The Fascist Institute of Culture and, even more substantially, the Ente Autonomo[126] of the city of Rapallo added their encouragement. We owe to the Marchesa Imperiali the two concerts of the singer Fino Savio, who was accompanied at the piano by the Marchesa herself.

Highlights of the Tigullians' concerts were the participation of the Gertler Quartet, Anno XIV [1935], and of the Hungarian-American composer Tibor Serly, who was our first link with Hungary and to whom we owe the unforgettable appearance of the New Hungarian Quartet (two concerts in Anno XV and the one last night). And we must also remember the performance of William Young's sonatas for several violins, played by Luigi Sansoni and others; the repeated performances of Mozart's sonatas by Miss Rudge and Gerhart Münch; and the Vivaldi studies (to be continued) transcribed by Münch.

Owing to masterly and authoritative interpretations and the system by which we chose the programs, the Tigullian concerts aroused the interest of reviewers of well-known foreign periodicals in London, Paris, Chicago, Barcelona, Berlin and even Tokyo, who noted our system of contrasting old masterpieces with new experimental compositions; and approved and commended our desire to present whole programs of works by composers able to capture and maintain the interest of connoisseurs, instead of presenting works by composers capable only of momentarily dazzling the audience.   EZRA POUND

In 1938 Ronald Duncan started a new publication entitled *Townsman,* to which Pound contributed a number of short pieces on music. Following his university studies, Duncan had gone to visit Pound in Rapallo, and Gandhi in India, then returned to England to gain some considerable distinction as a poet and playwright. A close friend of Benjamin Britten, for whom he produced some libretti, Duncan was a sensitive music enthusiast. Pound had given him a note of introduction to Stravinsky, and

---

[126] A local agency similar to the American chamber of commerce, but concerned exclusively with tourism.

following his visit to Stravinsky in Paris, Duncan conceived a plan for an antiwar concert with one of the London orchestras, at which Stravinsky would conduct his own works. Stravinsky was ready to donate his services, but the plan fell through when the orchestral managers, and even Stravinsky's British publisher, were indifferent. Pound wrote Duncan, in a letter already quoted (page 236), assuring him that Rapallo at least stood ready.

Pound also saw Duncan in London in 1938 when he went to sort out the affairs of his mother-in-law, Olivia Shakespear, who had died in October of that year. According to Noel Stock, Pound "wanted badly to see a Noh play performed in a theatre and to this end Ronald Duncan persuaded Ashley Dukes to lend them the Mercury Theatre. Benjamin Britten produced a musician who could play gongs and another of Duncan's friends, Henry Boys, suggested a female dancer by the name of Suria Magito. One afternoon, with Duncan as audience, Pound recited one of his own Noh translations while the girl danced."[127]

Duncan and Pound corresponded frequently on musical subjects. "I remember we spent some time trying to define melody," Duncan wrote me in 1968. The whole collection is in the University of Texas, but I have not been able to consult it in the preparation of this volume.

For the first issue of *Townsman* Pound wrote a short piece, "Janequin, Francesco da Milano," supplemented with the violin line of Gerhart Münch's arrangement of the *Chant des Oiseaux*, the same as that which appears in Canto LXXV. For the same issue Olga Rudge wrote "Music as a Process." The second issue of *Townsman* contained a short Pound piece entitled "Villon and Comment," together with Olga Rudge's reduction of the "Heaulmière" aria from *Le Testament* for voice and violin. These were both reprinted at the end of *Guide to Kulchur*. Two further short pieces, "Muzik as Mistaught" and "Musicians; God Help 'em," complete the *Townsman* redaction.

JANEQUIN, FRANCESCO DA MILANO[128]

> "Clement Janequin wrote a chorus... when Francesco da Milano reduced it for the lute, the birds were still with the music. And when Münch transcribed it for modern instruments the birds were still there." *A.B.C. of Reading*, p. 38.

[127] Noel Stock, *The Life of Ezra Pound*, p. 356.
[128] *Townsman*, Vol. I, No. 1, January, 1938, p. 18.

The two pages of Janequin are there, indestructible, and as indisputable as Pisanello's portrait of Miss Este, indisputable, no one can ever have misunderstood them any more than you can misunderstand the flowers and the butterfly in Pisanello's paint. More indestructible in that no calamity to a single exemplar can obliterate their statement. And that statement did not begin with the French master. It is there in Arnaut Daniel's prosody in the canzoni "L'aura amara" and "Autet e bas."

Neither Vivaldi nor Couperin in any way superseded it. There are in the arts certain maxima. There has been little comparative objective criticism in music. Cocteau and De Schloezer and Sauzay, and Richter who wrote about counterpoint may have cleared up a good deal but haven't stolen my thunder on this point. The ideogram of real composition is in Münch two pages, which belong to no man. They are abbreviated out of Francesco da Milano's transcription for the lute. Something has happened to the Janequin. The casual reader of Henry Expert's edition won't immediately identify the notes. In the Münch MS. before me he has given Francesco's name with perhaps greater justice than Chilesotti's reference to the choral work. At any rate there was something I did not hear when I heard the song done by chorus.

In one sense I don't care a hoot about the authorship. The gist, the pith, the unbreakable fact is there in the two pages of violin part (whether Münch has shown greater talent in his later editing of Vivaldi is beside the point). The point is "not one bird but a lot of birds" as our violinist said on first playing it.

The undeformable objects in music comparatively few. Compare Casella in conversation: "I just can't remember bad music."

Objectivity? the presentation in one art of what cannot be given in any other. It can imply, it can concentrate into itself any amount of implication, and does "epitomize" etc. Thus the two pages are mediaeval and nothing can make 'em renaissance or ornamental, or take 'em into the realm of applied ornament. I doubt if choral performance underlines the thing that I mean. I doubt if Francesco da Milano's lute quite so concentrated the statement. The statement is in the violin part, which stands as food for the critical eye (or ear, better say ear) even without the "accompaniment."

Arnaut's lost music existed before or about A.D. 1200. Expert dates Janequin "attaignant 1529" Besard wanted a portable Dowland that he could play himself. Idem Francesco da Milano for Janequin's chorus. Idem Bach when he put Vivaldi into a transcript that could be done from a keyboard.

The bed rock in any art is composed of such solids. You could construct music again from a few dozen such proofs of invention.

MUZIK, AS MISTAUGHT[129]

Melody, said Boris de Schloezer, is the most artificial thing in all music, i.e. it is furthest from anything a man can just find there in nature.[130]

He was writing about uncle Igor. The Dial printed the translation. The state of public inertia is judged by Eng/ and Am/ pubrs to be too low to make edtn/ in bk/ form a tempting business operation.

The slop of the damned XIX century derived from a psychosis which neglected melody. The study of a conservatoire curriculum ought to make any sane man vomit. The way to LEARN composition is:

A. Melody. Study of melody. Comparison of melodies from the earliest known up to now. Comparison of melodic development in the orient with that of the occident.

B. Almost as a sub-head, the study of simultaneous rhythms, say in oriental dance music.

C. What was done during the clean and decent periods of European music, namely the filling in of parts from melody and base.

This had, has or can have, an enormously enlightening effect on any student ever worth preserving.

At one period, and a long one, the keyboard player was supposed to, and did, know enough to play the intermediate parts at sight.

No process with pen in hand teaches a man so much both of the thought and of the actual idiom; of the actual way to *write down* the sound desired and the durations desired as the copying out of work of genius.

In no other way does the learner pay the same degree of attention. AND as not one musician in a million has creative faculty in excess of what is needed to devise intermediate parts. The natural and justifiable instinct to "create" has here a decent, proportioned outlet. The man who is not a mere pianola roll, the maker, the artisan of high quality, can here be artifex without cluttering the earth with inferior products.

All that is skill, all that is taste and sensibility can find outlet. The quality of the performer is established.

The one with understanding takes his due rank above the monkey-fingered executant. The novelty, the invention is left to the artifex who can write melody BETTER than his forerunners who has something to add to the plenum of music.

In any art there is a great part of virtue which consists simply in not

---

[129] *Townsman*, Vol. I, No. 3, July, 1938, pp. 8–9.

[130] The literal quotation, in Pound's own translation, runs: "Melody is the form of organizing sonority which is furthest removed from reality, the most artificial, and precisely the form by which the sonorous world acquires a specific character." Boris de Schloezer, "A Classic Art," translated by Ezra Pound, *Dial*, July, 1929, p. 473.

doing evil. *La lingua s'affecta* with pointing to the effects in fresco when the craftsmen worked each to his capacity under a leader.

In the creation of music: FIRST, melody. The melody whether its maker be conscious of it or not HAS a base, it is written willi-nilly ABOVE certain simple progressions of fundamental.

Bach may have heard the whole lot, parts, etc/ all together. In listening to a Vivaldi melody I have myself had the illusion of hearing the lower permutations "fall into place" as the tumblers are supposed to be felt falling into place by the sand-papered fingers of Ed Wallace's cracksmen.

(That don't mean to say I even think I cd/ have written them down. The layman probably does not sufficiently demark the difference between composing and writing music. Writing it implies the capacity to make the true, not the merely approximate, graph of the sounds imagined.)

In dead music the intervening parts do NOT aid the lateral movement. Take these bastards who are such nuts on harmony. Take W., supposed to be so correct and so skilled, *magari* learned, in harmony. His damned music does not move. On the other hand the man who said: harmony is perpendicular melody said a mouthful, though it be a bit sibylline. The intervening parts CAN draw on the future notes of the melody, and DO so in great music. They are parts of a living organism that gets up and travels.

Naturally if the student never learns to know a good melody from a bad one, he or she will remain the kind of pest that infects the concert platform or conduces ultimately to crooning, the last disease of poxblistered decadence.

E. P.

MUSICIANS; GOD HELP 'EM[131]

What they don't know is the FIRST page of the exercise book. Namely, that a whole note equals a whole note; or 2 halves or 4 quarters etc. not approx but exactly.

And if I could DO it? That takes us back to Aristotle's *TeXne*, which the lecturing lice omitted from the curriculum.

Then there is the effect of counting in the English language, where *three* is a longer word, I mean takes longer to SAY than, *one* or *two*. Hence that god-awful drag on the third beat in a four beat bar which has castrated and sunk so much British performance.

[131] *Townsman*, Vol. I, No. 4, October, 1938, pp. 8–9.

I can myself understand the complicated stuff, the theories, etc. If I could play two or four measures in time I shd/ be astounding the public from the platform. As it is I grope and try to warn others. Poor brutes who have nothing but performance to stand on, and who get started wrong.

There is, I am glad to learn, ONE piano school (address, Hirzel LANGENHAN, Schloss Berg, bei Weinfelden, Kanton Thurgau, in Switzerland) where the pupil is first taught that the PYANO is an instrument played with the hands. (Simple and one might think obvious starting point, neglected in institutions.)

Secondly the pew-PILL is taught that a composition has a main form and articulations, that is a root, a main structure, and details. To remember ONE main fact and not a hundred separate notes...

There is nothing new in this doctrine. It is rediscovered from time to time, but taught inadequately, that is, it is taught in general not in particular.

Whether I shd/ apologize for beginning the preceding lesson with melody and not with the "first page" of the exercise book, can be debated. I doubt if any one CAN understand the first page until they are interested, I mean really and acutely interested, in melody...

When their hunger for melody and their melodic hate (as well as love) is sufficiently keen, then they may get round to noticing bar length, to disliking accordion bars which stretch and contract unintentionally, which are (in how many god damned editions) loaded with "*poco rit.*" and similar marks of ineptitude, in season and out.

And if the editor hasn't put in these indications in wrong places or all over the place, the purr-former performs 'em gratis and without indication.

After the first stumbles and the instinctive sense that a form must contain UNEVEN elements, one suffers and learns that an even measure if long enough, has room for all sorts of oddities and uneven figures and units.

This is a long time learning. People might be told, but would they learn it?

The learnèd and expert have such difficulty in understanding what the unlearned do NOT understand when told with an even voice.

PART TWO

An open air show in this village indicates, perhaps, another chance for a little sanity. Lo Monaco (conducting), Anita de Alba, G. Guidi, in Rossini's Barbiere di Siviglia, emphasized in August various points that Lavignac knew and that the public and bad composers have forgotten.

Rossini is, in this opera, unsurpassed by anyone I know of, in combining orchestra with songs.

This is not the same thing as fitting words to melody or making an unity of words and melody in a song or an aria, nevertheless, Lavignac in his condensed and insufficiently meditated vade mecum makes two points. First, that Rossini had told him that he (Rossini) learned his job copying the parts of Haydn's quartettes, and second, that Rossini STOPPED writing operas after his Wm. Tell (1829).

Which STOP, in the fear of doing something worse, was probably an act of genius, the master from Pesaro consciously or unconsciously refusing dead to participate in the general DOWN-SLOSH of the god blithering and bemessed ottocento.

England damned, since Cromwell brought in his usurers, to an avoidance of technique and of verbal clarity; to be obfuscation of all values and all honesty, lost the art of, and care for, singing WORDS.

That art persisted in Italian libretti, which are SINGING matter; which are NOT reading matter.

That art I did have the decency to notice, in "The Spirit of Romance," if I remember, in a brief reference to Metastasio. Or at any rate I have referred now and again to Metastasio. And there are probably fifty librettists who knew the job better than ANY of the bleeding literary gents who committed book-poetry in England from the time of Waller to the occasional heaves of Mr. Browning when he did an occasional lyric.

This technique, which includes and very largely consists in vowel sequence, COULD be revived by a hundred or so poetasters IF the term poetaster didn't exclude the idea of honest work.

The YOUNG have little to say. Adolescence is, in decent social orders, a time of preparation. Labour on the TECHNIQUE of singable words is honourable labour. God knows I worked in the dark from 1905 onwards, and the light has come very slowly.

I don't really care a hang about verse drama to be spoken on the stage. Anyway it is Mr. Eliot's job, and his fragments of an Agon are worth all his stage successes, but verse to be sung is something vastly worth reviving, and verse to be sung in opera, if it could be as good as Sterbini's in the "Barbiere" would be an addition to life as we suffer it.

It need NOT be reading matter. A great deal of Sterbini's don't even need to be looked up in the book of words for the simple reason that one can HEAR it when sung, I mean hear the words and grasp their simple meaning.

This note is in the nature of a prayer for the continuance of the open air opera in Rapallo. Damn Puccini, and my ingress into one other open air performance in another province only resulted in tracing

Mickey Mouse to his lair in Boito (doubtless of historic and philological import but not part of my private agenda). I shd/ like to hear all of Rossini (to find out what is good) plus another hundred operas pre/ Traviata.

There is nothing inherently impossible in their happening a few per year in Rapallo, or even in other of the numerous open air revivals now proceding in Italy. The price here was from fifteen lire down to three lire, with voices audible over the fence for those reluctant to disburse.

The guild system is, or was from the 1st to the 4th of August, working quite nicely in orchestra in Liguria.

EZRA POUND

By "accordion bars" I do NOT mean deliberate use of bars of SPECIFICALLY different lengths, that is, specifically measured changes in the great bass tone, but the undersigned and not specifically calculated playing off the great bass, as a bad singer sings out of tune.

MUSICIANS[132]

The betrayal of English musicians (vide protest in *Action* for June 18) began with the betrayal of English music.

England HAD (past tense) a music that asked and needed no favours. Then you got Herr Haendel and boiled potatoes. He was a composer above the average, and no one cried havoc. In those days no one was on the watch for the cancer of usury. Nobody thought of connecting art and economics. In came the Dutch banking system. OUT went critical acumen. The usurer has never subsidized a free press. Under usuriocracy there is one kind of art, namely art that does NOT cause the beholder to "NOTICE." As usury rises, perception declines. As long as people look at art or really listen to music they notice the design. The habit of noticing anything is prejudicial to the moneylender. Man asking: "WHY?" is not Shylock's meat. If a man notices the FORM of a melody he may notice something else, he may notice, in fact, anything. And when that starts, good-bye to Baldwins, Sieffs, Baruchs, and Normans.

ROTTING THE ARTS

Mercantilism rots the arts. When a musician starts worrying about pay instead of music, good-bye music. In the foetid hell of a mercantilist

[132] *Action*, July 16, 1938, p. 13. The reference in paragraph one is to an article entitled "A Place for English Writers," *Action*, June 18, 1938, p. 13. There Pound related the growth of the British Empire to the retreat of English literature, identifying the 1690s as the critical turning point. The theory is plausible for music also. Henry Purcell, the last great English composer, died in 1695.

age, he HAS to think about costs, payment, and "overhead" in the concert hall.

If he is a mere average player he is drawn into worry about competition, whether from better or worse players. Criticism gets a black eye. And, not because it should be so, but because it just happens, he starts trying to sell his own stuff regardless of quality. Also the player is put above the composer. The player has to eat NOW.

Whether you accept my argument or not, the fact remains that no adequate critical effort is made for English music that COULD stand up to any music whatsoever in open court. Gerald Hayes manages to bring out a magnificent edition of "King's Music" as a coronation souvenir. I wonder how many copies are in circulation. I also wonder how much better a book he mightn't have made if he hadn't been making a coronation souvenir.

WHAT SUPPORT

What support has Dr. Whittaker had for his magnificent edition of William Young? He has upset the whole of musical history with English music, reprinted from a single copy preserved in Sweden, from the seventeenth century. We gave the music I think in Rapallo before it was given in England, Idem his "12 Purcell Sonatas." Here you have what many continentals consider the greatest English composer. At any rate a very English composer. The music of Dowland and Purcell is certainly soaked with racial characteristics. It cedes to no foreign music. Should Whittaker's edition have made it available to a Rapallo audience before you heard it in England?

Or need it, for that matter, have been published in Paris? The "Lyre Bird Press" has done a magnificent job, but would British Union England have forced that work out of the country.

ANITA DE ALBA—AND POSSIBILITIES FOR RAPALLO[133]

There are people who prefer Rossini's art to the nonclassical opera which prevailed after 1829. The gap between classicists or Rossinians and Puccinians is insurmountable, and we recognize sincerity on both sides.

The reasons for a classical preference need to be stressed again, and in particular with reference to the exceptionally lucid and interesting performances of *Il Barbiere di Siviglia* given in Rapallo on August 1 & 4.

Anita de Alba is a singer and actress who can take her place in any

---

[133] *Il Mare*, August 13, 1938; translated.

metropolis. Lo Monaco conducts with rare clarity, and his integral understanding of composition surpasses that of many conductors of greater celebrity. Even children testify to the vitality of Rossini's art, that of his librettist Sterbini, and Guido Guidi's ability to present this art; for as I was going home along the Boate after the performance, I heard them talk of Don Basilio as if he were a living creature.

Personally I hate the "star" system because often so-called great names disregard the values of the composer's artistic creation. Indeed I believe that such a convention, typical of a mercantile and decadent period, has ruined a great quantity of music, and above all has ruined contact and understanding between artists and public. With such a cast as Anita de Alba, the inimitable Don Basilio (Guido Guidi), Paterna (specialist in Pergolesi), De Cristina, Medici and Tarenzi (and here we must praise Mr. Tandini's discrimination in assembling such forces) we could begin to develop an opera season in Rapallo celebrated throughout Europe and America; and this could be accomplished without going beyond our means, without enormous staging expenses, etc. It would be in line with the sound and respectable taste shown by the Rapallo public who filled the less expensive seats at the performances of *Il Barbiere*.

Clarity, of the kind possessed by de Alba and the whole cast of *Il Barbiere*, seems to me to be the prerequisite for reviving eighteenth-century Italian opera, up to that fateful day when Rossini refused to write new music for fear of botching it.

With a grant we could try. I don't ask at all for the impossible. Wagner is beyond our means, Mozart's *Don Giovanni* requires a minimum of stage effects not at our disposal, Stravinsky and some Russian masterpieces are also not accessible to us. But a great number of eighteenth-century Italian operas are.

La Serva Padrona could easily be staged in our Teatro Reale.

With some providential help Rapallo could become a centre for musicophiles wishing to listen to a portion of Rossini's forty operas, including many unknown to the public both abroad and in Italy. How many have heard Vivaldi? And Paisiello's eighty-four operas, Cimarosa's eighty (with the exception of *Il Matrimonio Segreto*), how many know them?

Not only the scholars would be attracted by curiosity but also those who enjoyed *Il Barbiere* would become devotees of Donizetti, Mercadante and Bellini. To fill the most expensive seats we'd have to entice some queen or duchess from some more or less living state... and we'd sell out completely!

In November, 1938, a rather rambling piece appeared in *The Musical Times* under the title "Ad Libitum" by someone who signed himself "Feste." In reality this was Dr. Harvey Grace, editor of *The Musical Times*. It was a review of Pound's *Guide to Kulchur*, which had just appeared, specifically of those passages dealing with music. Feste's article is largely reportage, but (on p. 820) he had parted company over Pound's theories of Great Bass, claiming that if the great composers were aware at all of profound frequencies gathering and shaping their compositions, it was at an unconscious level only. Pound kept the argument alive with a letter to the editor of the *Times*, where he also went on to thump for a Vivaldi revival.

MR. POUND REPLIES[134]

Sir,—There are several points in "Feste's" kindly article which one or the other or both of us might further clarify. I shall attempt to treat them in order of importance.

1st. I wd. say to composers, that the really great composers have been INTERESTED in line, that is, in melody and in theme, and they have been diligent in expressing their ideas so that one, two or very small groups of players can represent them.

2ndly. To publishers I wd. say that from now on NO edition of old inedited music is valid or contemporary unless it be accompanied by the photographic verification now COMMERCIALLY possible by reason of the grainless film and new modes of photoprinting.

The better the editor the more he will WANT this proof of his skill, the more he will want the curious and expert player or reader of his edition to know what difficulties he has faced, what errors (if any) of the manuscript he has dealt with, and what necessary or voluntary additions and/or interpretations he has employed in deciphering a bass or allocating the parts to different instruments.

As corollary to, or emphasis on, point one, I wd. say that a composer who is any real good CAN make a musical statement in a violin and piano sonata that will distinguish him from duds, duffers, second-rate composers and the general soggy mess of nineteenth century music, as it slogged along after Chopin and Rossini.

As to "scientific bases" (*vide* Feste's article, p. 820, col. 2). I don't suppose Hawaiian and Javanese musicians are consciously worrying about scientific bases, but a cathode ray wd. probably record results that wd. prove quite satisfactory under the most rigid tests science cd. apply. Intelligence often causes a man to remain unconscious of the circum-

---

[134] *The Musical Times*, January, 1939, pp. 57–58.

pullulent idiocy and dullness of his fellows. I wholly agree with Feste's adverb "unconsciously." I must have said somewhere that Bach and his peers so took it for granted that composers would ACT on great bass that they never took the trouble to explain it, though I think earlier theoricians *thought* they had done so.

I don't quite know what "Feste" means by his sentence, " (Pound) won't admit that a composer's intentions are not adequately expressed on paper and that the performer must 'interpret'. . . them."

My point is that good composers WRITE down what they want played, but that duds (meaning most of the composers since Rossini) simply have NOT had any really accurate intentions as to the duration of their notes. Strawinsky has. The rest of 'em being too utterly and damnably incapable of HEARING the finer divisions of time HAVE, confound it, left a sort of general stage direction and the performer IF competent must "interpret," *i.e.,* do one of the most vital parts of the composer's job for him. Almost any ass or even a middle-aged literary gent like myself can hunt around on a clavichord until he finds the PITCH of the note he wants in a melody, but the job of WRITING music is something more than the mere imagining of a melodic line or an harmonic progression; it requires the capacity for registering the duration of notes and pauses. All of which most musicians will grant and not one in ten thousand realize. Any ass can draw a face, two eyes, a nose and slit beneath the latter, but we have very few Henry Gaudiers and Pablo Picassos.

What wd. you think of a painter who left a portrait vague and expected the photographer or engraver to put in the real likeness to the sitter when making the reproductions? The analogy is inexact, but may start some readers on the path toward what I am driving at.

As to my letch for Vivaldi, my minimum claim is that one can't be certain that Vivaldi is merely another composer like 60 others until one has at least heard or read through the 309 inedited concerti lying in Turin.

I admit that my acquaintance with his work has been favourably conditioned; I mean I have heard his line as rendered by a violinist exceptionally sensitive to certain qualities which are either there on the page or are suggested to the violinist by what IS on the page. ("Feste" may claim they are "interpreted" into it, but at any rate they differ from what is suggested to the violinist in question by the printed music of Bach or of Mozart.)

Bach was sufficiently interested to want some of Vivaldi's work in a form he himself cd. play without being bothered to train an ensemble. Distant from a reference library, I do not wish to mislead any reader, but my impression is that of the 12 or 16 concerti reduced by Bach (or some member of his family) for keyboard, only about six are Vivaldi's, some at least are known to be by other Italians (I think). I have heard Gerhart Münch get quite good results in performance of two that are certainly Vivaldi's and extant in Vivaldi MSS.

I am perfectly willing to admit a possible or even probable component of error in my present tentative (note the word *tentative*) hunch. Quite possible that a simple-minded bloke like myself, copying out the Dresden concerti note by note, and being pleased by the quality of Vivaldi's mind therein apparent, become more enthusiastic over the possibilities of the unpublished Vivaldi than I wd. if I heard even the same concerti played (as I have) by a heavy and heavily led orchestra. Piccardi said to me, of one of my efforts in another direction: "You will never get an orchestra to do it. With a few instruments you might get the effect."

As to the chances offered a reconstructor of Vivaldi, I can only adduce a bit of autobiography. A brilliant pianist playing from my grubby copy reproved me last summer for introducing my modern stunts into the piano part. Said stunts being found on examination IN THE MS and in no way due to my setting or adaptation.

I wd. readily admit that Vivaldi was in a sense "out of date," meaning out of fashion, out of the received ideas of the general public for a hundred and fifty years, and that he comes *into date* along with the Miro's painting, as that painting was in the years immediately following Miro's arrival in Paris.

I don't see how there can be very accurate estimate of Vivaldi's extent and variety until at least a few experts have seen or heard the 309 concerti and the 29 or more operas. Some of the Arie whereof are in various reprints. My impression is that Dandelot and Borrel are among his best modern condensers now on sale in the music shops. The first step toward a general estimate wd. be publication of the thematic catalogue now lying before me. Were musical archeology as active as several other less vital branches of what is miscalled "scholarship" this catalogue wd. have been in print three weeks after O. Rudge had made it. The Turin instrumental section (that is the list of the main incognita up to date) wd. require six pages of photo reproductions the size of the present page of *The Musical Times,* if done without margin.

I must already have overrun the space allowed to your correspondents, and must leave "Feste's" other points for another occasion. He has, in fact, raised so many that one wd. need a series of articles adequately to deal with them all.

Ezra Pound

In his article "Feste" had also queried Pound's Vivaldi figures (". . . 309 concerti of Vivaldi unplayed, lying in Turin . . ."), and took the trouble to look the matter up in Grove's *Dictionary*, where in the current edition he discovered listings for only seventy. This figure gives an idea of the state of affairs concerning this composer in 1938. But Gillies Whittaker came to Pound's rescue in a letter to the *Times*' editor (December, 1938, p. 930) and went on to give the Tigullians credit for some other musical insights as well.

> Sir,—*Re* "Feste"—Pound, November issue, pp. 819–822, Mr. Pound's Vivaldi figures are post-Grove. A young American musicologist, Miss Olga Rudge, has catalogued an immense quantity of Vivaldi's concertos which lie practically unknown in Turin, and Mr. Pound had been agitating to induce powers-that-be to have these microphotoed and made available to students. . . .
>
> "Feste" expresses surprise, in his delightful review (would that all reviews were as entertaining!), at "Ezra's" acquaintance with William Young's Sonatas. Mr. Pound not only knows them thoroughly, but has given all the eleven plus the First Set of Purcell's twelve string sonatas at his chamber concerts in Rapallo, a piece of enthusiasm not approached by the countrymen of these composers.—Yours, etc.,
>
> W. Gillies Whittaker

The final series of Rapallo concerts was held in March, 1939, and featured Olga Rudge, Renata Borgatti, and bass Guido Guidi. As in the previous year, an attractive broadside was printed, giving the programs, and this was also reprinted in *Il Mare*, February 25, on the front page. There were six concerts, of which four were devoted to Mozart sonatas, bringing the whole series full circle back to the point from which, in 1933, it had begun.

Sixteen Sonatas of Mozart
(Olga Rudge and Renata Borgatti)
And Arias Sung by Guido Guidi

First Evening: Thursday, March 2.
Sonata in D major (K. 306), 1778;
Sonata in G major (K. 379), 1781;
Sonata in A minor (K. 402), 1782;
Sonata in E-flat major (K. 380), 1781.

Second Evening: Saturday, March 4.
Two sonatas by J. Christian Bach (whom Leopold Mozart recommended to his son for study).
Sonata in F major (K. 377), 1781;
Sonata in E minor (K. 304), 1778;
Sonata in C major (K. 296), 1778.

Third Evening: Tuesday, March 7.
Sonata in F major (K. 376), 1781;
Sonata in A major (K. 305), 1778;
Sonata in B-flat major (K. 378), 1779;
Sonata in E-flat major (K. 481), 1785.

    Violin: Olga Rudge
    Piano: Renata Borgatti.

Fourth Evening: Thursday, March 9.
J. S. Bach: Partita in C minor; Renata Borgatti.
1. ALLESANDRO SCARLATTI: *Oh cessate di piagarmi;* ANTONIO CALDARA: *Sebben crudel;*
2. MOZART: *Magic Flute*—Aria by Sarastro in E major (Act II) "Qui sdegnio non s'accende"; Guido Guidi.
MOZART: Sonata in B-flat major (K. 454), composed in 1784; Olga Rudge—Renata Borgatti.
MOZART: 1. *Marriage of Figaro:* Aria in C major (Act I) "Non più andrai farfallone amoroso (Figaro's aria);
2. *Don Giovanni:* Aria in D major (Act I) "Madamina il catalogo è questo" (Leporello's aria); Guido Guidi.

Fifth Evening: Saturday, March 11.
Sonata in E-flat major (K. 302), 1778;
Sonata in G major (K. 301), 1778;
Sonata in C major (K. 303), 1778;
Sonata in A major (K. 526), 1787;
    Renata Borgatti, piano solo.

Sixth Evening: Monday, March 13.
J. S. Bach: Sonata in E major;
    Renata Borgatti, Olga Rudge.
HAYDN: Sonata in D major;
J. S. BACH: Toccata in F-sharp minor;
    Renata Borgatti.

M. RAVEL: *Gaspard de la Nuit;*
Renata Borgatti.
M. RAVEL: Sonata for violin and piano;
Renata Borgatti, Olga Rudge.

MOZART CONCERTS IN MARCH IN RAPALLO[135]

The assumption underlying our first concerts was that Mozart's sonatas for piano and violin constitute a source, a concentration of musical intelligence as unique in its way as Dante's *Paradiso* is in the realm of poetry.

The nucleus of Mozart's musical thought is in these sonatas, later to be developed in his larger compositions and finally in his full-sized operas. The sonatas, it is believed, were composed during three periods, in 1778, in 1781, and—the third stage—during the most decisive and fruitful years of his career.

It was the aim of our concerts that at least in one part of the world the public could periodically, every year, have the opportunity to hear and re-hear this series of sonatas in its entirety, sharpening its ear and training its critical judgment—that is, its ability to perceive the musical line and form of the sonata by measuring the difference between the melodic and thematic sensitivity of Mozart and other pre- and post-Mozartian composers—and to assess the place of the sonata as a musical structure in the history of music side by side with the development of other forms such as the concerto, the symphony etc.

This intention of ours was later modified for various reasons, notably by the publication by Dr. Whittaker of unknown or little known music (Wm. Young and Purcell); and our plans could be further modified by the appearance of other editions or transcriptions of early masterpieces. The first time we presented the sonatas in their order of composition; this year there will be four evenings, each of which will in itself offer the opportunity of observing the complete development of the composer's thought.

The March concerts will take place between March 2 and 13; the dates will be specified later and the programs may be subject to changes and additions.

[A tentative program then followed.]

A sixth evening to be added during the period of those already announced—will introduce us to the bass Guido Guidi, a former member of the Chicago Civic Opera, who was enthusiastically received

[135] *Il Mare,* February 11, 1939; translated.

during the open air operatic season in Rapallo last August (as Don Basilio in the *Barber of Seville*); he will sing Leporello's arias from *Don Giovanni* and other Mozart arias yet to be determined, probably from *The Magic Flute* and *The Marriage of Figaro*.

These were the last concerts to be held in Rapallo. In 1940 Pound wrote to Tibor Serly:

> Our public performances suspended now for duration of war, but editing, dechifrage, of Vivaldi goes on. Reduction to two or three instruments—pyanny and one or two violins so as to try 'em out and see which shd. be written out in partitur for orchestra. However, the Siena week shows where a small push can lead.[136]

In September 1939 the Accademia Musicale Chigiana of Siena had decided to give over the entire program of the third *Settimana musicale* to Vivaldi. For Pound and Olga Rudge it was a musical triumph. Olga was by this time, of course, very active in Siena as Secretary to the Academy, and in 1938 Pound had given Count Guido Chigi Saracini, the Academy's illustrious founder and benefactor, the microfilms he had obtained from Dresden for the library. Some of these were later to be transcribed and performed on *Settimana* programs, excellently performed, under the artistic direction of Alfredo Casella.

The idea of presenting great blocks of one composer's work in sequence was a long-standing Tigullian ideal, as was a particular passion for the composer in question, and Pound took pleasure in the fact that the Rapallo experiment had at least served as a useful prototype for the extended exercise now possible in Siena. To Tibor Serly he wrote:

> Note ours of 1933. Not indicating that Casella got it from us but steps in developing a demand *for* constructed program.
> The improvement of Italian festival programs. Siena now proposes to do one composer or groups of related composers, not merely mixed salad. Due mainly to O. R., but don't rub it in too hard, not tactful. Politeness to Casella will do you no harm. Easy enough to distribute the credit so as not to annoy anyone.[137]

The Vivaldi Week was celebrated in a number of articles. In the second of these, "Vocal or Verbal," discussion of the Siena

[136] Paige, *Letters*, New York, p. 344; London, p. 443.
[137] *Ibid.*

activities swerves into a consideration of the values of vocal versus verbal treatment of words in song settings. This is a subject with a long history for Pound. Most recently he had considered it in connection with the "verbal" felicities of Arnaut Daniel versus the "vocal" effects of Janequin in dealing with the same subject matter—birds (*vide: Il Mare,* April 25, 1936). I have also mentioned Pound's intention to investigate the work of the Florentine *Camerata,* and members of this group do get mentioned in the "Vocal or Verbal" article as well as in "A Letter from Rapallo" of a year later. The *Camerata* was a group of revolutionary poets and musicians who gathered together about 1590, at first to discuss the function of music in Greek drama. Their importance for music history is that out of these discussions they invented a new *genre:* opera. But their idea of opera was one in which music was definitely to be subservient to the text. Basically, they rebelled against the polyphonic music of the Renaissance and advocated a recitative style in which music was intended to become a vehicle for enhancing great poetry, a theory very much like Pound's own. The emergence of this *stile rappresentativo,* or recitative, dates from about 1600 when the first operas were written. The leading figures of the *Camerata* were Count Bardi, the poet Ottavio Rinunccini, the singer-composers Jacopo Peri and Giulio Caccini, and the theoretician Vincenzo Galilei, father of the astronomer.

THE VIVALDI REVIVAL[138]

We must not think that after the triumph of the Siena Week the revival of Vivaldi's music has come to an end, nor that the treasure of his unpublished manuscripts is exhausted. We must say at once that this treasure has hardly been tapped.

We lit our little spark four years ago during the days of the sanctions.[139] We have mentioned a Vivaldi-Bach axis, and we could also, if necessary, proclaim a musical autarchy of our own.

I don't see any need for employing the antinomy "an Italian Bach." Vivaldi was a true Italian, who often had the self-assurance to leave his lines blank and unembellished wherever he or a contemporary would

---

[138] *Il Mare,* November 25, 1939; translated.

[139] The reference here is to sanctions imposed by the League of Nations against Italy after Mussolini's attack on Ethiopia in October, 1935. Italy was accordingly forced to fall back and establish a state of autarchy or cultural and economic self-sufficiency.

have immediately understood which notes needed to be added to his meagre indications. A week of his music (and recognition for its success must be given to Count Chigi and to the maestri Casella, Mortari and Frazzi) has still left three hundred concerti unpublished and a quantity of sacred and operatic music untouched!

In Rapallo we are studying several dozen "repatriated" compositions, and I don't know how many, and what else besides, we will be able to offer this year to our faithful colleagues. But we will certainly do something, and the dates will be announced in due time, whether there are sanctions or not, and regardless of mercantile considerations.

So as to be able to make comparisons and to have a point of reference, our musicians will present some Bach masterpieces, especially the partita containing the Chaconne. Then, if other supporters will back the request I have already received, I will add some of Corelli's sonatas, even though I do so somewhat against my will, because—without question—I find Corelli inferior to Vivaldi just as Handel is inferior to Bach. In any case we will be performing unpublished or little known music by Vivaldi that is much more stimulating than the sonatas by Corelli available in current editions.

Further, in support of Italian musical autarchy we have enough unpublished music by Vivaldi and Boccherini to last for ten years of musical weeks and festivals, and of operatic music by Rossini, which must again become a part, if not of the regular repertoire, at least of the listening experience of the few connoisseurs and perhaps of the curious.

EZRA POUND

VOCAL OR VERBAL[140]

In the art of making enemies I know of no more efficient method than to praise those memorable moments, those exceptional triumphs which cannot be repeated. All who have not shared in them are indignant because they can't use such publicity for their own benefit.

And when we get down to details, even the subjects of our praises are dissatisfied. The struggle towards perfection is tiring, even to the most faithful.

I must say that the Vivaldi Week in Siena was the most serious musical celebration I have witnessed in Italy, and the program one of the most interesting I have discovered. It was a triumph of organization. Casella's, Frazzi's, and particularly Mortari's work was excellent. The

---

[140] *Meridiano di Roma,* November 26, 1939; translated.

performances overcame so many immediate difficulties that we must remember them as we do the supreme moments of past festivals, such as the Hungarian Quartet in Venice three years ago, Stravinsky's *Capriccio* in Venice the previous year, etc.

A system of perfect preservation does not exist in any country, and an archive by definition has no capacity for choosing interesting dates.

Since Italian music criticism has Della Corte, the author of an analysis of Stravinsky's *Oedipus,* I am convinced of the inutility of adding more notes.

And in fact I have no intention of writing a critique of the Vivaldi Week. I'll only add some observations.

The first concert was magnificiently built. For years I have been insisting that the *program* of a musical evening must have a form complete in itself, no less well planned than a fugue. Such a form has been conscientiously studied in Rapallo. I think the example offered by Siena should be quoted for general study as a typical model to follow. The credit goes to Alfredo Casella. Take note:

> *Vivaldi.* 1. Sinfonia in D major; 2. Concerto in G minor; 3. Concerto in B minor; 4. Aria "Non posso lasciar"; 5. Concerto in A minor, i.e., Vivaldi's B minor transcribed by Bach for harpsichords; 6. *Concert'alla Rustica,* in which the parts were magnificently distributed by Casella among the instruments of an orchestra *not too large* for this music.

Composition No. 3 bears repetition as No. 5 because the whole history of music contains few works of such outstanding value that they have been adapted or submitted to variations by another composer of equal stature.

I had in Siena the same impression another critic had in Munich, namely that the great German composer did not improve Vivaldi's concerto. But this does not mean his service was useless. I maintain against the academicians that a conscientious study may be of educational value even if the result is negative, as happened with Busoni's adaptation of Bach's *Chaconne.* I have not yet heard Casella's orchestration of this masterpiece and I won't defend it on principle because I doubt the result.[141]

In art one single vice is forbidden: cowardice. After producing a week which can stand comparison with any other music festival in the world, Siena promises to repeat the event every year. So we must not

---

141 Compare: "Without having heard Casella's resetting of the Chaconne for orchestra. I wd. defend even that *on principle.*" Guide to Kulchur, p. 251.

be content with short-range hopes. It is legitimate to make various suggestions, in fact more legitimate than retrospective comments.

In the *Meridiano* of September 3 I find a quotation from the qualified musicologist S. A. Luciani. His autochthonous name ought to protect me from any accusation by our editor that I present "things invented and that do not exist." Nevertheless the article in the *Meridiano* omits Luciani's most explicit sentence.

Everything Luciani says concerning *Bel Canto* on p. 74 of his *Mille anni di musica* must be considered in relationship to what he says on p. 45 on polyphony.

"The art of *Bel Canto* consists simply of turning the human voice into an instrument to compete with the flute etc." Page 45: "The polyphonic production of the XVth and XVIth centuries is essentially vocal . . . etc. . . . But this does not mean that it is verbal. The diversity and independence of the voices often hinders the comprehension of the text."

There may be *two* crimes against verbal values. The first has a musical merit, or may have one in a contrapuntal structure. In first-rate counterpoint it may be permissible to sacrifice verbal values, particularly if they are undistinguished. But when melody adds nothing to the verbal value it is not laudable to warp valid and interesting verbal rhythm or sense.

When sung, the text often has no value in itself. Here too we must distinguish. If the protagonist sings only "Proud of myself," repeating it six or more times, the text as poetry doesn't matter.

But we have neglected the distinctions too much. It is permissible to dream of a first-rate text set to first-rate music, a music which intensifies or illustrates the values of very great poetry.

When the poet has been lazy, ignorant or clumsy, he doesn't deserve such an addition, and can't obtain it; for the musician, given a poem lacking technical and vocal values worth singing, is forced either to abandon the words or ruin his music.

It is an act of cowardice to hide archetypes. We need, need greatly, to hear the experiments of Caccini and Vincenzo Galilei again, to determine whether they are dry and pedantic exercises, precursors only of a new form, or if "le Nuove Musiche" of 1600 contained real masterpieces neglected by subsequent audiences lacking sufficient and precise general culture. Are they worth reviving in our time?

In the Fascist "Era Nuova" (year XVIII) perhaps we are better equipped to hear and appreciate them than the public of the accursed and porcine nineteenth century, the century of "usura" and of all the aesthetic vices accompanying its nefarious tolerance, which blunted the perception of *all* truth.

If Caccini and Galilei have failed, an excellent field of *possibility* remains open for us and our successors.

I do not speak without experience for I have set to music Villon's and Cavalcanti's best poems with one merit at least. That is, when my work on Villon's text was broadcast by the London radio I could understand every word with its proper sense and weight sitting in the electrician's kitchen in Rapallo, and I ought to achieve the same result with Cavalcanti's and Sordello's words. I don't say this for the benefit of other composers, and I am not discussing my possible lack, etc., of musical talent. I rest my case.[142] Let the judges have the verdict. I don't expect to start a craze since the amount of poetry susceptible to such treatment is limited. Few poets have the necessary skill, the substance and rhythmic variety to offer such scope to a musician.

Both Antheil and Tibor Serly, convinced of the value of my scheme, have asked me to find them texts. And I have not been able to do so because even Shakespeare's *Pericles* presents the same difficulties as the works mentioned by Luciani (pp. 62–64).

The verbal material of *Pericles* was put together to be declaimed on stage, not to be sung. Shakespeare's greatness as a playwright has obscured his talent as a lyrical technician. Note that he wrote short poems to be sung in his plays, and that when he wanted to provide material for the human voice as an instrument "to compete with the flute, the violin, etc.," he wrote meaningless syllables like "hey, nonny nonny" etc., with high vocal value to allow short descants.

The English language, compared to Spanish and Italian, is short on poetry that can be sung. Or rather it had a brilliant period but with limited rhythmic variety. After Villon, Cavalcanti, Sordello, I went to Catullus's epithalamium, but he was not the first expatriate of language.

Henry Lawes, praised by the poet Waller for the way he had set his poems to music, went back, at the end of his third collection, to the Greek and Latin poets, for lack, in my opinion, of English verbal material offering wider rhythmic and melodic variety. In other words, English lyrical poetry is built on a verbal range of few themes and variations which soon become monotonous. Whereas in Italy literary snobbishness has neglected the merits of Sterbini and perhaps of other librettists. Everyone knows *Il Barbiere di Siviglia* is a masterpiece but I am afraid very few appreciate the mastery of Rossini's librettist, the megalomania of that damned nineteenth century having obscured a finer greatness.

In fact, for words sung with orchestra, Rossini was the *miglior fabbro*. Forget the blockheads who admire operas beloved of the public.

---

142 English in original.

There is no greater misfortune in art than prestige which clouds the landscape and hinders clear perception of the *limitations* of great artists. Gregorio balefully said "greatness" obscures. He did not have verbal intuitions. Bach did not have verbal intuition. Very well! Let us admire him, but not as a musical verbalist any more than for his capacity to paint portraits.

In short, the organizers of the Vivaldi Week have beneficiently presented music for harpsichord; which is more than Gerlin could do when he returned to Venice from Paris, leaving his position to the Machiavellians of "usura" and the sale of war materials. Gerlin has had the courage to *represent* music for harpsichord on the piano (opening of the Society for Old Music, Venice, October 15). But Italy must not leave such an artist, a man so sensitive to the values of the texture of old music, without an instrument of his own.

It is impossible to listen properly to XVIIth and XVIIIth century music if we substitute the piano for the vintage qualities we have enjoyed in Siena. Autarchy lacks not the means of providing harpsichords for every conservatory on the peninsula.

A LETTER FROM RAPALLO[143]
Annual Music Week Proposed to Introduce Each Year Insufficiently Known Composer

At the beginning of the war in Ethiopia, as we could not expect a concert audience, the Rapallo group resolved itself into a study circle with the immediate intention of hearing as many of the 310 concerti of Vivaldi as were available in printed editions and executable by one or two violinists and a piano. Having done that, two Americans, Olga Rudge and David Nixon, gave a concert in Venice, made up entirely from Vivaldi's *Estro Armonico* (Op. 3) and an abortive Vivaldi society was started in his own city. Miss Rudge then made the first thematic catalog of the unpublished Vivaldi lying in the Turin Library (309 concerti) and other works, which catalog has now been printed by Count Chigi of Siena in the *Note e Documenti* for the full-dress Vivaldi Week given there.

That festival marks a definite advance in the Italian official method in treating their music. We have for some time been insisting that the whole of an evening's program should have a form in itself, which need not be inferior in structure to that of, say, a fugue or any other art form. And we have insisted that the auditor cannot get a clear or

[143] *Japan Times Weekly*, Tokyo, Sunday, January 7, 1940, p. 8.

adequate conception of a great composer's meaning unless he hears a lot of that composer's work all at once.

We also, as Katue Kitasono noted some time ago in VOU, suggested various methods of contrast between musical compositions, intended to test their real value and to demonstrate what modern compositions could stand comparison with past master-work.

Yeats long ago pointed out that minor poets often show up very well in anthologies, but that the difference between them and the greater poets is quickly apparent if you contrast whole books of their work.

The Sienese Week was admirable in various ways. Their first program was a model of construction (due I think to Alfredo Casella). And as Mr. Kitasono has cited some Rapallo examples, I shall perhaps be permitted to cite the Siena evening in detail though the reader will have to verify what I say of it, by future experiment on his own part. The program contained six items, five by Vivaldi and one transcribed from Vivaldi by his better known contemporary J. S. Bach. Given in this order:

> 1. Sinfonia in Do. magg. 2. Concerto in Sol min. 3. Concerto in si min. 4. Aria, from "La Fida Ninfa." 5. Bach's transcription from the concerto in Si. min, reworked that is by Bach for four harpsichords, and in the key of la min. 6. Concerto "Alla Rustica."

The Week's music was ably varied: these were instrumental works, a revival of the opera *Olimpiade,* probably the first performance since Vivaldi's death in 1741, and choral works given in the Church of S. Francesco with full orchestra.

The Week amply testified to Vivaldi's being a major composer not simply "another" Italian composer of his period to be remembered by the often reprinted "Cucco" movement from one of his violin concerti, or by the single aria "Un Certo non se che" which had been the only bit of his vocal music available in a modern edition.

All this being in accord with the beliefs printed by the violinist Rudge and by Cobbett, who had said a few years ago that Vivaldi was a composer with a future. Of course this doesn't mean that one has "discovered" Vivaldi. His name has long been in every encyclopedia or dictionary of music, but it does mean that musical history is undergoing a revision in its estimate of him. A number of general questions rise and or have been raised.

There is a timeliness in all resurrections in art; whether it be in painting, literature or in music. In Miss Rudge's own rendering of the concerto I have found a close kinship with the line of the surrealist Dali. I don't know whether this comes from the manuscript or from the executant. I have long blamed or at least teased the surrealists for their naive belief that they had invented something which had already been present in Guido Cavalcanti's poetry when Dante was 10 years old. There is plenty of surrealism in medieval poetry. The human spirit has recurring needs of expression.

Even before one knew the detail of Vivaldi's life one could hear certain qualities in his music, and possibly one exaggerates one's own perceptivity when one learns the personal and human background from which the Venetian master produced his music. He was priest, professor of music to a girl's convent school and then in later life ran an opera company, presenting his own operas and travelling from Mantua to Vienna in company with a barber's daughter, whom he had taught to sing with great success, and with assistant nymphs or whatever. Goldoni describes visiting the old man who was scribbling musical phrases on his desk and dipping into his breviary.

All of which is complementary to the qualities of his musical phrasing.

As composer his mind was furnished with the thoughts of Dante's Paradise and with the gaiety of his home city. At any rate the qualities registered in his music extend from one of these frontiers to the other. And the greatest of European composers J. S. Bach was sufficiently interested in six of his (Vivaldi's) concerti to transpose them for his own use without perhaps having improved them. The work of fitting this music to modern orchestra for the Siena festival was admirably performed by Casella, Frazzi, and Virgilio Mortari under the general direction of Casella. Count Chigi and the Italian authorities propose to proceed to an annual music week devoted each year to the work of one insufficiently known Italian creator or to a group of related composers. Possibly in 1940 we shall hear the two Scarlatti, and in 1941 possibly, on the bicentennial of Vivaldi's death, a second week of Vivaldi simply justified by the results of this year's performance.

It all means a much more serious presentation of old Italian music than we have yet had. It means a much more intelligent study of the enormous treasure of Italian musical composition.

Both the eminent musicologue S. A. Luciani[144] and the violinist Rudge[145] have raised another basic issue, namely the distinction and proper criteria for "musica vocale and musica verbale."

Which merely means: can one understand the words when they are sung? And this question can be divided into two aesthetic questions,

---

[144] *Mille anni di musica*, vol. 1, published by Hoepli of Milan [1935]. (Pound's note.) Editor's note: Pound knew Luciani. He was active at the *Accademia Chigiana* in Siena, where he founded, with Olga Rudge, the *Centro di Studi Vivaldiani*.

[145] Article in *Meridiano di Roma*, September 3, 1939. (Pound's note.)

namely: Has the musician preserved or has he ruined the rhythm and phonetic qualities of the poetry?

Or, on the other hand, did the poet know his job well enough to write with such qualities of sound and movement that his words are worth preserving or illustrating and emphasizing? In the twelfth century the troubadours tried to fit words and music to each other. Dante animadverted on this subject.

When it came to a question of theater and sung drama along about the year 1600 a.d. Vincenzo Galilei, Giulio Caccini and a literary circle in Firenze tried to make opera that would keep the verbal values as such. Then came stage music which used the voice mostly as an "instrument to rival the flute" etc. The words then usually of no great interest in themselves, gave way to vocalization and the intellectual qualities of opera, or at any rate the literary values of libretti are often dubious. Rossini attained a very high degree of mastery, in fact I know of no opera where the words and orchestra are so well combined as they are in the *Barbiere di Seviglia*.

On the other hand the French café-concert songs usually emphasize their words and the sharp meaning of the phrases.

The ideal or an idea, or call it merely my desire, if you like, is an opera where the singer sings great poetry to a fine music which emphasizes and illuminates the significance of the word, and, to do this, makes them clearly audible and comprehensible to the listener.

I have made a few attempts in this direction. No one is compelled to like my music, but I have at any rate set some of the greatest European poetry, namely that of Villon, and of Guido Cavalcanti with a few bits of Sordello. When the Villon was transmitted by the London radio I sat in the electrician's kitchen in Rapallo and could understand every one of the words.

Antheil and Tibor Serly both wanted to work on these lines: but it is very difficult to find poetry sufficiently well written to stand such musical treatment. Especially in English the amount of poetry that can be sung without either distorting the words or damaging the musician's invention is limited. Shakespeare wrote for declamation. He wrote a few lyrics to be sung in his plays. He solved the problem of using the voice merely as instrument by writing in such meaningless syllables as "Hey, nonny nonny" on which the singer cd. turn loose, without damaging the sense of the rest of the poem. The syllables have no meaning in themselves but have good sounds for the singer, and guide the musician in rhythm. In Italian there is a vast amount of libretto writing that is probably singable. But literary snobbism may or may not have obscured it.

However all this battle field is now again laid open.

If the Italians start again listening to two kinds of singing it can hardly fail to stimulate discrimination, and with the proper exposition of seventeenth century and, let us hope, also of sixteenth and fifteenth century music, we should have a musical reform in Italy or a new and valid movement in which fine musical line and strongly active invention will replace the sloppiness of the XIXth century composition.

At any rate, thanks to Count Guido Chigi Saracini and his associates the Sienese annual week of music, has started something and opened up possibilities. It is to be followed with increasing attention by critics of music in general, from all countries.

VIVALDI AND SIENA[146]

The Scarlatti week at Siena last year proved that three or five Scarlattis don't make a Vivaldi. This conclusion was a recompense for the expenses of that week. Every time I have tried to analyze, criticize, or jot down my impressions of that week, alien affairs, the necessity of confronting the syphilitic economic situation in the USA and the determination of the Morgenthau-Roosevelts to extend the armed conflict, has distracted me from paying homage to the Muses. But now that we are talking of a week dedicated to Vivaldi, I feel it my duty to register my experiences and speculations in case they may be of some use.

A most noticeable improvement in the performance standard of music in Siena has to be reported. The admirers of Scarlatti, particularly of his operatic work, have had a great advantage over the admirers of Vivaldi. All his merits and praises were sung and consecrated by the press last year. In my opinion, future developments of the Siena event must avoid a confusion, or confusions, of aims. It is useless to have at Siena a social event more or less like the "Maggio Musicale Fiorentino." When I say "social event" I mean a festival of music pandering to public taste.

This is legitimate, even eminently legitimate, often feasible, and, under the old mercantile system, almost everywhere necessary.

But the Siena Festival is in a different class. It should be able to attract international attention, permanently or increasingly, as long as it maintains its *own* style. The idea was to present a neglected or inadequately known composer comprehensively enough to enable the critic, the enthusiast, and the musicologist to form an accurate judgment of his merits and historical position.

[146] *Meridiano di Roma*, June 15, 1941; translated.

Vivaldi, with his 309 unpublished concerti in the Turin library, was an apt choice for the first Festival. But the idea was diluted by adding composers from the Scarlatti *family*. The result justified this deviation. The vast uncharted territory of Vivaldi's work still offers great possibilities for exploration.

The miracle in 1939 was that the Festival took place at all; tenors had to be called up at the last moment from the army. In 1940, under Maestro Guarnieri's direction, the works of Scarlatti proved charming, but didn't dazzle the audience to the point of obscuring the gap separating Vivaldi's melodic and thematic genius from Scarlatti's.

I note that the Salzburg Festival has acquired an international reputation because it focuses *adequate* attention on Mozart's music; the same is true of the Bethlehem Festival in the USA because it concentrates all its energies on Bach's music. But let's not exaggerate. I see the possibility for at least two types of music festival: the usual "social" one where a pot-pourri of diverse music is presented with whatever seriousness such circumstances will allow. In this case, I think, the festival that can count on the biggest budget will attract the widest audience, assisted by snobbery, press publicity, fashion, etc.

The Venice Festival (which was biennial) and the "Maggio Fiorentino" are of this type. In Venice it was customary to dedicate one entire evening to old music. But now I hear that future festivals in Venice will deal with contemporary music, giving special attention to premières of new works. That's fine, even if the old music was usually what gave most pleasure to the devotees. One week a year at least must be dedicated to the efforts of living composers. It would be useless for Siena to compete in this field. It is most desirable—at least this is what the more serious audience desires—that Siena should maintain its own style, that is, that it should present music, if not unknown, at least inaccessible and very seldom performed.

If financial problems arise, I can see two solutions. One composer's instrumental music could be featured and, if he hasn't written operas, the item chosen should simply be the most interesting among those unperformed for one or more centuries, or simply the best that we have not heard for a long time. Measured by certain standards Rossini had a mastery that his fame has eclipsed. But no serious composer should remain insensitive to Rossini's *technical* skill for combining and interweaving the melodic lines of instruments and human voices. How many of us have heard all Rossini's operas? (Even if they were all inferior to the *Barbiere,* how many of us are sure of it? Have serious listeners not more curiosity for Rossini?)

Guido Guidi once rightly said to me: "But the people have chosen certain operas from the rest of his repertoire, and this choice in itself is a criticism."

I agree that this form of criticism has its value, perhaps greater than that of a fanatic who loves music for personal reasons; but from time to time *every* evaluation, every hierarchy of values, needs to be revised. Nine times out of ten the revaluation confirms the judgment of "history." But the tenth time one discovers a treasure, and perhaps a revolution or renaissance in art is born.

The Siena Festival must go on and must not be diluted. It must not lose its character and descend to the level of a medley, a pot-pourri of diverse music.

If the means for stage production are lacking, our efforts should concentrate on neglected music that can be performed at less expense.

At Rapallo, for seven consecutive years up to the beginning of the present war, we persisted in a "narrow-gauge" experiment, more specialized than the Siena Festival. It was not our aim to be popular.

Let us say that Florence and Venice have social festivals, and that Siena, for the musicians, is a laboratory which may be of interest exclusively to musicologists, but this too may not be without value. If money is lacking, a group of players and scholars can still get together, and we can at least ask them to perform the results of their labours for a larger group of music lovers.

At Rapallo the first aim was to gratify my personal desire to hear all the Mozart sonatas for piano and violin, all of them one after the other, and frequently enough to imprint a good idea of the meaning Mozart gave to the word "sonata." In three years of writing concert reviews in London I never had that chance.

Having achieved this aim, the Rapallo group continued an examination of the "sonata" for two instruments, trying to establish a line between "first-rate," i.e., sonatas by truly great composers, and "second-rate," i.e., popular sonatas deserving *less* esteem, even if almost everyone likes them.

Experimenting with well-known music against the standard of Bach and Mozart, then widening the field with the help of the Gertler and the Hungarian Quartets with Vegh, Halmos, Koromzay, Palotai (and Székely the following year), we heard four quartets by Bartók, the little-known sonatas by Wm. Young and the ten sonatas by Purcell, newly illuminated in Whittaker's edition, all to the great pleasure and profit of a limited audience. It is not necessary for Siena to adopt such modest dimensions, but whenever the money is limited, a group of serious musicians can do something similar. It could also be done at

Siena if expenses had to be cut, without diminishing the intellectual level of the rest of the Festival.

We must not confuse two *different* types of experiment. The "Accademia Chigiana" is a school by definition. This suggests a great number of performers. An academy of this kind does not have to solve the problem of a "limited group."

The experienced listener derives more pleasure from a perfect performance by two players than from the stew of a mediocre orchestra. Very often a delicate talent is ruined by the mercantile system. Thus, for example, if a fine talent plays four or eight hours a day with the London BBC Orchestra, his organism will wear out and the quality of his performance will deteriorate. The touring life of the Hungarian musicians I mentioned above requires herculean strength to enable them to travel interminable hours by train and then perform wonders.

A humane system will conserve many talents that the mercantile system has shattered. It will be at the same time more demanding and more benevolent. It will not tolerate incompetence and especially lack of sensitivity on the part of the players.

But it will demand that particularly sensitive talents be given special treatment and receive assistance (material) to help them develop.

The hierarchy of musical values will be much more accurate and the steps better defined.

In recent times the bestiality of the music industry has extolled the performer over the composer. In London-Sodom posters twelve-by-eighteen feet carry only the name of the performer and almost no detail of the program. Naturally whoever goes to hear a coxcomb whacking a piano, in the end becomes less sensitive to the value-shadings of the music itself. This enlarges indifference to the internal *meaning* of the music, as well as to the quality of the performance.

The dream of the music lover is to be able to choose the program.

Of those music lovers of the last century who were also performers, only a few were able to choose their *own* program. Let us say that five per cent of all musicians have had clear or valid preferences, but even they have been restricted by "circumstance," by the necessity of making a living, and by the taste, real or imagined, of the public. The "superstar" system had the infamous effect of progressively reducing the concert repertoire. Only when the performers (in music or in drama) remain in one city or town can they expand their repertoire.

At this moment I don't know where in Italy I could hear a series of concerts containing a dozen first-rate sonatas or quartets, performed with real insight. And I am not at all sure whether it will be possible after the War to resume the kind of performances I described earlier at Rapallo. At Siena there is hope for a program without compromises, a program that will not be mistaken for *any* other.

En passant, I still have not been able to satisfy my curiosity to hear *L'Amfiparnasso* by Orazio Vecchi in Carlo Perinello's version.

This year is the bicentenary of the death of Antonio Vivaldi and I propose that a commemorative postage stamp be issued in his honor as has been done for Bellini, Pergolesi and Spontini.

5
Postscript 1942–1972

There is little more to add. The circumstances of Pound's life subsequent to the war are well known. Music continued to be recalled affectionately (particularly in *The Pisan Cantos*) but the making of music ceased, and even opportunities to listen to music were rare. On one of Louis Zukofsky's visits to Saint Elizabeths Hospital he took his son Paul, now a celebrated violinist, to play Bach, Mozart, and Corelli to the poet. Also played was the perennial *Chant des Oiseaux* in Münch's transcription. Another visitor was the conductor Robert Hughes, who visited him there in 1958 as the member of a recorder quartet from Buffalo, led by Forrest Read.

> We played Gabrieli Canzone out on the lawn for Pound and his wife, and Pound said it was only the second time he had heard live music during his incarceration there—the first time having been a pianist brought by Stokowski. In addition to the soprano recorder I had my bassoon along, and having read that Pound at one time had played the instrument I offered it to him. He declined, saying that he gave it up in the 1920s in order to take up boxing with Hemingway. I asked him about *Le Testament* and he said that, as a consequence of the war, he had no idea where the manuscript or a copy could be found. He did, however, say that he had a page or two of his unfinished opera *Cavalcanti* and promptly fetched it from his room. It looked like a Ruggles manuscript—very large notes scribbled on broad wrapping paper.

We played it for him: a simple troubadour-type tune, not terribly distinguished as a melody, but with a certain grace and ease for the voice.[1]

Although Pound was as active as ever, and even kept up a correspondence with some old musical acquaintances such as Agnes Bedford and Raymonde Collignon, the postwar period produced no more music reviews. A short note in *Edge*, October, 1957, signed W[illiam] A[theling] is not about music.

My own encounter with Pound dates from the summer of 1960. From London I had written asking if I could come to talk to him about poetry and music. I was particularly curious about the *Villon*, which I had seen mentioned in numerous critical studies, though no one seemed to know much about it. He wrote back that my proposal sounded "unvenomed and innocuous," then went on to tell me not to come. I went. Pound was at that time in Brunnenburg Castle near Merano in the Italian Tirol, the home of his daughter Mary and her husband Boris de Rachewiltz.

I knocked. No one seemed to be in. Then high above me from one of the towers Pound poked out his head and said simply, "So you've come." I went up. He was in his undershirt and quickly apologized for not having any of "the old vino" to offer me. He then promptly took to the horizontal on his bed and while I sat at his desk we had the most relaxed of our several conversations. We spoke of Arab music, which interested him because of its rhythms and its unharmonized melodies.[2] At one point he veered sharply off this theme and produced from one of his drawers a poem about Huey Long, which he thought would go well to music. "We've made a mess of the world for you people," he said, the only time he ever touched on the renunciation theme so often recounted by other visitors of these years, and then we returned to Arab music.

Pound was a generous conversationalist; he listened. He asked questions. There was no monologue but an exchange of ideas—at least one flattered oneself to think so.

On another day he "sang" portions of *Le Testament* while I studied some of the music, and I was astonished at his impeccable memory for the songs well over forty years after they had been

---

[1] Recounted in Ned Rorem's "Ezra Pound as Musician," *London Magazine*, January, 1968, p. 29.
[2] It will be recalled that Arab music was an ancient enthusiasm of Pound's. See the *New Age* article, April 15, 1920.

composed. On another occasion my wife and I were invited to tea. Dorothy Pound, Mary, and Boris were there. I noticed the Dolmetsch clavichord and mentioned it but was told it lacked strings, was out of tune, and no one played it. Pound was sullen, then after he reckoned we had chatted enough said in a plangent voice I shall never forget: "Schafer came here to talk music and the whole thing has degenerated into a goddamned tea-party." Immediately everyone left. Mary was asked to fetch "the books," but before she could do so the old man sprang out of his chair with a startling athleticism and went for them himself. He had marked places in each one, and for the next several hours he read poems and we talked about how or if they could be set to music. He favoured the *Odes*, which he insisted needed music to complete them more than the earlier poems. When asked which instruments he would like to see employed in settings of his poetry he mentioned the trombone, bassoon, percussion, and piano.

I have never set any of Pound's poems, though I once wrote a song about him to a text of my own. When I was leaving the castle I asked how I could obtain a copy of *Le Testament,* which I had proposed to the BBC for broadcast, and he quickly typed out a note to the Librarian of the Library of Congress:

> Give Schafer microfilm of the *Villon.*
> Ezra Pound.

Then with remarkable ingenuousness he handed me an open brown envelope. "Something to read on the train. When you get back to London give this to Tom." The package contained a neat typewritten draft of a set of Cantos, the last, I was later to learn, he ever completed.

Appendix I

THE DEVELOPING THEORIES OF ABSOLUTE RHYTHM AND GREAT BASS

Reviewing *Antheil and the Treatise on Harmony* in 1931 the American musicologist Carl Engel wrote:

> On the whole, however, Mr. Pound's observations on rhythm are neat and sensible rather than original. He believes in an absolute rhythm. So did Heraclitus. So do most of us, for that matter. But what the secret is of a flowing line of verse, or felicitous prose cadence, Mr. Pound does not pretend to divulge. . . .[1]

Mr. Engel was, of course, in no position to know the extent of Pound's obsession with this subject. The purpose of this appendix is simply to gather together many of the poet's statements concerning the concepts he called *absolute rhythm* and *Great Bass* in roughly chronological order, and to try to determine what he meant by them, a matter of some confusion. Most of the quotations have been drawn from the substance of this book itself, though a few important statements come from other Pound books. There are others still from other sources, but the present collection, I believe, shows the thrust of Pound's ideas clearly enough. His thought is not without ambiguities; no discussion of rhythm has ever been foolproof.

In its broadest sense rhythm organizes the parts into a whole. Rhythm articulates the journey. There are regular rhythms and irregular

---

[1] Carl Engel, "Poet as Prophet" in *Discords Mingled*, Freeport, New York, 1947, pp. 172-83.

rhythms. Some rhythms may be as imprecise as the flow of water, for rhythm and river are etymologically related: *rheō,* flow. Because of the propensity of Western man to organize time into regular pulsations (ticks, beats, accents), a lot of misunderstanding exists between rhythm and meter.

> Rhythm is in the year and its seasons recurrently flowing. Time is their marking off into days and hours. Calendars change, but the silent procession of the seasons goes on, regardless of man's reckoning. Was ever the Equinox changed by Gregory or Julian? Does Spring hop into Summer on a given day with an "accent"? Let flow our music as the seasons flow. . . . The great cosmic stream as it courses through the arts is called Rhythm. The channels by means of which it flows we call rhythms, and the measurement of those moulds that take the flow we call meter. . . . To measure Rhythm by its mould would be to confound the life of a man with his statue.[2]

This distinction, by Pound's friend Katherine Ruth Heyman, could have been suggested to her by Pound and may indeed have been. Because the confusion between rhythm and meter is persistent, Pound's theories of *absolute rhythm* and *Great Bass* are concerned to set the relationship between them straight. What is the relationship between temporal metrics and the living shapes of art? The first is mathematical, the second organic. One of the paradoxes is that music, which in principle employs discrete pitch and time units and has developed a quantified system of notation for their precise expression, has never claimed that the performance of music should be without its *tempo rubato,* while speech, which is of necessity unequal in stress and articulation, has in some of the highest forms of poetry been constrained by arbitrary systems of quantitative meter. Pound made much out of this when he quoted Thomas Mace, Rousseau, and Couperin from Dolmetsch's book *The Interpretation of the Music of the XVIIth and XVIIIth Centuries.*

> . . . you must Know, That, although in our First Undertakings, we ought to *strive,* for the most Exact Habit of *Time-keeping* that possibly we can attain unto . . . yet, when we come to be *Masters* . . . we Then *take Liberty* . . . to *Break Time*. . . .   [MACE]

> . . . At this word "movement" there are people who imagine that to give the movement is to follow and keep time; but there is a difference between the one and the other, for one may keep time without entering into the movement. . . .   [ROUSSEAU]

[2] Katheryn Ruth Heyman, *The Relation of Ultramodern to Archaic Music,* Boston, 1921, pp. 46–47.

> We write differently from what we play.... I find that we confuse Time, or Measure, with what is called Cadence or Movement. Measure defines the quantity and equality of beats; Cadence is properly the spirit, the soul that must be added to it.[3]
>
> [COUPERIN]

The condition of music was invoked to argue for *vers libre,* the liberation of poetry from metrical imprisonment to find its natural cadence. The term *absolute rhythm* was defined by Pound with great precision as early as 1910 in the introduction to his Cavalcanti translations.

> Rhythm is perhaps the most primal of all things known to us. It is basic in poetry and music mutually, their melodies depending on a variation of tone quality and of pitch respectively, as is commonly said, but if we look more closely we will see that music is, by further analysis, pure rhythm; rhythm and nothing else, for the variation of pitch is the variation in rhythms of the individual notes, and harmony the blending of these varied rhythms. When we know more of overtones we will see that the tempo of every masterpiece is absolute, and is exactly set by some further law of rhythmic accord. Whence it should be possible to show that any given rhythm implies about it a complete musical form—fugue, sonata, I cannot say what form, but a form, perfect, complete. Ergo, the rhythm set in a line of poetry connotes its symphony, which, had we a little more skill, we could score for orchestra.

The definition is repeated in the essay "Prologomena" from *Poetry Review* (I, 2, February, 1912).

> I believe in an "absolute rhythm," a rhythm, that is, in poetry which corresponds exactly to the emotion or shade of emotion to be expressed. A man's rhythm must be interpretative, it will be, therefore, in the end, his own, uncounterfeiting, uncounterfeitable.

Respect for the *absolute rhythm* theory in practice exists in Pound's 1911 translation of the *Seafarer* from the Old English, where he follows the original rhythms with "uncounterfeiting" accuracy.

Hugh Kenner has suggested that the term *absolute rhythm* may have been stimulated by Rémy de Gourmont's *Le Latin mystique* (Paris, 1892). Although the precise expression does not appear there, the idea may indeed have been suggested by certain remarks in that book, particularly those where de Gourmont is speaking of the birth of the sequence in medieval liturgical poetry through the procedure known as

---

[3] Katheryn Ruth Heyman also quotes this statement by Couperin in her book, *op. cit.*, p. 102.

troping, that is, adding new texts to the long melismatic passages of the plain chant, particularly the "Alleluia." The birth of the sequence is usually accredited to the St. Gall monk Notker Balbulus, sometimes known as Goddeschalk. De Gourmont writes:

> Pendant que les moines de Saint-Gall créaient cette forme absolument nouvelle, en poésie, la séquence irrégulière, l'hymne subissait des modifications intimes qui, lentement, la métamorphosaient. Moins par ignorance de la métrique que par raffinement musical, les poètes commencèrent, non plus à mesurer, mais à nombrer les syllabes: il n'y a plus ni brèves ni longues absolues; il n'y a que des brèves et des longues par position; la quantité est déterminée non plus par la morphologie de la syllabe, mais par la nécessité du rhythme.[4]

De Gourmont had previously pointed out that Notker and his colleague Wipo were both musicians and poets simultaneously, and a statement such as the following is an obvious fortification for Pound's own pronouncements on the importance of holding the two art forms in contiguity:

> Notker était musicien, composait ensemble les phrases verbales et les phrases vocales: ainsi, sans nulle doute, Wipo et presque tous les séquentaires.[5]

Pound had written in 1913:

> It is not intelligent to ignore the fact that both in Greece and in Provence the poetry attained its highest rhythmic and metrical brilliance at times when the arts of verse and music were most closely knit together, when each thing done by the poet had some definite musical urge or necessity bound up within it.[6]

It is this relationship between music and poetry that is at the heart of the following statements from the various music reviews of the London years, though we may, after reading them, feel no closer to a precise understanding of what constitutes *absolute rhythm*, a matter which we will pursue further in a moment.

> The music of the troubadour period is without bars in the modern sense. . . . One reads the words on which the notes indubitably depended; a rhythm comes to life—a rhythm which seems to explain the music and which is not a "musician's" rhythm. Yet it is possible to set this rhythm in a musician's

[4] Rémy de Gourmont, *Le Latin mystique*, Paris, 1922 edition, p. 163.
[5] *Ibid.*, p. 129.
[6] *Literary Essays*, p. 91.

rhythm without, from the poet's feeling in the matter, harming it or even "altering it," which means altering the part of it to which he is sensitive; which means again, that both poet and musician "feel around" the movement, "feel at it" from different angles. . . .

Yet it is quite certain that some people can hear and scan "by quantity," and more can do so "by stress," and fewer still feel rhythm by what I would call the inner form of the line. And it is this "inner form," I think, which must be preserved in music; it is only by mastery of this inner form that the great masters of rhythm—Milton, Yeats, whoever you like—are masters of it.[7]

That is the whole flaw of impressionist or "emotional" music as opposed to pattern music. It is like a drug; you must have more drug, and more noise each time, or this effect, this impression which works from the outside, in from the nerves and sensorium upon the self—is no use, its effect is constantly weaker and weaker. I do not mean that Bach is not emotional, but the early music starts with the mystery of pattern; if you like, with the vortex of pattern; with something which is, first of all, music, and which is capable of being, after that, many things. What I call emotional, or impressionist music, starts with being emotion or impression and then becomes only approximately music. It is, that is to say, something in the terms of something else. If it produces an effect, if from sounding as music it moves at all, it can only recede into the original emotion or impression. Programme music is merely a weaker, more flabby and descriptive sort of impressionist music, needing, perhaps, a guide and explanation.[8]

The tempo of every masterwork is definitely governed; and not only the general tempo of the whole work, but the variations in speed, the tempo of individual passages, the time interval between particular notes and chords. The actual sound of a given note or chord needs a certain time to round itself out before the next sound is imposed or shot after it. The masterly rendering of a piece depends almost wholly on the exact instants chosen for this imposition or suite of the arcs or spheres of succeeding sounds one on another. This affects not merely the rhythm of the piece, but it affects, more than people usually realise, the quality of the tone. . . . The sense of the real tempo may be instinctive and incommunicable.[9]

In affairs of tempo the *beat* is a knife-edge and *not* the surface of a rolling-pin.[10]

Rhythm-sense is not merely a *temps mesuré*, it is not merely a clock-work of the bar-lengths. Measured time is only one form of

---

[7] *The New Age*, February 8, 1912, p. 344.
[8] *Ibid.*, January 7, 1915, p. 247.
[9] *Ibid.*, January 3, 1918, p. 189.
[10] *Ibid.*, January 24, 1918, p. 249.

rhythm; but a true rhythm sense assimilates all sorts of uneven pieces of time, and keeps the music alive.[11]

Pattern may not be pattern in imitation of J. S. Bach, nor anything that he would have recognized under that designation. The most general faults of contemporary London instrumentalists seem to me to be (a) a neglect of main structure (b) a tendency to melt all composers, or at least very diverse composers, into a unity; to impose on rhythms written in diverse manners a sort of personal uniformity (probably bound up with the performer's own physique).[12]

The music of free period; of a constantly varying phrase-length and rhythm-length is a freedom from fixed lengths, but the symmetry must underlie, and the sense of this symmetry must be kept fresh and vivid, if not in the consciousness, at least in the sub-consciousness of the performer.[13]

A rhythm unit is a shape; it exists like the keel-line of a yacht, or the lines of an automobile-engine, for a definite purpose, and should exist with an efficiency as definite as that which we find in yachts and automobiles.[14]

As regarding rhythm: to compose in the sequence of the musical phrase, not in sequence of a metronome.[15]

Rhythm is a form cut into TIME, as a design is determined SPACE.[16]

The writer of bad verse is a bore because he does not perceive time and time relations, and cannot therefore delimit them in an interesting manner, by means of longer and shorter, heavier and lighter syllables, and the varying qualities of sound inseparable from the words of his speech.[17]

Most arts attain their effects by using a fixed element and a variable.[18]

Statements such as these, though they may not claim to be so explicitly, must be regarded as embellishments or workings-out of the *absolute rhythm* theme. What is remarkable about them is their adherence to the middle ground; they argue neither for the precision of the metrical paradigm nor for the validity of the uninhibited flow of material, but rather draw our attention consistently to *the relationship between the two*—"a fixed element and a variable"—the vine *and* the trellis. In 1910 the definition of *absolute rhythm* was absolute. But in

[11] *Ibid.*, March 7, 1918, p. 377.
[12] *Ibid.*, September 5, 1918, pp. 302–3.
[13] *Ibid.*, March 20, 1919, pp. 329–30.
[14] *Ibid.*, November 25, 1920, p. 44.
[15] *Pavannes and Divisions*, 1918; quoted from *Literary Essays*, p. 3.
[16] *ABC of Reading*, p. 198.
[17] *Ibid.*, p. 199.
[18] *Ibid.*, p. 201.

terms of practical work, or in the elaboration of critical standards for practical work, tensions and ambiguities resulted. It seems to me Pound enjoyed discussing these ambiguities and made good use of them. It is the tension created by playing on or against a tradition of metrical schemata which gave *vers libre* its audacity. It is the way counterpoint is produced out of a single line, by playing against a residuum of metrical expectations, a matter which Pound understood as well as anyone who has ever written in the English language.

I believe Pound first conceived of *absolute rhythm* as something existing above the abrasions of workaday art. It was the breath-pattern of the master artificer, above analysis. Maybe *absolute rhythm* is only possible to an artist who is enveloped and at ease in a culture or tradition, the kind of ease Cavalcanti enjoyed, or that which Pound claimed for Boccherini (in *Guide to Kulchur*) and contrasted against Bartók and himself, who worked in the conflictful *entre-temps* between traditions. In any case, the discussions of rhythm subsequent to the first idealized conception are notable for their contrapuntal tensions rather than their purity of statement. In a moment I will suggest that it was this difficulty between an ideal and the contingencies of practice which made it necessary to invent a new concept, that of *Great Bass*. Indeed some of the statements above, for instance that which introduces the metaphor of the ship's keel-line, adumbrate the later concept. For the moment let me merely fortify my assertion that during the early stages the tension of opposites was the operative outcome of the *absolute rhythm* theme. In a book much admired by Pound, Cocteau's *Cock and Harlequin*, the same concern for restraint versus freedom is present in numerous statements. This, for instance:

> The speed of a runaway horse counts for nothing . . .
> TACT IN AUDACITY CONSISTS IN KNOWING HOW FAR WE MAY GO TOO FAR.[19]

This is also at the root of Boris de Schloezer's discussion of Stravinsky's rhythmic concerns in his book *Stravinsky: His Technique*, translated by Pound.

> . . . Stravinsky has never destroyed the measured bar; he struggles against it, he disarticulates it, he multiplies and hooks up the different metres, but he never permits himself once, and for good and all, to get rid of this bothersome fiction, he needs the annoyance, the resistance, against which to leap and surge, for there is no rhythmic diversity without stability, in relation, precisely, to which the most complex movement is perceived.[20]

[19] Jean Cocteau, "Cock and Harlequin," in *A Call to Order*, London, 1926, pp. 7–8.
[20] Boris de Schloezer, *Stravinsky: His Technique*, Pound's translation, *Dial*, February, 1929, pp. 107–8.

Pound's footnote on this statement is: "At this point we have no disagreement."

The artist can obtain very special effects by insinuating freedoms into strict conventions of organization. It is this tension that is always present in the execution of music from its written score and is the reason Pound so assiduously cultivated friendship with performing musicians.

Antheil had a very special influence on the poet's thought, though it may not have been an entirely healthy influence. For Antheil was concerned with the precisioning of musical notation to a point where all ambiguity was eliminated between the printed shapes of music and their living sounds in performance. We will recall his editorial remark to *Le Testament,* where he denies the performers any interpretive leeway.

> This opera is made out of an entirely new musical technic, a technic, for certain, made of sheer music which upholds its line through inevitable rhythmic locks and new grips . . . a technic heretofore unknown, owing to the stupidity of the formal musical architects still busy with organizing square blocks of wornout and formal patterns . . . a powerful technic that grips musical phrases like the mouths of great poets grip words. . . .
>
> As the opera is written in such a manner so that nothing at all is left to the singer, the editor would be obliged if the singer would not let the least bit of temperament affect in the least the correct singing of this opera, which is written as it sounds! Please do not embarrass us by suddenly developing intelligence.

Pound accepted Antheil's "technic" in *Antheil and the Treatise on Harmony,* a contribution which he did not immediately see would lead up a cul-de-sac.

> Stravinsky's merit lies largely in taking hard bits of rhythm and noting them with great care. Antheil continues this; and these two composers mark a definite break with the "atmospheric" school. . . .

Following this statement he moved to an enthusiastic discussion of the precision of machines. In the same work he praises the discoveries of the fourteenth-century *Ars Nova* theorists Marchettus of Padua and Prosdocimus de Beldemandis, for they too were concerned with the perfection of musical notation, particularly in the area of rhythmic exactitude. But if notation becomes so precise that it eliminates interpretive freedom, an artificiality results, the same artificiality that confounded much *Ars Nova* music (which is practically unexecutable) as that which has confounded a great deal of contemporary music (also unexecutable). The eventual consequence of Pound's association with

Antheil's theories of notational exactitude and automated performance was the projected book on "Machine Art," which significantly he was unable to complete—or at least did not feel he should publish.[21] Thus, contemporary with this strained position, we find Pound in *Antheil and the Treatise on Harmony* reasserting in a footnote his faith in the 1910 definition of *absolute rhythm,* and in the text laying the foundations for a new ideal, that of *Great Bass.*

> You can use your beat as a third or fourth or Nth note in the harmony.
>
> To put it another way; the percussion of the rhythm can enter the harmony exactly as another note would. It enters usually as a Bassus, a still deeper bassus; giving the main form to the sound.
>
> It may be convenient to call these different degrees of the scale the megaphonic and microphonic parts of the harmony.
>
> Rhythm is nothing but the division of frequency plus an emphasis or phrasing of that division. [*Harmony* treatise, Chapter 4]

A statement from the "Varia" section of the same book moves forward a similar ideal:

> Nothing but the main form of a work will resist the vicissitudes and calamities of presentation.

In *Le Testament,* which was composed about the same time as this statement, there is a practical application of these ideas in the use of deep pedal notes and the incorporation of percussion into the fabric of the songs to give the work fundamental unity.

The term "Great Base," spelled that way, first makes its appearance in a footnote to the essay "Workshop Orchestration" in *New Masses,* March, 1927, at a point where the machine adulation reached its apex. But the definitive statements are not to be found until 1938 in *Guide to Kulchur,* though they must have been well in hand at least by 1934, for in that year four pages on *Great Bass* had been sent to the American

---

[21] I am indebted to Stephen Adams for drawing to my attention a small but possibly significant fact in accounting for Pound's strange about-face from an early mistrust in the metronome and all such mechanistic devices to his later fanatical respect for such instruments: namely the visits he paid to the French phonetician Abbé J. P. Rousselot. Rousselot invented a "phonoscope" for measuring vowel quantities. Pound mentions him in his Paris Letter in *Dial,* November, 1920; apparently on one of these visits he had his vowels "measured." Rousselot's work is described in his *Principes de phonétique experimentale,* two volumes, Paris, 1897 and 1908. Though this may indeed provide a bridge to his enthusiasm for technology it should not obscure the error of confusing a descriptive notation of an actual "performance" with a mechanized imposition on all possible performances; and I would suggest that when Rousselot makes his reappearance in Canto LXXVII, where he is said to have "fished for sound in the Seine," the reverence for such approaches to art may be assumed to have passed.

composer John Becker, editor of the quarterly *New Music,* with the hope they would be published, but they never were. This would make the *Great Bass* preoccupation more or less contemporaneous with Pound's second opera *Cavalcanti,* with its unusual reliance on the lower stringed instruments of the orchestra.

Chapter 7 of *Kulchur* is entitled *Great Bass: Part One.* In it Pound is concerned to make clear that *Great Bass* is to be regarded as the reduction of a composition to simple frequency ratios, a sort of heterodyne of inscrutable to scrutable elements, a matter he had discussed in detail in his *Harmony* treatise, and one which I have dealt with in the notes to that work.

> I assert at this point one thing without which I can not see music rightly received.
>
> I have put it in a dozen forms, I have printed it in one form, and sent it out by private letter more briefly.
>
> Certain sounds we accept as "pitch," we say that a certain note is do, re, mi, or B flat in the treble scale, meaning that it has a certain frequency of vibration.
>
> Down below the lowest note synthesized by the ear and "heard" there are slower vibrations. The ratio between these frequencies and those written to be executed by instruments is OBVIOUS in mathematics. The whole question of tempo, and of a main base in all musical structure resides in use of these frequencies.
>
> It is unlikely that great composers neglected this basis. I am convinced that it is unwise to wander into musical study without taking count of it.

He then goes on to discuss Leibnitz's "unsquashable monad" and Scottus Erigena's belief in authority, which he likens to Gaudier's sculpture, the unbendable, hammered-down artifact, reminding his readers in a concluding paragraph:

> These disjunct paragraphs belong together, Gaudier, Great Bass, Leibnitz, Erigena, are parts of one ideogram, they are not merely separate subjects.

Chapter 31 of *Kulchur* has some pertinent remarks under the title of "Time, Again."

> On the eve of his 21st birthday Gerhart M. packed a suitcase and silently left the parental mansion. His father had spoken of the nuances of Bach. The timing of the departure indicated determination to separate. It also indicated sensibility and conviction.
>
> A few days before his 30th birthday the younger Münch said: Now my father wd. know that at once. Meaning wd. know the

exact pace of playing indicated by the metronome signature, 80, 84, etc.

This I took as the first sign of middle age. I said so. I said you have admitted yr. father knows something.

I was also pleased at further confirmation of my own theory or belief in "great-bass." The really fine musician has this sense of time-division and/or duration. An alteration of it inadvisedly or needlessly, for any cause not inherent in the composer's pattern, is bad music, bad playing.

It ultimately reduces all composition to slush if not checked in season.

The theory of pleasing the audience, of wooing the audience, the theory that the audience really hears the performer not the composer, and that there can be no absolute rendering of the composer's design, ultimately destroys all composition, it undermines all values, all hierarchy of values.

The sweeter the poison, the more necessary the defence. If the composer doesn't know how to write down what he wants, that is his fault, not the performer's.

There is an enormous leeway even in the best graph, BUT it is a leeway of intensity, not of duration. It is a leeway in graduations of force and of quality, not of duration, or in the lapse of very small time intervals between the beginnings of notes.

Between a legato and a marked staccato, there are graduations, which do not mean that there is leeway about starting the notes.

Rubato, is compensated. In the direction for *"rubato"* the composer *could* indicate the limits wherein he intends the compensation to occur. Strictly speaking this is supposed to be inside the bar.

There is no doubt that lots of mediocre music is badly graphed, and a great deal *is* mediocre BECAUSE the bad graphing indicates very loose conception on the part of the composer.

We NEVER know enough. The good artist (I dare say even Strawinsky) is oppressed by his own ignorance—ignorance of simple fundamentals of his craft, even when he knows more than anyone else dead or living.

This doesn't mean that they have no pleasures. A man may enjoy playing his best in a game, and losing.

The simplicity of the arts is mystery and inviolable. I know two highbrow composers who agonized for months on a problem that the café-tango composer B. solves apparently without effort, whether from having been through a conservatory or playing jazz, I have not discovered. Mozart also wrote a great many notes between one bar line and another. OF course. "The trained never think." Like the school teacher in Frobenius' anecdote, they are scandalized when a pupil stops at a fundamental. It is so OBvious that if you use 64th notes or 32nds you can make more "funny shapes" than you can with ½s and ¼s, and still keep an even bar measure. Tell it to little children.

I strongly suspect that Rummel and I in 1910, following other students who were supposed then to know more than we did, failed to recognize what might have been supposed to be a ms. indication. I suggest that the next digger try to interpret troubadour tune on the hypothesis that the line (of verse) is the bar and can be graphed to best advantage as a (that is one single) bar.

Chapter 42 is entitled *Great Bass: Part Two.*

> The wobbling about by deficient musicians, the attempt to give life to a piece by abundant rallentandos and speedings up, results in reduction of all music to one doughy mass and all compositions to the one statement of the performing executant, said wobbly time is due to their NOT divining the real pace of the segment.
>
> The 60, 72, or 84, or 120 per minute is a BASS, or basis. It is the bottom note of the harmony.
>
> If the ear isn't true in its sense of this time-division the whole playing is bound to be molten, and doughy.
>
> The sense of high order and clarity is not due to sense pitch as between [musical notation] and [musical notation] alone but to the sense of proportion between all time divisions from 10 to the minute or era up to top harmonic 8vo and 32mo above treble stave.
>
> Failing to hit the proper great bass, the deficient musician fumbles about OFF the gt. bass key as a poor singer fumbles about a little flat or a ¼ tone too high.

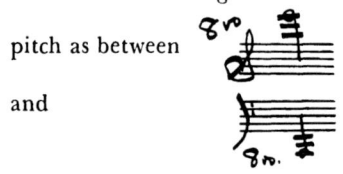

The first part of Chapter 43, entitled *Tone,* extends this theme.

> Everyone feels something about it. Plenty of players will admit in the theory that there is a right speed for a piece or movement, but "they let it go at that." There is probably a stricter sense sic: just as there is silence or dullness of sound produced by interference of sound waves in the middle stave, so there is an aid, reinforcement or interference from the great bass, according as the speed is right or not.
>
> Listening to the Bach A minor Concerto I have wondered whether the violin part is intended to flow through it as colourless

water. Impossible to know from hearing piano reduction of the orchestra. One wd. have to listen to a number of performances with orchestra to *know*. It wd. have been a legitimate and highly distinguished intention on the composer's part to make the binding-force of so great a composition almost imperceptible (locally).

Certainly in all work for strings the speed is of more importance than generally understood. (Lie down, Towser, "everyone knows" that the tempo has *some* importance. I am talking of its having *more* importance.)

A minuscule excess of speed is less emollient than a lack, as a singer singing sharp is less soupy and porridge-like than one singing flat.

We need to look for the underlying unity of these statements. I do not think too much account should be made of Pound's discussions of harmonics and overtone structure, except for his assertion that complex harmonic combinations can sometimes be reduced to very simple ratios, for instance, that of the octave—any octave—is 1:2, that of the perfect fifth is 2:3, etc. The whole principle of Fourier analysis of harmonic events assumes that any wave form no matter how complex can be reduced to simple sine waves, but this is not the same as saying that tuning forks produce great music. Nor should we pay too much attention to his insistence on the efficacy of the metronome for divining absolute tempi, a matter which as a nonpractising musician he simply did not understand (see note 38, page 303). I take it this fondness for figures is related to his infatuation with historical dates though we may be at a loss to know precisely why certain dates are invested with such epochal significance.

But we can still admire his tenacity in looking for elementary relationships, for purifying, for striking away the debris. *Great Bass* is again an idealized concept as was *absolute rhythm*. It does not merely imply a bass in the present sense of the lowest line of polyphony; likewise it has little to do with the ground bass or thorough bass of baroque music, and certainly has nothing to do with *basso ostinato,* which is merely embroidery for the left hand. Rather it is a basis which exists like the keel of a ship, exercising a centripetal pull over everything above it. It too, is a temporal, not a formal concept, or more correctly, a temporal concept governing form. I should think it is something more or less between the concepts of time and order. It is that precise and uncounterfeiting order which the material in any masterpiece achieves when the temporal flow of its elements is exactly sensed. *Absolute rhythm* governed the proportions of the elements of masterpieces; *Great Bass* links the elements into an indivisible whole. In this sense the final word on the subject is not to be found in *Kulchur* at all but in a casual piece entitled "Musicians; God Help 'Em," written the same year, 1938, for Ronald Duncan's magazine *Townsman:*

> ...a composition has a main form and articulations, that is a root, a main structure, and details. To remember ONE fact and not a hundred separate notes....

It is the realization of "one main fact" that causes Heracles in Pound's translation of Sophokles *Trachiniae* to cry out:

> SPLENDOUR, IT ALL COHERES.

Pound prints it large; it is the pivot on which everything balances. *Great Bass* reasserts Pound's idealistic faith, in spite of the imperfections of material or craftsman.

> i.e. it coheres all right
> > even if my notes do not cohere.
> > > [CANTO 116]

Appendix II

GLOSSARY OF IMPORTANT MUSICAL PERSONALITIES

This glossary comprises three groups of musicians: (1) those mentioned frequently by Pound in his reviews—at least twice; (2) those who were personal friends of the poet, even though they may not always have been professionals; and (3) figures in the history of music who seemed important to Pound in some special way. This list does not include historical figures mentioned by Pound only once; some of these are identified in the footnotes, while others are well known or easily locatable. It is not always possible to trace less celebrated performing musicians, so a few names are missing from the list for want of information.

ADAM DE LA HALLE (b. Arras, *circa* 1230—d. Naples, *circa* 1287), trouvère. Many of his works survive, including the pastoral music drama *Le Jeu de Robin et de Marion,* sometimes referred to as the precursor of comic opera. Pound's own opera *Le Testament* is not unlike this work in the sense that it consists of a collection of songs bound together by (frequently) comic dialogue.

D'ALVAREZ, MARGUERITE (b. Liverpool, 1886—d. Italy, 1953), contralto. Born in England of Peruvian parentage, she specialized in opera and was associated with Hammerstein's Manhattan Opera House from 1909 on, and also with the Chicago Opera Company.

ANTHEIL, GEORGE (b. Trenton, N.J., 1900—d. New York, 1959), American pianist and composer of Polish parentage. His controversial whirlwind tours of Europe, where he performed his own music with a revolver on the piano, are best studied in his autobiography *Bad Boy of Music* (New York, 1945). Pound met him in Paris in 1923 and wrote a number of articles about him, culminating in *Antheil and the Treatise on Harmony* (Paris, 1924). Antheil helped Pound edit his opera *Le Testament*, adding the orchestration which the composer could not handle. With Olga Rudge (*q.v.*) Antheil gave numerous concerts in Paris featuring Pound's violin music, and he participated in the première of *Le Testament* in the Salle Pleyel in 1926. In 1930 Antheil's opera *Transatlantic* was premièred in Frankfurt. Pound attended, but by this time the toughness of Antheil's music, which Pound had admired, had begun to become mollified, and the two artists were drifting apart. Antheil eventually pioneered backward to Hollywood where he ended up writing background music to films, but Pound continued throughout his writings to recall the excitement of the Paris days with nostalgia, (*vide: Guide to Kulchur*, pp. 94–95, and elsewhere). Antheil is also mentioned in Canto LXXIV.

D'ARANYI, JELLY (b. Budapest, 1895—d. Florence, 1966). Hungarian violinist. A notable exponent of modern violin music, she premièred several important compositions, including Bartok's sonatas, Ravel's *Tzigane*, and Vaughan Williams's concerto.

ARNAUT DANIEL (b. Perigord, *circa* 1150—d. *circa* 1200), troubadour. His poetry is characterized by word-play, onomatopoeia, and artifice. He was a favorite poet of Dante, who mentions him in *De vulgari eloquentia* (II.2) and in the Purgatory section of the *Divina Commedia*. Pound translated some of his verse. Two of his melodies are extant, and Pound traced these in the Ambrosiana Library in Milan for incorporation into his collaborative edition of troubadour songs with Walter Morse Rummel (*q.v.*). Arnaut Daniel is mentioned in Canto XCVII.

ARNAUT DE MAROILL (b. Perigord *circa* 1170—d. *circa* 1200), troubadour. Six pieces of his are extant with both text and music, and Pound transcribed some of these into modern musical notation when he was teaching himself to read neumes. He figures in the poem "Marvoil."

ARNE, THOMAS AUGUSTINE (b. London, 1710—d. London, 1778), English composer. Composer of "Rule Britannia" and numerous other songs, many to Shakespeare texts, as well as many now-forgotten operas.

ASTAFIEVA, SERAFIMA (b. 1876—d. 1934), Russian dancer. She was a member of the Diaghilev Company when they came to London. In Canto LXXIX there is a reference to "Astafieva inside the street doors of the Wigmore...." She appears later again in the same Canto. Also ". . . I took Parson Elyot to see the Prima Ballerina and it evoked 'Grushkin'; as you can see in that bewteeful poEM entytled 'Whispers of Immortality' " (*Pavannes and Divagations*, p. 161).

BACH, JOHANN SEBASTIAN (b. Eisenach, 1685—d. Leipzig, 1750), German composer. For Pound, Bach was the chief exponent of what he called "pattern music," which he contrasted against impressionistic or emotional music. He is mentioned frequently in the reviews and also in Cantos LIX and LXXX.

BANTOCK, SIR GRANVILLE (b. London, 1868—d. 1946), English composer, conductor, and editor. He was trained at the Royal Academy of Music, and later became chairman of Trinity College, London. Noted especially for his songs.

BARBIROLLI, SIR JOHN (b. 1899—d. 1970), English conductor. He made his début as a cellist at the age of eleven in the Queen's Hall. After the First World War he organized his own orchestra and then became conductor of the British National Opera Company. Atheling reviewed him first as a cellist on January 3, 1918, in *The New Age*.

BARILLI, BRUNO (b. Fano, 1880—d. Rome, 1952), Italian composer and music critic. An admirer of Stravinsky, he opposed the developments of the modern Italian school of composers. Mentioned in Canto LXXX.

BARTÓK, BÉLA (b. Hungary, 1881—d. New York, 1945), composer. Pound was introduced to his music by Tibor Serly (*q.v.*) and then by the Gertler and New Hungarian quartets (*q.v.*). On January 13, 1935, the Gertler Quartet gave Bartók's first and fourth quartets in Rapallo. But the work which made the biggest impact on Pound was the fifth quartet, which he heard first played by the New Hungarian group at the Venice Biennale in September, 1936, and later in Rapallo. He felt this work resembled his *Cantos* in the sense that it represented the struggle of a man working against traditions and culture. He wrote about it in *Guide to Kulchur*. Bartók's other music seems to have been known to him by name only. This composer is also mentioned in Canto LXXXIV.

BAX, SIR ARNOLD (b. London, 1883—d. Cork, 1953), British composer. He was trained as a pianist and composer at the Royal Academy of Music. Author of chamber music and songs, often inspired by Celtic folklore, as well as seven symphonies. In 1942 he became Master of the King's Musick.

BECKER, JOHN J. (b. Henderson, Ky., 1886—d. Wilmette, Ill., 1961). American composer. Becker was associate editor of the quarterly *New Music,* and wrote frequent articles for various journals advancing the cause of contemporary music in America. His own music is adventurous and employs many daring harmonic and contrapuntal devices. Sometime before 1934 Pound apparently sent Becker four pages on *Great Bass* (probably some variant of those which eventually appeared in *Kulchur*) with the hope that they might be published in *New Music* or some other avant-garde journal, but they never were. "The American composer John Becker tried vainly to get them printed in several musical periodicals, they serve just as well in carbon copies and in conversation as they could in print." (From "Date Line," originally published in *Make It New,* London, 1934, and reprinted in *Literary Essays,* 1954).

BEDFORD, AGNES (b. 1892—d. London, 1969), English pianist and vocal coach. She is first mentioned in Atheling's review of November 20, 1919, in *The New Age*. She was soon to become the poet's musical amanuensis for the first sketches of his opera *Le Testament* and a person to whom he was to turn throughout his life for musical advice and assistance. Their collaborative work began with *Five Troubadour Songs*, arranged by Agnes Bedford with "Original Provençal words and English words adapted by E. P. from Chaucer" (Boosey & Co., London, 1920). Soon Pound was dictating his own music to her, and he sent her the first draft of *Le Testament* for comment. Later he sent the score of his second opera, *Cavalcanti*, for the same purpose. It was she who selected the notes from the William Atheling *New Age* reviews for incorporation in the book *Antheil and the Treatise on Harmony*. Their correspondence on musical affairs extended up to 1959.

BÉDOS DE CELLES, DOM FRANCIS (b. 1709—d. 1779), French Benedictine monk and organ-builder. Pound encountered him in Arnold Dolmetsch's *The Interpretation of the Music of the XVIIth and XVIIIth Centuries*, and in his *Antheil* book quoted a remark from the famous treatise *L'Art du facteur d'orgues* to the effect that on mechanical instruments such as the organ, where stress was not possible for accented notes, compensations had to be made by slight temporal prolongations of important notes and diminutions of passing notes.

BEECHAM, SIR THOMAS (b. St. Helens, Lancashire, 1879—d. London, 1961), British conductor. In 1905 he gave his first orchestral concert in London with the Queen's Hall Orchestra, and in 1908 he founded his own orchestra, which a family fortune enabled him to do. In 1910 he leased Covent Garden and organized a season of operas, employing his own orchestra and a company of carefully selected singers. In 1913 he became associated with Diaghilev's Russian Ballet when it first appeared in England. In 1916 Pound translated the libretto of Massenet's *Cinderella* for Beecham's opera company and was given excellent seats for many of the productions that season.

BEETHOVEN, LUDWIG VAN (b. Bonn, 1770—d. Vienna, 1827), German composer. Pound tended to regard Beethoven's music as the record of a "struggle" against tradition and culture, a position he also accorded to Bartók's music and his own *Cantos (vide: Guide to Kulchur)*. As *The New Age* music critic William Atheling he once pronounced Beethoven's *Moonlight Sonata* "a bore." Beethoven is mentioned in Canto LXXIX.

BELLINI, VICENZO (b. Sicily, 1801—d. Paris, 1835), Italian composer, largely of operas in the so-called *bel canto* tradition.

BERG, ALBAN (b. Vienna, 1885—d. Vienna, 1935), Austrian composer. One of Schoenberg's early students, Berg, while embracing the twelve-tone method, nevertheless remained faithful to the spirit of late Romanticism and is in many ways closer to figures like Mahler than to the forward thrust of twentieth-century musical thought. The only Berg piece which Pound seems to have heard was his *Lyric Suite* for string quartet (composed 1926) at the Venice Biennale in 1936, played by the Gertler Quartet. He found the work "sticky and aimless" and, at least by comparison with other works he heard at that festival, he did not like it.

BÉSARD, JEAN BAPTISTE (b. circa 1567—d. circa 1625), French lutenist and composer. Bésard lived in Germany and published in 1603 in Cologne a famous international collection of lute pieces under the title *Thesaurus harmonicus*. Pound made his acquaintance in Oscar Chilesotti's article on Italian lute music of the sixteenth and seventeenth centuries in Lavignac and Laurencie's *Encyclopédie de la musique et dictionaire du conservatoire*. When Chilesotti's unpublished papers came into the hands of Gerhart Münch, he arranged several Bésard pieces, and they were performed in the Rapallo concerts during the early years. Pound felt that the date of Bésard's collection, 1603, was significant as it coincided with the birth of the *Monte dei Paschi*, the Italian bank mentioned in Cantos XLII through XLIV.

BIANCHI, GABRIELE (b. Verona, 1901), Italian composer. He studied with Malipiero and in 1925 began teaching at the Venice Conservatory. Since 1960 he has been its director. Olga Rudge was accompanied by Bianchi in a Venice concert featuring Mozart, Bach, and Debussy in 1927; and in 1934 his sonata for violin and piano was featured in a Rapallo concert (see *Il Mare*, October 6, 1934).

BLOCH, ERNEST (b. Geneva, 1880—d. Portland, Oregon 1959), Swiss-American composer. Bloch set out consciously to reflect Jewish themes in his music, which is rich and nostalgic. He was known to Pound as George Antheil's composition teacher; this accounts for the unusual deference shown toward him in *Antheil and the Treatise on Harmony*.

BLOM, ERIC (b. Bern, 1888—d. London, 1959), English music critic and editor. He would have been known to Atheling first as the author of the program notes for the Queen's Hall concerts (1919–26). Later he became music critic for the *Manchester Guardian* and in 1937 editor of *Music and Letters*. Pound had some correspondence with him over his article "Ligurian View of a Venetian Festival," which appeared in *Music and Letters* in January, 1937 (see his letter to Agnes Bedford, December, 1936, in *Letters*). In 1946 Blom undertook the monumental task of preparing a new edition of *Grove's Dictionary of Music and Musicians* (1954), for which he asked Olga Rudge (*q.v.*) to contribute the article on Vivaldi.

BOCCHERINI, LUIGI (b. Lucca, 1743—d. Madrid, 1805), Italian cellist and composer. Most of Boccherini's works are in chamber music form and there are a great many of them: over one hundred string quartets, over one hundred string quintets, nearly fifty string trios, etc., many of which are still not published. Boccherini's music in spirit and technique has much in common with that of Joseph Haydn, who was almost his exact contemporary. Pound admired the effortlessness of Boccherini's music (as natural as the jokes in Boccaccio) and contrasted this with the music of Bartók (*q.v.*) which was the result of great struggle (see *Guide to Kulchur*). Bartók and Boccherini had been performed together by the New Hungarian Quartet in Rapallo in March, 1937.

BORGATTI, RENATA (b. Bologna, 1894—d. 1968), Italian pianist. She was the daughter of the famous Italian tenor Giuseppe Borgatti. She studied in Bologna, Munich, and Switzerland. She performed throughout Europe and became known particularly as a Debussy and Bach specialist. Pound heard her first in a London concert where she accompanied Olga Rudge (see *The New Age,* November 25, 1920). She later performed frequently in the Rapallo concerts, both as soloist and as accompanist to Miss Rudge. In 1948 she accepted a position at the Accademia Chigiana in Siena, where Olga Rudge was also employed as Secretary.

BORODIN, ALEXANDER (b. St. Petersburg, 1833—d. St. Petersburg, 1887), Russian composer. Pound knew and particularly appreciated his songs, heard in recitals in London about 1918 by Vladimir Rosing (*q.v.*) (see *The New Age* reviews).

BOWEN, EDWIN YORK (b. London, 1884—d. Hampstead, 1961), English composer. Educated at the Royal Academy of Music. He was a fine pianist and a composer of chamber music and songs. But William Atheling did not like his music, which he referred to as "usual 'école' of 'Narcissus,' ripple, etc."

BUXTEHUDE, DIETRICH (b. Sweden, 1637—d. Lübeck, 1707), German organist and composer, much admired by Bach. He is mentioned in Canto LXXV.

CACCINI, GIULIO (b. Rome, 1558—d. 1615), Italian composer. One of the members of the Florentine *Camerata,* the group that began by studying the function of music in ancient Greek drama and ended up discovering opera. About 1939 Pound began showing considerable interest in studying their theories on the relationship between poetry and music (the *stile rappresentativo*). Caccini seems to be mentioned indirectly in Canto LXXIX by the inclusion of an aria from his collection *Le Nuove Musiche* (1602) entitled "Amarilli," which William Atheling had heard sung by Stroesco in London (see *The New Age* review, June 5, 1919). Pound probably learned about Caccini first from Arnold Dolmetsch's book *The Interpretation of the Music of the XVIIth and XVIIIth Centuries.*

CALDARA, ANTONIO (b. Venice, 1670—d. Vienna, 1738), Italian composer. He wrote over seventy operas and numerous oratorios, motets, masses, string sonatas, etc. A member of the so-called *bel canto* school, William Atheling enjoyed his music in London concerts.

CAMPION, THOMAS (b. London, 1567—d. London, 1620), English physician, poet, and composer. The details of his life are incomplete. He was educated at Cambridge. In 1602 he published his first set of "ayres." His total collection of songs comprises about one hundred items. They are on the whole simpler than those of his contemporaries, for example, Dowland. He also wrote a critical study of *English Poesie* (1602) and a treatise on counterpoint (1613). For Pound he represented the highest achievement of the English poetry-music tradition.

CARISSIMI, GIACOMO (b. Rome, 1605—d. Rome, 1674), Italian composer. He belongs to the second generation of opera composers and is especially noted for his excellent handling of the recitative principle as well as for a few arias which are still performed. William Atheling enjoyed his music in the London concerts.

CASELLA, ALFREDO (b. Turin, 1883—d. Rome, 1947), Italian composer. He studied at the Paris Conservatory under Fauré and made an early reputation as a pianist and conductor. Much of his music belongs to the neoclassical school of twentieth-century composition. On May 6, 1926, he accompanied Olga Rudge in a recital in Rome which featured a work by Pound entitled "Hommage à Froissart." Pound knew the composer and his music (he had reviewed his *Sinfonia* favourably when he heard it at the Venice Biennale in 1936), and in 1939 Casella was director of the *Settimana musicale* of the Siena Academy when the first Vivaldi festival was held, an event to which both Pound and Olga Rudge had substantially contributed.

CERNIKOFF, VLADIMIR (b. Paris, 1882—d. London, 1940), pianist. He studied in Geneva, Malta, and Berlin. He made his London debut in February, 1908, and subsequently toured widely. Cernikoff (Atheling usually spells his name "Czernikoff") was a great favorite of Pound's during *The New Age* days.

CHILESOTTI, OSCAR (b. Bassano, 1848—d. Bassano, 1916), Italian musician and historiographer. He was educated at the University of Padua, studying law and music. He transcribed considerable lute music from the tablature and wrote several historical studies of early Italian music. For many years he made Milan his home and wrote regularly for the *Gazzetta Musicale*. Much of his editorial work appeared in *Biblioteca de Rarità musicali* (1883, etc., 9 vols.). For Lavignac's *Encyclopédie de la musique et dictionaire du conservatoire* (Paris, 1920) he contributed an elaborate essay on tablatures: "Italy: XVIth and XVIIth Centuries," (Vol. II, pp. 636–84). He was also editor of *Di G. B. Besardo e del suo Thesaurus harmonicus* (Milan, 1886). These works were both known to Pound, and he refers to them in his *Il Mare* article of November 11, 1933, and elsewhere. Chilesotti's unpublished papers were turned over to Gerhart Münch, and they formed the basis of many of the Rapallo *Inverno musicale* concerts.

CHOPIN, FRÉDÉRIC FRANÇOIS (b. Poland, 1810—d. Paris, 1849), Polish composer. He was featured in numerous Rapallo concerts, though Pound seems to have made every attempt to keep his popularity with the audience from getting out of hand.

COLLIGNON, RAYMONDE (b. Blois, France, 1894), French soprano. She gained great celebrity in London during the early decades of the century for her interpretations of French folk songs, which she performed in costume. Ernest Newman said of her talents: "Her voice is not at all large, but it is pure and delightful . . . and as with her voice, so with her movements and gestures." Atheling also reviewed her enthusiastically on several occasions beginning with his review in *The New Age,* January 3, 1918. She premièred the Pound/Rummel Troubadour Songs on April 27, 1918, and Atheling reviewed them in *The New Age* on May 16. It was after one of Miss Collignon's recitals that Pound wrote the poem "Vergier," included in *Personae.* In the BBC 1931 broadcast of *Le Testament* she sang the "Mère au Saveur" aria. Pound continued to remember her affectionately, and in an unpublished 1958 letter to Agnes Bedford he expressed the hope that she might be available to participate in the second (1962) BBC performance of the work. Pound also continued to correspond with Miss Collignon from Saint Elizabeths Hospital. Jo Brantley Berryman (*Paideuma,* Vol. 2, No. 3, 1973) has suggested that Raymonde Collignon is the artist who sang Pound that song of Lawes in the "Envoi" of *Mauberley.* A small body of unpublished correspondence between Pound and Miss Collignon contains nothing to confirm or deny this suggestion.

COUPERIN, FRANÇOIS (b. Paris, 1668—d. Paris, 1733), French composer. At the age of twenty-five he became organist in the private chapel of Louis XIV at Versailles and at twenty-eight was also appointed organist at St. Gervais in Paris. His chief contribution to music was his large body of harpsichord pieces, often with programmatic titles and contents, and his treatise *L'Art de toucher le Clavecin* (1717). Pound knew this book through Dolmetsch's *The Interpretation of the Music of the XVIIth and XVIIIth Centuries* (London, 1915), and frequently quoted the passage (Dolmetsch, p. 20) "We write differently from what we play" in his defense of *vers libre.*

CZERNIKOFF, VLADIMIR, *See:* CERNIKOFF, VLADIMIR.

DANIEL, ARNAUT, *See:* ARNAUT DANIEL.

DANIEL, SALVADOR (b. Bourges, 1830—d. Paris, 1871), French writer on music. He was for some years teacher of music at an Arabic school in Algiers, and he published a monograph, *La musique arabe* (1863), which was translated into English in 1915. Pound had always been an enthusiast for Arabic music and probably knew this volume. He refers to Salvador Daniel's theories in *The New Age,* April 15, 1920.

DEBUSSY, CLAUDE ACHILLE (b. near Paris, 1862—d. Paris, 1918), French composer. Throughout his life Pound had an ambivalent relationship with this composer. Certainly his impressionism was far removed from the "pattern music" Pound consistently demanded, but he respected Debussy nevertheless, largely because Walter Morse Rummel (*q.v.*) had been a member of his "intimate circle." Pound attended the première of *Le Martyre de Saint-Sébastien* in Paris in 1911, and found the music "wonderful," though D'Annunzio's libretto did not please him. He had also seen Debussy conduct his Charles d'Orléans songs in Paris, and may also have seen him conduct in London. Whether he ever met Debussy through Rummel is not known. Debussy is mentioned in Canto LXXX.

DEFAUW, DÉSIRÉ (b. Ghent, 1885—d. Indiana, 1960), Belgian violinist and conductor. During the First World War he founded the Allied String Quartet, with Lionel Tertis, Charles Woodhouse, and Emile Doehard. Atheling heard this group in London. Defauw became a professor at the Antwerp conservatory and conducted frequently in Brussels. In 1943 he was appointed conductor of the Chicago Symphony Orchestra.

DIAGHILEV, SERGEI (b. Novgorod, 1872—d. Venice, 1929), Russian ballet impresario. In 1909 he inaugurated his Russian Ballet in Paris and gathered about him an impressive array of musicians and dancers. Ravel, Stravinsky, Falla, Prokofiev, Milhaud, and Poulenc wrote music specially for his productions. From 1911 on the Diaghilev Ballet performed frequently in London, often in association with Beecham's opera seasons. Pound attended the London premières of numerous Diaghilev ballets, including Stravinsky's *Rite of Spring* and Satie's *Parade*.

DI VEROLI, MANLIO (b. Rome, 1888—d. London, 1960), Italian pianist, accompanist, and composer. Educated at the Academy of St. Cecilia, Rome, he lived in London where he acted as Vladimir Rosing's (*q.v.*) accompanist. He is the composer of numerous songs and piano pieces.

DIEREN, BERNARD VAN, *See:* VAN DIEREN, BERNARD.

DOLMETSCH, ARNOLD (b. France, 1858—d. Haslemere, 1940), English music antiquarian and scholar. He studied in Brussels and at the Royal College of Music, London. His father was a piano-maker. After being aroused by the collections of old instruments in the British Museum, he began to build his own clavichords and harpsichords, first for Chickering of Boston, then for Gaveau of Paris. He later built and revived the playing of almost every instrument of the fifteenth to the eighteenth centuries, training the members of his family to play them. He established his workshop in Haslemere, Surrey, and gave frequent concerts in London. In 1925 he founded an annual chamber music festival for old music in Haslemere. His book *The Interpretation of the Music of the XVIIth and XVIIIth Centuries* (London, 1915) is a landmark in the revival of the performance practices of ancient music. Pound must have met Dolmetsch about 1914; at least on November 30 of that year he wrote to his father (unpublished letter), "Dolmetsch is about to have concert." Of their meeting Mrs. Dolmetsch wrote to Pound's biographer Charles Norman:

> Ezra Pound, then a budding poet of rather flamboyant appearance, was immediately attracted to Arnold Dolmetsch; and through their continued intercourse he became deeply interested in the English music of former centuries. He delighted in listening to Arnold's performances on the *clavichord*. For this reason he became possessed of one. (Charles Norman, *Ezra Pound*, New York, 1969, p. 124.)

Pound asked Dolmetsch to make him a duplicate of his own clavichord, but Dolmetsch sold him the original. It accompanied him later to Rapallo and finally ended up in the castle at Brunnenburg. Pound wrote numerous articles about Dolmetsch, beginning with that in *The New Age,* January 7, 1915. He was particularly influenced by Dolmetsch's study of rhythm and tempo in the old music (see Chapters II and III of the *Interpretation*). Dolmetsch is mentioned in Cantos LXXX, LXXXI, and XCIX.

DOWLAND, JOHN (b. London, 1563—d. London, 1626), English composer. He was the greatest lutenist of his age and held the position of Court Lutenist to the King of Denmark, and later to Charles I of Britain. His songs with lute accompaniment are the most accomplished works of their kind and have been revived in the twentieth century to become once again recital favorites with modern audiences. Pound knew the songs from his London days as *The New Age* critic, and he later got to know at least some of the lute music via Jean Bésard's collection *Thesaurus harmonicus*, from which Gerhart Münch made some arrangements for the Rapallo concerts. Dowland is mentioned in Canto LXXXI.

DULAC, EDMOND (b. Toulouse—d. 1953). French artist and illustrator. Greatly interested in European and Oriental folk music, he was a maker of instruments, particularly Polynesian bamboo nose-flutes, one of which is mentioned in the score of Pound's *Le Testament.* In 1916 he created costumes, masks, sets, and incidental music for the first performance of Yeats's *At the Hawk's Well*, which Pound attended in the company of T. S. Eliot. He is named in Canto LXXX.

ELGAR, SIR EDWARD (b. Broadheath, 1857—d. Worcester, 1934), English composer. Although he was a central influence in British musical life after the turn of the century, William Atheling never hesitated to denigrate his music, often amusingly. For instance Elgar's "Capricieuse" reminded Atheling of the "schoolboy's Latin verb 'fleebo, fleerie, itchee, scratchum' " (*The New Age,* May 30, 1918).

EVANS, EDWIN (b. 1874—d. 1945), English writer and lecturer on music. Critic of the *Pall Mall Gazette*, 1914–23, and organizer of numerous lecture-recitals at which musicians such as Raymonde Collignon (*q.v.*) appeared. A progressive musician, Evans later became President of the International Society for Contemporary Music.

FAIDIT, GAUCELM (b. Limousin *circa* 1180—d. 1216), troubadour. There are about sixty of his poems extant, and fourteen of these include both words and music. Pound transcribed some of his songs into modern musical notation when he was teaching himself to read neumes. One of Faidit's songs is included in the collection on which he collaborated with Agnes Bedford (*q.v.*).

FERRARI, GUSTAVE (b. Geneva, 1872—d. Geneva, 1948), baritone singer, conductor, composer, and arranger. He broadcast frequently on the BBC and was a conductor of *Chu Chin Chow*, the amazingly successful musical version of the *Arabian Nights*. He was Yvette Guilbert's accompanist. He also made several collections of harmonizations of old French songs, including the *Selection Yvette Guilbert* for which Pound provided the English translations. He took the part of Villon in the 1931 BBC broadcast of *Le Testament*, and Pound hoped he might also perform the lead in the anticipated broadcast of *Cavalcanti*, which, however, never materialized.

FERROUD, PIERRE-OCTAVE (b. 1900—d. 1936), French conductor, critic, and composer, principally of ballet music. Pound heard his string quartet in C at the Venice Biennale in 1936 and liked it. (See "Mostly Quartets," *The Listener*, October 14, 1936.)

FÉTIS, FRANÇOIS JOSEPH (b. 1784—d. 1871), French pianist, organist, violinist, critic, and historian. He founded the *Revue Musicale* in 1827, and in 1833 became director of the Brussels Conservatory. His chief work was the monumental *Biographie Universelle des Musiciens* (1837-44) in eight volumes. Pound was familiar with this work and consulted it in connection with the Rapallo concerts. In the *Antheil* book he quotes from Fétis' *Manuel des compositeurs, directeurs de musique, chefs d'orchestre et de musique militaire* (Paris, 1837).

FINO SAVIO, CHIARINA (b. Turin, 1878—d. Turin 1969), Italin soprano. After having studied harp and piano, she devoted herself to singing. During the 1930s she performed in numerous concerts organized by Pound in Rapallo. She later continued her career up to the age of seventy as a teacher of singing at the Pesara Liceo Musicale and at the Turin Conservatory.

FOLQUET DE MARSEILLES (b. between 1180 and 1195—d. 1231), troubadour who later became Bishop of Toulouse. Pound transcribed some of his songs into modern musical notation when he was teaching himself to read neumes.

FRANCESCO DA MILANO (b. 1497—d. *circa* 1543), Italian lutenist, composer, and arranger. Sometimes called "il divino" by his admirers, he was employed at the ducal court of Mantua as well as by Ippolito de' Medici. Eight books of *Intravolatura di liuto* by him were published in Venice from 1536 to 1563, containing mostly *ricercari* and fantasias. Like many other lutenists of the period he arranged numerous compositions by other composers for that instrument. He was known to Pound through the work of Oscar Chilesotti (*q.v.*) and his arrangement of Janequin's *Chant des Oiseaux* (originally a choral piece) was further elaborated by Gerhart Münch for violin and piano and became a perennial favorite in the Rapallo concerts. It is the violin line of this work in Münch's handwriting that appears in Canto LXXV.

FRAZZI, VITO (b. Secondo Parmense, 1888), Italian composer. He taught composition first at the Conservatory of Florence and later at the *Accademia musicale Chigiana* in Siena, where Olga Rudge (*q.v.*) was Secretary. He was the composition teacher of Luigi Dallapiccola and numerous other important twentieth-century Italian composers.

FRID, GÉSA (b. Hungary, 1904), Hungarian pianist and composer. He studied with both Bartók and Kodály and since 1929 has made Amsterdam his home. In the summer of 1933 he visited Rapallo with his friend Tibor Serly (*q.v.*), and Pound wrote an article to celebrate their visit (*Il Mare*, August 20).

GALILEI, VINCENZO (b. Florence, *circa* 1533—d. Florence, 1591), Italian singer, violist, lutenist, composer, and theoretician. He was a member of the celebrated *Camerata* group which invented opera. Pound began to become intrigued with the ideas of the *Camerata* about 1939, but Galilei's lute compositions were known to him earlier than this through the Chilesotti (*q.v.*) manuscripts, which were used as a basis for the early Rapallo concerts. Galilei was the father of the astronomer Galileo Galilei.

GALUPPI, BALDASSARE (b. near Venice, 1706—d. Venice, 1785), Italian composer mostly of operas but also of harpsichord music. Browning had written a poem on a imaginary *Toccata of Galuppi's*. Renata Borgatti played a sonata by Galuppi on a Rapallo concert, February 3, 1938. Pound seems to have had more than a passing interest in Galuppi's music. In an article "B. Galuppi, detto 'Il Buranello,'" by Olga Rudge in *Note e documenti raccolta in occasione della Settimana celebrativa* (20–26 Settembre 1948), Ticci, Siena, 1948, we read: "La Sinfonia in re, (probabilmente del Re Pastore) eseguita nel concerto del 20 settembre è stata messa in partitura da parti mss dell'epoca appartenenti a Ezra Pound." Pound's interest in Galuppi may have been aroused by Browning's poem.

GERTLER, ENDRÉ (or ANDRÉ) (b. Budapest, 1907), Hungarian violinist, who has spent most of his life in Brussels. He has appeared as soloist and as leader of the Gertler String Quartet (*q.v.*) which he founded in 1931. In 1967 he won the Grand Prix du Disque for his recording of the complete violin works of Bela Bartók.

GERTLER STRING QUARTET, founded in 1931 in Brussels by Endré Gertler (*q.v.*). Members: Endré Gertler and Pierre de Groot, violins, Làszlo Revesz, viola, and Marcel Lounon, cello. They performed in a

Rapallo concert in 1935, playing Bartók's first and fourth quartets, and Pound heard them again at the Venice Biennale in 1936.

GIORDANO, UMBERTO (b. Foggia, 1867—d. Milan, 1948), Italian composer of operas, of which *Andrea Chenier* (1896) is his most popular. In an article for *Music and Letters* Pound apparently called Giordano "a garbage can" but then deleted the comment (see letter to Agnes Bedford, December, 1936).

GLUCK, CHRISTOPH WILLIBALD VON (b. Bavaria, 1714—d. Vienna, 1787), German composer, particularly of operas. He was an important reformer in that, in a time of highly ornamental and extravagant vocal writing, he returned to the principles of the original opera composers of the early seventeenth century. In the preface to his *Alcestis* he sets out his reform as follows: 1) The music was to be secondary to the poetry and drama, and was not to weaken them by unnecessary ornaments; 2) Halts in the poetry and action for the sake of any kind of display were to be particularly avoided. Gluck is mentioned in Pound's Canto LXXX.

GODDESCHALK, *See:* NOTKER BALBULUS.

GREEF, ARTHUR DE (b. Louvain, 1862—d. Brussels, 1940), Belgian composer and pianist. He was professor of piano at the Conservatory of Brussels and a well-known virtuoso during Atheling's London days.

GREENE, HARRY PLUNKET (b. Dublin, 1865—d. London, 1936), Irish bass. Especially noted as a recitalist, he toured Canada and the U.S.A. Celebrated for his interpretations of Schumann and Brahms. He also wrote a number of books on music.

GRETCHANINOFF, ALEXANDER (b. Moscow, 1864—d. New York, 1956), Russian composer, particularly of songs and children's music. Pound heard many of his songs during the London days, sung by Vladimir Rosing (*q.v.*).

DE GROOT, PIERRE, *See:* GERTLER STRING QUARTET.

GUARNIERI, ANTONIO (b. Venice, 1883—d. Milan, 1952), Italian cellist, conductor, and composer. Conducted at *La Scala,* Milan, and at the Vienna State Opera. Pound heard him at the Venice Biennale in 1936 and liked his work.

GUIDO (or GUI) D'AREZZO (b. *circa* 995—d. *circa* 1050), Benedictine monk and musician. An important theoretician, in his treatise *Micrologus* he outlines the principles of a system of solmization of which he was the inventor, and of staff notation of which, if he was not the inventor, he was certainly the first to employ to full advantage. Pound was early aware of his contribution to notation (see: the "Arnold Dolmetsch" article, *The Egoist,* August, 1917) and refers to him in Canto LXXIX where he sees the birds on the telephone wires above his cage at Pisa as neumes on a staff invented by Guido.

GUILBERT, YVETTE (b. Paris, 1865—d. Aix-en-Provence, 1944), French singer, actress, and diseuse. She began her career in café concerts and later appeared in the leading vaudeville houses of Paris, London, Berlin, Vienna, and Rome. She toured extensively presenting historical and genre cycles of French chansons. Her accompanist was Gustav Ferrari (*q.v.*) and he arranged the songs of the *Selection Yvette Guilbert* (London, 1912) for which Pound provided the English translations. She wrote a book of memoirs, *The Song of My Life* (1929).

HAHN, REYNALDO (b. Venezuela, 1875—d. Paris, 1947). Venezuelan composer, particularly of songs. He lived much of his life in Paris and was a close friend of Proust.

HALEY, OLGA (b. Huddersfield, 1898), English mezzo-soprano. Studied at the Royal College of Music, London, and in Switzerland. Made her début at the Albert Hall, London, in 1916, and her operatic début at Covent Garden in 1922 as Carmen.

HALMOS, LÁSZLÓ, *See:* HUNGARIAN STRING QUARTET.

HANDEL, GEORGE FREDERICK (b. Halle in Saxony, 1685—d. London, 1759), German-English composer. In *Guide to Kulchur* Pound calls him "Handel (the dull)," but the performance practices of the English oratorio school at the time doubtless affected Pound's evaluation.

HAYDN, FRANZ JOSEPH (b. Rohrau, 1732—d. Vienna, 1809), Austrian composer. Pound believed that Haydn, like Boccherini (*q.v.*) whom he so much resembles, had the advantage of being able to move effortlessly within a culture, by contrast with Bartók (*q.v.*) and Beethoven (also himself) who had to work *against* culture. Haydn quartets were performed at the Rapallo concerts between those of Bartók to serve as an "engine cooler."

HAYES, GERALD RAVENSCOURT (b. London, 1889—d. London, 1955), English writer on musical subjects. He was an editor at Oxford University Press and corresponded with Pound about various editions of old music available in print during the years of the Rapallo concerts. He became one of the founders of the Dolmetsch Foundation.

HAYES, ROLAND (b. 1887), American Negro tenor. Noted for his lyrical interpretations of German Lieder as well as for Negro spirituals. Dorothy Pound recalled (in a letter to the editor) that he visited them in their London flat about 1914 or 1915. Atheling reviewed his series of London recitals for *The New Age*, November 25 and December 23, 1920. In a notebook Pound later jotted down his name as the favored singer for the "Je renye Amours" aria from *Le Testament*.

HEYMAN, KATHERINE RUTH (b. 1887—d. 1944), American pianist. She made her début as soloist in 1899 with the Boston Symphony Orchestra. Pound had met her about 1904. From 1905 until 1915 she toured Europe and the U.S.A. giving concerts, and in 1908 for a short time in Venice Pound acted as her manager. She was the inspiration for at least two of Pound's early poems. Among her specialties as a pianist was the music of Scriabin. In 1921 she published a book *The Relation of Ultramodern to Archaic Music,* which shows some signs of Pound's influence on her conception of music. In 1934 she founded the "Scriabin Circle" in New York, which she conducted until her death. She is mentioned in Canto LXXVI (as K.H.). The poem "Scriptor Ignotus" in *A Lume Spento* is dedicated to her.

HINDEMITH, PAUL (b. Hanau, 1895—d. Frankfurt, 1963), German composer. Pound had heard Hindemith play his *Schwanendreher* (viola concerto) at the Venice Biennale in 1936 and had been much impressed. To Tibor Serly he had written "And say bo!! can yr. li'l friend Hindemith play the VI-olahhh?! I'll say he can *play* the viola." He also wrote to Gerhart Münch to ask him to persuade Hindemith to come to Rapallo (see letters to Serly and Münch, September and December, 1936). Unfortunately he did not come. With their insistence on craft in composition, the two artists would have had much to discuss. Hindemith's *Marienleben* for voice and piano and his *Klaviermusik* (1926–27) were performed in a Rapallo concert on April 27, 1934, and were reviewed by Pound in *Il Mare,* May 5. The same composer's *Sonatina* for piano was performed in a Rapallo concert on February 5, 1938.

HOLBROOKE, JOSEPH (or JOSEF) (b. London, 1870—d. London, 1958), British composer. He wrote a large quantity of music in all forms, including an opera trilogy. As a controversialist he used to be vigorous and even violent. Holbrooke sometimes signed his name "Joseph" and sometimes "Josef," concerning which, see Atheling's humorous letter in *The New Age,* July 24, 1919.

HONEGGER, ARTHUR (b. Havre, 1892—d. Paris, 1955), Swiss composer. In Paris he had been a member of "Les Six," who had derived inspiration from Eric Satie and had Jean Cocteau as their propagandist. Pound had heard the première of Honegger's second string quartet at the Venice Biennale of 1936, played by the Gertler Quartet, and in January, 1938, the same work, it appears, was given in Rapallo, this time performed by the New Hungarian Quartet.

HUNGARIAN STRING QUARTET, founded with the title of New Hungarian String Quartet in 1933. The original members were Sándor Végh, first violin, Peter Szervansky, second violin, Denes Koromzay, viola, and Vilmos Palotai, cello. By 1936 László Halmos had joined the group as second violin. Pound heard them first at the Venice Biennale in 1936 and was very impressed (see his letter to Tibor Serly in September, 1936). They performed in Rapallo concerts in 1937 and 1938, and Pound wrote several enthusiastic articles about them. In 1938 the quartet was reorganized; the "New" was dropped and the members became Zoltan Székely, first violin, Alexander Moskowsky, second violin, Koromzay, and Palotai. This ensemble remained unchanged until 1956 and gained worldwide fame.

JANEQUIN, CLÉMENT (sixteenth century), French composer. Very few facts are known about his life. He took part in the Italian campaigns of Francis I and witnessed the Battle of Marignano, which he later celebrated in a remarkable chanson. His choral compositions are fascinating for their programmatic descriptions. The best known of these are *Le Chant des Oiseaux, La Chasse, La Bataille de Marignan,* all of which were known to Pound in both their original choral versions and in instrumental versions by Janequin's Italian contemporaries. *Le Chant des Oiseaux* in a lute version by Francesco da Milano (*q.v.*), further elaborated by Gerhart Münch (*q.v.*) for violin and piano, became a perennial favourite in the Rapallo concerts. It is the violin line of this work in Münch's handwriting that appears in Canto LXXV. Janequin is also mentioned in Canto LXXIX.

JENKINS, JOHN (b. Maidstone, 1592—d. Norfolk, 1678), British composer. A much-valued musician in his day, he was employed by numerous noble families throughout England. He composed a great many sonatas for two violins, bass bowed instrument, and keyboard, as well as fancies, catches, songs, etc. His work owes much to Henry Lawes (*q.v.*), his older contemporary, who also interested Pound. Just how Pound developed his intense interest in Jenkins is not known, though it could have been through Dolmetsch, who certainly was concerned about his revival. In any case, he returned to the name of Jenkins repeatedly throughout his life, apparently without ever having heard much (or perhaps any) of his music. Agnes Bedford (*q.v.*) recalled how, during the London days, Pound attempted to organize a "Jenkins Evening," but when the musicians arrived no one knew anything about Jenkins. To Gerald Hayes, the editor, he wrote (November 30, 1937), "I know nowt of Jenk, save what you have told me." While *The Oxford Companion to Music* was still able to report in 1950, "A revival of interest in this once celebrated composer seems to be overdue ...," very little progress seems to have been made to date in this direction. Pound mentions Jenkins in Canto LXXXI.

KENNEDY, DAISY (b. Australia, 1893), Australian violinist. For a time she was married to the pianist Benno Moiseiwitsch and toured England and Europe.

KENNEDY-FRASER, MARJORY (b. Perth. 1857—d. Edinburgh, 1930), collector and arranger of folk songs. Her life work became her collection of *Songs of the Hebrides* (London, 3 vols., 1909, 1917, 1921). Pound seems to have known her personally, at least from 1912, for Brigit Patmore remembers meeting her at Pound's flat in Church Walk in that year; they possibly could have met first at one of W. B. Yeats's evenings of poetry reading as early as 1909. William Atheling frequently attended her London concerts, and called her frankly "a genius," a word which he almost never employed, for her efforts to revive Hebridean folk music. Pound once tried to fit *Beowulf* to some of this music (see *ABC of Reading*, Chapter Five).

KIDDLE, FREDERICK B. (b. Frome, Somerset), English organist and pianist.

He studied at the Royal College of Music under Parratt and Rockstro, and later became especially noted as an accompanist.

KOLISCH STRING QUARTET, Austrian quartet founded in Vienna, 1922, by Rudolf Kolisch. They made their American début in 1935 at the Library of Congress premièring Bartók's fifth string quartet, a work which Pound was to hear played a year later by the New Hungarian Quartet in Venice.

KOROMZAY, DENES, *See:* HUNGARIAN STRING QUARTET.

LAMOND, FREDERIC A. (b. Glasgow, 1868—d. Stirling, 1948), Scottish pianist. He toured Europe extensively, specializing in the late sonatas of Beethoven. Eventually he made his home in Berlin.

LAVIGNAC, ALBERT (b. 1846—d. 1916), French theoretician and historian who taught at the Paris Conservatory. In the *Harmony* treatise Pound quotes from his *La Musique et Les Musiciens* (Paris, 1895). Together with Laurencie he edited the monumental *Encyclopédie de la musique et dictionaire du conservatoire.* Pound knew this work also, particularly sections of it, such as Oscar Chilesotti's article on Italian lute music and an article on Greek music, which he recommended to Mary Barnard (letter of February 23, 1934) as "the only book of any use on rhythm." In a notebook from the London period Lavignac's encyclopedia is mentioned together with some transcriptions of troubadour songs into modern notation, indicating that it may have been the source he used to teach himself how to read neumes.

LAWES, HENRY (b. Dinton, 1596—d. London, 1662), English composer. He was a Gentleman of Charles I's Chapel Royal, and wrote music for Milton's masque of *Comus,* the songs for Herrick's *Hesperides,* and made numerous settings of poems by contemporary poets. His settings were much appreciated by the poets; Milton addressed a sonnet "To Mr. H. Lawes on his Aires," beginning:

> Harry, whose tuneful and well-measured song
> First taught our English music how to span
> Words with just note and accent....

Edmund Waller also dedicated a poem "To Mr. Henry Lawes, who had then newly set a song of mine, in the year 1635," which concluded:

> The writer's and the setter's skill
> At once the ravished ears do fill.
> Let those which only warble long,
> And gargle in their throats a song,
> Content themselves with *ut, re, mi:*
> Let words, and sense, be set by thee.

William Atheling referred repeatedly to Henry Lawes's settings when confronted with vocal pyrotechnics in the London recital halls, and continued to invoke his name in the *ABC of Reading, Guide to Kulchur,* and elsewhere. He is mentioned, together with Dowland, Jenkins, and Dolmetsch, in the *libretto* of Canto LXXXI. Lawes is also mentioned in *Mauberley.*

DE LENS, MARIE-THÉRÈSE, French singer and writer on music. William Atheling, in *The New Age* review for April 15, 1920, claims she had been commissioned by the French government to collect and study the traditional music of Morocco. Pound had always been interested in Arabic music, and he was familiar with the theories of Salvador Daniel (*q.v.*), expressed in his book *La musique arabe.* Marie-Thérèse de Lens was a close friend of Arnold and Mabel Dolmetsch, and Pound may have met her through them.

LIDDLE, SAMUEL (b. Leeds, 1868), English pianist and song writer. He studied at the Royal College of Music, London. Composer of *Abide with Me.*

LISZT, FERENCZ (or FRANZ) (b. Raiding, 1811—d. Beyreuth, 1886), Hungarian pianist and composer. Liszt is mentioned in Canto XXVII as a visitor to the home of the parents of Clara Leonora, a graduate student at the University of Pennsylvania during Pound's university days.

LOUNON, MARCEL, *See:* GERTLER STRING QUARTET.

LUCIANI, SABASTIANO ARTURO (b. Acquaviva delle Fonti, 1884—d. there, 1950), Italian musicologist active at the Siena Accademia Chigiana, where he founded with Olga Rudge the Centro di Studi Vivaldiani. He edited *Antonio Vivaldi: note e documenti sulla vita e sulle opere,* published by the academy in 1939, to which Olga Rudge also contributed. Pound was also familiar with his book *Mille anni di musica* (Milan, 1935), which formed the basis for his article "Vocal or Verbal" in *Meridiano di Roma,* November 26, 1939.

MACKINLAY, JEAN STERLING (b. London), singer of folk songs and old ballads. Devised the Jean Sterling Mackinlay Christmas Matinées for Children and Grown-ups. She was the daughter of a noted contralto, Antoinette Sterling.

MACKINNON, LILIAS (b. Aberdeen), Scottish pianist. Studied at the Royal Academy of Music with Tobias Matthay, where she won a gold medal. She gave concerts and lectures in London and in the U.S.A.

MAINARDI, ENRICO (b. Milan, 1897), Italian cellist and composer. Well known as a soloist, in 1949 he founded a trio with Edwin Fischer and Wolfgang Schneiderhan. He was at the Florence concert given by Olga Rudge and Gerhart Münch in May, 1935, and is mentioned in Pound's review (*Il Mare,* May 18, 1935).

MAITLAND, ROBERT (b. Lancashire, 1875), English bass-baritone. He began his career with the Edinburgh Orchestral Society in Gordon Craig's production of Handel's *Acis and Galatea* in 1896. He appeared in Wagner's *Ring* under Hans Richter in London, 1903, and in Queen's Hall Wagner concerts under Sir Henry Wood. In 1910 he took part in Beecham's opera season. From 1914 on he began singing more frequently in France, the U.S.A. and elsewhere. He sang in the première of *Le Testament* in Paris on June 29, 1926, dividing the arias with Yves Tinayre (*q.v.*), and again in the London 1931 BBC broadcast of the opera, where he took the part of "Bozo," the drunken brothel-keeper.

MARCHESI, BLANCHE ELIZABETH (b. Paris, 1869—d. London, 1940), French soprano. Educated at the Vienna Conservatory, she gave her début in Paris in 1895 and in London in 1896. She sang at Covent Garden for a time and following a successful career became extremely influential as a teacher of singing.

MARCHETTUS OF PADUA (fl. fourteenth century), Italian theoretician of the Ars Nova period. In his treatise *Pomerium musicae mensurate* (written sometime between 1309 and 1343) he provided music with a neatly classified system of rhythmic notation. Pound was familiar with his work through Guido Gasperini's "L'Art Musical Italien au XIV siècle," from Lavignac's *Encyclopédie de la musique et dictionaire du conservatoire,* and refers to it in his article on George Antheil for *The Criterion,* March, 1924, later incorporated into the *Antheil* book.

MAROILL, ARNAUT DE, *See:* ARNAUT DE MAROILL.

MARQUESITA, VIOLET (b. Buenos Aires, 1896), contralto. Born of a Scottish father and a French mother, her real name was Violet Hume, and the name "Marquesita" was given to her by her teacher, Blanche Marchesi (*q.v*). She had great fame in the 1920s as Lucy Lockit in the Lyric Theatre Hammersmith production of *The Beggar's Opera,* and she performed in numerous other operettas and musicals. Equally well known as a performer of folk song with gesture (in English, French, and Spanish), she coached with Agnes Bedford (*q.v.*), and through her Pound became interested in her work. She sang the part of Villon's mother in the BBC 1931 broadcast of Pound's *Le Testament.*

MARVOIL, ARNAUT DE, *See:* ARNAUT DE MAROILL.

MAYER, LONNY (b. Zürich—d. U.S.A., 1940), Swiss soprano. She studied in Zürich and in Germany and was active giving recitals in Switzerland, Germany and Italy during the 1930s, frequently performing little-known music from the Middle Ages and early Baroque. Pound wrote an introductory piece for her Rapallo concert of May 8, 1934, in *Il Mare* for May 5. In this concert she performed the arias "Tos temps serai" and "Ailas!" from Pound's opera *Cavalcanti,* and this was presumably the only time any portion of that opera was given public performance.

MENOTTI, GIAN CARLO (b. Cadegliano, 1911), Italian-American composer. Educated at the Milan Conservatory and at the Curtis Institute of Music in Philadelphia, he gained fame largely as an opera composer. In 1958 he founded the Festival of Two Worlds at Spoleto, Italy, where on July 14, 1965, the first stage performance of Pound's opera *Le Testament* was given.

METASTASIO, THE ABBE—real name, PIETRO TRAPASSI (b. Rome, 1698—d. Vienna, 1782), Italian librettist. His libretti were accepted as models of perfection in his time and numerous composers (Gluck, Handel, Haydn, and Mozart) set them. Hasse even set all his libretti once and some of them twice. Metastasio is mentioned in Canto LXXVIII and frequently in Pound's prose.

MOISEIWITSCH, BENNO (b. Odessa, 1890—d. London 1963), Russian pianist, long resident of England. His first appearance in England was in 1908. In 1914 he married the Australian violinist Daisy Kennedy (*q.v.*). He represented the traditional school of piano playing, excelling mostly in Romantic repertoire.

MORTARI, VIRGILIO (b. Milan, 1902), Italian composer. Educated at the Milan Conservatory, having studied under Pizzetti. In 1940 he assumed a position at the Rome Conservatory. In 1939 he had been associated with the Vivaldi week of the Siena Festival and Pound knew him there. In 1963 he became vice-president of the Accademia di Santa Cecilia.

MOSKOWSKY, ALEXANDER, *See:* HUNGARIAN STRING QUARTET.

MOZART, WOLFGANG AMADEUS (b. Salzburg, 1756—d. Vienna, 1791), Austrian composer. Mozart was one of Pound's perennially favorite composers. It will be recalled that all, or at least a great many, of Mozart's violin sonatas were performed in the Rapallo concerts on more than one occasion, and that in a program note Pound had likened them to Dante's *Paradiso*. Pound had also enjoyed visits to the Mozart Festival in Salzburg during the 1930s. Mozart is mentioned in Cantos XXVI, XLI, LXXVI, LXXVIII, CV, CXIII, and CXV. That Pound was familiar with some intimate details of Mozart's life is demonstrated in the last line of Canto XXVI, an explanation for which can be found in the *Annotated Index to the Cantos of Ezra Pound* (Berkeley and Los Angeles, 1959).

MULLINGS, FRANK CONINGSBY (b. Walsall, 1881—d. Manchester, 1953). English tenor and later choral director and professor of singing at the Birmingham Midland Institute.

MÜNCH, GERHARD, German pianist, arranger, and composer. Münch was originally from Dresden where, according to Pound, he had given a Liszt piano concerto with the Dresden Philharmonic at the age of thirteen, and had then performed the same piece in Berlin, Leipzig, Munich, Paris, Brussels, and Zurich. (See *Il Mare,* broadside, 1933.) Münch spent considerable periods of time in Rapallo during the 1930s, where he became one of the principal performers in the series of concerts organized by Pound under the title *Inverno musicale.* The papers of the Italian musicologist Oscar Chilesotti had come into his hands, and from these he arranged numerous pieces of ancient music for the Rapallo concerts. It is the violin line from Münch's arrangement of Janequin's *Chant des Oiseaux* which appears (also in Münch's autography) in Canto LXXV. After the Second World War Münch emigrated to California and later went to Mexico City, where he was active as a teacher as late as 1954. He is mentioned in Cantos LXXV and LXXX.

MURDOCH, WILLIAM DAVID (b. Australia, 1888—d. Surrey, 1942), Australian pianist and piano professor at the Royal Academy of Music in London. He published an analytical study of the piano works of Brahms.

MUSSORGSKY, MODESTE (b. Pskov, 1839—d. St. Petersburg, 1881), Russian composer. William Atheling had heard many of his songs sung in London by Vladimir Rosing (*q.v.*) and had "preferred their Russian bareness to the upholsteries of XIXth century Europe. Mussorgsky," he had written, "has his place beyond all the other Russians."

NEVADA, MIGNON (b. Paris, 1886), French soprano who lived in London, where she sang at the Royal Opera, Covent Garden. Daughter of soprano Emma Nevada.

NEVIN, ETHELBERT WOODBRIDGE (b. Edgeworth, Pa., 1862—d. New Haven, Conn., 1901), American composer, mostly of songs. His song "The Rosary" had an enormous vogue, selling six million copies in the first thirty years after its composition (1898).

NEW HUNGARIAN STRING QUARTET, *See:* HUNGARIAN STRING QUARTET.

NOTKER BALBULUS (d. 912), (Pound sometimes calls him GODDESCHALK). A monk of St. Gall, Switzerland, he was one of the originators of the Sequence, or as Pound has it, the Sequaire. It began as one of the many forms of interpolation in the ordinary of the Mass. As the melismatic character of certain portions of the Mass increased, texts, at first in prose, and later in poetry, were fitted to the extended melodies, rendering them again into syllabic types of song. Pound learned about Balbulus via Rémy de Gourmont's *Le Latin mystique.* As a maker of words and melodies simultaneously he was appreciated. "Notker était musicien, composait ensemble les phrases verbales et les phrases vocales: ainsi . . . tous les séquentaires." (*Le Latin mystique,* Paris, 1922, p. 129.)

OTTONE, MARCO (b. Chiavari, 1901), Italian cellist. He took his diploma in 1929 at Milan, then returned to Chiavari. In his article "Money versus Music" (*The Delphian Quarterly,* January, 1936) Pound says he was "a man who had taken degrees, et cetera, but was of old family and had no need to make any money, and in particular not a fighter who could on his own impose high grade music on his home town." He performed frequently in the Rapallo concerts, and the success of these stimulated him to participate with other music lovers in his home town of Chiavari—fifteen miles down the coast from Rapallo—in instituting a similar series there.

OXENFORD, EDWARD, English librettist. Son of John Oxenford (1812-77), English dramatist, poet, and general writer. Edward's libretti and lyrical pieces were set by numerous British composers. Atheling considered him a bad poet.

PALOTAI, VILMOS, *See:* HUNGARIAN STRING QUARTET.
PARLOW, KATHLEEN (b. Calgary, 1890—d. Toronto, 1963), Canadian violinist. She gave her London début in 1905 at the Bechstein Hall, and in 1906 she played with the London Symphony Orchestra. Between 1906 and 1908 she studied in St. Petersburg with Leopold Auer and gave many recitals there. She toured Europe and America extensively and in 1941 accepted an appointment at the Royal Conservatory of Toronto.
PEIROL (b. Auvergne, *circa* 1180—d. Montpellier, *circa* 1220), troubadour. Pound transcribed some of his songs into modern musical notation when he was teaching himself to read neumes. One of his seventeen known songs is included in the collection on which Pound collaborated with Walter Morse Rummel *(q.v.)*.
PIZZETTI, ILDEBRANDO (b. Parma, 1880—d. Rome. 1968), Italian composer. He was a professor of harmony in the Florence Conservatory and became its director in 1942. He composed several operas, a volume of church music and songs, etc. Olga Rudge had worked with him and, according to Pound, gave the first performance of his violin sonata outside Italy.
PONS DE CAPDOILL (b. *circa* 1180/1190), troubadour. Pound transcribed some of his songs into modern musical notation when he was teaching himself to read neumes. One of his songs is included in the collection on which he collaborated with Agnes Bedford *(q.v.)*.
PUCCINI, GIACOMO (b. Lucca, 1858—d. Brussels, 1924), Italian composer of operas. As may be expected, Pound did not like him. He appears in Canto LXXX as "Spewcini".
PURCELL, HENRY (b. London, 1658—d. London, 1695), English composer. He was organist at Westminster Abbey and Composer in Ordinary at the Chapel Royal. The last, perhaps, of the great British composers, at least until the present century, Purcell's music runs to string sonatas and fantasias, harpsichord suites, a large amount of polyphonic church music, and a quantity of royal odes and theater pieces. Pound had always been fond of Purcell's music, and in 1938 he organized for the Rapallo concerts performances of ten trio sonatas for two violins and continuo, which had been edited by W. Gillies Whittaker *(q.v.)* and published by L'Oiseau Lyre in Paris.
RADFORD, ROBERT (b. Nottingham, 1874—d. London, 1933), English bass. Studied at the Royal Academy of Music. Sang in numerous European opera houses and at Covent Garden.
RESPIGHI, OTTORINO (b. Bologna, 1879—d. Rome, 1936), Italian composer. Pound was not pleased with Respighi's suites of old music for modern orchestra: "Respighi shows us a wrong way in his attempts to set chamber music for large orchestra" *(Kulchur,* p. 251).
REVESZ, LÀSZLO, *See:* GERTLER STRING QUARTET.
RONALD, SIR LANDON (b. London, 1873—d. London, 1938), English con-

ductor. Educated at the Royal College of Music in London, he specialized in conducting the music of his friend Edward Elgar, and later became Principal of the Guildhall School of Music in London.

ROOTHAM, CYRIL BRADLEY (b. Bristol, 1875—d. Cambridge, 1938), English composer and music lecturer. He exercised a strong influence on the musical life of St. John's College, Cambridge, where he taught and conducted.

ROSING, VLADIMIR (b. St. Petersburg, 1890—d. Los Angeles, 1963), Russian tenor and opera director. He studied in St. Petersburg, making his début there in 1912. In 1913 he made his début at the Royal Albert Hall, London, and subsequently undertook tours of Europe and North America. One of Atheling's favorite performers, Rosing gave frequent recitals in London in which he undertook surveys of Russian vocal music. He recorded for His Master's Voice, Vocalion, Parlaphone, and Decca records. In 1923 he went to the U.S.A. as director of the Opera Department of the Eastman School of Music. He later became artistic director of the American Opera Company and stage director of the City Centre Opera Company in New York City.

RUBINSTEIN, ANTON (b. Podolsk, 1830—d. Peterhof, 1894), Russian composer and pianist. A few of his piano pieces and songs are still performed.

RUBINSTEIN, ARTHUR (b. Lódz, 1886), Polish-American pianist, one of the most eminent of the twentieth century.

RUDGE, OLGA (b. Youngstown, Ohio, 1895), American violinist. Daughter of a singer, she came to Europe at the age of nine and studied violin in Paris. During the first decades of the century she gave numerous violin recitals in the various capitals of Europe: London, Paris, Vienna, Rome. Her early London recitals are reviewed in the London *Times,* November 9, 1916; November 29, 1916; October 30, 1919; November 12, 1920; November 19, 1921; May 12, 1924; June 3, 1929. The following samples from these early reviews give a general idea of the quality of her playing: ". . . her really strong point, a flowing *cantabile;* not to the exclusion of other matters that usually interest expert violinists, but no stress was laid on these," ". . . excellent technique and fine taste. . . ." "The technical success in Sarasate's Spanish Dance, No. 8, was not great, but she managed to minimize its vulgarity." Before meeting Pound, Olga already showed an adventurous repertoire, performing not only standard violin works like Lalo's *Symphonie Espagnole,* but modern works by Pizzetti *(q.v.),* Respighi *(q.v.),* Malipiero, Castelnuovo-Tedesco, Paul Paray, and Lili Boulanger. William Atheling first reviewed one of Olga Rudge's London concerts in *The New Age,* November 25, 1920, where she performed with the Italian pianist Renata Borgatti. Atheling was charmed by Olga's playing, but did not care for Renata's "piano whack." The poet was later to meet Olga in Paris. The meeting is described in Pound's article in *Il Mare,* September 30, 1933. Soon she was performing music by George Antheil and Pound in various Paris concerts. Antheil described her as "a dark, pretty, Irish-looking girl, about twenty-five years old and, as I discovered when we commenced playing a Mozart sonata together, a consummate violinist. I have heard many violinists, but none with the superb lower register of the D and G strings that was Olga's exclusivity." (George Antheil, *Bad Boy of Music,* p. 121.) On December 11, 1923, Antheil and Rudge gave a joint recital in the Salle du Conservatoire in Paris in which they played two violin sonatas by Antheil and a Pound arrangement for solo violin of a twelfth-century air by Gaucelm Faidit, as well as a short original composition entitled *Sujet pour violon (Resineux).* Miss Rudge repeated the *Sujet pour violon* in an Aeolian Hall recital in London on May 10, 1924. On this occasion she also introduced Pound's *Fiddle Music, First Suite.* On July 7 of the same year Miss Rudge again participated in a Paris concert featuring some Pound music, and on May 6, 1926, she premièred Pound's *Hommage à Froissart* in the Sala Sgambati in Rome with Alfredo Casella at the keyboard. She also played a leading role in the miniature orchestra which was employed for the première of Pound's opera *Le Testament* in Paris on June 19, 1926. After the Pounds moved to Rapallo, Miss Rudge followed and moved into a small apartment in Sant'Ambrogio, the village above Rapallo. She became one of the principal performers in the series of concerts which Pound organized in Rapallo between 1933 and 1939 under the title of *Inverno musicale.* In 1936, at Pound's instigation, she catalogued the three hundred and nine Vivaldi instrumental pieces in manuscript in the National Library in Turin; and following this she became one of the leading figures in Vivaldi's twentieth-century revival, eventually accepting a position as Secretary of the Accademia Chigiana in Siena, where she founded, together with the Italian musicologist S.A. Luciani *(q.v.),* the Centro di Studi Vivaldiani.

RUMMEL, WALTER MORSE (b. Berlin, 1887—d. Bordeaux, 1953), German pianist and composer. He was the grandson of Morse, the inventor of the telegraph. He was educated in Paris and became a member of Debussy's inner circle, giving the première of Debussy's *Twelve Studies* in 1916 to the approval of the composer. Pound appears to have met him first about 1908, perhaps through an introduction by Katherine Ruth Heyman *(q.v.),* and saw him frequently during the early London years. "I lived with Rummel several times for months at a stretch in Paris" (letter to Iris Barry, August 29, 1916). In 1912 he collaborated with Rummel by providing English translations and some of the original music for a collection of troubadour songs: *Hesternae [sic] Rosae, Serta II, Neuf Chansons de troubadours des XIIième et XIIIième Siecles pour voix avec accom-*

pagnement de piano (Paris, London, Boston, 1913). Rummel at the same time set four of Pound's poems to music (published by Augener, 1913); his music for "The Return" Pound called "the best comment on that poem that has appeared" (*This Quarter,* Fall, 1925). Rummel's other productions include a travel book in German, *Die Provenze* (1911), an early edition of Vivaldi's cello sonatas (1916), and incidental music for Yeats's *The Dreaming of the Bones* (1917). It is obviously to Rummel that we may ascribe Pound's leniency toward Debussy. To Rummel, Pound dedicated his "Maestro di Tocar" from *Canzoni.* There is an article on Rummel's piano style in *The Spectator,* July 1, 1922, beginning:

> In London, at least, no pianist of to-day has a more debated position among executants than Mr. Rummel. Abroad he is highly esteemed. Here he is as enthusiastically received by some as he is depreciated by others. There is a Rummel coterie and there is an anti-Rummel coterie. To the first he is the most individual of pianists. To the second he is the most debased of thumpers, who adds to his crimes by playing in a darkened hall. . . .

Rummel is mentioned in Canto LXXX, sitting in the Rapallo coffeehouse Finlandia, and in Canto CIV (as "Walter").

SALMOND, FELIX (b. London, 1888—d. New York, 1952), English cellist and teacher. He studied at the Royal College of Music in London and in Brussels. He later went to the U.S.A. where he taught cello at the Curtis Institute and at the Juilliard School of Music.

SAMMONS, ALBERT EDWARD (b. London, 1886—d. London, 1957), English violinist. From 1908 to 1913 he was leader of the Beecham orchestra and also of the London Philharmonic. He was also first violinist of the London String Quartet, which Atheling heard.

SANSONI, LUIGI (b. Pescia, 1888—d. Rapallo, 1956), Italian violinist and conductor. For a number of years he was director of the Rapallo Orchestra and of various salon-music ensembles. He became one of the principal performers in the Rapallo concerts organized by Pound. In his article "Money versus Music" (*The Delphian Quarterly,* January, 1936) Pound says Sansoni "had been in Rapallo 15 years, an excellent musician though not very powerful, a composer who had had a few things published, who lived by leading the small town orchestra playing jazz, dance music, *anything* but with complete submergence."

SARASATE, PABLO DE (b. Pampolona, 1844—d. Biarritz, 1908), Spanish violinist and composer. He is mentioned in Canto LXXX.

SATIE, ERIC (b. Honfleur, 1866—d. Paris, 1925), French composer. A musical curiosity, Satie had studied music briefly as a young man and returned to study further at the age of forty. His compositions are highly idiosyncratic, often whimsical in nature, with droll titles such as *Pieces in the Shape of a Pear,* or *Limp Preludes for a Dog.* He was a friend of Debussy and is said to have influenced that composer in terms of inducing a more simplified style. His music also greatly influenced "Les Six", a group of young French composers including Poulenc, Honegger, and Milhaud, in their reaction against Impressionism. He was accepted by them as their spiritual mentor and Jean Cocteau, in his book *A Call to Order,* acclaimed Satie as the new leader of the anti-Romantic movement. Pound had been familiar with Satie's music from the London days when he had heard the ballet *Parade* (See *The New Age* review, December 18, 1919). He met Satie in Paris and in an *Il Mare* article (September 30, 1933) he describes sitting next to him at the première of George Antheil's *Ballet mécanique.* Several of Satie's piano compositions were presented in a Rapallo concert of April 4, 1935.

SAVIO, CHIARINA FINO, *See:* FINO SAVIO, CHIARINA.

SCHLOEZER, BORIS DE (b. Vitebsk, 1884—d. 1969), Russian-French critic and author. An early champion of Scriabin, who was his brother-in-law, de Schloezer wrote a book about him in 1922. A philosophical critic who had studied Husserl's phenomenology and the Berlin school of Gestalt psychologists, he was chiefly interested in trying to work out some precise terminology for the study of form, structure, language, melody, etc., as they applied to contemporary music. He made his home in Paris after 1920, where he was active on the staff of *La Revue Musicale.* In 1929 he published a book on Stravinsky in French which Pound translated in seven installments for *Dial* (October, 1928, pp. 271-83; January, 1929, pp. 9-26; February, 1929, pp. 105-15; April, 1929, pp. 298-303; May, 1929, pp. 394-403; June, 1929, pp. 463-74; July, 1929, pp. 597-608). Pound was particularly pleased with his commentary on "melody" and his ideas on rhythm may have also influenced his own theory of *Great Bass (*see Appendix I).

SCHMIDT, FLORENCE, English singer. Pound translated some programs for a concert given by her in 1910 in Bechstein Hall, London. The details are given in Donald Gallup's "The Search for Mrs. Wood's Program" in *Ezra Pound Perspectives,* edited by Noel Stock (Chicago, 1965). According to a letter from Florence Schmidt, reprinted in Gallup's article, Pound had visited her for discussions on music in the company of D.H. Lawrence.

SCHOENBERG (or SCHÖNBERG), ARNOLD (b. Vienna, 1874—d. Los Angeles, 1951), Austrian composer. The leading figure in the so-called "Neo-Viennese school," Schoenberg's early music is characterized by a progressive abandonment of tonality and by various expressionistic devices (he was a close friend of Kandinsky); later he began to elaborate the celebrated twelve-tone or serial method of composition which has been very influential in twentieth-century musical thought. Pound seems to have been aware of his *Harmonielehre*

(1911), but he does not appear to have heard much, or any, of Schoenberg's music. However, since he did hear some of Alban Berg's and did not enjoy it, we may assume that the music of Berg's teacher would have been likewise dismissed as emotionally excessive.

SCRIABIN, ALEXANDER (b. Moscow, 1872—d. Moscow, 1915), Russian composer. A romanticist with interests in uniting mystical theories, religion, and cosmology, Scriabin's music, while influenced by Chopin and Liszt, expresses a unique personality. His works include a great quantity of piano music and the orchestral works, *The Poem of Ecstasy* and *Prometheus* (or *The Poem of Fire*). Pound had an oblique association with this composer through Katherine Ruth Heyman (*q.v.*), who had been a great champion of his music. His ambivalent feelings are best set forward in the article "Anti-Scriabin" (*Il Mare,* July 8, 1933).

SERLY, TIBOR (b. Losonc, 1900), Hungarian-American composer and violist. Serly was brought to America as a child in 1905 but returned to Hungary in 1923 to study music at the Budapest Academy. He graduated in 1925 with top honors, having studied composition with Kodály. He played the viola in the Cincinnati Symphony, the Philadelphia Symphony, and the NBC Symphony under Toscanini. In 1937 he settled in New York. He has written a symphony, a viola concerto, and other orchestral works, songs, etc. His association with Pound dates from 1929, when he wrote a "scathing" letter attacking *Antheil and the Treatise on Harmony*. During the 1930s, up to 1938, he spent portions of several summers in Rapallo and Siena en route to Budapest to visit old friends. He is largely responsible for introducing Pound to the music of Bartók. In fact, Serly was very close to Bartók and befriended him toward the end of his life, in New York. After his death he completed and orchestrated Bartók's unfinished viola concerto. Serly's music was performed on several Rapallo concerts, and he also performed there on his viola (March 3, 1935). Pound wrote several promotional pieces on behalf of Serly's music. To him he also gave the manuscript of his *Ghuidonis Sonata,* and Serly orchestrated it for string orchestra and performed it for the poet privately when he was in New York in 1939. For Serly, Pound translated from Hungarian the text of a Transylvanian folk song entitled "The Monstrous Flea." The text is given in a letter dated October, 1939, and the music has been published by Serly (MCA Music Corporation, New York, 1952).

SHARP, MARY ELIZABETH (BETTY) (b. Alma, Mich. 1890), American coloratura soprano. She studied singing in Vienna and made her début in 1914.

SOCIUS, RAPHAEL, *See:* ZARLINO, GIOSOFFO.

STRAVINSKY, IGOR (b. Oranienbaum, 1882—d. New York, 1971), Russian composer. Pound had a great respect for Stravinsky, and with their sense of craftsmanship and rhythmic daring the two artists possess much in common. "Among composers whose work I have heard Stravinsky is the only living musician from whom I can learn my own job." (*The New English Weekly,* March 28, 1935, p. 495.) He heard much of Stravinsky's music, including the London première of *Le Sacre du Printemps,* the London première of the *Three Pieces for String Quartet,* the *Capriccio* for piano and orchestra, shortly after it was written, the *Game of Cards* (in London with Ronald Duncan) etc. Stravinsky's *Pulcinella* suite was a favorite in the Rapallo concerts. In a sense one may regret that the two figures did not make more emphatic contact while in Paris together. The reason is probably that Pound was forced into the Antheil camp when Antheil and Stravinsky quarreled (see note 25, p. 262). He gave a note of introduction to Stravinsky to Ronald Duncan and was anxious to secure him for a Rapallo concert when Duncan was trying to organize a Stravinsky appearance in London (letter of January 17, 1939).

STROESCO, CONSTANTIN (b. 1886), Rumanian tenor. Studied at the Iassy Conservatory, graduating in 1905. He sang leads at the Bucharest Opera, the Opéra Comique in Paris, and in London and the United States. He was particularly celebrated for his roles in Debussy's *Pelléas et Mélisande,* Delibes' *Lakmé,* and Puccini's *Madame Butterfly.* He performed in René Clair's film *The Million.* There are many enthusiastic reviews of his London concerts in the Atheling columns in *The New Age.* Pound also hoped he would sing the aria "Mort, j'appelle" from *Le Testament,* though he never did. Returning to Rumania, he was appointed singing professor at the Bucharest Conservatory.

SZÉKELY, ZOLTAN (b. Kocs, 1903), Hungarian violinist and composer. He studied with Jenö Hubay and Zoltan Kodály. In 1938 he joined the Hungarian String Quartet *(q.v.)* as first violinist.

SZERVANSKY, PETER, *See:* HUNGARIAN STRING QUARTET.

TAGORE, RABINDRANATH (b. Calcutta, 1861—d. Bolpura, 1941), Bengali poet and musician. Pound had been an early admirer of Tagore in London. They had met in 1912, and Pound had heard Tagore recite and sing the poems of his *Gitanjali.* He recognized immediately the relation between the Bengali's work and that of the medieval troubadours. Later, when Tagore had been "discovered" and won the Nobel Prize, an estrangement developed between the two figures.

TERTIS, LIONEL (b. West Hartlepool, 1876—d. London, 1975), English viola player. He studied in Leipzig and at the Royal College of Music in London, and toured Europe and America as solo violist. He persuaded a number of British composers (Cyril Scott, Arthur Bliss, Arnold Bax, etc.) to write sonatas and concerti for the viola.

TEYTE, MAGGIE (b. Wolverhampton, 1888), English soprano. She studied at the Royal College of Music in London, and later sang at the

Opéra Comique in Paris, having first made her appearance as Mélisande in *Pelléas et Mélisande,* under Debussy's supervision. She later sang in London, then at the Chicago Opera Company, the Boston Opera Company, and the New York City Opera. She returned to London and gave numerous recitals of French songs during World War II.

THOMSON, VIRGIL (b. Kansas City, 1896), American composer. He went to Paris in 1921, returned briefly to the U.S.A., then went back and stayed until the beginning of World War II. Paris has never ceased to be his spiritual home. Since he was a close friend of Gertrude Stein he was more or less excluded from the Pound-Antheil camp, though he did attend the première of *Le Testament* in 1926 and liked it. (See *Virgil Thomson,* by Virgil Thomson, New York, 1966, p. 83.)

THURSFIELD, ANNE (b. New York, 1885—d. London, 1945), English mezzosoprano. She began giving song recitals in London during World War I. Giving preference to modern and unknown music, her exceptional gifts as a linguist enabled her to sing songs of many nations in the original.

TINAYRE, YVES (b. Paris, 1891), French lyric tenor and musical scholar. He studied singing in London and Milan and later appeared as soloist in concerts throughout Europe, usually specializing in forgotten music from the past. It was this which attracted him immediately to William Atheling, and there are numerous reviews of his London recitals in the columns of *The New Age,* beginning November 14, 1918. The two artists formed a friendship which lasted many years. Tinayre was later to sing in the Paris première of Pound's opera *Le Testament* in 1926. He also incorporated the aria "Mort, j'appelle" from that work into his repertoire and sang it on his tours during the years following. Pound kept in touch with him by letter from Italy and hoped he would come to give a concert of ancient music in the Rapallo series, though he never did. Tinayre's researches took him to many libraries throughout Europe, and he did much to revive the vocal music of the Middle Ages and Renaissance. He was made president of "Les Musiciens de la Vieille France."

TOYE, GEOFFREY (b. London, 1889—d. London, 1942), British conductor. Following studies at the Royal College of Music, he conducted the Beecham Opera Company and concerts of the Royal Philharmonic Society (1918-19). He also conducted the D'Oyly Carte Opera Company in the Gilbert and Sullivan repertory.

VAN DIEREN, BERNARD (b. Holland, 1884—d. London, 1936), Dutch-English composer. Van Dieren had developed a style of free dissonance quite his own, contemporary with Schoenberg's early work and although he was not very well respected in England, Pound appreciated his art well enough to declare (*The New Age,* November 14, 1918) "here is a composer seriously interested in his art. . . ."

At any rate he prized Van Dieren's music above that of most of his British contemporaries. They also had a mutual friend in the sculptor Jacob Epstein, about whom Van Dieren wrote a book.

VECCHI, ORAZIO (b. Modena, 1550—d. Modena, 1605), Italian composer of motets and madrigals. He printed a series of madrigals in the form of a drama entitled *L'Amfiparnasso,* a copy of which Pound possessed and hoped to get performed in the Rapallo concerts, but this never materialized. He is mentioned in Canto LXXIX.

VÉGH, SÁNDOR (b. Klausenburg, 1912), Hungarian violinist. He joined the Hungarian String Quartet *(q.v.)* in 1933. In 1940 he became a professor at the Budapest Hochschule der Musik and founded his own quartet, which became known as the Végh Quartet and quickly established itself as a first-class ensemble.

VENTADOUR, BERNART DE (b. Limousin, 1145—d. Limousin, 1195), troubadour. He was born the son of a poor servant in the Ventadour castle, and later served Eleanor of Acquitaine. According to his razo he was "able to compose and sing well." Much of his music is extant, and Pound transcribed some of it when he was teaching himself to read the musical notation of the troubadours. His songs are included in the two collections of troubadour music on which Pound collaborated: that with Walter Morse Rummel *(q.v.)* and that with Agnes Bedford *(q.v.).* The words and neumes at the beginning of Canto XCI appear to be a telescoping of Bernart de Ventadour's "per la doussor c'al cor li vai" and Guillem de Poitou's "ab lo dolchor del temps novel".

VERDI, GIUSEPPE (b. near Busseto, 1813—d. near Busseto, 1901), Italian opera composer. He is mentioned in "Moeurs Contemporaines," Canto LXXXIV, and Addendum for Canto C ("la donna é mobile").

VEROLI, MANLIO DI, *See:* DI VEROLI, MANLIO.

VIDAL, PEIRE (b. Toulouse, *circa* 1175—d. *circa* 1215), troubadour. Pound translated some of his verse in *The Spirit of Romance* (London, 1910), and transcribed some of his songs when he was teaching himself to read medieval musical notation. Altogether music for about a dozen of his songs is extant. Vidal figures in Canto IV.

VIVALDI, ANTONIO (b. probably Venice, 1675–78—d. Vienna, 1741), Italian composer and violinist. Pound and Olga Rudge began to become interested in reviving Vivaldi about 1936, well in advance of the heavy thrust of musicological attention he has since received. In that year Olga, at Pound's instigation, began her catalogue of the Vivaldi material in the Turin National Library. Pound initiated the Vivaldi studies with an article in *Il Mare,* March 14, 1936, and from that time on for several years Vivaldi was the principal focus of interest in the Rapallo concerts, climaxing in the *Settimana musicale* devoted to Vivaldi by the Accademia Musicale Chigiana of Siena in 1939. By this time Olga Rudge had become

Secretary to the academy, where she was to become one of the leading researchers in the Vivaldi field. (For a partial list of her Vivaldi publications see page 330.) In 1937 Pound ordered several microfilms of Vivaldi manuscripts from the Sächsische Landesbibliotek in Dresden, and in 1938 he gave these to Count Guido Chigi Saracini for inclusion in the holdings of the Siena Academy library. The frequently repeated story that the originals were destroyed during World War II, leaving Pound's microfilms as the only extant copies of these treasures, is not true. Vivaldi is mentioned in Canto XCII.

WHITEHOUSE, WILLIAM EDWARD (b. London, 1859—d. London, 1935), English cellist. He studied at the Royal Academy of Music in London. He toured England, France, and Italy as a member of the London Trio, and in 1886 he became a professor at Cambridge. He also taught at the Royal College of Music from 1895.

WHITTAKER, WILLIAM GILLIES (b. Newcastle-on-Tyne, 1876—d. Orkney Islands, 1944), Scottish choral conductor, editor, and arranger. He conducted the Newcastle and Gateshead Choral Union and the Newcastle Bach Choir, taking the latter on successful tours of England and Germany. In 1929 he became Director of the Scottish National Academy of Music, and was also simultaneously Professor of Music at Armstrong College, University of Durham. In 1924 he undertook the first complete performance of William Byrd's *Great Service*. He was an important editor of Bach's music and wrote a large study of the cantatas. He corresponded with Pound in the early 1930s concerning the latter's interest in the music of William Young *(q.v.)*, which he was then editing. The eleven sonatas of William Young from the Uppsala manuscript were issued separately in the Oxford orchestral series (Nos. 81-91, Oxford University Press, London, 1930). Whittaker sent Pound this collection in December, 1933, and in 1934 six of the sonatas were presented in Rapallo, apparently in advance of the British "première" at Oxford under Whittaker's own direction (see *Il Mare* article, March 3, 1934). In February, 1938, Whittaker's edition of Purcell's ten trio sonatas for two violins and continuo (L'Oiseau Lyre, Paris) were also given in Rapallo concerts.

WOOD, HENRY (b. London, 1869—d. London, 1944), British conductor particularly at the famous Promenade Concerts in the Queen's Hall, where Atheling frequently heard him conduct.

WOODGATE, HUBERT LESLIE (b. London, 1902), English choral conductor and organist. Educated at the Royal College of Music in London, he became Chorus Master of the BBC Chorus in 1928 and also founded and conducted the BBC Theatre Orchestra. He conducted the orchestra in the first broadcast performance of Pound's opera *Le Testament* on the BBC in 1931.

YOUNG, WILLIAM (d. 1672), British composer. Much remains to be discovered about the early part of his career. He appears to have been in the service of the Archduke of Austria, and he published the partbooks of a collection of eleven sonatas in Innsbruck in 1653. The single surviving copy of this printing is in the Uppsala library in Sweden. In 1660 he entered the band of Charles II of England, first as a flute player and later as a violinist. His work is in a style which might be called Purcellian, though he died when Purcell was but a boy. As the two musicians were in the same royal service it is presumed they were acquainted. During the Rapallo years Pound became very interested in Young's music and corresponded with his editor, the Scottish musician William Gillies Whittaker *(q.v.)*. Whittaker sent him his edition of the sonatas, and six of them were performed at Rapallo in advance of their official British "première" at Oxford under the editor's direction.

YSAYE, EUGÈNE (b. Liège, 1858—d. 1931), Belgian violinist and composer. He is mentioned in Canto LXXX.

ZARLINO, GIOSOFFO (b. 1517—d. 1590), Italian music theorist. There is a curious reference in Pound's *Harmony* treatise to a certain Raphael Socius who [sic] about 1556 catalogued the intervals which were considered pleasing and respectable. This can only refer to Zarlino's famous treatise *Institutioni harmoniche* (1558) where, in Book III, he discusses the intervals available to the composer, laying special emphasis on the major and minor third.

Appendix III

WHY A POET QUIT THE MUSES[1]

GEORGE ANTHEIL

Ezra Pound's music reminds me of Rousseau going out at a late age and painting the leaves of the trees all a little larger so that one does not have to paint so many leaves.

Ezra Pound starts out upon the art of music a little frantically; a little hectically; a tree is to him a tree with a certain technical capacity as a tree; the same with a telegraph pole. And he is always concerned with some musical lion or tiger with which he invariably gives a marvellous meaning to a whole landscape; his colors are glaring and glassy; the octave takes on the piercing quality that we have expected eventually from Strawinsky's music and have not received while that worthy has been for sometime engaged in easier fields.

Pound's whole music has a mediaeval intelligence, a brilliant intelligence although it is not intellectual. Nothing could be quite so plainly music and so free from intellectualism. But it is mediaeval by preference; by thought. I am convinced that no other music today is so completely free from the developments of music during the last three or four hundred years, yet the music is as tight and as built up upon inner and strict laws of its own, as if it were built upon hundreds of years of musical tradition.

Ezra Pound was, as those who know his poetry know, a musician from the beginning. There is nothing extraordinary about his abandoning (temporarily at least) poetry for music. To those who know his new musical technic and his last poetry, the break is imperceptible;

[1] From the *Chicago Tribune*, "Sunday Magazine" (Paris Edition), September 14, 1924, p. 9.

513

the music gains and does not lose in rhythm; in fact the whole rhythmic technic is a new invention and not a simple, but a complicated invention, whereby music for the first time in the history of its notation at least attains the rhythmic heights of poetry and does not confine itself to the falsely conceived metrical systems (from the viewpoint of great poetry) of the music of the past. Technically there is grand liberation, and excitement for the musicians alone; for the rest remain the stark words of Villon sung and annotated by another great poet some centuries later, with no fashionable musical gew-gaws now so in fashion in this period, but as simply as it might have been conceived musically by Villon himself.

This does not necessarily indicate that the music is "simple" in our conception. I am certain that the "simple" music of the France of today is complicated beyond measure in comparison to the stronger and easier conceived music of decades past when the complicated clowneries of M. Erik Satie did not "purify" music. I do not mean this ironically, but simply to indicate that intellectual purification does not remain musical purification; it is far easier for the intelligence to err than the intuition in producing a work of art. Erik Satie and his latest and most important victim and follower, Igor Strawinsky (I speak of the last works of Strawinsky of the past two years) to say nothing of Les Six and the still younger Ecole; all come to nothing whatsoever; their musical significance is nil and we do not know whither to turn for the moment; the impotence of the musical situation is superb. The last gallery of Picasso shows that he is more and more upon the sheerly virtuous path, and his present "arty" Twiddledum counterpart, Strawinsky, makes a dull brown portrait of his wife in the new piano concerto a few months afterwards. Constipation reigns. Twiddledee bows (Mr. Picasso); Twiddledum bows (Mr. Strawinsky); Les Six go into ecstasies of intellectual musical revolutionaryism, giving birth in thunderbolts to increditably boring works sounding like dispirited Chaminade and Godard ... composers whom we long since have found out for their complete shallowness and tinsel charm; an earthquake occurs and gives birth to the new Ecole calmly and "talentedly" tiddling away at Debussy. Gracious! ... the perverted audacity with which they are meek and impotent. Enough of them. They are in fashion. The having of "a day" indicates nothing whatsoever.

Just a little point of insistence, if you don't mind ... we do not want literature for musical talent ... sheer musical kernel. And music Ezra Pound gives us ... not a senseless set of gee-gaws. He gives us the music that knocks about in his own head, and which he dares to write down as simply as Moussorgsky dared to write down the music that was knocking about in his head. Every art epoch after a certain time of working out its fundamental phenomena becomes constipated, and a knocking about in a head here and a knocking about in a head there is far more precious than all the "intellectual purifying" in the world while no art is built up upon an intellectual basis, otherwise we should content ourselves with theses. Satie and Co. contents itself with theses and collections and ideas and examples. Pound, like Rousseau, is interested in making something that locks itself up in one piece.

I have insisted that Pound is mediaeval by preference and by thought. I have seldom read such a clear and simple statement of the theory of harmony as recently appeared in his article recently published in the *Transatlantic Review*. With one stroke it brushes away a world of imbecilities carefully cultivated and cherished by impotents since the times of Bach. And there it makes for once the clear and bright statement of what "harmony" really is and means, and its sole practical significance. "Of course!" One always finds a man of talent very much "of course." The thing has always existed. And so did Rousseau's trees, carriages, and basket-ball players. And with this clarity about rhythm, which was born in him, and harmony, which he could see as "of course" as the nose on his face, as clearly as Rousseau could see that trees were round ... it is with this that Ezra Pound makes a kind of music that is quite as different from other precious things of this time as anything I know of... as different as the members of Satie and Co. are alike to one another... as different as Rousseau was from the theoreticians of an age just past... and their piles of sunlight, resembling one another from a slight distance like so many new peas.

I find Pound's analogy in Rousseau. He seems the only man of the age who has started out writing music *round* so that there is air behind it... as he can clearly hear... and as Rousseau could clearly see. Pound's music, coming as it has, from a technically untrained musical talent that has been festering to express itself in real music all of his life, is a phenomena existing outside of our sphere of music for some time yet to come. To those musicians who have half an eye, it will be quite clear that the technical side of "Le Testament" is hectic, gawky, and from a viewpoint of modern musical technic, really annoying; nevertheless it will be apparent that it is a work of colossal talent; a genial work; a work gaunt and bare, but with a new richness, and an approach that is as new as new planets. The chief interest to young musicians is: Ezra Pound, musically, is a poet who wanted all of his life to become a musician, and has become one in such a curious manner that his music seems to have no connection with the last three or four hundred years at all! Every moment one is reminded of Rousseau painting his trees and telegraph poles round ... just because the others were too stupid, in their mathematical filteration of light, to see things as they were ... at any rate the way Rousseau saw them which was after all the most important. Musically Pound has with Rousseau, in the present mixed and impotent period of the world's musical history, an identicality which will in the course of time have some little influence upon the world of creative music ... in fact, I feel safe in saying, a great deal. Every really new work which brings an entire new technical world into being is sure of influencing the work of the future, for it seems that from the technical manner of approach artists can most easily steal from one another, for technicality is the uppermost, the most superficial manifestation of an artist, and if he be a great artist beneath and outwardly rich in technical inventions . . . he will be robbed grandly and hilariously for years to come. Pound is a gold-mine of new technical means, and stands out sharply against the whole sum and substance of the present moderns in musical composition, who are at best a bunch of false-noters on the old masters who were true musical genuises and inventors. Even Strawinsky has taken his place among them . . . his new pianoforte concerto sounds like a stupid new German work influenced by a second-rate or third-rate German "ultra-modern" who is jinking up the good old hearty counterpoint of Bach with a couple of "just stinkingly ultra" (as the Café du Dôme phrase has it) discords now and then. They are all of no account.

Anti-Romanticism? Faugh! I assure you that the present period in fashionable Paris' excitement over the fashionable Six . . . and the rest of Satie and Co. is quite the height of "Romanticism." I offer you a glass of clear water in its stead, the consideration of this: *the age of two dimensional music has passed forever*. If you write it you will be repeating yourself for some Debussy, Scriabine, Ornstein, Bloch, Rachmaninoff, Beethoven, Mozart, or Bach you heard the summer before last. The big wavy, sprawling, and idealistic line à la Bloch, Ornstein, etc. has left us. So has the jolly, pumping Rossini-line of the Six, etc. . . . if you don't believe it, listen to yourself, after coming over from London in a few hours instead of a few days. Time and not "times" has changed . . . that is, *our* conception of it, no matter be the subject mediaeval or fifty thousand years hence. We want new and tight projections into space. We want music that locks itself and that one can put one's hand about. We want music, sheerly and physically music, without a literature, or a mythical "purification".

With a simple gesture Pound gives us a real music, although there has been a great deal of shaking and batting about from the closed tent where he has given birth to it. The situation, perhaps, has the element of the comic. Sometimes I sit at supper tables and I am drawn into a discussion of Pound's opera, of which it is known I edited, and the skeptics declare that Pound is no musician but a poet . . . and there is a great deal of amusement in contemplation of what his opera will be like. I tell them, when pressed, about his ideas and his manner of approach . . . and there is still more amusement. No one is more amused than I. Fancy Rousseau going out to paint trees round, and capturing those marvellous lions, tigers, carts, and basketball players. Fancy him gripping everything by the ears, for once! I have not had such a good time since grandpapa "Mavra" fell downstairs and broke his neck. No one can be more amused, more polite, more hilarious than I.

INDEX OF PROPER NAMES

Abrahams, Edith, 67
Achron, Joseph, 137
Adam de la Halle, 95, 100, 105, 119, 133, 481
Adams, Stephen, 18n, 316n, 329n, 475n
Adowska, Ilma, 95
Albeniz, Isaac, 107, 238, 350
Albert, Heinrich, 361
Aldington, Richard, 28f
Ali Khan, 228
Allied String Quartet, 158, 178, 181, 489
Altmann, W., 329n, 385
Anacreon, 86, 271
Anderson, Margaret, 250
Ansermet, Ernest, 61n
Antheil, George, 19, 24, 41, 59, 195n, 242, 243ff, 253ff, 271, 276n, 293, 295n, 305, 307, 311ff, 333, 344, 345f, 378, 405, 454, 458, 474, 481f, 485, 499, 504, 506, 508, 509, 513ff
Antonius, Marcus, 393
Apollinaire, Guillaume, 416
Aragon, Louis, 242
Aranyi, Jelly d', 201f, 482
Arden, Evelyn, 94
Arensky, Antony, 144
Ariosto, Ludovico, 74
Aristotle, 30, 298, 305, 413, 437
Arkandy, Katherine, 146
Arnaud, Yvonne, 180f
Arnaut Daniel, 6, 11, 12, 27n, 34, 258, 391, 396, 435, 450, 482

Arnaut de Maroill, 482
Arne, Thomas, 116, 170, 205, 285, 482
Arnold, Matthew, 85
Ashbrooke, Philip, 91
Ashton, Leopold, 103, 160, 176, 179, 194
Assurbanipal, 46
Astafieva, Serafima, 482
Attey, John, 139
Aubert, Louis, 215, 216, 229
Aubry, Pierre, 368n
Auer, Leopold, 502
Auric, Georges, 242

Bach, C. P. E., 294, 396, 426
Bach, J. C., 447
Bach, J. S., 10, 18, 19, 20, 22, 33, 35, 38, 58, 67, 74, 81, 83f, 87, 98, 103, 109, 111, 112, 116, 120n, 122, 129, 130, 132, 143, 146, 157, 164, 165, 169, 175, 177, 186, 202, 205, 220, 223, 224, 234, 237, 241, 247, 254, 259, 268, 273, 275, 280, 287, 288, 292, 293, 294, 297, 298, 299, 315, 333, 338, 340, 342, 346, 347, 349, 350, 351, 353, 354, 355, 356, 358, 359, 360, 361, 362, 364, 366, 367, 369, 370, 376, 378, 380, 381, 384, 385, 387, 388, 389, 392, 394, 403, 408, 411, 414, 416, 419, 423, 424, 425, 435, 437, 444, 445, 447, 450, 451, 452, 455, 456, 457, 460, 461, 464, 471, 472, 476, 478, 482f, 485, 486, 511, 515, 516

517

Bacigalupo, Dott., 336
Backhouse, Rhoda, 67
Bagrinovsky (composer), 99
Baildon, Joseph, 204
Bantock, Granville, 85, 194, 232, 483
Barbirolli, Giovanni (Sir John), 67, 483
Bardi, Count, 450
Barilli, Bruno, 483
Barnard, Mary, 497
Barnes, Djuna, 250, 312
Barnes, Winifred, 181
Barney, Natalie, 336
Barrett, Elizabeth, 409
Barry, Iris, 25, 27, 50, 504
Bartholdi, 88
Bartlett, Ethel, 67
Bartók, Béla, 19, 25, 62, 263, 264, 323, 324, 334f, 364, 365, 366, 367, 372, 373, 376, 399, 400, 401, 403f, 410, 411, 414f, 419, 420ff, 425, 428n, 473, 482, 483, 486, 492, 493, 494, 497, 507
Bassani, Giovanni, 215, 216, 337, 338
Bassiano, Princess, 311
Baudelaire, Charles, 118, 167, 211
Bax, Sir Arnold, 60, 94, 102, 138, 221, 239, 483, 508
Beach, Sylvia, 250, 251, 311, 316n
Beardsley, Aubrey, 96n
Beaumarchais, Pierre de, 63
Becker, Hugo, 421
Becker, John J., 476, 483
Bedells, Phyllis, 52
Bedford, Agnes, 28n, 60, 195, 240, 243, 265, 384, 417, 465, 484, 485, 488, 491, 493, 496, 499, 502, 510
Bédos de Celles, Dom Francis, 258, 484
Beecham, Sir Thomas, 25, 66ff, 90, 124, 181, 187, 226, 484, 489, 498, 505, 509
Beethoven, Ludwig van, 60, 66, 73f, 85, 88f, 95, 97, 101, 105, 106, 113f, 116, 129, 131, 134, 149, 158, 159, 162f, 165, 180f, 186, 187, 205, 212, 214, 229, 238, 246, 255, 273, 284, 315, 351, 383, 397, 398, 413, 420n, 422n, 484, 494, 497, 516
Behrend, A. H., 211
Belgian String Quartet, 110
Bellini, Vicenzo, 442, 463, 484
Belloc, Hilaire, 144
Benda, Georg, 385
Bennet, William Sterndale, 101
Benoit, Clary, 366, 367, 368, 432
Benson, Renée, 165
Berg, Alban, 399, 401, 402, 405, 411, 415, 417, 484f, 507

Bergham, Jachet de, 361
Berlin Philharmonic Orchestra, 264
Berlioz, Hector, 111, 204, 284
Bernard, Anthony, 394
Bernhardt, Sarah, 406
Berryman, Jo Brantley, 488
Bésard, Jean Baptiste, 347, 348, 352, 360, 376, 378, 435, 485, 487, 490
Bianchi, Gabriele, 346, 364, 365, 485
Bice Berino, Gentil Donna, 336
Biggs, Claud, 146f
Bird, William, 251, 252
Birkett, Gwenhilda, 216
Bizet, Georges, 148, 155, 173, 174, 178
Blake, William, 85, 408
Bleichmann, Yuly Ivanovitch, 140, 162, 202
Bliss, Sir Arthur, 240, 508
Bloch, Ernest, 263, 264, 485, 516
Blom, Eric, 485
Bloomfield, Gertrude, 234
Blow, John, 327, 364
Boccherini, Luigi, 323, 421n, 429, 431, 451, 473, 485f, 494
Boëllmann, Léon, 164
Boito, Arrigo, 440
Boivan, Mme. (engraver), 389
Bonell, Julien, 105
Booth, John, 205
Booth, John Wilkes, 342
Bordes, Charles, 178, 179f
Borgatti, Giuseppe, 430, 486
Borgatti, Renata, 234, 325, 341, 428, 429ff, 432, 446, 447, 448, 486, 492, 503
Borlee, V., 179
Borodin, Alexander, 105, 140, 157, 183, 189, 190, 224, 225f, 288, 486
Borrel, E., 386, 445
Bortckiewicz, Sergei Eduardovitch, 174
Bosdorf family, 126
Botticelli, Sandro, 291, 299n, 306, 388, 390, 391, 395, 399
Boulanger, Lili, 503
Boult, Sir Adrian, 188, 189
Bowen, York, 60, 106, 108, 144, 486
Bowers, Faubion, 27n
Bowers, John, 67n
Boys, Henry, 434
Brahms, Johannes, 35, 73, 85, 98f, 101, 114, 118, 126, 129, 131, 147, 149, 154, 157, 158, 165, 178, 179, 187, 192, 193, 213, 214, 239, 255, 280, 493, 501
Brancusi, Constantin, 256, 257, 269
Bréville, Pierre, 160
Bridge, Frank, 60, 67, 72, 76f, 87, 99, 107, 133, 140, 198, 221, 231

Bristol, Jessie, 69
Britten, Benjamin, 433, 434
Brizzolari, Mario, 360
Brooks, Mrs. Romain, 336
Brown, John Lackay, 18n
Brown, Kathleen, 66
Browning, Robert, 123, 230, 408f, 413, 439, 492
Brunel, Mme. (reciter), 230
Brunova, Mlle. (dancer), 56
Brunskill, Muriel, 210
Bullock, Ernest, 144
Bunting, Basil, 321, 330, 332, 333, 337, 338, 348, 349, 364, 380
Burleigh, Henry Thacker, 238
Burns, Robert, 230
Busoni, Ferruccio, 81, 159, 175, 206, 212, 229, 268, 342, 452
Butler, Charles, 357
Butler, Samuel, 100, 153
Butsova, Hilda, 56
Buxtehude, Dietrich, 486
Byrd, William, 356, 511
Byron, Lord, 51, 214

Caccini, Giulio, 181, 195, 450, 453, 454, 458, 486
Cadman, Charles Wakefield, 237
Cagney, James, 344
Caldara, Antonio, 58, 76, 136, 195, 232, 239, 266, 388, 447, 486
Campion, Thomas, 24, 60, 61, 76, 100, 102, 312, 396, 487
Carey-Foster, Phyllis, 238
Carissimi, Giacomo, 58, 239, 266, 358, 487
Carnegie, Austin, 115
Carpaccio, Vittore, 388
Carpenter, J. A., 221
Carr, Howard, 124f
Casella, Alfredo, 270, 310, 325, 329, 333, 372, 399, 400, 409, 410, 414, 422, 449, 451, 452, 456, 457, 487, 504
Castelnuovo-Tedesco, Mario, 503
Catalani, Alfredo, 72
Catterall Quartet, 88f
Catullus, 254, 454
Cavalcanti, Guido, 12, 295, 396, 417, 454, 457, 458, 469, 473
Cavalli, Pietro Francesco, 104
Cellini, G. Lenghi, 194
Cene, Roger le, 387
Cernikoff, Vladimir, 26, 58, 167, 169f, 171, 186, 203, 212f, 215, 218, 240, 286, 388, 487
Cesti, Marcantonio, 136, 158
Cézanne, Paul, 256
Chaigneau, Marguerite, 389
Chaliapin, Fyodor Ivanovich, 49

Challoner, Bromley, 55
Chambard, Jehanne, 167, 174f, 180
Chamberlain, Neville, 375, 377
Chaminade, Cécile, 95, 514
Chaplin, Charles, 216f
Charles I, 497
Charles V, 179, 281
Charles d'Orléans, 70, 96n, 391, 410, 489
Charpentier, Gustave, 115
Chaucer, Geoffrey, 28n, 195n, 484
Chausson, Ernest, 67, 136, 139, 214
Cherubini, Luigi, 429
Chigi Saracini, Count Guido, 329, 449, 451, 457, 459, 460f, 511
Chilesotti, Oscar, 328, 336, 337, 340, 341, 347, 354, 355, 365, 376, 378, 435, 485, 487, 492, 497, 500
Chilton-Griffen, Miss (pianist), 148
Chopin, Frédéric 66, 72, 76, 81, 89, 90, 108, 113f, 129, 138, 146, 147, 149, 157, 159, 164, 174, 175, 176, 185, 189, 212, 218, 234, 237, 241, 265, 268, 272, 273, 279, 282, 293, 315, 324, 338, 351, 354, 358, 367, 370, 380, 388, 408, 424, 431, 443, 488, 507
Chute, Rev. Desmond, 324, 327n, 333, 336, 360, 363f, 383, 425
Ciampi, Legrenzio Vincenzo, 232
Cimara, Pietro, 194
Cimarosa, Domenico, 76, 442
Cinelli, Delfini, 369
Clapperton, Mr., 171
Clegg, Edith, 90
Clérambault, Louis Nicholas, 186
Clouet, Jean, 50
Clustine, Ivan, 56
Coates, Albert, 207, 209, 285, 417
Coates, Henry, 204
Coates, John, 166
Cobbett, Walter Willson, 456
Cochrane, Elsie, 192
Cocteau, Jean, 188n, 242, 243, 250f, 320, 371, 402, 435, 473, 495, 506
Coleman, Joseph, 182
Coleridge, Samuel Taylor (poet), 275
Coleridge-Taylor, Samuel (composer), 111, 203
Colles, Henry Cope, 35
Collet, Henri, 242
Collier O., 115
Collignon, Raymonde, 28n, 58, 67ff, 97, 102, 119, 153, 158, 161, 197, 225, 228, 239, 465, 488, 491
Colson, Percy, 91
Colum, Padriac, 19n
Comisarjevsky (dancer), 52f
Compinsky, Emanuel, 101

519

Confucius, 408
Consolo, Ernesto, 345
Constantine, Emperor, 393
Conus, George, 229
Cooke, Evelin, 67
Cooper, John, *See:* Coperario, John
Cooper, Margaret, 101
Coopman, Frances, 203
Coperario, John, 186, 201, 357
Copland, Aaron, 242, 245
Corder, Frederick, 148
Corelli, Arcangelo, 87, 95, 338, 340, 353, 359, 451, 464
Corfe, Joseph, 254, 297
Corneille, Pierre, 51
Corrado, Giorgio, 232
Cortot, Alfred, 206
Coucy (composer), 160
Couperin, François, 15, 44, 45, 46, 121, 146n, 186, 258, 292, 390, 411, 435, 468, 469, 488
Cousins, J. H., 221
Cowley, Malcolm, 242
Cox (composer), 74
Craig, Edward Gordon, 498
Cras, Jean Emile Paul, 160
Craxton, Harold, 116, 203, 205
Criscuolo, Leandro, 349f, 351
De Cristina (singer), 442
Croce, Giovanni, 409
Cromwell, Oliver, 142, 274, 439
Croze, le Comte de, 114
Cui, César, 91, 203, 222
Cummings, E. E., 335
Czarada, Mme., 336
Czernikoff, Vladimir, *See:* Cernikoff, Vladimir

Dainton, Mario, 55
D'Albert, Eugene, 234
Dale, B., 108
Dali, Salvador, 415, 456
Dallapiccola, Luigi, 492
Dalliba, Gerda, 369
Dalliba, Mrs. John, 368f
D'Alvarez, Marguerite, 59, 74ff, 88, 119f, 143, 146, 158, 161, 171f, 481
Dandelot, Georges, 386, 445
Daniel, Arnaut, *See:* Arnaut Daniel
Daniel, Salvador, 195, 224, 288, 488, 498
D'Annunzio Gabriele, 70, 96n, 152, 489
Dante Alighieri, 9, 10, 22, 31, 33, 224, 289, 332, 361, 391, 394, 396, 448, 457, 458, 482, 500
Da Parma (composer), 152
Daquin, Louis Claude, 147, 390

Dargomyzhsky, Alexander Sergeyevitch, 156, 157, 162
Darke, Harold Edwin, 198
Davey, Murray, 76
David, F., 386
David, Jacques-Louis, 50
Davidoff, Charles, 164, 165
Davies, Henry Walford, 60, 101f, 127, 198, 199
Dazzi, Manlio, 322
Dearth, Harry, 79
Debussy, Claude, 27f, 33, 61, 66, 70f, 75, 90, 94, 96f, 99, 106 *passim*, 135, 138, 147, 158, 160, 175, 176, 184, 187, 192, 194, 199, 200, 211, 214, 219, 222, 229, 237, 238, 242, 243, 253, 255, 256, 259, 263, 265, 273, 279, 307, 308, 323, 333f, 338, 340, 346 *passim*, 367, 369, 370, 388, 391, 410, 425, 426, 428, 432, 485, 486, 488f, 504, 505, 506, 508, 509, 514, 516
Dedekind, Constantin Christian, 361
Defauw, Désiré, 103, 110, 158, 178, 489
Defosse, Henri, 160
Degas, Edgar, 55
Delage, Maurice, 173, 182
De Lange, Daniel, 228
Delayrac (composer), 172
Delibes, Léo, 508
Delius, Frederick, 172
Della Corte (critic), 452
Del Leuto (composer), 136
Derain, André, 188n, 189, 190, 218
d'Erlanger, Frederick, 158
Descartes, René, 309
Desmond, Astra, 233
Dessauer, Alice, 180
De-Villi, Umberto, 167
Diaghilev Ballet, 55n, 188n, 482, 484, 489
Diaghilev, Serge, 201, 242, 489
di Alba, Anita, 438, 441f
Dickinson, Emily, 166
Dieren, Bernard Van, *See:* Van Dieren, Bernard
Dina (composer), 173
Dini, Ferruccio, 166f
Di Veroli, Manlio, 74, 76f, 88, 92, 95, 99, 100, 106, 109, 111, 117, 118, 119, 134, 140, 153 *passim*, 173, 178, 181, 182, 184, 202, 209, 218, 226, 489
Dixon (violinist), 198
Dobson, Austin, 53
Dodsworth, Edmondo, 408
Doehard, Emile, 110, 146, 149, 158, 178
Doenau, Miss (pianist), 84

Dohnányi, Erno von, 336, 371
Dolmetsch, Arnold, 15, 24, 27n, 29n, 35ff, 60, 69, 121, 146n, 174, 182, 184ff, 201, 240, 254, 255n, 258n, 259, 266, 282, 291, 296, 306, 327, 466, 468, 484, 486, 488, 489f, 496, 498
Dolmetsch, Mrs. Arnold, 27n, 41, 490, 498
Dolmetsch, Natalie, 201
Donato, Baldassare, 409
Doni, Giovanni, Battista, 305
Donizetti, Gaetano, 111, 114, 226, 228, 232, 442
Dorgominsky, See: Dargomyzhsky
Dostoievsky, Fyodor, 209
Dowland, John, 19, 139, 215, 216, 240, 327, 347, 348n, 351, 352, 360, 376, 397, 428, 435, 441, 487, 490, 498
D'Oyley Carte, 52, 187
Dressel, Detmar, 60, 115
Dryden, John, 45
Dufay, Guillaume, 394
Dulac, Edmond, 490
Dunbar, Lawrence, 233
Duncan, Ronald, 321, 326, 433f, 479, 508
Dunhill, Thomas Frederick, 111, 113
Duparc, Henri, 94, 111, 114, 118, 154, 160
Dupin, Paul, 176, 279
Durante, Francesco, 58, 86, 266
Dürer, Albrecht, 388
Durey, Louis, 242
Duse, Eleonora, 142, 274
Dvořák, Antonin, 149, 183, 192
Dyer, Mrs. (music publisher), 428

Eaton, Sybil, 67
Edmonds, Paul, 198f
Egerton, Helen, 180f
Einstein, Alfred, 262, 301
Eisdell, Hubert, 216
Eitner, Robert, 305n, 385
Elgar, Sir Edward, 1, 15, 23f, 35, 60, 75, 103, 107, 198, 211, 266, 490, 503
Eliot, T. S., 6, 311, 312, 371, 439, 466, 482, 490
Elkin, Robert, 24f
Elwes, Gervase, 101, 165, 173
Emery, Mrs., See: Farr, Florence
Enesco, Georges, 173
Engel, Carl, 306, 467
Epstein, Jacob, 510
Ernst, Max, 415
Euclid, 309
Evans, Edwin, 67ff, 107, 112, 161, 171, 227, 310, 490f

Evans, W., 127
Eveline, Beatrice, 222
Expert, Henry, 357, 389

Faidit, Gaucelm, 28n, 247, 258, 291, 396, 408, 491, 504
Fairless, Margaret, 87
Falconieri, Andrea, 221, 229
Falla, Manuel de, 188n, 189, 234, 489
Fanelli, Ernest, 263, 307ff
Fanelli, Mme., 307
Farr, Florence, 29n
Farrell, James T., 330
Fauré, Gabriel, 77, 91, 139, 160, 164, 487
Felizzano, Marchesa Carola Colli di, 334
Fenellosa, Ernest, 323
Ferdinando Carlo, Archduke of Austria, 359
Fergusson, G., 105, 114
Ferola, Maestro, 357f
Ferrari, Gustave, 491, 494
Ferroud, Pierre Octave, 401, 402f, 410, 411, 414, 415, 491
Fétis, François Joseph, 254, 385, 491
Field, John, 103, 212, 213
Fiesole, Mino da, 417
Filippini (musician), 369
Fino Savio, Chiarino, 325, 355, 356, 358, 377, 433, 491
Fischer, Edwin, 498
Flaubert, Gustave, 390, 415
Foch, Mareschal, 155
Fokine, Michel, 55
Folquet de Marseilles, 491
Ford, Ford Maddox, 242, 253
Ford, Thomas, 139
Forrest, Ada, 148
Foster, Ivor, 214, 216
Foster, Megan, 214
Foster, Muriel, 72, 128
Fourdrain, Felix, 210f
Fourier, Jean-Baptiste Joseph, 479
Fra Angelico, 390
France, Anatole, 343
Francescatti, Zino, 397
Francesco da Milano, 328, 337, 338, 340, 348, 351, 357, 360, 376, 378, 390, 392, 399, 416, 434f, 491f, 496
Franchetti, Luigi, 325, 384, 406f, 418, 419
Francis I, 496
Franck, César, 72, 73, 99, 107, 108f, 111, 159, 160, 175, 181, 234, 419
Franco of Cologne, 297
Frazzi, Vito, 451, 457, 492
Freer, Dawson, 232
Frescobaldi, Girolamo, 360

521

Frid, Geza, 334ff, 492
Frobenius, Leo, 318, 344f, 395, 477
Fryer, Herbert, 87
Fuller Maitland, J. A., 204

Gabrieli, Giovanni, 464
Gabrilovitch, Ossip Solomonovitch, 369
Gaillard, Rodolphe, 100
Galilei, Galileo, 492
Galilei, Vincenzo, 337, 340, 347, 450, 453, 454, 458, 492
Gallup, Donald, 57n, 69n, 331, 506
Galuppi, Baldassare, 426, 431, 492
Gardener, Edmund, 33
Garelli, Nina, 76f, 106
Gasperini, Guido, 257n, 499
Gaudier-Brzeska, Henri, 27n, 245, 253, 256, 262, 321, 444, 476
Gautier, Judith, 343
Gautier, Théophile, 208, 285, 343
Geminiani, Francesco, 255n
Gentili, Alberto, 329n, 386
Gerlin (pianist), 455
German, Edward, 100
Gertler, Endré (or André), 401, 405, 411, 415, 492
Gertler Quartet, 325, 364, 365, 367, 372, 377, 379, 400, 401, 404, 411, 414f, 420, 422, 433, 461, 483, 485, 492f, 495
Gibbons, Orlando, 357
Gide, André, 343
Gigli, Beniamino, 418
Gilbert, Stuart, 17, 311
Gilbert and Sullivan, 50ff, 187f, 193, 509
Gilliand, Helen, 51f, 187, 188
Giordano, Umberto, 417, 493
Glazounov, Alexander, 91, 99, 108f, 149
Glinka, Michael, 109, 162, 191, 209
Gluck, C. W. von, 94, 172, 182, 207, 210, 493, 500
Godard, Benjamin, 514
Goddeschalk, See: Notker Balbulas
Goethe, Johann Wolfgang von, 6, 12, 426
Golding, Arthur, 335
Goldoni, Carlo, 457
Goldsmith, Katie, 91
Golschmann, Vladimir, 311
Goodson, Katherine, 165
Goodwin, A., 145, 210
Goossens, Eugene, 94, 221, 228
Gordon, Miss, 336
Gorzanis (composer), 337
Gounod, Charles François, 94, 114

Gourmont, Rémy de, 16n, 220n, 343, 377, 469f, 501
Goya, Francisco, 419
Grace, Dr. Harvey, 443
Granados, Enrique, 228
Granville, Sydney, 51f, 187, 188
Graves, A. P., 111
Gray, Cecil, 120n
Greef, Arthur de, 127, 148, 206, 493
Greene, Harry Plunket, 92, 111, 121, 144, 191, 220, 493
Gregorio, 455
Gregory, Lady Augusta, 29
Gregory I, Pope, 93, 217, 468
Gretchaninoff, Alexander, 99, 149, 156, 157, 162, 173, 174, 178, 202, 231, 493
Grétry, André, 112, 171, 200, 227
Grieg, Edvard, 127, 147f, 174, 206, 215, 216
Griffiths, Dorothy, 144
Groot, Pierre de, 405, 411, 415, 492
Gross, Mrs. Christian, 346
Grünewald, Matthias, 364
Guarnieri, Antonio, 410, 413, 422, 460, 493
Guarnieri, F. de, 386
Guidi, Guido, 438, 442, 446, 447, 448
Guido (or Gui) d'Arezzo, 48, 121, 493
Guilbert, Yvette, 68, 161, 195, 196, 240, 491, 493f
Guillem de Poitou, 510
Guinicello, Guido, 396

Haas, Eugen, 337, 338, 363, 380
Hahn, Renaldo, 77, 112, 173, 174, 182, 494
Haics, Geza, 371
Haley, Mrs. Edward, 152f
Haley, Olga, 91, 121, 152f, 494
Halford (cellist), 198
Hall, Elsie, 165
Halmos, Laszlò, 411, 421, 423, 431, 461, 495
Hamaton, Adela, 238
Hambourg, Mark, 60, 67, 266
Handel, G. F., 67, 74, 89, 100, 115f, 153, 177, 221, 227, 440, 451, 494, 498, 500
Hare, Amy, 144, 165f
Harris, Sir Augustus, 128
Harty, Hamilton, 204, 216
Hasse, Johann Adolph, 500
Hastwell (violist), 198
Hawley, Stanley, 85
Haydn, F. J., 89, 338, 371, 419, 421, 431, 439, 447, 486, 494
Hayes, Gerald, 326f, 357, 441, 494, 496

Hayes, Roland, 232, 233, 237f, 310, 494
Hayward, Marjorie, 140, 149
Heap, Jane, 250
Heine, Heinrich, 133, 180, 281
Helmholtz, Hermann von, 18
Hemingway, Ernest, 242, 250, 253, 312, 464
Henley, W. E., 128
Henry VIII, 115
Heraclitus, 467, 480
Herrick, Robert, 144, 199, 497
Heseltine, Philip, *See:* Warlock, Peter
Hess, Myra, 72, 98f, 119, 167, 175f
Heyden, Johann, 304n
Heymen, Katherine Ruth, 26, 27, 468, 494f, 504, 507
Hill, Carmen, 124
Hinchcliff, Mr. (oboist), 103
Hindemith, Paul, 326, 360, 362, 371, 399, 400, 402, 404ff, 410, 411, 412, 415f, 420, 422, 426, 428, 495
Hinton, Arthur, 144
Hislop (singer), 310
Hobday, Ethel, 193, 214
Holbrooke, Joseph, 61, 76, 104f, 183, 186n, 200, 211f, 495
Holding, F., 183
Hollander, B., 74, 338
Homer, 18, 93, 175, 246, 352
Honegger, Arthur, 242, 399, 401, 403f, 410, 411, 415, 422, 425, 428, 495, 506
Housman, A. E., 85
Hubay, Jenö, 421, 508
Hué, Georges Adolphe, 111, 177, 222
Hughes, Robert, 464
Hughes, Vivien, 112
Hume, Violet, 103
Hummel, Johann Nepomuk, 212
Hungarian String Quartet, 325, 400ff, 411, 415, 418, 419, 420ff, 422, 423, 424, 425, 428, 429, 431, 432, 433, 452, 461, 483, 486, 495, 497, 508, 510
Hurwitz, Harold M., 35n
Husserl, Edmund, 506

Illersberg, Antonio, 414
Imperiali, Marchesa, 336, 433
Ingres, Jean Auguste Dominique, 50
Ireland, John, 24, 60, 72, 94, 104, 106, 108, 133, 140, 178, 222
Izard, Constance, 191

James, Henry, 171, 181, 207, 285
Janáček, Leoš, 294
Janequin, Clément, 12n, 19, 21, 324, 328, 340, 348, 351, 357, 360, 376, 378f, 387, 390, 391, 392, 397, 399, 416, 417, 434f, 450, 492, 495f, 500
Janigro, Antonio, 417
Jassy (composer), 173, 174
Jefferson, Thomas, 205, 284
Jenkins, John, 60, 326f, 357, 428, 496, 498
Jeremy, R., 178, 183
Jones, Robert, 214
Jonson, Ben, 100
Jordan, Arthur, 92
Josquin des Prés, 337
Joyce, Georgio, 250
Joyce, James, 12n, 16ff, 22, 41, 242, 250, 311, 312, 316n, 326
Julian, Emperor, 468
Julius Caesar, 393
Jung, Hans Rudolf, 329n
Justinian, Emperor, 393
Juta, Lula, 67

Kalinnikof, Wassily, 140, 162, 202
Kandinsky, Wassily, 506
Kanevskaya, Lilia, 147
Karsavina, Tamar, 190, 201
Katue, Kitasano, 419n, 456
Kaufferath, Fernanda, 164
Kay, R. C., 110, 158, 178
Keats, John, 230, 275, 313, 408
Keith, Charlton, 145
Kennedy, Daisy, 83, 122, 496, 500
Kennedy, Margaret, 197
Kennedy-Fraser, Marjory, 58, 61, 80, 92f, 121, 135, 141ff, 164, 166, 171, 180, 194, 197f, 212, 215, 220, 222f, 225, 227, 240, 266, 274, 275, 276, 287, 496
Kennedy-Fraser, Patuffa, 92f, 166, 171, 197f, 222, 225, 274
Kenner, Hugh, 13, 469
Kiddle, Frederick, 88, 95, 127, 143, 158, 165, 171, 172, 216, 496f
Kindler, Frida, 138
Kipling, Rudyard, 54, 81, 82, 100, 198, 203, 268, 284
Kirkby Lunn, Mme. (singer), 84
Klingsor, Tristan, 111, 177
Knocker, E. H., 67, 202
Kodaly, Zoltán, 334, 335, 372, 377, 428n, 492, 507, 508
Kolisch, Rudolf, 497
Kolisch String Quartet, 400, 420n, 423, 497
Konody, P. G., 373
Koromzay, Denes, 411, 415, 420n, 421, 423, 428, 461, 495
Korsakoff, *See:* Rimsky-Korsakoff
Koshitz, Alexander, 217
Koussevitsky, Sergei, 25, 314, 336

523

Krein, Grigory, 104
Kreisler, Fritz, 193
Krettly, Monsieur (violinist), 314
Krettly Quatuor, 313

Laforgue, Jules, 171
Lalo, Édouard, 95, 124, 164, 503
Lamond, Frederic, 158, 159, 162f, 164, 174, 176, 187, 212, 497
Lancare, (composer), 185
Landor, Walter Savage, 254
Landowska, Wanda, 336
Lansbury, Oscar, 184
L'Anson, Miss (singer), 171
Lasserson, Sascha, 137
Lauder, Harry, 97, 195
Laughlin, James, 397
Laurencie, Lionel de la, 257n, 485, 497
Lavignac, Albert, 257n, 306, 438, 485, 487, 497, 499
Lawes, Henry, 24, 58, 60, 61, 85, 86, 91, 100, 104, 123, 148, 180, 182f, 185, 240, 266, 281, 282, 327, 396, 454, 488, 496, 497f
Lawrence, D. H., 506
Lawson, Malcolm, 110
Lawson, Winifred, 95
Lebell (cellist), 113
Leclerc (music engraver), 389
Lecouvreur, Adriana, 342
Léger, Fernand, 311
Legrenzi, Giovanni, 91, 136
Leibnitz, Gottfried Wilhelm, 476
Leighton, Sir Frederic, 81, 268
Le Marchant, Ada, 103
Lens, Thérèse de, 223f, 498
Leonardo da Vinci, 388
Leonora, Clara, 498
Leschetizky, Theodor, 234
Lett, Phyllis, 79
Levenson (composer), 232
Levi, Giorgio, 427, 429
Lévy, Emil, 28n
Lewis, Wyndham, 27n, 57, 253, 256, 257, 259, 265
Liapounow, Serge, 113
Liddle, Samuel, 144, 230f, 498
Linder, Edwin, 333
Liszt, Franz, 60, 89, 101, 111, 129f, 146, 148, 159, 170, 218, 226, 238, 278, 333, 350, 351, 364, 498, 500, 507
Litante, Judith, 231f, 234, 238f
Liuzzi, Fernando, 362, 364
Livens, Leo, 203
Lockspeiser, Edward, 96n
Loewe, Carl, 191
Loggins, Vernon, 312

Lo Monaco (conductor), 438, 442
London String Quartet, 75f, 505
London Symphony Orchestra, 126n, 188, 216
London Trio, 145, 210
Long, Huey, 465
Lorain, J., 160
Lotti, Antonio, 86, 173, 409
Lounon, Marcel, 411, 492
Louÿs, Pierre, 104
Lowenson (composer), 219
Loy, Mina, 312
Lualdi, Adriano, 410
Lübeck, Vincent, 338, 361, 363, 367
Luciani, S. A., 330n, 453, 454, 457, 498, 504
Luck, Margot, 53
Ludovico Magnifico, 106
Lulli, Jean-Baptiste, 221
Lyne, Felice, 107f, 114
Lytton, Henry, 51f, 187, 188

McAlmon, Robert, 312, 316n, 330
Macaulay, Thomas Babbington, 155
Macbride, Winifred, 186f
McCormack, John, 19
McDonald, Annabel, 79f
Macdonald, George, 205
MacDowell, Edward, 89, 125
Mace, Thomas, 15, 43, 468
McEwan, John Blackwood, 106
Machaut, Guillaume de, 394
Machiavelli, 33
McKail, 105
Mackinlay, Jean Sterling, 97, 204, 224, 498
Mackinlay, Kenneth, 98
Mackinnon, Lilias, 108f, 121, 232, 498
McLean, Allan, 336
McLelland, Miss, (singer), 171
McLeod, Fiona, 73
MacVane, Miss, 55
Magito, Suria, 434
Maharini of Tikari, 234
Mahler, Gustav, 485
Mainardi, Enrico, 369, 498
Maitland, Robert, 312, 498f
Malatesta, Sigismundo, 322, 348
Malipiero, Francesco, 160, 176, 270, 485, 503
Mallarmé, Stéphane, 96n, 211, 219
Mälzel, Johann Nepomuk, 303n
Mancinelli, Luigi, 194
Manet, Édouard, 255, 256
Mangeot, André, 180
Mann, Adolph, 103, 146
Mantegna, Andrea, 320, 387, 388, 419

Marais, Marin, 103
Marcello, Benedetto, 86, 104, 193, 196, 358, 388, 389, 409, 414
Marchesi, Blanche, 114f, 195, 499
Marchettus of Padua, 257, 474, 499
Marconi, Alfonso, 392
Marconi, Gugliemo, 392
Marguerite, Victor, 176, 279
Marinetti, F. T., 252, 253, 330
Maroill, Arnaut de, See: Arnaut de Maroill
Marot, Clément, 133, 173
Marquesita, Violet, 194f, 227, 499
Marshall, Douglas, 215f, 219, 220, 221, 229, 230
Marshall, George, 336
Martin, Easthope, 136, 200
Mascagni, Pietro, 172, 184
Masefield, John, 214
Massenet, Jules, 25, 75, 111, 119, 197, 233, 238, 484
Massine, Léonide, 56, 188n, 189
Matelart, J., 423
Mather, Mr. (poet), 230
Mathers, Gwen, 150, 152
Matisse, Henri, 218, 256
Matthay, Tobias, 498
Mavon Ibbs, P., 192
Mayer, Lonny, 325, 360ff, 364, 365, 377, 499
Medici, Ippolito de', 491
Medici (singer), 442
Méhul, Etienne Nicolas, 173, 200
Meller, Raquel, 226
Mellers, Wilfred, 312
Melozzo da Forlì, 390
Mendelssohn, Felix, 76, 89, 178, 213, 214, 264, 266, 279, 286
Menotti, Gian Carlo, 499
Mercadante, Saverio, 442
Meredyll, Marguerite, 149
Mérimée, Prosper, 155
Metastasio, The Abbé, 112, 136, 283, 439, 500
Meymott, H. A., 55
Milano, Francesco da, See: Francesco da Milano
Milhaud, Darius, 242, 489, 506
Millar, Webster, 90
Milton, John, 33, 471, 497
Miró, Joan, 415, 445
Mischa-Leon, Harry Haurowitz, 191, 210ff
Moffat, Alfred, 136, 386
Moger, Gladys, 91
Moiseiwitsch, Benno, 75f, 113, 119, 128ff, 175, 186, 496, 500
Molinari, Bernardino, 398
Molinaro, S., 337

Monnier, Adrienne, 250
Monroe, Harriet, 34, 173
Montale, Eugenio, 369
Monteith, Brydon, 203, 205
Monteux, Pierre, 336
Monteverdi, Claudio, 86, 105, 176, 221, 355, 358, 409
Montrave, Doris, 221f
Moore, Tom, 123, 232
Morley, Rose, 206
Morley, Thomas, 148, 198
Morse, Samuel, 504
Mortari, Virgilio, 429, 451, 457, 500
Mosiewitsch, Benno, See: Moiseiwitsch, Benno
Moskowsky, Alexander, 495
Moullé (composer), 102
Moulton, Dorothy, 110f
Mozart, Leopold, 447
Mozart, W. A., 19, 37, 51, 61, 62ff, 71, 74, 85, 87, 90, 93, 111, 119, 124, 136, 139, 154, 158, 170, 187, 191, 202, 218, 223, 227, 229, 232, 248, 283, 287, 291, 293, 303, 323, 324, 331f, 333, 334, 336, 338, 346, 349, 350, 352, 353, 354, 364, 365, 367, 371, 376, 378, 380, 383, 388, 389, 392, 394, 396, 397, 398, 407, 408, 419, 425, 426, 428, 430, 431, 432, 433, 442, 444, 446ff, 460, 461, 464, 477, 485, 500, 504. 516
Müller, Wilhelm, 6
Mulligan, Miss, 71f
Mullings, Frank, 64, 93, 121, 152, 228, 500
Münch, Gerhart, 322, 324n, 325, 326, 327, 328, 331, 332f, 334, 337, 338, 340f, 346ff, 376ff, 387, 391, 392, 400, 406f, 416, 418, 422ff, 445, 464, 476, 487, 490, 492, 495, 496, 498, 500f
Munro, Miss (pianist), 101
Murdoch, William David, 73, 107, 183, 203, 501
Murger, Henri, 71, 81, 268
Murray Lambert, Miss, 67, 115f
Musset, Alfred de, 171, 175, 279
Mussolini, Benito, 384n, 450n
Mussorgsky, Modeste, 58, 95, 109, 114, 117f, 131, 134, 140, 141, 150, 153ff, 161, 162, 164, 167, 171, 193, 198, 200, 202, 209, 214, 218, 219, 223, 225, 229, 232, 266, 273, 275, 377, 388, 501, 514

Napravnik, Edward, 154
Nardi, Alfredo, 170f
Nardini, Pietro, 362, 369, 370
Negri Milanese, Cesare, 423

525

Nevada, Emma, 501
Nevada, Mignon, 112, 119, 167, 171f, 227f, 501
Nevin, Ethelbert, 116, 501
Nevine, Nin, 145
Nevstruoff (composer), 99, 118, 140, 141, 157, 273, 276
New Hungarian String Quartet, *See:* Hungarian String Quartet
Newman, Ernest, 488
Newmarch, Rosa, 126
New Russian Choir, 229
Nielka, Marguerite, 207
Nigrini, Nic., 337
Nijinski, Vaslav, 52
Nikisch, Arthur, 106
Nixon, David, 427, 429, 455
Norman, Charles, 41n, 243, 312, 329n, 490
Notker Balbulas, 48, 220, 288, 470, 501
Novello, Vincent, 200

Oakes, Loisann, 12n
O'Neill, Norman, 227
Orage, A. R., 57, 370, 373
Oriana Madrigal Society, 115
Ornstein, Leo, 263, 516
Ortmans, Réne, 74
Ottone, Marco, 322, 338, 350, 360, 369, 377, 429, 501
Ovid, 18, 335
Oxenford, Edward, 232, 501
Oxenford, John, 84, 140, 501

Paige, D. D., 357n
Paisiello, Giovanni, 136, 388, 389, 442
Palestrina, Giovanni Pierluigi da, 358, 361
Palmgren, Selim, 147, 221
Palotai, Vilmos, 401, 402, 411, 415, 421, 423, 428, 432, 461, 495
Paquin (couturier), 219
Paradies, Pietro Domenico, 136, 175
Paray, Paul, 503
Parisotti, Silvia, 107, 239
Parker, George, 139f
Parker, Robert, 93, 121
Parlow, Kathleen, 145, 228f, 502
Parratt, Walter, 497
Parry, Sir Hubert, 107, 145, 192, 221f
Pater, Walter, 73, 96n
Paterna (singer), 442
Paterson (cellist), 368
Patmore, Brigit, 496
Pavlova, Ludmilla, 52, 55f, 226
Pawlo, George, 128
Peake, Ethel, 117

Peatfield, T., 183
Pecskai (violinist), 210
Peirol (troubador), 502
Pepusch, Dr. John Christopher, 139
Pepys, Samuel, 37
Pergolesi, Giovanni Battista, 86, 118, 136, 176, 232, 239, 338, 355, 367, 368, 389, 407, 423, 463
Peri, Jacopo, 450
Pericles, 377
Perinello, Carlo, 427, 463
Peterson, Thelma, 126
Petrides, Petro, 99
Peyrot, J., 387
Philharmonic String Quartet, 110, 162, 183, 192
Philipoff (folk music collector), 140, 162, 202
Philipp, Isidore, 113
Phillipe, Charles Louis, 207, 285
Phillopowsky, Ivan, 188, 208
Picasso, Pablo, 188n, 189, 190, 201, 237, 242, 253, 256, 265, 388, 416, 444, 514
Piccardi, Maestro, 418, 445
Picchi, Giovanni, 337, 423
Piedmont, Prince of, 414n
Pier della Francesca, 388, 390, 407
Pierné, Gabriel, 113, 172, 173, 174
Pincerle, Marc, 329n
Pisanello, Antonio, 379, 390, 435
Pitsch, G., 180
Pizzetti, Ildebrando, 228f, 231, 333, 345, 346, 369, 430, 500, 502, 503
Plato, 30, 36, 107
Playfair, Nigel, 65
Poe, Edgar Allan, 211
Poldowski *(psued.* Lady Dean Paul), 104, 200, 215, 222
Polignac, Princesse Edmond de, 328, 357n
Pomilio, Signora, 336
Pons de Capdoill, 502
Poole, Monique, 149
Pope, Alexander, 175
Porrino, Ennio, 417
Poulenc, Francis, 234, 242, 489, 506
Pound, Dorothy, 325, 336, 466, 494
Pound, Homer, 57, 69, 336
Pound, Omar, 25
Primrose, William, 373
Prokofieff, Serge, 234, 270, 489
Prosdocimus de Beldemandis, 257, 474
Proust, Marcel, 494
Prudhomme, Sully, 176, 279
Ptolemy, 305
Puccini, Giacomo, 19, 118, 184, 197, 364, 379, 381, 439, 502, 508

Pugnani, Gaetano, 91
Puliti-Santoliquido, Ornella, 414n, 422
Purcell, Henry, 37, 59, 64, 72, 87, 91, 103, 104, 107, 116, 171, 172, 209, 228, 241, 326, 327, 338, 349, 350, 354, 359, 397, 425, 426, 427, 428, 432, 440n, 441, 446, 448, 461, 502, 511, 512
Purnell, Winifred, 89f, 112f, 119, 125, 170

Quantz, Johann Joachim, 45, 385
Quartetto Silvestri (Quartetto di Genova), 429
Quilter, Roger, 111f, 310
Quinn, John, 28n

Rachewiltz, Boris de, 465, 466
Rachewiltz, Mary de, 330, 465, 466
Rachilde, 343
Rachmaninoff, Serge, 80, 104, 146, 156, 178, 516
Racine, Jean, 51
Radford, Robert, 64, 121, 502
Raibin, Mr. (singing teacher), 239
Rameau, Jean Philippe, 175, 294
Rangoni, Luigi, 230f
Rans, Dom Nicholas de, 304n
Raphael, 82, 268, 390
Raphael Socius, *See:* Zarlino, Giosoffo
Ravel, Maurice, 25, 102f, 110, 121, 139, 151, 176, 214, 219, 238, 239, 242, 307, 310, 323, 338, 351, 353, 355, 358, 367, 410, 448, 482, 489
Rawlins, Bessie, 193
Raymer, Douglas, 219, 226
Read, Forrest, 464
Reimbautz de Vaquieras, 368n
Reinken, Johann Adam, 360
Rellstab, Ludwig, 6
Renaud, Albert, 219
Respighi, Ottorino, 188n, 348, 386, 413, 502, 503
Revesz, Laszlo, 411, 492
Rhené-Baton, 94, 211
Richter, Ernst Friedrich Eduard, 254, 297, 435
Richter, Hans, 498
Ricketts (critic), 371
Rimsky-Korsakoff, Nicholas, 104, 114, 131, 134, 140, 156, 162, 173, 174, 207, 209, 218, 221, 278, 285
Rinunccini, Ottavio, 450
Roberts, A., 55
Robertson, John, 230
Robilant, Conte Nicolis di, 336
Robinson, Forbes, 342
Robson, Dorothy, 213

Rockstro, William Smyth, 497
Ronald, Sir Landon, 128, 148, 231, 502f
Roncelli, Ludovico, 337, 354, 355
Rootham, Cyril, 126f, 214, 503
Rootham, Helen, 137
Ropartz, Guy, 214f
Rorem, Ned, 253n
Rosenmüller, Johann, 368
Rosing, Vladimir, 52f, 94ff, 105, 109f, 113, 114, 117f, 119, 128, 131, 133ff, 140f, 143, 144, 150f, 153, 158, 160f, 162, 164, 167, 171, 177, 178, 180, 188, 191 *passim*, 215 *passim*, 273, 275, 279, 377, 388n, 486, 489, 501, 503ff
Rosowsky, Zoia, 104, 156, 184, 190, 197
Rossi, Lemme, 305
Rossi, Luigi, 394
Rossetti, Christina, 85
Rossetti, D. G., 30, 37
Rossini, Gioachino Antonio, 77, 107, 188n, 189, 190, 219, 232, 263, 438ff, 441, 442, 443, 444, 451, 454, 458, 460
Rothenstein, William, 34
Rousseau, Le Douanier, 256, 416, 513ff
Rousseau, Jean-Jacques, 15, 43f, 145f, 468
Roussel, Albert, 211
Rousselot, Abbé J. P., 475n
Rubinstein, Anton, 76, 105, 140, 503
Rubinstein, Arthur, 206, 234f, 238, 241, 503
Rückert, Friedrich, 191
Rudge, Olga, 233f, 246ff, 310, 312, 316, 322, 325, 328ff, 331, 332f, 337 *passim*, 376 *passim*, 385n, 390, 397, 419, 422 *passim*, 445 *passim*, 482, 485, 486, 487, 492, 498, 502, 503f, 510
Ruggles, Carl, 464
Rummel, Walter Morse, 6, 27ff, 41, 62, 69, 70, 96n, 102, 121, 153, 240, 387, 389, 478, 482, 488, 489, 502, 504f, 510
Ruskin, John, 408f
Russolo, Luigi, 252, 253n, 260n, 312
Rust, Wilhelm, 426, 432
Ryley, T., 55

Sachse, William, 193
Sadero, Gene, 358
Sahnovsky (composer), 157
Saint Francis, 218, 226
Saint-Saëns, Camille, 95, 97, 103, 159, 228

527

Salmond, Felix, 67, 79f, 84, 102, 104, 105, 107, 113, 119, 214, 505
Salvini (actor), 342
Saminski, Lazare, 229
Sammons, A. E., 73, 106, 145, 505
Samuel, H., 80
Sansoni, Luigi, 322, 337f, 349, 350, 352, 355, 356, 364, 368, 377, 381, 382, 427, 428, 432, 433, 505
Sarasate, Pablo de, 67, 503, 505
Satie, Eric, 188n, 242f, 245, 260n, 262, 263, 307, 310, 312, 324, 338, 344, 367, 489, 495, 505f, 514, 515, 516
Sauret, Émile, 140
Sauzay, Eugène, 254, 298, 299, 403, 435
Savile, Jeremy, 115
Saviotti, Gino, 424
Scarlatti, Allesandro, 174, 221, 355, 356, 358, 447, 457, 459f
Scarlatti, Domenico, 144, 208, 366, 457, 459f
Schenker, Heinrich, 293f
Schering, Arnold, 329n
Schiff, Ernest Wilton, 78
Schiffer (cellist), 421
Schloezer, Boris de, 320, 402, 435, 473, 506, 536
Schmidt, Florence, 506
Schneiderhan, Wolfgang, 498
Schoenberg, Arnold, 25, 62, 120n, 256, 258n, 262, 264, 293f, 297, 303, 333, 371, 405, 411, 417, 506f
Scholes, Percy A., 60n
Schubert, Franz, 6, 85, 105, 146, 155, 157, 180, 181, 192, 210, 239, 281
Schumann, Robert, 76, 81, 85, 95, 105, 110, 113, 118, 129, 133f, 182, 190, 192, 205, 208, 213, 219, 231, 268, 272, 285, 286, 364, 431, 493
Schwerke, Irving, 247
Scott, Cyril, 133, 153, 172, 268, 508
Scott, Harold, 102
Scotus, Erigena, 395, 476
Scriabin, Alexander, 25, 60, 146, 170, 207f, 232, 263, 264, 285, 333f, 338, 351, 352, 494, 506, 507, 516
Sealy, Helen, 165
Segovia, Andrés, 358
Serato, Arigo, 338
Serly, Tibor, 321, 323f, 325, 331, 334ff, 364, 365, 366, 367, 370ff, 373, 376, 379, 400, 422, 433, 449, 454, 458, 483, 492, 495, 507
Sévérac, Déodat de, 146
Severi, Francesco, 354, 355, 378
Shakespear, Olivia, 434
Shakespeare, William, 45, 120n, 136, 140, 283, 342, 395, 454, 458, 482

Shannon (critic), 371
Sharpe, Betty, 183, 186n, 507
Sharpe, Cecil James, 183
Sharrer, Irene, 119
Shaw, George Bernard, 58
Shelly, Percy Bysshe, 408
Shostakovitch, Dmitri, 417
Sickert, Walter, 50
Simonati, A., 377, 381
Simpson, Christopher, 45
Smetana, Bedřich, 91
Snow, Jessie, 216
Socius, Raphael, *See:* Zarlino, Giosoffo
Solari, Mayor, 337
Sonzogno (musician), 417
Sophokles, 480
Sordello, 362, 454, 458
Sottacasa, Contessa Gabriella, 336
Spinola, Marchesa Solferina, 336, 433
Spontini, Gasparo Luigi Pacifico, 463
Sraffa, Grand 'Uff. Angelo, 336
Stanford, C. V., 35, 214
Steibelt, Daniel, 88, 213
Stein, Gertrude, 242, 320, 509
Sterbini, Cesare, 439, 442, 454
Sterling, Antoinette, 498
Sternberg, Constantine von, 264, 307
Sterne, Laurence, 153
Stevenson, R. L., 182, 216
Stier, T., 226
Stock, Noel, 329, 397n
Stokowsky, Leopold, 335, 366, 464
Stone (violinist), 198
Strachey, Lytton, 52
Stralia, Elsa, 106
Strauss, Richard, 278, 310, 413
Stravinsky, Igor, 14, 25, 59, 61, 162, 183, 242, 251, 252, 253, 257n, 258, 262, 264, 265, 273, 276, 278, 312, 315, 316, 326, 333, 338, 364, 365, 366, 367, 368, 369, 370, 372, 376, 379, 387, 394, 399, 402, 405, 410, 411, 412f, 416, 423, 428, 431, 433f, 436, 442, 444, 452, 473, 474, 477, 483, 489, 506, 507f, 513, 514, 516
Strockoff (violinist), 117
Stroesco, Constantin, 26, 58, 91, 110f, 119, 131, 135f, 144, 151, 152, 161, 167, 172ff, 177, 180, 181, 182, 184, 200, 209, 219, 220, 222, 226, 228, 231, 279, 486, 508
Suggio, Guilhermina, 144, 150
Swinburne, Algernon Charles, 53
Symons, Arthur, 96n, 403
Székeli, Zoltan, 428, 431, 461, 495, 508
Szervansky, Peter, 495
Szigeti, Joseph, 322

Szolc (dancer), 190
Szymanowski, Karol, 263, 264

Tagore, Rabindranath, 5, 34f, 221, 508
Tailleferre, Germaine, 234, 237, 242
Tallis, Thomas, 356
Tandini (manager), 442
Tarenzi (singer), 442
Tartini, Giuseppe, 67, 103, 366
Tasso, Torquato, 74
Tchelitchew, Pavel, 404
Tchernicheva, Lubov, 190
Telemann, Georg Philipp, 361, 363, 365
Templars Quartet, 198
Tennyson, Alfred Lord, 105, 148, 150, 212
Tertis, Lionel, 106, 110, 158, 165, 178, 489, 508
Terzi, Giovanni, 337, 338, 340, 347
Tetrazzini, Luisa, 194
Teyte, Maggie, 200f, 508f
Thomas, V., 172
Thomson, Virgil, 242, 245n, 246n, 312, 320n, 509
Thursfield, Anne, 143, 162, 193, 194, 203f, 221, 509
Tiersot, Julien, 105, 157, 239
Tilly, Margaret, 203
Tinayre, Yves, 58, 61, 114, 135, 139f, 144, 159f, 161, 162, 167, 173, 176ff, 180, 197, 203, 208, 228, 243, 250, 279, 312, 364, 366, 388n, 393, 394ff, 498, 509
Toscanini, Arturo, 371, 383, 397, 398, 407, 422, 507
Townley, Mrs. Ephra, 336, 337, 349
Toye, Geoffrey, 51, 187, 509
Tryer, Anderson, 203, 205
Tschaikovsky, Peter Ilich, 60, 118, 131, 149, 153 passim, 177, 191, 193, 209, 219, 239, 276
Tscherepnine, Nicholas, 99, 157, 178, 218
Tubb, Carrie, 84ff
Tuckfield, Ellen, 107
Tussaud, Mme., 75, 77
Tzara, Tristan, 242

Ukrainian National Choir, 217, 229

Valéry, Paul, 343
Valette, Alfred, 343
Van Dieren, Bernard, 60, 120, 137ff, 509f
Van Eyck, Jan, 388
Van Loo, Emil, 374

Vassilenko (Wassilenko), Sergey, 99, 218
Vaughan Williams, Ralph, 24, 85, 133, 216, 482
Vecchi, Orazio, 427, 463, 510
Vegh, Sándor, 411, 415, 421, 423, 428, 431, 461, 495, 510
Velasquez, Diego, 388, 407
Ventadour, Bernart de, 102, 510
Veracini, Francesco, 117, 338, 360
Verdi, Giuseppe, 64, 171, 310, 383, 398, 510
Veress, Sándor, 428, 431
Verlaine, Paul, 131, 172, 174
Verne, Adele, 226
Verne, Mathilde, 214
Veroli, Manlio di, See: Di Veroli, Manlio
Vidal, Peire, 510
Vigliani, Francesco, 70ff, 95
Vigliani String Quartet, 70ff, 75, 120
Villon, François, 5, 70, 138, 200, 232, 243, 295, 417, 454, 458, 491, 499, 514
Viotti, Giovanni Battista, 388
Vitali, Tommaso Antonio, 145
Vitri, Phillipe de, 257n
Vittoria, Tomás Luis de, 358, 361
Vivaldi, Antonio, 19, 61, 195, 232, 239, 323, 325, 327, 328ff, 338, 383 passim, 409, 424 passim, 443 passim, 463, 485, 487, 500, 504, 510f
Vlaminck, Maurice, 237
Volinin (dancer), 56

Wadsworth, Edward, 27n
Wagenseil, G. Ch., 368
Wagner, Richard, 33, 64, 71, 80, 95, 97, 109, 118, 134, 141, 150, 155, 204, 209, 255, 263, 264, 273, 284, 310, 315, 358, 398, 413, 442, 498
Waldbauer, Imre, 421
Walenn (musician), 101
Wallace, Edgar, 404, 437
Waller, Edmund, 24, 61, 85, 108, 123, 180, 182f, 198, 230, 240, 281, 282, 439, 454, 497
Walter, Bruno, 383, 397, 398
Walton, Sir William, 120n
Ward, Leo, 163
Waring, Miss (dancer), 55
Warlock, Peter, 120n
Watkinson, Mrs., 336
Watteau, Antoine, 118, 131, 313
Weaver, Harriet, 17n
Webb, Dorothea, 201
Webbe, Samuel, 139
Weckerlin, Jean Baptiste Théodore, 178, 239

529

Weckmann, Matthias, 360, 365
Weinwurstel, Eva, 251
Weitz (composer), 102
Whistler, James McNeill, 354, 403
Whitehouse, W. E., 103, 104, 113, 119, 145, 210, 511
Whitman, Walt, 144
Whittaker, W. Gillies, 326, 327, 355f, 357n, 359, 364, 366, 399, 419n, 427, 428, 441, 446, 448, 461, 502, 511, 512
Wieniawski, Henri, 88, 101, 182, 216
Wilbye, John, 204
Wilcox, Ella Wheeler, 111, 156, 158f, 166, 276
Williams, Arthur, 104f, 113f, 119, 165, 180
Williams, Capt. A., 79
Williams, William Carlos, 29, 290, 371
Willis, Joan, 165
Wilson, Helen, 149
Wipo of St. Gall, 470
Witt, Danina de, 358
Wolf-Ferrari, Ermanno, 414
Wolstenholme, William, 106
Wood, Charles, 144

Wood, Sir Henry, 63, 85, 124ff, 127, 192, 498, 511
Woodgate, Hubert Leslie, 511
Woodhouse, Charles, 489
Woof, Rowsby, 91
Wordsworth, William, 200
Wyatt, Thomas, 228

Yeats, W. B., 12, 18, 19n, 29, 33, 34, 93, 111, 321, 406, 456, 471, 490, 496, 505
Yorke, Yvonne, 103, 188
Young, William, 327, 356, 357, 358ff, 364, 366, 376, 381, 397, 399, 417, 433, 441, 446, 448, 461, 511f
Ysaye, Eugène, 406, 512

Zanolli, Maria Chiara, 330
Zarlino, Giosoffo, 302n, 512
Zedlitz, Josef, 191
Ziemska, Hela, 234
Zimbalist, Efrem, 369
Zolotareff, Vassily Andreyevich, 190
Zukofsky, Louis, 18n, 321, 330, 371, 464
Zukofsky, Paul, 464